RESEARCH METHODOLOGY

(Concepts, Methods, Techniques and SPSS)
(Text and Cases)

Dr. Priti Ranajan Majhi

M.A., MBA, M.Phil., Ph.D. (Operations Management),
Professor and Asso. Dean (Research and Fellow Programmes),
Regional College of Management Autonomous ***(RCMA)****,*
Bhubaneswar, Odisha, India

Dr. Prafull Kumar Khatua

M.Com., MBA, Ph.D.
Reader in Commerce,
Institute of Management and Information Technology ***(IMIT)****,*
Cuttack, Odisha, India.

ISO 9001:2015 CERTIFIED

First Edition : 2011
Second Revised Edition : 2013
Reprint : 2024
Reprint : 2025

Published by : Mrs. Meena Pandey
for **HIMALAYA PUBLISHING HOUSE PVT. LTD.,**
"Ramdoot", Dr. Bhalerao Marg, Girgaon, Mumbai - 400 004.
Phone: 022-23860170, 23863863; **Fax:** 022-23877178
E-mail: himpub@bharatmail.co.in; **Website:** www.himpub.com

Branch Offices :

New Delhi : "Pooja Apartments", 4-B, Murari Lal Street, Ansari Road, Darya Ganj, New Delhi - 110 002.
Phone: 011-23270392, 23278631; Fax: 011-23256286

Nagpur : Kundanlal Chandak Industrial Estate, Ghat Road, Nagpur - 440 018.
Phone: 0712-2721215, 2721216

Bengaluru : Plot No. 91-33, 2nd Main Road, Seshadripuram, Behind Nataraja Theatre,
Bengaluru - 560 020. Phone: 080-41138821; Mobile: 09379847017, 09379847005

Hyderabad : No. 3-4-184, Lingampally, Besides Raghavendra Swamy Matham, Kachiguda,
Hyderabad - 500 027. Phone: 040-27560041, 27550139

Chennai : No. 34/44, Motilal Street, T. Nagar, Chennai - 600 017. Mobile: 09380460419

Pune : "Laksha" Apartment, First Floor, No. 527, Mehunpura,
Shaniwarpeth (Near Prabhat Theatre), Pune - 411 030.
Phone: 020-24496323, 24496333; Mobile: 09370579333

Cuttack : Plot No. 5F-755/4, Sector-9, CDA Markat Nagar, Cuttack - 753 014,
Odisha. Mobile: 09338746007

Kolkata : 3, S.M. Bose Road, Near Gate No. 5, Agarpara Railway Station,
North 24 Parganas, West Bengal - 700 109. Mobile: 09674536325

DTP by : HPH, Editorial Office, Bhandup (Piryanka M.)

Printed at : Geetanjali Press Pvt. Ltd., Nagpur. On behalf of HPH.

Dedicated to

My Parents

For their unselfish love

Lord Baba Gokuleswar

For his spirit and blessing

My Loving Wife

My inspiration and strength

and

My Dear Students

For their continuous encouragement

Dr. Priti Ranjan Majhi

Preface to the Second Revised Edition

In recent years, the role of research in various fields of management related to economics, commerce, business, industry, trade or the economy as a whole, has greatly increased. The complex nature of business and economy has shifted our attention on the use of research in solving the existing problems. One of the obstacles in the way of self-knowledge and desirable change is the separation between knowing and doing. The need of the hour is for greater interaction between societies, industries and organizations with universities or institutions.

As the world of business and economy are changing drastically and speedily, one cannot wait for changes at the institutional level. Keeping in mind all these aspects, the present book entitled **"Research Methodology"** aims at a lucid exposition of various fundamental concepts and techniques of research that would be useful, particularly to the Indian students and practitioners.

This book is aimed primarily at academic researchers, management and doctoral students, teachers and graduate students of mathematics, management science and various other science and social science disciplines, practicing managers and marketing research professionals. The objective is to make the reader understand how they can use various statistical techniques for their research problems. The book covers the theoretical and practical aspects of research methodology, text and cases and the use of SPSS in a clear and exhaustive manner. Every chapter in this book explains the principles through appropriate descriptive and analytical explanations, for scientific method of research.

We are deeply indebted to various authors and publishers whose books we have referred to.

We are grateful to our friends, colleagues for their valuable suggestions and students for their constant encouragements for revision and updated edition of the book.

At last our hearty thanks to **Mr. Neeraj Pandey** and **Mr. B.K. Ojha** of **Himalaya Publishing House Pvt. Ltd.**, Mumbai, for their wholehearted support and cooperation in bringing out this edition in an elegant form.

We welcome suggestions and constructive criticisms for further improvement of the book.

Dr. Priti Ranajan Majhi
drpritiranjan@gmail.com

Dr. Prafull Kumar Khatua

Preface to the First Edition

In recent years, the role of research in various fields of management related to economics, commerce, business, industry, trade or the economy as a whole has greatly increased. The complex nature of business and economy has shifted our attention on the use of research in solving the existing problems. One of the obstacles in the way of self-knowledge and desirable change is the separation between knowing and doing. The need of the hour is for greater interaction between societies, industries and organizations with universities or institutions. As the world of business and economy are changing drastically and speedily, one cannot wait for changes at the institutional level. Keeping in mind all these aspects, the present book entitled **"Research Methodology for Management"** aims at a lucid exposition of various fundamental concepts and techniques of research that would be useful, particularly to the Indian students and practitioners.

The book is aimed primarily at academic researchers, management and doctoral students, teachers and graduate students of mathematics, management science and various other science and social science disciplines, practicing managers and marketing research professionals. The objective is to make the reader understand how they can use various statistical techniques for their research problems. The book covers the theoretical, practical aspects of research methodology and the use of SPSS in a clear and exhaustive manner. Every chapter in this book explains the principles through appropriate descriptive and analytical explanations, for scientific method of research.

We are deeply indebted to various authors and publishers whose books have been referred to.

We are thankful to our parents and family members for their active support and encouragement during the preparation of manuscripts.

We are grateful to our friends, colleagues for their valuable suggestions and students for their constant encouragement.

At last our hearty thanks to Mr. Neeraj Pandey and Mr. B.K. Ojha of Himalaya Publishing House (Pvt.) Ltd., Mumbai, for their wholehearted support and cooperation in bringing out this edition in an elegant form.

We welcome suggestions and constructive criticisms for further improvement of the book.

Dr. Priti Ranajan Majhi
drpritiranjan@gmail.com

Dr. Prafull Kumar Khatua

Contents

Detailed Contents

CHAPTER 1

RESEARCH METHODOLOGY: AN INTRODUCTION

Chapter Outline

Learning Objectives

- *Explain the meaning of research in the context of making intelligent decisions.*
- *Discuss the need for research in decision making.*
- *Explain the actual process of research and its role in managerial decisions.*
- *Distinguish between the various types of research.*
- *Identify various topics for business research.*

1.1 MEANING OF RESEARCH

Research is defined as the creation of new knowledge and/or the use of existing knowledge in a new and creative way so as to generate new concepts, methodologies and understandings. This could include synthesis and analysis of previous research to the extent that it leads to new and creative outcomes.

Research is consistent with a broad notion of research and experimental development (R&D) as comprising of creative work undertaken on a systematic basis in order to increase the stock of knowledge, including knowledge of humanity, culture and society, and the use of this stock of knowledge to devise new applications.

Research is the systematic process of collecting and analyzing information to increase our understanding of the phenomenon under study. It is the function of the researcher to contribute to the understanding of the phenomenon and to communicate that understanding to others.

"Research comprises defining and redefining problems, formulating hypothesis or suggested solutions; collecting, organizing and evaluating data; making deductions and reaching conclusion; and at last carefully testing the conclusions to determine whether they fit the formulating hypothesis" — **Clifford Woody.**

"The manipulation of things, concepts or symbols for the purpose of generalizing to extend, correct or verify knowledge, whether that knowledge aids in construction of theory or in the practice of an art" — **D. Slesinger and M. Stephenson.**

There are many different ways to carry out research but roughly speaking there are two main approaches, namely qualitative and quantitative. Qualitative studies concentrate mainly on words and meanings and aim to capture the richness and complexity of human experience, whereas quantitative studies involve recording information obtained from participants in numerical form so as to enable statistical analysis of the findings and the generalization of those findings to the wider population. Behind these two main approaches, there are important theoretical differences and philosophical assumptions about the nature of knowledge, truth and reality, how this should be recorded, what kinds of methods should be used and the role of the researcher in this process.

Research is a thorough, orderly, organized, efficient and logical investigation of an area of knowledge or of a problem.

Curiosity: Science is knowledge of the physical or material world gained through observation and experiment. Research begins with a broad question that needs an answer. A review of similar research narrows the scope of the research to a manageable, realistic question.

Theory (Hypothesis): Research creates a theory (hypothesis) to be proved from the question; the researcher maintains an awareness of the limitations of budget, time and technology on experiments needed to answer the question.

Experiment: Researchers design an experiment with steps to test and evaluate the theory (hypothesis) and generate analyzable data. Experiments have controls and a large enough sample group to provide statistically valid results.

Observation: Observing and recording the results of the experiment generates raw data to prove or disprove the theory.

Analysis: Statistical analysis on the data and organizing it so that it is understandable generates answers to the initial question. Data may show trends that allow for the broadening of the research.

Conclusions: Research following the scientific method will either prove or disprove the theory (hypothesis). What happened and why needs to be explained by the researcher. Even when a theory (hypothesis) is disproved, valuable data collected in the research may lead to further research. The results are usually published and shared.

1.2 OBJECTIVES OF RESEARCH

The objectives of research can be broadly classified as under in scientific way:

1. To seek insight into an observed phenomenon and explain its logic and reasoning of happening.
2. To explore the possibility and methodology of doing things which have not been done so far.
3. To improve the effectiveness of present systems and procedures in any field continuously.
4. To explore into new areas that might have become relevant or even might become relevant in the near future.

5. To test a hypothesis of a casual relationship between variables.
6. To analyze the past data for discovering trends, patterns and relationships.

1.3 PURPOSES OF RESEARCH

Research in whatever field of inquiry has four purposes, i.e., describing, explaining and predicting phenomena and ultimately controlling events.

A. Describing and Explaining

This is the attempt to understand the world we live in. Research is concerned with acquiring knowledge, establishing facts and developing new methods. The way this understanding is shown is through the theories developed and their efficacy at explaining the world in which we live.

B. Prediction

In research, predictions are usually stated as hypotheses, i.e., clear unambiguous statements which can be subjected to scientific verification or refutation. When the hypotheses are accepted or rejected, we are able to make generalizations or theories concerning various situations. We are able to say that given these conditions then this is likely to happen.

C. Control

This follows from our knowledge and the successful verification of hypotheses. Control represents the way in which research can be applied to real problems and situations, thus helping us to shape our environment. When we understand the relationship between variables, we are able to control our environment to suit our interests. This can be exemplified by research to find effective ways to deal with indiscipline in schools. Once identified, the effective strategies can be employed to reduce the incidence of indiscipline in schools and thus improve achievement. People do research for different reasons. In doing a particular research, a researcher may be motivated by one or more of the following among other reasons:

1. To fulfill an academic requirement for example as partial fulfillment for the award of a doctorate degree.
2. In an effort to solve practical problems of the society; for example to find a teaching approach that yields best performance in a given subject among students.
3. For enjoyment; some people enjoy the intellectual challenge of creative work.
4. Delegation by some authority; a researcher may be called upon to study a specified phenomenon by some higher authority. For example, the minister of education can commission a group to carry out research to find out why and how examination irregularities occur and what can be done to reduce their incidence.
5. To generate new theories, confirm existing ones or disapprove them.
6. To be informed; to contribute to the existing body of knowledge. This is mainly triggered by curiosity about a subject.

The increasingly complex nature of our society has focused attention on the use of research in solving operational problems. Research as an aid to policy and planning has gained importance, both in government and business. Research provides the basis for nearly all government policies in our economic system. In this context, research becomes a tool for policy decision making.

1.4 TYPES OF RESEARCH

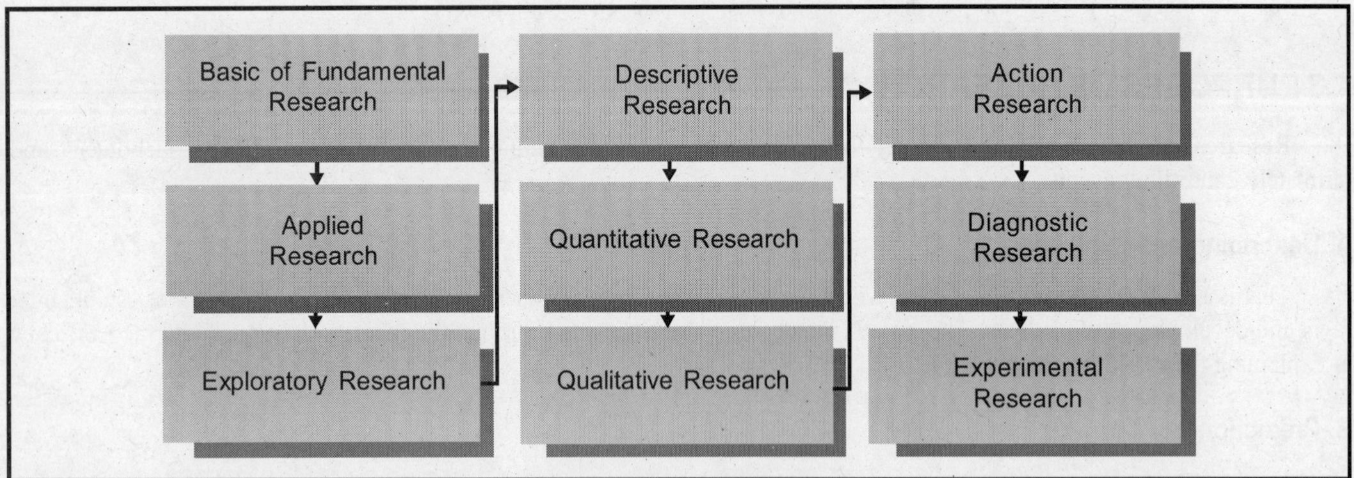

Fig. 1.1: Types of Research

1.4.1 Basic or Fundamental Research

Basic research is also called **fundamental** or **pure research,** and is conducted primarily to improve our understanding of general issues, without any emphasis on its immediate application. It is regarded as the most academic form of research since the principal aim is to make a contribution to knowledge, usually for the general good, rather than to solve a specific problem for one organization. This may take the form of the following:

- **Discovery:** where a totally new idea or explanation emerges from empirical research which may revolutionize thinking on that particular topic. An example of this would be the Hawthorne experiments (Gillespie, 1991).
- **Invention:** where a new technique or method is created. An example of this would be the invention of TQM (total quality management).
- **Reflection:** where an existing theory, technique or group of ideas is re-examined possibly in a different organizational or social context. For example, to what extent can Herzberg's theory of motivation be applied to front-line workers in the contract catering sector?

For an undergraduate dissertation, it is most likely that you will be concentrating on reflection, as the scope of the project is unlikely to be large enough to consider discovery or invention.

1.4.2 Applied Research

Applied research is a form of systematic inquiry involving the practical application of science. It accesses and uses some part of the research communities' (the academy's) accumulated theories, knowledge, methods, and techniques, for a specific, often state, business, or client driven purpose. Applied research is compared to pure research (basic research) in discussion about research ideals, methodologies, programs, and projects. Applied research deals with solving practical problems and generally employs empirical methodologies. Because applied research resides in the messy real world, strict research protocols may need to be relaxed. For example, it may be impossible to use a random sample. Thus, transparency in the methodology is crucial. Implications for interpretation of results brought about by relaxing an otherwise strict canon of methodology should also be considered.

Applied research is problem-oriented as the research is carried out to solve a specific problem that requires a decision, for example, the improvement of safety in the workplace, or market research. For your dissertation it is not usually acceptable to carry out applied research as it is very much limited to one establishment or company and you are required to look at issues of wider significance, perhaps to your industry as a whole or to a sector of it. You may have already carried out a problem-based piece of research related to your placement. It is important to understand that the dissertation requires you to carry out some form of basic research.

Applied research is designed to solve practical problems of the modern world, rather than to acquire knowledge for knowledge's sake. One might say that the goal of the applied scientist is to improve the human condition.

For example, applied researchers may investigate ways to:

- improve agricultural crop production
- treat or cure a specific disease
- improve the energy efficiency of homes, offices, or modes of transportation

Some scientists feel that the time has come for a shift in emphasis away from purely basic research and toward applied science. This trend, they feel, is necessitated by the problems resulting from global overpopulation, pollution, and the overuse of the earth's natural resources.

1.4.3 Exploratory Research

Exploratory research is conducted to clarify ambiguous problems. Management may have discovered general problems, but research is needed to gain better understanding of the dimensions of the problems. Exploratory studies provide information to use in analyzing a situation, but uncovering conclusive evidence to determine a particular course of action is not the purpose of exploratory research. Usually, exploratory research is conducted with the expectation that subsequent research will be required to provide conclusive evidence. It is a serious mistake to rush into detailed surveys before less expensive and more readily available sources of information have been exhausted.

In an organization considering a program to help employees with childcare needs, for example, exploratory research with a small number of employees who have children might determine that many of them have spouses who also work and that these employees have positive reactions to the possibility of an on-site childcare program. In such a case, exploratory research helps to crystallize a problem and identify information needs for future research.

1. Literature Search

This refers to "referring to a literature to develop a new hypothesis". The literature referred are – trade journals, professional journals, market research finding publications, statistical publications etc. Example: Suppose a problem is "Why are sales down?" This can quickly be analyzed with the help of published data which should indicate "whether the problem is an "industry problem" or a "firm problem". Three possibilities exist to formulate the hypothesis.

- The company's market share has declined but industry's figures are normal.
- The industry is declining and hence the company's market share is also declining.
- The industry's share is going up but the company's share is declining.

If we accept the situation that our company's sales are down despite the market showing an upward trend, then we need to analyze the marketing mix variables.

Example 1: A TV manufacturing company feels that its market share is declining whereas the overall television industry is doing very well.

Example 2: Due to a trade embargo imposed by a country, textiles exports are down and hence sales of a company making garment for exports is on the decline.

2. Experience Survey

In experience surveys, it is desirable to talk to persons who are well informed in the area being investigated. These people may be company executives or persons outside the organization. Here, no questionnaire is required. The approach adopted in an experience survey should be highly unstructured, so that the respondent can give divergent views. Since the idea of using experience survey is to undertake problem formulation, and not conclusion, probability sample need not be used. Those who cannot speak freely should be excluded from the sample.

Examples:

(i) A group of housewives may be approached for their choice for a "ready-to-cook product".

(ii) A publisher might want to find out the reason for poor circulation of newspaper introduced recently. He might meet: (a) Newspaper sellers, (b) Public reading room, (c) General public, (d) Business community; etc. These are experienced persons whose knowledge researcher can use.

3. Focus Group

Another widely used technique in exploratory research is the focus group. In a focus group, a small number of individuals are brought together to study and talk about some topic of interest. The discussion is co-ordinated by a moderator. The group usually is of 8-12 persons. While selecting these persons, care has to be taken to see that they should have a common background and have similar experiences in buying. This is required because there should not be a conflict among the group members on the common issues that are being discussed. During the discussion, future buying attitudes, present buying opinion etc., are gathered.

Most of the companies conducting the focus groups, first screen the candidates to determine who will compose the particular group. Firms also take care to avoid groups, in which some of the participants have their friends and relatives, because this leads to a biased discussion. Normally, a number of such groups are constituted and the final conclusions of various groups are taken for formulating the hypothesis. Therefore, a key factor in focus group is to have similar groups. Normally, there are 4-5 groups. Some of them may even have 6-8 groups. The guiding criteria are to see whether the latter groups are generating additional ideas or repeating the same with respect to the subject under study. When this shows a diminishing return from the group, the discussions stopped. The typical focus group lasts for 1-30 hours to 2 hours. The moderator under the focus group has a key role. His job is to guide the group to proceed in the right direction.

4. Analysis of Selected Cases

Analyzing a selected case sometimes gives an insight into the problem which is being researched. Case histories of companies which have undergone a similar situation may be available. These case studies are well suited to carry out exploratory research. However, the result of investigation of case histories are always considered suggestive, rather than conclusive. In case of preference to "ready-to- eat food", many case histories may be available in the form of previous studies made by competitors. We must carefully examine the already published case studies with regard to other variables such as price, advertisement, changes in the taste, etc.

1.4.4 Descriptive Research

Descriptive research is used to obtain information concerning the current status of the phenomena to describe "what exists" with respect to variables or conditions in a situation. The methods involved range from the survey which describes the status quo, the correlation study which investigates the relationship between variables, to developmental studies which seek to determine changes over time.

1. Case Studies

Detailed analysis of a single (or limited number) of people or events. Case studies are usually interesting because of the unusualness of the case. The major problem with case studies is the problem of objectivity. The person who is presenting the case usually has some theoretical orientation. It is acceptable for a theoretical orientation to affect one's interpretation of events. In a case study, the theoretical orientation can also lead to the selection of the facts to include in the case. It is not surprising that case studies often seem to provide very compelling evidence for a theory.

Case studies can therefore assist psychology by illustrating how a theory could be applied to a person or events and by assisting with the development of hypotheses for more systematic testing.

2. Observational Research

Accounts of the natural behavior of individuals or groups in some setting. Unless the observation is unobtrusive, there may be some subject reactivity to being observed. This often decreases with time, a process called habituation. Observers cannot usually observe all behaviors all of the time. They may use a behavioral checklist and may also use time sampling or event sampling procedures. It is important to assess observer bias by the use of inter-observer reliability. Observational research may also pose ethical problems. These can arise when the behaviors being observed are not public behaviors and when the observer joins a group in order to observe the members' behavior-participant's observation.

3. Survey Research

Structured questions to assess people's beliefs, attitudes, and self-reports of behavior. If the researcher wishes to generalize the responses to a population, it is important to have a representative sample. Surveys that rely on self-selection (respond if you are interested) produce non-generalizable results. Surveys also provide information for correlational research. One can correlate responses to some questions (often demographic questions) with responses to other questions (often attitudes or reports of behavior). Survey question must be clear and unambiguous. Even if the questions are unambiguous and non-leading, people may display a social desirability bias and give positive or socially acceptable and desirable answers. Survey methods include: (1) the interview or face-to-face method which is generally viewed as the best method for obtaining a high rate of responses but is also very costly; (2) phone surveys, which are less expensive but have a higher non-response rate (which has probably increased with caller ID); and (3) written or mail surveys, which are least expensive but have a very high non-response rate. Follow-up messages can help increase the response rate.

4. Archival Research

Analysis of pre-existing data or records. Archival research often involves content analysis, a qualitative analysis of material. For example, one would use content analysis to determine whether there had been an increase in the frequency with which women and minorities were mentioned in US history books between 1920 and 2000. Some archival research is quasi-experimental.

1.4.5 Quantitative Research

Quantitative research involves a collection of numerical data to answer a specific research question. Taking this definition one step further, Christiansen goes on to note that quantitative research is a descriptive type of research where the goal is to attempt to provide an accurate description or picture of a particular situation or phenomenon. Rather than utilizing the cause and effect relationships that are common to quantitative methodologies, qualitative investigations attempt to identify variables that exist in a given situation and, at times, to describe the relationship that exists between these variables. To accomplish this task, statistical data is typically utilized.

With a basic understanding of quantitative research clearly elucidated, it is now possible to consider the specific methodologies that are utilized in this context. Through a careful consideration of the various methods that utilize quantitative research, it will be possible to demonstrate not only the differences between quantitative and qualitative research but also the importance of this type of research to scholarly investigation. Although statistical data is a linchpin of qualitative research methods, it is evident that there are a myriad of ways in which to acquire data.

1. Correlational Study

Defining the basic context of the correlational study, you may observe that this method involves measuring two specific variables and attempting to quantify the relationship that exists between these variables. Correlational studies are important because they demonstrate the specific relationships that exist between two variables. If A can be correlated with B, other variables correlated with B may also have relationships to A. Thus, by delineating the specific relationships that exist between two variables, researchers can make a number of predictions about the impact of other variables in the same or similar situation.

What is perhaps interesting about the correlational study is that it provides a mechanism for ensuring internal validity. Fraenkel and Wallen go on to argue that a correlational study poses no possibility of manipulating implementers. As such, the results obtained in this context can be stringently verified with regard to statistical analysis. For this reason, the correlational study provides one of the most salient means for the quantification of data in a given experiment. The ability to statistically quantify results serves as the basis for promoting the integrity of data collected through this process.

2. Ex-post Facto Study

The ex-post facto study is unique because it requires the investigator to determine the specific variables for analysis after the research has been completed. The ex-post facto study utilizes a sample population that is similar to that of the general population. In this context, a similar variable is identified that links the subject population together. Subjects are broken into various groups and exposed to the same experimental conditions. Observations are made by the researcher to discern if there are differences in behavior based upon the notable differences among individuals in the population. Through this process, the researcher is able to investigate subjects in a naturalistic environment and to draw conclusions about what specific variables will influence behavior and outcomes.

3. Longitudinal Study

A longitudinal studies makes the following observations, longitudinal studies investigate developmental changes that take place at the time. The longitudinal study involves choosing a single group of participants and measuring them repeatedly at selected time intervals to note the changes that occur over time in the specified characteristics. The longitudinal study provides a salient means for collecting data with respect to the age and development of the subject. In particular, longitudinal studies often involve children, as researchers seek to discern how specific variables change through the course of growth and development. In this context, the longitudinal approach can provide marked insight into the process of change.

4. Meta-analysis

Meta-analysis can be used to synthesize the large volume of data describing numerous independent variables and their correlations with reference accuracy. Meta-analysis enables researchers to utilize information from past studies to better understand the specific variables that impact a subject. Typically, meta-analyses are undertaken for the purpose of synthesizing extensive amounts of work on a particular subject. Utilizing the data that has been collected in previous investigations, researchers can synthesize information to better understand the subject and to develop new research methodologies that specifically target the gaps in information that are identified through the process of meta-analysis.

5. Survey

The survey is defined as a method of collecting standardized information by interviewing a representative sample of some population. Although the survey is one of the most popular methods for quantitative investigation, over the course of the last several years, the integrity of this method has been questioned. In most cases, surveys involve direct contact with the population under investigation. Although well-established survey methods can be utilized for investigation, in many cases researchers seeking to understand a new facet of a particular population will develop a survey whose validity and reliability have not been proven. Even though specific methods for the development of surveys have been presented in the literature, utilizing a survey that has not been validated can serve as the basis for corrupting the integrity of data collection.

1.4.6 Qualitative Research

The alternative tradition is the qualitative approach. Here the investigator views the phenomena to be investigated as more personal and softer. He or she will use methods such as personal accounts, unstructured interviews and participant observation to gain an understanding of the underlying reasons and motivations for peoples' attitudes, preferences or behaviors. With this approach, the emphasis is more on generating hypotheses from the data collection rather than testing a hypothesis.

In reading around the subject, you will find many alternative names for qualitative and quantitative research. It is good to have an understanding of these and to recognize them when you see them in research method textbooks.

Qualitative research is a type of scientific research. In general terms, scientific research consists of an investigation that:

1. Seeks answers to a question.
2. Systematically uses a predefined set of procedures to answer the question.
3. Collects evidence.
4. Produces findings that were not determined in advance.
5. Produces findings that are applicable beyond the immediate boundaries of the study.

Qualitative research shares these characteristics. Additionally, it seeks to understand a given research problem or topic from the perspectives of the local population it involves. Qualitative research is especially effective in obtaining culturally specific information about the values, opinions, behaviors, and social contexts of particular populations.

The three most common qualitative methods, explained in detail in their respective modules, are participant observation, in-depth interviews, and focus groups. Each method is particularly suited for obtaining a specific type of data.

1. **Participant observation** is appropriate for collecting data on naturally occurring behaviors in their usual contexts.
2. **In-depth interviews** are optimal for collecting data on individuals' personal histories, perspectives, and experiences, particularly when sensitive topics are being explored.
3. **Focus groups** are effective in eliciting data on the cultural norms of a group and in generating broad overviews of issues of concern to the cultural groups or subgroups represented.

Quantitative and qualitative research methods differ primarily in:

1. Their analytical objectives.
2. The types of questions they pose.
3. The types of data collection instruments they use.
4. The forms of data they produce.
5. The degree of flexibility built into study design.
6. Qualitative and quantitative research methods are not clear-cut nor mutually exclusive – most research draws on both methods.
7. Both approaches can generate quantitative and qualitative data.
8. The difference between the two methods is in the overall form and in the emphasis and objectives of the study.

Table 1.1: Basic Differences between Quantitative and Qualitative Research Methods

	Qualitative approach	Quantitative approach
Usage	Find out what to investigate. When research ideas are needed. Emphasis on understanding. Focus on understanding from respondents' point of view.	Know what to investigate. When research results are needed. Emphasis on testing and verification. Focus on facts and/or reasons.
Approach	Flexible and informal. Do not need to know in advance specific topics or questions – these should 'emerge'. Small sample size.	Structured and formal. Must know in advance what questions to ask/areas to cover – they are 'imposed'. Large sample size.
Techniques	Unstructured interviews. Document analysis. Particular observation (called ethnographic studies). Diaries. Case studies.	Surveys — [Structured interviews and Questionnaires]. Non-participant observation. Experiments. Tests.
Responses	Explanatory and give depth. Verbal. Not easily processed.	Not explanatory and lack depth. Mainly numerical. More easily processed, for example, coding.
Outcome	Hypotheses and ideas. Not firm. Danger of subjective interpretation.	Results. Can be quantified. Interpretation more objective.

1.4.7 Action Research

This is a form of research where action is both an outcome and a part of the research. The researcher 'interferes' with or changes – deliberately – what is being researched. The critics of action research argue that since the researcher is changing what is being researched during the process of research, the work cannot be replicated. If it cannot be replicated, its findings cannot be tested in other situations. This prevents general knowledge being developed and thus it cannot contribute to theory. Also, as the researcher is involved in the change process there is a loss of critical, detached objectivity. There are two approaches to action research:

1. **Classical action research** begins with the idea that if you want to understand something you should try changing it.
2. **New paradigm research** is based on a new model or framework for research. It claims that research can never be neutral and that even the most static and conventional research exposes the need for change in what is being researched. It involves inquiry into persons and relations between persons, and is based on a close relationship between researcher and those being researched. The research is a mutual activity of a 'co-ownership' involving shared power with respect to the process and the outcomes of the research. Those being researched can, for example, decide how the research will be undertaken, in what form and with what questions being asked. The researcher is a member of a 'community' and brings to it special skills and expertise. The researcher does not dictate what will happen. This type of research is most easily carried out when working with individuals or small groups. It means that the researcher must be highly skilled not only in research methods but also in the interpersonal skills of facilitating others. It is not, therefore, usually appropriate for an undergraduate student who is carrying out a major piece of research for the first time. Action research is often used by educationalists who are trying to improve their own practice by making changes to the delivery of their classes and by observing and asking students which actions work best.

As you can see, there are a number of types of research and not all may be suitable for you in your dissertation. The key points to remember are as follows:

(a) While the purpose of your dissertation may have some elements of exploratory or descriptive research, you should concentrate on research that will mainly fall into the explanatory area, or perhaps predictive research if you are very confident. Explanatory research gives you the opportunity to demonstrate the skills of analysis and evaluation which will help you to score highly in your final marks.

(b) The process of your research can either be quantitative or qualitative and the different methods that can help you to carry out your research in this way are outlined more fully in Unit 3.

(c) It is likely that you will be carrying out basic or pure research in the reflection mode (rather than applied or action research) as this will give you the best chance of showing that you can test out a theory in a new situation.

1.4.8 Diagnostic Research

Diagnostic research study is similar to descriptive research study but with a different focus. It is directed towards discovering what is happening, why is it happening and what can be done about. It aims at identifying the causes of a problem and the possible solutions for it. A diagnostic research study may also be concerned with discovering and testing whether certain variables are associated. The basic focuses of the diagnostic research study are:

1. Formulating the objective of the study.
2. Designing the methods of data collection.
3. Selecting the sample.
4. Collecting the data.
5. Processing and analyzing the data.
6. Reporting the findings.

1.4.9 Experimental Research

Science revolves around experiments, and learning the best way of conducting an experiment is crucial to obtaining useful and valid results. When scientists speak of experiments, in the strictest sense of the word, they mean a true experiment, where the scientist controls all of the factors and conditions. Real world observations, and case studies, should be referred to as observational research, rather than experiments. For example, observing animals in the wild is not a true experiment, because it does not isolate and manipulate an independent variable.

The Basic of Conducting an Experiment

With an experiment, the researcher is trying to learn something new about the world, an explanation of 'why' something happens. The experiment must maintain internal and external validity, or the results will be useless. When designing an experiment, a researcher must follow all of the steps of the scientific method, from making sure that the hypothesis is valid and testable, to using controls and statistical tests.

Whilst all scientists use reasoning, operationalization and the steps of the scientific process, it is not always a conscious process. Experience and practice mean that many scientists follow an instinctive process of conducting an experiment, the 'streamlined' scientific process. Following the basic steps will usually generate valid results, but where experiments are complex and expensive, it is always advisable to follow the rigorous scientific protocols.

Conducting a experiment has a number of stages, where the parameters and structure of the experiment are made clear. Whilst it is rarely practical to follow each step strictly, any aberrations must be justified, whether they arise because of budget, impracticality or ethics.

Stage-1

After deciding upon a hypothesis, and making predictions, the first stage of conducting an experiment is to specify the sample groups. These should be large enough to give a statistically viable study, but small enough to be practical. Ideally, groups should be selected at random, from a wide selection of the sample population. This allows results to be generalized to the population as a whole. In the physical sciences, this is fairly easy, but the biological and behavioral sciences are often limited by other factors.

For example, medical trials often cannot find random groups. Such research often relies upon volunteers, so it is difficult to apply any realistic randomization. This is not a problem, as long as the process is justified, and the results are not applied to the population as a whole. If a psychological researcher used volunteers who were male students, aged between 18 and 24, the findings can only be generalized to that specific demographic group within society.

Stage-2

The sample groups should be divided, into a control group and a test group, to reduce the possibility of confounding variables. This, again, should be random, and the assigning of subjects to groups should be blind or double blind. This will reduce the chances of experimental error, or bias, when conducting an experiment.

Ethics are often a barrier to this process, because deliberately withholding treatment is not permitted. Again, any deviations from this process must be explained in the conclusion. There is nothing wrong with compromising upon randomness, where necessary, as long as other scientists are aware of how, and why, the researcher selected groups on that basis.

Stage-3

This stage of conducting an experiment involves determining the time scale and frequency of sampling, to fit the type of experiment. For example, researchers studying the effectiveness of a cure for colds would take frequent samples, over a period of days. Researchers testing a cure for Parkinson's disease would use less frequent tests, over a period of months or years.

Stage-4

The penultimate stage of the experiment involves performing the experiment according to the methods stipulated during the design phase. The independent variable is manipulated, generating a usable data set for the dependent variable.

Stage-5

The raw data from the results should be gathered, and analyzed, by statistical means. This allows the researcher to establish if there is any relationship between the variables and accept, or reject, the null hypothesis. These steps are essential to providing excellent results. Whilst many researchers do not want to become involved in the exact processes of inductive reasoning, deductive reasoning and operationalization, they all follow the basic steps of conducting an experiment. This ensures that their results are valid.

Table 1.2: Other Types of Research

Descriptive vs. Analytical	1. Descriptive research includes surveys and fact-finding enquiries of different kinds. The major purpose of descriptive research is description of the state of affairs as it exists at present. 2. In social science and business research, we quite often use the term ex-post facto research for descriptive research studies. 3. The main characteristic of this method is that the researcher has no control over the variables. 4. In analytical research, the researcher has to use facts or information already available, and analyze these to make a critical evaluation of the material.
Applied vs. Fundamental	1. Applied research aims at finding a solution for an immediate problem facing a society or an industrial/business organization, whereas fundamental research is mainly concerned with generalizations and with the formulation of a theory. 2. Research concerning some natural phenomenon or relating to pure mathematics are examples of fundamental research. 3. Research aimed at certain conclusions facing a concrete social or business problem is an example of applied research. 4. The central aim of applied research is to discover a solution for some pressing practical problems whereas basic research is directed towards finding information that has a broad base of applications.
Quantitative vs. Qualitative	1. Quantitative research is based on the measurement of quantity or amount. It is applicable to phenomena that can be expressed in terms of quantity. 2. Qualitative research is concerned with qualitative phenomenon, i.e., phenomena relating to or involving quality or kind. 'Motivation Research', an important type of qualitative research. 3. Qualitative research aims at discovering the underlying motives and desires, using in-depth interviews for the purpose. 4. Qualitative research is especially important in the behavioral sciences where the aim is to discover the underlying motives of human behavior.
Conceptual vs. Empirical	1. Conceptual research is that related to some abstract idea(s) or theory. It is generally used by philosophers and thinkers to develop new concepts or to reinterpret existing ones. 2. Empirical research relies an experience or observation alone, often without due regard for system and theory. It is data-based research, coming up with conclusions which are capable of being verified by observation or experiment. 3. Empirical research is necessary to get at facts firsthand, at their source, and actively to go about doing certain things to stimulate the production of desired information. 4. Empirical research is appropriate when proof is sought that certain variables affect other variables in some way. 5. Evidence gathered through experiments or empirical studies is today considered to be the most powerful support possible for a given hypothesis.

1.5 SIGNIFICANCE OF RESEARCH

Research is essential in all businesses, whether small or big. Based on research, management can make intelligent and informed decisions. Companies need to research which products to make, how to make them, the quantities thereof, how to market them, entice customers, motivate employees and run more effective systems. In the research mechanism, the analyst collects data, organizes and tabulates it, then presents it to top management in the form of text and charts.

A. Function: Research is necessary for managerial decision making. All strategic business areas are scrutinized and evaluated; then tactics for more efficient operations are developed. Every business often has several means of performing a task. Through research, the organization is able to choose the most efficient, productive and profitable one. Research could be applied to marketing, production, finance, IT and HR. Through research, the organization is able to gauge initially whether getting into a new line of trade would be a profitable venture. Ongoing research is essential to improve and improvize the product as per customer specifications. The company must also research ways and means to keep its employees happy and motivated.

B. Features: The research mechanism enables the organization to better understand and comprehend the market, its customers and competitors. The organization knows exactly what their customers need and desire, and takes the appropriate steps to deliver that to them. Also, the company can classify customers on the basis of demographics, such as gender, age, income and level of education. Once the company determine its customers' primary demographic group, it takes steps to service them better. Through research, competitors' moves and strategies are highlighted, and the company can then be proactive to preempt them.

C. Types: There are two types of research. The first type, primary research, is when the individuals who are the company's present or potential customers are asked to define their specifications on the kind of product they desire. The interviewer usually has a preset format or questionnaire when he goes to respondents to ask for feedback. This type of research is primarily conducted to gauge the customers' perceptions on a specific product. Secondary research uses an analyst to compile previously published data. This study is useful in understanding the broad market and industry situation.

D. Benefits: There are many benefits of conducting research. The company can understand what its customers actually want and can deliver that product to them. When the company is planning to diversify its product range, it will know at the very outset, through the research mechanism, whether or not there is a demand for such a product. When the company knows about what feature in the product attracts customers and what repels them, the company is able to take the appropriate steps. The company then accentuates its strengths more aggressively while allaying its weaknesses.

E. Considerations: Companies must apportion a chunk of their yearly budgets for research and development purposes. Also, many companies entrust the work of carrying out research to market research companies.

These companies may not be fully aware of the work ethos and ethics prevailing in the organization; hence there is always the possibility that they may not research that pertinent aspect of the company desired. Therefore, the research company must be made fully aware of the parameters of the research.

1.6 CHARACTERISTICS OF RESEARCH

The following definitions reveal the various characteristics of research:

1. Research is a systematic and critical investigation into a phenomenon.
2. It is not a mere compilation, but a purposive investigation; it aims at describing, interpreting and explaining a phenomenon.
3. It adopts scientific method.
4. It is objective and logical, applying possible tests to validate the measuring tools and the conclusions reached.
5. It is based upon observable experience or empirical evidence.
6. Research is directed towards finding answers to pertinent questions and solutions to problems.
7. It emphasizes the development of generalization, principles or theories.
8. The purpose of research is not to arrive at an answer, which is personally pleasing to the researcher, but rather one that will stand up the test of criticism.

(a) Systematic Approach: Each step of your investigation must be so planned that it leads to the next step. Planning and organization are part of this approach. A planned and organized research saves your time and money.

(b) Objectivity: It implies that true research should attempt to find an unbiased answer to the decision making problem.

(c) Reproducible: A reproducible research procedure is one, which an equally competent researcher could duplicate, and from it deduces approximately the same results. Precise information regarding samples-methods, collection etc., should be specified.

(d) Relevancy: It furnishes three important tasks:

(i) It avoids collection of irrelevant information and saves time and money.

(ii) It compares the information to be collected with researcher's criteria for action.

(iii) It enables to see whether the research is proceeding in the right direction.

(e) Control: Research is not only affected by the factors, which one is investigating but some other extraneous factors also. It is impossible to control all the factors. All the factors that we think may affect the study have to be controlled and accounted for.

1.7 CRITERIA OF GOOD RESEARCH

1. The research should be clearly defined – both conceptually as well as practically.
2. The research should be translated into clearly defined problem amenable to be resolved through a research study.
3. The research should have systematic characteristic inclusive of creative thinking.
4. The research should be logical reasoning and the logical process of induction and deduction. Logical reasoning makes research more meaningful in the context of decision making.
5. The research should be empirical that research is related basically to one or more aspects of a real situation and deals with concrete data to research results.
6. The research should be replicable that is the characteristic allows research to be verified by replicating the study.
7. To ensure comprehensiveness of the study, the research process should be detailed one.
8. The research design should be selected based on sound logic and realistic assumption.
9. The research procedure should be described in sufficient detail to permit another researcher.
10. The sources of secondary data should be indicated to establish credibility.
11. The data should be valid and reliable for research study.
12. The analysis of data should be sufficiently adequate and the methods of analysis should be appropriate for decision making.
13. Statistical terminology should be explained so as to appropriate the level of confidence and reliability by the decision maker.
14. All the assumptions for the study should be expressively mentioned.
15. The findings and conclusions should be confined and justified without adding extraneous views.

1.8 RESEARCH ETHICS

1. **Verifiability** – Research projects must fully document the methods, original motivations, and hypotheses. Research in progress must be clearly labeled as such.
2. **Honesty** – Research results are always honestly reported and without omissions, even if the results are undesirable, don't fit predetermined beliefs, or proposed hypotheses. Don't lead participants into drawing specific conclusions.
3. **Transparency** – Research reports must clearly explain everything done in the course of the research in an open and transparent manner so that other participants can draw their own independent conclusions.
4. **Objectivity** – Strive to conduct and report research in a way that allows experts to independently test, verify and confirm the validity of the research.
5. **Subjectivity** – You are free to express your views and opinions, but they should be clearly identified as such.

6. **Sources** – When sources of previous knowledge, data or other information are relied on cite your sources. This allows examination of those works too. Be clear to distinguish previous knowledge from new knowledge.
7. **Safety** – Research must be conducted in a safe and lawful manner. Do no harm.
8. **Consensual** – Inform and ask for consent before involving others in your research. People, groups, and organizations must be willing participants of your research.
9. **Disclosures** – Declare any biases or potential conflicts of interests that you are aware of at the start of research projects.
10. **Review process** – The peer review process contributes to quality control and is an essential step to ascertain the standing and originality of a research project.

1.9 MARKETING RESEARCH

According to **American Marketing Association,** "Marketing Research is the function that links the consumer, customer and public to the marketer through information — information used to identify and define marketing opportunities and problems, generate, refine and evaluate marketing actions; monitor marketing performance; and improve understanding of marketing as a process."

Marketing Research is systematic problem analysis, model building and fact finding for the purpose of important decision making and control in the marketing of goods and services.

Marketing Research is a well-planned, systematic process which implies that it needs planning at all the stages. It uses scientific method. It is an objective process as it attempts to provide accurate authentic information. Marketing Research is sometimes defined as the application of scientific method in the solution of marketing problems. Marketing Research plays a very significant role in identifying the needs of customers and meeting them in best possible way. The main task of Marketing Research is systematic gathering and analysis of information.

Before we proceed further, it is essential to clarify the relationship and difference between Marketing Research and Marketing Information System (MIS). Whatever information are generated by Marketing Research from internal sources, external sources, marketing intelligence agencies — consist the part of MIS.

MIS is a set of formalized procedures for generating, analyzing, storing and distributing information to marketing decision makers on an ongoing basis.

1. While Marketing Research is done with a specific purpose in mind with information being generated when it is conducted, MIS information is generated continuously.
2. MIS is continuous entity while Marketing Research is an ad-hoc system.
3. While in Marketing Research information is for specific purpose, so it is not rigid; in MIS information is more rigid and structured.

Marketing Research is essential for strategic market planning and decision making. It helps a firm in identifying what are the market opportunities and constraints, in developing and implementing market strategies, and in evaluating the effectiveness of marketing plans.

Marketing Research is a growing and widely used business activity as the sellers need to know more about their final consumers but are generally widely separated from those consumers. Marketing Research is a necessary link between marketing decision makers and the markets in which they operate.

Marketing Research includes various important principles for generating information which is useful to managers. These principles relate to the timeliness and importance of data, the significance of defining objectives cautiously and clearly, and the need to avoid conducting research to support decisions already made.

Marketing Research is of use to the following:

1. Producers

(a) To know about his product potential in the market *vis-à-vis* the total product;

(b) New products;

(c) Various brands;

(d) Pricing;

(e) Market structures and selection of product strategy, etc.

2. Business and Government

Marketing Research helps business and government in focusing attention on the complex nature of problems faced by them. For example:

(a) Determination of Gross National Product; Price indices, and per capita income;

(b) Expenditure levels and budgeting;

(c) Agricultural Pricing;

(d) The economic policies of Government; and

(e) Operational and planning problems of business and industry.

3. Market Research Agencies

Marketing Research is being used extensively by professionals to help conducting various studies in Marketing Research. Most prominent agencies being:

(a) Lintas India Ltd.;

(b) British Market Research Bureau (BMRB);

(c) Hindustan Thompson Associate Ltd.;

(d) eSurveysPro.com;

(e) MARG

1.10 LIMITATIONS OF MARKETING RESEARCH

Following are the main limitations of Marketing Research:

1. Marketing Research is not an exact science though it uses the techniques of science. Thus, the results and conclusions drawn upon by using Marketing Research are not very accurate.
2. The results of Marketing Research are very vague as Marketing Research is carried out on consumers, suppliers, intermediaries, etc. who are humans. Humans have a tendency to behave artificially when they know that they are being observed. Thus, the consumers and respondents upon whom the research is carried behave artificially when they are aware that their attitudes, beliefs, views, etc. are being observed.
3. Marketing Research is not a complete solution to any marketing issue as there are many dominant variables between research conclusions and market response.
4. Marketing Research is not free from bias. The research conclusions cannot be verified. The reproduction of the same project on the same class of respondents give different research results.
5. Inappropriate training to researchers can lead to misapprehension of questions to be asked for data collection.
6. Many business executives and researchers have ambiguity about the research problem and its objectives. They have limited experience of the notion of the decision-making process. This leads to carelessness in research and researchers are not able to do anything real.
7. There is less interaction between the Marketing Research department and the main research executives. The research department is in segregation. This all makes research ineffective.
8. Marketing Research faces time constraint. The firms are required to maintain a balance between the requirement for having a broader perspective of customer needs and the need for quick decision making so as to have competitive advantage.

9. Huge cost is involved in Marketing Research as collection and processing of data can be costly. Many firms do not have the proficiency to carry wide surveys for collecting primary data, and might not also able to hire specialized market experts and research agencies to collect primary data. Thus, in that case, they go for obtaining secondary data that is cheaper to obtain.
10. Marketing Research is conducted in open marketplace where numerous variables act on research settings.

1.11 BUSINESS RESEARCH

Business Research is a systematic and objective process of gathering, recording and analyzing data for aid in making business decisions. In general, business research refers to any type of researching done when starting or running any kind of business. For example, starting any type of business requires research into the target customer and the competition to create a business plan.

In general, business research refers to any type of researching done when starting or running any kind of business. For example, starting any type of business requires research into the target customers and the competition to create a business plan. Conducting business market research in existing businesses is helpful in keeping in touch with consumer demand. Small business research begins with researching an idea and a name and continues with research begins on customer demand and other business offering similar products or services. All business research is done to learn information that could make the company more successful.

Business research is an important management activity that helps companies to determine which products will be most profitable for companies to produce. Several steps are necessary when conducting business research; each step must be thoroughly reviewed to ensure that the best decision is made for the company.

A. Product Analysis: Product analysis is the first step of business research. Companies must find a product that meets or exceeds consumer demand, or the product will fail in the economic marketplace. One type of analysis is to find an existing product that can be improved through design or features. Another type of product analysis will find emerging markets with high demand and low supply, which allows for companies to sell new products to meet consumer demand.

B. Market Analysis: Companies will conduct a market analysis to determine how much profit may be earned from current demand. Management will look at which stage of the business cycle the market is currently in, whether emerging, plateau, or declining. Each stage has its own level of profitability, with the first stage being the highest and the last stage being the lowest profitability. A market analysis will also determine the price points at which products can be sold; for example, high quality products at a higher price may not tempt consumers to start buying the product based on quality itself.

C. Financial Analysis: A financial analysis determines the cost of each production item used to produce goods and services. High costs may not allow companies to price goods or services competitively, leading to an unprofitable situation. Management will examine the costs of raw materials, labor, and manufacturing overhead to find the best raw goods available to produce the most profitable product. Management will also review the best cost application methods, ensuring that all production costs are properly applied to each product or service produced.

D. Competitor Analysis: Analyzing the current competitors of a market is an important part of business research. Knowing which companies have the best production methods or customer loyalty helps new companies understand how they can create a competitive advantage when entering a new market. Proper business research will also indicate how financially stable companies are and if they can be purchased outright by a company wanting to enter the industry. Buying a competitor may be cheaper than starting new operations for a company.

E. Growth Analysis: Business research usually includes forecasting the growth and direction of the current industry or market. Knowing which direction the market is headed helps companies determine the stability of new business operations. Entering a slow-growth industry may be unprofitable early on but have better long-term growth potential. High-growth industries will sometimes face a quick downfall, such as the dot.com boom of 2000-2001. Strong growth early in the business cycle quickly gave way to record losses, leading many businesses into bankruptcy from poor growth analysis.

1.12 NATURE AND SCOPE OF BUSINESS RESEARCH

Research methods provide you with the knowledge and skills you need to solve the problems and meet the challenges of a fast-paced decision making environment. Business research courses are a recognition that students in business, not-for-profit, and public organizations – in all functional areas – need training in the scientific method and its application to decision making. Two factors stimulate an interest in more scientific decision making: (1) the manager's increased need for more and better information and (2) the availability of improved techniques and tools to meet this need.

During the last two decades, we have witnessed dramatic changes in the business environment. Emerging from a historically economic role, the business organization has evolved in response to the social and political mandates of national public policy, explosive technology growth, and continuing innovations in global communications. These changes have created new knowledge needs for the manager. Other knowledge demands have arisen from problems with mergers, trade policies, protected markets, technology transfers, and macroeconomic savings – investment issues.

The trend toward complexity has increased the risks associated with business decisions, making it more important to have a sound information base. Increased complexity means there are more variables to consider. The competition is more vigorous, with many businesses downsizing to make competitive gains. Workers, shareholders, customers, and the public are better informed and more sensitive to their self-interest. Government continues to show concern with all aspects of society.

Each of these factors demands that managers have more and better information upon which to base decisions.

To do well in such an environment, you will need to be equipped with an understanding of scientific methods and a means of incorporating them into decision making. You will need to know how to identify good research and how to conduct it.

As the complexity of the business environment has increased, there has been a commensurate of increase in the number and power of the tools to conduct research. There is vastly more knowledge in all fields of management. We have begun to build better theories. The computer has given us a quantum leap in the ability to deal with problems. New techniques of quantitative analysis take advantage of this power. Communication and measurement techniques have also been enhanced. These trends reinforce each other and are having a massive impact on business management.

1.13 LIMITATIONS OF BUSINESS RESEARCH

- Access to information
- Access to resources
- Time management
- Access to exports for editing, proofreading, and guidance
- Support from organizations and participants

1.14 ROLE OF RESEARCH IN BUSINESS AND INDUSTRY

Through research, an executive can quickly get a synopsis of the current scenario which improves his information base for making sound decisions affecting future operations of the enterprise. The following are the major areas in which research plays a key role in making effective decisions.

A. Marketing: Marketing research has become very crucial in taking sound marketing decisions. Marketing research involves the process of systematic collection, compilation, analysis, and interpretation of relevant data for marketing decisions. Research tools are applied effectively for studies involving demand forecasting, consumer buying behavior, measuring advertising effectiveness, media selection, test marketing, product positioning, and new product potential.

B. Production: Research enables an organization to decide on what to produce, how much to produce, when to produce, and for whom to produce in the field of production. Research tools are also of immense help in quality control, and setting up optimum inventory level.

C. Banking: Banking institutions have found it useful to set up research departments for the purpose of gathering and analyzing information both for their internal operations and for making in-depth studies on economic conditions of business. Reserve Bank of India has set up an excellent research department for planning and management reporting.

D. Materials: The materials department uses research to frame suitable policies regarding where to buy, how much to buy, when to buy, and at what price to buy.

E. Human Resource Development: The human resource development department uses research to study wage rates, incentive schemes, cost of living, employee turnover rates, employment trends, and performance appraisal. It also uses research effectively for its most important activity namely manpower planning.

F. Government: Research lays the foundation for all government policies in our economic system. For example, research is applied for evolving the union finance budget and railway budget every year. Research is used for economic planning and optimum utilization of resources for the development of the nation. Research is also needed for systematic collection of information on the economic and social structure of the nation. Such information indicates what is happening to the economy and what changes are taking place.

1.15 RESEARCH METHODS VS. RESEARCH METHODOLOGY

Research Methods are the methods or techniques employed by researchers in conducting research operations for collection of data, establishing relationship and evaluating accuracy of the results.

Research Methodology is a scientific and systematic approach to solve research problems. The methodology adopted for different types of problems are different from one another. Thus, the scope of research methodology is broader than research methods.

Methodology should include:

1. Recapitulation of the research problem.
2. The sample or test population.
3. Data collection methods.
4. Statistical tools.
5. Data analysis techniques.
6. Presentation of findings.

1.16 FRAMEWORK FOR RESEARCH METHODOLOGY

1.16.1 Problem Finding

(a) Formal Approaches

Prior research	Inductive fact finding that leads to generating a theory. Deductive relates to testing a theory.
Analog method	Using knowledge gained in one problem area to formulate a research question in a related area.
Renovation	Replacing defective components of a theory. This requires training in structural analysis, i.e., the ability to diagnose a system to find the defective part.
Dialectic method	Developing counter-plans for challenging, refining or deposing an existing theory. Price level adjustments to financial statement are mentioned as an example.
Extrapolation	Extending stable trends into the future and posing questions related to predicted outcomes.
Teratological analysis	Similar to extrapolation, but involves unstable trends, or unexpected futures. Radical what if questions related to contingences.
Morphology	A method of formalizing combinational possibilities in complex problems.

Decomposition	Breaking problems into component parts. Dichotomy – separating a problem into questions that can be answered yes or no. Examples include flow charting, network analysis, algorithms, and computer programming.
Aggregation	Aggregate research findings and apply them to more complex problems. Example: Applying input-output analysis, utility theory and motivational theory to measuring managerial performance.

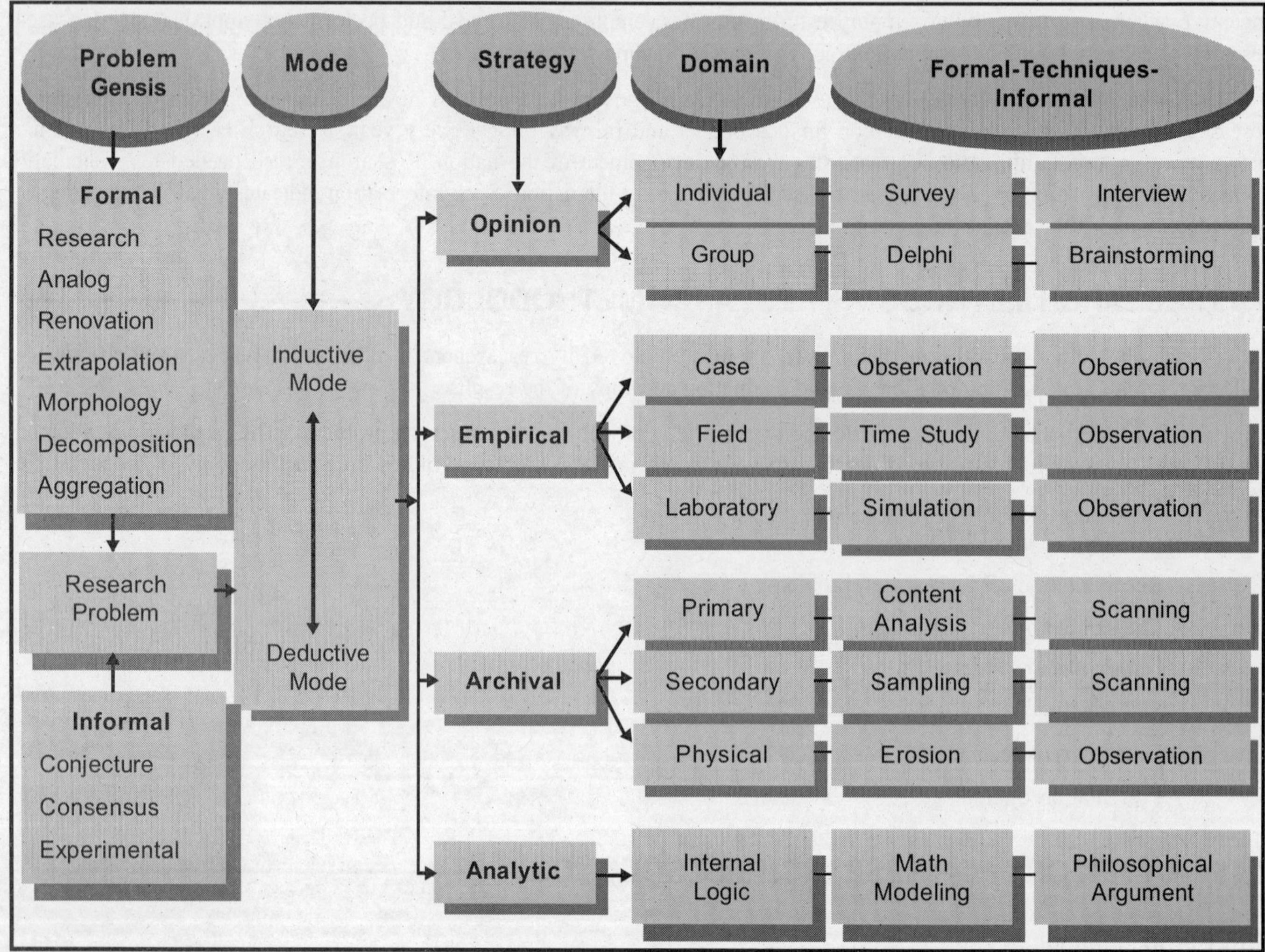

Fig. 1.2: Framework of Research Methodology

(b) Informal Approaches

Conjecture	Based on intuition or hunch.
Phenomenology	Research problems created by a phenomenon, e.g., computers, conglomerates, environmentalism, etc.
Consensus	Group agreement that there is a problem. The FASB approach is given as an example.
Experiential	Research to find ways to avoid a reoccurrence of a problem, e.g., lawsuits, liquidity problem, customer complaints.

1.16.2 Research Problem

A research problem:

1. Must be defined properly.
2. Must be posed in solvable terms.
3. Must be logically connected to the environment from which it was drawn so that the solution can be applied to that environment.
4. Has been screened against existing body of knowledge, i.e., not been solved.
5. Has a potential significant contribution.

Examples of deficiencies in defining the research problem include:

1. Mislabeling the problem. Confusing descriptive with normative. Descriptive questions relate to empirical research, observing **what is**. Normative questions involve opinion research, i.e., **what should be**. Applying past or future problems to the present. Using students to study the behavior of business people.
2. Defining a problem that is unsolvable such as how businessmen solve problems.

1.16.3 Research Mode

A researcher needs to know which mode they are in to understand the consequences of the methods.

Induction: the process of generating theory – from specific facts to generalizations. Relevant questions search for truth, e.g., which, where, who, why, whether, how, and what. Avoid one's own theories or opinions.

Deduction: the process of testing theory – testing a hypothesis against theory – from general to specific. Relevant questions include; **will** questions such as 'will it work?', **is** questions such as, 'is it a good idea?', set-response questions such as how do people feel?, **task-response** questions such as 'did he do a good job', and **if** questions such as 'will this occur if we do that'?

Research Strategies, Domains and Techniques: Research methodology includes a set of strategies, domains and techniques used in generating or testing theory or problem solving.

1.16.4 Research Strategy

Research strategy refers to the nature of the data, the process of obtaining the data and the way we go about generating or testing theory. Research strategies include: opinion, empirical, archival and analytic.

Opinion: Includes views, judgments or appraisals of individuals or groups. There is no direct observation of the facts. Techniques Include questionnaires, opinion polls, interviews, Delphi (for groups where opinions are stated, if no consensus, then circulate and include invitation to revise, continue until a consensus is reached or appears infeasible) and brainstorming.

Empirical: Based on observation or experience. Direct access to the facts. The researcher either experiences the phenomena or is an eye-witness to the events.

1.17 SCIENTIFIC RESEARCH METHOD

A scientific method takes into consideration the application of valid and reliable methods of research. It has three distinct characteristics:

1. Objectivity: The scientific method should enable us to classify facts accurately and carefully, without any bias.

2. Accuracy of Measurement: A mere collection and classification of the facts may not be sufficient; one must be able to make observations of their correlation and sequence.

3. Self-criticism: Scientists should critically examine their own research as they are a group of people who are never sure that they have found the ultimate truth, thus their studies are continuing and exhaustive. If researchers are completely objective, their measurements are accurate and their studies are exhaustive, then their result will be valid and reliable.

Scientific method is the pursuit of truth as determined by logical considerations based on certain basic postulates having empirical evidence, utilizing objective considerations and ethical neutrality. It results into predictions and testing the conclusions through replication. The scientific method, as practice in business research, guides our approach to problem solving. The essential tenets of the scientific methods are:

1. Direct observation of phenomena.
2. Clear definition of variables, methods and procedures.
3. Empirically testable hypotheses.
4. The ability to rule out rival hypotheses.
5. Statistical rather than linguistic justification of conclusions.

A. What is the Purpose of the Scientific Method?

The scientific method is the means by which researchers are able to make conclusive statements about their studies with a minimum of bias. The interpretation of data, for example the result of a new drug study, can be laden with bias. The researcher often has a personal stake in the results of his work. As any skilled debater knows, just about any opinion can be justified and presented as fact. In order to minimize the influence of personal stakes and biased opinions, a standard method of testing a hypothesis is expected to be used by all members of the scientific community.

B. How does the Scientific Method Work?

The first step to using the scientific method is to have some basis for conducting your research. This is based on observed phenomena that are either directly or indirectly related to the specific subject matter of your proposed research. For example, you may have observed that Drug A is effective in treating an illness (Disease A) caused by Virus A. A new illness (Disease B) has arisen that mimics some symptoms of Disease A, but with variation (such as the patient with Disease B has swollen lymph nodes and a low grade fever instead of no swelling and a high grade fever). Outbreaks of Disease B occur near outbreaks of Disease A. These are the observations you make in your first step of using the Scientific Method.

The next step is to form a hypothesis to explain some aspect of your observations. You speculate that the virus that causes Disease B is either Virus A or it is related to Virus A. Your hypothesis is that the cause of Disease A and Disease B is the same virus.

Now that you have a hypothesis, you are ready to test it. You must now use your hypothesis to predict other phenomena that have not yet been observed. You know that Drug A will wipe out Disease A. If Disease B is caused by the same virus, you reason that the same drug should be effective.

The final step of the scientific method is to rigorously test your prediction. Remember, you cannot "prove" your hypothesis. You can only fail to disprove it. While this is an example of how the scientific method is used in everyday research and hypothesis testing, it is also the basis of creating theories and laws.

The scientific method requires a hypothesis to be eliminated if experiments repeatedly contradict predictions. No matter how great a hypothesis sounds, it is only as good as its ability to consistently predict experimental results. It should also be noted that a theory or hypothesis is not meaningful if it is not quantitative and testable. If a theory does not allow for predictions and experimental research to confirm these predictions, then it is not a scientific theory.

C. Misapplications of the Scientific Method

A common error encountered by people who claim to use the scientific method is a lack of testing. A hypothesis brought about by common observations or common sense does not have scientific validity. As stated above, even though a good debater may be quite convincing as he conveys the merits of his theory, logical arguments are not an acceptable replacement for experimental testing.

Although the purpose of the scientific method is to eliminate researcher bias, an investigation of the raw data from an experiment is always a good idea. Researchers sometimes toss out data that does not support their hypothesis. This isn't necessarily done with the intent of deception, it is sometimes done because the researcher so passionately believes in his hypothesis that he assumes unsupportive data must have been obtained in error. Other times, outside forces (such as the corporation sponsoring and conducting the research) may put extreme pressure on the researcher to get specific results.

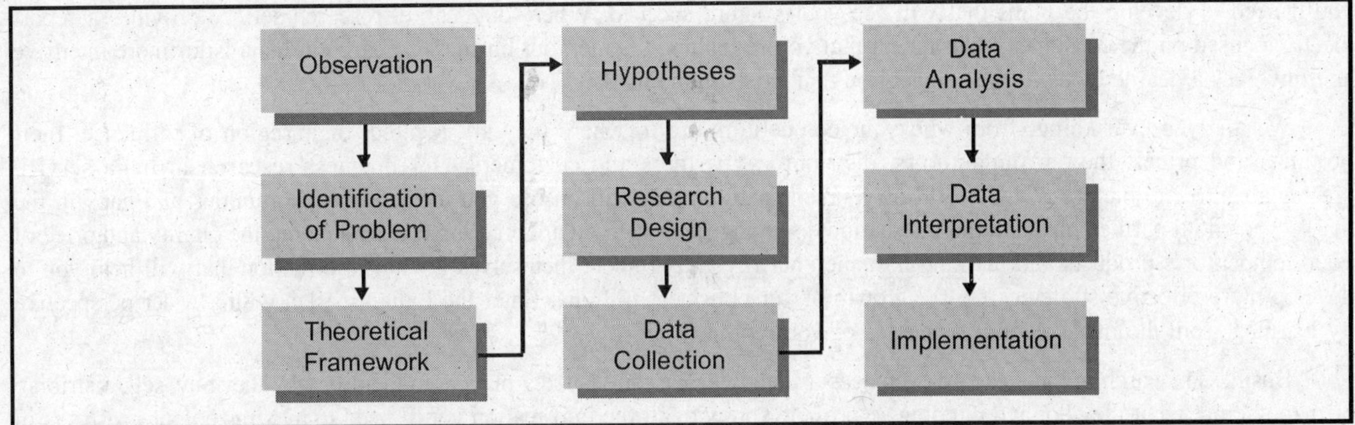

Fig. 1.3: Scientific Investigation

1.18 DISTINCTION BETWEEN SCIENTIFIC AND NON-SCIENTIFIC METHODS

Three major differences between scientific and non-scientific methods that affect the reliability and validity of results are:

1. Objectivity of the investigator
2. Accuracy of measurement
3. Continuing and exhaustive nature of investigation

1. Objectivity of the Investigator

- Researcher must base their judgment on facts, not on perceived notions or intuition.
- If an investigator is not completely objective in his thinking, if he is not just as anxious to find facts supporting one outcome of his study, it is unlikely his work will be scientific.
- Marketing researcher often report to strong-willed executives and they pressurize the researcher to confirm their views.

2. Accuracy of Measurement

- The scientific method attempts to obtain the most accurate measurement possible.
- In the Physical Sciences, electronic measuring devices of great accuracy are available for some measurements.
- In marketing researches, typical scales used are.

  I like a lot.

  I like it little.

  I dislike it.

  I dislike it little.

3. Continuing and Exhaustive Nature of Investigation

- Considers all the facts pertinent to the problem at hand.
- It is aggressive searching for additional evidence to support or confound the existing conclusion.

1.19 CURRENT STATUS OF BUSINESS/MARKET RESEARCH IN INDIA

As one of the fastest-growing consumer markets on the planet, India has much to offer European businesses. But to fully exploit this potential, information is key. Our thorough business research in India will provide you with all the intelligence you'll need to develop the plans that will see your venture succeed. Where our market research service provides a report mostly focused on the consumer environment that you're looking to enter, our business research in India is far more intensive as it involves a detailed look at the competition that exists in the market.

We analyze everything, from who your competitors are to where they are located, their region of influence, their products and prices, their manufacturers, distributors, partners and customers. Our business research in India service creates an intricate picture of the world of your competition that will enable you to identify opportunities and gaps in the market, potential partnerships and the international playing field that you are entering. Understanding the quality and price of your competitor's products and learning how they portray and promote themselves is vital information that will help you to develop more effective strategies for the growth of your business in India. Enter the Indian market with a wiser perspective by learning from the mistakes and successes of your competition.

Business research in India can go even deeper than this. We can visit key players to identify why they buy, sell, distribute or manufacture what they do, and in doing so provide you with all the information you'll need to maximize your prospects in the Indian marketplace.

India Market Research provides an idea of the business and the consumer market pattern. They pave the way to economic and business development and help to generate profit for the country. An extensive Market Research in India takes care of all the queries of the marketers — giving them the required information for a smooth marketing journey. Market research involves giving insight to all the categories of marketing — valuation, distribution, promotion of product and services. For betterment and improvement, market research is absolutely essential.

There are loads of Market Research agencies and consulting firms that gives excellent report, provides a helping hand to the Indian and international companies. Out of the lot, IMRB (Indian Market Research Bureau) International is the ground breaker in Indian Market Research. The market research agencies pan India; cover all the main areas of marketing — spanning B2B and industrial research, social research, media research, brand research, corporate and employee research, channel and retail research, product and packaging research, pricing research and business-specialized consumer research.

1.20 GLOBAL BUSINESS RESEARCH

Global business is an integral part of our modern economy. Most companies — large or small, international or local — are affected by the global marketplace. The growing number of agents in the international market creates strong demand for timely and insightful scholarship in the field. Concepts, Tools, and Methodologies is designed to provide students and scholars with an in-depth body of knowledge from the cutting-edge of modern business research. This multi-volume reference examines critical issues and emerging trends in global business. With topics ranging from managing new information technology in global business operations to ethics and communication strategies, this collection is a valuable reference tool for academics and practitioners alike.

Information Resources Management Association (IRMA) is a research-based professional organization dedicated to advancing the concepts and practices of information resources management in modern organizations. IRMA's primary purpose is to promote the understanding, development and practice of managing information resources as key enterprise assets among IRM/IT professionals. IRMA brings together researchers, practitioners, academicians, and policymakers in information technology management from over 50 countries.

1.21 SUMMARY

Research is the systematic process of collecting and analyzing information to increase our understanding of the phenomenon under study. Business research is the systematic and objective process for gathering, recording and analyzing data for decision making. The research must be systematic not haphazard. It must be objective to avoid the distorting effects of personal bias. The objective of applied business research is to facilitate managerial decision making. Basic or pure research is used to increase knowledge about theories and concepts.

Manager can use business research in all stages of the decision making process: to define problem, to identify opportunities, to diagnose causal factors, and to clarify alternatives. Research is also used to evaluate current programs and course of action, to explain what went wrong with managerial effort in the past, and to forecast future conditions. Business research plays a major role in total quality management programs.

1.22 KEY TERMS

Business Research: Business Research is a systematic and objective process of gathering, recording and analyzing data for aid in making business decisions.

Curiosity: Science is knowledge of the physical or material world gained through observation and experiment.

Theory (Hypothesis): Research creates a theory (hypothesis) to be proved from the question; the researcher maintains an awareness of the limitations of budget, time and technology on experiments needed to answer the question.

Experiment: Researchers design an experiment with steps to test and evaluate the theory (hypothesis) and generate analyzable data.

Observation: Observing and recording the results of the experiment generates raw data to prove or disprove the theory.

Analysis: Statistical analysis on the data and organizing it so that it is understandable generates answers to the initial question.

Prediction: Predictions are usually stated as hypotheses, i.e., clear unambiguous statements which can be subjected to scientific verification or refutation.

Control: Control represents the way in which research can be applied to real problems and situations, thus helping us to shape our environment.

Basic (Fundamental or **Pure) Research:** Basic research is conducted primarily to improve our understanding of general issues, without any emphasis on its immediate application.

Applied Research: Applied research is the problem-oriented to solve a specific problem that requires a decision.

Exploratory Research: Exploratory research is conducted to clarify ambiguous problems and to gain better understanding of the dimensions of the problems.

Focus Group: Focus group is a small number of individuals brought together to study and talk about some topic of interest.

Descriptive Research: Descriptive research is used to obtain information concerning the current status of the phenomena to describe "what exists" with respect to variables or conditions in a situation.

Ex-post Facto Research: Ex-post facto research is the investigator to determine the specific variables for analysis after the research has been completed.

Meta-analysis: Meta-analysis is to synthesize the large volume of data describing numerous independent variables and their correlations with reference accuracy.

Survey: Survey is a method of collecting standardized information by interviewing a representative sample of some population.

Scientific Method: Scientific method is a systematic method of investigation, evaluation, experimentation, interpretation and theorizing.

1.23 MULTIPLE OBJECTIVE TYPE QUESTIONS

1. Research is the systematic process of collecting and analyzing information to increase the understanding of the phenomenon under study.

   (a) True (b) False

2. Business research is a systematic and objective process of gathering, recording and analyzing data for aid in making business decisions.

   (a) True (b) False

3. Product analysis is the first step of social research.
   (a) True (b) False
4. Research methods provide the knowledge and skills to solve the problems and meet the challenges of a fast-paced decision-making environment.
   (a) True (b) False
5. Exploratory research is problem-oriented as the research is carried out to solve a specific problem that requires a decision.
   (a) True (b) False
6. Literature search refers to "referring to a literature to develop a new theory".
   (a) True (b) False
7. Descriptive research is used to obtain information concerning the future status of the phenomena.
   (a) True (b) False
8. Archival research is the analysis of pre-existing data or records.
   (a) True (b) False
9. Ex-post facto study is requires the investigator to determine the specific variables for analysis after the research has been completed.
   (a) True (b) False
10. Research Methodology is a scientific and systematic approach to solve business problem.
   (a) True (b) False
11. Which research is the problem oriented to solve a specific problem that requires a decision?
   (a) Fundamental research (b) Applied research
   (c) Exploratory research (d) Descriptive research
12. Which is a systematic method of investigation, evaluation, experimentation, interpretation and theorizing?
   (a) Survey (b) Experiment
   (c) Scientific method (d) Meta-analysis
13. Which one is the limitation of business research?
   (a) Access to information (b) Time management
   (c) Access to resources (d) All the above
14. Which analysis is the first step of business research?
   (a) Product analysis (b) Market analysis
   (c) Financial analysis (d) Competitor analysis
15. Which research is a well-planned, systematic process which implies that it needs planning at all the stages?
   (a) Marketing research (b) Business research
   (c) Social research (d) Scientific research
16. What is research ethics?
   (a) Safety (b) Honesty
   (c) Transparency (d) All the above
17. Which study is similar to descriptive research study but with a different focus?
   (a) Experimental research (b) Diagnostic research
   (c) Qualitative research (d) All the above

18. Which study is required by the investigator to determine the specific variables for analysis after the research has been completed?
    (a) Correlational study
    (b) Ex-post facto study
    (c) Longitudinal study
    (d) Meta analysis
19. Which one of the following is the criterion of good research?
    (a) Research is a systematic and critical investigation into a phenomenon
    (b) Research is based upon observable experience
    (c) All the assumptions for the study should be expressively mentioned
    (d) Research is not to arrive at an answer
20. Research methodology is a scientific approach to solve
    (a) Research methods
    (b) Research problem
    (c) Research operations
    (d) All the above

Answers to Multiple Objective Type Questions

Questions	1	2	3	4	5	6	7	8	9	10
Answers	T	T	F	T	F	T	F	T	T	F
Questions	11	12	13	14	15	16	17	18	19	20
Answers	b	c	d	a	a	d	b	b	c	b

1.24 CONCEPTUAL QUESTIONS

1. What is research and its objectives? How scientific method is useful for all types of research?
2. What do you mean by Business research? Explain its nature and scope.
3. What are the different types of Business research? Explain Details.
4. What are the significance of research and its characteristics? Explain.
5. Explain in detail the roles of research in business and industry.
6. Distinguish between Research Methods and Research Methodology.
7. What is scientific method? Distinguish between research and scientific method.
8. What are the differences between scientific and non-scientific methods? Explain.
9. Describe the different types of research, clearly pointing out the difference between an experiment and a survey.
10. Distinguish between qualitative research and quantitative research.
11. What are the criteria of the good research? Explain.
12. Explain in detail the current status of business research in India.
13. "Empirical research in India in particular creates so many problems for the researchers". Explain.
14. "Research is much concerned with proper fact finding, analysis and evaluation". Discuss.
15. Write short notes:
    (a) Fundamental Research
    (b) Applied Research
    (c) Exploratory Research
    (d) Focus Group
    (e) Descriptive Research
    (f) Qualitative Research
    (g) Quantitative Research
    (h) Meta Analysis
    (i) Action Research
    (j) Diagnostic Research
    (k) Experimental Research
    (l) Ex-post-facto Research

* * * * *

APPENDIX 1.1

HOW TO WRITE RESEARCH PAPER?

In a research paper, the universally accepted written structure carries out a dual purpose. First, it allows the writer to state the objectives of the research and to reinforce their importance from different perspectives in different sections. Second, this structure facilitates the interaction between the writer and the reader and helps the latter to follow the development of ideas to the paper's culmination.

Research Paper Structure:

The outline below highlights the essence of each structural section of the research paper:

The Introduction: The introduction initiates the conversation on the issue; and a strong thesis statement recaps the problem and the author's plan of action.

The Literature Review: The literature review states the importance of the problem. In addition, it talks about previous attempts to resolve the issue and about historical trends that can inform the current investigation. This section proves to the reader that the author is a credible researcher with broad knowledge and in-depth understanding of the subject area.

The Methods and Procedures: The methods and procedure section can focus on secondary data study, primary data collection and analysis, or a combination of both. Regardless of the approach, the writer has to justify their choices and give a detailed account of the people and the activities involved in the research.

The Discussion: The discussion section is a culmination of the research and the most important part of the paper. This is the place to present a business proposition and to discuss its practical value. This section is the reason for doing the research; its value for the reader is the acquisition of new knowledge.

Conclusion: Conclusion provides an overview of the entire paper while highlighting the focal points of the discussion.

CHAPTER 2

RESEARCH PROCESS

R E S E A R C H M E T H O D O L O G Y

Chapter Outline

Learning Objectives

- *Identify the primary stages of research process.*
- *Explain the various steps in research process for managerial decisions.*
- *Discuss the business research process in decision making.*

2.1 PRIMARY STAGES OF RESEARCH PROCESS

Research is a source which can be drawn upon to make a substantial contribution to the body of the knowledge; research should be followed by some sort of original contribution. The primary stage of any research process includes:

1. **Observation:** Research starts with observation, which leads to curiosity to learn more about what has been observed. Observation can either be unaided visual observation or guided and controlled observation. Sometimes a casual or associated observation leads to substantial research and a great invention. Deliberate and guided observation can also form the basis for research. While observation leads to research, research results in elaborate observation and convulsions; or even further research observation can either be subjective or objective. These are participant observation, on-participant observation, controlled observation and non-controlled observation.
2. **Interest:** The observation of certain occurrences creates an interest and inquisitiveness in the mind of the researcher to study it further. This is the basis of interest to study the subject matter of observation. It may be self-interest or group interest. The interest is the guiding force behind any research.
3. **Crystallization:** Crystallization is the process of designing the definite form of research to be undertaken for the purpose of studying the subject matter. It is the formulation of the research project, defining of its objectives, rationale, scope, methodology, limitations, including financial commitments and sources. It is at this stage that the research project is given a concrete shape and structure, forming a basis of further investigation.
4. **Formulation of Hypothesis:** At this stage, the hypothesis is formed on the basis of observation. Hypothesis is a part of the scientific method, and has been dealt with in detail in the chapter on "Scientific Method and Hypothesis".
5. **Primary Synopsis:** Synopsis is a summary/outline/brief of any subject. It is not a complete subject till formalization of a subject/replica of a subject. It saves time. It will give an idea of time required for presentation of the main subject. Once the subject is decided, you can arrange titles like main headings, paragraph heading – elaborate the paragraph with importance of main issues.
6. **Conceptual Clarity:** Any researcher should have in-depth background knowledge of the topic of his study. He can gain such basic knowledge only by an extensive reading of text books, specialized books and publications on the topic in addition to articles and research papers published in journals and periodicals, reports of the past studies, etc. He can also gain knowledge by detail discussion with the people concerned and by his own observation. However, it is imperative for a researcher to gain a deep knowledge from any reliable source prior to actually plunging himself into a research, so that he may have clear knowledge of the concepts which would be of value to him in his task.
7. **Documentation:** The documentary sources are important sources of information for a researcher. A document is anything in writing – a record, files or diaries, published or unpublished – which can be extracted and used in research. It is a very valuable source of information for research either in management or in social science. It may comprises office files, business and legal papers, biographies, official and unofficial records, letters, proceedings of any courts, committees, societies, assemblies and parliaments, enactments, constitution, reports of surveys or research of commissions, official statistics, newspapers editorials, special articles, company news, cases or company directors reports etc. Documentation is the process of collecting and extracting the documents with relevant research. Documents may be classified into personal documents, company documents, consultants report and published materials and public documents.
8. **Bibliography:** At the end of any research report, a bibliography is generally added. This is the list of books publication, periodicals, journals, reports, etc. which are used by the researcher in connection with the study. It is a description of books, their authorship, editions, publishers, year of publication, place of publication etc. In ordinary circumstance, a researcher reads, and makes notes from, many books and publications at the primary stage of research in order to gain conceptual clarity. He prepares a list of such publications and reports then and there, which helps him in the course of his research. Some mistakenly believe that a bibliography is merely a list of publication compiled at the end of report writing like an appendix. On the contrary, a bibliography contains and is composed of the details of publications that the researcher has used in connection with his study. These facilitates any further reference to the matter either by the researcher himself or anybody who goes through the researcher's report.

2.2 STEPS IN RESEARCH PROCESS

1. Formulating the research problems, aims and objectives
2. Extensive literature survey
3. Development working hypothesis
4. Preparing research design
5. Determining sample design
6. Collecting the data
7. Execution of the project
8. Analysis of the data
9. Hypothesis Testing
10. Generalizations and interpretation
11. Preparation of the report or thesis

2.2.1 Formulating Research Problems, Aims and Objectives

Step 1: Identify a broad field or subject area of interest to you

Step 2: Dissect the broad area into sub-areas

Step 3: Select what is the most interesting to you

Step 4: Raise research question

Step 5: Formulate objectives

Step 6: Assess your objectives

Step 7: Double-check

Aims of Research Problem

1. are broad statements of desired outcomes, or the general intentions of the research, which 'paint the picture' of your research proposal.
2. emphasize what is to be accomplished, not how it is to be accomplished.
3. address the long-term project outcomes, i.e., they should reflect the aspirations and expectations of the research topic.
4. do not need to be numbered.

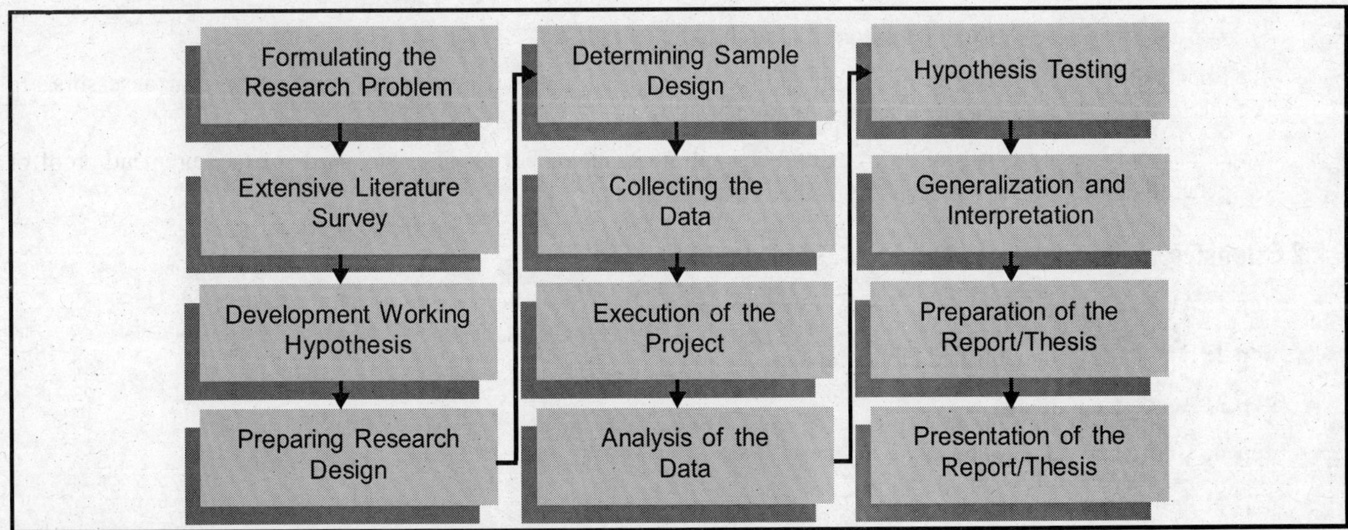

Fig. 2.1: Research Process

Once aims have been established, the next task is to formulate the objectives. Generally, a project should have no more than two or three aims statements, while it may include a number of objectives consistent with them.

Objectives of Research Problem

1. are the steps you are going to take to answer your research questions or a specific list of tasks needed to accomplish the goals of the project.
2. emphasize how aims are to be accomplished.
3. must be highly focused and feasible.
4. address the more immediate project outcomes.
5. make accurate use of concepts and be sensible and precisely described.
6. are usually numbered so that each objective reads as an 'individual' statement to convey your intentions.

For each specific objective, you must have a method to attempt to achieve it. The development of a realistic time schedule may help to prioritize your objectives and help to minimize wasted time and effort.

Aims and Objectives should

1. Be presented concisely and briefly.
2. Be interrelated. The aim is what you want to achieve, and the objective describes how you are going to achieve that aim, i.e., make sure that each aim is matched with specific objectives.
3. Be realistic about what you can accomplish in the duration of the project and the other commitments you have, i.e., the scope of your project must be consistent with the time frame and level of effort available to you.
4. Provide you and your assessors with indicators of how you:
   (a) intend to approach the literature and theoretical issues related to you project
   (b) intend to access your chosen subjects, respondents, units, goods or services and develop a sampling frame and strategy or a rationale for their selection
   (c) will develop a strategy and design for data collection and analysis
   (d) you will deal with ethical and practical problems in your research

Aims and Objectives should not

1. Be too vague, ambitious or broad in scope: Though aims are more general in nature than objectives, it is the viability and feasibility of your study that you have to demonstrate and aims often present an over-optimistic picture of what the project can achieve.
2. Just repeat each other in different terms.
3. Just be a list of things related to your research topic.
4. Spend time discussing details of your job or research site, i.e., it is your research study your assessors are interested in and you should keep this in mind at all times.
5. Contradict methods, that is, they should not imply methodological goals or standards of measurement, proof or generalizability of findings that the methods cannot sustain.

2.2.2 Extensive Literature Review/Survey

Step 1: Abstracting and indexing journals

Step 2: Published or unpublished bibliographies

Step 3: Academic journals

Step 4: Conference proceedings

Step 5: Government reports

Step 6: Books

A. What is a Literature Review?

A literature review uses as its database reports of primary or original scholarship, and does not report new primary scholarship itself. The primary reports used in the literature may be oral, but in the vast majority of cases reports are written documents. The types of scholarship may be empirical, theoretical, critical/analytic, or methodological in nature. Second, a literature review seeks to describe, summarize, evaluate, clarify and/or integrate the content of primary reports.

The review of relevant literature is nearly always a standard chapter of a thesis or dissertation. The review forms an important chapter in a thesis where its purpose is to provide the background to and justification for the research undertaken. Who has published widely on the topic of the literature review, has identified six elements of a literature review. These elements comprise a list; a search; a survey; a vehicle for learning; a research facilitator; and a report.

B. Why is Literature Review Done?

A crucial element of all research degrees is the review of relevant literature. So important is this chapter that its omission represents a void or absence of a major element in research. According to **Bourner (1996),** there are good reasons for spending time and effort on a review of the literature before embarking on a research project. These reasons include:

1. To identify gaps in the literature.
2. To avoid reinventing the wheel (at the very least this will save time and it can stop you from making the same mistakes as others)
3. To carry on from where others have already reached (reviewing the field allows you to build on the platform of existing knowledge and ideas)
4. To identify other people working in the same fields (a researcher network is a valuable resource)
5. To increase your breadth of knowledge of your subject area
6. To identify seminal works in your area
7. To provide the intellectual context for your own work, enabling you to position your project relative to other work
8. To identify opposing views
9. To put your work into perspective
10. To demonstrate that you can access previous work in an area
11. To identify information and ideas that may be relevant to your project
12. To identify methods that could be relevant to your project

A good literature review requires knowledge of the use of indexes and abstracts, the ability to conduct exhaustive bibliographic searches, ability to organize the collected data meaningfully, describe, critique and relate each source to the subject of the inquiry, and present the organized review logically, and last, but by no means least, to correctly cite all sources. The Library offers a range of training for research students that will assist with the production of literature reviews including sessions on electronic databases, using the bibliographic management software, End Note to download records, Internet searching using Netscape, Library catalogue searching, off-campus student orientation, subject resources, and research skills.

2.2.3 Developing Working Hypothesis

Step 1: Guide the researcher by delimiting the area of research.

Step 2: Keep the person on right track.

Step 3: Sharpens the thinking.

Step 4: Focus attention on more important points.

A **working hypothesis** is a **hypothesis** that is provisionally accepted when no alternatives are available, or when the philosophical implications of the alternatives are considered to be absurd or otherwise undesirable. Like all hypotheses, a working hypothesis can be constructed as a statement of expectations. They can be linked to the **exploratory research** purpose in empirical investigation, and are also often used as a **conceptual framework** as they are well suited to qualitative research methods. Working hypotheses are a "provisional, working means of advancing investigation" and lead to the discovery of other important facts.

Scientific study designed to increase our knowledge of natural phenomena can follow at least three different intellectual methods. These can be called the method of the ruling theory, the method of the working hypothesis, and the method of multiple working hypotheses. The first two are the most popular but they can, and often do, lead to ineffective research that overlooks relevant data. Instead, the method of multiple working hypotheses offers a more effective way of organizing one's research.

A. Ruling Theories

Our desire to reach an interpretation or explanation commonly leads us to a tentative interpretation that is based on relatively hasty examination of a single example or case. Our tentative explanation, as such, is not a threat to objectivity, but if we then begin to trust it without further testing, we can be blinded to other possibilities that we ignored at first glance. Our premature explanation can become a tentative theory and then a ruling theory, and our research becomes focused on proving that ruling theory. The result is a blindness to evidence that disproves the ruling theory or supports an alternate explanation. Only if the original tentative hypothesis was by chance correct does our research lead to any meaningful contribution to knowledge.

B. Working Hypotheses

The working hypothesis, is a hypothesis to be tested, not in order to prove the hypothesis, but as a stimulus for study and fact-finding. Nonetheless, the single working hypothesis can imperceptibly degenerate into a ruling theory, and our desire to prove the working hypothesis, despite evidence to the contrary, can become as strong as the desire to prove the ruling theory.

Multiple Working Hypotheses

The method of multiple working hypotheses involves the development, prior to our research, of several hypotheses that might explain the phenomenon we want to study. Many of these hypotheses will be contradictory, so that some, if not all, will prove to be false. However, the development of multiple hypotheses prior to the research lets us avoid the trap of the ruling hypothesis and thus makes it more likely that our research will lead to meaningful results.

The method of multiple working hypotheses has several other beneficial effects on one's research. Careful study often shows that a phenomenon is the result of several causes, not just one, and the method of multiple working hypotheses obviously makes it more likely that we will see the interaction of the several causes. The method also promotes much greater thoroughness than research directed toward one hypothesis, leading to lines of inquiry that we might otherwise overlook, and thus to evidence and insights that single-minded research might never have encountered. Thirdly, the method makes us much more likely to see the imperfections in our knowledge and thus to avoid the pitfall of accepting weak or flawed evidence for one hypothesis when another provides a more elegant solution.

2.2.4 Preparing Research Design

Step 1: Means of obtaining the information

- Availability of skills of researcher and staff.
- Time available for research
- Cost factor relating to the research.

Step 2: Research Purposes

- Exploration
- Descriptive
- Diagnosis
- Experimentation

Step 3: Research Design

- Experimental design
- Non-experimental design

Even formulating a design for your research would require you to acquire many resources that can act as your references. These references may be helpful in educating you on related topics such as types, methods, specialists, examples, definitions, etc. Here are some points that you should take before creating a research design.

1. It is a plan that covers the implementation of a research effort.
2. It is where the steps to be taken in achieving the expected results are confirmed in detail.
3. It states the objective and the problem or issue to be dealt with, the needed information, and the methods to be employed in order to get the most accurate findings from which a conclusion can be based.
4. There are two types of research designs. One is the quantitative type while the other is qualitative. The former has the most advantages that can make a study scientifically precise because of its research techniques, while the latter is most useful when dealing with more complex data resources such as human emotions.

Research design is best approached by thinking through the research process in a sequential, step-by-step process. There will inevitably be some iteration and adjustments between steps, but the following is a useful starting point.

The Principal Steps are:

1. Identify a problem
2. Ask a clear question
3. Limit the scope of the research
4. Say what is known and not known about the problem
5. Identify the skills and information needed to answer the question
6. Select the methods needed to collect and analyze the data
7. Explain the kind of results expected and how they will be presented
8. Specify the timetable and budget

2.2.5 Determining Sample Design

Step 1: Define the Population

Step 2: Specify the Sampling Frame

Step 3: Specify Sampling Unit

Step 4: Selection of Sampling Method

Step 5: Determination of the Sample Size

Step 6: Specify the Sampling Plan

Step 7: Select the Sample

A **sample design** can be described by two factors.

- **Sampling method.** Sampling method refers to the rules and procedures by which some elements of the population are included in the sample. Some common sampling methods are described elsewhere in the tutorial (see **simple random sampling, stratified sampling,** and **cluster sampling.**)
- **Estimator.** The estimation process for calculating sample statistics is called the estimator. Different sampling methods may use different estimators. For example, the formula for computing a mean score with a simple random sample is different from the formula for computing a mean score with a stratified sample.

A. Non-probability Sampling Methods

Two of the main types of non-probability sampling methods are voluntary samples and convenience samples.

- **Voluntary sample.** A voluntary sample is made up of people who self-select into the survey. Often, these folks have a strong interest in the main topic of the survey.

  Suppose, for example, that a news show asks viewers to participate in an online poll. This would be a volunteer sample. The sample is chosen by the viewers, not by the survey administrator.

- **Convenience sample.** A convenience sample is made up of people who are easy to reach.

  Consider the following example. A pollster interviews shoppers at a local mall. If the mall was chosen because it was a convenient site from which to solicit survey participants and/or because it was close to the pollster's home or business, this would be a convenience sample.

B. Probability Sampling Methods

The main types of probability sampling methods are simple random sampling, stratified sampling, cluster sampling, multistage sampling, and systematic random sampling. The key benefit of probability sampling methods is that they guarantee that the sample chosen is representative of the population. This ensures that the statistical conclusions will be valid.

1. **Simple random sampling.** Simple random sampling refers to any sampling method that has the following properties:
   - The population consists of *n* objects.
   - The sample consists of *n* objects.
   - If all possible samples of *n* objects are equally likely to occur, the sampling method is called simple random sampling.

   There are many ways to obtain a simple random sample. One way would be the lottery method. Each of the n population members is assigned a unique number. The numbers are placed in a bowl and thoroughly mixed. Then, a blind-folded researcher selects n numbers. Population members having the selected numbers are included in the sample.
2. **Stratified sampling.** With stratified sampling, the population is divided into groups, based on some characteristic. Then, within each group, a probability sample (often a simple random sample) is selected. In stratified sampling, the groups are called **strata.** As an example, suppose we conduct a national survey. We might divide the population into groups or strata, based on geography – north, east, south, and west. Then, within each stratum, we might randomly select survey respondents.
3. **Cluster sampling.** With cluster sampling, every member of the population is assigned to one, and only one, group. Each group is called a cluster. A sample of clusters is chosen, using a probability method (often simple random sampling). Only individuals within sampled clusters are surveyed.
4. **Multistage sampling.** With multistage sampling, we select a sample by using combinations of different sampling methods.
5. **Systematic random sampling.** With systematic random sampling, we create a list of every member of the population. From the list, we randomly select the first sample element from the first *k* elements on the population list. Thereafter, we select every k^{th} element on the list.

This method is different from simple random sampling since every possible sample of *n* elements is not equally likely.

2.2.6 Collecting the Data

Step 1: By observation

Step 2: Through personal interview

Step 3: Through telephone interview

Step 4: By mailing of questionnaires

Step 5: Through schedules

Data collection is a term used to describe a process of preparing and collecting data. The purpose of data collection is to obtain information to keep on record, to make decisions about important issues, to pass information on to others. Primarily, data is collected to provide information regarding a specific topic. Data Collection is an important aspect of any type of research study. Inaccurate data collection can impact the results of a study and ultimately lead to invalid results. Data collection methods for impact evaluation vary along a continuum. There are four main methods of data collection.

1. **Census.** A census is a study that obtains data from every member of a **population.** In most studies, a census is not practical, because of the cost and/or time required.
2. **Sample survey.** A sample survey is a study that obtains data from a subset of a population, in order to estimate population attributes.
3. **Experiment.** An experiment is a controlled study in which the researcher attempts to understand cause-and-effect relationships. The study is "controlled" in the sense that the researcher controls (i) how subjects are assigned to groups and (ii) which treatments each group receives. In the analysis phase, the researcher compares group scores on some **dependent variable.** Based on the analysis, the researcher draws a conclusion about whether the treatment (**independent variable**) had a causal effect on the dependent variable.
4. **Observational study.** Like experiments, observational studies attempt to understand cause-and-effect relationships. However, unlike experiments, the researcher is not able to control (i) how subjects are assigned to groups and/or (ii) which treatments each group receives.

Quantitative and Qualitative Methods

The **Quantitative data collection methods**, rely on random sampling and structured data collection instruments that fit diverse experiences into predetermined response categories. They produce results that are easy to summarize, compare, and generalize.

Quantitative research is concerned with testing hypotheses derived from theory and/or being able to estimate the size of a phenomenon of interest. Depending on the research question, participants may be randomly assigned to different treatments. If this is not feasible, the researcher may collect data on participant and situational characteristics in order to statistically control for their influence on the dependent, or outcome, variable. If the intent is to generalize from the research participants to a larger population, the researcher will employ probability sampling to select participants.

Typical Quantitative Data Gathering Strategies Include:

1. Experiments/clinical trials.
2. Observing and recording well-defined events (e.g., counting the number of patients waiting in emergency at specified times of the day).
3. Obtaining relevant data from management information systems.
4. Administering surveys with closed-ended questions (e.g., face-to face and telephonic interviews, questionnaires etc.).

A. Interviews

1. **Face-to-face interviews** have a distinct advantage of enabling the researcher to establish rapport with potential participants and therefore gain their co-operation. These interviews yield highest response rates in survey research. They also allow the researcher to clarify ambiguous answers and when appropriate, seek follow-up information. Disadvantages include impractical when large samples are involved time consuming and expensive.
2. **Telephonic interviews** are less time-consuming and less expensive and the researcher has ready access to anyone on the planet who has a telephone. Disadvantages are that the response rate is not as high as the face-to-face interview but considerably higher than the mailed questionnaire. The sample may be biased to the extent that people without phones are part of the population about whom the researcher wants to draw inferences.
3. **Computer Assisted Personal Interviewing (CAPI)** is a form of personal interviewing, but instead of completing a questionnaire, the interviewer brings along a laptop or handheld computer to enter the information directly into the database. This method saves time involved in processing the data, as well as saving the interviewer from carrying around hundreds of questionnaires. However, this type of data collection method can be expensive to set up and requires that interviewers have computer and typing skills.

B. Questionnaires

1. **Paper-pencil questionnaires:** can be sent to a large number of people and saves the researcher time and money. People are more truthful while responding to the questionnaires regarding controversial issues in particular due to the fact that their responses are anonymous. But they also have drawbacks. Majority of the people who receive questionnaires don't return them and those who do might not be representative of the originally selected sample.
2. **Web based questionnaires:** A new and inevitably growing methodology is the use of Internet based research. This would mean receiving an e-mail on which you would click on an address that would take you to a secure web-site to fill in a questionnaire. This type of research is often quicker and less detailed. Some disadvantages of this method include the exclusion of people who do not have a computer or are unable to access a computer. Also the validity of such surveys are in question as people might be in a hurry to complete it and so might not give accurate responses.
3. **Qualitative data collection methods:** play an important role in impact evaluation by providing information useful to understand the processes behind observed results and assess changes in people's perceptions of their well-being. Furthermore qualitative methods can be used to improve the quality of survey-based quantitative evaluations by helping generate evaluation hypothesis; strengthening the design of survey questionnaires and expanding or clarifying quantitative evaluation findings. These methods are characterized by the following attributes:
   (a) they tend to be open-ended and have less structured protocols (i.e., researchers may change the data collection strategy by adding, refining, or dropping techniques or informants).
   (b) they rely more heavily on interactive interviews; respondents may be interviewed several times to follow up on a particular issue, clarify concepts or check the reliability of data.
   (c) they use triangulation to increase the credibility of their findings (i.e., researchers rely on multiple data collection methods to check the authenticity of their results).
   (d) generally their findings are not generalizable to any specific population, rather each case study produces a single piece of evidence that can be used to seek general patterns among different studies of the same issue.

The qualitative methods most commonly used in evaluation can be classified in three broad categories: **(1) in-depth interview; (2) observation methods and (3) document review.**

C. Schedules and Questionnaires

An important method for the collection of data followed usually by private individuals, research workers, non-official institutions and sometimes the Government also, is that of schedules and questionnaires. In this method a list of questions relating to the problem under investigation is prepared and printed and information is collected from various in any of the following ways:

1. By sending the questionnaire to the persons concerned and requesting them to answer the questions and return the questionnaire.
2. By sending the questionnaire through enumerators to help the informants in filling the answers.

2.2.7 Execution of the Project

Step 1: Should be conducted in the systematic manner.

Step 2: Proper arrangement should be made according to the requirement.

Step 3: Methods should be adopted for securing the response from the people who are not co-operated.

The **Project Execution Plan** (PEP) is a document which acts as a primary manner by which the Project is planned, monitored and managed. It assists the management in ensuring the effectiveness and control of their day-to-day functions. It should be noted that the Project Execution Plan is a dynamic document, and so for it to serve as a **communication** tool, it has to be kept updated as the project progresses through its design stages.

To meet the particular state of affairs of a project, the Project Execution Plan needs to be modified accordingly. However, a typical PEP should include plans pertaining to the project as a whole; **product purchasing, product development** and **risk management.**

To make sure that everyone understands and carries out their responsibilities, the Project Execution Plan should **clearly define** the roles, responsibilities and authorities. It should set out the mechanisms and procedures concerning the quality and reporting. Finally, the PEP should cover the major schedules and budgets of the project and resources applicable to it.

An effective Project Execution Plan brings with it various benefits for the project. It highlights the **critical drivers** and accordingly helps management focus on a clear path forward to support the project effort. It establishes a support for valuable decision making and communication, thus assisting the management in implementing the planned strategies and policies.

2.2.8 Analysis of the Data

Step 1: Data transformation and coding

Step 2: Editing

Step 3: Tabulation

Step 4: Statistical inference

Analysis of data involves the application of raw data into categories through coding and tabulation. The unwieldy data is condensed into manageable categories for further analysis. The researcher attempts to classify the raw data into some purposeful and usable categories. In coding, the categories of data are transformed into symbols that may be tabulated and counted. Use of computers is helpful especially when dealing with large amounts of data. Analysis work after tabulation is usually based on computation of various statistical measures. Data entry and analysis software such as SPSS, EPI info, Excel and Access are helpful at this stage. In analysis, relationships or differences that support or conflict the original hypothesis are subjected to tests of significance to determine the validity with which conclusions can be made. If there are no hypotheses, the researcher seeks to explain the findings.

A. Data Transformation and Coding

Transformation of data may be carried out to achieve one or all of the following objectives:

(a) equalization of variances

(b) normalization of observations

(c) selection of appropriate regression variables

The overall aim, however, is to ensure the use of correct statistical procedures. Common transformations include the square root and logarithm for counts and the angular for percentages.

Data coding is different from data transformation. Ranking of data from original observations, reducing or increasing all data by a common factor are common forms of data coding. Sometimes this is done to simplify the arithmetic computations or in the case of species coding, to facilitate the use of conventional statistical procedures.

Coding is the process of classifying responses into meaningful categories. It involves combining/pooling detailed information into a limited number of categories that enable simple description of the data and allow for statistical analysis. Coding refers to the process of assigning numerals or other symbols to answers that responses can be put into a limited number of categories or classes (Pre-coding and Post-coding).

Basic Principles of Coding

1. Link to Theory
2. Exhaustiveness
3. Mutual Exclusiveness
4. Detail

B. Editing

Editing is a process of examining the collected raw data (especially in surveys) to detect errors, options, inadequate entries and to correct these when possible.

Basic Principles of Editing

1. Checking of the number of schedules/questionnaire
2. Completeness (completed in filling of questions)
3. Legibility
4. To avoid inconsistencies in answers
5. To maintain degree of uniformity
6. To eliminate irrelevant responses

Field Editing: While the data collection is in the process, the supervisor is responsible to collect the correct information. Normally, it will be done at the same day or next day. Here, two types of problems may be avoided: Recording the Answer to Questions and Illegible Hand Writing.

Central Editing: At the Office mostly after data collection or at during data collection, editor must keep the following points in mind while editing the data familiar with instructions given to the interviewer and coder. While crossing out the original entry, there should be just one line, so as the original is visible.

C. Tabulation

Tabulation is the process of summarizing raw data and same in compact form (i.e., in the form of statistical table) for further analysis. When mass data has been assembled, it becomes necessary for the researcher to arrange the same in some kind of concise logical order, which may be called tabulation. The orderly and systematic presentation of numerical data in a form designated to elucidate the problem under consideration.

Tabulation is Essential Because:

1. It conserves space and reduces explanatory and descriptive statement to a minimum
2. It facilitates the process of comparison
3. It facilitates the summation of items and the detection of errors and omissions
4. It provides a basis for various statistical computations

2.2.9 Hypothesis Testing

Step 1: Identify the null hypothesis H_0 and the alternate hypothesis H_a.

Step 2: Choose a. The value should be small, usually less than 10%. It is important to consider the consequences of both types of errors.

Step 3: Select the test statistic and determine its value from the sample data.

Step 4: Compare the observed value of the statistic to the critical value obtained for the chosen a.

Step 5: Make a decision.

(a) **If the test statistic falls in the critical region:** Reject H_0 in favor of H_a.

(b) **If the test statistic does not fall in the critical region:** Conclude that there is not enough evidence to reject H_0.

Step 6: Hypothesis testing is done to check whether the facts support the hypothesis or not.

In a research hypothesis testing, a hypothesis is an optional detail of a phenomenon. A null hypothesis is a hypothesis that a researcher aims to challenge. Usually, the null hypothesis denotes the current vision/explanation of a feature of the world that the researcher needs to test. Research methodologies involve the researcher provided that an optional hypothesis, a research hypothesis, as an optional method to give details of the phenomenon.

Hypothesis Benefits

A hypothesis testing gives the following benefits:

1. They establish the focus and track for a research effort.
2. Their development services the researcher to shape the purpose of the research movement.
3. They establish what variables will not be measured in a study, similarly those will be considered.
4. They need the researcher should contain the operational explanation of the variables of interest.

Process of hypothesis testing:

1. State the hypotheses of importance.
2. Conclude the suitable test statistic.
3. State the stage of statistical significance.
4. State the decision regulation for rejecting/not rejecting the null hypothesis.
5. Collect the data and complete the needed calculations.
6. Choose to reject/not reject the null hypothesis.

2.2.10 Generalizations and Interpretation

Step 1: Generalization refers to build a theory when the hypothesis is also there.

Step 2: Interpretation is based on the theory when there is no hypothesis.

A. Meaning of Interpretation

Interpretation refers to the task of drawing inferences from the collected facts after an analytical and/or experimental study. In fact, it is a search for broader meaning of research findings. The task of interpretation has two major aspects, viz.,

- The effort to establish continuity in research through linking the results of a given study with those of another, and
- The establishment of some explained concepts.

"In one sense, interpretation is concerned with relationships within the collected data, partially overlapping analysis. Interpretation also extends beyond the data of the study to inch the results of other research, theory and hypotheses." Thus, interpenetration is the device through which the factors that seem to explain what has been observed by researcher in the course of the study can be better understood and it also provides a theoretical conception which can serve as a guide for further researches.

B. Why Interpretation?

Interpretation is essential for the simple reason that the usefulness and utility of research findings lie in proper interpretation. It is being considered a basic component of research process because of the following reasons:

1. It is through interpretation that the researcher can well understand the abstract principle that works beneath his findings. Through this, he can link up his findings with those of other studies, having the same abstract principle, and thereby can predict about the concrete world of events. Fresh inquiries can test these predictions later on. This way the continuity in research can be maintained.
2. Interpretation leads to the establishment of explanatory concepts that can serve as a guide for future research studies; it opens new avenues of intellectual adventure and stimulates the quest for more knowledge.
3. Researcher can better appreciate only through interpretation why his findings are what they are and can make others to understand the real significance of his research findings.
4. The interpretation of the findings of exploratory research study often results into hypotheses for experimental research and as such interpretation is involved in the transition from exploratory to experimental research. Since an exploratory study does not have a hypothesis to start with, the findings of such a study have to be interpreted on a *post factum* basis in which case the interpretation is technically described as *'post factum'* interpretation.

C. Technique of Interpretation

The task of interpretation is not an easy job, rather it requires a great skill and dexterity on the part of the researcher. Interpretation is an art that one learns through practice and experience. The researcher may, at times, seek the guidance from experts for accomplishing the task of interpretation. The technique of interpretation often involves the following steps:

1. Researcher must give reasonable explanations of the relations which he has found and he must interpret the lines of relationship in terms of the underlying processes and must try to find out the thread of uniformity that lies under the surface layer of his diversified research findings. In fact, this is the technique of how generalization should be done and concepts be formulated.
2. Extraneous information, if collected during the study, must be considered while interpreting the final results of research study, for it may prove to be a key factor in understanding the problem under consideration.
3. It is advisable, before embarking upon final interpretation, to consult someone having insight into the study and who is frank and honest and will not hesitate to point out omissions and errors in logical argumentation. Such a consultation will result in correct interpretation and, thus, will enhance the utility of research results.
4. Researcher must accomplish the task of interpretation only after considering all relevant factors affecting the problem to avoid false generalization. He must be in no hurry while interpreting results, for quite often the conclusions, which appear to be all right at the beginning, may not at all be accurate.

2.2.11 Preparation of the Report or Thesis

Step 1: Report should include preliminary pages, main text, end matter.

Step 2: Report should be concise and simple.

Step 3: Charts and illustrations should be used.

Step 4: Include experience during the research.

The scientific method of inquiry requires that the researcher should document all details about his study. This helps other researchers who might want to repeat similar studies to confirm the findings. The research report should be detailed enough to communicate all aspects of the investigation. Aspects to be covered should include a statement of the problem under investigation, methodology used, scope of the study and the limitations. The report should also communicate the findings, conclusions and the recommendations arrived at. All the elements in a research report should be presented in a logical sequence and broken down into readily identifiable sections.

A. Preliminary Section

1. Title Page: Some Basic Considerations

The title page usually includes:

- The name of the topic
- The name of the author
- The relationship of the report to a course or degree requirement
- The name of the institution where the report is submitted
- The date and place of the presentation

Any research work starts with a title that will almost certainly change before the research is completed and reported. It is very wise, therefore, to think of an effective title that will be finally adopted. So it is a good idea to keep notes of alternative titles or ideas as you proceed in preparing and writing the research report. The title should catch the readers' attention while informing them about the main thesis of the study. First impressions are strong and can attract attention. The title should be concise and should give a precise indication of what is to come. It should not claim more than what the study actually delivers. The title should be typed in capital letters, single spaced and centered between the right and left margins of the page.

2. Acknowledgement (if any)

An acknowledgement page is included if the writer has received unusual assistance in the conduct of the study. The author gives credit for external support received during the conduct of the study. Acknowledgement also expresses gratitude for the use of copyrighted or otherwise restricted materials. A doctoral candidate may choose to dedicate the dissertation to a person(s) who has had significant impact on his work.

3. Table of contents

A good table of contents serves as an important purpose in providing an outline of the content of the report. The relationship between principal and minor divisions is indicated by capitalization of chapter numbers and titles, with sub-headings in small letters and with capitalized principal letters.

B. Main Body of the Report

1. Introduction

- As in the proposal, the introduction presents the problem addressed by the research.
- Gives sufficient background information to allow readers to understand the results of the study.
- It is written in such a way that readers will know the current status of research conclusions on the topic, the theoretical implications associated with the results of previous research on the subject, and the statement of a hypothetical resolution of the issues to be tested by the research described.
- As in the proposal, the introduction should describe the nature and purpose of the study, present the guiding research questions, and explain the significance of and justification for conducting the study. Terms likely to be used throughout the paper should be defined in this section.
- A statement of objectives is included and a research hypothesis.

2. Review of Related Literature

A literature review must be organized in relation to the research topic you are developing. In the process, you should synthesize results into a summary of what is and is not known; identify areas of controversy in the literature; formulate questions that need further research.

3. Materials and Methods (Methodology)

The methodology section is used to describe what the researcher did and how the study was conducted. One important purpose is to enable others repeat the experiment and verify the results if they wish to. In doing so, you should summarize the procedures in the execution of each of the stage of your work. This section should build on the description of methods outlined in the proposal. You should label sub-sections similar to those in the proposal. It may include sub-sections describing participants or subjects, another describing testing or measurement procedures undertaken with the participants, and a section describing limitations of the methodology. These are all done in the past tense or past perfect tense.

This section should present the following:

1. Procedures used and kind of design
2. Sources of data
3. Methods of gathering data
4. Description of data gathering instruments used

4. Analysis of Data/Results

- This section summarizes the data collected and details the statistical treatment of that data.
- Present your results in a logical sequence using only observations pertinent to your stated objectives.
- After a brief statement of the main results or findings of the study, the data are reported in sufficient detail to justify the conclusions.

- Tables and illustrations may be used to report data when these methods are seen to present the data more clearly and economically.
- Do not replicate observations in your tables. Give only means and measures of variability.
- Use tables to present exact values and figures to show trends and relationships.
- All tables and illustrations should be mentioned in the text, with appropriate titles or captions and enough explanations to make them readily identifiable.
- Avoid repetition of numerical data from the tables and figures in the text.

5. Discussion

This section should reflect the implications of the study. Here the researcher evaluates the data and interprets the findings in the context of the research questions or hypothesis. He is guided by questions like the following:

- What do my results mean and what are their implications?
- Should interpret your results clearly, concisely and logically. For each objective, describe how your results relate to meeting the objectives.
- Here, the major results are picked or summarized, evaluated, and interpreted with respect to the original research questions and hypotheses and related with previous works.
- Theoretical and practical consequences of the results and the validity of conclusions may appropriately be discussed in this section.
- The limitations of the study and suggestions for future work may also be included.
- Emphasize on new results and suggest new lines of work or further research.

6. Conclusions and Recommendations

In this section you should describe briefly what you did, the main results and recommendations for further research or applicability. Implications what the findings of the research imply (consider suggestions).

7. References

At the end of your report, you need to list all the sources cited in the text. Details regarding citations and references are given in part four.

2.3 BUSINESS RESEARCH PROCESS

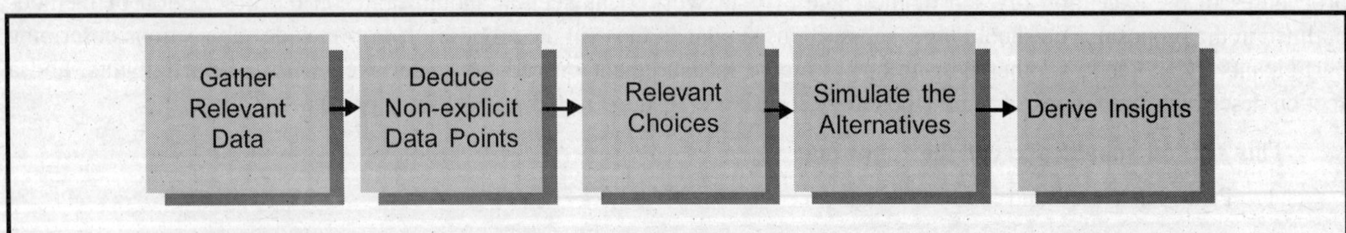

Fig. 2.2: Business Research Process

Step 1: Gather relevant data. Using primary and secondary research techniques, assemble both structured and unstructured (tacit) data and information. Accumulate a wide array of leading secondary data sources and also to a pool of well-regarded industry, academic, and functional experts. For Web-based research, use proprietary software tools and protocols efficiently and effectively to collect the most relevant data. For primary research, utilize comprehensive survey and data collection methodologies. Finally, apply multiple filters to arrive at data that is relevant, consistent, and reliable.

Step 2: Deduce non-explicit data points. Data and information are not always available via primary and secondary research. In cases where there are gaps in the data, employ assumptive methodologies such as devising intelligent proxies and statistical techniques. Assumptions should always be clearly stated.

Step 3: Relevant choices. Once all data has been gathered and filtered, use advanced analytical techniques to structure and analyze data for patterns, trends, and outliers. Using the proprietary multidimensional databases, one can intelligently observe structured data sets in comparative and cross-relational formats.

Step 4: Simulate the alternatives. Leveraging the significant modelling expertise, input structured data into customized predictive models. The models constructed to serve as point-and-click tools to simulate scenario-based business case outcomes. Simulated outcomes are driven by leading indicators such as changes in industry/sector dynamics, shifts in innovation and business model cycles, changes in operating paradigms, movements of macroeconomic drivers, etc.

Step 5: Drive insights. The aim is to provide with continuous, complete, and error-free knowledge and insight that support rapid, effective decision making. Combining outputs from steps 1-4 with the creative frameworks and third-party objectivity, Dolcera drives the insights to rely upon to stay ahead of the curve in a knowledge-intensive business environment. Because the information is so thoroughly synthesized and analyzed, clients rarely require additional processing or even formatting. That's what we reckon as the Advantage of Knowledge.

2.4 SUMMARY

A major problem facing students of business research is that it is difficult to consider each stage in the research process separately. However, without concentrated emphasis on each stage of the total process, it is difficult to understand the individual stages. Thus, the primary stage of any research process includes: observation, interest and crystallization, formulation of hypothesis, primary synopsis, conceptual clarity, documentation and bibliography. Decision making is the process of resolving a problem or choosing from alternative opportunities. Decision makers must recognize the nature of the problem; identify how much information is available and what information is needed. Thus, the research process proceeds in a series of eleven interrelated stages. They are: (1) Formulating the research problems, (2) Extensive literature survey, (3) Development working hypothesis, (4) Preparing research design, (5) Determining sample design, (6) Collecting the data, (7) Execution of the project, (8) Analysis of the data, (9) Hypothesis Testing, (10) Generalizations and interpretation, and (11) Preparation of the report or thesis.

2.5 KEY TERMS

Crystallization: Crystallization is the process of designing the definite form of research to be undertaken for the purpose of studying the subject matter.

Bibliography: Bibliography is the list of books publication, periodicals, journals, reports, etc. which are used by researcher in the connection with the study.

Working Hypothesis: Working hypothesis is a **hypothesis** that is provisionally accepted when no alternatives are available, or when the philosophical implications of the alternatives are considered to be absurd or otherwise undesirable.

Sampling Method: Sampling method refers to the rules and procedures by which some elements of the population are included in the sample.

Estimator: The estimation process for calculating sample statistics is called the estimator.

Voluntary Sample: A voluntary sample is made up of people who self-select into the survey.

Convenience Sample: A convenience sample is made up of people who are easy to reach.

Census: A census is a study that obtains data from every member of a **population**.

Sample Survey: A sample survey is a study that obtains data from a subset of a population, in order to estimate population attributes.

Experiment: An experiment is a controlled study in which the researcher attempts to understand cause-and-effect relationships.

Project Execution Plan (PEP): Project Execution Plan is a document which acts as a primary manner by which the project is planned, monitored and managed.

Editing: Editing is a process of examining the collected raw data (especially in surveys) to detect errors, options, inadequate entries and to correct these when possible.

Tabulation: Tabulation is the process of summarizing raw data and displaying the same in compact form (i.e., in the form of statistical table) for further analysis.

2.6 MULTIPLE OBJECTIVE TYPE QUESTIONS

1. Crystallization is the process of designing the definite form of research to be undertaken for the purpose of studying the subject matter.
(a) True (b) False
2. Research problem address the long-term project outcomes, i.e., that should reflect the aspirations and expectations of the research topic.
(a) True (b) False
3. A working hypothesis is a hypothesis that is provisionally accepted when alternatives are available, or when the philosophical implications of the alternatives are considered to be absurd or otherwise undesirable.
(a) True (b) False
4. Research design is best approached by thinking through the research process in a sequential, step-by-step process.
(a) True (b) False
5. Sampling method refers to the rules and procedures by which one elements of the population are included in the sample.
(a) True (b) False
6. In cluster sampling, every member of the population is assigned to one, and only one, group.
(a) True (b) False
7. A sample survey is a study that obtains data from a subset of a population, in order to estimate sample attributes.
(a) True (b) False
8. An experiment is a controlled study in which the researcher attempts to understand cause-and-effect relationships.
(a) True (b) False
9. Computer Assisted Personal Interviewing (CAPI) is a form of personal interviewing, but instead of completing a questionnaire, the interviewer brings along a laptop or handheld computer to enter the information directly into the database.
(a) True (b) False
10. The Project Execution Plan (PEP) is a document which acts as a primary manner by which the project is planned, monitored and managed.
(a) True (b) False
11. Which stage of research process, the research project is given a concrete shape and structure forming a basis of further investigation.
(a) Observation (b) Interest
(c) Crystallization (d) Documentation
12. Which one is the objective of research problem?
(a) Must be highly focused and feasible (b) Address the less immediate project outcomes.
(c) Not presented consciously and briefly (d) None of the above.

13. Which of the following are good reasons for spending time and effort on a review of the literature before embarking on a research project?
    (a) To identify gaps in the literature
    (b) To increase the breadth of knowledge of your subject area
    (c) To put your work into prospective
    (d) All the above.
14. "Scientific study designed to increase our knowledge of natural phenomena can follow at least three different intellectual methods". These method is called
    (a) Working hypothesis (b) Multiple working hypothesis
    (c) Ruling theory (d) All of the above
15. Which of the following can be sent to large number of people and saves the researcher's time and money?
    (a) Web-based questionnaires (b) Paper-pencil questionnaires
    (c) Qualitative data collection method (d) None of the above
16. Which plan is a document which acts a primary manner by which the project is planned, monitored and managed?
    (a) Product purchasing (b) Product development
    (c) Risk management (d) Project execution
17. Which one is the basic principle of coding?
    (a) Exhaustiveness (b) Legibility
    (c) Completeness (d) All of the above
18. Which one of the basic principle of editing?
    (a) Link to the theory (b) Degree of uniformity
    (c) Mutually Exhaustiveness (d) All of the above
19. Which one obtains the data from a subset of population, in order to estimate population attributes?
    (a) Census (b) Experiment
    (c) Sample survey (d) Sampling
20. Which is the process of summarizing raw data and displaying the same in compact from for further analysis?
    (a) Tabulation (b) Coding
    (c) Editing (d) Interpretation

Answers to Multiple Objective Type Questions

Questions	1	2	3	4	5	6	7	8	9	10
Answers	T	T	F	T	F	T	F	T	T	T
Questions	11	12	13	14	15	16	17	18	19	20
Answers	c	a	d	c	b	d	a	b	c	a

2.7 CONCEPTUAL QUESTIONS

1. What is research process? Explain in detail the primary stages of research process.
2. Explain in detail the various steps in research process.
3. Distinguish between probability and non-probability sampling methods.
4. What is business research process? Explain.

5. Write short notes on:
   (a) Formulating the research problems
   (b) Extensive literature survey
   (c) Development working hypothesis
   (d) Preparing research design
   (e) Determining sample design
   (f) Collecting the data
   (g) Execution of the project
   (h) Analysis of the data
   (i) Hypothesis Testing
   (j) Generalizations and interpretation
   (k) Tabulation
   (l) Preparation of the report or thesis

* * * * *

CHAPTER 3

RESEARCH PROBLEM

Chapter Outline

Learning Objectives

- *Explain clearly the distinguishing features of research problem.*
- *Discuss the significance and importance of the elements that make up the complete research problem.*
- *Formulate research problem in terms of a hypothesis to be tested.*

3.1 MEANING OF RESEARCH PROBLEM

A research problem is the situation that causes the researcher to feel apprehensive, confused and ill at ease. It is the demarcation of a problem area within a certain context involving the WHO or WHAT, the WHERE, the WHEN and the WHY of the problem situation.

There are many problem situations that may give rise to research. Three sources usually contribute to problem identification. Own experience or the experience of others may be a source of problem supply. A second source could be scientific literature. You may read about certain findings and notice that a certain field was not covered. This could lead to a research problem. Theories could be a third source. Shortcomings in theories could be researched.

Research can thus be aimed at clarifying or substantiating an existing theory, at clarifying contradictory findings, at correcting a faulty methodology, at correcting the inadequate or unsuitable use of statistical techniques, at reconciling conflicting opinions, or at solving existing practical problems.

3.2 STATEMENT OF THE RESEARCH PROBLEM

For some students this is the most difficult phase of the research process. Quite often the Research Problem is vague. It is either too scanty or too lengthy but not precise. Despite having written so many paragraphs, the student is unable to state clearly and convincingly:

(i) What is the problem?

(ii) Why it is important?

(iii) What should be done?

Perhaps, the following guidelines on the right may help you with this task.

(i) What is the problem?

You begin by first stating the problem. It is some aspect that your are worried about, think about and want to find a solution, for e.g., Graduate are poor critical thinkers.

(ii) Why is it important that the problem be investigated, i.e., give a rationale for why it is of concern?

For example: Employers are complaining about the poor critical thinking skills of graduates they employ.

Questions about this problem have not been answered convincingly or are inconclusive or answers have not been found up to the present – e.g., very few studies have addressed the critical thinking ability of university students as most studies continue to focus on primary and secondary school students.

(iii) What should be done, i.e., the purpose?

- Your purpose is to solve the problem, i.e., find answers to questions put forward.
- State what should be done clearly and grammatically correct. Avoid meaningless words.
- There should be no doubt in your mind what are your intentions.
- It is good practice to divide you problem into sub-problems which are called research questions.
- Research Questions guide the solution of the problem.

Example: Specifically, this study aims to answer the following research questions:

(a) Is there a difference in critical thinking male and female students?

(b) Is there a relationship between academic performance and critical thinking?

3.3 RESEARCH QUESTIONS

The word "research" means 'finding out' or 'discovery' using a systematic method. You "research" by asking questions and searching for answers to the questions. You cannot "research" if you do not want to know anything, that is, you must have something you would like to know more about before you can do "research".

You begin with QUESTIONS. If you have none, you will find no answers or will not know when you have found one. Your task is to conduct RESEARCH. A study without a question in mind will NOT be a RESEARCH study. You should MAKE SURE that:

1. The research question is clear, straightforward and easily understood by others.
2. The research question states the relationship between two or more variables.
3. The variables mentioned in the research question should be measurable.
4. The answer to the research question is not immediately obvious.
5. The research question indicates the method that is to be adopted, i.e., the data collection techniques.
6. The research question can be answered in the time available to you.
7. The research question can be answered with the resources available to you.

3.4 TYPES OF RESEARCH QUESTIONS

Generally there are three basic types of questions that research projects can address:

A. Descriptive Research Questions

Here you describe what is going on or what exists. For example, you may want to find the proportion of teachers who support the teaching of sex education in secondary school. You are simply interested in describing something.

Statistical Tools

- Mean, median and mode
- Frequency tables
- Histograms, Line graphs

B. Relational Research Questions

Here you want to know the relationships between two or more variables. For example, you want to know the proportion of males and females who support the teaching of sex education in secondary school. In other words, you are interested in studying the relationship between gender and preference for teaching of sex education.

Statistical Tools

- Simple correlation
- Linear regression
- Multiple regressions

C. Causal Research Questions

Here, you want to know whether one or more variables (e.g., a programme or treatment variable) causes or affects one or more outcome variables. For example, you conduct a workshop to the group of teachers to determine whether their opinion about teaching sex education to secondary school students has changed.

Statistical Tools

- t-test
- Analysis of Variance (ANOVA)
- Multiple Analyses of Variance (MANOVA)

Checklist for Testing the Feasibility of the Research Problem

YES

NO

1. Is the problem of current interest? Will the research results have social, educational or scientific value?
2. Will it be possible to apply the results in practice?
3. Does the research contribute to the science of education?
4. Will the research opt new problems and lead to further research?
5. Is the research problem important? Will you be proud of the result?
6. Is there enough scope left within the area of research (field of research)?
7. Can you find an answer to the problem through research? Will you be able to handle the research problem?
8. Will it be practically possible to undertake the research?
9. Will it be possible for another researcher to repeat the research?
10. Is the research free of any ethical problems and limitations?
11. Will it have any value?
12. Do you have the necessary knowledge and skills to do the research? Are you qualified to undertake the research?
13. Is the problem important to you and are you motivated to undertake the research?
14. Is the research viable in your situation? Do you have enough time and energy to complete the project?
15. Do you have the necessary funds for the research?
16. Will you be able to complete the project within the time available?
17. Do you have access to the administrative, statistic and computer facilities the research necessitates?

3.5 IDENTIFICATION OF RESEARCH PROBLEM

The identification of research problem is the first and foremost step that every researcher has to undertake. At times, it becomes rather difficult for an inexperienced researcher or a novice/beginner in research to conceptualize a research problem. In general, a research problem should be understood as some difficulty, unclear situation which a researcher experiences in practical or theoretical context and wants to obtain a tangible explanation, clarification or offer solution to it. For students, this problem may be as a result of theoretical encounter in the area of specialization. As such, before embarking on any research, you should identify the major research area of your interest, mostly the area of your specialization. For instance from:

- Education
- Social sciences
- Humanities
- Business administration

The prospective researcher should think what caused the need to do the research (problem identification). The question that he/she should ask is: Are there questions about this problem to which answers have not been found up to the present?

Research originates from a need that arises. A clear distinction between the PROBLEM and the PURPOSE should be made. The problem is the aspect the researcher worries about, thinks about, wants to find a solution for. The purpose is to solve the problem, i.e., find answers to the question(s). If there is no clear problem formulation, the purposes and methods are meaningless.

Keep the following in mind:

1. Outline the general context of the problem area.
2. Highlight key theories, concepts and ideas current in this area.
3. What appear to be some of the underlying assumptions of this area?
4. Why are these issues identified important?
5. What needs to be solved?

6. Read round the area (subject) to get to know the background and to identify unanswered questions or controversies, and/or to identify the most significant issues for further exploration.

The research problem should be stated in such a way that it would lead to analytical thinking on the part of the researcher with the aim of possible concluding solutions to the stated problem. Research problems can be stated in the form of either questions or statements.

1. The research problem should always be formulated grammatically correct and as completely as possible. You should bear in mind the wordings (expressions) you use. Avoid meaningless words. There should be no doubt in the mind of the reader what your intentions are.
2. Demarcating the research field into manageable parts by dividing the main problem into sub-problems is of the utmost importance.

3.6 CHARACTERISTICS OF A GOOD RESEARCH PROBLEM

The following are some of the characteristics of a good research problem:

1. It should be one that can be investigated through the collection and data analysis.
2. The problem can be stated clearly and concisely.
3. It generates a number of more specific research questions.
4. It relates to academic discipline.
5. It has basis in research literature.
6. It should have potential significance.
7. It should be one that can be carried out within the set time frame and budget.
8. It should be the one that has sufficient data.
9. It should be the one that you can adequately investigate given your research skills, available resources and time.

3.7 SELECTING RESEARCH PROBLEM

The selection of a problem is the first step in research. The term 'problem' means a question or issue to be examined. The selection of a problem for research is not an easy task; itself is a problem. It is least amenable to formal methodological treatment. Vision, an imaginative insight, plays an important role in this process. This problem of selection arises when a student has to undertake research as a part of his course requirement and the student has to select a problem for his research.

3.7.1 The Mode of Selection

The students who undertake research as a course requirement do their research work under the guidance of a professor. What should be the mode of selection in their cases? Should a problem be suggested by the guide or be selected by the researcher himself? One with a critical, curious and imaginative mind and is sensitive to practical problems could easily identify problems for study.

Sources of Problems

1. **Academic Experience:** Classroom lectures, class discussions, seminar discussions and out-of-class exchanges of ideas with fellow students and professors will suggest many stimulating problems to be studied.
2. **Daily Experience:** Life is dynamic. We learn new things and undergo new experiences every day. If we are alert, inquisitive and sensitive to life situations, we may hit upon questions worth of investigation. "It is a mark of scientific genius to be sensitive to difficulties where less gifted people pass untroubled by doubt".
3. **Exposure to field situations:** Field visits; internship training and extension work provide exposure to practical problems that call for study.
4. **Consultations:** Discussions with experts, researchers, administrators and business executives will help a researcher to identify meaningful problems for research.

5. **Brainstorming:** Intensified discussion within a group of interested persons may often be a means of identifying pertinent questions, and of developing new ideas about a problem.
6. **Research:** Research on one problem may suggest problems for further research.
7. **Intuition:** Sometimes new ideas may strike one's mind like a flash. Reflective mind is a spring of knowledge.

3.7.2 Formulation of the Selected Problem

The problem selected for research may initially be a vague topic. The question to be studied or the problem to be solved may not be known. Why the answer/solution is wanted also may not be known. Hence, the selected problem should be defined and formulated. This is a difficult process. It requires intensive reading of a few selected articles or chapters in books in order to understand the nature of the selected problem. The researcher should read selected literature, digest, think and reflect upon what is read and digested. He should also discuss with learned persons. Then only can he gain insight into the selected problem and be able to define and formulate it.

Formulation means translating and transforming the selected research problem/topic into a scientifically researchable question. It is concerned with specifying exactly what the research problem is and why is it studied. The formulation should include both what and why aspects.

Formulation Process

The process of formulation involves the following steps:

1. Developing title.
2. Building a conceptual model.
3. Defining the objectives of the study.
4. Setting investigative questions.
5. Formulation of hypotheses.
6. Operational definition of concepts.
7. Delimiting the scope of the study.

3.8 HOW TO SELECT THE RESEARCH PROBLEM?

1. **Prevention of unnecessary duplication.** The problem must not have been investigated before. If the problem is investigated before, it may be the subject of another study but with different assumptions, different methods, or different ways of analyzing data.
2. **Practical value of the problem.** The result of the research study should use to improve practices and concepts. It can use of those who may want to make use it.
3. **Researcher's interest in the problem.** The researcher should select a problem not because of research popularity or someone wants him to investigate it but because it appeals to his interest.
4. **Availability of data on the problem.** A fruitful results yield if data on the problem is available.
5. **Personal choice of the researcher problem or topic.** This is to prevent from blaming others or offering excuses for any problem encountered.
6. **Researchable and manageable research problem or topic.** All the data used should be accessible as well as equipment and instruments for research are available and can give valid and reliable results. Also, the hypothesis formulated are testable and the research problem or topic should be able to meet the standards of accuracy, objectivity and verifiability.
7. **Within period of time.** Research topic should be completed within a reasonable period of time. There must be a project timetable.
8. **Relevant to the present time.** Research topic should be significant, important and relevant to the present time and situation, and of current interest. In addition, it should be able to arouse people's interest.

9. **Add human knowledge.** Research topic must contribute a new bit of knowledge to what we already have since all the facts and knowledge are the products of research.
10. **Solve problems.** Prove the way for the solution of the problems or problems intended to be solved. After research or project have been conducted, recommendations are made for the solution and if implemented can solve the problems.
11. **Moral and spiritual values.** Research topic must promote divine values and admirable human values including love, peace, goodwill, etc.
12. **Quality of human life.** Research topic must improve the quality of human life or show how to improve unsatisfactory conditions.

3.9 TECHNIQUES INVOLVED IN DEFINING RESEARCH PROBLEM

The following steps are to be involved:

1. Statement of the problem
2. Nature of the problem
3. Literature Survey
4. Rephrasing the research problem

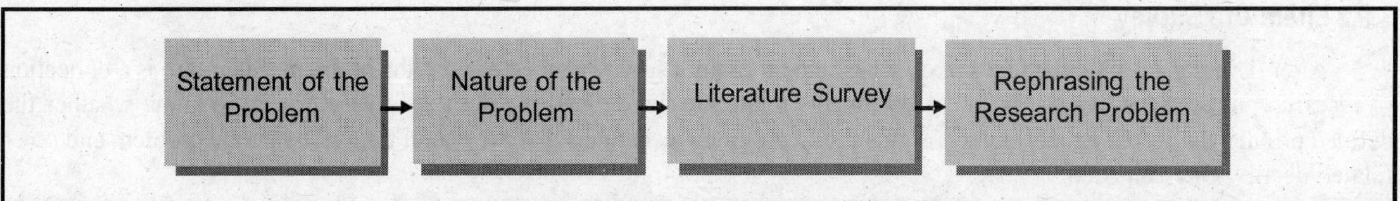

Fig. 3.1: Techniques Involved Research Problem

3.9.1 Statement of the Problem

A **problem statement** is a concise description of the issues that need to be addressed by a problem solving team and should be presented to them (or created by them) before they try to solve the problem. A good statement should answer these questions:

1. What is the problem? This should explain why the team is needed.
2. Who has the problem or who is the client/customer? This should explain who needs the solution and who will decide the problem to be solved.
3. What are the scope and limitations to solve the problem?

The primary purpose of a problem statement is to focus the attention of the problem solving team. However, if the focus of the problem is too narrow or the scope of the solution too limited, the creativity and innovation of the solution can be stifled.

A **research-worthy problem statement** is the description of an active challenge (i.e., problem) faced by researchers and/or practitioners that does not have adequate solutions available including the argumentation for its viability based on solid peer-reviewed sources as well as theoretical foundation. The worthy problem statement should address all six questions: what, how, where, when, why, and who. On the other hand, statement of the problem is one or two sentences claim that outlines the problem that the study addresses. The statement of the problem should briefly address the question: What is the problem that the research will address?

Functions of Problem Statement

In order to demonstrate that your problem is researchable, the statement of research problem should perform the following functions:

1. The context of research;
2. The focus of research;
3. The significance of research;
4. The framework for results and conclusions.

3.9.2 Nature of the Problem

Understanding the nature of the problem is to discuss it with those who first raised it in order to find out how the problem originally came about and with what objectives in view. If the researcher has stated the problem himself, he should consider once again all those points that induced him to make a general statement concerning the problem. The following points are to better understand the research problem:

1. Understand the nature and origin of the problem in clear terms.
2. For better understanding of the nature of the problem involved, he can enter into discussion with those who have good knowledge of the problem concerned or similar other problems.
3. By discussion and consultation with experts keeping in view the objectives of the study he should make a general statement relating to the problem.
4. The researcher should also keep in view the environment within which the problem is to be studied and understood.

3.9.3 Literature Survey

After defining a problem, the researcher has to do literature survey connected with the problem. Literature is a collection of research publications, books and other documents related to the defined problem. It is very crucial to know whether the defined problem has already been solved, status of the problem, techniques that are useful to investigate the problem and other related details. One can survey

1. the journals which publish abstracts of papers published in various journals,
2. review articles related to the topic chosen,
3. journals which publish research articles,
4. advanced level books on the chosen topic,
5. proceedings of conferences, workshops, etc.,
6. reprint/preprint collections available with the supervisor and nearby experts working on the topic chosen,
7. Internet.

No research shall be complete unless we make use of the knowledge available in books, journals and internet. Review of the literature in the area of research is a preliminary step before attempting to plan the study.

Literature Survey Helps Us:

(a) sharpen the problem, reformulate it or even leads to defining other closely related problems,

(b) get proper understanding of the problem chosen,

(c) acquire proper theoretical and practical knowledge to investigate the problem,

(d) show how the problem under study relates to the previous research studies,

(e) know whether the proposed problem had already been solved.

Through survey, one can collect relevant information about the problem. Clarity of ideas can be acquired through study of literature.

- Before defining or rephrasing the research problem, all available research literature should be surveyed and examined thoroughly.
- The type of difficulties that may be encountered for the present study may be ascertained.

- If there is any gap or inconsistency in existing theories of different studies, they should be integrated.
- All possible analytical shortcomings should be indicated.

3.9.5 Rephrasing the Research Problem

Once the nature of the problem has been clearly understood, the environment has been defined, discussions over the problem have taken place and the available literature has been surveyed and examined. Through rephrasing, the researcher puts the research problem in as specific terms as possible so that it may become operationally viable and may help in the development of working hypotheses.

The following points must also be observed while defining a research problem:

1. To rephrase the research problem into a working proposition.
2. The statement of the problem should be clearly defined.
3. The problem should be specified so that it becomes operationally viable which may lead to help the development of working hypotheses.
4. Basic assumptions to the research problem should be clearly stated.
5. A straightforward statement of the value of the investigation should be provided.
6. The suitability of the time-period and the sources of data available must also be considered by the researcher in defining the problem.

3.10 TYPES OF VARIABLE

There are many ways of classifying variables but in educational research, the two most common methods of classification are as follows:

1. Independent and Dependent Variables
2. Continuous and Categorical Variables

3.10.1 Independent and Dependent Variables

An independent variable (IV) is the variable that is presumed to cause a change in the dependent variable (DV). The independent variables is the antecedent while the dependent variable is the consequent, which describes a study to determine which teaching method (independent variable) is effective in enhancing the academic performance (dependent variable) of students.

The independent variable (teaching method) can be manipulated. 'Manipulated' means the variable can maneuvered, and in this case it is divided into 'discussion method' and 'lecture method'. Other examples of independent variables are gender (male-female), race (Malay, Chinese, Indian), socio-economic status (high, middle, low). Other names for the independent variable are treatment, factor and predictor variable.

The dependent variable in this study is academic performance which cannot be manipulated by the researcher. Academic performance is a score and other examples of dependent variables are IQ (score from IQ tests), attitude (score on an attitude scale), self-esteem (score from a self-esteem test) and so forth. Other names for the dependent variable are outcome variable, results variable and criterion variable.

3.10.2 Continuous and Categorical Variables

A **continuous variable** (also called ordinal variable) is capable of taking on an ordered set of values within a certain range. For example, an attitude scale towards smoking may have values ranging from 5 to 20 which expresses differing amounts of attitude towards smoking. A **categorical variable** (also called nominal variable) may be made up of two or more subsets or categories. Each subset or category possess certain characteristics and individuals are categorized by their possession of those characteristics that defines a subset. For example, the variable socio-economic class (SES) may consist of three values such as high SES, middle SES and low SES.

3.11 SUMMARY

A research problem is the situation that causes the researcher to feel apprehensive, confused and ill at ease. Three sources usually contribute to problem identification, i.e., own experience or the experience of others may be a source of problem supply. Source could be scientific literature and shortcomings in theories could be researched. The identification of research problem is the first and foremost step that every researcher has to undertake. The prospective researcher should think on what caused the need to do the research (problem identification). The techniques involved in defining research problems are: (1) Statement of the problem in a general way; (2) Understanding the nature of the problem; (3) Surveying the available literature; (4) Developing the ideas through discussions; and (5) Rephrasing the research problem into a working proposition.

3.12 KEY TERMS

Research Problem: Research problem is the situation that causes the researcher to feel apprehensive, confused and ill at ease.

Consultations: Discussions with experts, researchers, administrators and business executives will help a researcher to identify meaningful problems for research.

Brainstorming: Intensified discussion within a group of interested persons may often be a means of identifying pertinent questions, and of developing new ideas about a problem.

Intuition: Sometimes, new ideas may strike one's mind like a flash. Reflective mind is a spring of knowledge.

Formulation: Formulation means translating and transforming the selected research problem/topic into a scientifically researchable question and it is concerned with specifying exactly what the research problem is and why is it studied.

Continuous Variable: Continuous variable is capable of taking on an ordered set of values within a certain range.

3.13 MULTIPLE OBJECTIVE TYPE QUESTIONS

1. Research problem should be investigated through the collection and data analysis.
   (a) True (b) False
2. Research problem should be carried out within the set of time frame and budget.
   (a) True (b) False
3. Formulation means translating and transforming the selected research problem/topic into a scientifically researchable question.
   (a) True (b) False
4. Formulation of the research problem does not require primary data collection.
   (a) True (b) False
5. The research problem or topic should be within the interest of the researcher so that the researcher will focus his full attention on the research work.
   (a) True (b) False
6. The dependent variable is the antecedent while the dependent variable is the consequent.
   (a) True (b) False
7. Independent variable is academic performance which cannot be manipulated by the researcher.
   (a) True (b) False
8. A continuous variable is capable of taking on an ordered set of values within a certain range.
   (a) True (b) False
9. Research topic should be completed within a reasonable period of time.
   (a) True (b) False

10. Research topic should not contribute a new bit of knowledge.
    (a) True (b) False
11. Which statistical tools belong to descriptive research questions?
    (a) Average (b) Correlation and regression
    (c) Analysis of variance (d) All of the above
12. Which statistical tools belong to relational research questions?
    (a) Average (b) Correlation and regression
    (c) Analysis of variance (d) All of the above
13. Which statistical tools belong to causal research questions?
    (a) Average (b) Correlation and regression
    (c) Analysis of variance (d) All of the above
14. Which variable is presumed to cause a change in the dependent variable?
    (a) Dependent (b) Independent
    (c) Continuous (d) Categorical
15. Which variable is capable of talking on an ordered set of values within a certain range?
    (a) Dependent (b) Independent
    (c) Continuous (d) Categorical
16. Which of the following must be observed while defining research problem?
    (a) To rephrase the research problem into a working proposition
    (b) The statement of the problem should be clearly defined
    (c) Basic assumptions to the research problem should be clearly stated
    (d) All the above
17. Which are the characteristics of a good research problem?
    (a) The problem can be stated clearly and concisely
    (b) It should have potential significance
    (c) It should be the one that has sufficient data
    (d) All the above
18. Which of the following is to better understand the research problem?
    (a) Understand the nature and origin of the problem
    (b) By discussion and consultation with expert
    (c) Both (a) and (b)
    (d) None of the above
19. Research problems can be stated in the form of
    (a) Only questions (b) Only statements
    (c) Neither questions nor statements (d) Either questions or statements
20. Before defining or rephrasing the research problem, all available literature should be
    (a) Surveyed thoroughly (b) Examined thoroughly
    (c) Surveyed and examined thoroughly (d) None of the above

Answers to Multiple Objective Type Questions

Questions	1	2	3	4	5	6	7	8	9	10
Answers	T	T	T	F	T	F	F	T	T	F
Questions	11	12	13	14	15	16	17	18	19	20
Answers	a	b	c	b	c	d	d	c	d	c

3.14 CONCEPTUAL QUESTIONS

1. What is research problem? Describe the techniques of defining a research problem.
2. Define the main issues which should receive the attention of the researcher in formulating the research problem. Give suitable examples to elucidate your points.
3. How do you define a research problem? Give three examples to illustrate your answer.
4. What is the necessity of defining a research problem? Explain.
5. "The task of defining the research problem often follows a sequential pattern". Explain.
6. "Knowing what data are available often serves to narrow down the problem itself as well as the technique that might be used". Explain the underlying idea in this statement in the context of defining a research problem.
7. Write short notes on:
   (a) Experience survey
   (b) Pilot survey
   (c) Components of research problem
   (d) Rephrasing the research problem
   (e) Statement of the problem in a general way
   (f) Understanding the nature of the problem
   (g) Surveying the available literature
   (h) Developing the ideas through discussions
   (i) Independent and dependent variable.

CHAPTER 4

RESEARCH DESIGN

Chapter Outline

Learning Objectives

- *Discuss the various experimental design as powerful tools to study the cause. and effect relationship amongst variables in research.*
- *Explain the assumptions embodied in the design models.*
- *Choose the appropriate design model for a specific research problem.*

4.1 MEANING OF RESEARCH DESIGN

A research design is a logical and systematic plan prepared for directing a research study. It specifies the objectives of the study, the methodology and techniques to be adopted for achieving the objectives. It constitutes the blueprint for the collection, measurement and analysis of data. A research design is the program that guides the investigator in the process of collecting, analyzing and interpreting observations. It "provides a systematic plan of procedure for the researcher to follow."

Essentials of a Good Research Design

1. It is a plan that specifies the objectives of the study and the hypotheses to be tested.
2. It is an outline that specifies the sources and types of information relevant to the research questions.
3. It is a blueprint specifying the methods to be adopted for gathering and analyzing the data.

4.1.1 Nature of Research Design

A research design is indispensable for a research project. However, it is not a precise and specific plan like a building plan to be followed without deviations, but rather a series of guideposts to keep one going in the right direction. It is a tentative plan which undergoes modifications, as circumstances demand, when the study progresses, new aspects, new conditions and new relationships come to light and insight into the study deepens. Thus, a research design "represents a compromise dictated by many practical considerations."

4.1.2 Importance of Research Plan

The preparation of a research plan for a study aids in establishing direction to the study and in knowing exactly what has to be done and how and when it has to be done at every stage. It enables the researcher to consider beforehand the various decisions to be made: What are the objectives of the study? What are the investigative questions? What are the sources of data? What is the universe of the study? What sampling method is appropriate? and so on.

Without a plan, research work becomes unfocussed and aimless empirical wandering, the researcher would find it difficult, laborious and time-consuming to make adequate discrimination in the complex interplay of factors before him; he may not be able to decide which is relevant and which is not, and may get lost in a welter of irrelevancies. The use of a research design guides to proceed in the right direction.

- A research plan prescribes the boundaries of research activities and enables the researcher to channel his energies in the right work.
- With clear research objectives in view, the researcher can proceed systematically toward their achievement.
- The design also enables the researcher to anticipate potential problems of data gathering, operationalization of concepts, measurement, etc.

4.1.3 Preparation of the Research Design

Planning involves deciding things in advance. Accordingly, the preparation of a research plan involves a careful consideration of the following questions and making appropriate decisions on them:

1	What the study is about?
2	Why is the 'study' made?
3	What is its scope?
4	What are the 'Objectives' of the study?
5	What are the propositions to be tested?
6	What are the major concepts to be defined operationally?
7	On the basis of what criteria or measurements, the operational definitions to be made?
8	When or in what place the study will be conducted?
9	What is the reference period of the study?

10	What is the typology of the design?
11	What kinds of data are needed?
12	What are the sources of data?
13	What is the universe from which the sample has to be drawn?
14	What is the sample size?
15	What sampling techniques can be used?
16	What methods are to be adopted for collecting data?
17	What tools are to be used for collecting data?
18	How the data are to be processed?
19	What techniques of analysis are to be adopted?
20	What is the significance of the study?
21	To what target audience the reporting of the findings is meant?
22	What is the type of report to be prepared?
23	What is the time period required for each stage of research work?
24	What is the time limit within which the whole work should be completed?
25	What is the cost involved?

These questions should be considered with reference to the researcher's interest, competence, time and other resources, and the requirements of sponsoring agency, if any. "Thus, the considerations which enter into making decisions regarding what, where, when, how much, by what means constitute a plan of study or a study design".

4.1.4 The Contents of a Research Plan/Design

After making decisions on the above questions, a formal research plan is drafted, incorporating those decisions. The format may vary depending on the "purpose" for which the study is undertaken, but, in general, the research plan of a research student/academicians may cover the following essential sections:

1. **Introduction:** The introduction of a research plan or proposal should place the research problem in its historical perspective; state the need for studying it, and the researcher's precise interests in the study of the problem.
2. **Statement of the Problem:** The research problem should be defined, pointing out its core nature and its importance. The issue relating to the problem may also be stated. This statement gives direction to the research process.
3. **Review of the Previous Studies:** The selected theme, others might have previously made some studies. A review of available literature will bring out information on them.
4. **Scope of the Study:** A complete study of any problem is well nigh non-manageable. It would entail such an overwhelming mountain of data that it would require more than a student's lifetime to comprehend and complete the study. Therefore, the scope and dimensions of the study should be delimited with reference to the topical scope — breadth and depth, geographical area to be covered, reference period, the type of institutions/respondents to be studied, the issues to be analyzed, etc. The purpose of this demarcation is to make the study manageable in terms of the researcher's aim, interest and competence and available techniques, time, finance and facilities.
5. **Objective of the Study:** The specific objectives of the study should be stated clearly. These refer to the questions to which the researcher proposes to seek answers through the study. Although there is no limit to the number of research objectives, it is desirable to limit the objectives to a reasonable number. What is reasonable depends upon the time limitations, resource constraints, capability etc. It is wise to pick objectives that are challenging but not impossible to achieve.

   The objectives may be stated as under:

   - to study the extent of ...
   - to identify the factors which influence ...

- to examine the nature of relation between ...
- to investigate the impact of ...
- to identify the causes of...

The statement of objective may be followed by a statement of the investigative questions relating to each of the research objectives.

6. **Conceptual Model:** This section is the heart of the research plan. This is where the researcher formulates and develops the structure of relationships among the variables he is investigating.
7. **Hypotheses:** These are logically deduced from the theoretical framework above. These refer to the anticipated outcome or possible answers to the research questions. They should be conceptually clear, specific and simple.
8. **Operational Definition of Concepts:** The major concepts used in the title of the study, its objectives, the investigative questions and the hypotheses should be identified. Each of them should be defined in operational terms pertinent to the measurement criteria or operations.
9. **The Significance of the Study:** It is important to point out the relevance and significance of the investigation. What would be the value of the findings of the study for policy formulation, theory or practice? Can the findings contribute to the enrichment of theory and/or to the solution of some practical problems? A careful statement of the value of the study and the possible applications of its finding helps to justify its importance and social relevance.
10. **Geographical area to be covered:** The territorial area to be covered by the study should be decided and specified in the plan. The area to be chosen depends on the purpose of the study and time and other resources available.
11. **Reference Period:** This period may be one year or two or more years depending on the nature of the study and availability of data. The period should be longer, say 5 or 10 years, if the study aims at making a trend analysis of an activity like production or sale or profitability.
12. **Methodology:** In this section, the overall typology of the design, experimental, descriptive, survey, case study or historical study – is specified. Further, the method or methods to be adopted for collection of data – observation, interviewing or mailing – are specified.
13. **Sampling Plan:** If the study requires collection of primary data from the field, the universe must be delineated, and the methods of sampling to be used for drawing the sample from the universe and the sample size must be stated.
14. **Tools for gathering data:** In this section, the tools, to be used for gathering data – interview schedule/guide or questionnaire or checklist, etc. – are listed and each of them is described. The tools chosen should be appropriate to the methods to be adopted for gathering data.
15. **Plan of Analysis:** The statistical techniques to be used for analyzing the various techniques should be specified. The application of appropriate techniques is essential for testing hypothesis and drawing inferences.
16. **Chapter Scheme:** The chapter scheme of the report/dissertation to be prepared for communicating the findings of the study to the academic community and the users should be outlined and the purpose of each chapter should be stated.
17. **Time Budget:** The time period required for each stage of work and the total time duration of the study are specified.
18. **Financial Budget:** This should include as estimate of the expected costs of the project under various major categories like salary (if any), printing and stationery, postage, travel expenses, computation, secretarial and typing etc.

4.2 CONCEPTS RELATING TO RESEARCH DESIGN

1. Dependent and Independent Variable

An independent variable is the variable that the researchers systematically manipulate in the experiment. An independent variable is measured, manipulated, or selected by the experimenter to determine its relationship to an observed phenomenon.

This might be a variable that you control, like a treatment, or a variable not under your control, like an exposure. Dependent variable is the factor which is observed and measured to determine the effect of the independent variable, that is, the factor appears, disappears, or varies as the experimenter introduces, removes, or varies as the independent variable. The dependent variable is the participant's response. The dependent variable is the outcome of experiment. One variable depends upon or is a consequence of other variable, it is termed as a dependent variable, and the variable that is antecedent to the dependent variable is termed as independent variable. For example: if height depends on age, then height is dependent variable and age is independent variable.

2. Extraneous Variable

Extraneous variables are undesirable variables that influence the relationship between the variables that an experimenter is examining. These variables are undesirable because they add error to an experiment. A major goal in research design is to decrease or control the influence of extraneous variables as much as possible. The researcher wants to test the hypothesis that there is relationship between children's gains in social studies achievement and their self-concepts. In this case, self-concept is an independent variable and social studies achievement is a dependent variable. Intelligence may as well affect the social studies achievement, but since it is not related to the purpose of the study undertaken by the researcher, it will be termed as an extraneous variable.

3. Control Variable

A control variable is a variable that affects the dependent variable. When we "control a variable", we wish to balance its effect across subjects and groups so that we can ignore it, and just study the relationship between the independent and the dependent variables. The technical term 'control' is used when we design the study minimizing the effects of extraneous independent variables. In experimental searches, the term 'control' is used to refer to restrain experimental conditions.

4. Research Hypothesis

A research hypothesis is the statement created by a researcher when they speculate upon the outcome of a research or experiment. The research hypothesis is a paring down of the problem into something testable and falsifiable. Scientists must generate a realistic and testable hypothesis around which they can build the experiment. When a prediction or hypothesized relationship is to be tested by scientific methods, is it termed as research hypothesis? It is a predictive statement that relates an independent variable to a dependent variable.

5. Experimental and Non-experimental Hypothesis-testing Research

In this case, the purpose of research is to test a research hypothesis. It can be of the experimental design and/or of the non experimental design. Research in which the independent variable is manipulated is termed 'experimental hypothesis-testing research' and a research in which an independent is not manipulated is called 'non experimental hypothesis-testing research'.

6. Experimental and Control Group

A control group is the experimental group tested without changing the variable. In this research when a group is exposed to usual conditions, it is termed as a control group, but when a group is exposed to some special conditions, it is termed as experimental group.

7. Treatments

Treatments refer to the different conditions under which experimental and control groups are placed.

8. Experiment

An experiment usually refers to observations in which conditions are artificially controlled and manipulated by the experimenter to eliminate extraneous factors. It denotes the process of examining the truth of a statistical hypothesis, relating to research problem. Experiments can be of two types, viz., absolute experiment and comparative experiment.

9. Experimental Unit(s)

An experimental unit is the portion of experimental material to which a treatment is applied. Randomization of treatments or the predetermined plots or the blocks, where different treatments are used, are known as experimental units.

4.3 QUALITATIVE RESEARCH DESIGN VS. QUANTITATIVE RESEARCH DESIGN

Table 4.1: Qualitative and Quantitative Research Designs

	Qualitative Research Designs
Descriptive	• Describe phenomena as they exist. Descriptive studies generally take raw data and summarize it in a useable form. • Can also be qualitative in nature if the sample size is small and data are collected from questionnaires, interviews or observations.
Experimental	• The art of planning and implementing an experiment in which the research has control over some of the conditions where the study takes place and control over some aspects of the independent variable(s) (presumed cause or variable used to predict another variable).
Quasi-experimental	• A form of experimental research. One in which the researcher cannot control at least one of the three elements of an experimental design: – Environment – Intervention (program or practice) – Assignment to experimental and control groups
	Quantitative Research Designs
Historical	• Collection and evaluation of data related to past events that are used to describe causes, effects and trends that may explain present or future events. Data are often archival. • Data includes interviews.
Ethnographic	• The collection of extensive narrative data over an extended period of time in natural settings to gain insights about other types of research. • Data are collected through observations at particular points of time over a sustained period. • Data include observations, records and interpretations of what is seen.
Case Studies	• An in-depth study of an individual group, institution, organization or program. • Data include interviews, field notes of observations, archival data and biographical data.

Advantages and Disadvantages of Quantitative Research Design

Advantages

1. Quantitative research design is an excellent way of finalizing results and proving or disproving a hypothesis.
2. The structure has not changed for centuries, so is standard across many scientific fields and disciplines.
3. After statistical analysis of the results, a comprehensive answer is reached, and the results can be legitimately discussed and published.
4. Quantitative experiments also filter out external factors, if properly designed, and so the results gained can be seen as real and unbiased.
5. Quantitative experiments are useful for testing the results gained by a series of qualitative experiments, leading to a final answer, and narrowing down of possible directions for follow-up research to take.

Disadvantages

1. Quantitative experiments can be difficult and expensive and require a lot of time to perform.
2. They must be carefully planned to ensure that there is complete randomization and correct designation of control groups.
3. Quantitative studies usually require extensive statistical analysis, which can be difficult, due to most scientists not being statisticians.
4. The field of statistical study is a whole scientific discipline and can be difficult for non-mathematicians.
5. The requirements for the successful statistical confirmation of results are very stringent, with very few experiments comprehensively proving a hypothesis; there is usually some ambiguity, which requires retesting and refinement to the design. This means another investment of time and resources must be committed to fine-tune the results.
6. Quantitative research design also tends to generate only proven or unproven results, with there being very little room for grey areas and uncertainty. For the social sciences, education, anthropology and psychology, human nature is a lot more complex than just a simple yes or no response.

4.4 TYPES OF RESEARCH DESIGNS

The different research designs are meant for different type of studies:

1. Exploratory Research Studies.
2. Descriptive and Diagnostic Research Studies
3. Experimental Studies (Hypothesis-testing Research Studies)

Following are the details of different research designs:

4.4.1 Exploratory Research Studies

Exploratory research is the first step in research process and is formulating a problem for more precise investigation. Research design has to be flexible enough to provide opportunity for considering different aspects of a problem under study. The main objective of the exploratory research is to manage the broad problem into specific problem statement and generate possible hypothesis.

The exploratory studies are mainly used for:

(a) Providing information to enable a more precise problem definition.
(b) Establishing research priorities.
(c) Making researcher aware of the problem situation.
(d) Data collecting information like tools, methods and techniques.

The generally used methods in exploratory research are:

1. Survey of existing research: The researcher explores the published and unpublished books, journals, magazines and other literature available on the problem definition. This usually does not provide solution to the problem but it can certainly provide direction to the research process.

2. Survey of experienced individuals: The professionals, academicians, experts, managers etc. are the individuals who can provide substantial data on the research problem.

3. Analysis of selected case situations: Sometimes the popular cases are gone through to develop understanding on the given research problem.

4.4.2 Descriptive and Diagnostic Research Studies

Descriptive research studies are concerned with describing the characteristics of certain individuals or a group. Descriptive research studies are used for preliminary and exploratory studies in addition to their frequent use as conductive studies. This study is typically guided by an initial hypothesis. Diagnostic research studies determine the frequency with which something occurs or its association with something else. These studies are concerned with specific predictions and characteristics concerning individual, group or situation. The descriptive as well as diagnostic research studies share common requirements. In both the studies, the researcher must be able to define clearly, what he wants to measure and must find adequate methods of measuring it.

Following are the steps involved in both the studies:

1. Data collection must be relevant with sufficient precision.
2. Techniques of data must be devised and questions must be well examined and must be unambiguous.
3. Designing samples should be accurate information with a minimum amount of research effort.
4. Data should be error free and collected data should be examined for completeness, comprehensibility, consistency and reliability.
5. The data collected must be processed and analyzed.
6. The processing and analyzing procedure should be planned in detail before actual work is started.
7. To avoid error in coding, the reliability of coders needs to be checked.
8. The accuracy of tabulation may be checked by having a sample of tables redone.
9. Communicating the findings must be in efficient manner.
10. The layout of the report needs to be well planned so that all things relating to the research study may be well presented in a simple and effective style.

4.4.3 Experimental Studies (Hypothesis-testing Research Studies)

Before we attempt to understand the experimental studies or hypothesis-testing research studies, it is very essential to know what experiment is as it has a specific meaning for a researcher. This study is a method of making statistical decisions from and about experimental data. Null-hypothesis testing just answers the question of "how well the findings fit the possibility that chance factors alone might be responsible." This is done by asking and answering a hypothetical question. Under this process of experimentation, the experimenter indicates that the experiments systematically manipulating some factor or factors to elicit a response from the subject or respondent.

Experimental Design Objectives

1. Comparative objective: If you have one or several factors under investigation, but the primary goal of your experiment is to make a conclusion about one a-priori important factor (in the presence of, and/or in spite of the existence of the other factors), and the question of interest is whether or not that factor is "significant" (i.e., whether or not there is a significant change in the response for different levels of that factor), then you have a *comparative problem and* you need a *comparative design* solution.

2. Screening objective: The primary purpose of the experiment is to select or *screen out* the few important main effects from the many less important ones. These *screening designs* are also termed main effects designs.

3. Response Surface (method) objective: The experiment is designed to allow us to estimate interaction and even quadratic effects, and therefore give us an idea of the (local) shape of the response surface we are investigating. For this reason, they are termed *response surface method (RSM) designs*. RSM designs are used to:

- Find improved or optimal process settings
- Troubleshoot process problems and weak points
- Make a product or process more *robust* against external and non-controllable influences. "Robust" means relatively insensitive to these influences.

4. Optimizing responses when factors are proportions of a mixture objective: If you have factors that are proportions of a mixture and you want to know what the "best" proportions of the factors are so as to maximize (or minimize) a response, then you need a *mixture design*.

5. Optimal fitting of a regression model objective: If you want to model a response as a mathematical function (either known or empirical) of a few continuous factors and you desire "good" model parameter estimates (i.e., unbiased and minimum variance), then you need a *regression design*.

Applications of Experimental Design

Design of Experiment is applicable to almost every problem whether to improve the problem or just to optimize the problem. It has found wide application in industry especially in the agricultural sector. An experimental plan is developed to collect data to find answer for issues like ways to improve the quality of certain combination or to find what factor should be controlled to have a robust process. This is why the usage of experimental design in statistics increases the effectiveness of the research experiment.

Experimental design has six basic areas of application in industrial research. These areas are:

1. Optimization of manufacturing process
2. Optimization of analytical instruments
3. Screening and identification of important factors
4. Robustness testing of methods
5. Robustness of products
6. Formulation experiments

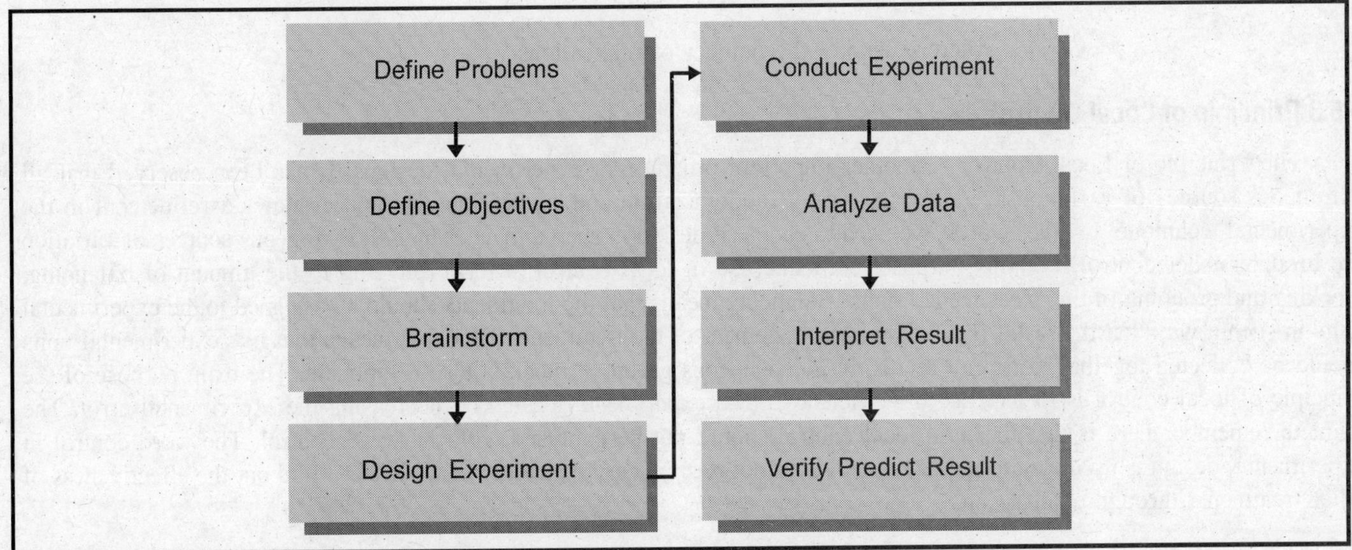

Fig. 4.1: Experimental Design Process

4.5 PRINCIPLES OR EXPERIMENTAL DESIGNS

Experimental Designs are basically based on the various types of designs of experiments and how an experiment looks nice if it is designed in a better way. The basic principles of experimental designs are: (1) Randomization, (2) Replication and (3) Local control. These principles make a valid test of significance possible. Each of them is described briefly in the following:

4.5.1 Principle of Randomization

The first principle of an experimental design is randomization, which is a random process of assigning treatments to the experimental units. The random process implies that every possible allotment of treatments has the same probability. An experimental unit is the smallest division of the experimental material and a treatment means an experimental condition whose effect is to be measured and compared. The purpose of randomization is to remove bias and other sources of extraneous variation, which are not controllable. Another advantage of randomization (accompanied by replication) is that it forms the basis of any valid statistical test. Hence, the treatments must be assigned at random to the experimental units. Randomization is usually done by drawing numbered cards from a well-shuffled pack of cards, or by drawing numbered balls from a well-shaken container or by using tables of random numbers.

4.5.2 Principle of Replication

The second principle of an experimental design is replication; which is a repetition of the basic experiment. In other words, it is a complete run for all the treatments to be tested in the experiment. In all experiments, some variation is introduced because of the fact that the experimental units such as individuals or plots of land in agricultural experiments cannot be physically identical. This type of variation can be removed by using a number of experimental units. We therefore perform the experiment more than once, i.e., we repeat the basic experiment. An individual repetition is called a replicate. The number, the shape and the size of replicates depend upon the nature of the experimental material. A replication is used:

1. to secure more accurate estimate of the experimental error, a term which represents the differences that would be observed if the same treatments were applied several times to the same experimental units;
2. to decrease the experimental error and thereby to increase precision, which is a measure of the variability of the experimental error; and
3. to obtain more precise estimate of the mean effect of a treatment, since

$$\sigma_{\bar{y}}^2 = \frac{\sigma^2}{n},$$

where *n* denotes the number of replications.

4.5.3 Principle of Local Control

The Principle of Local Control is another important principle of experimental designs. It has been observed that all extraneous sources of variation are not removed by randomization and replication. This necessitates a refinement in the experimental technique. In other words, we need to choose a design in such a manner that all extraneous sources of variation are brought under control. For this purpose, we make use of local control, a term referring to the amount of balancing, blocking and grouping of the experimental units. Balancing means that the treatments should be assigned to the experimental units in such a way that the result is a balanced arrangement of the treatments. Blocking means that like experimental units should be collected together to form a relatively homogeneous group. A block is also a replicate. The main purpose of the principle of local control is to increase the efficiency of an experimental design by decreasing the experimental error. The point to remember here is that the term local control should not be confused with the word control. The word control in experimental design is used for a treatment which does not receive any treatment but we need to find out the effectiveness of other treatments through comparison.

4.6 IMPORTANT EXPERIMENTAL DESIGN

Experimental design is a planned interference in the natural order of events by the researcher. Experimental design refers to the framework or structure of an experiment and as such there are several experimental designs.

Experimental Design Terminology

1. Treatment Group and Control Group: The group in an experiment which receives the specified treatment is called the *Treatment Group* or the experimental group. However, the term *Control Group* refers to another group assigned to the experiment, but not for the purpose of being exposed to the treatment. Thus, the performance of the control group usually serves as a baseline against which to measure the effect of the full treatment on the treatment group randomly assigned to groups. *Random assignment* of subjects to groups tend to spread out differences between subjects in unsystematic (random) ways so that there is no tendency to give an edge to any group.

2. Variable: A *variable* refers to almost anything under the sun. There are only two kinds of stuff in the world for researchers: variables and constants. As a result, almost any concept, or thing, or event they are interested in, that varies or can be made to vary, and that is related to their research can be called a variable.

3. Extraneous Variables: *Extraneous variables* (external to the experiment) are variables that may influence or affect the results of the treatment on the subject.

4. Factor: A variable of specific experimental interest is sometimes referred to as a *factor*. The term is used when an experiment involves more than one variable. These variables are often identified as factors and are labeled "Factor A" and "Factor B," etc.

5. Level: *Level* refers to the degree or intensity of a factor. Any factor may be presented in one or more of several levels, including a zero level.

6. Randomness: *Randomness* refers to the property of completely chance events that are not predictable (except in the sense that they are random). If they are truly random, examining past instances of occurrence should give the researcher no clues as to future occurrences. Randomness becomes important in the design of the experiments primarily in the assignment of subjects to groups. Researchers feel more secure about the results of their studies if subjects have been randomly assigned to groups. *Random assignment* of subjects to groups tends to spread out differences between subjects in unsystematic (random) ways so that there is no tendency to give an edge to any group.

7. *Ex-post Facto*: *Ex-post facto* refers to causal inferences drawn "after the fact." For example, in the *ex-post facto* study, the causal event of interest has already happened. These are known as non-experimental studies and are often contrasted with experimental studies.

8. Variance: *Variance* refers to the variability of any event. If one uses a fine enough measuring device, one can find differences between any two objects or events.

9. Internal Validity: The inside logic of an experiment is referred to as *internal validity*. Primarily, it asks the question: Does it seem reasonable to assume that the treatment has really produced the measured effect? Extraneous variables which might have produced the effect with or without the treatment are often called "threats to validity."

10. External Validity: *External validity*, on the other hand, refers to the proposed interpretation of the results of the study. If one asks the question: With what other groups could we reasonably expect to get the same results if we used the same treatment? If Treatment X resulted in lowered blood pressure in middle age men, could you logically claim that it will produce the same effect in older women?

11. Blocks: *Blocks* usually refer to categories of subjects with a treatment group. Experimental designs can be of two broad categories namely, informal experimental designs and formal experimental designs. Informal experimental designs are normally use a less sophisticated form of analysis based on differences in magnitudes, whereas formal experimental designs offer relatively more control and use precise statistical procedures for analysis work. Important experimental designs are as follows:

1. **Informal experimental designs:**
   (a) Before-and-after without control
   (b) After-only with control
   (c) Before-and-after with control
   (d) *Ex-post facto* design
2. **Formal experimental designs:**
   (a) Completely Randomized Design
   (b) Randomized Block Design
   (c) Latin Square Design
   (d) Factorial Design

4.7 INFORMAL EXPERIMENTAL DESIGN

(a) Before-and-after without Control: The Before-and-after without control is the simplest design to be used in research. In this design, the researcher measures the test unit that is independent variable before and after it has been subjected to the treatment. It involves no control group. The dependent variable is measured again after the treatment has been introduced. The effect of the treatment would be equal to the level of the phenomenon after the treatment minus the level of the phenomenon before the treatment. This design is represented as in the following figure:

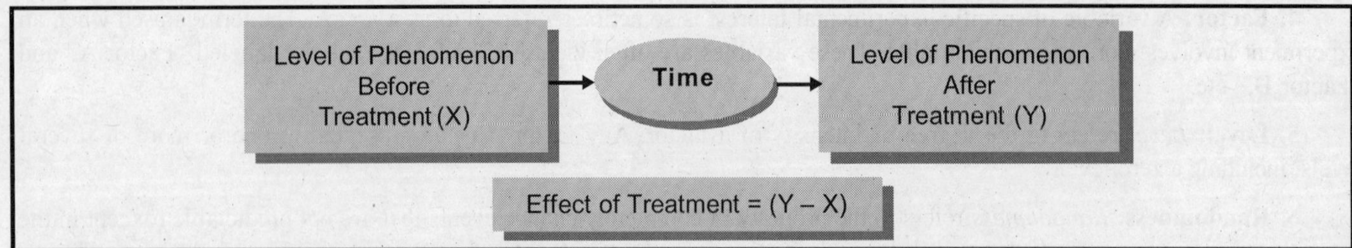

Fig. 4.2: Before-and-after without Control

The merits of this design are: (1) Reduced cost and (2) Lesser time needed.

(b) After-only with Control: The After-only with control design is most oftenly used in research. In this design, an experimental unit is selected and studied during the experimental period. Under this design, two groups are selected like control group and experimental group. The dependent variable is then measured in both the areas at the same time. In this design, the two areas are identical with respect to their behavior. This design is superior to before-and-after without control design and there are no before measurement of group involved. This design is represented as in the following figure:

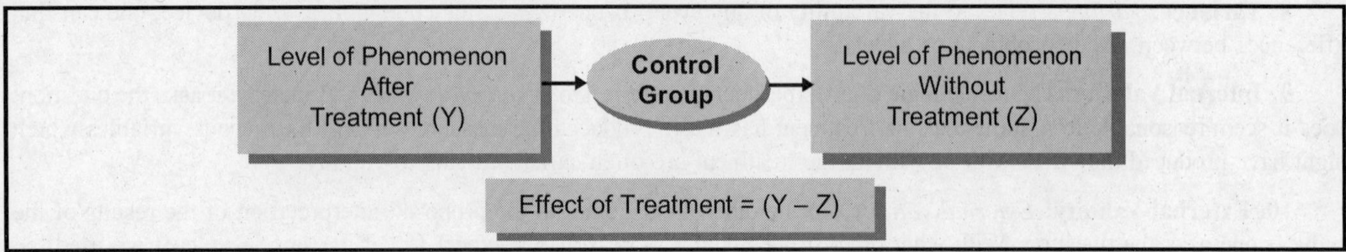

Fig. 4.3: After Only with Control

(c) Before-and-after with Control: In case of before-and-after with control design, an experimental unit is selected and studied during the experimental period. Under this design, two areas are selected and the dependent variable is measured in both time-periods after the introduction of the treatment. This design is superior to the above two designs because it avoids extraneous variation of the control areas. This design is represented as in the following figure:

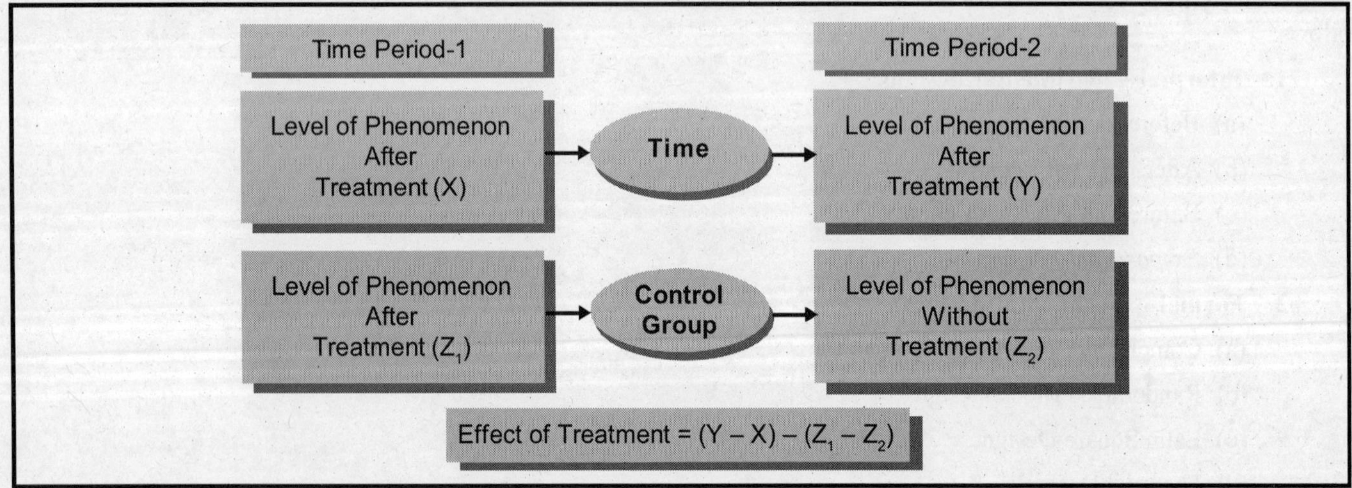

Fig. 4.4: Before-and-after with Control

(d) Ex-post Facto Design: This design is a variation of the after-only design. Here, instead of selecting the experimental design before the experiment none of the groups selected before experiment. The groups equivalent to experiment and control are identified only by the treatment given, after they are exposed to the experiment. In this approach, one cannot control the independent variable or variables because they have already occurred and cannot assign subjects or treatments at random. Under this design, an investigator starts by observing a dependent variable(s) and the possible causes for it, i.e., independent variable(s) and then he studies the independent variable(s) retrospectively for its possible effect on the dependent variable(s).

4.8 FORMAL EXPERIMENTAL DESIGN

(a) Completely Randomized Design

A Completely Randomized Design (CRD), which is the simplest type of the basic designs, may be defined as a design in which the treatments are assigned to experimental units completely at random, that is the randomization is done without any restrictions. The design is completely flexible, i.e., any number of treatments and any number of units per treatment may be used. Moreover, the number of units per treatment need not be equal. A completely randomized design is considered to be more useful in situations where (i) the experimental units are homogeneous, (ii) the experiments are small such as laboratory experiments, and (iii) some experimental units are likely to be destroyed or fail to respond. Completely Randomized Design involves only two principles, viz., the principle of replication and the principle of randomization of experimental designs. One-way analysis of variance (or one-way ANOVA) is used to analyze such a design.

Procedure for Randomization

1. Assign treatments to experimental units completely at random.
2. Verify that every experimental unit has the same probability of receiving any treatment.
3. Perform randomization by using a random number table, computer, program, etc.

Advantages of CRD

1. Experimental units are similar.
2. Several units may be destroyed or fail to respond.
3. It is a relatively small experiment.
4. CRD is flexible because it can be done even in a limited number of experimental subjects, however equal number of subjects for each treatment is encouraged.
5. Statistical analysis is simple and easy.
6. Statistical analysis is manageable even though some of the experimental subjects or treatments are lacking.

Disadvantages of CRD

1. Difficult to establish homogeneity of characteristics among subjects either experimental or control.

Table 4.2: The ANOVA table for the Completely Randomized Design (CRD)

Source	Degree of Freedom (df)	Sum of Square (SS)
Treatments	t – 1	SS_{Tr}
Error	t (n – 1)	SS_{Error}
Total	tn – 1	SS_{Total}

(b) Randomized Block Design

Randomized block design (RBD) takes advantage of grouping similar experimental units into blocks or replicates. One requirement of RBD is that the blocks of experimental units be as uniform as possible. The reason for grouping experimental units is so that the observed differences between treatments will be largely due to "true" differences between treatments and not random occurrences or chance. This is a randomized block design and should not be analyzed with the one-way ANOVA. Two-way analysis of variance (or two-way ANOVA) is used to analyze such a design.

Procedure for Randomization

1. Randomize each replicate separately.
2. Verify that each treatment has the same probability of being assigned to a given experimental unit within a replicate.
3. Have each treatment appear at least once per replicate.

Advantages of RBD

1. Generally more precise than the CRD.
2. No restriction on the number of treatments or replicates.
3. Some treatments may be replicated more times than others.
4. Missing plots are easily estimated.
5. Whole treatments or entire replicates may be deleted from the analysis.
6. If experimental error is heterogeneous, valid comparisons can still be made.

Disadvantages of the RBD

1. Error is smaller than that for the CRD (problem with a small number of treatments).
2. If there is a large variation between experimental units within a block, a large error term may result (this may be due to too many treatments).
3. If there are missing data, a RBD experiment may be less efficient than a CRD.

This is a randomized block design and should not be analyzed with the one-way ANOVA.

Table 4.3: The ANOVA Table for the Randomized Block Design

Source	Degree of Freedom (df)	Sum of Square (SS)
Block	n – 1	SS_{Block}
Treatments	t – 1	SS_{Tr}
Error	(t – 1) (n – 1)	SS_{Error}
Total	tn – 1	SS_{Total}

(c) Latin Square Design

Latin Square Design (LSD) is more powerful than the randomized block design in that the Latin square design attempts to control or block out the effect of two extraneous factors. This design is so named because of the layout of the table representing the design is square. It is a complex design to set up and expensive too to execute. This design makes sure that the treatments on each subject are tested one at a time in some sequence in a effort to offset the effects of the extraneous factors. As a result of rotating the treatments, it is hoped that the extraneous factors will offset each other and washout.

Facts about LSD

With the Latin Square design, you are able to control variation in two directions:

(a) Treatments are arranged in rows and columns.

(b) Each row contains every treatment.

(c) Each column contains every treatment.

(d) The most common sizes of LS are 5 × 5 to 8 × 8.

Advantages of LSD

1. You can control variation in two directions.
2. Hopefully you increase efficiency as compared to the Randomized Completely Block Design (RCBD).

Disadvantages of LSD

1. The number of treatments must equal the number of replicates.
2. The experimental error is likely to increase with the size of the square.

3. Small squares have very few degrees of freedom for experimental error.
4. You can't evaluate interactions between:
   (a) Rows and columns
   (b) Rows and treatments
   (c) Columns and treatments.

Table 4.4: The ANOVA Table for a Latin Square Experiment

Source	Degree of (df)	Sum of Freedom (SS)	Mean Square Square (MS)	F
Treat	t – 1	SS_{Tr}	MS_{Tr}	MS_{Tr}/MSE
Block	t – 1	SS_{Row}	MS_{Row}	$MS_{Row}MSE$
Treatments	t – 1	SS_{Col}	MS_{Col}	MS_{Col}/MSE
Error	(t – 1) (t – 2)	SS_E	MS_E	
Total	$t^2 - 1$	SS_{Total}		

(d) Factorial Design

This is another use of rotated test units which is known as factorial design. Though it appears diagrammatically same as Latin-square design, it has a different purpose to achieve. In factorial design, the experimenter tries to measure the influence of interacting variables on dependent variables. Factorial designs are used in experiments where the effects of varying more than one factor are to be determined. They are especially important in several economics and social phenomena where usually a large number of factors affect a particular problem. Factorial deigns can be two types: (1) simple factorial design and (2) complex factorial design.

Advantages of Factorial Designs

1. A greater precision can be obtained in estimating the overall main factor effects.
2. Interaction between different factors can be explored.
3. Additional factors can help to extend validity of conclusions derived.

4.9 SUMMARY

A research design is a logical and systematic plan prepared for directing a research study. It specifies the objectives of the study, the methodology and techniques to be adopted for achieving the objectives. It constitutes the blueprint for the collection, measurement and analysis of data. The different research designs are meant for different type of studies: (1) Exploratory Research Studies; (2) Descriptive and Diagnostic Research Studies and (3) Experimental Studies (Hypothesis-testing Research Studies). Exploratory Research Studies is formulating a problem for more precise investigation. Major emphasis is on the discovery of ideas and insights. Research design has to be flexible enough to provide opportunity for considering different aspects of a problem under study. In the descriptive as well as diagnostic research studies, the researcher must be able to define clearly, what he wants to measure and must find adequate methods of measuring it. The aim is to obtain complete and accurate information; hence, the procedure to be used must be carefully planned. Experimental studies are a method of making statistical decisions from and about experimental data. In these studies, the researcher tests the hypothesis of casual relationship between variables. Such studies require procedures that will not only reduce bias and increase reliability, but will permit drawing inferences about causality. Designs are basically based on the various types of designs of experiments and how an experiment looks nice if it is designed in a better way. Professor Fisher has enumerated three principles of experimental designs: (1) Principle of Replication, (2) Principle of Randomization, and (3) Principle of Local Control.

4.10 KEY TERMS

Research Design: Research design is a logical and systematic plan prepared for directing a research study.

Extraneous Variable: Independent variables that are not related to the purpose of the study, but may affect the dependent variable are termed as extraneous variables.

Research Hypothesis: When a prediction or hypothesized relationship is to be tested by scientific methods, is it termed as research hypothesis. It is a predictive statement that relates an independent variable to a dependent variable.

Experimental and Control Group: When a group is exposed to usual conditions, it is termed as a control group, but when a group is exposed to some special conditions, it is termed as experimental group.

Experimental Unit(s): The pre-determined plots or the blocks, where different treatments are used, are known as experimental units.

Exploratory Research Studies: Exploratory research studies are formulating a problem for more precise investigation.

Descriptive Research Studies: Descriptive research studies are concerned with describing the characteristics of certain individuals or a group.

Diagnostic Research Studies: Diagnostic research studies are concerned with specific predictions, with narration of facts and characteristics concerning individual, group or situation.

Experimental Studies: Experimental studies are a method of making statistical decisions from and about experimental data.

Completely Randomized Design: Completely Randomized Design is the simplest type of the basic designs where the treatments are assigned to experimental units completely at random.

4.11 MULTIPLE OBJECTIVE TYPE QUESTIONS

1. Research design specifies the objectives of the study, the methodology and techniques to be adopted for achieving the objectives.

   (a) True (b) False

2. A good research design is a blueprint specifying the methods to be adopted for gathering and analyzing the data.

   (a) True (b) False

3. A research design prescribes the boundaries of research activities and enables the researcher to channel his energies in the right work.

   (a) True (b) False

4. Independent variables that are not related to the purpose of the study, but may affect the dependent variable are termed as extraneous variables.

   (a) True (b) False

5. The different conditions under which experimental and control groups are put are usually referred to as 'experiment'.

   (a) True (b) False

6. Qualitative research design is an excellent way of finalizing results and proving or disproving a hypothesis.

   (a) True (b) False

7. Quantitative experiments can be difficult and expensive and require a lot of time to perform.

   (a) True (b) False

8. Objective of the exploratory research is to manage the broad problem into specific problem statement and generate possible hypothesis.

   (a) True (b) False

9. The Principle of Randomization provides protection, when we conduct an experiment, against the effects of extraneous factors by randomization.
   (a) True (b) False
10. Completely Randomized Design involves the principle of replication and the principle of randomization of experimental designs.
   (a) True (b) False
11. Which is the program that guides the investigator in the process of collecting, analyzing and interpreting observation?
   (a) Research process (b) Research problem
   (c) Research design (d) All of the above
12. Research in which the independent variable is manipulated is called
   (a) Experimental hypothesis-testing research (b) Experimental and control group
   (c) Treatments (d) Experiment
13. Which is the advantage of the qualitative research design?
   (a) Can be difficult and expensive
   (b) An excellent way of finalizing results and proving a hypothesis
   (c) Require extensive statistical analysis which is difficult
   (d) None of the above
14. Exploratory research studies mainly used for
   (a) Providing information (b) Establishing research priorities
   (c) Data collecting information (d) All of the above
15. Which of the following group refers to another group assigned to the experiment?
   (a) Treatment group (b) Control group
   (c) Experimental group (d) Random group
16. Which one of the following are the principles of experimental design?
   (a) Principle of randomization (b) Principle of replication
   (c) Principle of local control (d) All of the above
17. Which one of the following is an informal experimental design?
   (a) Latin square design (b) Factorial design
   (c) *Ex-post facto* design (d) Randomized block design
18. Which one of the following is formal experimental design?
   (a) After with control (b) Before without control
   (c) *Ex-post facto* design (d) Completely Randomized block design
19. Which one of the following is the advantage of randomized block design?
   (a) Missing plot are easily estimated (b) No restriction on the number of treatment
   (c) Both (a) and (b) (d) None of the above
20. Which one the following are the advantages of latin square design?
   (a) You can control variation in two direction
   (b) The number of treatments must equal the number of replicates
   (c) The experimental error is likely to increase with the size of the square
   (d) All the above

Answers to Objective Type Questions

Questions	1	2	3	4	5	6	7	8	9	10
Answers	T	T	F	T	F	F	T	T	T	T
Questions	11	12	13	14	15	16	17	18	19	20
Answers	c	a	b	d	b	d	c	d	c	a

4.12 CONCEPTUAL QUESTIONS

1. Explain the meaning and importance of a Research design.
2. Describe the various concepts relating to the research design.
3. Distinguish between qualitative and quantitative research design. Write its advantages and disadvantages.
4. What are the types of research design? Explain in detail.
5. Describe the principle of experimental research design.
6. What are the importance of experimental design? Explain in detail.
7. Give your understanding of a good research design. Is single research design suitable in all research studies? If not, why?
8. What is the procedure of randomization in formal experiential design? Write its advantages and disadvantages.
9. "Research design in exploratory studies must be flexible but in descriptive studies, it must minimize bias and maximize reliability". Discuss.
10. Discuss the basis of satisfaction to be employed in sampling public opinion on inflation.
11. Explain the meaning of the following in the context of Research design:
    (a) Extraneous variables
    (b) Confounded relationship
    (c) Research hypothesis
    (d) Experimental and Control groups
    (e) Treatments
    (f) Formal experimental design
    (g) Informal experimental design
    (h) *Ex-post facto* design
    (i) Latin square design
    (j) Random replications design
    (k) Simple factorial design

CHAPTER 5

SAMPLING DESIGN

Chapter Outline

Learning Objectives

- *Identify the population, sample, sampling unit and sampling frame.*
- *Apply probabilistic consideration to use simple random sampling with or without replacement.*
- *Discuss the idea of stratification of a population and to use stratified sampling method to improve precision.*
- *Describe other sampling methods of data collection suitable in relevant cases; design a suitable.*

5.1 MEANING OF SAMPLE

A sample is a finite part of a statistical population whose properties are studied to gain information about the whole (Webster, 1985). When dealing with people, it can be defined as a set of respondents (people) selected from a larger population for the purpose of a survey. A population is a group of individual's persons, objects, or items from which samples are taken for measurement, for example, a population of presidents or professors, books or students.

Size of the Sample

How big a sample do I need? The size depends upon:

1. The Nature of the universe – homogeneous/heterogeneous.
2. Nature of the study, i.e., intensive/extensive.
3. Availability of finance, time and personnel.
4. Standard of accuracy.
5. Size of the schedule/questionnaire.
6. Nature of the cases to be contacted – geographically scattered.
7. Type of sampling used.

A sample will be a non-representative one due to:

1. Imperfect stratification.
2. Too small sample.
3. Purposive selection.
4. Selection of/by field wonders.
5. Convenient sampling.
6. Inadequate random.
7. Nature of the universe.

5.2 MEANING OF SURVEY

A survey is a data collection tool used to gather information about individuals. Surveys are commonly used in psychology research to collect self-report data from study participants. A survey may focus on factual information about individuals, or it might aim to collect the opinions of the survey takers.

A survey can be administered in a couple of different ways. In one method known as a structured interview, the researcher asks each participant the questions. In the other method known as a questionnaire, the participant fills out the survey on his or her own.

Surveys are generally standardized to ensure that they have reliability and validity. Standardization is also important so that the results can be generalized to the larger population.

Table 5.1: Conditions for a Survey

Before a Survey	• Define the questions to the answer. • Define the sampling strategy. • Design and test the questionnaire. • Train the field workers. • Define the technique for cross validation. • Define the final analysis.

During the Survey	• Verify and cross validate the questionnaire. • Check timetable and budget.
After the Survey	• Cross-check again all the data. • Perform the main analysis. • Perform any exploratory data analysis.

A. Advantages of Using Surveys

1. As in sample study few units are to be examined, detailed study of the survey can be done.
2. As few units are to be examined, the survey work requires less time. Thus, in this way, sample survey saves time.
3. As few units are to be examined, the survey work requires less money. Thus, in this way, sample survey saves lot of money.
4. In sample survey, few persons are required for the survey work so experts can be appointed for the survey. This will increase the reliability of the survey results.
5. When the test is of destructive nature, sampling is only the way out. In such cases, the population survey is not possible.
6. A large area can be covered under survey in the available time and money.
7. If proper method is employed under the survey, the results obtained will represent the population adequately. Surveys are relatively inexpensive (especially self-administered surveys).
8. Surveys are useful in describing the characteristics of a large population. No other method of observation can provide this general capability.
9. They can be administered from remote locations using mail, e-mail or telephone.
10. Consequently, very large samples are feasible, making the results statistically significant even when analyzing multiple variables.
11. Many questions can be asked about a given topic giving considerable flexibility to the analysis.
12. Sample survey make measurement more precise by enforcing uniform definitions upon the participants.
13. Sample survey means that similar data can be collected from groups then interpreted comparatively (between-group study).
14. Sample survey is also used to check the accuracy of the census data (population survey).
15. Surveys are an efficient way of collecting information from a large number of respondents. Very large samplings are possible. Statistical techniques can be used to determine validity, reliability, and statistical significance.
16. Surveys are flexible in the sense that a wide range of information can be collected. They can be used to study attitudes, values, beliefs, and past behaviors.
17. Because they are standardized, they are relatively free from several types of errors.
18. They are relatively easy to administer.
19. There is an economy in data collection due to the focus provided by standardized questions. Only questions of interest to the researcher are asked, recorded, codified, and analyzed. Time and money is not spent on tangential questions.
20. Sample surveys are usually cheaper to conduct than a full census.
21. Surveys allow researchers to collect a large amount of data in a relatively short period of time.
22. Surveys are less expensive than many other data collection techniques.
23. Surveys can be created quickly and administered easily.
24. Surveys can be used to collect information on a wide range of things, including personal facts, attitudes, past behaviors and opinions.

B. Disadvantages of Using Surveys

1. Poor survey construction and administration can undermine otherwise well-designed studies.
2. The answer choices provided on a survey may not be an accurate reflection of how the participant truly feels.
3. While random sampling is generally used to select participants, response rates can bias the results of a survey.
4. Subjects may not be aware of their reasons for any given action.
5. Structured surveys, particularly those with closed ended questions, may have low validity when researching affective variables.
6. The individuals chosen to participate in surveys are often randomly sampled, errors due to non-response may exist for more information on how to deal with non-responsed and biased data.
7. Survey question-answer choices could lead to vague data sets because at times they are relative only to a personal abstract notion concerning "strength of choice".

C. Types of Survey Data Collection

Surveys can be implemented in a number of different ways. Chances are good that you have participated in a number of different market research surveys in the past. Some of the most common ways to administer survey include:

1. **Mail:** An example might include an alumni survey distributed via direct mail by your almameter.
2. **Telephone:** An example of a telephone survey would be a market research call about your experiences with a certain consumer product.
3. **Online:** Online surveys might focus on your experience with a particular retailer, product or website.
4. **At-home interviews:** The Indian Census is a good example of an at-home interview survey administration.

5.2.1 Quality of Survey

When researchers describe the quality of survey results, they may use one or more of the following terms.

1. **Accuracy.** Accuracy refers to how close a sample **statistic** is to a population **parameter**. Thus, if you know that a sample mean is 99 and the true population mean is 100, you can make a statement about the sample accuracy. For example, you might say the sample mean is accurate to within 1 unit.
2. **Precision.** Precision refers to how close estimates from different samples are to each other. For example, the **standard error** is a measure of precision. When the standard error is small, estimates from different samples will be close in value; and *vice versa*. Precision is inversely related to standard error. When the standard error is small, sample estimates are more precise; when the standard error is large, sample estimates are less precise.
3. **Margin of error.** The margin of error expresses the maximum expected difference between the true population parameter and a sample estimate of that parameter. To be meaningful, the margin of error should be qualified by a probability statement. For example, a pollster might report that 50% of voters will choose the Democratic candidate. To indicate the quality of the survey result, the pollster might add that the margin of error is +5%, with a confidence level of 90%. This means that if the same sampling method were applied to different samples, the true percentage of Democratic voters would fall within the margin of error 90% of the time.

5.3 SAMPLE DESIGN

A **sample design** can be described by two factors.

- **Sampling method:** Sampling method refers to the rules and procedures by which some elements of the population are included in the sample.
- **Estimator:** The estimation process for calculating sample statistics is called the estimator. Different sampling methods may use different estimators. For example, the formula for computing a mean score with a simple random sample is different from the formula for computing a mean score with a stratified sample. Similarly, the formula for the **standard error** may vary from one sampling method to the next.

The "best" sample design depends on survey objectives and on survey resources. For example, a researcher might select the most economical design that provides a desired level of precision. Or, if the budget is limited, a researcher might choose the design that provides the greatest precision without going over budget. Or other factors might guide the choice of sample design.

Characteristics of Good Sample Design

1. Sample design must result in a truly representative sample.
2. Sample design must be such which results in a small sampling error.
3. Sample design must be viable in the context of funds available in the research study.
4. Sample design must be such so that systematic bias can be controlled in a better way.
5. Sample design must give the results of the sample study which can be applied in general for the universe with a reasonable level of confidence.

5.4 MEANING OF SAMPLING

A Sampling is a part of the total population. It can be an individual element or a group of elements selected from the population. Although it is a subset, it is representative of the population and suitable for research in terms of cost, convenience, and time. The sample group can be selected based on a probability or a non-probability approach. A sample usually consists of various units of the population. The size of the sample is represented by "n".

Sampling is the act, process, or technique of selecting a representative part of a population for the purpose of determining the characteristics of the whole population. In other words, the process of selecting a sample from a population using special sampling techniques is called sampling. It should be ensured in the sampling process itself that the sample selected is representative of the population.

1. **Population or Universe:** The entire aggregation of items from which samples can be drawn is known as a population. In sampling, the population may refer to the units, from which the sample is drawn. Population or populations of interest are interchangeable terms. The term "unit" is used, as in a business research process, samples are not necessarily people all the time. A population of interest may be the universe of nations or cities. This is one of the first things the analyst needs to define properly while conducting a business research. Therefore, population, contrary to its general notion as a nation's entire population has a much broader meaning in sampling. "N" represents the size of the population.
2. **Census:** A complete study of all the elements present in the population is known as a census. It is a time-consuming and costly process and is, therefore, seldom popular with researchers. The general notion that a census generates more accurate data than sampling is not always true. Limitations include failure in generating a complete and accurate list of all the members of the population and refusal of the elements to provide information. The national population census is an example of census survey.
3. **Precision:** Precision is a measure of how close an estimate is expected to be, to the true value of a parameter. Precision is a measure of similarity. Precision is usually expressed in terms of imprecision and related to the standard error of the estimate. Less precision is reflected by a larger standard error.
4. **Bias:** Bias is the term which refers to how far the average statistic lies from the parameter it is estimating, that is, the error, which arises when estimating a quantity. Errors from chance will cancel each other out in the long run, those from bias will not. Bias can take different forms.

Importance of Sampling in Social Research

1. A large number of units can be studied.
2. It saves a lot of time, energy and money.
3. Homogeneous universe sampling is very useful.
4. Intensive study is possible.

5. When the data are unlimited – highly useful.
6. When cent per cent accuracy is not required.
7. It makes easier for tabulation and analysis.

5.5 STEPS IN SAMPLING PROCESS

An operational sampling process can be divided into seven steps as given below:

1. Defining the target population.
2. Specifying the sampling frame.
3. Specifying the sampling unit.
4. Selection of the sampling method.
5. Determination of sample size.
6. Specifying the sampling plan.
7. Selecting the sample.

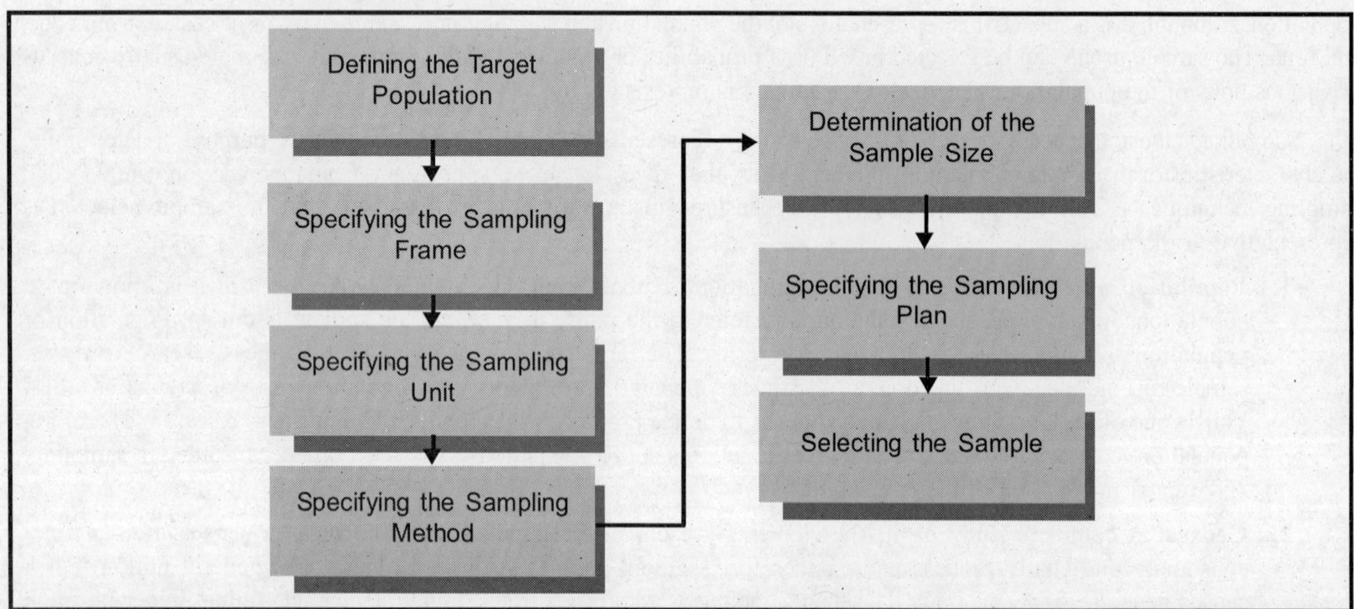

Fig. 5.1: Sampling Process

5.5.1 Defining the Target Population

Defining the population of interest, for business research, is the first step in sampling process. In general, target population is defined in terms of element, sampling unit, extent, and time frame. The definition should be in line with the objectives of the research study. For example, if a kitchen appliances firm wants to conduct a survey to ascertain the demand for its micro ovens, it may define the population as 'all women above the age of 20 who cook (assuming that very few men cook)'. However, this definition is too broad and will include every household in the country, in the population that is to be covered by the survey. Therefore, the definition can be further refined and defined at the sampling unit level, that, all women above the age 20, who cook and whose monthly household income exceeds ₹ 20,000. This reduces the target population size and makes the research more focused. The population definition can be refined further by specifying the area from where the researcher has to draw his sample, that is, households located in Hyderabad.

A well-defined population reduces the probability of including the respondents who do not fit the research objective of the company. For example, if the population is defined as all women above the age of 20, the researcher may end up taking the opinions of a large number of women who cannot afford to buy a micro oven.

5.5.2 Specifying the Sampling Frame

Once the definition of the population is clear, a researcher should decide on the sampling frame. A sampling frame is the list of elements from which the sample may be drawn. Continuing with the micro oven example, an ideal sampling frame would be a database that contains all the households that have a monthly income above ₹ 20,000. However, in practice, it is difficult to get an exhaustive sampling frame that exactly fits the requirements of a particular research. In general, researchers use easily available sampling frames like telephone directories and lists of credit card and mobile phone users. Various private players provide databases developed along various demographic and economic variables. Sometimes, maps and aerial pictures are also used as sampling frames. Whatever may be the case, an ideal sampling frame is one that of an entire population and which lists the names of its elements only once.

A sampling frame error pops up when the sampling frame does not accurately represent the total population or when some elements of the population are missing another drawback in the sampling frame is overrepresentation. A telephone directory can be overrepresented by names/household that have two or more connections.

5.5.3 Specifying the Sampling Unit

A sampling unit is a basic unit that contains a single element or a group of elements of the population to be sampled. In this case, a household becomes a sampling unit and all women above the age of 20 years living in that particular house become the sampling elements. If it is possible to identify the exact target audience of the business research, every individual element would be a sampling unit. This would present a case of primary sampling unit. However, a convenient and better means of sampling would be to select households as the sampling unit and interview all females above 20 years, who cook. This would present a case of secondary sampling unit:

(i) Geographical units like city, district, ward, and village

(ii) Construction units like house and flat

(iii) Special group units like family and college

(iv) Individual unit

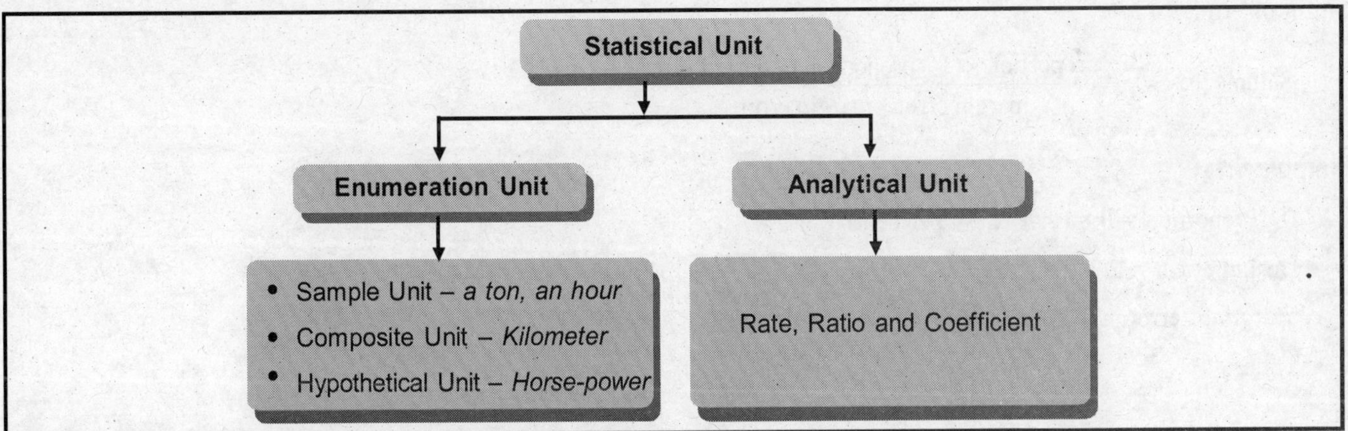

Applications of Statistical Unit

1. An experimental statistical unit is typically thought of as one number of a set of objects that are initially equivalent, with each object then subjected to one of several experimental treatments.
2. Universal examples of a unit would be a single person, animal, plant, or manufactured item that belongs to a larger collection of such entities being studied.
3. The sampling unit is characteristically thought of as an entity that has been sampled as of a statistical people.
4. It is the term, that is commonly used for the estimation poll and survey of sampling.
5. In some cases, the observed units may not be from a sample from any meaningful population, but rather constitute a convenience sample or may represent the entire population of interest.

6. In this statistical units descriptively or we may learning their dynamics above time.
7. In easy data sets, the unit is in one-to-one connection with the data values.
8. In extra or additional complex data sets, multiple dimensions are made for each one in the entire units.
9. At the same time as units is frequently lowest level at which explanation are made, further cases, a unit can be some rotten as a statistical gathering.

5.5.4 Selection of the Sampling Method

The sampling method outlines the way in which the sample units are to be selected. The choice of the sampling method is influenced by the objectives of the business research, availability of financial resources, time constraints, and the nature of the problem to be investigated. All sampling methods can be grouped under two distinct heads, that is, probability and non-probability sampling.

5.5.5 Determination of Sample Size

The sample size plays a crucial role in the sampling process. There are various ways of classifying the techniques used in determining the sample size. A couple those hold primary importance and are worth mentioning are whether the technique deals with fixed or sequential sampling and whether its logic is based on traditional or Bayesian methods. In non-probability sampling procedures, the allocation of budget, thumb rules and number of subgroups to be analyzed, importance of the decision, number of variables, nature of analysis, incidence rates, and completion rates play a major role in sample size determination. In the case of probability sampling, however, formulas are used to calculate the sample size after the levels of acceptable error and level of confidence are specified. The details of determination the sample size as follows:

Calculation of Sample Size

Sample size calculation is a simple procedure, yet many people are put off by its apparent complexity. Due to sampling error, this estimate is not an exact measurement. The use of probability sampling, however, allows us to calculate a range in which the actual indicator can be reasonably expected to fall. The upper and lower limits of this range are known as the margin of error.

$$\text{Sample Size} = \frac{4 \times \text{proportion} \times (1 - \text{proportion}) \times \text{design effect}}{\text{margin error} \times \text{margin error}}$$

Example 5.1:

If, Proportion = 0.8 (that is, 80 per cent)

Design effect = 2

Margin of error = 0.05 (±5 percentage points)

Then,

$$\text{Sample Size} = \frac{4 \times 0.8 \times (1 - 0.8) \times 2}{(0.05 \times 0.05)} = 512$$

So, the sample size should be 512. That is, to obtain an estimate with a margin of error of plus or minus five percentage points (a 95 per cent chance that the true rate falls within 75 per cent and 85 per cent). These calculations must be repeated for each of the indicators being measured in the survey.

Sample Size — Infinite Population (where the population is greater than 50,000)

$$\text{Sample Size} = \frac{Z^2 \times p \times (1 - p)}{C^2}$$

where,

Z = Z-value (e.g., 1.96 for a 95 per cent confidence level)

p = Percentage of population picking a choice, or proportion

C = Confidence interval or Marginal error, expressed as decimal (e.g., .04 = +/-4 percentage points)

Z-values (Cumulative Normal Probability Table) represent the probability that a sample will fall within a certain distribution.

The Z-values for confidence levels are:

1.645 = 90 per cent confidence level

1.96 = 95 per cent confidence level

2.576 = 99 per cent confidence level

Sample Size – Finite Population (where the population is less than 50,000)

Calculate the sample size using the infinite population formula first. Then use the sample size derived from that calculation to calculate a sample size for a finite population.

$$\text{New Sample Size} = \frac{\text{Sample Size}}{1 + \left(\frac{\text{Sample Size} - 1}{\text{Population}}\right)}$$

Example 5.2:

Calculate the sample size from the population 4,300 with 95% confidence level, 4% of confidence interval and 5% of proportion.

Solution:

Sample Size – Infinite Population:

$$\text{Sample Size} = \frac{Z^2 \times p \times (1-p)}{C^2} = \frac{3.8416 \times 0.5 \times 0.5}{0.04^2} = 600$$

Sample Size – Finite Population:

$$\text{New Sample Size} = \frac{\text{Sample Size}}{1 + \left(\frac{\text{Sample Size} - 1}{\text{Population}}\right)} = \frac{600}{1 + \left(\frac{600-1}{4,300}\right)} = 527$$

So, sample size from population 4,300 is 527.

Table 5.3: Calculation of Minimum Sample Size

Infinite Inverse	Finite Inverse
$\text{Sample size } n = \left(\frac{z\sigma}{\sigma_{\bar{x}}}\right)^2$	$\text{Sample size } n = \frac{\sigma^2}{\left(\frac{\sigma x^2}{z^2} + \frac{\sigma^2}{n}\right)}$
z = At a specified level of confidence	*n* = number of items in the universe
σ = Standard deviation of the population	
$\sigma_{\bar{x}}$ = Standard error of mean	

Table 5.4: The Ingredients in a Sample Size Calculation, for One or Two Groups

Type I Error (α)	Probability of rejecting the null hypothesis when it is true
Type II Error (β)	Probability of not rejecting the null hypothesis when it is false
Power = $1 - \beta$	Probability of rejecting the null hypothesis when it is false
σ_1^2 and σ_2^2	Variances under the null and alternative hypotheses (may be the same)
μ_1 and μ_2	Means under the null and alternative hypotheses
n_1 and n_2	Sample sizes in two groups (may be the same)

5.5.6 Specifying the Sampling Plan

In this step, the specifications and decisions regarding the implementation of the research process are outlined. Suppose, blocks in a city are the sampling units and the households are the sampling elements. This step outlines the *modus operandi* of the sampling plan in identifying houses based on specified characteristics. It includes issues like how is the interviewer going to take a systematic sample of the houses. What should the interviewer do when a house is vacant? What is the recontact procedure for respondents who were unavailable? All these and many other questions need to be answered for the smooth functioning of the research process. These are guidelines that would help the researcher in every step of the process. As the interviewers and their co-workers will be on field duty if most of the time, a proper specification of the sampling plans would make their work easy and they would not have to revert to their seniors when faced with operational problems.

5.5.7 Selecting the Sample

This is the final step in the sampling process, where the actual selection of the sample elements is carried out. At this stage, it is necessary that the interviewers stick to the rules outlined for the smooth implementation of the business research. This step involves implementing the sampling plan to select a sample required for the survey.

5.6 SAMPLING METHODS IN RESEARCH

Sampling method refers to the way that observations are selected from a **population** to be in the **sample** for a **sample survey**.

5.6.1 Population Parameter vs. Sample Statistic

The reason for conducting a sample survey is to estimate the value of some attribute of a population.

- **Population parameter.** A population parameter is the true value of a population attribute.
- **Sample statistic.** A sample statistic is an estimate, based on sample data, of a population parameter. Consider this example. A public opinion pollster wants to know the percentage of voters that favor a flat-rate income tax. The *actual* percentage of all the voters is a population parameter. The *estimate* of that percentage, based on sample data, is a sample statistic.

The quality of a sample statistic (i.e., accuracy, precision, representativeness) is strongly affected by the way that sample observations are chosen; that is, by the sampling method.

5.6.2 Probability vs. Non-probability Samples

As a group, sampling methods fall into one of two categories.

- **Probability samples.** With probability sampling methods, each population element has a known (non-zero) chance of being chosen for the sample.
- **Non-probability samples.** With non-probability sampling methods, we do not know the probability that each population element will be chosen, and/or we cannot be sure that each population element has a non-zero chance of being chosen.

Non-probability sampling methods offer two potential advantages — convenience and cost. The main disadvantage is that non-probability sampling methods do not allow you to estimate the extent to which sample statistics are likely to differ from population parameters. Only probability sampling methods permit that kind of analysis.

There are two basic approaches to sampling: probabilistic and non-probabilistic sampling. Let us look at the various types of sampling under each category:

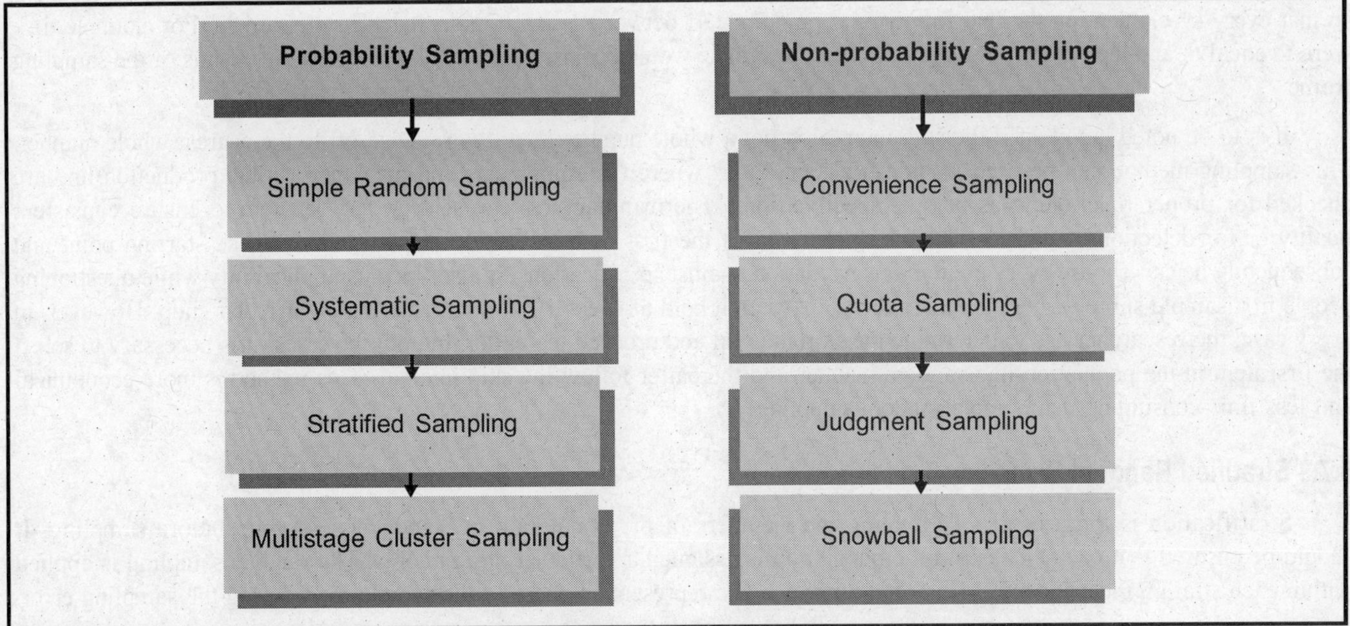

Fig. 5.2: Probability and Non-probability Sampling

5.7 PROBABILITY SAMPLING

A sampling in which every member of the population has a calculable and non-zero probability of being included in the sample is known as probability sampling. Methods of random selection consistent with both the probabilities of inclusion are used in forming estimates from the sample. The probability of selection need not be equal for members of the population. If the purpose of a research is to arrive at conclusions or make predictions affecting the population as a whole, then the choice of a probabilistic sampling approach is desirable.

5.7.1 Simple Random Sampling

A sampling process where each element in the target population has an equal chance or probability of inclusion in the sample is known as simple random sampling. For example, if a sample of 15000 names is to be drawn from the telephone directory, then there is equal chance for each number in the directory to be selected. These numbers (serial no. of name) could be randomly generated by the computer or picked out of a box. These numbers could be later matched with the corresponding names thus fulfilling the list. In small populations, random sampling is done without replacement to avoid the instance of a unit being sampled more than once.

The benefits of simple random sampling can be reaped when the target population size is small, homogeneous, sampling frame is clearly defined, and not much information is available regarding the population. It is advantageous in that it is free of classification error, and requires minimum advance knowledge of the population. Two striking features are the elimination of human bias and non-dependency on the availability of the element. It is seldom put into practice because of the application problem associated with it. This sampling method is generally not preferred as it becomes imperative to list every item in the population prior to the sampling and requires constructing a very large sampling frame, resulting in extensive sampling calculations and excessive costs.

5.7.2 Systematic Sampling

Systematic sampling involves the selection of every k^{th} element from a sampling frame. Here 'k' represents the skip interval and is calculated using the following formula.

Skip interval (k) = Population size/Sample size

Often used as a substitute to simple random sample, it involves the selection of units from a list using a skip interval (k) so that every k^{th} element on the list, following a random start between 1 and k, is included in the sample. For example, if k were to equal 6, and the random start were 2, then the sample would consist of 2nd, 8th, 14th, 20th.......elements of the sampling frame.

It is to be noted here that if the skip interval is not a whole number then it is rounded off to the nearest whole number. This sampling method can be used in industrial operations where the equipments and machinery in the production line are checked for proper functioning as per the specifications. The manufacturer can select every k^{th} item to ensure consistent quality or for detection of defects. Therefore, he requires the first item to be selected at random as the starting point and subsequently he can choose every k^{th} item for evaluation against specifications. It also finds its applicability while questioning people in a sample survey where the interviewer may catch hold of every 10th person entering a particular shop. However, in every case, the researcher has to determine the skip interval and proceed thereafter. In both the cases, it is necessary to select the first item in the population in a random manner and thereafter follow the skip interval. This method is more economical and less time-consuming than simple random sampling.

5.7.3 Stratified Random Sampling

Stratification is the process of grouping the members of the population in homogeneous group before sampling. It should be ensured that each element in the population is assigned a particular stratum only. The random sampling is applied within each stratum independently. This often improves the representativeness of the sample by reducing the sampling error.

The number of units drawn for sampling from each stratum depends on the homogeneity of the elements. A smaller sample can be drawn from those known to have the elements with the same value whereas a sample can be drawn in much higher proportion from another stratum where the values are known to differ. This is because in the former case the information from the smaller number of respondents can be enumerated to the whole sample stratum. However, in the latter case, with much variability among the elements the higher elements value will keep the sampling to minimum errors to minimum value. The smaller errors may be due to groups are appreciably represented when strata are combined.

5.7.4 Multistage Cluster Sampling

Clustering involves grouping the population into various clusters and selecting few clusters for study. Cluster sampling is suitable for conducting research studies that cover large geographic area. Once the cluster is formed, the researcher can either go for one-stage, two-stage, or multistage cluster sampling. In single stage, all the elements from each selected are studied, whereas in two stages, the researchers use random to select few elements from clusters. Multistage sampling involves selecting a sample in two or more successive stages. Here, the cluster selected in the first stage can be divided into cluster units.

For example, consider the case where a company decides to interview 400 households about the likeability of its new detergent in a metropolitan city. To minimize the resources and time researchers, divide the city into separate blocks say 40, each block consist of heterogeneous units. The researcher may opt for the two-stage cluster sampling if he finds that individual clusters have little heterogeneity to other clusters. Similarly, a multistage cluster sampling involves three or more sampling steps, it differs from stratified sampling that is done in cluster in contrast to elements within strata as is the case in the stratified sampling. Elements are randomly selected from each stratum in another stratum in case of stratified sampling whereas only selected clusters are studied in cluster sampling.

5.8 NON-PROBABILITY SAMPLING

It involves the selection of units based on factors other than random chance. It is also known as deliberate sampling and purposive sampling. For example, a scheme whereby units are selected purposefully would yield a non-random sample. In a general sense, it is an umbrella term, which includes any sample that does not conform to the requirements of a probability sampling. Convenience sampling, quota sampling, judgment sampling and snowball sampling are few examples of non-probability sampling.

5.8.1 Convenience Sampling

The selection of units from the population based on their easy availability and accessibility to the researcher is known as convenience sampling. For example, imagine a company, that surveys a sample of its employees to know the acceptance for a new flavor of potato chips that it plans to introduce in the market. This type of sampling is a typical example of convenience sampling as the criterion for selecting a sample is convenience and availability. Although this type of research is easy and cost-effective, the findings of the sample survey cannot be generalized to the entire population, as the sample is not representative. As there is no set criterion for selecting the sample, there is a scope for research being influenced by the bias of the researcher. As in the above example, the researcher may conduct a sample survey involving its own employees to find whether the market, would accept the product.

5.8.2 Quota Sampling

In quota sampling, the entire population is segmented into mutually exclusive groups. The number of respondents (quota) that are to be drawn from each of several categories is specified in advance and the final selection of respondents is left to the interviewer who proceeds until the quota for each category is filled. Quota sampling finds extensive use in commercial research where the main objective is to ensure that the sample represents in relative proportion, the people in the various categories if the researcher wants to segment the entire population based on gender, then he would have two categories of respondents, that is, males and females. If he plans to collect a sample of 30, he may allot a quota of 15 for male and 15 for female respondents. Therefore, the researcher will stop administering the questionnaire to females after he interviews the 15th female respondent, that is, when the quota of 15 males is filled.

Quota sampling is subject to interviewer bias that may result in:

1. The quota reflecting the population in terms of superficial characteristics.
2. The researcher selecting the respondents based on availability rather than on their suitability to the study.

5.8.3 Judgment Sampling

The selection of a unit, from the population based on the judgment of an experienced researcher, is known as judgment or purposive sampling. Here, the sample units are selected based on population's parameters. It is often noticed that companies frequently select certain preferred cities during test marketing their products. This is because they consider the population of that particular city to be representative of the total population of the country. The same is the case with the selection of specific shopping malls that according to the researcher's judgment attract a reasonable number of customers from different sections of the society. Polling results predicted on television is also a result of judgment sampling. Researchers select those districts that have voting patterns close to the overall state or country in the previous year. The judgment of the researcher is based on the assumption that the past voting trends of selected sample districts are still representative of the political behavior of the state's population. For example, certain companies test market their new product launches in cities like Mumbai and Bangalore, because the profile of these cities is representative of the total Indian population.

5.8.4 Snowball Sampling

Sampling procedures that involve the selection of additional respondents are known as snowball sampling. This sampling technique is used against low incidence or rare populations. Sampling is a big problem in this case, as the defined population from which the sample can be drawn is not available. Therefore, the process sampling depends on the chain system of referrals. Suppose, SG Sports Ltd., a manufacturer of sports equipment plans to survey 100 senior players through its new website for getting their feedback on the quality of its products.

However, getting track of such senior squash players can be very difficult, as their presence may be very rare or low. Therefore, it collects the details of the first 200 visitors to its website, to list if any of them is a squash player or knows a squash player. If the visitor is a squash player, then he is requested to refer the names of at least 3 other players known to him. The referred names of the squash players are then called upon for further referrals and this goes on until the sample size of 100 adult players is reached. Although small sample sizes and low costs are the clear advantages of snowball sampling, bias is one of its disadvantages. The referral names obtained from those sampled in the initial stages may be similar to those initially sampled. Therefore, the sample may not represent a cross-section of the total population. It may also happen that visitors to the site or interviewers may refuse to disclose the names of those whom they know.

5.9 SAMPLING VS. COMPLETE ENUMERATION

Data collection is the recording of one or more data variables (length, duration, etc.) from members of a population of "data-units" (the population of fishing vessels, fishing trips, etc.). Two basic data collection approaches are possible:

- by complete enumeration, where all members of the whole population are measured;
- by sampling, where only a proportion of members of the whole population are measured.

Fisheries data usually collected by complete enumeration include vessel registers and infrastructure data. Data sometimes collected by complete enumeration and sometimes by sample surveys include catch per unit effort, price per kilogram and costs and earnings of fishing units. Data usually collected by the sample-based approach include species composition and biological data (e.g., size frequency data). A complete enumeration may well refer to a subset, for example, one may make a complete enumeration of all vessels longer than 10 meters.

Both complete enumeration and sample-based approaches have as their objective the collection of data for a specified period, often over a calendar month, to determine some statistic of interest. For example, a total enumeration approach could be used to calculate the total catch where all landings were monitored. An example sample-based approach to estimate total catch would use the mean catch per fishing day from a landings sample and the mean number of fishing days per vessel from a vessel sample, which multiplied together give the mean catch per vessel. The total catch can then be obtained by multiplying this by the total number of vessels (a raising factor) obtained from a frame survey or vessel register. The applicability of either sampling or complete enumeration is determined by various criteria related to the type of data and to existing financial and human constraints.

Most data collection methods can be utilized under either complete enumeration or sampling approaches. For instance, logbook catch and effort information may be monitored by means of a complete reporting of landings. Catch and effort data from small-scale and subsistence fisheries generally are sampled. Biological and socio-cultural data are usually collected through a sample-based system, though demographics are collected by complete enumeration. Very large populations, like fish stocks, can be sampled only.

A complete enumeration-based survey is often preferred for certain types of data, solely because it is expected that it will provide complete statistical coverage over space and time. However, a well-designed sample-based survey can often provide good estimates of important parameters at a fraction of the cost. Complete enumeration of some variables (e.g., through a frame survey) is always needed to obtain raising factors when totals of variables like catch or effort are required. Which approach is used will depend on local circumstances. Complete enumeration sometimes may be seen as desirable, but not attainable for operational reasons. An existing sampling programme can be progressively expanded to provide more reliable and robust estimates, if human and logistics resources allow such expansion in a sustainable manner.

5.10 SAMPLING ERROR IN RESEARCH

Error is defined as, "an act, assertion, or belief that unintentionally deviates from what is correct, right, or true". In a business research process, there is sure to be some error in the results because there is the involvement of human intelligence and the use of sampling methods that may not be always accurate. The absolute value of the difference between an unbiased point estimate and the corresponding population parameter is known as a sampling error. It arises because the data is collected from a part, rather than the whole of the population. The sampling error can be more reliable by increasing the sample size. Total survey errors are of two types: Random sampling error and non-sampling error.

5.10.1 Sampling Error or Random Sampling Error

Random sampling error or sampling error is the difference between the sample results and the results of a census conducted by identical procedures. Although a representative sample is taken, there is always a slight deviation between the true population value and the sample value. This is because the sample selected is not perfectly representative of the test population. Therefore, a small random sampling error is evident. As the sampling error is the outcome of chance, the laws of probabilities are applicable to it. The sampling error is inversely proportional to the sample size. As the sample size increases, the sampling error decreases. Although sampling errors cannot be avoided altogether, they can be controlled through careful sample designs, large samples, and multiple contacts to assure representative response. Random sampling error represents how accurately the sample's true mean value (X sample), is representative of the population's true mean value (X population).

5.10.2 Non-sampling Error or Systematic Error

Non-sampling errors also known as systematic errors occur due to the nature of the study's design and the correctness of execution. Non-sampling error includes non-observation errors and measurement errors. Non-observational errors occur when data cannot be collected from the sampling unit or variable. Measurement errors arise from various sources like respondents, interviewers, supervisors, and even data processing systems. Non-observation error is further divided into non-coverage and non-response error. In probability sampling, each element of the population has a non-zero chance of selection into the sample. Non-coverage error occurs when an element in the target population has no chance of being selected into the sample. Non-response error occurs when data cannot be collected from the element actually selected into the sample. This may be due to the refusal of the element to cooperate because of language barrier, health limitation, or non-availability of the element during the survey period. Selection of faulty sampling frame may also result in a non-sampling error. Sampling frame error is said to occur when certain non-potential respondents are included in the sampling frame and certain deserving respondents are rejected.

5.11 STANDARD ERROR

The standard error or *standard error of the mean*, of multiple samples is the standard deviation of the sample means, and thus gives a measure of their spread. Thus, 68% of all sample means will be within one standard error of the population mean (and 95% within two standard errors).

What the standard error gives in particular is an indication of the likely accuracy of the sample mean as compared with the population mean. The smaller the standard error, the less the spread and the more likely it is that any sample mean is close to the population mean. A small standard error is thus a Good Thing.

Important Formulae for computing the standard errors concerning various measures based on samples are as under:

1. **In case of Sampling Attributes**

(i) Standard error of number of success = $\sqrt{n.p.q}$

where n = number of events in each sample

p = probability of success in each event

q = probability of failure in each event

(ii) Standard error of population of success = $\sqrt{(p.q)/n}$

(iii) Standard error of the difference between proportions of two samples:

$$\sigma_{(p2-p2)} = \sqrt{p.q\left(\frac{1}{n_2}+\frac{1}{n_2}\right)} \text{ or } \sqrt{\frac{p_1q_1}{n_1}+\frac{p_2q_2}{n_2}}$$

where p = best estimate of proportion in the population

and $$p = \sqrt{\left(\frac{n_1p_1+n_2p_2}{n_1+n_2}\right)}$$

$q = 1 - p$

n_1 and n_2 = number of events in sample one and sample two

2. In case of Sampling of Variables (Large Samples)

(i) Standard error of mean when population standard deviation is known:

$$SE = \sigma_{\bar{x}} = \frac{\sigma_s}{\sqrt{n}}$$

where, $\sigma_{\bar{x}}$ = standard deviation of the population and

n = number of items in the sample ($n \leq 30$)

(ii) Standard error of mean when population standard deviation is not known:

$$SE = \sigma_s = \frac{\sigma_s}{\sqrt{n}}$$

where, σ_s = standard deviation of the sample and $\sigma_s = \sqrt{\frac{\Sigma(x-\bar{x})^2}{n-1}}$

and n = number of items in the sample.

(iii) Standard error of standard deviation when population standard deviation is known:

$$\sigma_s = \sigma_p / \sqrt{2n}$$

(iv) Standard error of standard deviation when population standard deviation is not known:

$$\sigma_s = \sigma_s / \sqrt{2n}$$

(v) Standard error of the coefficient of simple correlation:

$$\sigma_r = \frac{1-r^2}{\sqrt{2}}$$

where, r = coefficient of simple correlation

n = number of items in the sample

(vi) Standard error of difference between two samples:

(a) From same population:

$$\sigma_{\bar{x}1-\bar{x}2} = \sigma_p \sqrt{\left(\frac{1}{n_1} + \frac{1}{n_2}\right)}$$

(b) From different population:

$$\sigma_{\bar{x}1-\bar{x}2} = \sigma_p \sqrt{\left(\frac{\sigma_{p2}{}^2}{n_1} + \frac{\sigma_{p2}{}^2}{n_2}\right)}$$

3. In case of Sampling of Variables (Small Samples)

(i) Standard error of mean when σ_p is unknown:

$$\sigma_{s_{1.2}} = \sqrt{\frac{n_1(\sigma_{s_2})^1 + n_2(\sigma_{s_2})^2 + n_1(\bar{x}_1 - \bar{x}_{1.2})^2 + n_2(\bar{x}_2 - \bar{x}_{1.2})}{n_1 + n_2}}$$

where, $\bar{x}_{1.2} = \frac{n_1\bar{x}_1 + n_2\bar{x}_2}{n_1 + n_2}$

(ii) Standard error of difference between two sample means when σ_p unknown:

$$t = \frac{\bar{x}_1 - \bar{x}_2}{\sqrt{\frac{\Sigma(x_1 - \bar{x}_1)^2 + \Sigma(x_2 - \bar{x}_2)^2}{n_1 + n_2 - 2}}} \times \frac{1}{\sqrt{\frac{1}{n_2} + \frac{1}{n_2}}}$$

5.12 SAMPLING DISTRIBUTION

Sampling distribution is the distribution of all possible values of a statistic from all the distinct possible samples of equal size drawn from a population or a process. The sampling distribution of the mean values has its own arithmetic mean denoted by $\mu_{\bar{x}}$ and standard deviation $\sigma_{\bar{x}}$ or s. The standard deviation of the sampling distribution indicates how different samples would be distributed. The calculation of these sampling distribution statistics is based on the following properties:

1. The arithmetic mean $\mu_{\bar{x}}$ sampling distribution of the mean values is equal to the population mean μ regardless of the form of population distribution, that is, $\mu_{\bar{x}} = \mu$.
2. The sampling distribution has a standard deviation (also called standard error or sampling error) equal to the population standard deviation divided by the square root of the sample size, that is, $\sigma_{\bar{x}} = \sigma/\sqrt{n}$.
3. The sampling distribution of sample mean values from normally distributed populations is the normal distribution for samples of all sizes.

Sampling error provides some idea of the precision of a statistical estimate. A low sampling error means a relatively less variability or range in sampling distribution. Since we never actually see the sampling distribution, calculation of sampling error is based on the calculation of the standard deviation of the sample. Thus, greater the sample's standard deviation, the greater the standard error (and the sampling error). The standard error is also related to the sample size: greater the sample size, smaller the standard error.

A sample of size $n > 30$ is generally considered to be a large sample for statistical analysis whereas a sample size $n \leq 30$ is considered to be a small sample. It may be noted from the formula of $\sigma_{\bar{x}}$ that value tends to be smaller as the size of sample *n* increases and *vice versa*.

When standard deviation σ of population is not known, the standard deviation *s* the sample, which closely approximates σ values, is used to compute standard error, that is, $\sigma_{\bar{x}} = \sigma/\sqrt{n}$.

5.13 IMPORTANCE OF SAMPLING DISTRIBUTION

Some important sampling distributions, which are commonly used, are:

1. Sampling distribution of mean
2. Sampling distribution of proportion
3. Students' t-distribution
4. Chi-square distribution
5. F-distribution

5.13.1 Sampling Distribution of Mean

Sampling distribution of mean refers to the probability distribution of all the possible means of random samples of a given size that we take from a population. If samples are taken from a normal population N (μ, σ_p), the sampling distribution of mean would be normal with mean $\mu_{\bar{x}} = \mu$ and standard deviation $n = \sigma_p \sqrt{n}$, where μ is the mean of the population, σ_p is the standard deviation of the population and n is the number of items in the samplc.

If the sampling distribution of mean to unit normal distribution, i.e., N(0,1), then the normal variate z for the sampling distribution of mean is given by:

$$z = \frac{\bar{x} - \mu}{\sigma_p / \sqrt{n}}$$

where, $\bar{x}$ = Sample mean

μ = Population mean

σ_p = Standard deviation of the population

n = Sample size

The characteristics of the sampling distribution of mean are very useful in several decision situations for accepting or rejection of hypothesis.

If standard deviation of the populations is known, and when two samples are drawn from the different population size, then the z for the distribution of two mean is given by:

$$z = \frac{(\bar{x}_1 - \bar{x}_2)}{\sqrt{\frac{\sigma_{p2}^2}{n_1} + \frac{\sigma_{p2}^2}{n_2}}} \sigma_{p1}^2$$

where, $(\bar{x}_1 - \bar{x}_2)$ = difference between two sample mean, i.e., sample statistics

σ_{p1}^2 and σ_{p1}^2 = variances of first population and second population

n_1 and n_2 = sample size of first sample and second sample

5.13.2 Sampling Distribution of Proportion

Like sample distribution of mean, we can as well have a sampling distribution of proportion. This happens in case of statistics of attributes. Usually, the statistics of attributes correspond to the conditions of binomial distribution that tends to become normal distribution as n becomes larger and larger. If *p* represents the proportion of successes and *q* the proportion of failures, i.e., $(q = 1 - p)$ and *p* is treated as a random variable, then the sampling distribution of proportion of success has a mean is:

p with standard deviation = $\sqrt{\frac{p.q}{n}}$ where n is the sample size

The normal distribution of large *n*, the normal variate of sampling distribution of proportion, *z* is given by:

$$z = \frac{(\bar{p} - p)}{\sqrt{pq/n}}$$

where $\bar{p}$ = the population or sample

and $\bar{p} = \frac{\text{Number of success in the sample}}{\text{Sample size}} = \frac{x}{n}$

The sample proportion of success can be used for testing of hypothesis.

5.13.3 Students' t-Distribution

When standard deviation of the population (σ_p) is known, population is normal and infinite and the sample is of a small size $(n \leq 30)$, then the t-distribution for the sampling distribution of mean is given by:

$$t = \frac{(\bar{x}-\mu)}{\sigma_s/\sqrt{n}} \times \frac{1}{\sqrt{(N-n)/(N-1)}}, \text{ with df} = (n-1)$$

where, x = Sample mean

μ = Population mean

σ_s = Standard deviation of the sample and $\sigma_s = \sqrt{\frac{\Sigma(x-\bar{x})^2}{n-1}}$

n = Sample size and df = degree of freedom

When the sample size gets larger, the shape of the t-distribution becomes approximately equal to the normal distribution. For sample sizes of more than 30, the t-distribution is so close to normal distribution and it is identical with normal distribution.

The confidence interval estimate of the population mean μ when unknown population standard deviation p is estimated by sample standard deviation σ_s, is:

$$\bar{x} \pm t\frac{\sigma_s}{\sqrt{n}} = \text{level of significance}$$

where t-test statistic value based on a t-distribution with (n – 1) degree of freedom and (1 – ∗) is the confidence coefficient.

If standard deviation of the population is not known, population is normal and finite, and then the t-distribution for the sampling distribution of mean is given by:

$$t = \frac{(\bar{x}-\mu)}{\sigma_s/\sqrt{n}} \times \frac{1}{\sqrt{(N-n)/(N-1)}}, \text{ with df} = (n-1)$$

If standard deviation of the population is not known, population is normal and finite, and then the t-distribution for the sampling distribution of mean is given by:

$$t = \frac{\bar{x}_1 - \bar{x}_2}{\sqrt{\frac{\Sigma(x_1-\bar{x}_1)^2 + \Sigma(x_2-\bar{x}_2)^2}{n_1+n_2-2}}} \times \frac{1}{\sqrt{\frac{1}{n_2}+\frac{1}{n_2}}}$$

with df = $(n_1 + n_2 - 1)$

The table value of t for given degrees of freedom at a certain level of significance is compared with the calculated value of t from the sample data, and if the latter is either equal to or exceeds, we infer that the null hypothesis cannot be accepted.

5.13.4 Chi-square (χ^2) Distribution

A sample of size *n* is taken from a population having a **normal distribution,** then there is a well-known result which allows a test to be made of whether the variance of the population has a predetermined value. The test statistic *t* of this instance could be set to be the sum of squares about the sample mean, divided by the nominal value for the variance then has a chi-square distribution with (n – 1) of freedom. Thus, the χ^2 distribution for a test of population variance is given by:

$$\chi^2 = \frac{\sigma_s^2}{\sigma_p^2}(n-1)$$

where σ_s^2 = Variance of the sample,

σ_p^2 = Variance of the population

(n – 1) = degrees of freedom, n being the number of items in the sample.

Chi-square distribution is not symmetrical and all the values are positive. This distribution may also be used for judging the significance of difference between observed and expected frequencies and also as a test of goodness of fit. The generalized shape of χ^2 distribution depends upon the df and the χ^2 distribution value is:

$$\chi^2 = \sum_{t=1}^{n} \frac{(O_i - E_i)}{E_i}$$

where, O_i = an observed frequency;

E_i = an expected (theoretical) frequency, asserted by the null hypothesis;

n = the number of cells in the table.

χ^2 distribution, which may be used at a desired level of significance for testing of hypothesis.

5.13.5 F-Distribution

The F-distribution is formed by the ratio of two independent Chi-square variables divided by their respective degrees of freedom.

Since F is formed by chi-square, many of the chi-square properties carry over to the F-distribution.

- The F-values are all non-negative.
- The distribution is non-symmetric.
- The mean is approximately 1.
- There are two independent degrees of freedom, one for the numerator, and one for the denominator.
- There are many different F-distributions, one for each pair of degrees of freedom.

If ($\sigma_{S_1}{}^2$) and ($\sigma_{S_2}{}^2$) are the variance of two independent samples of size n_1 and n_2 respectively taken from two independent normal population, having the same variance the F-test is given by:

$$F = \frac{\left(\sigma_{S_1}{}^2\right)}{\left(\sigma_{S_2}{}^2\right)}$$

where

$$\left(\sigma_{S_1}{}^2\right) = \frac{\Sigma\left(x_1 - \bar{x}_1\right)^2}{n_1 - 1} \text{ and } \left(\sigma_{S_2}{}^2\right) = \frac{\Sigma\left(x_1 - \bar{x}_1\right)^2}{n_2 - 1}, \text{ with } (n_1 - 1) \text{ and } (n_2 - 1) \text{ degree of freedom}$$

The hypothesis that, the means of several **normally distributed** populations, all having the same **standard deviation**, are equal. This is perhaps the best-known F-test, and plays an important role in the **analysis of variance** (ANOVA). The calculated value of F from the sample data is compared with the corresponding table value of F and if the former is equal to or exceeds the latter, then we infer that the null hypothesis of the variances being equal cannot be accepted. We shall make use of the F ratio in the context of hypothesis testing and also in the context of ANOVA techniques.

The advantage of the ANOVA F-test is that we do not need to pre-specify which treatments are to be compared, and we do not need to adjust for making **multiple comparisons**. The disadvantage of the ANOVA F-test is that if we reject the **null hypothesis**, we do not know which treatments can be said to be significantly different from the others if the F-test is performed at level α we cannot state that the treatment pair with the greatest mean difference is significantly different at level α.

5.14 SUMMARY

Sampling is a procedure that uses a small number of units of a given population as a basis for drawing conclusion about the whole population. Sampling is often necessary because it would be practically impossible to conduct a census to measure characteristics of all elements of a population. Samples are also needed in cases where measurement involves destruction of the unit measured. A sampling frame is a list of elements, or individual members, of the overall population from which the sample is drawn. A sampling unit is a single element or group of elements subject to selection in the sample.

Sampling process can be divided into seven steps as: (1) Defining the target population; (2) Specifying the sampling frame; (3) Specifying the sampling unit; (4) Selection of the sampling method; (5) Determination of sample size; (6) Specifying the sampling plan; and (7) Selecting the sample. The two major sampling methods are probability and non-probability techniques. The probability techniques includes Random sampling, Systematic sampling, Stratified sampling and Multistage cluster sampling and the non-probability techniques includes Convenience sampling, Quota sampling, Judgment sampling and Snowball sampling. With these techniques, random sampling error can be accurately predicted. Researchers who must take a decision concerning the most appropriate sample design for a specific project will identify a number of sampling criteria and evaluate the relevance importance of each criterion before selecting a sample design.

5.15 KEY TERMS

Sample: Sample is a finite part of a statistical population whose properties are studied to gain information about the whole.

Census: A complete study of all the elements present in the population is known as a census.

Sampling: Sampling is a part of the total population. It can be an individual element or a group of elements selected from the population.

Accuracy: Accuracy refers to how close a sample statistic is to a population parameter.

Precision: Precision refers to how close estimates from different samples are to each other.

Margin of Error: The margin of error expresses the maximum expected difference between the true population parameter and a sample estimate of that parameter.

Estimator: The estimation process for calculating sample statistics is called the estimator.

Precision: Precision is a measure of how close an estimate is expected to be, to the true value of a parameter.

Target Population: Target population is defined in terms of element, sampling unit, extent, and time frame.

Sampling Frame: Sampling frame is the list of elements from which the sample may be drawn.

Sampling Unit: Sampling unit is a basic unit that contains a single element or a group of elements of the population to be sampled.

Sampling Method: Sampling method refers to the way that observations are selected from a **population** to be in the sample for a sample survey.

Population Parameter: A population parameter is the true value of a population attribute.

Sample Statistic: A sample statistic is an estimate, based on sample data, of a population parameter.

Simple Random Sampling: A sampling process where each element in the target population has an equal chance or probability of inclusion in the sample is known as simple random sampling.

Systematic Sampling: Systematic sampling involves the selection of every k^{th} element from a sampling frame and 'k' represents the skip interval.

Stratified Random Sampling: The number of units drawn for sampling from each stratum depends on the homogeneity of the elements.

Multistage Clustering Sampling: Clustering involves grouping the population into various clusters and selecting few clusters for conducting research studies.

Convenience Sampling: The selection of units from the population based on their easy availability and accessibility to the researcher is known as convenience sampling.

Quota Sampling: In quota sampling, the entire population is segmented into mutually exclusive groups.

Judgment Sampling: The selection of a unit, from the population based on the judgment of an experienced researcher, is known as judgment or purposive sampling.

Snowball Sampling: Sampling procedures that involve the selection of additional respondents are known as snowball sampling. This sampling technique is used against low incidence or rare populations.

Sampling Error: Random sampling error or sampling error is the difference between the sample results and the results of a census conducted by identical procedures.

Non-sampling Errors: Non-sampling errors also known as systematic errors occur due to the nature of the study's design and the correctness of execution. Non-sampling error includes non-observation errors and measurement errors.

Standard Error: The standard error or *standard error of the mean* is the standard deviation of the sample means, and thus gives a measure of their spread.

Sampling Distribution: Sampling distribution is the distribution of all possible values of a statistic from all the distinct possible samples of equal size drawn from a population or a process.

5.16 MULTIPLE OBJECTIVE TYPE QUESTIONS

1. Sampling is the process of selecting a representative part of a population for the purpose of determining the characteristics of the whole sample.
   (a) True (b) False
2. Sampling method refers to the rules and procedures by which some elements of the population are included in the sample.
   (a) True (b) False
3. Sample design must give the results of the sample study and can be applied in general for the universe with a reasonable with a reasonable level of confidence.
   (a) True (b) False
4. Target population is defined in terms of element, sampling unit, extent, and time frame.
   (a) True (b) False
5. A sampling unit is a basic unit that contains a single element or a group of elements of the population to be sampled.
   (a) True (b) False
6. In non-probability sampling methods, each population element has a known (non-zero) chance of being chosen for the sample.
   (a) True (b) False
7. In simple random sampling, each element in the target population has an equal chance or probability of inclusion in the sample.
   (a) True (b) False
8. Stratification is the process of grouping the members of the population in non-homogenous group before sampling.
   (a) True (b) False
9. Quota sampling finds extensive use in commercial research where the main objective is to ensure that the sample represents in relative proportion, the people in the various categories in the population.
   (a) True (b) False
10. Systematic errors occur due to the nature of the study's design and the correctness of execution.
   (a) True (b) False
11. Which is a finite part of a statistical population whose properties are studied to gain information about the whole?
   (a) Sample (b) Population
   (c) Survey (d) Data collection

12. Which is a data collection tool used together information about individuals?
    (a) Sample (b) Survey
    (c) Measurement (d) Sampling
13. When researchers describe the quality of survey results, which of the following term they use?
    (a) Accuracy (b) Precision
    (c) Margin of error (d) All the above
14. Which of the following is the part of total population?
    (a) Sample (b) Survey
    (c) Sampling (d) Population
15. Which of the following is the least of elements from which the sample may be drawn?
    (a) Sampling plan (b) Sampling frame
    (c) Sampling unit (d) All of the above
16. A sampling in which every member of the population has a calculable and non-zero probability of being included in the sample is known as
    (a) Probability sampling (b) Non-probability sampling
    (c) Quota sampling (d) Multistage sampling
17. In which sampling the entire population is segmented into mutually exclusive groups?
    (a) Convenience sampling (b) Quota sampling
    (c) Judgment sampling (d) Snowball sampling
18. The absolute value of the difference between an unbiased point estimate and the corresponding population parameter is known as a
    (a) Population error (b) Standard error
    (c) Sampling error (d) None of the above
19. The sampling error is inversely proportional to the
    (a) Sample size (b) Population size
    (c) Systematic error (d) Sampling frame error
20. 68% of all samples mean will be within what standard error of the population mean?
    (a) One (b) Two
    (c) Three (d) None of these

Answers to Objective Type Questions

Questions	1	2	3	4	5	6	7	8	9	10
Answers	F	T	T	T	T	F	T	F	T	T
Questions	11	12	13	14	15	16	17	18	19	20
Answers	a	b	d	c	b	a	b	c	a	a

5.17 CONCEPTUAL QUESTIONS

1. What do you mean by sample and Sample Design? Describe the characteristics of sample design.
2. What is the meaning of survey? Write its merits and demerits.
3. What is the meaning of sampling? Write its importance both in social and scientific research.

4. What points should be taken into consideration by a researcher in developing a sample design for this research project.
5. Describe the various steps in sampling process.
6. Distinguish between probability sampling and non-probability sampling.
7. Why probability sampling is generally preferred in comparison to non-probability sampling? Explain the procedure of selecting a simple random sample.
8. Under what circumstances stratified random sampling design is considered appropriate? How would you select such sample?
9. What is sampling vs. complete enumeration? Explain in detail.
10. What are the sampling errors in research? Explain.
11. What is the importance of sampling distribution in sampling design? Describe briefly.
12. Write short notes:
    (a) Probability and non-probability samples
    (b) Sampling frame and sampling unit
    (c) Systematic and stratified sampling
    (d) Cluster and multistage sampling
    (e) Convenience sampling and quota sampling
    (f) Judgment sampling and Snowball sampling
    (g) Sampling error and non-sampling error
    (h) Non-probability sampling
    (i) Complete enumeration
    (j) Standard error

Chapter 6

ATTITUDE MEASUREMENT AND SCALING TECHNIQUE

Chapter Outline

Learning Objectives

- *Describe the type of managerial research problems which utilize the tools of attitude measurement.*
- *Discuss the type of issues which come up when one attempts the measurement of attitudes.*
- *Explain the different attitude measurement scales, along with their strengths and limitations.*
- *Decide for which type of research problems one should go in for specific scale or think of using multidimensional scaling.*

6.1 MEANING OF ATTITUDE

An attitude is a point of view about a situation. An attitude has three components. An attitude is made up of:

1. What you think?
2. What you do?
3. What you feel?

The dictionary definition of attitude includes such words as "feeling" and "position." This combination is interesting because, to most psychologists and to many in the working world, if a person feels a certain way it puts that person in a particular position from which to view the world.

According to most language research, the word has a history that dates back at least 500 years, with connection to the French "attitudine." While definitions of attitude usually include reference to positive attitude and negative attitude as the main states of mind, there are nuances and combination attitudes as well, according to psychological research.

The more clinical definition of attitude includes references to a person's like or dislike for something, whether it be a physical thing or a set of circumstances. Again, this leads to the positive/negative division. Yet, people are also said to have an attitude that is not completely positive or completely negative. In fact, some people actually maintain mixed feelings or almost no state of mind at all in certain situations.

In clinical psychology, the attitude is often described as having three parts, as a model for thinking about the issue. The parts are: affect, which is the response to the item or situation; behavior, which is the outward indication of the attitude; and cognitive, which is the resulting belief from having the experience.

In the business setting, management is well-served by having an understanding of attitude. This allows managers and supervisors to offer incentives along with training and work-related information, incentives that may alter attitudes in a positive way. The result may be higher quality products, more efficient production and a satisfied, loyal staff.

From the management viewpoint, as well as from the view of friends and family, what we do with and for another person is quite important. But, following that, the individual reaction to what we do ultimately determines attitude. Some people can maintain a positive attitude, and look at the world from a comfortable point of view in spite of what happens. There are those who argue that the resulting viewpoint can be controlled.

6.2 THE NATURE OF ATTITUDE

Research on attitudes has been popular in many disciplines. However, the construct is considered more central to Social Psychology than to any other academic area. The concept of attitude is probably the most distinctive and indispensable concept in contemporary American social psychology. This assessment is as appropriate today as it was then.

Attitude has been a difficult concept to define adequately, primarily because it has been defined by so many, but also because of the word's differing lay uses and connotations. Attitude defined as:

- A mental and neural state of readiness, organized through experience, exerting a directive or dynamic influence upon the individual's response to all objects and situations with which it is related.
- An evaluative disposition toward some object based upon cognitions, affective reactions, behavioral intentions, and past behaviors ... that can influence cognitions, affective responses, and future intentions and behaviors.

Attitudes are latent and not directly observable in themselves, but they act to organize or provide direction to actions and behaviors that are observable. Many refer to attitudes as "predispositions to respond". Attitudes are related to how people perceive the situations in which they find themselves. Also, attitudes vary in direction (either positive or negative), in degree (the amount of positiveness or negativeness), and in intensity (die amount of commitment with which a position is held).

Attitude Systems

Attitude positions are the summary aggregation of four components: (a) *affective responses,* (b) *cognitions,* (c) *behaviors,* and (d) *behavioral intentions.* The *affective* of attitude is said to consist of a person's evaluation of, liking of, or emotional response to some situation, object, or person. Affective responses reflect one's attitude with sensations of pleasure, sadness, or other levels of physical arousal. For example, for the attitude construct of *computer anxiety,* topic of current interest, the affective component would be a person's liking of the computer and his feeling of excitement, or dread, when she or he used one.

The *cognitive* of an attitude is conceptualized as a person's factual knowledge of the situation, object, or person, including oneself. In other words, the cognitive component refers to how much a person knows about a topic, such as computers. The cognitive component of computer anxiety would be based on how much a person knows about computers and her level of understanding of computer operation.

The *behavioral* of an attitude involves the person's overt behavior directed toward a situation, object, or person. For example, the behavioral component of computer anxiety would be related to how often a person had used a computer, and what kind of experience he had. Persons who routinely use computers, especially if they choose to use them freely, would be more likely to have positive attitudes toward computers, and be less anxious, than would others who have fewer experiences with computers.

Finally, the *behavioral intention* involves the person's plans to perform in a certain way, even if sometimes these plans are never acted upon." The behavioral intention component of this attitude construct would be the "apprehension felt by an individual when considering the implications of utilizing computer technology." In other words, if people knew that they were going to have to use computers in an upcoming class, this would partially shape their level of computer anxiety. If the class were to be a difficult one, say in statistics, then computer anxiety would be likely to be increased.

These four components of attitude form an attitude system. The components are not isolated but are interrelated and produce an organizing framework or mental representation of the attitude construct. Cognitive schemata provide structure to interrelated attitudes and guide the information processes of attending, interpreting, and reconstructing. Behavioral research supports the idea that actions lead to the formation of cognitive schemata, which lead to the creation of attitudes. It would seem that the opposite is also true. Attitudes help form cognitive relationships, which in turn predispose behaviors.

Attitude Formation

Situational stimuli or events in the environment directly influence behavior and the formation of attitudes. Strict behaviorists would argue that internal events that form attitudes are the result of observable actions. A change in attitude or beliefs occurs as a result of actions that have been influenced by reinforcers. Social learning theory expands this principle. According to social learning theorists, it is not essential to learn behaviors directly through action and reinforcement, as traditional behavioral psychologists would propose. Indirect learning through observing a model and receiving verbal instruction has a powerful impact on behavior and attitude formation.

Situations that include a change in the behavioral component of attitude lead to changes in attitudes. But there is also a reciprocal action. Since the components of attitude systems are interrelated, a change in liking (affect) may result in a change in behaviors. For example, the currently popular concept of the cognitive apprenticeship is based on the idea of learners participating as apprentices in real-world activities with those who are more knowledgeable than them. If designed correctly, these situations are perceived by learners as important and realistic, and learners come to value them. The overt activities of cognitive apprenticeships produce in students favorable dispositions (i.e., affects), which in turn promote a sense of value and often a desire to learn more.

6.3 IMPORTANCE OF ATTITUDE

Traditionally when instruction is designed, there are two categories of outcomes in mind: those directed toward cognitive goals, and those related to the attitudes of the learner. There is little necessity to argue the importance of the acquisition of knowledge by a student as a result of instruction. Achievement is the paramount objective of most instructional activities; however, it may also be important to recognize the need for establishing attitudinal goals and for planning activities designed to facilitate affective outcomes in learners as a consequence of an instructional situation. As a matter of fact, it has become increasingly apparent to those involved in educational technology research that one of the major, and possibly unique, consequences of instructional situations involving media is the likelihood of the development of positive attitudinal positions in students.

The impact of attitude on learning is only one reason for interest in attitudes. There are other arguments that explain why attitudes of learners are important. First, most educators would agree that there are times when it is legitimate, and important, for learners to accept the truth of certain ideas — in other words, to accept an attitudinal position. The importance of voting is an attitude position that most would agree is important. Civics teachers routinely "teach" this attitude.

Second, while the strength of the relationship between attitudes and achievement is unclear, it seems logical that students are more likely to remember information, seek new ideas, and continue studying when they react favorably to an instructional situation or like a certain content area. Students who like chemistry will tend to stay after class to work on experiments, read about chemistry outside of class, and be more likely to elect to take a chemistry course than will those who do not like chemistry. Learners tend to do what they like, not what they do not like. They gravitate toward their interests.

Third, there are some instances when influencing student's attitudes is not desirable, so educators should be aware of which techniques affect attitudes. In this way, possible bias can be recognized and eliminated. The gender biases found in textbooks are considered partially responsible for gender biases in people. For example, the use of the generic *he* was long considered appropriate by textbook authors and publishers. Now it is obvious that the use of this term helped form an inappropriate attitude position in both boys and girls that males were more important.

Last, student attitudes toward a situation can tell the teacher a great deal about the impact of that situation on the learning process. Obviously, attitudes need to be measured in order to know if they have been influenced. As a result of quantitatively and qualitatively assessing the opinions of students toward the learning activities in which they are participating, it may be possible to improve the quality of procedures. One of the most important techniques of evaluation is to ascertain attitudes toward some event, object, or person. End-of-course evaluations of attitude toward courses and course content are a standard activity in schools and training centers.

6.4 ATTITUDE MEASUREMENT

Measurement implies the process of obtaining information which can be subject to analysis. Attitude measurement relates to the process of measuring an individual's attitude towards an object. When we go for measurement of attitudes or any other parameter, one has to clearly sort out the following:

1. "what" has to be measured?
2. "who" is to be measured?
3. the accuracy desired in the measurement
4. the costs permissible
5. the choices available in the measurement/data collection techniques.

In attitude measurement, the researcher is primarily interested in measuring the "state of mind" of the respondent(s). It may include factors such as awareness, attitudes and decision processes. An interesting characteristic of these measures is that their verification is rather difficult. There is no way to determine whether the answer given by a respondent to the level of liking for a new product, such as ice-cream mix, represents the "truth" or not. The researcher, unless he is a "telepathist", cannot actually observe the states of mind like preference, likes and dislikes, etc. Such things can only be inferred.

It has been stated in the previous section, that attitudes are affected by attributes and beliefs. So, the first step, before embarking on an attitude-measurement exercise, is selecting the relevant attributes of the object under investigation. For instance, the salient attributes of a product like "Shrikhand" may be price, shelf life, flavour, and pack size. For a public distribution system, they may be quality of grains, prices, outlet working timings, and assurance of availability. It is clearly impossible to measure every attribute of the process/object under consideration. The researcher should settle for the relevant ones only. It is advisable to measure only those attributes which can be related to actions by the respondents. Exploratory research can be helpful in identifying attributes. The methods used could include non-disguised ones like depth interviews and disguised ones like projective techniques. The depth interviews are the most commonly used technique. They use no structured framework for gathering information. The respondents are encouraged to talk about the object under investigation and the investigator tries to uncover its salient attributes in this process. This procedure requires skilled investigators. It is also considered costly and the results are prone to bias errors. The projective techniques attempt to uncover the information from the respondent in an indirect manner. The subject is requested to respond to incomplete stimuli here. In doing so, he/she is believed to reveal elements of attitude towards the object that will not be revealed in response to direct queries. The projective techniques used may include a cartoon test, word association test, sentence completion test, etc. Though these techniques also have some disadvantages, they are used more than the non-disguised methods.

The next important issue in attitude measurement is that "who" is to be measured. It involves people. The question to be posed now is of what kind? Their education, age, sex, occupation, religion etc. may have a bearing on the choice of the measurement method. The measurement procedure must be designed with the characteristics of the respondents under consideration. For instance, using a mail questionnaire for disinterested or hostile respondents would hardly be the right choice as a research instrument.

The third major issue in attitude measurement is the choices in data collection and measurement techniques. The data collection techniques can be categorized into (a) Questionnaire methods, and (b) Observational methods. Usually questionnaires are used for measuring the attitudes.

The approaches for measuring attitudes are as follows:

1. Self-report inventories
2. Using psychological measures like galvanic skin response or pupillary response
3. Projective techniques like thematic and perception test.

The weaknesses of the self-report measures are that:

1. The results are limited to what the individuals know about their attitudes and are willing to relate.
2. The validity of the verbalized attitudes is questionable.

Finally, the last major issue for a managerial researcher here relates to the costs and accuracy desired in the measurement. As has been stated earlier, these type of measurements are never entirely free of inaccuracy. Moreover, cost and accuracy are generally reciprocal properties in measurement. The intimate knowledge of a research instrument can go a long way in the correct interpretation of the results.

6.5 MEASUREMENT SCALES

There are many types of scales and scaling techniques. We have to choose the most appropriate technique to suit the research being done. The statements contained therein have to be prepared in such a way that the answers received can easily be converted into numerical values. The three most commonly used scales are the Nominal scale, the Ordinal scale and the Interval scale. You will note later on that the appropriateness of a statistical method depends upon the type of scale used in data collection.

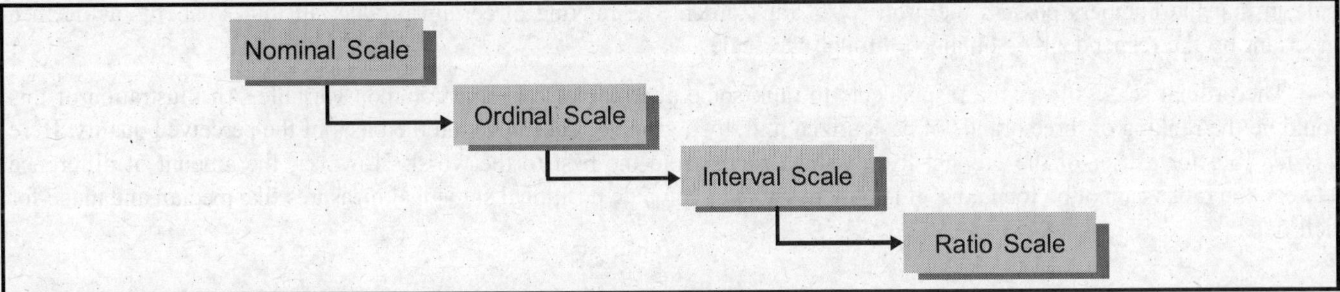

Fig. 6.1: Measurement of Scales

6.5.1 Nominal Scale

This is a very simple scale and least powerful level of measurement. It consists of assignment of facts/choices to various alternative categories which are usually exhaustive as well mutually exclusive. These scales are just numerical and are the least restrictive of all the scales. The nominal scale simply allows the categorization of responses into a number of mutually exclusive categories. There are no relationships between the categories, implying that there is no ranking or ordering. The typical applications of the nominal scale is in classification of responses by social class, "like" or "dislike", "yes" or ''no", "sex", and so on. The statistical operation possible for nominally scaled data is counting only.

Instances of Nominal Scale are – credit card numbers, bank account numbers, employee id numbers etc. It is simple and widely used when relationship between two variables is to be studied. In a Nominal Scale, numbers are no more than labels and are used specifically to identify different categories of responses. Following example illustrates:

What is your gender?

1. ☐ Male
2. ☐ Female

Another example is – a survey of retail stores done on two dimensions – way of maintaining stocks and daily turnover.

How do you stock items at present?

1. ☐ By product category
2. ☐ At a centralized store
3. ☐ Department wise
4. ☐ Single warehouse

Daily turnover of consumer is?

1. ☐ Between 100-200
2. ☐ Between 200-300
3. ☐ Above 300

In nominal scale, we split a set into subsets which are mutually exclusive and collectively exhaustive.

	No. of Students	
	Male	**Female**
Day Scholars	300	200
Hosteler	100	150
Total	400	350

6.5.2 Ordinal Scale

Ordinal scales are the simplest attitude measuring scale used in Marketing Research. It is more powerful than a nominal scale in that the numbers possess the property of rank order. The ranking of certain product attributes/benefits as deemed important by the respondents is obtained through the scale.

The ordinal scale allows the respondents to rank some alternatives by some common variable. An illustration of this would be the ranking of three brands of pasteurized milk by a group of consumers on the basis of the perceived quality. Here it is feasible for a user of the product to rank the brands from the best to the worst. However, the amount of difference between the ranks cannot be found out. It is only possible to compute positional statistical measures like median and mode for such data.

Example 6.1:

Rank the following attributes (1-5), on their importance in a microwave oven.

(a) Company Name

(b) Functions

(c) Price

(d) Comfort

(e) Design

The most important attribute is ranked 1 by the respondents and the least important is ranked 5. Instead of numbers, letters or symbols too can be used to rate in a ordinal scale. Such scale makes no attempt to measure the degree of favorability of different rankings.

One can ask respondents questions on the basis of one or more attributes such as flower, colour, etc., and ask about liking or disliking, e.g., whether the respondent likes soft drinks or not.

- I strongly like it
- I like it
- I am indifferent
- I dislike it
- I strongly dislike it

Example 6.2:

If there are 4 different types of fertilizers and if they are ordered on the basis of quality as Grade A, Grade B, Grade C, Grade D is again an Ordinal Scale.

Example 6.3:

	Judge's score x	Score minus 8 x – 8	Tripled score 3x	Cubed score x^3
Alice's cooking ability	10	2	30	1000
Bob's cooking ability	9	1	27	729
Claire's cooking ability	8.5	0.5	25.5	614.125
Dana's cooking ability	8	0	24	512
Edgar's cooking ability	5	–3	15	125

Since $x - 8$, $3x$, and x^3 are all monotonically increasing functions, replacing the ordinal judge's score by any of these alternate scores does not affect the relative ranking of the five people's cooking abilities. Each column of numbers is an equally legitimate ordinal scale for describing their abilities. However, the numerical (additive) difference between the various ordinal scores has no particular meaning.

6.5.3 Interval Scale

The deficiencies of the nominal and the ordinal scales are taken care of in the interval scale. The scale has an arbitrary zero point with numbers placed at equally appearing intervals. A number of statistical operations including addition, subtraction, and computation of the mean can be done on intervally scaled data.

Mostly, the nominal and the ordinal type of scales are used in attitude measurement. However, there are attempts to treat them or convert them into interval scales so as to make the data more amenable to statistical operations. But the reasonability of this assumption should be always tested before making inferences.

Most of the attitude measurement scales used are ordinal in nature, though there is attempt to treat the resulting data as intervally scaled. The simplest possible type of such scale has the respondent classifying the object/issue/product/himself into one among two dichotomous categories. Further refinements may include the provision of additional alternatives denoting the degrees of liking or disliking. These are listed in sequence so that the alternatives form a type of scale. These scales are basically self-report inventories, with a list of favorable and unfavorable statements towards the subject.

The attitude measurement scales can be categorized into those which are unidimensional in nature and those which are multidimensional. The different type of single dimensional attitude measurement scales which are available are graphical and numerical scales, summated scales, paired comparisons, equal-appearing intervals, etc. Some scales of the above-mentioned type will be discussed in the subsequent sections of this unit.

Example 6.4:

How do you rate your present refrigerator for the following qualities?

Company Name	Less Known	1	2	3	4	5	Well-known
Functions	Few	1	2	3	4	5	Many
Price	Low	1	2	3	4	5	High
Design	Poor	1	2	3	4	5	Good
Overall Satisfaction	Very Dissatisfied	1	2	3	4	5	Very Satisfied

Such a scale permits the researcher to say that position 5 on the scale is above position 4 and also the distance from 5 to 4 is same as distance from 4 to 3. Such a scale however does not permit conclusion that position 4 is twice as strong as position 2 because no zero position has been established. The data obtained from the Interval Scale can be used to calculate the Mean scores of each attributes over all respondents. The Standard Deviation (a measure of dispersion) can also be calculated.

6.5.4 Ratio Scale

Ratio Scales are not widely used in research unless a base item is made available for comparison. In the above example of Interval scale, a score of 4 in one quality does not necessarily mean that the respondent is twice more satisfied than the respondent who marks 2 on the scale. A Ratio scale has a natural zero point and further numbers are placed at equally appearing intervals. For example, scales for measuring physical quantities like – length, weight, etc.

Table 6.1: Scales of Measurement

Scale	Basic Characteristics Example Descriptive	Common Example	Marketing Statistics	Permissible
Nominal	Number of identity and classify objective	Social Security numbers, numbering of football players	Brand nos., Store type	Percentage, Mode
Ordinal	Nos. indicate the relative position of objects but not the magnitude of differences between them	Quality ranking, rankings of team in a tournament	Preference ranking, Market position, Social class	Percentile, Median
Interval	Differences between objectives	Temperatures options, Index	Attitudes, Standard Deviation	Range, Mean,
Ratio	Zero point is fixed, ratios of scale value can be compared	Length, Weight	Age, sales, Income, Costs	Geometric Mean, Harmonic Mean

OK to compute....	Nominal	Ordinal	Interval	Ratio
Frequency distribution.	Yes	Yes	Yes	Yes
Median and percentiles	No	Yes	Yes	Yes
Add or subtract	No	No	Yes	Yes
Mean, standard deviation, standard of the mean	No	No	Yes	Yes
Ratio or coefficient of variation	No	No	No	Yes

The ratio scales are very common in physical scenarios. Quantified responses forming a ratio scale analytically are the most versatile. Ratio scale possess all the characteristics of an interval scale, and the ratios of the numbers on these scales have meaningful interpretations. Data on certain demographic or descriptive attributes, if they are obtained through open-ended questions, will have ratio-scale properties. Consider the following questions:

1. What is your annual income before taxes?
2. How far is the Theater from your home?

Answers to these questions have a natural, unambiguous starting point, namely zero. Since starting point is not chosen arbitrarily, computing and interpreting ratio makes sense. For example, we can say that a respondent with an annual income of ₹ 40,000 earns twice as much as one with an annual income of ₹ 20,000.

6.6 TEST OF SOUND/GOOD MEASUREMENT

6.6.1 Test of Validity

Validity is the ability of an instrument (for example measuring an attitude) to measure what it is supposed to measure. That is, when we ask a set of questions (i.e., develop a **measuring instrument**) with the hope that we are tapping the concept, how can we be reasonably certain that we are indeed measuring the concept we set out to do and not something else? There is no quick answer.

Researchers have attempted to assess validity in different ways, including asking questions such as "Is there consensus among my colleagues that my attitude scale measures what it is supposed to measure?" and "Does my measure correlate with others' measures of the 'same' concept?" and "Does the behavior expected from my measure predict the actual observed behavior?" Researchers expect the answers to provide some evidence of a measure's validity.

What is relevant depends on the nature of the research problem and the researcher's judgment. One way to approach this question is to organize the answer according to measure-relevant types of validity. One widely accepted classification consists of three major types of validity: (1) content validity, (2) criterion-related validity, and (3) construct validity.

(1) Content Validity

The content validity of a **measuring instrument** (the composite of measurement scales) is the extent to which it provides adequate coverage of the investigative questions guiding the study. If the instrument contains a representative sample of the universe of subject matter of interest, then the content validity is good. To evaluate the content validity of an instrument, one must first agree on what dimensions and elements constitute adequate coverage. To put it differently, content validity is a function of how well the dimensions and elements of a concept have been delineated. Look at the concept of *feminism* which implies a person's commitment to a set of beliefs creating full equality between men and women in areas of the arts, intellectual pursuits, family, work, politics, and authority relations. Does this definition provide adequate coverage of the different dimensions of the concept? Then we have the following two questions to measure *feminism*:

1. Should men and women get equal pay for equal work?
2. Should men and women share household tasks?

These two questions do not provide coverage to all the dimensions delineated earlier. It definitely falls short of adequate content validity for measuring *feminism.*

A panel of persons to judge how well the instrument meets the standard can attest to the content validity of the instrument. A panel independently assesses the test items for a performance test. It judges each item to be essential, useful but not essential, or not necessary in assessing performance of a relevant behavior.

Face validity is considered as a basic and very minimum index of content validity. Face validity indicates that the items that are intended to measure a concept, do on the face of it look like they measure the concept. For example a few people would accept a measure of college student math ability using a question that asked students: 2 + 2 = ?. This is not a valid measure of college-level math ability on the face of it. Nevertheless, it is a subjective agreement among professionals that a scale logically appears to reflect accurately what it is supposed to measure. When it appears evident to experts that the measure provides adequate coverage of the concept, a measure has face validity.

(2) Criterion-related Validity

Criterion validity uses some standard or criterion to indicate a construct accurately. The validity of an indicator is verified by comparing it with another measure of the same construct in which research has confidence. There are two sub-types of this kind of validity.

A. Concurrent validity: To have concurrent validity, an indicator must be associated with a prior state of the respondents themselves – is indicative of its stability and low vulnerability to changes in the situation. This attests to its "**goodness**" because the concept is stably measured, no matter when it is done. Two tests of stability are test-retest reliability and parallel-form reliability.

(1) Test-retest Reliability

Test-retest method of determining reliability involves administering the same scale to the same respondents at two separate times to test for stability. If the measure is stable over time, the test, administered under the same conditions each time, should obtain similar results. For example, suppose a researcher measures job satisfaction and finds that 64 per cent of the population is satisfied with their jobs. If the study is repeated a few weeks later under similar conditions, and the researcher again finds that 64 per cent of the population is satisfied with their jobs, it appears that the measure has repeatability. The high stability correlation or consistency between the two measures at time 1 and at time 2 indicates high degree of reliability. This was at the aggregate level; the same exercise can be applied at the individual level. When the **measuring instrument** produces unpredictable results from one testing to the next, the results are said to be unreliable because of error in measurement.

There are two problems with measures of test-retest reliability that are common to all longitudinal studies. Firstly, the first measure may sensitize the respondents to their participation in a research project and subsequently influence the results of the second measure. Further if the time between the measures is long, there may be attitude change or other maturation of the subjects. Thus, it is possible for a reliable measure to indicate low or moderate correlation between the first and the second administration, but this low correlation may be due to an attitude change over time rather than to lack of reliability.

(2) Parallel-form Reliability

When responses on two comparable sets of measures tapping the same construct are highly correlated, we have parallel-form reliability. It is also called equivalent-form reliability. Both forms have similar items and same response format, the only changes being the wording and the order or sequence of the questions. What we try to establish here is the error variability resulting from wording and ordering of the questions. If two such comparable forms are highly correlated, we may be fairly certain that the measures are reasonably reliable, with minimal error variance caused by wording, ordering, or other factors.

B. Internal Consistency of Measures

Internal consistency of measures is indicative of the homogeneity of the items in the measure that tap the construct. In other words, the items should 'hang together as a set,' and be capable of independently measuring the same concept so that the respondents attach the same overall meaning to each of the items. This can be seen by examining if the items and the subsets of items in the **measuring instrument** are highly correlated. Consistency can be examined through the inter-item consistency reliability and split-half reliability.

(1) Inter-item Consistency Reliability: This is a test of consistency of respondents' answers to all the items in a measure. To the degree that items are independent measures of the same concept, they will be correlated with one another.

(2) Split-half Reliability: Split-half reliability reflects the correlations between two halves of an instrument. The estimates could vary depending on how the items in the measure are split into two halves. The technique of splitting halves is the most basic method for checking internal consistency when measures contain a large number of items. In the split-half method, the researcher may take the results obtained from one half of the scale items (e.g., odd-numbered items) and check them against the results from the other half of the items (e.g., even numbered items). The high correlation tells us there is similarity (or homogeneity) among its items.

It is important to note that reliability is a necessary but not sufficient condition of the test of **goodness** of a measure. For example, one could reliably measure a concept establishing high stability and consistency, but it may not be the concept that one had set out to measure. Validity ensures the ability of a scale to measure the intended concept.

6.6.3 Test of Sensitivity and Practicality

Sensitivity: The sensitivity of a scale is an important measurement concept, particularly when changes in attitudes or other hypothetical constructs are under investigation. Sensitivity refers to an instrument's ability to accurately measure variability in stimuli or responses. A dichotomous response category, such as "agree or disagree," does not allow the recording of subtle attitude changes. A more sensitive measure, with numerous items on the scale, may be needed. For example adding "strongly agree," "mildly agree," "neither agree nor disagree," "mildly disagree," and "strongly disagree" as categories increases a scale's sensitivity.

The sensitivity of a scale based on a single question or single item can also be increased by adding additional questions or items. In other words, because index measures allow for greater range of possible scores, they are more sensitive than single item.

Practicality: The scientific requirements of a project call for the measurement process to be reliable and valid, while the operational requirements call for it to be practical. Practicality has been defined as *economy*, *convenience*, and *interpretability*.

6.7 SCALING

The term scaling is applied to the attempts to measure the attitude objectively. Attitude is a resultant of number of external and internal factors. Depending upon the attitude to be measured, appropriate scales are designed. Scaling is a technique used for measuring qualitative responses of respondents such as those related to their feelings, perception, likes, dislikes, interests and preferences.

6.7.1 Scale Construction Techniques

Scale Construction Decisions

(1) What level of data is involved (nominal, ordinal, interval, or ratio)?

(2) What will the results be used for?

(3) Should you use a scale, index, or typology?

(4) What types of statistical analysis would be useful?

(5) Should you use a comparative scale or a non-comparative scale?

(6) How many scale divisions or categories should be used (1 to 10; 1 to 7; –3 to +3)?

(7) Should there be an odd or even number of divisions? (Odd gives neutral center value; even forces respondents to take a non-neutral position.)

(8) What should the nature and descriptiveness of the scale labels be?

(9) What should the physical form or layout of the scale be? (graphic, simple linear, vertical, horizontal)

(10) Should a response be forced or be left optional?

6.7.2 Classification of Scaling Techniques

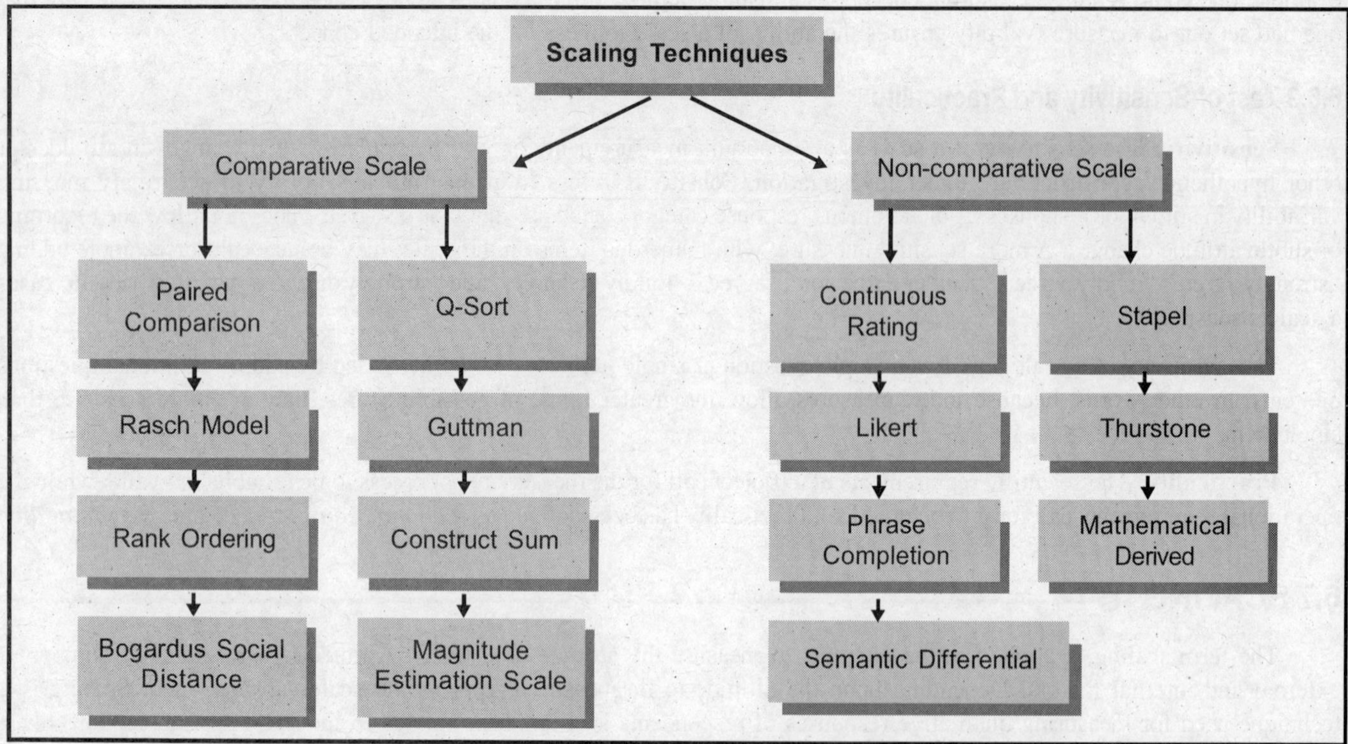

Fig. 6.2: Classification of Scaling Techniques

6.8 COMPARATIVE SCALING TECHNIQUES

(1) Pairwise comparison scale
(2) Rasch model scaling
(3) Rank ordering
(4) Bogardus social distance scale
(5) Q-Sort
(6) Guttman scale
(7) Constant sum scale
(8) Magnitude estimation scale

6.8.1 Pairwise Comparison Scale

Pairwise comparison generally refers to any process of comparing entities in pairs to judge which of each pair is preferred, or has a greater amount of some quantitative property. The method of pairwise comparison is used in the scientific study of preferences, attitudes, voting systems, social choice, public choice, and multi-agent AI systems. In psychology literature, it is often referred to as paired comparison.

If an individual or organization expresses a preference between two mutually distinct alternatives, this preference can be expressed as a pairwise comparison.

Table 6.2: Paired-comparison Data for 5 Brands of Cake Mix
Matrix A

	A	B	C	D	E
A	–	.90	.64	.14	.27
B	.10	--	.32	.02	.21
C	.36	.68	--	.15	.36
D	.86	.98	.85	--	.52
E	.73	.79	.64	.48	--

Table 6.3: Paired-comparison Data for 5 Brands of Cake Mix
Matrix B

	A	B	C	D	E
A	–	1	1	0	0
B	0	--	0	0	0
C	0	1	--	0	0
D	1	1	1	--	1
E	.1	1	1	0	--
Total	**2**	**4**	**3**	**0**	**1**

Entries represent proportion of respondents preferring "column" brand to "row" brand (i.e., 90 per cent prefer Brand B to Brand A)

6.8.2 Rasch Model Scaling

Rasch models are used for analyzing data from assessments to measure things such as abilities, attitudes, and personality traits. For example, they may be used to estimate a student's reading ability from answers to questions on a reading assessment, or the extremity of a person's attitude to capital punishment from responses on a questionnaire.

Rasch models are particularly used in **psychometrics,** the field concerned with the theory and technique of psychological and educational measurement. In addition, they are increasingly being used in other areas, including the **health profession** and market research because of their general applicability.

The mathematical theory underlying Rasch models is in some respects the same as **item response theory**. However, Rasch models have a specific measurement property that provides a criterion for successful measurement.

In the Rasch model, the probability of a specified response (e.g., right/wrong answer) is modeled as a function of person and item parameters. Specifically, in the simple Rasch model, the probability of a correct response is modeled as a **logistic function** of the difference between the person and item parameter. The mathematical form of the model is provided later in this article. In most contexts, the parameters of the model pertain to the level of a quantitative trait possessed by a person or item. For example, in educational tests, item parameters pertain to the difficulty of items while person parameters pertain to the ability or attainment level of people who are assessed. The higher a person's ability relative to the difficulty of an item is the higher the probability of a correct response on that item. When a person's location on the latent trait is equal to the difficulty of the item, there is by definition a 0.5 probability of a correct response in the Rasch model.

The purpose of applying the model is to obtain measurements from categorical response data. Estimation methods are used to obtain estimates from matrices of response data based on the model.

The Rasch model is a *model* in the sense that it represents the structure which data should exhibit in order to obtain measurements from the data, i.e., it provides a criterion for successful measurement. It is therefore a model in the sense of an *ideal* or standard. The perspective or paradigm underpinning the Rasch model is distinctly different from the perspective underpinning statistical modelling. Models are most often used with the intention of describing a set of data. Parameters are modified and accepted or rejected based on how well they fit the data. In contrast, when the Rasch model is employed, the objective is to obtain data which fit the model.

The brief outline above highlights certain distinctive and interrelated features of Rasch's perspective on social measurement, which are as follows:

1. He was concerned principally with the measurement of *individuals*, rather than with distributions among populations.
2. He was concerned with establishing a basis for meeting a prior *requirements* for measurement deduced from physics and, consequently, did not invoke any *assumptions* about the distribution of levels of a trait in a population.
3. Rasch's approach explicitly recognizes that it is a scientific hypothesis that a given trait is both quantitative and measurable, as operationalized in a particular experimental context.

6.8.3 Rank Ordering

A **ranking** is a relationship between a set of items such that, for any two items, the first is either 'ranked higher than', 'ranked lower than' or 'ranked equal to' the second. In **mathematics**, this is known as a **weak order or total preorder** of objects. It is not necessarily a **total order** of objects because two different objects can have the same ranking. The rankings themselves are totally ordered.

Example 6.5:

Rank the various brands of toothpaste in order of preference. Begin by picking out the one brand that you like most and assign it a number 1. Then find the second most preferred brand and assign it a number 2. Continue this procedure until you have ranked all the brands of toothpaste in order of preference. The least preferred brand should be assigned a rank of 8.

No two brands should receive the same rank number.

	Brand	Rank Order
1.	Colgate	5
2.	Pepsodent	4
3.	Close Up	3
4.	Plus White	--
5.	Meshwak	2
6.	Neem	--
7.	Babul	1
8.	Prestige	--

The criterion of preference is entirely up to you. There is no right or wrong answer. Just try to be consistent.

Assumptions

1. All the observations from both groups are independent of each other,
2. The responses are ordinal or continuous measurements (i.e., one can at least say, of any two observations, which is the greater),
3. Under the null hypothesis, the distributions of both groups are equal, so that the probability of an observation from one population (X) exceeding an observation from the second population (Y) equals the probability of an observation from Y exceeding an observation from X, that is, there is a symmetry between populations with respect to probability of random drawing of a larger observation.
4. Under the alternative hypothesis, the probability of an observation from one population (X) exceeding an observation from the second population (Y) (after correcting for ties) is not equal to 0.5. The alternative may also be stated in terms of a one-sided test, for example: $P(X > Y) + 0.5\ P(X = Y) > 0.5$.

6.8.4 Bogardus Social Distance Scale

The **Bogardus Social Distance Scale** is a **psychological testing scale** created by **Emory S. Bogardus** to empirically **measure** people's willingness to participate in social contacts of varying degrees of closeness with members of diverse social groups, such as other **racial** and **ethnic groups**, **sex offenders,** and **homosexuals.**

The scale asks people the extent to which they would be accepting of each group (a score of 1.00 for a group is taken to indicate no social distance):

(1) As close relatives by **marriage** (score 1.00)

(2) As my close personal **friends** (2.00)

(3) As **neighbors** on the same street (3.00)

(4) As **co-workers** in the same occupation (4.00)

(5) As **citizens** in my country (5.00)

(6) As only **visitors** in my country (6.00)

(7) Would **exclude** from my country (7.00)

The Bogardus Social Distance Scale is a cumulative scale (a Guttman scale), because agreement with any item implies agreement with all preceding items. The scale has been criticized as too simple because the social interactions and attitudes in close familial or friendship-type relationships may be qualitatively different from social interactions with and attitudes toward relationships with far-away contacts such as citizens or visitors in one's country.

The Bogardus Social Distance Scale measures attitudes about how close or distant people feel towards other people.

Example 6.6:

Place a check-mark against all statements with which you agree.

It is ok for people to immigrate to this county	[ ]
It is ok for people to immigrate to this town	[ ]
It is ok for people to immigrate and live in this street	[ ]
It is ok for people to immigrate and live next door	[ ]

6.8.5 Q-Sort

The Q-Sort technique is used to discriminate among large number of objectives quickly. It uses a rank order procedure and the objectives are sorted into piles based on similarity with respect to some criteria. Where respondents are asked to sort a given number of items or statements and classify them into a predetermined number of sets according to some criterion such as preference, attitude, or behavioral intent, this is the most popular and simplest method to use in the sorting process.

Example 6.7:

The deck in front of you contains pictures of 75 magazines. Please choose the 9 magazines you most prefer of the 75. Once you have selected the 9 you most prefer, please list the magazine names on the form provided under the column "Prefer Most." Now, we would like you to select the 9 magazines you *least* prefer from the remaining 66 magazines. Please list these nine under the column "Prefer Least." Of the remaining 57 magazines, please select the 15 you like most and list these 15 under the column labeled "Like." Of the remaining 42 magazines, please choose the 15 you like the least and place these names under the column "Dislike." There should be 27 magazines remaining; please list the titles of these magazines under the column "Neutral."

Tabulation Sheet

Prefer Most	Like	Neutral	Dislike	Prefer Least
(9)	(15)	(27)	(15)	(9)

6.8.6 Guttman Scale

The Guttman scale was first described by Louis Guttman in 1944. It allows progressive investigation in the nature of interview probing, such that you can find out *to what degree* respondents agree with a concept or principle. The group of questions seek to investigate just one factor or trait.

There is a danger with this that respondents feel committed by earlier questions and seek to sustain **consistency** and thus agree with more than they really believe. They may also fear being drawn into an extreme position and hence hold back. This can be mitigated by using the concealed form, interleaving the questions with random numbers of other questions (that may or may not be needed in the survey). Guttman scaling is also known as *cumulative scaling* or *scalogram analysis.*

A Guttman scale presents a number of items to which the person is requested to agree or not agree. This is typically done in a 'Yes/No' **dichotomous** format. It is also possible to use a **Likert** scale, although this is less commonly used. Questions in a Guttman scale gradually increase in specificity. The intent of the scale is that the person will agree with all statements up to a point and then will stop agreeing. The scale may be used to determine how extreme a view is, with successive statements showing increasingly extremist positions. If needed, the escalation can be concealed by using intermediate questions.

Example 6.8:

Place a check-mark against all statements' with which you agree.

I like eating out	[ ]
I like going to restaurants	[ ]
I like going to themed restaurants	[ ]
I like going to Chinese restaurants	[ ]
I like going to Beijing-style Chinese restaurants	[ ]

Example 6.9:

Concealed example (hardening attitude towards crime), using Likert scale:

	Strongly agree	**Tend to agree**	**Neither agree nor disagree**	**Tend to disagree**	**Strongly disagree**
Criminals should be punished	[ ]	[ ]	[ ]	[ ]	[ ]
Litter is a problem in the street	[ ]	[ ]	[ ]	[ ]	[ ]
Sentences for many crimes should be longer	[ ]	[ ]	[ ]	[ ]	[ ]
Streets in this town are not well lit	[ ]	[ ]	[ ]	[ ]	[ ]
More criminals deserve the death penalty	[ ]	[ ]	[ ]	[ ]	[ ]

6.8.7 Constant Sum Scale

Constant Sum Scaling is a scaling method used to organize and sort a variety of options. The respondent is presented with a few options and given a number of points to allocate to each option. Aside from being used in surveys and questionnaires, constant sum scaling can also be used in more qualitative settings such as **focus groups** or **in-depth interviews**, as a way to spark discussion. Here is a basic example of a constant sum scaling question that might be included in a survey (see below). This particular question tries to uncover buying behavior behind purchasing a vehicle. The respondent is asked to allocate 100 points among 4 key features of purchasing a vehicle based on their importance of each.

Performance	40
Safety	10
Body style	20
Interior Design	30
Total	**100 points**

By entering the relative value of each feature into the equation, constant sum scaling can be used as a way to understand comparative importance when respondents are presented with multiple options. By adding more points to one feature, the respondent is in a sense taking away from points that could be allocated to other features – as the constant sum is 100 points.

6.8.8 Magnitude Estimation Scale

Magnitude estimation was developed in 2003 as a new method for measuring usability. The magnitude estimation method is the classical measuring method in psychophysics for making a direct quantitative estimate of sensory magnitude in response to a series of physical stimuli. Here, numerical values provide relative assessments without the use of unit.

In the prototypical case, people are asked to assign numbers in proportion to the magnitude of the stimulus. This psychometric function of the geometric means of their numbers is often a **power law** with stable, replicable exponent. Although contexts can change the law and exponent, that change too is stable and replicable. Instead of numbers, other sensory or cognitive dimensions can be used to match a stimulus and the method then becomes "magnitude production" or "cross-modality matching". The exponents of those dimensions found in numerical magnitude estimation predict the exponents found in magnitude production. Magnitude estimation generally finds lower exponents for the psychophysical function than Likert scaling, because of the restricted range of the categorical **Likert** scales.

6.9 NON-COMPARATIVE SCALING TECHNIQUES

(1) Continuous Rating Scale/Graphic Rating Scale
(2) Likert Scale
(3) Phrase Completion Scales
(4) Semantic Differential Scale
(5) Stapel Scale
(6) Thurstone Scale
(7) Mathematically Derived Scale

6.9.1 Continuous Rating Scale/Graphic Rating Scale

The Continuous rating scale is a form on which the manager simply checks off the employee's level of performance. This is the oldest and most widely method used for performance appraisal.

The scales may specify five points, so a factor such as job knowledge might be rated 1 (poorly informed about work duties) to 5 (has complete mastery of all phases of the job).

Example 6.10:

Rating scales can include 5 elements as follows:

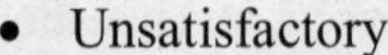

- Unsatisfactory
- Fair
- Satisfactory
- Good
- Outstanding

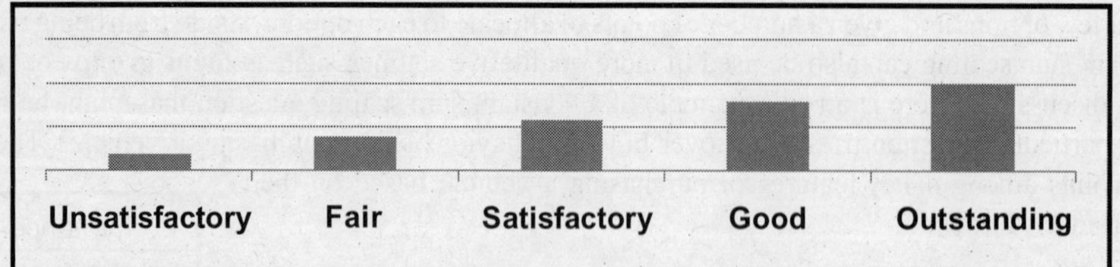

Advantages of the rating scales

(1) Graphic rating scales are less time-consuming to develop.

(2) They also allow for quantitative comparison.

Disadvantages of the rating scales

(1) Different supervisors will use the same graphic scales in slightly different ways.

(2) One way to get around the ambiguity inherent in graphic rating scales is to use behavior based scales, in which specific work related behaviors are assessed.

(3) More validity comparing workers ratings from a single supervisor than comparing two workers who were rated by different supervisors.

6.9.2 Likert Scale

Likert scale was developed by Rensis Likert. Here, the respondents are asked to indicate a degree of agreement and disagreement with each of a series of statement. Each scale item has 5 responses categories ranging from strongly agree to strongly disagree.

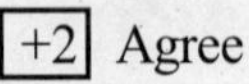

+1 Strongly agree

+2 Agree

0 Indifferent

-1 Disagree

-2 Strongly Disagree

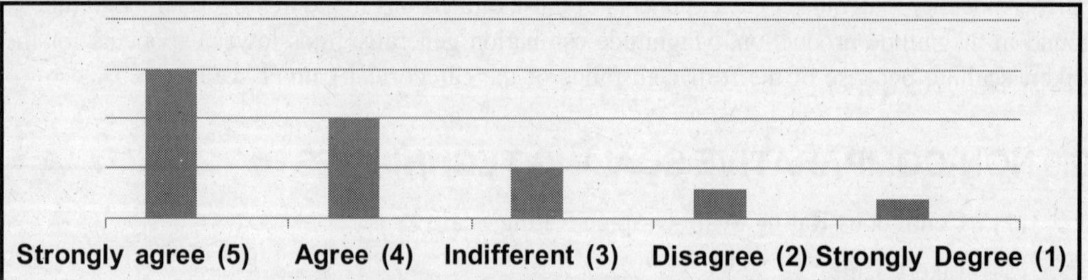

Each degree of agreement is given a numerical score and the respondents' total score is computed by summing these scores. This total score of respondent reveals the particular opinion of a person. Likert scale are of ordinal type, they enable one to rank attitudes, but not to measure the difference between attitudes. They take about the same amount of efforts to create as Thurston scale and are considered more discriminating and reliable because of the larger of responses typically given in Likert scale.

Advantages

(1) It is relatively easy to construct and administer.

(2) Instructions that accompany the scale are easily understood; hence it can be used for mail surveys and interviews with children.

Disadvantages

(1) It takes a longer time to complete as compared to Semantic Differential Scales, etc.

(2) Care needs to be taken when using Likert Scales in cross-cultural research, as there may be cultural variations in willingness to express disagreement.

6.9.3 Phrase Completion Scale

Phrase completion scales are a type of **psychometric** scale used in **questionnaires.** Developed in response to the problems associated with **Likert scales,** Phrase completions are concise, unidimensional measures that tap ordinal level data in a manner that approximates interval level data. Phrase completions consist of a phrase followed by an 11-point response key. The phrase introduces part of the concept.

Marking a reply on the response key completes the concept. The response key represents the underlying theoretical continuum. Zero (0) indicates the absence of the construct. Ten (10) indicates the theorized maximum amount of the construct. Response keys are reversed on alternate items to mitigate response set bias.

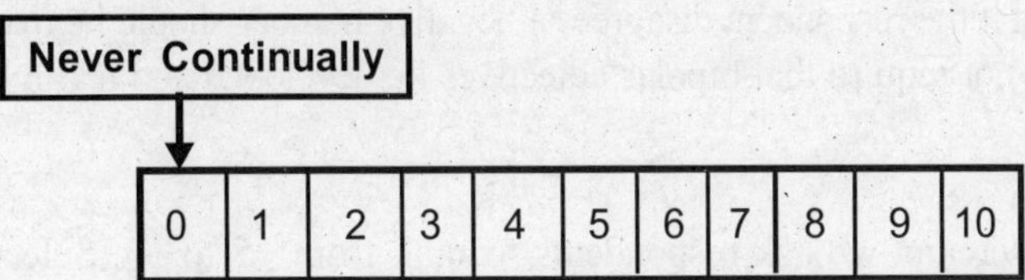

After the questionnaire is completed, the score on each item is summed together, to create a test score for the respondent. Hence, Phrase Completions, like Likert scales, are often considered to be summative scales. The response categories represent an ordinal level of measurement. Ordinal level data, however, varies in terms of how closely it approximates interval level data. By using a numerical continuum as the response key instead of sentiments that reflect intensity of agreement, respondents may be able to quantify their responses in more equal units.

Research designed to inform practice and policy decisions is based upon the reliability and validity of the measures used. Although Likert scales are perhaps the most widely used method for constructing scales, a number of little known problems are associated with their use, including multidimensionality and relatively coarse ordinal level data that taps only a portion of the underlying theoretical construct. To circumvent the problems associated with Likert scales, phrase completion scales were developed. Phrase completion scales are concise, unidimensional measures designed to tap ordinal level data in a manner that approximates interval level data. The validity and reliability coefficients were higher for the phrase completion items relative to the Likert items while the levels of measurement error were lower. The results suggest that scales constructed using the phrase completion method may offer a better method of measurement compared to similarly Likert items, at least in some situations.

6.9.4 Semantic Differential Scale

The Semantic Differential question scale offers a bipolar pair of adjectives between which the respondent must choose along some form of scaling (typically a five-point scale). The pairs of words need not be opposite and may be used to discover fine differences in viewpoint. They are often adjectives. This is a relatively unusual form of question that is used in more specialist surveys where the connotative meaning is being explored.

Pairs of words are often clear opposites. This is not always the case, in which case there is more cognitive challenge. This style can be used to test interpretation of words or subconscious perception. It is also possible people will ignore or select random response. Unmarked scales are more difficult to code afterwards, although this can be done with a Likert-type overlay. The advantage of these is that they are not dependent on the interpretation of words (for example, 'somewhat' can mean a lot or a little to different people). Respondents will tend to score these relatively — thus if they feel less strongly about a question than the previous one, they will mark the scale in a more central position.

Example 6.11:

Please indicate your opinions about the 'Jolly Boys' TV show by checking one box in each row below:

	Very much	Some-what	Neither	Some-what	Very much	
Enjoyable	[ ]	[ ]	[ ]	[ ]	[ ]	Boring
Likeable	[ ]	[ ]	[ ]	[ ]	[ ]	Challenging
Noisy	[ ]	[ ]	[ ]	[ ]	[ ]	Fascinating
Silly	[ ]	[ ]	[ ]	[ ]	[ ]	Ridiculous

6.9.5 Stapel Scale

Stapel scale has some distinct features:

1. Each item has only one ward/phrase indicating the dimension it represents.
2. Each item has ten response categories.
3. Each item has even number categories.
4. The response categories have numerical labels but no verbal labels.

Stapel Scale – similar to the semantic differential scale except that (1) points on the scale are identified by numbers, (2) only one statement is used and if the respondent disagrees a negative number should be marked, and (3) there are 10 positions instead of seven. This scale does not require that bipolar adjectives be developed and it can be administered by telephone.

Example 6.12:

Suppose for quality of ice-cream, we ask respondents to rank from +5 to –5. Select a plus number for words which best describe the ice-cream accurately. Select a minus number for wards you think do not describe the ice-cream accurately. Thus, we can select any number from +5, for wards we think are very accurate, to –5, for wards we think are very inaccurate. This scale is usually present vertically.

+5	+5
+4	+4
+3	+3
+2	+2
+1	+1
High Quality	**Poor Quality**
–1	–1
–2	–2
–3	–3
–4	–4
–5	–5

This is a unipolar rating scale.

6.9.6 Thurston Scale

It is one of the Multi Item Scales developed by L.L. Thurstone's method of Equal Appearing Intervals on the concept that, even though people could not assign quantitative measures to their own attitudes, they could tell the difference between the attitude represented by two different statements and could identify items that were approximately halfway between the two. The procedure is as follows:

1. Collect a large number of statements (perhaps as many as several hundred) related to the attitude in question.
2. Have a number of judges (perhaps 20 or more) sort the statements independently into 11 piles that vary from the most favorable statement to neutral statements to most unfavorable statements.
3. Study the frequency distribution of ratings for each statement and eliminate those statements that the different judges have given widely scattered ratings – that are in a number of different piles.
4. Determine the scale value of each of the remaining statements – that is, the number of the pile in which the median of the distribution falls.
5. Select one of the two statements from each of the 11 piles for the final scale. Those statements with the narrowest range of rating are preferred as the most reliable.

Advantage

1. It is important to note that there are 11 attitude positions because in a scale with odd number of parameters, it is easier to identify a neutral position.

Disadvantages

1. Thurstone scales are not widely used for Marketing Research because they are time-consuming during preparation.
2. The ratings may be influenced by the judges' personal attitude.
3. Different individuals can obtain exactly the same score from agreeing with quite different items.
4. It does not obtain information about the intensity of agreement with the ratings.

This technique for developing an attitude scale compensates for the limitation of the Likert scale in that the strength of the individual items is taken into account in computing the attitude score. It also can accommodate neutral statements.

Example 6.13:

Constructing the scale

Step 1: Collect statements on the topic from people holding a wide range of attitudes, from extremely favorable to extremely unfavorable. For this example, we will use **attitude toward the use of marijuana.** Example statements are:

- It has its place.
- Its use by an individual could be the beginning of a sad situation.
- It is perfectly healthy; it should be legalized.

Step 2: Duplicates and irrelevant statements are omitted. The rest are typed on 3/5 cards and given to a group of people who will serve as judges.

Step 3: Originally, judges were asked to sort the statements into eleven (11) stacks representing the entire range of attitudes from **extremely unfavorable (1)** to **extremely unfavorable (11)**. The middle stack is for statements which are **neither favorable nor unfavorable (6)**. Only the end points (extremely favorable and extremely unfavorable) and the midpoint are labeled. The assumption is the intervening stacks will represent equal steps along the underlying attitude dimension. With a large number of judges, for example, using a class or some other group to do the preliminary ratings, it is easier to create a paper-and-pencil version.

*Rate each of the following statements indicating the degree to which the statement is unfavorable or favorable to marijuana use. Do **not** respond in terms of your own agreement or disagreement with the statements; rather, respond in terms of the judged degree of favorableness or unfavorableness. Place an **X** in the interval that best reflects your judgment. For example: **Marijuana is OK** for* **most people, but a few people, may have problems with it.**

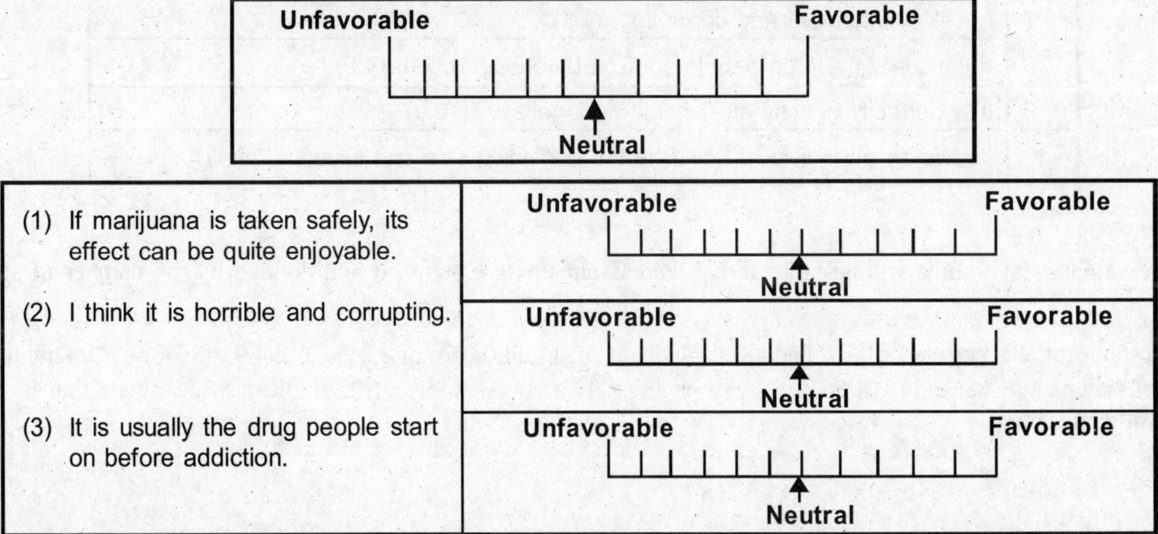

Remind the judges to rate favorability with regard to the target (marijuana), not to give their opinion as whether they agree or disagree with the statement.

Step 4: Each statement will have a numerical rating (1 to 11) from each judge, based on the stack in which it was placed. The number or weight assigned to the statement is the average of the ratings it received from the judges.

Statement	Average rating from 20 judges (11 = extremely favorable)
If marijuana is taken safely, its effect can be quite enjoyable.	8.9
I think it is horrible and corrupting.	1.6
It is usually the drug people start on before addiction.	4.9

If the judges cannot rate the item on its favorability or show a high degree of variability in their judgments, the item is eliminated. For example, the statement "Marijuana use should be taxed heavily" was rejected because it was ambiguous. Some judges thought it was pro-marijuana as it implied legalization; others though it was anti-marijuana because it advocated a heavy tax.

Administering the Scale

Here is the final form. The respondents check only the statements with which they agree. The average ratings by the judges are shown in parentheses. These would **not** be included on the actual form given to respondents. Note that the more positive statements have a higher weight.

This is a scale to measure your attitude toward marijuana. It does *not* deal with any other drug, so please consider that the items pertain to marijuana exclusively. We want to know how students feel about this topic. In order to get honest answers, the questionnaires are to be filled out anonymously. Do *not* sign your name.

Please check all those statements with which you agree.

1	I don't approve of something that puts you out of a normal state of mind. (3.0)
2	It has its place. (7.1)
3	It corrupts the individual. (2.2)
4	Marijuana does some people a lot of good. (7.9).
5	Having never tried marijuana, I can't say what effects it would have. (6.0)
6	If marijuana is taken safely, its effect can be quite enjoyable. (8.9)
7	I think it is horrible and corrupting. (1.6)
8	It is usually the drug people start on before addiction. (4.9)
9	It is perfectly healthy and should be legalized. (10.0)
10	Its use by an individual could be the beginning of a sad situation. (4.1)

Scoring

The weights (favorability rating) for the checked statements are summed and divided by the number of statements checked.

A respondent who selected #3, #7, and #8 would have an attitude score of 2.2 + 1.6 + 4.9 = 8.7/3 = 2.9. Dividing by the number of statements checked (3) puts the score on the 1-11 scale. A score of 2.9 indicates an attitude that is definitely unfavorable to marijuana.

6.9.7 Mathematically Derived Scale

A scale in which researchers infer respondents' answers mathematically as in the case of multidimensional scaling and conjoint analysis.

6.10 SUMMARY

Attitude measurement is particularly important in behavioral research. Attitudes are enduring dispositions to respond consistently, in a given manner, to various aspects of the world, including persons, events and objects. Three components of attitudes are the affective (emotion or feelings involved), the cognitive (awareness or knowledge), and the behavioral (predisposition to action). Attitudes are hypothetical constructs; that is, they are variables that are not directly observable but must be measured indirectly.

Several scales, such as the behavioral differential have been developed to measure the behavioral component of an attitude. The three most commonly used scales are the Nominal scale, the Ordinal scale and the Interval scale. The nominal scale simply allows the categorization of responses into a number of mutually exclusive categories. There are no relationships between the categories, implying that there is no ranking or ordering. The ordinal scale allows the respondents to rank some alternatives by some common variable. In the interval scale, the respondent has classifying the object/issue/product/himself into one among two dichotomous categories. These scales are basically self-report inventories, with a list of favorable and unfavorable statements towards the subject.

The business researcher can choose from a number of attitude scales. Making a decision among the alternatives requires that the researcher to consider several questions, each of which is generally answered by comparing the advantages of each alternative to the problem. Scaling is a technique used for measuring qualitative responses of respondents such as those related to their feelings, perceptions, likes, dislikes, interests and preferences. The classification of scaling techniques in two types: comparative scale and non-comparative scale. Comparative scale consists: (1) **Pairwise comparison scale**; (2) **Rasch model scaling**; (3) **Rank-ordering**; (4) **Bogardus social distance scale**; (5) **Q-Sort**; (6) **Guttman scale**; (7) **Constant sum scale** and (8) **Magnitude estimation scale.** Non-comparative scale consists: (1) **Continuous Rating Scale/Graphic Rating Scale**; (2) **Likert Scale**; (3) **Phrase Completion Scales**; (4) **Semantic Differential Scale**; (5) **Stapel Scale**; (6) **Thurstone Scale** and (7) **Mathematically Derived Scale.**

6.11 KEY TERMS

Attitude: Attitude is a mental and neural state of readiness, organized through experience, exerting a directive or dynamic influence upon the individual's response to all objects and situations.

Measurement: Measurement implies the process of obtaining information which can be subject to analysis.

Attitude Measurement: Attitude measurement relates to the process of measuring an individual's attitude towards an object.

Nominal Scale: The nominal scale simply allows the categorization of responses into a number of mutually exclusive categories. There are no relationships between the categories, implying that there is no ranking or ordering.

Ordinal Scale: The ordinal scale, allows the respondents to rank some alternatives by some common variable.

Interval Scale: In the interval scale the respondent classifies the object/issue/product/himself into one among two dichotomous categories.

Ratio Scale: A Ratio scale has a natural zero point and further numbers are placed at equally appearing intervals.

Validity: Validity is the ability of an instrument to measure what it is supposed to measure.

Content Validity: The content validity of a measuring instrument (the composite of measurement scales) is the extent to which it provides adequate coverage of the investigative questions guiding the study.

Face Validity: Face validity is considered as a basic and very minimum index of content validity.

Convergent Validity: Convergent validity means that multiple measures of the same construct hang together or operate in similar ways.

Reliability: The reliability of a measure is an indication of the *stability* and *consistency* with which the instrument measures the concept and helps to assess the **"goodness"** of measure.

Parallel-form Reliability: Parallel-form reliability reflects when responses on two comparable sets of measures tapping the same construct are highly correlated.

Split-half Reliability: Split-half reliability reflects the correlations between two halves of an instrument.

Sensitivity: Sensitivity refers to an instrument's ability to accurately measure variability in stimuli or responses.

Practicality: Practicality has been defined as *economy*, *convenience*, and *interpretability.*

Pairwise Comparison Scale: Pairwise comparison scale refers to any process of comparing entities in pairs to judge which of each pair is preferred, or has a greater amount of some quantitative property.

Rasch Model: The Rasch model is a *model* in the sense that it represents the structure which data should exhibit in order to obtain measurements from the data.

Rank Ordering: Rank ordering is a relationship between a set of items such that, for any two items, the first is either 'ranked higher than', 'ranked lower than' or 'ranked equal to' the second.

Q-Sort: The Q-Sort technique is used to discriminate among large number of objectives quickly. It uses a rank order procedure and the objectives are sorted into piles based on similarity with respect to some criteria.

Likert Scale: Likert scale is that the respondents are asked to indicate a degree of agreement and disagreement with each of a series of statement.

6.12 MULTIPLE OBJECTIVE TYPE QUESTIONS

1. Attitude is defined as a mental and neural state of readiness.

   (a) True (b) False

2. A change in attitude or beliefs occurs as a result of actions that have been influenced by reinforcers.

   (a) True (b) False

3. Measurement implies the process of obtaining information which can be subject to analysis.

   (a) True (b) False

4. Attitude measurement relates to the process of measuring an individual's attitude towards an object.

   (a) True (b) False

5. The validity of the verbalized attitudes is questionable.

   (a) True (b) False

6. Nominal scale consists of assignment of facts/choices to various alternative categories which are usually exhaustive as well mutually exclusive.

   (a) True (b) False

7. Ordinal scales are the simplest attitude measuring scale used in Marketing Research and it is more powerful than a nominal scale.

   (a) True (b) False

8. Ratio scales are widely used in research unless a base item is made available for comparison.

   (a) True (b) False

9. Validity is the ability of an instrument to measure what it is supposed to measure.

   (a) True (b) False

10. In Constant Sum Scaling, the respondent is presented with a few options and given a number of points to allocate to each option.

    (a) True (b) False

11. Which scale of the following allows the categorization of responses into a number of mutually exhaustive categories?
    (a) Nominal (b) Ordinal
    (c) Ratio (d) Interval
12. Which scale is simplest attitude measuring scale used in marketing research?
    (a) Nominal (b) Ordinal
    (c) Interval (d) Ratio
13. The deficiencies of the nominal and the ordinal scales are taken care of in which scale?
    (a) Nominal (b) Ordinal
    (c) Ratio (d) Interval
14. In which scale has a natural zero point and further numbers are placed at equally appearing intervals?
    (a) Nominal (b) Ordinal
    (c) Ratio (d) Interval
15. Face validity is considered as a basic and very minimum index of
    (a) Content validity (b) Criteria-related validity
    (c) Concurrent validity (d) None of the above
16. Which is a necessary but not sufficient condition of the test of goodness of measures?
    (a) Test of validity (b) Reliability
    (c) Measurement (d) Test of sensitivity
17. Which technique is used to discriminate among large number of objectives quickly?
    (a) Rash model (b) Rank ordering
    (c) Q-sort (d) Likert scale
18. Which one is the advantage of Likert scale?
    (a) It is easy to construct and administer (b) It cannot be used in easy survey
    (c) It takes longer time to complete (d) All of the above
19. Which scaling used to organize and sort a variety of options?
    (a) Q-sort (b) Guttman
    (c) Constant sum (d) Rash model
20. Attitude measurement is particularly important in which research?
    (a) Scientific research (b) Social research
    (c) Historical research (d) Behavioral research

Answers to Multiple Objective Type Questions

Questions	1	2	3	4	5	6	7	8	9	10
Answers	T	T	T	T	T	T	T	F	T	T
Questions	11	12	13	14	15	16	17	18	19	20
Answers	a	b	d	c	a	b	c	a	c	d

6.13 CONCEPTUAL QUESTIONS

1. What do you mean by attitude and nature of attitude? Describe its importance.
2. What is the meaning of attitude measurement in research?
3. What are scales of measurement? What are the differences between nominal, ordinal, interval and ratio scale? Explain giving examples.
4. Point out the possible sources of error in measurement. Describe the tests of good measurement.
5. Distinguish between test of reliability and test of sensibility.
6. What is scaling? How to construct the scale? Explain.
7. What are comparative scaling techniques? Explain in detail.
8. What are non-comparative scaling techniques? Explain.
9. Distinguish between comparative scaling and non-comparative scaling.
10. Describe the different methods of scale construction, pointing out the merits and demerits of each.
11. "Scaling describes the procedures by which numbers are assigned to various degrees of opinion, attitude and other concepts". Also point out the bases for scale classification.
12. Write short notes:
    (a) Pairwise comparison scale
    (b) Rasch model scaling
    (c) Rank-ordering
    (d) Bogardus social distance scale
    (e) Q-Sort
    (f) Guttman scale
    (g) Constant sum scale
    (h) Continuous Rating Scale
    (i) Graphic Rating Scale
    (j) Likert Scale
    (k) Phrase Completion Scales
    (l) Semantic Differential Scale
    (m) Stapel Scale
    (n) Thurstone Scale
    (o) Mathematically Derived Scale
    (p) Magnitude estimation scale

CHAPTER 7

METHODS OF DATA COLLECTION

RESEARCH METHODOLOGY

Chapter Outline

Learning Objectives

- *Discuss the necessity and usefulness of data collection.*
- *Distinguish between primary and secondary data.*
- *Describe different methods of collecting primary data with their merits and demerits.*
- *Design questionnaire for collection of primary data.*
- *Develop skills in conducing interview.*
- *Identify the sources of secondary data.*
- *Examine the reliability, suitability and adequacy of secondary data.*

7.1 TYPES OF DATA

7.1.1 Primary Data

Primary data means original data that have been collected specially for the purpose in mind. It means when an authorized organization or an investigator or an enumerator collects the data for the first time himself or with the help of an institution or an expert then the data thus collected are called primary data.

*Research where one gathers this kind of data is referred to as **field research.***

For example: a questionnaire.

Primary data is important for all areas of research because it is unvarnished information about the results of an experiment or observation. It is like the eyewitness testimony at a trial. No one has tarnished it or spun it by adding their own opinion or bias so it can form the basis of objective conclusions.

Identification: Primary data is the specific information collected by the person who is doing the research. It can be obtained through clinical trials, case studies, true experiments and randomized controlled studies. This information can be analyzed by other experts who may decide to test the validity of the data by repeating the same experiments.

Significance: Suppose that you are researching the effects of a certain new substance on the nervous system of mice. Because yours will be the first such experiment, the data that you collect will be considered prospective in nature. It can be used to establish a baseline from which other follow-up experiments can be devised. In the education context, prospective primary data about the kindergartners in a **school** district might be to collect the actual test results from the first day of school showing how many could write their names, count to 20, and retell a simple story in a logical way. The information forms the baseline from which the district must move their students so that they can meet the state standards for entering first graders within the next 180 days.

Types: Primary data can also be retrospective, interventional and observational in nature. Retrospective primary data gathers information about past conditions or behaviors. The researcher may be investigating a cause of a preventable disease, for instant as in the connection between smoking and lung cancer. Interventional primary data may be gathered to see the effect of a new drug or therapy. A recent study reported in the Journal of Ophthalmology, for example, described an interventional study about treatments for convergence insufficiency. Patients with this diagnosis received one of three treatments over a 12-week period to determine which intervention would be the most effective. Observational studies gather primary data by means of case studies such as the work done by naturalists like Jane Goodall on chimpanzees in the wild.

Features: Two strategies are commonly employed when researchers gather primary data: randomizing and blinding. Both of these strategies serve to keep the results objective. Both involve limiting the information given either to the researcher or the subject about which test group a subject has been assigned. The researcher is prevented from imposing her bias on the data so she may be a more careful observer. The subject is prevented from becoming either encouraged or discouraged by any previous opinions about the treatment, in a drug trial for example, that he may have started with.

Potential: Once the primary data has been gathered, analysts study it using other research methods. They look for **relationships** between factors that may suggest the designs for new studies. When they combine the primary data from more than one study, they are using integrative methods. Their findings present secondary data, a synthesis of several streams of primary data.

Advantages of Primary Data

(1) Degree of accuracy is quite high.

(2) It does not require extra caution.

(3) It depicts the data in great detail.

(4) Primary source of data collection frequently includes definitions of various terms and units used.

(5) For some investigations, secondary data are not available.

Disadvantages of Primary Data

(1) Collection of data requires a lot of time.

(2) It requires lot of finance.

(3) In some enquires it, is not possible to collect primary data.

(4) It requires a lot of labour.

7.1.2 Secondary Data

Secondary data are data that have been collected for another purpose and where we will use Statistical Method with the Primary Data. It means that after performing statistical operations on Primary Data the results become known as Secondary Data.

Research where one gathers this kind of data is referred to as desk research.

For example: data from a book.

Secondary data is the data that have been already collected by and readily available from other sources. Such data are cheaper and more quickly obtainable than the primary data and also may be available when primary data cannot be obtained at all.

Advantages of Secondary Data

(1) It is economical. It saves efforts and expenses.

(2) It is time saving.

(3) It helps to make primary data collection more specific since with the help of secondary data, we are able to make out what are the gaps and deficiencies and what additional information needs to be collected.

(4) It helps to improve the understanding of the problem.

(5) It provides a basis for comparison for the data that is collected by the researcher.

Disadvantages of Secondary Data

(1) Secondary data is something that seldom fits in the framework of the marketing research factors. Reasons for its non-fitting are:

  (a) Unit of secondary data collection – Suppose you want information on disposable income, but the data is available on gross income. The information may not be same as we require.

  (b) Class Boundaries may be different when units are same.

  (c) Thus, the data collected earlier is of no use to you.

(2) Accuracy of secondary data is not known.

(3) Data may be outdated.

Evaluation of Secondary Data

Because of the above mentioned disadvantages of secondary data, we will lead to evaluation of secondary data. Evaluation means the following four requirements must be satisfied:

(1) Availability: It has to be seen that the kind of data you want is available or not. If it is not available, then you have to go for primary data.

(2) Relevance: It should be meeting the requirements of the problem. For this, we have two criterion:

  (a) Units of measurement should be the same.

  (b) Concepts used must be same and currency of data should not be outdated.

(3) Accuracy: In order to find how accurate the data is, the following points must be considered:

(a) Specification and methodology used;

(b) Margin of error should be examined;

(c) The dependability of the source must be seen.

(4) Sufficiency: Adequate data should be available.

7.1.3 Differences between Primary Data and Secondary Data

Research can be carried out with 2 different types of data; primary and secondary data. What type of data is best is really determined by the research goal. Companies should use both types of information, as secondary data can be used to create a new question, while the primary data can determine the answer to the question.

Source: Primary data is collected firsthand by a researcher. It normally is collected through experiments, surveys, questionnaires, focus groups, interviews and taking measurements. Secondary data has already been collected and is available to the public. The sources of secondary data include books, journals, census data, biographies, articles and databases.

Accuracy: Primary research is tailored specifically for the project and tends to be more accurate. While secondary data can provide plenty of information, it is less accurate because the data collected was not collected specifically for the questions. Primary data is customized while secondary data is not.

Scientific Method: Primary data follows the scientific method. A hypothesis is formed, data is collected from an experiment based on the hypothesis and the hypothesis is proven correct or not. Secondary data does not start with a hypothesis as the data is already collected. Patterns and insights are found within the secondary data and then the observation on that data is made.

Cost: The cost of obtaining primary data is typically more than secondary. This cost includes monetary values as well as time. Primary data will include the chemicals needed to perform the experiment, any scientific analysis, and most importantly the time needed to carry out the data collection, determine the results and conclusions and then write up the data for publication. Secondary data is typically available for free or for the subscription fee to the database, magazine or journal. Once the subscription is obtained, the data can be obtained immediately so it takes much less time to collect secondary data.

Types of Science: Primary data is used by all branches of science but especially for what is known as the "hard" sciences: chemistry, biology, physics, agriculture and more. The vast majority of papers published in these fields consist of primary data. It is the social sciences where secondary data is used extensively. Social science research will frequently take secondary data to find patterns within the area of study.

Table 7.1: Difference between Primary Data and Secondary Data

Primary Data	Secondary Data
(1) Needs more funds	(1) Needs comparatively less funds
(2) Investing Agency collects the data	(2) Some other investing agency collects it for its own use
(3) Requires longer time for collection	(3) Requires less time for collection
(4) More reliable and suitable to the enquiry because the investor himself collects it	(4) Less reliable and suitable as someone else does collection which may not set the purpose
(5) Requires elaborate organization	(5) No need of any organizational set-up
(6) No extra precautions are required	

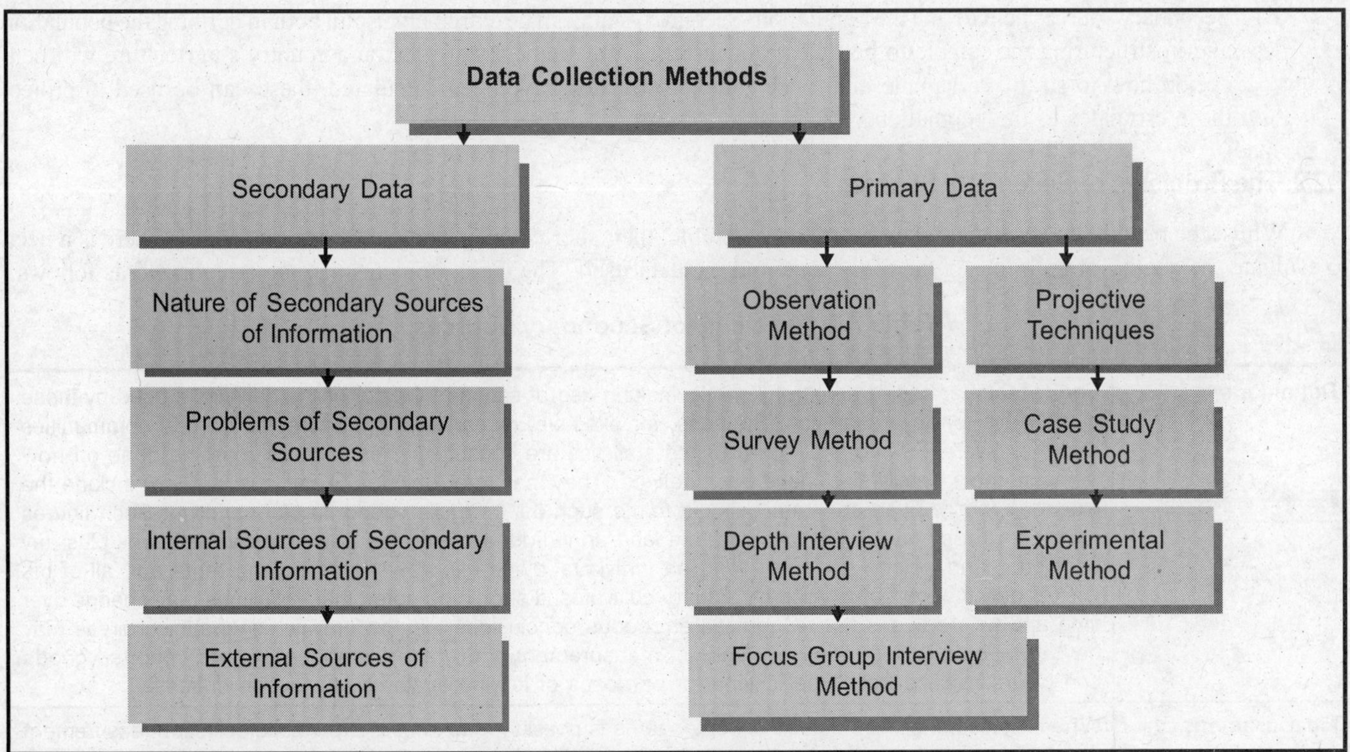

Fig. 7.1: Data Collection Methods

7.2 SECONDARY DATA COLLECTION METHODS

7.2.1 The Nature of Secondary Sources of Information

Secondary data is data which has been collected by individuals or agencies for purposes other than those of our particular research study. For example, if a government department has conducted a survey of, say, family food expenditures, then a food manufacturer might use this data in the organization's evaluations of the total potential market for a new product. Similarly, statistics prepared by a ministry on agricultural production will prove useful to a whole host of people and organizations, including those marketing agricultural supplies.

No marketing research study should be undertaken without a prior search of secondary sources (also termed desk research). There are several grounds for making such a bold statement.

(1) Secondary data may be available which is entirely appropriate and wholly adequate to draw conclusions and answer the question or solve the problem. Sometimes primary data collection simply is not necessary.

(2) It is far cheaper to collect secondary data than to obtain primary data. For the same level of research budget, a thorough examination of secondary sources can yield a great deal more information than can be had through a primary data collection exercise.

(3) The time involved in searching secondary sources is much less than that needed to complete primary data collection.

(4) Secondary sources of information can yield more accurate data than that obtained through primary research. This is not always true but where a government or international agency has undertaken a large scale survey, or even a census, this is likely to yield far more accurate results than custom designed and executed surveys when these are based on relatively small sample sizes.

(5) It should not be forgotten that secondary data can play a substantial role in the exploratory phase of the research when the task at hand is to define the research problem and to generate hypotheses. The assembly and analysis of secondary data almost invariably improves the researcher's understanding of the marketing problem, the various lines of inquiry that could or should be followed and the alternative courses of action which might be pursued.

(6) Secondary sources help define the population. Secondary data can be extremely useful both in defining the population and in structuring the sample to be taken. For instance, government statistics on a country's agriculture will help decide how to stratify a sample and, once sample estimates have been calculated, these can be used to project those estimates to the population.

7.2.2. The Problems of Secondary Sources

Whilst the benefits of secondary sources are considerable, their shortcomings have to be acknowledged. There is a need to evaluate the quality of both the source of the data and the data itself. The main problems may be categorized as follows:

Table 7.2: Problems of Secondary Sources

Definitions	The researcher has to be careful, when making use of secondary data, of the definitions used by those responsible for its preparation. Suppose, for example, researchers are interested in rural communities and their average family size. If published statistics are consulted, then a check must be done on how terms such as "family size" have been defined. They may refer only to the nucleus family or include the extended family. Even apparently simple terms such as 'farm size' need careful handling. Such figures may refer to any one of the following: the land an individual owns, the land an individual owns plus any additional land he/she rents, the land an individual owns minus any land he/she rents out, all of his land or only that part of it which he actually cultivates. It should be noted that definitions may change over time and where this is not recognized erroneous conclusions may be drawn. Geographical areas may have their boundaries redefined, units of measurement and grades may change and imported goods can be reclassified from time to time for purposes of levying customs and excise duties.
Measurement error	When a researcher conducts field work, she/he is possibly able to estimate inaccuracies in measurement through the standard deviation and standard error, but these are sometimes not published in secondary sources. The only solution is to try to speak to the individuals involved in the collection of the data to obtain some guidance on the level of accuracy of the data. The problem is sometimes not so much 'error' but differences in levels of accuracy required by decision makers. When the research has to do with large investments in, say, food manufacturing, management will want to set very tight margins of error in making market demand estimates. In other cases, having a high level of accuracy is not so critical. For instance, if a food manufacturer is merely assessing the prospects for one more flavour for a snack food already produced by the company then there is no need for highly accurate estimates in order to make the investment decision.
Source bias	Researchers have to be aware of vested interests when they consult secondary sources. Those responsible for their compilation may have reasons for wishing to present a more optimistic or pessimistic set of results for their organization. It is not unknown, for example, for officials responsible for estimating food shortages to exaggerate figures before sending aid requests to potential donors. Similarly, and with equal frequency, commercial organizations have been known to inflate estimates of their market shares.
Reliability	The reliability of published statistics may vary over time. It is not uncommon, for example, for the systems of collecting data to have changed over time but without any indication of this to the reader of published statistics. Geographical or administrative boundaries may be changed by government, or the basis for stratifying a sample may have altered. Other aspects of research methodology that affect the reliability of secondary data is the sample size, response rate, questionnaire design and modes of analysis.
Time scale	Most censuses take place at 10 year intervals, so data from this and other published sources may be out-of-date at the time the researcher wants to make use of the statistics. The time period during which secondary data was first compiled may have a substantial effect upon the nature of the data. For instance, the significant increase in the price obtained for Ugandan coffee in the mid-90s could be interpreted as evidence of the effectiveness of the rehabilitation programme that set out to restore coffee estates which had fallen into a state of disrepair. However, more knowledgeable coffee market experts would interpret the rise in Ugandan coffee prices in the context of large scale destruction of the Brazilian coffee crop, due to heavy frosts, in 1994, Brazil being the largest coffee producer in the world.

Whenever possible, marketing researchers ought to use multiple sources of secondary data. In this way, these different sources can be cross-checked as confirmation of one another. Where differences occur, an explanation for these must be found or the data should be set aside.

7.2.3 Internal Sources of Secondary Information

Sales data: All organizations collect information in the course of their everyday operations. Orders are received and delivered, costs are recorded, sales personnel submit visit reports, invoices are sent out, returned goods are recorded and so on. Much of this information is of potential use in marketing research but a surprising amount of it is actually used. Organizations frequently overlook this valuable resource by not beginning their search of secondary sources with an internal audit of sales invoices, orders, inquiries about products not stocked, returns from customers and sales force customer calling sheets. For example, consider how much information can be obtained from sales orders and invoices:

(a) Sales by territory

(b) Sales by customer type

(c) Prices and discounts

(d) Average size of order by customer, customer type, geographical area

(e) Average sales by sales person and

(f) Sales by pack size and pack type, etc.

This type of data is useful for identifying an organization's most profitable product and customers. It can also serve to track trends within the enterprise's existing customer group.

Financial data: An organization has a great deal of data within its files on the cost of producing, storing, transporting and marketing each of its products and product lines. Such data has many uses in marketing research including allowing measurement of the efficiency of marketing operations. It can also be used to estimate the costs attached to new products under consideration, of particular utilization (in production, storage and transportation) at which an organization's unit costs begin to fall.

Transport data: Companies that keep good records relating to their transport operations are well placed to establish which are the most profitable routes, and loads, as well as the most cost-effective routing patterns. Good data on transport operations enables the enterprise to perform trade-off analysis and thereby establish whether it makes economic sense to own or hire vehicles, or the point at which a balance of the two gives the best financial outcome.

Storage data: The rate of stock turn, stock handling costs, assessing the efficiency of certain marketing operations and the efficiency of the marketing system as a whole. More sophisticated accounting systems assign costs to the cubic space occupied by individual products and the time period over which the product occupies the space. These systems can be further refined so that the profitability per unit, and rate of sale, are added. In this way, the direct product profitability can be calculated.

7.2.4 External Sources of Secondary Information

The marketing researcher who seriously seeks after useful secondary data is more often surprised by its abundance than by its scarcity. Too often, the researcher has secretly (sometimes subconsciously) concluded from the outset that his/her topic of study is so unique or specialized that a research of secondary sources is futile. Consequently, only a specified search is made with no real expectation of sources. Cursory researches become a self-fulfilling prophecy. Dillon *et al.* give the following advice:

"You should never begin a half-hearted search with the assumption that what is being sought is so unique that no one else has ever bothered to collect it and publish it. On the contrary, assume there are scrolling secondary data that should help provide definition and scope for the primary research effort."

The same authors support their advice by citing the large numbers of organizations that provide marketing information including national and local government agencies, quasi-government agencies, trade associations, universities, research institutes, financial institutions, specialist suppliers of secondary marketing data and professional marketing research enterprises. Dillon *et al.,* further advise that searches of printed sources of secondary data begin with referral texts such as directories, indexes, handbooks and guides. These sorts of publications rarely provide the data in which the researcher is interested but serve in helping him/her locate potentially useful data sources.

The main sources of external secondary sources are: (1) government (federal, state and local), (2) trade associations, (3) commercial services and (4) national and international institutions.

Table 7.3: External Sources of Secondary Information

Government statistics	These may include all or some of the following: (1) Population censuses (2) Social surveys, family expenditure surveys (3) Import/export statistics (4) Production statistics (5) Agricultural statistics.
Trade associations	Trade associations differ widely in the extent of their data collection and information dissemination activities. However, it is worth checking with them to determine what they do publish. At the very least, one would normally expect that they would produce a trade directory and, perhaps, a yearbook.
Commercial services	Published market research reports and other publications are available from a wide range of organizations which charge for their information. Typically, marketing people are interested in media statistics and consumer information which has been obtained from large scale consumer or farmer panels. The commercial organization funds the collection of the data, which is wide ranging in its content, and hopes to make its money from selling this data to interested parties.
National and international institutions	Bank economic reviews, university research reports, journals and articles are all useful sources to contact. International agencies such as World Bank, IMF, IFAD, UNDP, ITC, FAO and ILO produce a plethora of secondary data which can prove extremely useful to the marketing researcher.

7.3 PRIMARY DATA COLLECTION METHOD

The primary data can be collected through:

(1) Observation Method
(2) Survey Method
(3) Depth Interview Method
(4) Focus Group Interview Method
(5) Projective Techniques
(6) Case Studies Method
(7) Experimental Method

7.3.1 Observation Method

The observation method involves human or mechanical observation of what people actually do or what events take place during a buying or consumption situation. "Information is collected by observing process at work." The following are a few situations:

(1) Service Stations – Pose as a customer, go to a service station and observe.
(2) To evaluate the effectiveness of display of Dunlop Pillow Cushions – In a departmental store, observer notes: (a) How many pass by; (b) How many stopped to look at the display and (c) How many decide to buy.
(3) Super Market-Which is the best location in the shelf? Hidden cameras are used.
(4) To determine typical sales arrangement and find out sales enthusiasm shown by various salesmen – Normally, this is done by an investigator using a concealed tape-recorder.

A. Advantages of Observation Method

(1) If the researcher observes and records events, it is not necessary to rely on the willingness and ability of respondents to report accurately.

(2) The biasing effect of interviewers is either eliminated or reduced. Data collected by observation are, thus, more objective and generally more accurate.

B. Disadvantages of Observation Method

(1) The most limiting factor in the use of observation method is the inability to observe things such as attitudes, motivations, customers/consumers state of mind, their buying motives and their images.

(2) It also takes time for the investigator to wait for a particular action to take place.

(3) Personal and intimate activities, such as watching television late at night, are more easily discussed with questionnaires than they are observed.

(4) Cost is the final disadvantage of observation method. Under most circumstances, observational data are more expensive to obtain than other survey data. The observer has to wait doing nothing, between events to be observed. The unproductive time is an increased cost.

7.3.2 Survey Method

The Survey method is the technique of gathering data by asking questions to people who are thought to have desired information. A formal list of questionnaire is prepared. Generally, a non-disguised approach is used. The respondents are asked questions on their demographic interest opinion.

A. Advantages of Survey Method

(1) As compared to other methods (direct observation, experimentation), survey yield a broader range of information. Surveys are effective to produce information on socio-economic characteristics, attitudes, opinions, motives etc. and to gather information for planning product features, advertising media, sales promotion, channels of distribution and other marketing variables.

(2) Questioning is usually faster and cheaper than Observation.

(3) Questions are simple to administer.

(4) Data is reliable.

(5) The variability of results is reduced.

(6) It is relatively simple to analyze, quote and interrelate the data obtained by survey method.

B. Disadvantages of Survey Method

(1) Unwillingness of respondents to provide information – This requires salesmanship on the part of the interviewer. The interviewer may assure that the information will be kept secret or apply the technique of offering some presents.

(2) Inability of the respondents to provide information – This may be due to:

(a) Lack of knowledge

(b) Lapse of memory

(c) Inability to identify their motives and provide "reasons why?" for their actions

(3) Human biases of the respondents are there, for e.g., "Ego".

(4) Semantic difficulties are there – it is difficult, if not impossible, to state a given question in such a way that it will mean exactly same thing to each respondent. Similarly two different wordings of the same question will frequently produce quite different results.

C. How to Overcome the Limitations of Survey Method?

(1) Careful framing and phrasing of questions.

(2) Careful control of data gathering by employing specially trained investigators who will observe carefully report on subtle reactions of persons interviewed.

(3) Cautious interpretations by a clear recognition of the limitations of the data and understating of what exactly the data represents. This is especially true of responses to questions like – "What price would you be willing to pay for this product?"

(4) Looking at facts in relative rather than absolute terms. For e.g. – A survey by a dentist team showed that the number of families in the middle income group used toothpaste taken by itself in the absolute sense, the results of the survey are in some doubt. Even though the individual group readings shall differ say for e.g.: for upper income group families it could be 90%. Hence, we should look at the facts in relative rather than in absolute terms.

D. Techniques of Survey Methods

There are mainly four methods by which we can collect data through the Survey Method.

(1) Telephonic Interview

(2) Personal Interview

(3) Mail Interview

(4) Electronic Interview

1. Telephonic Interview

Telephone Interviewing stands out as the best method for gathering quickly needed information. Responses are collected from the respondents by the researcher on telephone.

Advantages of Telephonic Interview

(1) It is a very fast method of data collection.

(2) It has the advantage over "Mail Questionnaire" of permitting the interviewer to talk to one or more persons and to clarifying his questions if they are not understood.

(3) Response rate of telephone interviewing seems to be a little better than mail questionnaires.

(4) The quality of information is better.

(5) It is a less costly method and there are less administration problems.

Disadvantages of Telephonic Interview

(1) They can't handle interviews which need props.

(2) It can't handle unstructured interview.

(3) It can't be used for those questions which requires long descriptive answers.

(4) Respondents cannot be observed.

(5) People are reluctant to disclose personal information on telephone.

(6) People who don't have telephone facility cannot be approached.

2. Personal Interviewing

It is the most versatile of the all methods. They are used when props are required along with the verbal response, non-verbal responses can also be observed.

Advantages of Personal Interview

(1) The person interviewed can ask more questions and can supplement the interview with personal observation.

(2) They are more flexible. Order of questions can be changed.

(3) Knowledge of past and future is possible.

(4) In-depth research is possible.

(5) Verification of data from other sources is possible.

(6) The information obtained is very reliable and dependable and helps in establishing cause and effect relationship very early.

Disadvantages of Personal Interview

(1) It requires much more technical and administrative planning and supervision.

(2) It is more expensive.

(3) It is time-consuming.

(4) The accuracy of data is influenced by the interviewer.

(5) A number of call banks may be required.

(6) Some people are not approachable.

3. Mail Survey

Questionnaires are sent to the respondents, they fill it up and send it back.

Advantages of Mail Survey

(1) It can reach all types of people.

(2) Response rate can be improved by offering certain incentives.

Disadvantages of Mail Survey

(1) It cannot be used for unstructured study.

(2) It is costly.

(3) It requires established mailing list.

(4) It is time-consuming.

(5) There is problem in case of complex questions.

4. Electronic Interview

Electronic interviewing is a process of recognizing and noting people, objects, occurrences rather than asking for information. For example, when you go to store, you notice which product people like to use. The Universal Product Code (UPC) is also a method of observing what people are buying.

Advantages of Electronic Interview

(1) There is no relying on willingness or ability of respondent.

(2) The data is more accurate and objective.

Disadvantages of Electronic Interview

(1) Attitudes cannot be observed.

(2) Those events which are of long duration cannot be observed.

(3) There is observer bias. It is not purely objective.

(4) If the respondents know that they are being observed, their response can be biased.

(5) It is a costly method.

7.3.3 Depth Interview Method

They generally use small samples and also conduct direct one-to-one personal interviews. A detailed background is provided by the respondents and elaborate data concerning the respondents opinions, values, motivation, expression, feeling etc. are obtained. Even their non-verbal expressions are observed. They take long time, therefore lengthy observations are involved.

These are conducted to customize individual responses. The questions will depend on what kind of answers are given. Even interview climate influences the respondents. The success of interviews depends on the rapport of the interviewers established with the respondents.

A. Advantages of Depth Interview

(1) Lot of detail is provided.

(2) Information obtained is comparatively more accurate.

(3) Personal or intimate topic can also be discussed since the personal rapport is established between the respondent and the interviewer.

B. Disadvantages of Depth Interview

(1) It is difficult to generalize since the interviewers are non-standardized.

(2) Since the success depends on the interviewer, there are chances of bias.

(3) Data analysis takes a lot of time.

7.3.4 Focus Group Interview Method

Focus groups are also known as group interviews or group discussions. They are used to understand the attitude or behavior of the audience. Six to twelve individuals are selected and either one or two moderators (those who lead the discussions) are selected. If there are two moderators, they will adopt opposite positions. It is the moderator who introduces the topic. Discussion is controlled through these moderators. The group is watched from adjacent rooms. There are various devices which are used to record these discussions.

A. Objectives of Focus Group

(1) To gather primary information for research project.

(2) To help developing questionnaires in terms of survey research.

(3) To understand reason behind a particular phenomenon.

(4) To see how people interpret certain phenomenon.

(5) To test primarily ideas or plan.

B. Steps Involved in Conducting Focus Group

(1) Define the problem.

(2) Select a sample.

(3) Determine the number of groups necessary (minimum number should be two).

(4) Prepare the study mechanics. Arrange the respondents place where the focus group is to be assembled.

(5) Select moderators and brief them.

(6) Prepare the focus group material.

(7) Conduct the session.

(8) Analyze the data and prepare summary report.

C. Advantages of Focus Group

(1) It is used to collect primary information and therefore it can conduct a pilot study also.

(2) Relative cost is not much.

(3) It can be conducted quickly.

(4) It has flexibility.

(5) Moderator can detect the opinion and certificates of those who cannot speak well by facial expression and other non-verbal behavior.

(6) We can get the questionnaire filled up either before or after the discussion.

D. Disadvantages of Focus Group

(1) It is inappropriate for gathering quantitative data.

(2) Self-appointed group leader may impose his/her opinion on other members. Moderators can restrict people.

(3) It depends heavily on skills of moderator.

(4) Respondents in the focus group may or may not represent the population from which they are drawn.

(5) Recording equipments are likely to restrict respondents. Location of recording equipment is very important.

7.3.5 Projective Techniques

Projective Techniques are indirect and unstructured methods of investigation which have been developed by the psychologists and use projection of respondents for inferring about underline motives, urges or intentions which cannot be secured through direct questioning as the respondent either resists to reveal them or is unable to figure out himself. These techniques are useful in giving respondents opportunities to express their attitudes without personal embarrassment. These techniques help the respondents to project his own attitude and feelings unconsciously on the subject under study. Thus, Projective Techniques play an important role in motivational researches or in attitude surveys.

A. Important Projective Techniques

(1) Word Association Test

(2) Completion Test

(3) Construction Techniques

(4) Expression Techniques

1. Word Association Test: An individual is given a clue or hint and asked to respond to the first thing that comes to mind. The association can take the shape of a picture or a word. There can be many interpretations of the same thing. A list of words is given and you don't know in which word they are most interested. The interviewer records the responses which reveal the inner feeling of the respondents. The frequency with which any word is given a response and the amount of time that elapses before the response is given are important for the researcher. For e.g., Out of 50 respondents 20 people associate the word "Fair" with "Complexion".

2. Completion Test: In this, the respondents are asked to complete an incomplete sentence or story. The completion will reflect their attitude and state of mind.

3. Construction Test: This is more or less like completion test. They can give you a picture and you are asked to write a story about it. The initial structure is limited and not detailed like the completion test. For e.g., 2 cartoons are given and a dialogue is to written.

4. Expression Techniques: In this, the people are asked to express the feeling or attitude of other people.

B. Disadvantages of Projective Techniques

(1) Highly trained interviewers and skilled interpreters are needed.

(2) Interpreter's bias can be there.

(3) It is a costly method.

(4) The respondent selected may not be representative of the entire population.

7.3.6 Case Study Method

Case study research is a time-honored, traditional approach to the study of topics in social science and management. Because only a few instances are normally studied, the case researcher will typically uncover more variables than he or she has data points, making statistical control (example, through multiple regression) an impossibility. This, however, may be considered a strength of case study research: it has the capability of uncovering causal paths and mechanisms, and through richness of detail, identifying causal influences and interaction effects which might not be treated as operationalized variables in a statistical study. As such, it may be particularly helpful in generating hypotheses and theories in developing fields of inquiry.

In recent years, there has been increased attention to implementation of case studies in a systematic, stand-alone manner which increases the validity of associated findings. However, although case study research may be used in its own right, it is more often recommended as part of a multimethod approach ("triangulation") in which the same dependent variable is investigated using multiple additional procedures.

Types of Case Studies:

(1) **Snapshot case studies:** Detailed, objective study of one research entity at one point in time. Hypothesis testing by comparing patterns across sub-entities (example, comparing departments within the case study agency).

(2) **Longitudinal case studies:** Quantitative and/or qualitative study of one research entity at multiple time points.

(3) **Pre-post case studies:** Study of one research entity at two time points separated by a critical event. A critical event is one which on the basis of a theory under study would be expected to impact case observations significantly.

(4) **Patchwork case studies:** A set of multiple case studies of the same research entity, using snapshot, longitudinal, and/or pre-post designs. This multi-design approach is intended to provide a more holistic view of the dynamics of the research subject.

(5) **Comparative case studies:** A set of multiple case studies of multiple research entities for the purpose of cross-unit comparison. Both qualitative and quantitative comparisons are generally made.

Advantages of Case Study

(1) Accurate data is provided.

(2) There is detailed analysis.

Disadvantages of Case Study

(1) It is difficult to generalize.

(2) It consumes lot of time.

(3) Confidential and sensitive information may not be given.

(4) Interviewer bias is there.

7.3.7 Experimental Method

There are number of experimental designs that are used in carrying out an experiment. However, market researchers have used four experimental designs most frequently. These are:

1. **CRD – Completely Randomized Design:** A Completely Randomized Design (CRD), which is the simplest type of the basic designs, may be defined as a design in which the treatments are assigned to experimental units completely at random, that is the randomization is done without any restrictions. The design is completely flexible, i.e., any number of treatments and any number of units per treatment may be used. Moreover, the number of units per treatment need not be equal. A completely randomized design is considered to be most useful in situations where (i) the experimental units are homogeneous, (ii) the experiments are small such as laboratory experiments, and (iii) some experimental units are likely to be destroyed or to tail to respond.

2. **RBD – Randomized Block Design:** The term Randomized Block Design has originated from agricultural research. In this design, several treatments of variables are applied to different blocks of land to ascertain their effect on the yield of the crop. Blocks are formed in such a manner that each block contains as many plots as a number of treatments so that one plot from each is selected at random for each treatment. The production of each plot is measured after the treatment is given. These data are then interpreted and inferences are drawn by using the analysis of Variance Technique so as to know the effect of various treatments like different doses of fertilizers, different types of irrigation etc.

3. **LSD – Latin Square Design:** A Latin square is one of the experimental designs which has a balanced two-way classification scheme say for example – 4 × 4 arrangement. In this scheme, each letter from A to D occurs only once in each row and also only once in each column. The balance arrangement, it may be noted that, will not get disturbed if any row gets changed with the other. The balance arrangement achieved in a Latin Square is its main

strength. In this design, the comparisons among treatments, will be free from both differences between rows and columns. Thus, the magnitude of error will be smaller than any other design.

4. **FD – Factorial Design:** This design allows the experimenter to test two or more variables simultaneously. It also measures interaction effects of the variables and analyzes the impacts of each of the variables.

In a true experiment, randomization is essential so that the experimenter can infer cause and effect without any bias.

7.4 COLLECTION OF DATA THROUGH QUESTIONNAIRES

A good questionnaire should not be too lengthy. Simple English should be used and the question shouldn't be difficult to answer. A good questionnaire requires sensible language, editing, assessment, and redrafting.

7.4.1 Questionnaire Design Process

1. **State the information required:** This will depend upon the nature of the problem, the purpose of the study and hypothesis framed. The target audience must be concentrated on.
2. **State the kind of interviewing technique:** Interviewing method can be telephone, mails, personal interview or electronic interview. Telephonic interview can be computer assisted. Personal interview can be conducted at respondent's place or at mall or shopping place. Mail interview can take the form of mail panel. Electronic interview takes place either through electronic mails or through the internet.
3. **Decide the matter/content of individual questions:** There are two deciding factors for this:

   (a) Is the question significant? – Observe contribution of each question. Does the question contribute for the objective of the study?

   (b) Is there a need for several questions or a single question? – Several questions are asked in the following cases:

   - When there is a need for cross-checking
   - When the answers are ambiguous
   - When people are hesitant to give correct information.
4. **Overcome the respondents' inability and unwillingness to answer:** The respondents may be unable to answer the questions because of the following reasons:

   (a) The respondent may not be fully informed.

   (b) The respondent may not remember.

   (c) He may be unable to express or articulate.

   The respondent may be unwilling to answer due to:

   (d) There may be sensitive information which may cause embarrassment or harm the respondent's image.

   (e) The respondent may not be familiar with the genuine purpose.

   (f) The question may appear to be irrelevant to the respondent.

   (g) The respondent will not be willing to reveal traits like aggressiveness (For instance – if he is asked "Do you hit your wife, sister", etc.).

   To overcome the respondent's unwillingness to answer:

   (a) Place the sensitive topics at the end of the questionnaire.

   (b) Preface the question with a statement.

   (c) Use the third person technique (For example – Mark needed a job badly and he used wrong means to get it – Is it right? Different people will have different opinions depending upon the situation).

   (d) Categorize the responses rather than asking a specific response figure (For example – Group for income levels 0-25,000, 25,000-50,000, 50,000 and above).

7.4.2 Decide on the Structure of the Question

Questions can be of two types:

(a) Structured questions: These specify the set of response alternatives and the response format. These can be classified into multiple choice questions (having various response categories), dichotomous questions (having only 2 response categories such as "Yes" or "No") and scales (discussed already).

(b) Unstructured questions: These are also known as open-ended question. No alternatives are suggested and the respondents are free to answer these questions in any way they like.

Determine the question language/phrasing: If the questions are poorly worded, then either the respondents will refuse to answer the question or they may give incorrect answers. Thus, the words of the question should be carefully chosen. Ordinary and unambiguous words should be used. Avoid implicit assumptions, generalizations and implicit alternatives. Avoid biased questions. Define the issue in terms of who the questionnaire is being addressed to, what information is required, when is the information required, why the question is being asked, etc.

Properly arrange the questions: To determine the order of the question, take decisions on aspects like opening questions (simple, interesting questions should be used as opening questions to gain co-operation and confidence of respondents), type of information (basic information relates to the research issue, classification information relates to social and demographic characteristics, and identification information relates to personal information such as name, address, contact number of respondents), difficult questions (complex, embarrassing, dull and sensitive questions could be difficult), effect on subsequent questions, logical sequence, etc.

Recognize the form and layout of the questionnaire: This is very essential for self-administered questionnaire. The questions should be numbered and pre-coded. The layout should be such that it appears to be neat and orderly, and not cluttered.

Reproduce the questionnaire: Paper quality should be good. Questionnaire should appear to be professional. The required space for the answers to the question should be sufficient. The font type and size should be appropriate. Vertical response questions should be used, for example:

Do you use brand X of shampoo?

(h) Yes

(i) No

Pre-test the questionnaire: The questionnaire should be pre-tested on a small number of respondents to identify the likely problems and to eliminate them. Each and every dimension of the questionnaire should be pre-tested. The sample respondents should be similar to the target respondents of the survey.

Finalize the questionnaire: Check the final draft questionnaire. Ask yourself how much will the information obtained from each question contribute to the study. Make sure that irrelevant questions are not asked. Obtain feedback of the respondents on the questionnaire.

7.4.3 The Qualities of a Good Questionnaire

The design of a questionnaire will depend on whether the researcher wishes to collect exploratory information (i.e., qualitative information for the purposes of better understanding or the generation of hypotheses on a subject) or quantitative information (to test specific hypotheses that have previously been generated).

Exploratory questionnaires: If the data to be collected is qualitative or is not to be statistically evaluated, it may be that no formal questionnaire is needed. For example, in interviewing the female head of the household to find out how decisions are made within the family when purchasing breakfast foodstuffs, a formal questionnaire may restrict the discussion and prevent a full exploration of the woman's views and processes. Instead one might prepare a brief guide, listing perhaps ten major open-ended questions, with appropriate probes/prompts listed under each.

Formal standardized questionnaires: If the researcher is looking to test and quantify hypotheses and the data is to be analyzed statistically, a formal standardized questionnaire is designed. Such questionnaires are generally characterized by:

(1) prescribed wording and order of questions, to ensure that each respondent receives the same stimuli

(2) prescribed definitions or explanations for each question, to ensure interviewers handle questions consistently and can answer respondents' requests for clarification if they occur

(3) prescribed response format, to enable rapid completion of the questionnaire during the interviewing process.

Given the same task and the same hypotheses, six different people will probably come up with six different questionnaires that differ widely in their choice of questions, line of questioning, use of open-ended questions and length. There are no hard-and-fast rules about how to design a questionnaire, but there are a number of points that can be borne in mind:

(1) A well-designed questionnaire should meet the research objectives. This may seem obvious, but many research surveys omit important aspects due to inadequate preparatory work, and do not adequately probe particular issues due to poor understanding. To a certain degree, some of this is inevitable. Every survey is bound to leave some questions unanswered and provide a need for further research but the objective of good questionnaire design is to 'minimize' these problems.

(2) It should obtain the most complete and accurate information possible. The questionnaire designer needs to ensure that respondents fully understand the questions and are not likely to refuse to answer, lie to the interviewer or try to conceal their attitudes. A good questionnaire is organized and worded to encourage respondents to provide accurate, unbiased and complete information.

(3) A well-designed questionnaire should make it easy for respondents to give the necessary information and for the interviewer to record the answer, and it should be arranged so that sound analysis and interpretation are possible.

(4) It would keep the interview brief and to the point and be so arranged that the respondent(s) remain interested throughout the interview.

Each of these points will be further discussed throughout the following sections. Figure 4.1 shows how questionnaire design fits into the overall process of research design that was described in chapter 1 of this textbook. It emphasizes that writing of the questionnaire proper should not begin before an exploratory research phase has been completed.

Even after the exploratory phase, two key steps remain to be completed before the task of designing the questionnaire should commence. The first of these is to articulate the questions that research is intended to address. The second step is to determine the hypotheses around which the questionnaire is to be designed.

It is possible for the piloting exercise to be used to make necessary adjustments to administrative aspects of the study. This would include, for example, an assessment of the length of time an interview actually takes, in comparison to the planned length of the interview; or, in the same way, the time needed to complete questionnaires. Moreover, checks can be made on the appropriateness of the timing of the study in relation to contemporary events such as avoiding farm visits during busy harvesting periods.

7.5 PRELIMINARY DECISIONS IN QUESTIONNAIRE DESIGN

There are nine steps involved in the development of a questionnaire:

(1) Decide the information required.

(2) Define the target respondents.

(3) Choose the method(s) of reaching your target respondents.

(4) Decide on question content.

(5) Develop the question wording.

(6) Put questions into a meaningful order and format.

(7) Check the length of the questionnaire.

(8) Pre-test the questionnaire.

(9) Develop the final survey form.

7.5.1 Deciding on the Information Required

It should be noted that one does not start by writing questions. The first step is to decide 'what are the things one needs to know from the respondent in order to meet the survey's objectives?' These, as has been indicated in the opening chapter of this textbook, should appear in the research brief and the research proposal.

One may already have an idea about the kind of information to be collected, but additional help can be obtained from secondary data, previous rapid rural appraisals and exploratory research. In respect of secondary data, the researcher should be aware of what work has been done on the same or similar problems in the past, what factors have not yet been examined, and how the present survey questionnaire can build on what has already been discovered. Further, a small number of preliminary informal interviews with target respondents will give a glimpse of reality that may help clarify ideas about what information is required.

7.5.2 Define the Target Respondents

At the outset, the researcher must define the population about which he/she wishes to generalize from the sample data to be collected. For example, in marketing research, researchers often have to decide whether they should cover only existing users of the generic product type or whether to also include non-users. Secondly, researchers have to draw up a sampling frame. Thirdly, in designing the questionnaire, we must take into account factors such as the age, education, etc. of the target respondents.

7.5.3 Choose the Method(s) of Reaching Target Respondents

It may seem strange to be suggesting that the method of reaching the intended respondents should constitute part of the questionnaire design process. However, a moment's reflection is sufficient to conclude that the method of contact will influence not only the questions the researcher is able to ask but the phrasing of those questions. The main methods available in survey research are:

(1) Personal interviews

(2) Group or focus interviews

(3) Mailed questionnaires

(4) Telephone interviews.

Within this region, the first two mentioned are used much more extensively than the second pair. However, each has its advantages and disadvantages. A general rule is that the more sensitive or personal the information, the more personal the form of data collection should be.

7.5.4 Decide on Question Content

Researchers must always be prepared to ask, "Is this question really needed?" The temptation to include questions without critically evaluating their contribution towards the achievement of the research objectives, as they are specified in the research proposal, is surprisingly strong. No question should be included unless the data it gives rise to is directly of use in testing one or more of the hypotheses established during the research design.

There are only two occasions when seemingly "redundant" questions might be included:

(1) Opening questions that are easy to answer and which are not perceived as being "threatening", and/or are perceived as being interesting, can greatly assist in gaining the respondent's involvement in the survey and help to establish a rapport. This, however, should not be an approach that should be overly used. It is almost always the case that questions which are of use in testing hypotheses can also serve the same functions.

(2) "Dummy" questions can disguise the purpose of the survey and/or the sponsorship of a study. For example, if a manufacturer wanted to find out whether its distributors were giving the consumers or end-users of its products a reasonable level of service, the researcher would want to disguise the fact that the distributors' service level was being investigated. If he/she did not, then rumors would abound that there was something wrong with the distributor.

7.5.5 Develop the Question Wording

Survey questions can be classified into three forms, i.e., closed, open-ended and open response-option questions. So far only the first of these, i.e., closed questions has been discussed. This type of questioning has a number of important advantages and disadvantages:

Advantages

(1) It provides the respondent with an easy method of indicating his answer – he does not have to think about how to articulate his answer.

(2) It 'prompts' the respondent so that the respondent has to rely less on memory in answering a question.

(3) Responses can be easily classified, making analysis very straightforward.

(4) It permits the respondent to specify the answer categories most suitable for their purposes.

Disadvantages

(1) They do not allow the respondent the opportunity to give a different response to those suggested.

(2) They 'suggest' answers that respondents may not have considered before.

With open-ended questions, the respondent is asked to give a reply to a question in his/her own words. No answers are suggested.

Example: What do you like most about this implement?

Open-ended questions have a number of advantages when utilized in a questionnaire:

(1) They allow the respondent to answer in his own words, with no influence by any specific alternatives suggested by the interviewer.

(2) They often reveal the issues which are most important to the respondent, and this may reveal findings which were not originally anticipated when the survey was initiated.

(3) Respondents can 'qualify' their answers or emphasize the strength of their opinions.

However, open-ended questions also have inherent problems which mean they must be treated with considerable caution. For example:

(1) Respondents may find it difficult to 'articulate' their responses, i.e., to properly and fully explain their attitudes or motivations.

(2) Respondents may not give a full answer simply because they may forget to mention important points. Some respondents need prompting or reminding of the types of answer they could give.

(3) Data collected is in the form of verbatim comments – it has to be coded and reduced to manageable categories. This can be time consuming for analysis and there are numerous opportunities for error in recording and interpreting the answers given on the part of interviewers.

(4) Respondents will tend to answer open questions in different 'dimensions'. For example, the question: "When did you purchase your tractor?", could elicit one of several responses, viz.:

(a) "A short while ago".

(b) "Last year".

(c) "When I sold my last tractor".

(d) "When I bought the farm".

Such responses need to be probed further unless the researcher is to be confronted with responses that cannot be aggregated or compared.

It has been suggested that the open response-option questions largely eliminate the disadvantages of both the aforementioned types of question. An open response-option is a form of question which is both open-ended and includes specific response-options as well. For example,

What features of this implement do you like?

(1) Performance

(2) Quality

(3) Price

(4) Weight

(5) Others mentioned

The advantages of this type of question are twofold:

(1) The researcher can avoid the potential problems of poor memory or poor articulation by then subsequently being able to prompt the respondent into considering particular response options.

(2) Recording during interview is relatively straightforward.

The one disadvantage of this form of question is that it requires the researcher to have a good prior knowledge of the subject in order to generate realistic/likely response options before printing the questionnaire. However, if this understanding is achieved the data collection and analysis process can be significantly eased.

Clearly there are going to be situations in which a questionnaire will need to incorporate all three forms of question, because some forms are more appropriate for seeking particular forms of response. In instances where it is felt the respondent needs assistance to articulate answers or provide answers on a preferred dimension determined by the researcher, then closed questions should be used. Open-ended questions should be used where there are likely to be a very large number of possible different responses (e.g., farm size), where one is seeking a response described in the respondent's own words, and when one is unsure about the possible answer options. The mixed type of question would be advantageous in most instances where most potential response-options are known; where unprompted and prompted responses are valuable, and where the survey needs to allow for unanticipated responses.

There are a series of questions that should be posed as the researchers develop the survey questions themselves:

"Is this question sufficient to generate the required information?"

For example, asking the question "Which product do you prefer?" in a taste panel exercise will reveal nothing about the attribute(s) the product was judged upon. Nor will this question reveal the degree of preference. In such cases, a series of questions would be more appropriate.

"Can the respondent answer the question correctly?"

An inability to answer a question arises from three sources:

(1) Having never been exposed to the answer, e.g., "How much does your husband earn?"

(2) Forgetting, e.g., "What price did you pay when you last bought maize meal?"

(3) An inability to articulate the answer, e.g., "What improvements would you want to see in food preparation equipment?"

"Are there any external events that might bias response to the question?"

For example, judging the popularity of beef products shortly after a foot and mouth epidemic is likely to have an effect on the responses.

"Do the words have the same meaning to all respondents?"

For example, "How many members are there in your family?"

There is room for ambiguity in such a question since it is open to interpretation as to whether one is speaking of the immediate or extended family.

"Are any of the words or phrases loaded or leading in any way?"

For example, "What did you dislike about the product you have just tried?"

The respondent is not given the opportunity to indicate that there was nothing he/she disliked about the product. A less biased approach would have been to ask a preliminary question along the lines of, "Did you dislike any aspect of the product you have just tried?", and allow him/her to answer yes or no.

The respondent is given the opportunity to answer only 'yes' or 'no', whereas he might like the speed, but not the reliability, or *vice versa.* Thus, it is difficult for the respondent to answer and equally difficult for the researcher to interpret the response.

The use of ambiguous words should also be avoided. For example: "Do you regularly service your tractor?"

The respondents' understanding and interpretation of the term 'regularly' will differ. Some may consider that regularly means once a week, others may think once a year is regular. The inclusion of such words again present interpretation difficulties for the researcher.

"Are any words or phrases vague?"

Questions such as 'What is your income?' are vague and one is likely to get many different responses with different dimensions. Respondents may interpret the question in different terms, for example:

- hourly pay?
- weekly pay?
- yearly pay?
- income before tax?
- income after tax?
- income in kind as well as cash?
- income for self or family?
- all income or just farm income?

The researcher needs to specify the 'term' within which the respondent is to answer.

7.5.6 Putting Questions into a Meaningful Order and Format

Opening questions: Opening questions should be easy to answer and not in any way threatening to the respondents. The first question is crucial because it is the respondent's first exposure to the interview and sets the tone for the nature of the task to be performed. If they find the first question difficult to understand, or beyond their knowledge and experience, or embarrassing in some way, they are likely to break off immediately. If, on the other hand, they find the opening question easy and pleasant to answer, they are encouraged to continue.

Question flow: Questions should flow in some kind of psychological order, so that one leads easily and naturally to the next. Questions on one subject, or one particular aspect of a subject, should be grouped together. Respondents may feel it disconcerting to keep shifting from one topic to another, or to be asked to return to some subject they thought they gave their opinions about earlier.

Question variety: Respondents become bored quickly and restless when asked similar questions for half an hour or so. It usually improves response, therefore, to vary the respondent's task from time to time. An open-ended question here and there (even if it is not analyzed) may provide much-needed relief from a long series of questions in which respondents have been forced to limit their replies to pre-coded categories. Questions involving showing cards/pictures to respondents can help vary the pace and increase interest.

7.5.7 Closing Questions

It is natural for a respondent to become increasingly indifferent to the questionnaire as it nears the end. Because of impatience or fatigue, he may give careless answers to the later questions. Those questions, therefore, that are of special importance should, if possible, be included in the earlier part of the questionnaire. Potentially sensitive questions should be left to the end, to avoid respondents cutting off the interview before important information is collected.

In developing the questionnaire, the researcher should pay particular attention to the presentation and layout of the interview form itself. The interviewer's task needs to be made as straightforward as possible.

(1) Questions should be clearly worded and response options clearly identified.

(2) Prescribed definitions and explanations should be provided.

(3) This ensures that the questions are handled consistently by all interviewers and that during the interview process the interviewer can answer/clarify respondents' queries.

Ample writing space should be allowed to record open-ended answers, and to cater for differences in handwriting between interviewers.

7.5.8 Physical Appearance of the Questionnaire

The physical appearance of a questionnaire can have a significant effect upon both the quantity and quality of marketing data obtained. The quantity of data is a function of the response rate. Ill-designed questionnaires can give an impression of complexity, medium and too big a time commitment. Data quality can also be affected by the physical appearance of the questionnaire with unnecessarily confusing layouts making it more difficult for interviewers, or respondents in the case of self-completion questionnaires, to complete this task accurately. Attention to just a few basic details can have a disproportionately advantageous impact on the data obtained through a questionnaire.

Table 7.4: Physical Appearance of the Questionnaire

Use of booklets	The use of booklets, in the place of loose or stapled sheets of paper, make it easier for interviewer or respondent to progress through the document. Moreover, fewer pages tend to get lost.
Simple, clear formats	The clarity of questionnaire presentation can also help to improve the ease with which interviewers or respondents are able to complete a questionnaire.
Creative use of space and typeface	In their anxiety to reduce the number of pages of a questionnaire, these is a tendency to put too much information on a page. This is counter-productive since it gives the questionnaire the appearance of being complicated. Questionnaires that make use of blank space appear easier to use, enjoy higher response rates and contain fewer errors when completed.
Use of colour coding	Colour coding can help in the administration of questionnaires. It is often the case that several types of respondents are included within a single survey (e.g., wholesalers and retailers). Printing the questionnaires on two different colours of paper can make the handling easier.
Interviewer instructions	Interviewer instructions should be placed alongside the questions to which they pertain. Instructions on where the interviewers should probe for more information or how replies should be recorded are placed after the question.

In general, it is best for a questionnaire to be as short as possible. A long questionnaire leads to a long interview and this is open to the dangers of boredom on the part of the respondent (and poorly considered, hurried answers), interruptions by third parties and greater costs in terms of interviewing time and resources. In a rural situation, an interview should not last longer than 30-45 minutes.

7.5.9 Piloting the Questionnaires

Even after the researcher has proceeded along the lines suggested, the draft questionnaire is a product evolved by one or two minds only. Until it has actually been used in interviews and with respondents, it is impossible to say whether it is going to achieve the desired results. For this reason, it is necessary to pre-test the questionnaire before it is used in a full-scale survey, to identify any mistakes that need correcting.

The purpose of pre-testing the questionnaire is to determine:

(1) whether the questions as they are worded will achieve the desired results

(2) whether the questions have been placed in the best order

(3) whether the questions are understood by all classes of respondent

(4) whether additional or specifying questions are needed or whether some questions should be eliminated

(5) whether the instructions to interviewers are adequate.

Usually a small number of respondents are selected for the pre-test. The respondents selected for the pilot survey should be broadly representative of the type of respondent to be interviewed in the main survey.

If the questionnaire has been subjected to a thorough pilot test, the final form of the questions and questionnaire will have evolved into its final form. All that remains to be done is the mechanical process of laying out and setting up the questionnaire in its final form. This will involve grouping and sequencing questions into an appropriate order, numbering questions, and inserting interviewer instructions.

7.6 CONSTRUCTING QUESTIONNAIRE/SCHEDULE

7.6.1 How to Construct Questionnaires?

When constructing each question, think about the words you use. Avoid jargon and technical terms whenever possible. Try not to use words which may have a double meaning or be misinterpreted, as some words have different meanings for different groups of people. Don't use emotive words. Make sure the question is not ambiguous. And, above all, avoid questions which will cause annoyance, frustration, offense, embarrassment or sadness. You should never make someone feel uncomfortable, for whatever reason, as a result of filling in your questionnaire.

(1) Questions should be kept short and simple. This will avoid many of the problems outlined above. Check that a question is not double-barreled, that is, two questions in one. If it is, ask two questions rather than one. Also, avoid negative questions – the type which have 'not' in them as this can be confusing, especially when a respondent is asked to agree or disagree.

(2) Make sure that your questions don't contain some type of prestige bias. This phrase refers to questions which could embarrass or force respondents into giving a false answer. They might do this if they do not want to look 'bad' in front of the researcher, or they might do it because it is expected behavior. Questions about income or educational qualifications might illicit this type of response, so you need to be careful about how you try to obtain this information.

(3) Some issues may be very sensitive and you might be better asking an indirect question rather than a direct question. Promising confidentiality and anonymity may help, but many respondents can, understandably, be skeptical about these promises. If you ask an indirect question in which respondents can relate their answer to other people, they may be more willing to answer the question.

7.6.2 Using Closed-ended Questions

If you are constructing a closed-ended question, try to make sure that all possible answers are covered. This is particularly important for time and frequency questions such as 'how often do you'. You need to make sure that all the frequencies are covered so that respondents aren't constrained in their answers and tick a box which isn't right for them. Also, you want to make sure that you don't artificially create opinions by asking someone a question about which they don't know, or don't care. You need to make sure that you include a 'don't know' category in this case.

7.6.3 Avoiding Leading Questions

Don't asking leading questions. The question 'How often do you wash your car?' might seem innocuous enough. However, it makes two assumptions. Firstly, it assumes that the respondent has a car and secondly, it assumes the respondent washes his car. It could be considered a prestige bias question. Would a respondent feel bad if they didn't have a car and therefore would tick 'four times a week' anyway? Would they feel bad if they don't ever wash their car but feel the researcher expects them to? If you need to ask this question, you should ask a filter question first to find out whether the respondent actually owned a car. Then you would need to ask: 'If you wash your car, how many times a year?' By wording the question in this way and by being careful about the frequency list, you're not leading the respondent into answering in a certain way.

7.6.4 Questionnaire Construction Issues

(1) Know how (and whether) you will use the results of your research before you start. If, for example, the results won't influence your decision or you can't afford to implement the findings or the cost of the research outweighs its usefulness, then save your time and money; don't bother doing the research.

(2) The research objectives and frame of reference should be defined beforehand, including the questionnaire's context of time, budget, manpower, intrusion and privacy.

(3) How (randomly or not) and from where (your sampling frame) you select the respondents will determine whether you will be able to generalize your findings to the larger population.

(4) The nature of the expected responses should be defined and retained for interpretation of the responses, be it preferences (of products or services), facts, beliefs, feelings, descriptions of past behavior, or standards of action.

(5) Unimportant questions are an expense to the researcher and an unwelcome imposition on the respondents. All questions should contribute to the objective(s) of the research.

(6) If you "research backwards" and determine what you want to say in the report (i.e., Package A is more/less preferred by X% of the sample vs. Package B, and Y% compared to Package C), then even though you don't know the exact answers yet, you will be certain to ask all the questions you need – and only the ones you need – in such a way (metrics) to write your report.

(7) The topics should fit the respondents' frame of reference. Their background may affect their interpretation of the questions. Respondents should have enough information or expertise to answer the questions truthfully.

(8) The type of scale, index, or typology to be used shall be determined.

(9) The level of measurement you use will determine what you can do with and conclude from the data. If the response option is yes/no, then you will only know how many or what per cent of your sample answered yes/no. You cannot, however, conclude what the average respondent answered.

(10) The types of questions (closed, multiple-choice, open) should fit the statistical data analysis techniques available and your goals.

(11) Questions and prepared responses to choose from should be neutral as to intended outcome. A biased question or questionnaire encourages respondents to answer one way rather than another. Even questions without bias may leave respondents with expectations.

(12) The order or "natural" grouping of questions is often relevant. Prior previous questions may bias later questions.

(13) The wording should be kept simple: no technical or specialized words.

(14) The meaning should be clear. Ambiguous words, equivocal sentence structures and negatives may cause misunderstanding, possibly invalidating questionnaire results. Double negatives should be reworded as positives.

(15) If a survey question actually contains more than one issue, the researcher will not know which one the respondent is answering. Care should be taken to ask one question at a time.

(16) The list of possible responses should be collectively exhaustive. Respondents should not find themselves with no category that fits their situation. One solution is to use a final category for "other ________".

(17) The possible responses should also be mutually exclusive. Categories should not overlap. Respondents should not find themselves in more than one category, for example in both the "married" category and the "single" category – there may be need for separate questions on marital status and living situation.

(18) Writing style should be conversational, yet concise and accurate and appropriate to the target audience.

(19) Many people will not answer personal or intimate questions. For this reason, questions about age, income, marital status, etc. are generally placed at the end of the survey. This way, even if the respondent refuses to answer these "personal" questions, he/she will have already answered the research questions.

(20) "Loaded" questions evoke emotional responses and may skew results.

(21) Presentation of the questions on the page (or computer screen) and use of white space, colors, pictures, charts, or other graphics may affect respondent's interest or distract from the questions.

(22) Numbering of questions may be helpful.

(23) Questionnaires can be administered by research staff, by volunteers or self-administered by the respondents. Clear, detailed instructions are needed in either case, matching the needs of each audience.

7.6.5 Types of Questions

1. Contingency questions: A question that is answered only if the respondent gives a particular response to a previous question. This avoids asking questions of people that do not apply to them (for example, asking men if they have ever been pregnant).

2. Matrix questions: Identical response categories are assigned to multiple questions. The questions are placed one under the other, forming a matrix with response categories along the top and a list of questions down the side. This is an efficient use of page space and respondents' time.

3. Closed-ended questions: Respondents' answers are limited to a fixed set of responses. Most scales are closed-ended. Other types of closed-ended questions include:

(a) **Yes/no questions:** The respondent answers with a "yes" or a "no".

(b) **Multiple choice:** The respondent has several options from which to choose.

(c) **Scaled questions:** Responses are graded on a continuum (example: rate the appearance of the product on a scale from 1 to 10, with 10 being the most preferred appearance). Examples of types of scales include the Likert scale, semantic differential scale, and rank order scale (See scale for a complete list of scaling techniques.).

4. Open-ended questions: No options or predefined categories are suggested. The respondent supplies their own answer without being constrained by a fixed set of possible responses. Examples of types of open-ended questions include:

(a) **Completely unstructured:** For example, "What is your opinion of questionnaires?"

(b) **Word association:** Words are presented and the respondent mentions the first word that comes to mind.

(c) **Sentence completion:** Respondents complete an incomplete sentence. For example, "The most important consideration in my decision to buy a new house is . . ."

(d) **Story completion:** Respondents complete an incomplete story.

(e) **Picture completion:** Respondents fill in an empty conversation balloon.

(f) **Thematic Apperception Test:** Respondents explain a picture or make up a story about what they think is happening in the picture.

7.6.6 Question Sequence

(1) Questions should flow logically from one to the next.

(2) The researcher must ensure that the answer to a question is not influenced by previous questions.

(3) Questions should flow from the more general to the more specific.

(4) Questions should flow from the least sensitive to the most sensitive.

(5) Questions should flow from factual and behavioral questions to attitudinal and opinion questions.

(6) Questions should flow from unaided to aided questions.

(7) According to the three stage theory (also called the sandwich theory), initial questions should be screening and rapport questions. Then in the second stage, you ask all the product specific questions. In the last stage, you ask **demographic** questions.

The following points should be kept in mind while drafting a questionnaire:

1. The questionnaire should not be lengthy.
2. A decent paper and printing is to be chosen.
3. The questions asked should be well warded and should not be ambiguous.
4. The questions asked should be in proper sequence.
5. Irrelevant questions to the study should be avoided.
6. Questions should be free from personal bias. These should not injure the feelings of the respondents.
7. Questions should be such that respondent has to do the minimum of writing work.

Method of Collecting Questionnaire

- This method has a low cost.
- Survey participants can choose to remain anonymous.
- It is not labour-intensive.

Telephone

- Questionnaires can be conducted swiftly.
- Rapport with respondents.
- High response rate.
- Be careful that your sampling frame (i.e., where you get the phone numbers from) doesn't skew your sample. For example, if you select the phone numbers from a phone book, you are necessarily excluding people who only have a mobile phone, those who requested an unpublished phone number, and individuals who have recently moved to the area because none of these people will be in the book.

Electronic

- This method has a low cost, and on most surveys costs nothing for the participants and little for the surveyors.
- Questionnaires can be conducted swiftly.
- Survey participants can choose to remain anonymous.
- It is not labour-intensive.
- Questions can be more detailed, as opposed to the limits of paper or telephones.
- This method works well if your survey contains several branching questions.
- Sample may "self select" and thus not be representative of the population.

Personally Administered

- Questions can be more detailed, as opposed to the limits of paper or telephones.
- Rapport with respondents.
- High response rate.
- Usually, a convenience (vs. a statistical) sample so you cannot generalize your results.

7.7 DIFFERENCE BETWEEN QUESTIONNAIRES AND SCHEDULE

In practical life, schedule or questionnaires have same meaning. But in theoretical aspect, difference is made between a schedule or questionnaire. If an investigator himself fills the form by asking face-to-face questions to informants, it will be called a schedule, but on the other hand, if the same work is done by sending the form to the informant and informant himself fills the form and sends it back, the form is called questionnaire. The important points of differences are as under:

(1) Questionnaire is filled by informants but schedule is filled by enumerators, who are specially appointed for this purpose.

(2) In questionnaire, if the questions are complex, there are chances of non-response but in schedule there is no chance of non-response.

(3) Questionnaire is the list or series of questions prepared to be asked but schedules is scheduled events or plans to be executed on specific days or dates.

(4) To collect data through questionnaire is relatively cheap and economical but through schedules is relatively more expensive.

(5) In case of questionnaire, it is not always clear as to who replies, but in case of schedule the identity of respondent is known.

(6) Personal contact is generally not possible in case of questionnaire method but in case of schedules direct personal contact is established with respondents.

(7) The questionnaire method is likely to be very slow but in case of schedules the information is collected well in time.

(8) Questionnaire method can be used only when respondents are literate and cooperative, but in case of schedules the information can be gathered even when the respondents happen to be illiterate.

(9) In the questionnaire method, wider and more representative distribution of sample is possible but in schedules there usually remains the difficulty in sending enumerators over a relatively wider area.

(10) In the questionnaire method, incomplete and wrong information is relatively more but in case of schedules the information is relatively more accurate.

(11) The success of questionnaire method lies more on the quality of the questionnaire itself, but in case of schedules much depends upon the honesty.

(12) Both questionnaire method and schedules observation method is not possible for collecting the data.

7.8 SUMMARY

Primary data is important for all areas of research because it is unvarnished information about the results of an experiment or observation. Primary data is the specific information collected by the person who is doing the research. Primary data can also be retrospective, interventional and observational in nature. Retrospective primary data gathers information about past conditions or behaviors. The primary data can be collected through: (1) Observation Method; (2) Survey Method; (3) Depth interview method; (4) Focus group interview method; (5) Projective Techniques; (6) Case studies method and (7) Experimental Method. The observation method involves human or mechanical observation of what people actually do or what events take place during a buying or consumption situation. The Survey method is the technique of gathering data by asking questions to people who are thought to have desired information. In depth interview, detailed background is provided by the respondents and elaborate data concerning the respondents' opinions, values, motivation, expression, feeling etc. are obtained. Focus groups are used to understand the attitude or behavior of the audience. Projective techniques are useful in giving respondents opportunities to express their attitudes without personal embarrassment. Case study method is particularly helpful in generating hypotheses and theories in developing fields of inquiry.

Secondary data is the data that have been already collected by and readily available from other sources. Such data are cheaper and more quickly obtainable than the primary data and also may be available when primary data cannot be obtained at all. Secondary data is data which has been collected by individuals or agencies for purposes other than those of our particular research study. The secondary data can be collected through: (1) Sales data; (2) Financial data; (3) Transport data; (4) Storage data; (5) Government (federal, state and local); (6) Trade associations; (7) Commercial services and (8) National and international institutions. The chief advantages of secondary data is that they are almost always less expensive than primary data. The main disadvantage of secondary data is that they were not designed specially to meet the researcher's needs.

7.9 KEY TERMS

Primary Data: Primary data means when an authorized organization or an investigator or an enumerator collects the data for the first time himself or with the help of an institution or an expert then the data thus collected are called primary data.

Secondary Data: Secondary data means that after performing statistical operations on Primary Data the results become known as Secondary Data.

Observation Method: The observation method involves human or mechanical observation of what people actually do or what events take place during a buying or consumption situation.

Survey Method: The Survey method is the technique of gathering data by asking questions to people who are thought to have desired information.

Depth Interview: In depth interview, detailed background is provided by the respondents and elaborate data concerning the respondents' opinions, values, motivation, expression, feeling etc. are obtained.

Focus Group: Focus groups are used to understand the attitude or behavior of the audience.

Projective Techniques: Projective techniques are useful in giving respondents opportunities to express their attitudes without personal embarrassment.

Case Study Method: Case study method is particularly helpful in generating hypotheses and theories in developing fields of inquiry.

Closed-ended Questions: Respondents' answers are limited to a fixed set of responses.

Open-ended Questions: No options or predefined categories are suggested. The respondent supplies their own answer without being constrained by a fixed set of possible responses.

Thematic Apperception Test: Respondents explain a picture or make up a story about what they think is happening in the picture.

7.10 MULTIPLE OBJECTIVE TYPE QUESTIONS

1. Secondary data is important for all areas of research because it is unvarnished information about the results of an experiment or observation.
   (a) True (b) False
2. Primary data can be retrospective, interventional and observational in nature.
   (a) True (b) False
3. Retrospective primary data gathers information about past conditions or behavior.
   (a) True (b) False
4. After performing statistical operations on primary data the results become known as secondary data.
   (a) True (b) False
5. Secondary data is normally collected through experiments, survey questionnaires, focus groups, interviews and taking measurements.
   (a) True (b) False
6. Secondary data is data which has been collected by individuals or agencies.
   (a) True (b) False
7. When a researcher conduct field work, she/he is possibly able to estimate inaccuracies in measurement through the standard deviation and standard error.
   (a) True (b) False
8. The survey method is the technique of gathering data by asking questions to people who are thought to have desired information.
   (a) True (b) False
9. Depth interview method is used to understand the attitude or behavior of the audience.
   (a) True (b) False
10. A good questionnaire requires sensible language, editing, assessment and redrafting.
    (a) True (b) False
11. Which following data is internal source of secondary information?
    (a) Sales data (b) Financial data
    (c) Storage data (d) All of the above

12. Which one of the following is the advantage of the primary data?
    (a) Degree of accuracy is quite high
    (b) It require lot of finance
    (c) Collection of data requires a lot of time
    (d) None of the above
13. Which one of the following is the advantage of the secondary data?
    (a) The information may not be same
    (b) Data may be outdated
    (c) It helps to improve the understanding of the problem
    (d) None of the above
14. Which research is a time-honored, traditional approach to the study of topics in social science and management?
    (a) Survey
    (b) Case study
    (c) Focus group
    (d) None of the above
15. Which questionnaire is designed if the researchers are looking to test and quantify hypothesis and the data is to be analyzed statistically?
    (a) Exploratory
    (b) Pre-test
    (c) Formal standardized
    (d) None of the above
16. Which of the following is classified into multiple choice questions?
    (a) Structured questions
    (b) Unstructured questions
    (c) Pre-test questions
    (d) None of the above
17. Which one of the following is the preliminary decision in questionnaire design?
    (a) Define target respondent
    (b) Decide question content
    (c) Pre-test questionnaire
    (d) All of the above
18. Survey questions can be classified into which forms?
    (a) Closed
    (b) Open-ended
    (c) Open response-open questions
    (d) All the above
19. Which questionnaire is more necessary before using a full scale survey to identify the mistake?
    (a) Survey
    (b) Pre-test
    (c) Exploratory
    (d) Formal
20. Which of the following techniques are useful in giving respondents opportunities to express their attitudes without personal embarrassment?
    (a) Projective techniques
    (b) Focus group
    (c) Case study method
    (d) Depth interview

Answers to Multiple Objective Type Questions

Questions	1	2	3	4	5	6	7	8	9	10
Answers	F	T	T	T	F	T	T	T	F	T
Questions	11	12	13	14	15	16	17	18	19	20
Answers	d	a	c	b	c	a	d	d	b	a

2.11 CONCEPTUAL QUESTIONS

1. What do you mean by primary data and secondary data?
2. Distinguish between primary data and secondary data. Write their advantages and disadvantages?
3. Enumerate the different methods of data collection. How data collection is important in business organization? Discuss its advantages and disadvantages.
4. What is secondary data collection method? Explain in detail.
5. What are primary data collection methods? Explain.
6. How to collect the data through the questionnaire?
7. What are the guiding considerations in the construction of questionnaire? Explain.
8. Clearly explain the difference between collection of data through questionnaires and schedules.
9. What is the quality of good questionnaire? How to construct the questionnaire? Explain with suitable example.
10. What are the preliminary decisions in questionnaire design?
11. How does the case study method differ from the survey method?
12. "Experimental method of research is not suitable in management research". Discuss.
13. Write short notes:
    (a) Observation method
    (b) Survey method
    (c) Depth interview method
    (d) Focus group interview method
    (e) Projective techniques
    (f) Case studies method
    (g) Experimental method

* * * * *

APPENDIX 7.1

Sample Questionnaire
Insurance Survey

General Information:

(a) Name of the policy holder : ______________________

(b) Full Address : ______________________

(c) Phone Number : ______________________

(d) Date of Birth : ____________ Age: ______

(e) E-mail id : ______________________

Q.1. Have you taken any insurance policy?

(a) Yes (b) No

Q.2. If the answer to the above question is 'Yes', please mention the details of the insurance policy

Term : ______________

Maturity year : ______________

Premium : ______________

Insurance coverage amount: ____________

Q.3. Are you happy with your insurance plan?

(a) Yes (b) No

Q.4. Please provide your suggestions on the insurance plan below:

____

Q.5. What financial constraints guided you to opt for this plan?

(a) Returns and dividends (b) Higher return at the end of maturity

(c) Lesser risk (d) Any others, please mention

____

Q.6. What do you do with the amount that you receive from the insurance policy?

(a) Reinvest (b) Spend on financial expenditures

(c) Others please mention ______________________

Q.7. What are your financial goals?

(a) Income generation (b) Capital appreciation and income generation

(c) Capital preservation (d) Other ______________________

Q.8. What are your financial constraints in the short term (1-5 years)?

____

Q.9. What are your financial considerations in the long term (>5 years)?

____

Q.10. Mention your satisfaction level with this insurance policy.

(a) Very dissatisfied (b) Dissatisfied

(c) Moderately satisfied (d) Satisfied

(e) Highly satisfied

Sample Questionnaire
Customer Satisfaction

General Information:

(a) Name of customer : ______________

(b) Age : ______________

(c) Sex : ______________

(d) Contact number : ______________

Q.1. How do you rate your overall consumption experience with this product?

(a) Excellent (b) Very good

(c) Good (d) Somewhat satisfactory

Q.2. Tell us about the number of complaints have you fired against your dissatisfactory experience?

(a) Once (b) Twice

(c) Thrice (d) More than this

(e) Never fired a complaint

Q.3. What sort of dissatisfaction did you experience with our products?

(a) Poor quality (b) Inadequate quantity

(c) High price (d) Weak performance

(e) Others, please mention ______________

Q.4. Where did you lodge your complaint?

(a) With the regional customer service office (b) With national customer support centre

(c) International customer support centre

Q.5. Did you receive a customer complaint number after submitting your complaints?

(a) Yes (b) No

(c) Not sure

Q.6. How satisfied are you with our customer support department?

(a) Very happy (b) Good

(c) Reasonably satisfied (d) Dissatisfied

Q.7. Do you think that the designing and packaging of our products is effective?

(a) Yes (b) No

c) Not sure

Q.8. As per your opinion, what is the current customer strength of our brand in the market?

(a) Excellent (b) Very good

(c) Good (d) Average

(e) Poor

Q.9. What changes would you like to see in our product so as to increase your satisfaction level?

____

Sample Questionnaire
New Product in Marketing

General Information:

(a) Name : ____________________

(b) Date of Birth : ____________________

(c) Residential address : ____________________

(d) Office address : ____________________

(e) Telephone no. : ____________________

(f) E-mail Id : ____________________

Q.1. How would you rate the attractiveness of our product?

(a) Very attractive (b) Attractive

(c) Neutral (d) Not attractive at all

Q.2. Do you find our product touch sensitive?

(a) Yes (b) No

Q.3. Do you find the product easy to handle?

(a) Yes (b) No

Q.4. How advanced do you find the technology of our product?

(a) Very advanced (b) Advanced

(c) Normal (d) Not so advanced

(e) Outdated

Q.5. What is the least attractive factor about our product?

(a) Design (b) Handling options

(c) Installation options (d) Technology

(e) Price (f) Other

Q.6. Have you used similar product of another brand?

(a) Yes (b) No

Q.7. What is the most attractive feature of our product?

(a) Design (b) Handling options

(c) Installation options (d) Technology

(e) Price (f) Other

Q.8. Do you find the price of the product reasonable?

(a) Yes (b) No

Q.9. How would you rate your experience of using our product?

(a) Excellent (b) Good

(c) Satisfactory (d) Bad

(e) Terrible

Q.10. Would you like to use our product again?

(a) Yes (b) No

Q.11. Would you recommend our product to your friends or relatives?

(a) Yes (b) No

Sample Questionnaire
Consumer Buying Behavior Regarding the Different Brands of Mobile Handsets

General Information:

Name : ________________

Age : ________________

Gender : ________________

Address : ____

Contact No. : ________________

Q.1. Do you have a mobile phone?

(a) Yes ☐ (b) No ☐

Q.2. Which brand of mobile handset do you have? (Please Tick)

(a) Nokia _______ (b) Sony Ericsson

(c) Motorola _______ (d) Samsung _______

(e) Any other (please specify) _______

If it is your first mobile phone, then skip Q.3?

Q.3.(i) Did you have the same brand earlier?

(a) Yes ☐ (b) No ☐

(ii) If NO, then which brand you had earlier? (Please specify)

____

(iii) Because of features you switched from earlier brand to latest one?

Items	Not True	Somewhat True	Neutral	Almost True	True
Advanced technology					
New features					
Inefficiency in earlier mobile					

Q.4. Why have you bought the mobile? (Tick one option)

(a) Communication purpose (b) Status

(c) Don't have landline phone (d) Any other (please specify) ____________

Q.5. Which of the following factors you considered while choosing the mobile handset? (Can tick more than one option)

(a) Price (b) Appearance

(c) Brand (d) Features

(e) Easy to carry/Weight

Q.6. Who influenced you to buy this brand? (Tick one option)

(a) Friend (b) Family member

(c) Advertisement (d) Dealer

(e) Any other (please specify) ________________

Q.7. For which different purposes, do you use your mobile? (Can tick more than one option)

(a) Receiving/making calls (b) SMS/MMS

(c) Games (d) E-mail/Internet

(e) Music (f) Camera

Q.8. Rank the following features of your handset according to your preference. (Rank 1 to most preferred and rank 6 to least preferred)

(a) Bluetooth (b) MP3 Player/Video Player

(c) Camera (d) Data Storage Capacity

(e) GPRS (f) Personal information management

Q.9. Tick the range of price you would like to spend on a mobile handset?

(a) Below 5,000 (b) 5,000-15,000

(c) 15,000-25,000 (d) Above 25,000

Q.10. Tick the following features you like. (Can tick more than one option)

(a) Camera (b) Bluetooth

(c) Music Player (d) Memory

(e) Any other (Please Specify) ____________________

Q.11. Tick the following brand you like.

(a) Nokia (b) Motorola

(c) Sony Ericsson (d) Samsung

(e) Any other (Please Specify) ____________________

Q.12. Rank the factors you consider in an accessing order during purchasing of a mobile handset as per their priority.

(a) Price (b) Durability

(c) Style and looking (d) Colour

(e) Battery longibility (f) Reparability

(g) Availability of spare-parts (h) Proximity to service station

(i) Sales promotional activities attached used

Q.13. What additional features do you want in your mobile handset? (Can tick more than one option)

(a) Wi-Fi (b) TV

(c) Video Conferencing (d) Windows

Q.14. Are you satisfied with your existing mobile handset?

(a) Yes ☐ (b) No ☐

If Yes, why?

____

If No, why?

____

Sample Questionnaire
Identifying the Needs of Women and the Current Car Design

General Information:

(a) Name : ______________
(b) Date of Birth : ______________
(c) Residential address : ______________
(d) Office address : ______________
(e) Telephone no : ______________
(f) E-mail id : ______________

Q.1. Car manufacturers have ignored the likes and dislikes of women in car design.
(a) Strongly agree (b) Agree
(c) Undecided (d) Disagree
(e) Strongly disagree

Q.2. Which of the below best matches your perception of a car? (Choose any one)
(a) A mode of transport (b) A status symbol
(c) A speed machine (d) A family vehicle
(e) A style quotient

Q.3. What is the most appealing aspect to you in car design? (Choose any one)
(a) Exterior Looks (b) Engine power
(c) Mileage (d) Cabin space
(e) Other (please specify) ______________

Q.4. Which feminine feature according to you is missing in the cars available in the Indian market?
(a) ______________ (b) ______________
(c) ______________

Q.5. Which type of car would you consider buying? (Choose any one)
(a) Hatchback (b) Sedan
(c) SUV (d) Compact (2 door)

Q.6. The budget perceived for your car would be in the range (in lakh).
(a) 0.0-4.0 (b) 4.0-6.0
(c) 6.0-8.0 (d) 8.0-10.0

Q.7. Which space in your car do you think is highly underutilized? (Rank 1 to 4, 1 has highest rank)
(a) Legroom in the front row seats as you/driver is not very tall ______________
(b) Legroom in the back row seats as your family doesn't have a Michael Jordan ______________
(c) Boot-space as you generally do not carry luggage ______________
(d) Cabin-height (headroom) because tall boy concepts look ugly ______________

Q.8. What would be the favorite colour for your car? (Choose any one)
(a) Red (b) Pink
(c) Blue (d) Silver
(e) Other (please specify) ________

Q.9. What are the most important accessories you would like in your car? (Rank 1 to 4, 1 has highest rank)

(a) A built in voice activated audio, video and GPS navigation system ____________

(b) A pull out vanity kit with lipstick, nail polish holders (instead of glove-box) ____________

(c) A portable wardrobe case for your party clothes ____________

(d) A refrigerated compartment for holding bottles ____________

Q.10. According to you, presently which car model best serves all your needs to the extent possible?

(a) ____________ (b) ____________

(c) ____________ (d) No one suits my taste

Q.11. Specify your preference in car engine type. (Choose any one)

(a) Petrol (low noise and maintenance) (b) Diesel (cheaper fuel)

(c) CNG (d) Electric (cheap and convenient)

Q.12. The most dull thing to do in car driving (Rank 1 to 4, 1 has highest rank)

(a) Open the car doors manually (wish you had automatic doors) ____________

(b) Crank the car (wish you had push start button) ____________

(c) Open the bonnet to check the level oil, coolant and battery (wish you had electronic fault indicators) ____________

(d) Crammed parking space (wish you had parking sensors) ____________

Q.13. What kind of upholstery would you prefer inside your car? (Choose any one)

(a) Plush like your drawing room (b) Leather finished

(c) Soft fabric with cushions (d) Other (please specify) ____________

Q.14. Your biggest fear in car driving would be (Rank 1 to 4, 1 has highest rank)

(a) Having to change flat tyres ____________

(b) Worried about having an accident ____________

(c) Coordinate between steering, gears, clutch, brake and accelerator

(d) Car breakdown in the middle of nowhere ____________

APPENDIX 7.2

Conducting a Case Study in Eight Steps

Step 1: Establish the Broad Case to Investigate

Your lecturer may give you a specific case to investigate. If on the other hand, you have to choose one, first ask yourself:

- Can I gain access to the company? (Is it local or offshore? Is the data available or subject to commercial confidence?)
- Is there enough published information on the company?
- Is too much information already available?
- Will I be able to conduct the study in the time I have available?

Step 2: Establish the Research Question(s)

After you establish the case you want to investigate, you need a question or series of questions to answer. Note that most research questions begin with: how, why, what or can and they are clearly formulated, narrow and researchable.

You can also use a research statement to guide your investigation. Research statements can be conditional or non-conditional, directional or non-directional or expressed as a null hypothesis. Research Essentials and The Research Process for further assistance. Below is an example of a testable research statement:

There is a difference between the work ethic values of Australian and Asian employees working in the Mitsubishi Car Company in Adelaide and Japan. Once you have a hypothesis or research question/statement, you need to do an extensive literature review to find what others have done in this area.

Step 3: Select the Precise Case(s) to be Used

You then need to choose a precise case (or cases) to study. A single case might be, for example, the operation of a certain private hospital. A multiple case might involve looking at several different companies operating in the wine industry.

When using multiple cases, you need to treat each case as a single case. You would best devote a chapter or section of your study to each case. The conclusions from each part can then be used as information contributing to the whole study, but each case should remain separate in your treatment.

It is useful to select cases that:

- represent a variety of geographic regions
- represent a variety of size parameters (i.e., big and small companies with a large and small client base)
- represent different market segments
- use different raw materials, etc.

In other words, choose cases that are unique in different ways.

Step 4: Determine Data Gathering and Analysis Techniques

Good case studies use a number of different research tools to increase validity. For example, you can use both quantitative and qualitative approaches and different data collection instruments (surveys, interviews, documentation review, and artifact collection).

You should aim to "triangulate" your research instruments or techniques so they provide different views of the case. This avoids the problem of observer bias, i.e., your choice of instrument measuring what you want to see and not what is really there.

It is best to use multiple cases in your study as this provides more evidence. If, however, you are analyzing a single case study, make sure that you look at different levels of analysis, for example, a firm which is part of an industry and the industry itself (e.g., Mitsubishi in Australia and the car industry at large). This type of case study increases the complexity and amount of data that can be evaluated. Remember that your aim should be to collect data from many different sources so that light will be shed on your research question from many angles.

When researching, you must ensure construct validity, internal validity, external validity, and reliability.

Construct validity means selecting the most appropriate measurement tool for the concepts being studied. Does your tool really measure what you want to assess?

Internal validity is another term for using different methodological tools to "triangulate" the data. What other methods can you use to check for the same phenomenon?

External validity refers to how well the data can be applied beyond the circumstances of the case to more general situations. Can you apply your data across the industry and to others?

Reliability means the extent to which the results can be repeated in ways that yield the same results. That is, the extent to which the results are accurate and stable. Are you confident that your study can be repeated by others and the results will be the same?

Step 5: Prepare to Collect the Data

You need a method of coding, categorizing and sorting your data. It is no good conducting your study and then finding that all the good data was not recorded properly or that you missed opportunities. You might consider establishing any or all of the following:

- Databases designed to codify data
- Protocols for interviews and surveys
- Pilot studies that capture the concepts and data needed
- Formats for narrative reporting
- Field notes
- Procedures for tape or video recordings

When carrying out the study, be flexible in real-life situations and have contingency plans for things that may go wrong. Specifically:

- Anticipate key events and problems
- Have a plan for unexpected changes, delayed appointments, lack of office space, unavailability of staff, etc.
- Be open to contrary findings and unexpected events or interview responses
- Approach people who feel threatened or unsure about the case study in a delicate manner
- Be prepared to revise the research design.

Step 6: Collect the Data

Several points need to be kept in mind when collecting data:

- Evidence must be collected systematically. While the case study methodology is very flexible, it must be clear how the data from various sources contribute to the overall aims of the study.
- You should not collect data randomly. There needs to be a purpose for collecting certain data. Refine your research question/statement, if necessary.
- Data must be stored in formats that can be referenced so that the patterns of information are clear.
- Researchers should be able to see causal factors associated with the information collected (How is X related to Y?)
- If changes need to be made to the data collection procedure, these changes need to be recorded and documented.
- You need to be able to record anecdotes, comments and illustrations/examples easily — these might turn out to be vital pieces of qualitative information.
- Notes should be kept recording the thoughts you have about the evolving case study (e.g., in a case diary).

Step 7: Analyze the Data

In case study research, data is used to find relationships between the object of study and the research questions posed. A few pointers about doing this follow:

- One can quickly get lost in a web of complex data unless you have a clear research objective. You should aim to seek data that answers this objective from as many different sources as possible. Don't try to establish thirty different things: establish one thing well with data from different areas that confirm it.
- Good researchers cross-check the facts and discrepancies their data. They also tabulate information so that it can be checked easily.
- Focus interviews may be needed to re-confirm existing data.
- Flow charts or other displays, and tabulating frequency of events are a good way of recording and analyzing information.
- Quantitative data can be used to corroborate and support the qualitative data obtained and *vice-versa.*
- Multiple investigators can assist in seeing the patterns in the data. This can ensure confidence in the data. If there are discrepancies in how the data is viewed, then the researchers need to investigate again.
- You should also investigate across case studies (from one company to another). Don't just settle on one example from one case.

Step 8: Prepare the Report

The report format is generally followed in writing up case studies. However, this format can be modified as appropriate.

- Qualitative data: stories, anecdotes, quotations, interview transcripts, artifacts, recordings, etc. are placed in the Results section along with empirical data.
- Where possible, empirical evaluation techniques are used. The standard empirical report style is usually modified to make it clear how the data from different sources answer and/or illuminate the research question(s).
- Generally, the writer refers back to the research questions(s) with quotations or other qualitative/quantitative evidence collected.
- The report also includes evidence from published literature that confirms and disconfirms the data collected. This is generally placed in the Discussion section, and analyzed carefully.

CHAPTER 8

EDITING, CODING AND CLASSIFICATION OF DATA

RESEARCH METHODOLOGY

Chapter Outline

Learning Objectives

- *Discuss the necessity and usefulness of data editing and editing rules.*
- *Discuss the necessity and usefulness of coding and coding techniques.*
- *Describe various types of data classification.*

8.1 EDITING

8.1.1 Meaning of Editing

After data are obtained through questionnaire, interviews, observation or through secondary sources, they need to be edited. The blank responses, if any, have to be handled in some way, the data coded, and categorizing scheme has to be set up. The data will then have to be keyed in, and some software program used to analyze them.

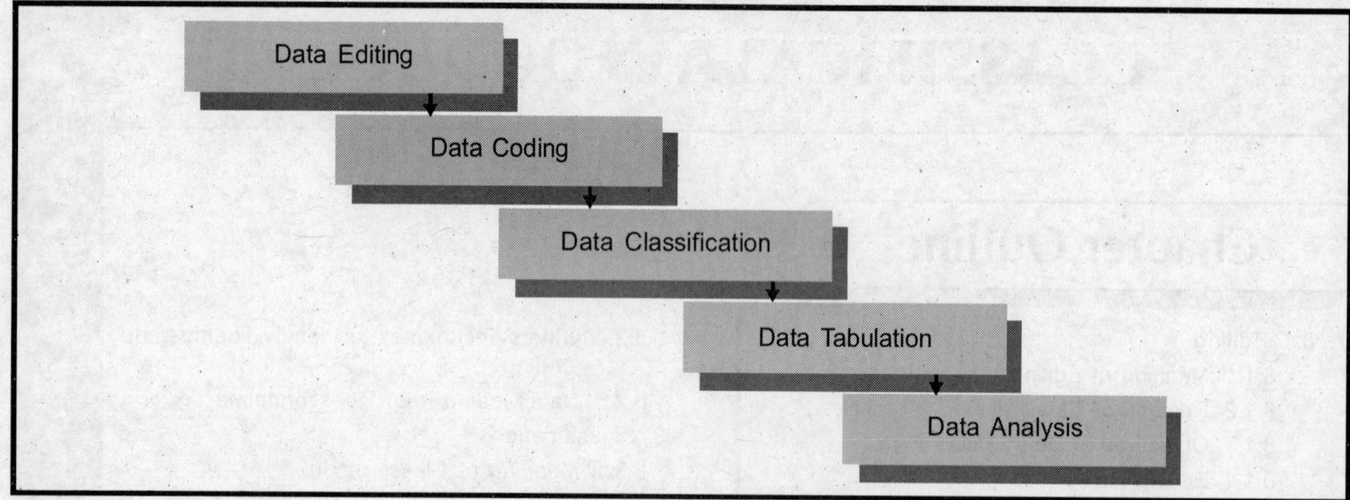

Fig. 8.1: Data Preparation Process

Why is Data Editing a Focal Point?

Data editing is a step in the preparation of statistics, the goal of which is to improve the quality of the statistical information. Data have to be edited, especially when they relate to responses to open-ended questions of interviews and questionnaires, or unstructured observations. In other words, information that may have been noted down by the interviewer, observer, or researcher in a hurry must be clearly deciphered so that it may be coded systematically in its entirety. Lack of clarity at this stage will result later in confusion. The edited data should be identifiable through the use of a different color pencil or ink so that original information is still available in case of further doubts.

Incoming mailed questionnaire data have to be checked for incompleteness and inconsistencies, if any, by designated members of research staff. Inconsistencies that can be logically corrected should be rectified and edited at this stage. Much of the editing is automatically taken care of in the case of computer-assisted telephone interviews and electronically administered questionnaires, even as the respondent is answering the question.

We might ask the question "Why are there errors in our files?" There are several situations where errors can be introduced into the data, and the following list gives some of them:

(1) A respondent could have misunderstood a question.

(2) A respondent or an interviewer could have checked the wrong response.

(3) An interviewer could have miscoded or misunderstood a written response.

(4) An interviewer could have forgotten to ask a question or record the answer.

(5) A respondent could have provided inaccurate responses.

8.1.2 Reasons of Data Editing

(1) Consistency

(2) Completeness

(3) Uniformity

(4) Accuracy

8.2.5 Data Coding from Questionnaires

We have questionnaire data and we would like to analyze the data. The first step of data analysis is **data coding**. Data coding is transformation of our questionnaire data into another format that computer (in this case we are going to use Microsoft Excel) could understand. Thus, we convert our questionnaire data into *numbers one for each of value.*

The original data from questionnaire is shown in the Table below:

Table 8.2: Data Coding from Questionnaires

Family	Time	Mode	Activity	Satisfaction	Playground
1	30	1	1, 2, 3	0	N
2	30	3	4, 6	1	Y
3	60	2	1, 2	2	Y
4	45	1	5	-1	N
5	30	1	6	1	N
6	60	2	2	2	Y
7	30	3	4	1	N
8	45	2	3, 4	-1	N
9	15	1	6	1	Y
10	60	2	2	2	Y
11	180	4	1, 2, 3, 4	2	Y
12	120	2	1, 2, 4	2	Y

Out of six variables in the questionnaire, only variable *Activity* and *Playground* need modifications while the others are already in the correct format (i.e., one number for each value). Variable *Activities* need to be converted to binary format (1 and 0, 1 = chose that activity, 0 = did not do that activity) for each value. Thus, we will convert it into 6 columns according to the number of values in the variable *Activity* . Variable *Playground* need to be converted to binary (1 = yes, and 0 = no) so that we can use **Data Analysis** tool in MS excel that can only accept numerical data.

8.3 CLASSIFICATION

8.3.1 Meaning of Classification

Data classification, in the context of information security, is the classification of data based on its level of sensitivity and the impact to the University should that data be disclosed, altered or destroyed without authorization. The classification of data helps determine what baseline security controls are appropriate for safeguarding that data. All institutional data should be classified into one of three sensitivity levels, or classifications:

1. Restricted Data

Data should be classified as Restricted when the unauthorized disclosure, alteration or destruction of that data could cause a significant level of risk to the University or its affiliates. Examples of Restricted data include data protected by state or federal privacy regulations and data protected by confidentiality agreements. The highest level of security controls should be applied to Restricted data.

2. Private Data

Data should be classified as Private when the unauthorized disclosure, alteration or destruction of that data could result in a moderate level of risk to the University or its affiliates. By default, all Institutional Data that is not explicitly classified as Restricted or Public data should be treated as Private data. A reasonable level of security controls should be applied to Private data.

3. Public Data

Data should be classified as Public when the unauthorized disclosure, alteration or destruction of that data would results in little or no risk to the University and its affiliates. Examples of Public data include press releases, course information and research publications. While little or no controls are required to protect the confidentiality of Public data, some level of control is required to prevent unauthorized modification or destruction of Public data.

8.3.2 Data Classification in Research

Classification is the way of arranging the data in different classes in order to give a definite form and a coherent structure to the data collected, facilitating their use in the most systematic and effective manner. It is the process of grouping the statistical data under various understandable homogeneous groups for the purpose of convenient interpretation. A uniformity of attributes is the basis criterion for classification; and the grouping of data is made according to similarity. Classification becomes necessary when there is diversity in the data collected for meaningful presentation and analysis. However, in respect of homogeneous presentation of data, classification may be unnecessary.

8.3.3 Objectives of Classification of Data

(1) To group heterogeneous data under the homogeneous group of common characteristics;

(2) To facilitate similarity of various group;

(3) To facilitate effective comparison;

(4) To present complex, haphazard and scattered dates in a concise, logical, homogeneous, and intelligible form;

(5) To maintain clarity and simplicity of complex data;

(6) To identify independent and dependent variables and establish their relationship;

(7) To establish a cohesive nature for the diverse data for effective and logical analysis;

(8) To make logical and effective quantification.

A good classification should have the characteristics of clarity, homogeneity, equality of scale, purposefulness, accuracy, stability, flexibility, and unambiguity.

Classification is of two types, viz., quantitative classification, which is on the basis of variables or quantity; and qualitative classification (classification according to attributes). The former is the way of grouping the variables, say quantifying the variables in cohesive groups, while the latter groups the data on the basis of attributes or qualities. Again, it may be multiple classification or dichotomous classification. The former is the way of making many (more than two) groups on the basis of some quality or attributes, while the latter is the classification into two groups on the basis of the presence or absence of a certain quality. Grouping the workers of a factory under various income (class intervals) groups comes under multiple classifications; and making two groups into skilled workers and unskilled workers is dichotomous classification. The tabular form of such classification is known as statistical series, which may be inclusive or exclusive.

The classified data may be arranged in tabular forms (tables) in columns and rows. Tabulation is the simplest way of arranging the data, so that anybody can understand it in the easiest way. It is the most systematic way of presenting numerical data in an easily understandable form. It facilitates a clear and simple presentation of the data, a clear expression of the implication, and an easier and more convenient comparison. There can be simple or complex tables, and general purpose or summary tables. Classification and tabulation are interdependent events in a research.

8.3.4 Characteristics of Classification

(1) **Exhaustive:** There must be no item which cannot find a class, for each item there is a class.

(2) **Mutually Exclusive:** There must be no item which can find its way into more than one class.

(3) **Stability:** Every stage of classification must be made with one principle.

(4) **Flexibility:** It should be flexible and must be capable of adjustment to new situations.

(5) **Arithmetical Accuracy:** The total of the items should be equal with the number of items in universe.

(6) **Suitability:** It should conform to the objects of query.

8.4 SUMMARY

Data editing is a step in the preparation of statistics, which is to improve the quality of the statistical information. Data have to be edited, especially when they relate to responses to open-ended questions of interviews and questionnaires, or unstructured observations. In several situations where errors can be introduced into the data: (1) A respondent could have misunderstood a question, (2) A respondent or an interviewer could have checked the wrong response, (3) An interviewer could have miscoded or misunderstood a written response, (4) An interviewer could have forgotten to ask a question or record the answer and (5) A respondent could have provided inaccurate responses. Reasons of Data Editing are: Consistency, Completeness, Uniformity and Accuracy. The Objectives of Data Editing are: (1) To ensure the accuracy of data; (2) To establish the consistency of data; (3) To determine whether or not the data are complete; (4) To ensure the coherence of aggregated data; and (5) To obtain the best possible data available.

Coding is the process of combing the data for themes, ideas and categories and then marking similar passages of text with a code label so that they can easily be retrieved at a later stage for further comparison and analysis. Coding is the development and use of a language that will be used to transfer data from the instrument which was employed in the data collection process to a **"codebook"** or directly to the computer in a form that is appropriate for data analysis and reporting results. The purpose of coding is making decisions about how to represent the data you collected on questionnaires in a way that the **SPSS** program will use effectively to do analysis. *Codes can be based on:* Themes, Topics, Ideas, Concepts, Terms, Phrases and Keywords.

The classification of data helps determine what baseline security controls are appropriate for safeguarding that data. Classification is the way of arranging the data in different classes in order to give a definite form and a coherent structure to the data collected, facilitating their use in the most systematic and effective manner. It is the process of grouping the statistical data under various understandable homogeneous groups for the purpose of convenient interpretation. A good classification should have the characteristics of clarity, homogeneity, equality of scale, purposefulness, accuracy, stability, flexibility, and unambiguity. Classification is of two types, viz., quantitative classification, which is on the basis of variables or quantity; and qualitative classification (classification according to attributes).

8.5 KEY TERMS

Data Editing: Data editing is a step in the preparation of statistics, the goal of which is to improve the quality of the statistical information.

Validity Edits: Validity edits are check to ensure the record identifiers, invalid characters, and values have been accounted for; essential fields have been completed specified units of measure have been properly used; and the reporting time is within the specified limits.

Range Edits: Range edits are similar to validity edits in that they look at one field at a time. The purpose of this type of edit is to ensure that the values, ratios and calculations fall within the pre-established limits.

Duplication Edits: Duplicate edits are checks to ensure that the respondent does not appear in the survey universe more than once, especially if there has been a name change.

Statistical Edits: Statistical edit is performed only after all other edits have been applied and the data have been corrected. The data are compiled and all extreme values, suspicious data and outliers are rejected.

Complexity: Complexity refers to the length as well as the number of questions asked. It also includes the detail of questions and the range of subject matter that the questionnaire may cover.

Coding: Coding is the process of combing the data for themes, ideas and categories and then marking similar passages of text with a code label so that they can easily be retrieved at a later stage for further comparison and analysis.

Pawing (Handling): Pawing is marking the text and eyeballing or scanning the text. Circle words, underline, use coloured highlighters, run coloured lines down the margins to indicate different meanings and coding. Then look for patterns and significances.

Cutting and Sorting: Cutting and sorting is the traditional technique of cutting up transcripts and collecting all those coded the same way into files, envelopes or folders or pasting them onto cards.

Data Classification: Data classification is the classification of data based on its level of sensitivity and the impact to the University should that data be disclosed, altered or destroyed without authorization. The classification of data helps determine what baseline security controls are appropriate for safeguarding that data.

Restricted Data: Data should be classified as Restricted when the unauthorized disclosure, alteration or destruction of that data could cause a significant level of risk to the University or its affiliates.

8.6 MULTIPLE OBJECTIVE TYPE QUESTIONS

1. Data have to be edited, especially when they relate to responses to open-ended questions of interviews and questionnaires or unstructured observations.
   (a) True (b) False
2. Data editing is influenced by the complexity of the questionnaire.
   (a) True (b) False
3. Editing the data makes it easier to search the data, to make comparisons and to identify any patterns that require further investigation.
   (a) True (b) False
4. The purpose of range edit is to ensure that the values, ratios and calculations fall within the pre-established limits.
   (a) True (b) False
5. Statistical edits is performed only after all other edits have been applied and the data have been corrected.
   (a) True (b) False
6. Data editing is influenced by the complexity of the ________.
   (a) Data (b) Questionnaire
   (c) Schedule (d) None of these
7. Which one of the traditional technique of cutting up transcripts and collecting all those coded the same way into files, envelopes or folders or pasting them onto cards?
   (a) Connectors (b) Pawing
   (c) Cutting and sorting (d) All of these
8. The highest level of security controls should be applied to which data.
   (a) Restricted data (b) Private data
   (c) Public data (d) All of the data
9. The classified data may be arranged in which form?
   (a) Raw form (b) Column form
   (c) Tabular form (d) None of the above
10. Which one of the following is the characteristic of Classification?
   (a) Exhaustive (b) Mutually exclusive
   (c) Stability (d) All the above

Answers to Multiple Objective Type Questions

Questions	1	2	3	4	5	6	7	8	9	10
Answers	T	T	F	T	T	b	c	a	c	d

8.7 CONCEPTUAL QUESTIONS

1. What is the meaning of data editing and its objectives? Why is data editing is a focal point?
2. What is editing rules? Explain the difference type of data editing.
3. What is coding? Explain the different techniques in coding.
4. What do you mean by data coding in questionnaire? Explain.
5. What is the meaning of data classification? Write its objectives and characteristics. How classification is done in research? Explain.
6. "Processing of data implies editing, coding, classification and tabulation". Describe.
7. Write short notes:
   (a) Editing
   (b) Range edits
   (c) Duplication edits
   (d) Data errors
   (e) Coding
   (f) Deductive approach
   (g) Inductive approach
   (h) Data Classification
   (i) Pawing
   (j) Cutting and sorting

APPENDIX 8.1

Questionnaire along with Coding

1. Age (X1)

Age	Coding
< 20	1
21-30	2
31-40	3
41-50	4
50-60	5
>60	6

2. Sex (X2)

Sex	Coding
Male	1
Female	2

3. Marital Status (X3)

Marital Status	Coding
Single	1
Married	2

4. Profession (X4)

Profession	Coding
Student	1
Professional	2
Self-employed	3
Retired	4
Housewife	5

5. What is your family's average monthly income? (X5)

Income	Coding
0-10,000	1
10,000-20,000	2
20,000-30,000	3
30,000-40,000	4
40,000-50,000	5
50,000+	6

6. How many times do you eat out in a week? (X6)

Eat out	Coding
Only 1	1
2-3	2
4-6	3
7-10	4
11+	5

7. Which of the following categories eateries do you prefer? (X7)

Categories	Coding
Restaurant	1
Fast food	2
Dhaba	3
Home food	4

8. With whom do you eat frequently? (X8)

Whom	Coding
Alone	1
With Partner	2
With Family	3
With Friends	4
With Collegious	5

9. Which meal of the day do you prefer to eat out? (X9)

Meal	Coding
Breakfast	1
Lunch	2
Dinner	3
Snacks	4
50-60	5
>60	6

10. Approximately how much do you spend per week on eating? (X10)

How much	Coding
0-200	1
200-500	2
500-1000	3
1000-2000	4
2000+	5

11. When do you prefer to eat out? (X11)

Prefer	Coding
Weekdays (X11a)	0 = No
	1 = Yes
Weekends (X11b)	0 = No
	1 = Yes
Any day (X11c)	0 = No
	1 = Yes

12. For what reason do you eat out? (X12)

Reason	Coding
No option of home food (X12a)	0 = No
	1 = Yes
Special Occasion (X12b)	0 = No
	1 = Yes
Leisure (X12c)	0 = No
	1 = Yes
To spend time with friends and family (X12d)	0 = No
	1 = Yes
Others, specify (X12e)	0 = No
	1 = Yes

13. Rank the following factors from 1-6 (X13). (Rank 1 = Most Important and rank 6 = Least Important).

Ranked from 1-6, Coded as 1-6 (X13a, X13b, X13c, X13d, X13e, X13f).

Parameter	Coding
Quality Food (X13a)	
Price (X13b)	
Service (X13c)	
Friends (X13d)	
Location (X13e)	
Brand (X13f)	

14. How you rate the following when you decide to eat? (X14)

Factors	Extremely Important	Important	Neither Important nor Unimportant	Unimportant	Extremely Unimportant
	(1)	(2)	(3)	(4)	(5)
Taste of food (X14a)					
Menu-item variety (X14b)					
Presentation of food (X14c)					
Price (X14d)					
Speed of service (X14e)					
Cleanliness (X14f)					
Brand (X14g)					
Recommendation from friends (X14h)					
Payment option offered (X14i)					

CHAPTER 9

TABULATION AND PRESENTATION OF DATA

RESEARCH METHODOLOGY

Chapter Outline

Learning Objectives

- *Develop appropriate data tabulation and its rule.*
- *Discuss the need for data interpretation in research.*
- *Explain the significance of data presentation and construction of graphs.*

9.1 TABULATION

9.1.1 Meaning of Tabulation

Tabulation refers to the systematic arrangement of the information in rows and columns. In simple words, tabulation is layout of figures in rectangular from with appropriate headings to explain different rows and columns. The main purpose of the table is to simplify the presentation and facilitate comparisons.

According to Neiswanger, "A statistical table is a systematic organization of data in columns and rows."

According to Connor, "Tabulation involves the orderly and systematic presentation of numerical data in a form designed to elucidate the problem under consideration."

From the above cited definitions, it is clear that tabulation refers to the systematic arrangement of data in rows and columns. Rows are horizontal arrangements whereas columns are vertical arrangements. It may be simple, double or complex depending upon the type of classification.

If questionnaire data are not collected on scanner answer sheets, which can be directly entered into the computer as a data file, the raw data will have to be manually keyed into the computer. Raw data can be entered through a software program. For instance, the SPSS Data Editor, which looks like a spread-editor represents a case, and each column represents a variable. All missing values will appear with a period (dot) in the cell. It is possible to add, change, or delete values after the data have been entered.

9.1.2 Types of Tabulation

(1) Simple Tabulation or One-way Tabulation

When the data are tabulated to one characteristic, it is said to be simple tabulation or one-way tabulation.

For example: Tabulation of data on population of world classified by one characteristic like Religion is an example of simple tabulation.

(2) Double Tabulation or Two-way Tabulation

When the data are tabulated according to two characteristics, it is said to be double tabulation or two-way tabulation.

For example: Tabulation of data on population of world classified by two characteristics like Religion and Sex is example of double tabulation.

(3) Complex Tabulation

When the data are tabulated according to many characteristics, it is said to be complex tabulation.

For example: Tabulation of data on population of world classified by two characteristics like Religion, Sex and Literacy etc. is example of complex tabulation.

9.1.3 Objectives and Importance of Tabulation

Tabulation is a technique to present and interpret the complex information in a simple and systematic form. The main objectives of the process of tabulation are as follows:

(1) The main purpose of the tabulation is to simplify the complex information so that it can be easily understood.

(2) Under tabulation, data is divided into various parts and for each part there are totals and subtotals. Therefore, relationship between different parts can be easily known.

(3) Since data are arranged in a table with a title and a number, these can be easily identified and used for the required purpose.

(4) Tabulation makes the data brief. Therefore, it can be easily presented in the form of graphs.

(5) Tabulation presents the numerical figures in an attractive form.

(6) Tabulation makes complex data simple and as a result of this, it becomes easy to understand the data.

(7) This form of the presentation of data is helpful in finding mistakes.

(8) Tabulation is useful in condensing the collected data.

(9) Tabulation makes it easy to analyze the data from tables.

(10) Tabulation is a very cheap mode to present the data. It saves time as well as space.

(11) Tabulation is a device to summarize the large scattered data. So, the maximum information may be collected from these tables.

9.1.4 Rules of Tabulation

There are no hard and fast rules for the tabulation of data but for constructing a good table, following general rules should be observed while tabulating statistical data:

(1) First of all, there should be a proper title to each table. Table number and title of table must be written above the table.

(2) The table should suit the size of the paper and, therefore, the width of the column should be decided before hand.

(3) Number of columns and rows should neither be too large nor too small.

(4) Captions, heading or sub-headings of columns and heading and sub-headings of rows must be self-explanatory.

(5) Each column and row must be given a title. Title of column is called caption and title of the row is called stub.

(6) As far as possible, figures should be approximated before tabulation. This would reduce unnecessary details.

(7) Items should be arranged either in alphabetical, chronological or geographical order or according to size.

(8) The units of measurement under each heading or sub-heading must always be indicated.

(9) Footnote can be written if necessary, by using signs like X etc.

(10) The sub-total and total of the items of the table must be written.

(11) Percentages are given in the tables, if necessary.

(12) Ditto marks should not be used in a table because sometimes it can create confusion.

(13) Table should be simple and attractive.

9.1.5 Preparation of a Table

Preparation of a table is an art which needs an expert handling of data. Following general principles may be followed for the purpose of preparing a perfect table:

(1) Table Number: When a table or a book contains more than one table, each table must have a number. The tables are numbered in a sequence so that they may be easily referred to. The number of the table should be placed at the middle on the top of the table.

(2) Title: Every table must have a suitable heading. The heading should be short, clear and convey the purpose of the table. It should contain four types of information:

(a) The subject matter

(b) Time

(c) Basis of classification

(d) Sources.

Besides, the main heading, there may be some sub-heading also.

The title should be so worded that it permits one and only one interpretation. Its letters should be the most prominent of any lettering on the table. Long titles cannot be read as promptly as short titles, but they may have to be used for the sake of clarity when necessary. In such a situation, a "catch title" may be given above the main title.

(3) **Captions and stubs:** Captions refer to the vertical column's headings, whereas stubs refer to the horizontal row's headings. Captions generally give the basis of classification, e.g., sex, occupation, meters, kms, etc. It may consists of one or more column headings. Under a column heading, there may be sub-heads. The captions should be clearly defined and placed at the middle of the column. It is desirable to number each column and row for reference and to facilitate comparisons.

(4) **Head notes:** Head Note is a statement given below the title which clarifies the contents of the table. It gives an explanation concerning the entire table or main parts of it, e.g., the units of measurement are usually expressed in a head note such as 'in hectares', 'in millions', 'in quintals' etc.

(5) **Body:** The body of the table contains the figures that are to be presented to the readers. The table must contain sub-totals of each separate class of data and grand total for the combined classes.

(6) **Source:** The source is given in case of secondary data. It gives the sources from which the data were obtained. The source should give the name of the book, page number, table number etc. from which the data have been collected.

9.1.6 Limitations of Tabulation

Tabulation suffers from the following limitations:

(a) Tables contain only numerical data. They do not contain details.

(b) Qualitative expression is not possible through tables.

(c) Tables can be used by experts only to draw conclusions. Common men do not understand them properly.

9.1.7 Cross Tabulation

A cross-tabulation table represents the joint frequency distribution of two discrete variables. Rows and columns correspond to the possible values of the first and the second variables, the cells contain frequencies (numbers) of occurrence of the corresponding pairs of values of the 1st and 2nd variable. Cross tabulation tables can be also used for more than two variables.

The use of cross tabulation is also sometimes referred to as a chi-square. The way these tables are set up shows the results of multiple variables when compared against each other. For example, a person may be creating a table of how many men and women drive green cars versus blue cars. To gather the data, this person would have to interview several people and write the information down. If he interviewed 40 people, the table he created from this data may look something like this:

Gender	Green Car	Blue Car
Male	9	13
Female	12	6

Cross tabulation has benefits even in everyday life. A person may use it to track her family's monthly spending over a period of time, and even school children are often taught to compile simple data this way. A visual representation of large amounts of variable data is typically easier for people to understand than pages and pages of written data.

In industry, data like this is very important when attempting to forecast markets trends, review financial variables over a long period of time and even track the health records of an entire country. It is very common for these tables to include many variables, and several different tables may even be grouped together which compare and contrast dozens of elements. Cross tabulation has use in many areas like marketing, product management and sometimes even in staff research.

The process of cross tabulation tends to give a more complete picture of past and current trends as well as possible future outcomes. It helps those analyzing the data gain an understanding of what factors affect their given elements, form hypothesis of what may happen if new information or an element is added, and see what information is not in their forecasts that should be.

9.1.8 Tabulation Applications

(1) Market research surveys

(2) Customer satisfaction

(3) Demographic studies

(4) Business to business assessments
(5) Multi-store analysis
(6) Brand tracking
(7) Performance Benchmarking
(8) Political and public opinion

9.2 TESTING GOODNESS OF DATA

The reliability and validity of the measures can now be tested.

Reliability: The reliability of a measure is established by testing for both consistency and stability. Consistency indicates how well the items measuring a concept hang together as a set. Cronbach's alpha is a reliability coefficient that indicates how well the items in a set are positively correlated to one another. Cronbach's alpha is computed in terms of the average intercorrelations among the items measuring the concept. The closer Cronbach's alpha is to 1, the higher the internal consistency reliability.

Another measure of consistency reliability used in specific situations is the split-half reliability coefficient. Since this reflects the correlations between two halves of a set of items, the coefficients obtained will vary depending on how a scale is split. Sometimes split-half reliability is obtained to test for consistency when more than one scale, dimension, or factor, is assessed. The items across each of the dimensions or factors are split, based on some predetermined logic. In almost every case, Cronbach's alpha is an adequate test of internal consistency reliability.

The stability of a measure can be assessed through parallel from reliability and test-retest reliability. When a high correlation between two similar forms of a measure is obtained, parallel form reliability is established. Test-retest reliability can be established by computing the correlation between the same tests administered at two different time periods.

Validity: Factorial validity can be established by submitting the data for factor analysis. The results of factor analysis (a multivariate technique) will confirm whether or not the theorized dimensions emerge. Measures are developed by first delineating the dimensions so as to operationalize the concept. Factor analysis would reveal whether the dimensions are indeed tapped by the items in the measure, as theorizes. Criterion-related validity can be established by testing for the power of the measure to differentiate individuals who are known to be different. Convergent validity can be established when there is high degree of correlation between two different sources responding to the same measure. Discriminate validity can be established when two distinctly different concepts are not correlated to each other.

9.3 DATA INTERPRETATION

After the data has been completely analyzed, its results have to be properly interpreted and presented. That interpretation of results is the most meaningful to the organization.

Data Interpretation can be defined as "the application of statistical procedures to analyze specific observed or assumed facts from a particular study". Data interpretation is something that is pretty common in education circles. They come as questions in tests to understand how much a student has understood the subject at hand. In school, college, university and higher educational levels, data interpretation is common. In various entrance exams for colleges too, data interpretation is used as a means to understand a student's grasp of the subject.

It is very important to understand how to interpret data in order to do well in these tests. It is especially important in case of students planning to study finance and mathematics. An interpretation question will usually contain a chart or a graph. It will also contain some data or even sets of data which the student has to analyze and come to a conclusion. When you are solving an interpretation question, you will have to understand what the graph or chart means. If there are numbers involved (most probably they will be), you will have to find out what they stand for. Next, you need to draw a data set that represents the graph or chart in question. Now you have to look at the data set and come to a conclusion about what it means.

9.3.1 Principles of Data Interpretation

(1) Do the arithmetic.

(2) Show the data.

(3) Look for and beware of selectivity in groups.

(4) When comparing groups, make sure the groups are comparable.

(5) Be sure the rhetoric and the numbers match.

(6) Beware of convenient claims that, whatever the calamity, public schools are to blame.

(7) Beware of simple explanations for complex phenomena.

(8) Making certain you know what statistic is being used when someone is talking about the "average."

(9) Be aware of whether you are dealing with *rates* or *numbers*. Similarly, be aware of whether you are dealing with *rates* or *scores*.

(10) When comparing rates or scores over time, make sure the groups remain comparable as the years go by.

(11) Be aware of whether you are dealing with *ranks* or *scores*.

(12) Watch for Simpson's paradox.

(13) Do not confuse statistical significance and practical significance.

(14) Make no causal inferences from correlation coefficients.

(15) Any two variables can be correlated. The resultant correlation coefficient might or might not be meaningful.

(16) Learn to be "see through" graphs to determine what information they actually contain.

(17) Make certain that any test aligned with a standard, comprehensively tests the material called for by the standard.

(18) Any attempt to set a passing score or a cut score on a test will be arbitrary.

(19) Ensure that it is arbitrary in the sense of arbitration, not in the sense of being capricious.

(20) Make certain that descriptions of data do not include improper statements about the type of scale being used.

(21) Do not use a test for a purpose other than the one it was designed for without taking care to ensure it is appropriate for the other purpose.

(22) Do not make important decisions about individuals or groups on the basis of a single test.

9.4 DATA PRESENTATION

9.4.1 Graphic Presentation

A graph refers to the plotting of different values of the variables on a graph paper which gives the movement or a change in the variable over a period of time. Diagrams can present the data in an attractive style but still there is a method more reliable than this. Diagrams are often used for publicity purposes but are not of much use in statistical analysis. Hence, graphic presentation is more effective, result oriented and meaningful.

According to A.L. Boddington, "The wandering of a line is more powerful in its effect on the mind than a tabulated statement; it shows what is happening and what is likely to take place, just as quickly as the eye is capable of working."

Advantages of Graphs

The presentation of statistics in the form of graphs facilitates many processes in economics. The main uses of graphs are as under:

(1) **Attractive and Effective Presentation of Data:** The statistics can be presented in an attractive and effective way by graphs. A fact that an ordinary man cannot understand easily, could understand in a better way by graphs. Therefore, it is said that a picture is worth of a thousand words.

(2) **Simple and Understandable Presentation of Data:** Graphs help to present complex data in a simple and understandable way. Therefore, graphs help to remove the complex nature of statistics.

(3) **Useful in Comparison:** Graphs also help to compare the statistics. If investment made in two different ventures is presented through graphs, then it becomes easy to understand the difference between the two.

(4) **Useful for Interpretation:** Graphs also help to interpret the conclusion. It saves time as well as labour.

(5) **Remembrance for Long Period:** Graphs help to remember the facts for a long time and they cannot be forgotten.

(6) **Helpful in Predictions:** Through graphs, tendencies that could occur in near future can be predicted in a better way.

(7) **Universal Utility:** In modern era, graphs can be used in all spheres such as trade, economics, government departments, advertisement, etc.

(8) **Information as well as Entertainment:** Graphs help us in entertainment as well as for providing information. By graphs, there occurs no hindrance in the deep analysis of every information.

(9) **Helpful in Transmission of Information:** Graphs help in the process of transmission as well as information of facts.

(10) **No Need for Training:** When facts are presented through graphs, there is any need for special training for these interpretations.

9.4.2 Rules of the Construction of Graph

The following are the main rules to construct a graph:

(1) Every graph must have a suitable title which should clearly convey the idea, the graph intends to portray.

(2) The graph must suit the size of the paper.

(3) The scale of the graph should be in even numbers or in multiples.

(4) Footnotes should be given at the bottom to illustrate the main points about the graph.

(5) Graph should be as simple as possible.

(6) In order to show many items in a graph, index for identification should be given.

(7) A graph should be neat and clean and it should be appealing to the eyes.

(8) Every graph should be given with a table to ensure whether the data has been presented accurately or not.

(9) The test of good graph depends on the case with which the observer can interpret it. Thus, the economy in cost and energy should be exercised in drawing the graph.

9.4.3 Limitations of Graph

1. **Limited Application:** Graphic representation is useful for a common man but for an expert, its utility is limited.
2. **Lack of Accuracy:** Graphs do not measure the magnitude of the data. Theory only depict the fluctuations in them.
3. **Subjective:** Graphs are subjective in character. Their interpretation varies from person to person.
4. **Misleading Conclusions:** The person who lacks knowledge can draw misleading conclusions from graphs.
5. **Simplicity:** Graph should be as simple as possible.
6. **Index:** In order to show many items in a graph, index for identification should be given.

Table 9.1: Graph Check List

What Makes for a Good Graph?	For a Good Graph, You Should Answer "Yes" to Every Question
Have you selected the appropriate graph type for the data you are displaying?	Yes/No
Does your graph have a title?	Yes/No
Have you placed the independent variable on the X-axis and the dependent variable on the Y-axis?	Yes/No
Have you labeled the axes correctly and specified the units of measurement?	Yes/No
Does your graph have the proper scale (the appropriate high and low values on the axes)?	Yes/No
Is your data plotted correctly and clearly?	Yes/No

9.5 TYPES OF DIAGRAMS

9.5.1 Bar Diagrams

Bar diagrams are commonly used to show the number or proportion of nominal or ordinal data which possess a particular attribute. They depict the frequency of each category of data points as a bar rising vertically from the horizontal axis. Bar diagrams most often represent the number of observations in a given category, such as the number of people in a sample falling into a given income or ethnic group. They can be used to show the proportion of such data points, but the pie chart is more commonly used for this purpose. Bar diagrams are especially good for showing how nominal data change over time.

Types of bar diagrams are possible:

(a) Simple Bar Diagram

(b) Double Bar Diagram

(c) Divided Bar Diagram

(d) Multiple Bar Diagram

(a) Simple Bar Diagram

Example 9.1:

Construct the Simple Bar Diagram from the following data:

Class	IX-A	IX-B	IX-C	IX-D
No. of Students	22	26	30	40

Solution:

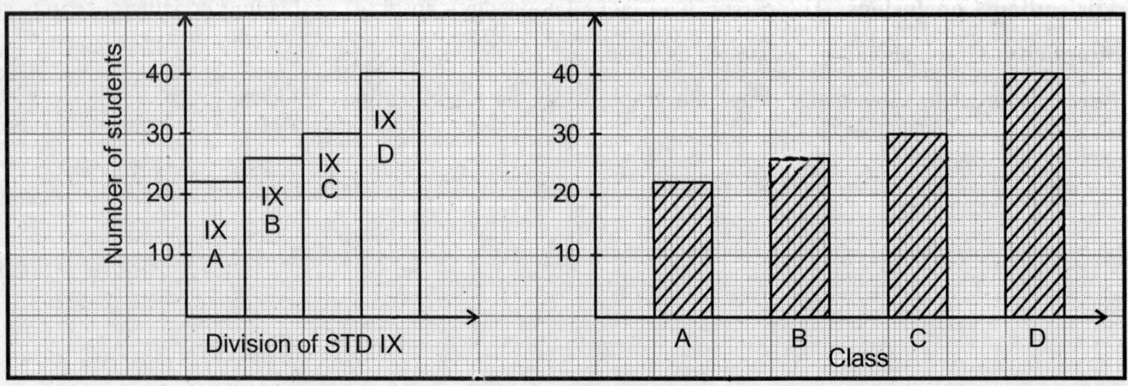

Simple Bar Diagram

Note:

(1) All bars have the same thickness.

(2) Distance between two consecutive bars is the same. The bars can touch each other.

(3) The height of each bar represents the frequency number of students.

(4) The thickness has no significance.

(5) Bar graphs are preferred when each item of data is separate from the other.

(b) Double Bar Diagram

Example 9.2:

Construct double bar diagram from the following data:

Class	IX-A	IX-B	IX-C	IX-D
Girls	10	26	18	16
Boys	12	20	12	24
Total	22	46	30	40

Solution:

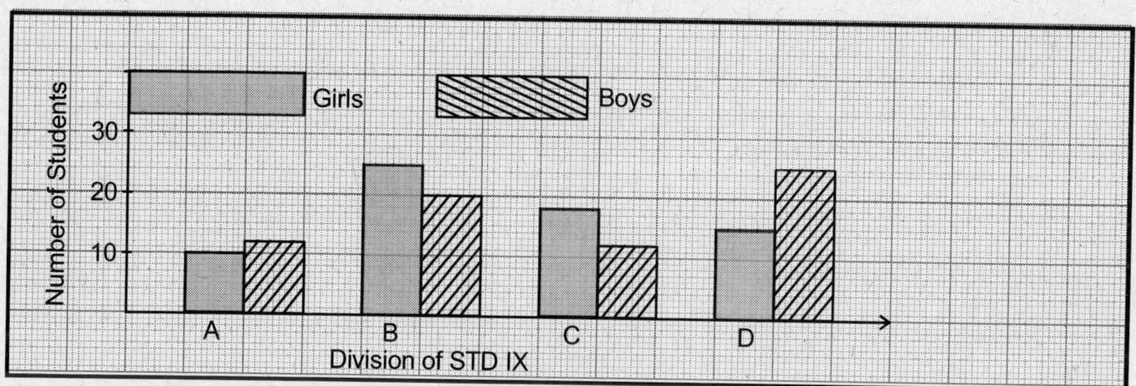

Double Bar Diagram

(c) Divided Bar Diagram

Example 9.3:

Construct Divided bar diagram from the following data:

Class	IX-A	IX-B	IX-C	IX-D
Girls	10	26	18	16
Boys	12	20	12	24
Total	22	46	30	40

Solution:

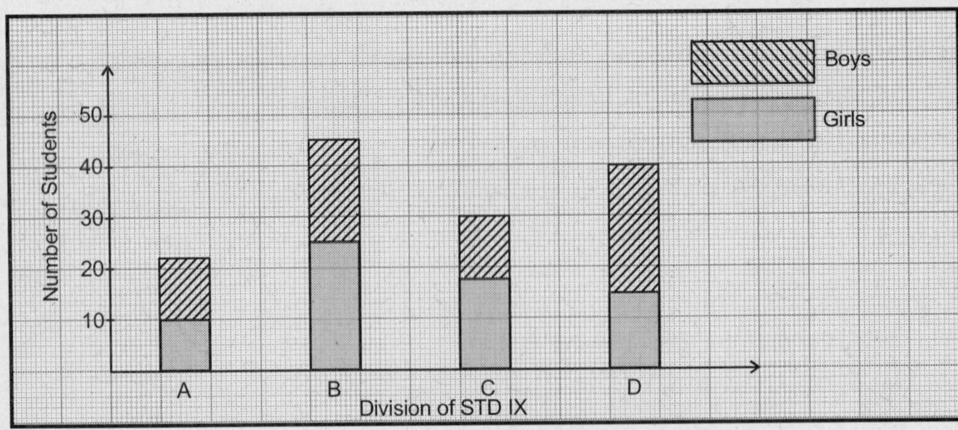

Divided Bar Diagram

Note:

Double bar or divided bar graph is preferred when we want to compare two sets of related data.

(d) Multiple Bar Diagram

Example 9.4:

Construct the Multiple bar diagram from the following data:

Literacy Rate in Percentage

Census Year	Person	Male	Female
1951	18	27	9
1961	27	40	14
1971	34	46	22
1981	43	56	30
1991	52	64	40
2001	64	76	52

Solution:

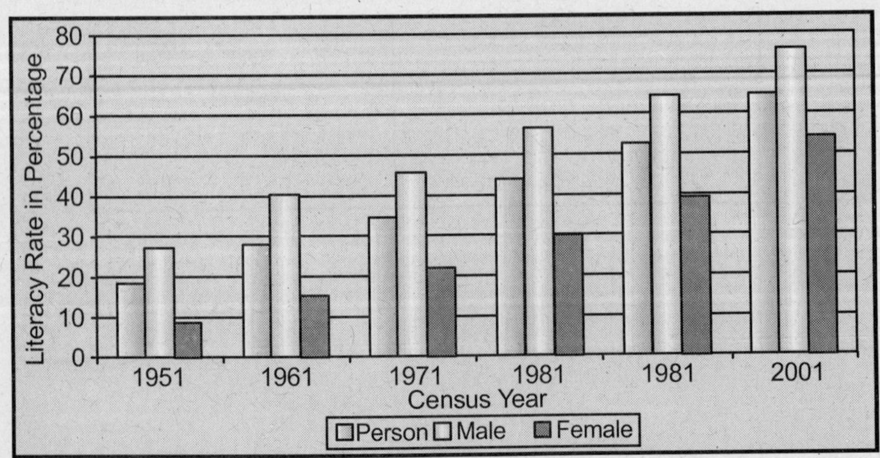

Multiple Bar Diagram

Advantages

(1) Show each nominal or ordinal category in a frequency distribution.

(2) Display relative numbers or proportions of multiple categories.

(3) Summarize a large data set in visual form.

(4) Clarify trends better than do tables or arrays.

(5) Estimate key values at a glance.

(6) Permit a visual check of the accuracy and reasonableness of calculations.

(7) Be easily understood due to widespread use in business and the media.

Disadvantages

(1) Require additional written or verbal explanation.

(2) Be easily manipulated to yield false impressions.

(3) Be inadequate to describe the attribute, behavior, or condition of interest.

(4) Fail to reveal key assumptions, norms, causes, effects, or patterns.

9.5.2 Frequency Polygons

Frequency polygons are the preferred way to graph the frequency distribution of ungrouped (raw) interval data. They represent the frequency of each class of data points as a line connecting the midpoints of the bars of a histogram. The normal (bell) curve is the most common type of frequency polygon. Frequency polygons can describe the behavior of the same interval variable under different circumstances, as in before-after situations, if superimposed on each other.

Example 9.5:

The marks scored by 120 students in an examination are as given in the table. Construct a frequency polygon.

Marks	0 – 10	10 – 20	20 – 30	30 – 40	40 – 50	50 – 60	60 – 70	70 – 80	80 – 90
Frequency	2	8	10	15	24	36	14	6	5

Solution:

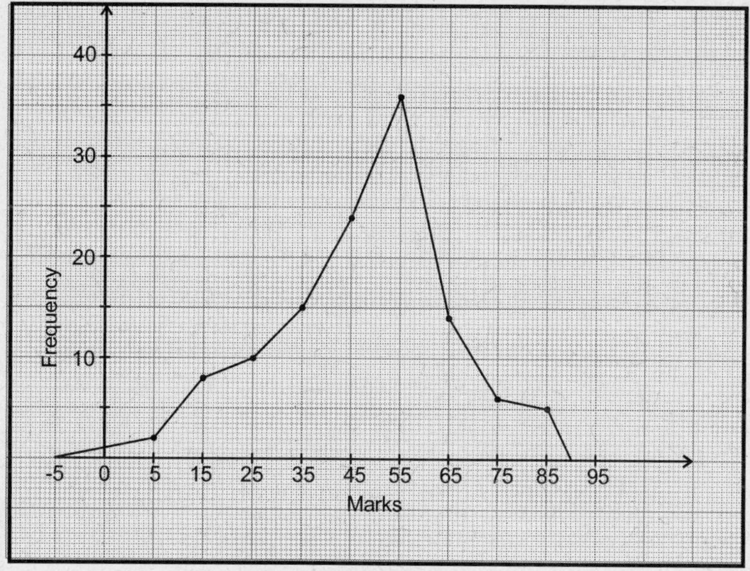

Frequency Polygon

Example 9.6:

The weight of 50 students is recorded below. Draw a frequency polygon for this data.

Class	Mid-mark	Frequency
40 – 44	42	3
45 – 49	47	10
50 – 54	52	12
55 – 59	57	15
60 – 64	62	7
65 – 69	67	5

Solution:

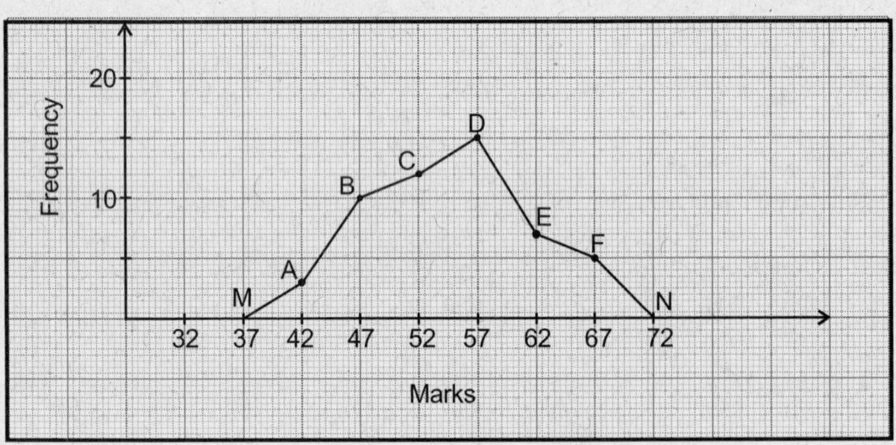

Frequency Polygon

Note:

If the above graph is joined by a smooth curve, then it is known as frequency curve.

Advantages

(1) Good to show central tendency, dispersion, and clustering/modality.

(2) Estimate key values, especially the mean, and show skew and kurtosis.

(3) Summarize a large data set in visual form.

(4) Clarify trends better than do tables, arrays, and most other graphs.

(5) Show the behavior and distribution of a variable.

(6) Become more smooth as classes or data points are added.

(7) Be easily understood due to widespread use in business and the media.

Disadvantages

(1) Fail to delineate each interval in a frequency distribution.

(2) Lose details on relative numbers and proportions *vis-a-vis* the histogram.

(3) Require additional written or verbal explanation.

(4) Be inadequate to describe the attribute, behavior, or condition of interest.

(5) Fail to reveal key assumptions, norms, causes, effects, or patterns.

(6) Be easily manipulated to yield false impressions.

(7) Fail as a visual check of the accuracy or reasonableness of calculations.

9.5.3 Histograms

Histograms are the preferred method for graphing grouped interval data. They depict the number or proportion of data points falling into a given class. For example, a histogram would be appropriate for depicting the number of people in a sample aged 18 – 35, 36 – 60, and over 65. While both bar graphs and histograms use bars rising vertically from the horizontal axis, histograms depict continuous classes of data rather than the discrete categories found in bar charts. Thus, there should be no space between the bars of a histogram.

Example 9.7:

Draw a histogram for the following data:

Class Interval	Frequency
0 – 5	4
5 – 10	10
10 – 15	18
15 – 20	8
20 – 25	6

Solution:

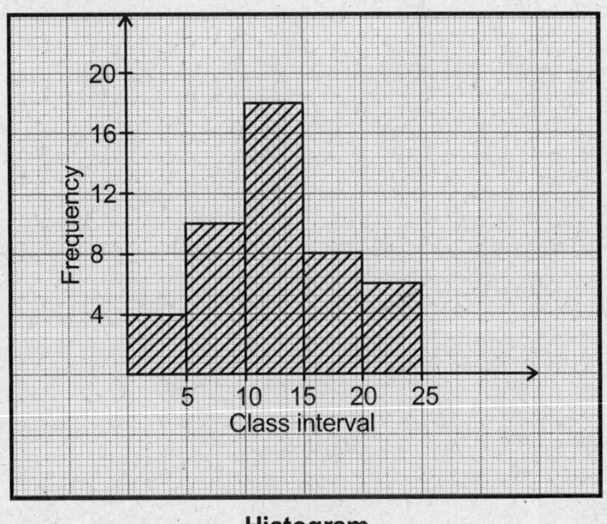

Histogram

Example 9.8:

The daily wages of 50 workers, in rupees, are given below. Draw a histogram for the following data:

Wages (in ₹)	Frequency
51 – 60	4
61 – 70	12
71 – 80	8
81 – 90	16
91 – 100	4
101 – 110	6

Solution:

The daily wages of 50 workers, in rupees in table, the class intervals are inclusive. So, we convert them to the exclusive form as shown in following table.

Wages (in ₹)	Frequency
50.5 – 60.5	4
60.5 – 70.5	12
70.5 – 80.5	8
80.5 – 90.5	16
90.5 – 100.5	4
100.5 – 110.5	6

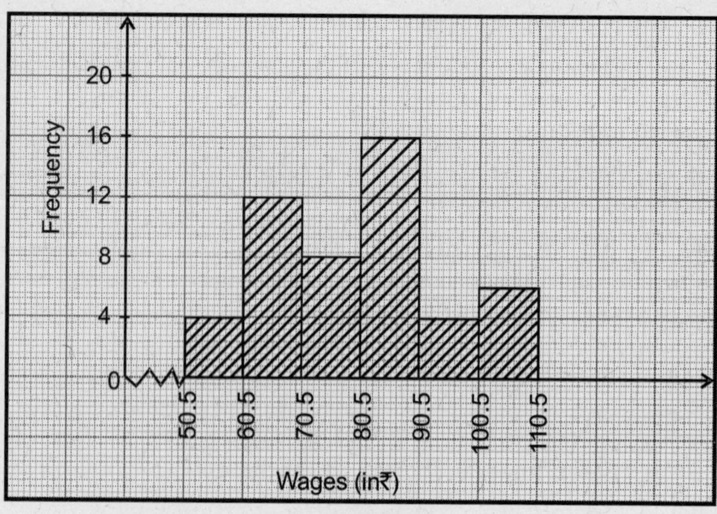

Histogram

Example 9.9:

Distribution of shops according to the number of wage-earners employed at a shopping complex is given below:

Number of Wage-earners	Number of Shops	Frequency Density
40 – 44	42	3
45 – 49	47	10
50 – 54	52	12
55 – 59	57	15
60 – 64	62	7
65 – 69	67	5

Illustrate the above table by a histogram, showing clearly how you deal with the unequal class intervals.

Solution:

When the intervals are unequal, we construct each rectangle with the class intervals as base and frequency density as height.

$$\text{Frequency density} = \frac{\text{Frequency of the class interval}}{\text{Class size of the interval}}$$

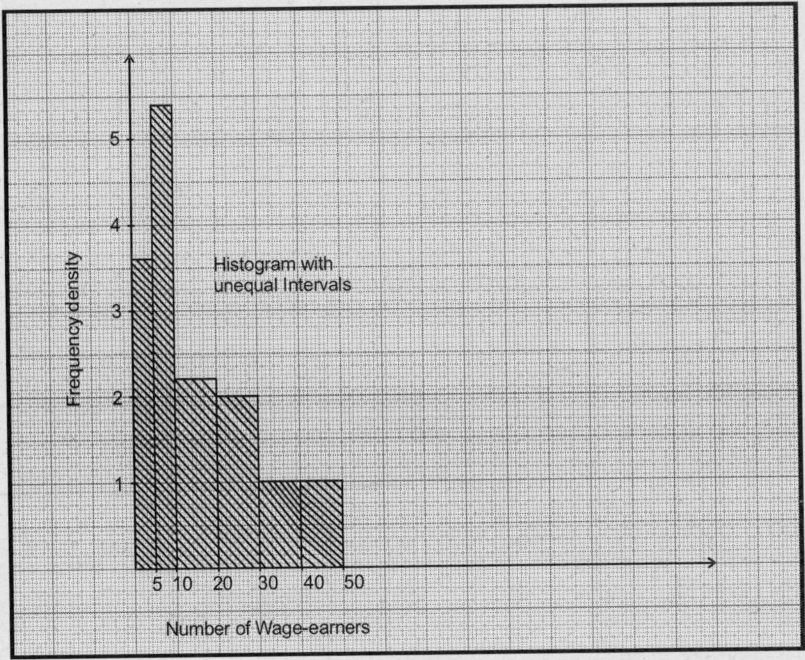

Histogram

Table 9.2: Comparison of Histogram and Bar Graph

Histogram	Bar Graph
1. It consists of rectangles touching each other.	1. It consists of rectangle, normally separated from each other with equal space.
2. The frequency is represented by the area of each rectangle	2. The frequency is represented by height. The width has no significance.
3. It is two-dimensional (width and height are considered).	3. It is one-dimensional (only height is considered).
	4. It is used as visual aid to represent data.

Advantages

(1) Shows the central tendency and dispersion of a data set.

(2) Closely resembles the bell curve if sufficient data and classes are used.

(3) Shows each interval in the frequency distribution.

(4) Summarizes a large data set in visual form.

(5) Clarifies trends better than do tables or arrays.

(6) Estimates key values at a glance.

(7) Permit a visual check of the accuracy and reasonableness of calculations.

(8) Be easily understood due to widespread use in business and the media.

(9) Use bars whose areas reflect the proportion of data points in each class.

Disadvantages

(1) Require additional written or verbal explanation.

(2) Be easily manipulated to yield false impressions.

(3) Be inadequate to describe the attribute, behavior, or condition of interest.

(4) Fail to reveal key assumptions, norms, causes, effects, or patterns.

9.5.4 Line Graphs

Line graphs use a single line to connect plotted points of interval and, at times, nominal data. Since they are most commonly used to visually represent trends over time, they are sometimes referred to as time-series charts.

Example 9.10:

Children like munchies. 75% children's like biscuits, 95% children's like ice-creams, 65% children like chocolates and 94% children like cool drinks. Solve the line graphs.

Solution:

The line graph is declared below. The line graph is drawn among children and their rate of liking things.

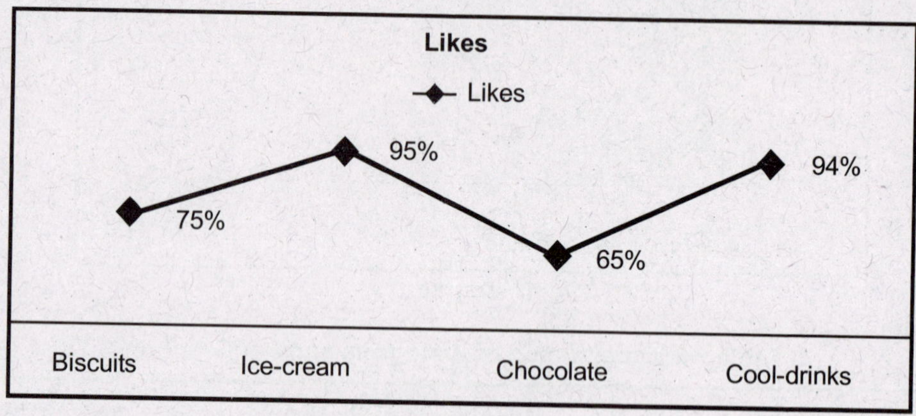

Line Graph

Example 9.11:

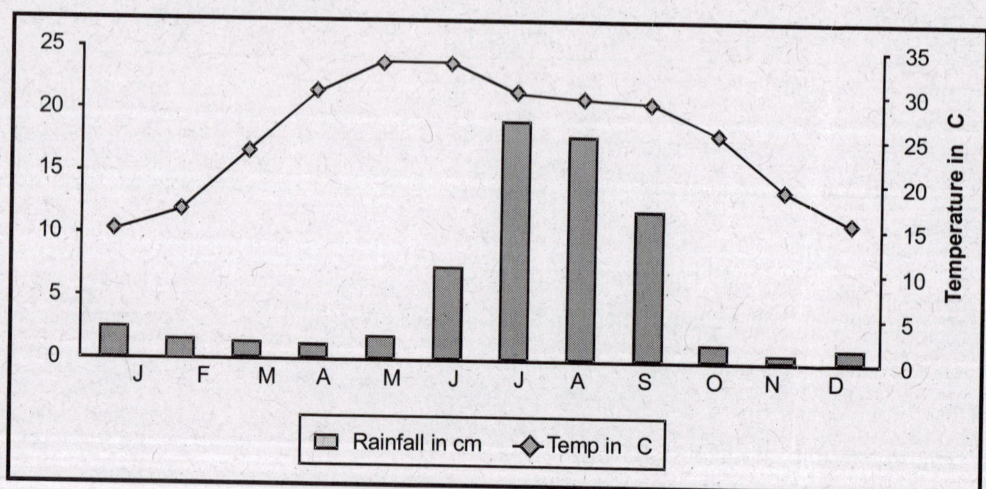

Construct a Line and Bar Graph

Advantages

(1) Clarify patterns and trends over time better than most other graphs.

(2) Be visually simpler than bar graphs or histograms.

(3) Summarize a large data set in visual form.

(4) Become more smooth as data points and categories are added.

(5) Be easily understood due to widespread use in business and the media.

(6) Require minimal additional written or verbal explanation.

Disadvantages

(1) Be inadequate to describe the attribute, behavior, or condition of interest.

(2) Fail to reveal key assumptions, norms, or causes in the data.

(3) Be easily manipulated to yield false impressions.

(4) Reveal little about key descriptive statistics, skew, or kurtosis.

(5) Fail to provide a check of the accuracy or reasonableness of calculations.

9.5.5 Ogives

Ogives are a type of frequency polygon used to depict the cumulative number or cumulative proportion of grouped interval data. They represent the cumulative frequency of each class of data points as a line connecting the upper limit of each class. Ogives let us make such statements as "X number (or X%) of the people sampled make below "Y." They are also quite useful for discussing rates of change between classes in a data set by measuring how quickly the effect of a variable accumulates across groups of data points.

Example 9.12:

Construct a 'less than' Ogive curve for the following data:

Marks	Frequency	Cumulative Frequency
0 - 10	2	2
10 - 20	8	10
20 - 30	12	22
30 - 40	18	40
40 - 50	28	68
50 - 60	22	90
60 - 70	6	96
70 - 80	4	100

Solution:

(1) We plot the points with coordinates having abscissa as actual limits and ordinates as the cumulative frequencies, (10, 2), (20, 10), (30, 22), (40, 40), (50, 68), (60, 90), (70, 96) and (80, 100) are the coordinates of the points.

(2) Join the points plotted by a smooth curve.

(3) An Ogive is connected to a point on the X-axis representing the actual lower limit of the first class.

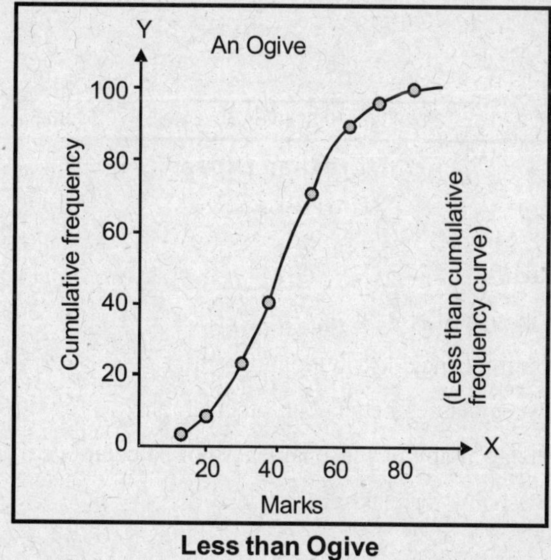

Less than Ogive

Example 9.13:

Using the data given below, construct a 'more than' cumulative frequency table and draw the Ogive.

Marks	1 - 10	11 - 20	21 - 30	31 - 40	41 - 50	51 - 60	61 - 70	71 - 80
Frequency	3	8	12	14	10	6	5	2

Marks	Frequency	Cumulative Frequency (more than)
More than 1	3	60
More than 11	8	57
More than 21	12	49
More than 31	14	37
More than 41	10	23
More than 51	6	13
More than 61	5	7
More than 71	2	2

Solution:

(1) We plot the points with coordinates having abscissa as actual lower limits and ordinates as the cumulative frequencies, (70.5, 2), (60.5, 7), (50.5, 13), (40.5, 23), (30.5, 37), (20.5, 49), (10.5, 57), (0.5, 60) are the coordinates of the points.

(2) Join the points by a smooth curve.

(3) An Ogive is connected to a point on the X-axis representing the actual upper limit of the last class [in this case), i.e., point (80.5, 0)].

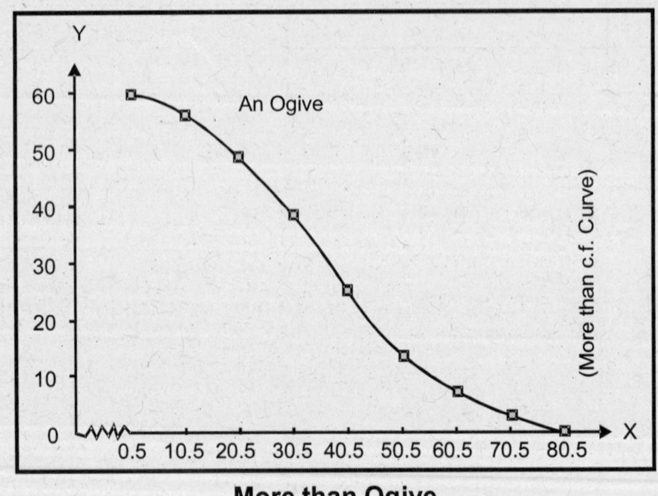

More than Ogive

Advantages

(1) Visually approximate raw data.

(2) Summarize a large data set in visual form.

(3) Delineate each interval in the frequency distribution.

(4) Clarify rates of change between classes better than other graphs.

(5) Provide a visual check of the accuracy or reasonableness of calculations.

(6) Become more smooth as data points or classes are added.

(7) Be easily understood due to widespread use in business and the media.

(8) Show the number or proportion of the data points above/below a particular value.

Disadvantages

(1) Be somewhat complicated to prepare.

(2) Fail to reflect all data points in a data set.

(3) Reveal little about central tendency, dispersion, skew, or kurtosis.

(4) Often require additional written or verbal explanation.

(5) Be inadequate to describe the attribute, behavior, or condition of interest.

(6) Fail to reveal key assumptions, norms, causes or effects.

(7) Be somewhat easily manipulated to yield false impressions.

9.5.6 Pie Charts

Pie charts are circles subdivided into a number of "slices." The area of each represents the relative proportion data points falling into a given category. Pie charts are the preferred method for graphing both nominal data and percentages.

Example 9.14:

The proportions of a budget for advertising: 45% television, 40% newspaper, and 15% yelling on an avenue corner. Construct a Pie Chart.

Solution:

The figure below shows the pie chart, in which the circle is divided into three parts as 45% for television, 40% for newspaper and 15% for yelling. Each part is labeled with its corresponding percentage.

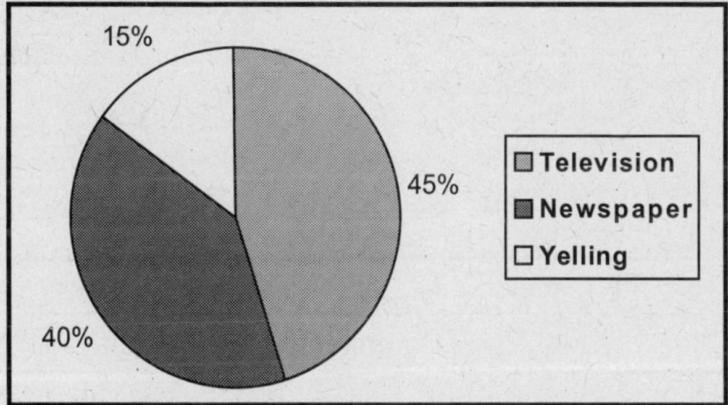

Example 9.15:

In a tenth grade, 15 students pass in Math, 23 students pass in English, 9 students pass in Science, 25 students pass Chemistry, 17 students pass in Biology. For this detail, draw a pie chart.

Solution:

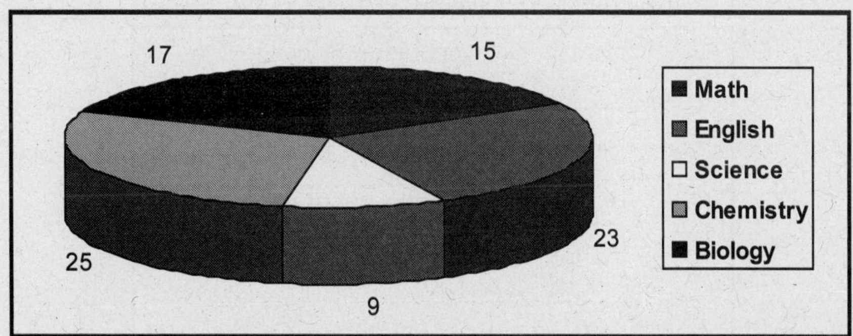

The above pie chart figure is divided into five parts as Math, English, Science, Chemistry, Biology.

Advantages

(1) Display relative proportions of multiple classes of data.

(2) Show areas proportional to the number of data points in each category.

(3) Summarize a large data set in visual form.

(4) Be visually simpler than other types of graphs.

(5) Permit a visual check of the reasonableness or accuracy of calculations.

(6) Require minimal additional verbal or written explanation.

(7) Be easily understood due to widespread use in business and the media.

Disadvantages

(1) Reveal little about central tendency, dispersion, skew, or kurtosis.

(2) Fail to reveal key assumptions, norms, causes, effects, or patterns.

(3) Fail to describe the attribute, behavior, or condition of interest.

(4) Be easily manipulated to yield false impressions.

9.5.7 Stacked Bar Diagrams

Stacked bar diagrams (component bar diagrams) add information to standard bar graphs by representing multiple categories of data in a single bar. Each bar is divided into sections whose heights indicate the proportion of observations falling into a given category. Since they deal with categories, these diagrams are generally used for nominal data.

Stacked bar graphs are useful for comparing the contributions of different groups to the total value of a variable. They can also compare two identical nominal data sets under different conditions, especially at different times. Stacked bar diagrams are often a good alternative to using multiple pie charts since they depict how much the size of a given category changes under varying circumstances.

Such diagrams also eliminate the need to construct a separate bar for each category, as would occur when using multiple bar diagrams.

Example 9.16:

From the following data, construct the Stacked Bar Diagram:

No. of Students	38	35	30
Favorite Sport	Basket Ball	Badminton	Volleyball
Girls	16	15	10
Boys	22	20	20

Solution:

In the given below, example each bar of the stacked bar graph is divided into two categories: girls and boys. Each of the three bars represents a whole. That is: about 38 students like Basket Ball, out of which 16 are girls.

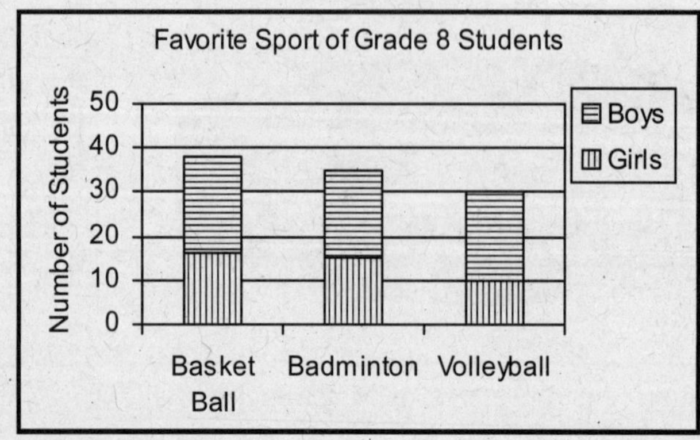

Example 9.17:

The table shows the maximum marks scored by grade 6, 7, and 8 students in Math. Which of the following is the correct stacked bar graph for the table shown?

Maximum Mark Scored in Math

Grade	Girls	Boys
6	10	19
7	15	20
8	10	30

Solution:

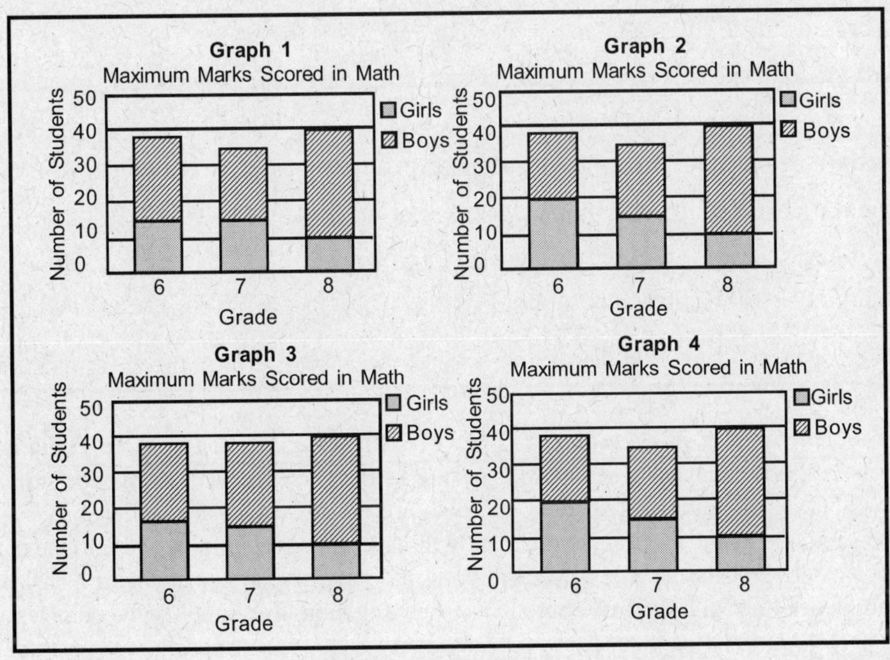

Advantages

(1) Combine richer information than bar graphs or multiple pie charts.

(2) Show how each category contributes to the overall value of a variable.

(3) Show each nominal or ordinal category in frequency distribution.

(4) Display relative proportions of multiple categories.

(5) Summarize a large data set in visual form.

(6) Clarify trends better than do tables or arrays.

(7) Estimate key values at a glance.

(8) Permit a visual check of the accuracy and reasonableness of calculations.

(9) Be easily understood due to widespread use in business and the media.

Disadvantages

(1) Be visually intimidating.

(2) Require additional verbal or written explanation.

(3) Be somewhat complicated to prepare.

(4) Be easily manipulated to yield false impressions.

(5) Be inadequate to describe the attribute, behavior, or condition of interest.

(6) Fail to reveal key assumptions, norms, causes, effects, or patterns.

(7) Reveal little about central tendency, dispersion, skew, or kurtosis.

9.6 DATA MANAGEMENT AND ANALYSIS WITH SPSS

Software (SPSS) can help the researcher with data management and analysis at different stages in the research process, as follows:

(1) **Word processing:** writing up and editing field notes.

(2) **Coding:** attaching codes to segments of the text for later retrieval.

(3) **Storing:** keeping text in an organized database.

(4) **Search and retrieval:** locating text segments when required.

(5) **Linking data:** assembling relevant data into clusters, categories and networks.

(6) **Memoing:** writing reflective comments on various segments of the data.

(7) **Analyzing content:** counting frequencies, sequences, or locations of words or phrases.

(8) **Displaying data:** condensing and organizing data for display.

(9) **Theory building:** developing coherent explanations of findings.

(10) **Graphic mapping:** creating diagrams.

9.7 SUMMARY

Tabulation is layout of figures in rectangular form with appropriate headings to explain different rows and columns. Rows are horizontal arrangements whereas columns are vertical arrangements. It may be simple, double or complex depending upon the type of classification. If questionnaire data are not collected on scanner answer sheets, which can be directly entered into the computer as a data file, the raw data will have to be manually keyed into the computer. Tabulation is a technique to present and interpret the complex information in a simple and systematic form. The main objectives of the process of tabulation are as follows: (1) The main purpose of the tabulation is to simplify the complex information so that it can be easily understood. (2) Under tabulation, data is divided into various parts and for each part there are totals and sub-totals. Therefore, relationship between different parts can be easily known. (3) Since data are arranged in a table with a title and a number so these can be easily identified and used for the required purpose.

Preparation of a table is an art which needs an expert handling of data. Following general principles may be followed for the purpose of preparing a perfect table: (1) Table Number, (2) Title, (3) Captions and stubs, (4) Head notes, (5) Body and (6) Source. Tabulation suffers from the following limitations: (a) Tables contain only numerical data, (b) Qualitative expression is not possible through tables and (c) Tables can be used by experts only to draw conclusions. Common men do not understand them properly.

A cross tabulation table represents the joint frequency distribution of two discrete variables. Rows and columns correspond to the possible values of the first and the second variables, the cells contain frequencies (numbers) of occurrence of the corresponding pairs of values of the 1st and 2nd variable. Cross tabulation tables can be also used for more than two variables. Data Interpretation can be defined as "the application of statistical procedures to analyze specific observed or assumed facts from a particular study". Data interpretation is something that is pretty common in education circles. They come as questions in tests to understand how much a student has understood the subject at hand.

Diagrams can present the data in an attractive style but still there is a method more reliable than this. Diagrams are often used for publicity purposes but are not of much use in statistical analysis. Hence, graphic presentation is more effective and meaningful. The main rules to construct a graph are: (1) Every graph must a suitable title which should clearly convey the idea, the graph intends to portray. (2) The graph must suit to the size of the paper. (3) The scale of the graph should be in even numbers or in multiples. (4) Footnotes should be given at the bottom to illustrate the main points about the graph. (5) Graph should be as simple as possible.

9.8 KEY TERMS

Tabulation: Tabulation is layout of figures in rectangular form with appropriate headings to explain different rows and columns.

Simple Tabulation or One-way Tabulation: When the data are tabulated to one characteristic, it is said to be simple tabulation or one-way tabulation.

Double Tabulation or Two-way Tabulation: When the data are tabulated according to two characteristics, it is said to be double tabulation or two-way tabulation.

Complex Tabulation: When the data are tabulated according to many characteristics, it is said to be complex tabulation.

Captions and Stubs: Captions refer to the vertical column's headings, whereas stubs refer to the horizontal row's headings.

Head Note: Head note is a statement given below the title which clarifies the contents of the table.

Cross tabulation: Cross tabulation table represents the joint **frequency distribution** of two discrete variables. Rows and columns correspond to the possible values of the first and the second variables.

Reliability: The reliability of a measure is established by testing for both consistency and stability. Consistency indicates how well the items measuring a concept hang together as a set and reliability indicates how well the items in a set are positively correlated to one another.

Graph: Graph refers to the plotting of different values of the variables on a graph paper which gives the movement or a change in the variable over a period of time.

Bar Diagram: Bar diagram is commonly used to show the number or proportion of nominal or ordinal data which possess a particular attribute.

Frequency Polygon: Frequency polygon is the preferred way to graph the frequency distribution of ungrouped (raw) interval data. They represent the frequency of each class of data points as a line connecting the midpoints of the bars of a histogram.

Histogram: Histogram is the preferred method for graphing grouped interval data. They depict the number or proportion of data points falling into a given class.

Ogive: Ogive is a type of frequency polygon used to depict the cumulative number or cumulative proportion of grouped interval data. They represent the cumulative frequency of each class of data points as a line connecting the upper limit of each class.

9.9 MULTIPLE OBJECTIVE TYPE QUESTIONS

1. Tabulation involves the orderly and systematic presentation of numerical data in a form designed to elucidate the problem under consideration.

   (a) True (b) False

2. When the data are tabulated to one characteristic, it is said to be simple tabulation or two-way tabulation.

   (a) True (b) False

3. When the data are tabulated according to many characteristics, it is said to be complex tabulation.

   (a) True (b) False

4. Tables cannot be used by experts only to draw conclusions. Common men do not understand them properly.

   (a) True (b) False

5. A cross tabulation table represents the joint frequency distribution of two discrete variables.

   (a) True (b) False

6. Which one of the following is the objective and importance of tabulation?
   (a) Tabulation presents the numerical figures in an attractive form
   (b) Tabulation is useful in condensing the collected data
   (c) Tabulation makes it easy to analyze the data from tables
   (d) All of the above
7. Captions refer to the
   (a) Vertical column's headings (b) Horizontal row's headings
   (c) Both column and row heading (d) None of the above
8. The reliability of a measure is established by testing for
   (a) Stability (b) Consistency
   (c) Both consistency and stability (d) None of the above
9. Which of the following is commonly used to show the number or proportion of nominal or ordinal data which possess a particular attribute?
   (a) Bar diagram (b) Histogram
   (c) Pie Chart (d) Ogive
10. Which of the following is the preferred way to graph the frequency distribution of ungrouped (raw) interval data?
   (a) Multiple Bar Diagram (b) Frequency Polygon
   (c) Stacked Bar Diagrams (d) None of the Above

Answers to Multiple Objective Type Questions

Questions	1	2	3	4	5	6	7	8	9	10
Answers	T	F	T	F	T	d	a	c	a	b

9.10 CONCEPTUAL QUESTIONS

1. What is tabulation? Write its objective and importance.
2. Why tabulation is more essential in research study? Briefly explain the rules of tabulation.
3. Differentiate between tabulation and cross tabulation. How to prepare a table? Explain.
4. What do you mean by testing goodness of data? Explain.
5. What is meant by data interpretation? Briefly explain its principle.
6. What is data presentation? Write its advantages and disadvantages.
7. What are the rules and limitations of construction of graphs?
8. How diagrams are more essential for conducting research? Explain with suitable examples.
9. What is data management? How it is important for research studies? Discuss.
10. Write short notes:
    (a) Tabulation (b) Cross tabulation
    (c) Complex tabulation (d) Reliability
    (e) Validity (f) Graph
    (g) Bar diagram (h) Histogram
    (i) Stacked bar diagram

* * * * *

Chapter 10

HYPOTHESIS TESTING: PARAMETRIC TEST

Chapter Outline

Learning Objectives

- *Explain the meaning of hypothesis and basic concepts in the context of making intelligent decisions.*
- *Discuss the need for hypothesis testing for large and small samples in decision making.*
- *Explain the actual process of research and its role in managerial decisions for difference between two population mean.*

10.1 MEANING OF HYPOTHESIS

A hypothesis is an explanation for a phenomenon which can be tested in some way which ideally either proves or disproves the hypothesis. For the duration of testing, the hypothesis is taken to be true, and the goal of the researcher is to rigorously test the terms of the hypothesis. The concept of the hypothesis is a very important part of the scientific method, and it also holds true in other disciplines as well.

When someone formulates a hypothesis, he or she does so with the intention of testing it, and he or she should not know the outcome of potential tests before the hypothesis is made. When formulating a hypothesis, the ideals of the scientific method are often kept in mind, so the hypothesis is designed to be testable in a way which could be replicated by other people. It is also kept clear and simple, and the hypothesis relies on known information and reasoning. A hypothesis does not have to be right or wrong, but the person formulating the hypothesis does have to be prepared to test the theory to its limits. When scientists publish results which support a hypothesis, they often detail the steps they took to disprove the hypothesis as well as the steps which confirmed it, to make the case that much stronger.

According to Schick and Vaughn, researchers weighing up alternative hypotheses may take into consideration:

(1) Testability

(2) Simplicity

(3) Scope

(4) Fruitfulness

(5) Conservatism

Table 10.1: Basic Features of Hypothesis

1.	It is clear and precise.
2.	It is capable of being tested.
3.	Marks the relationship between variables.
4.	It is specific and compact.
5.	Expressed in simple terms.
6.	It is consistent.
7.	It is amenable to testing.
8.	It has empirical evidence.

10.2 CHARACTERISTICS OF HYPOTHESIS

(1) Hypothesis must be conceptually clear and precise. If the hypothesis is not clear and precise, the inferences drawn on its basis cannot be taken as reliable.

(2) Hypothesis should be empirical realities. In case these are not empirical realities, then it will not be possible to make the observations.

(3) Hypothesis should state relationship between variables, if it happens to be a relational hypothesis.

(4) Hypothesis must be specific. The hypothesis should not only be specific to a place and situation but also these should be narrowed down with respect to its operation.

(5) Hypothesis should be stated as far as possible in most simple terms so that the same as easily understandable by all concerned.

(6) Hypothesis should be consistent with most known facts.

(7) Hypothesis should be amenable to testing within the suitable time.

(8) Hypothesis should be related to a body of theory. For the development of a framework, the researcher shall depend on the existing body of knowledge.

(9) Hypothesis has to be supported by theoretical argumentation. For this purpose, the researcher may develop his/her theoretical framework which could help in the generation of relevant hypothesis.

(10) Hypothesis must explain the facts that give rise to the need for explanation.

Table 10.2: Characteristics of a Good Hypothesis

1. A good hypothesis is based on sound reasoning.
   - Your hypothesis should be based on previous research.
   - The hypothesis should follow the most likely outcome, not the exceptional outcome.
2. A good hypothesis provides a reasonable explanation for the predicted outcome.
   - Do not look for unrealistic explanations.
3. A good hypothesis clearly states the relationship between the defined variables.
   - Clear, simply written hypothesis is easier to test.
   - Do not be vague.
4. A good hypothesis defines the variables in easy to measure terms.
   - Who are the participants?
   - What is different or will be different in your test?
   - What is the effect?
5. A good hypothesis is testable in a reasonable amount of time.
   - Do not plan a test that will take longer than your class project.

10.3 GENERAL PROCEDURE FOR HYPOTHESIS TEST

All hypothesis tests are conducted the same way. The researcher states a hypothesis to be tested, formulates an analysis plan, analyzes sample data according to the plan, and accepts or rejects the null hypothesis, based on results of the analysis.

(1) **Formulate the hypothesis:** Every hypothesis test requires the analyst to state a null hypothesis (H_0) and an alternative hypothesis (H_a). If one hypothesis is true, the other is false. The hypotheses are stated in such a way that they are mutually exclusive. If μ is the population mean and μ_0 represents the hypothesized value of μ and $\bar{x}$ is the sample mean, then:

Consequently $H_a: \mu < \mu_0$ or $H_a: \mu > \mu_0$

and The null hypothesis $H_0: \mu = \mu_0$

Alternative hypothesis $H_a: \mu \neq \mu_0$

(2) **Test the hypothesis:** Test the hypothesis indicates that whether the hypothesis is one-tailed test or two-tailed test. If the alternative hypothesis, H_a is of the type greater than or smaller than, we use a one-tailed test, and if H_a is of the type whether greater than or smaller than (i.e., not equal to), then we use a two-tailed test.

(3) **Significance level:** Once the hypothesis is formulated, it is followed by testing its validity at certain level of significance. That is, the confidence with which a null hypothesis is rejected or accepted depends on the significance level. Researchers choose significance levels (α) equal to 5%, 1% or 10%; but any value between 0 and 1 can be used.

(4) **Deciding the distribution/Test statistics:** After deciding the level of significance, hypothesis testing is to determine the appropriate sampling distribution and test statistics. Computed from sample data, the test statistic might be a mean score, proportion, difference between means, difference between proportions, z-score, t-score, chi-square, etc. If sample size (n) is more than 30 (i.e., $n > 30$), z-test is applicable and if sample size (n) is less than equal to 30 (i.e., $n \leq 30$) t-test is applicable.

(5) **Analyze sample data and compute the value:** To select the random sample(s) and compute an appropriate value from the sample data concerning the test statistic utilizing the relevant distribution.

(6) Test statistic: When the null hypothesis involves a mean or proportion, use either of the following equations to compute the test statistic.

Test statistic = (Statistic – Parameter)/(Standard deviation of statistic)

Test statistic = (Statistic – Parameter)/(Standard error of statistic)

where *Parameter* is the value appearing in the null hypothesis and *Statistic* is the point estimate of *Parameter*. When the parameter in the null hypothesis involves categorical data, you may use a chi-square statistic as the test statistic.

(7) P-value: The P-value is the probability of observing a sample statistic as extreme as the test statistic, assuming the null hypothesis is true.

(8) Interpret the results: If the sample findings are unlikely, given the null hypothesis, the researcher rejects the null hypothesis. If calculation value is less than the critical value or tabulated value, then null hypothesis H_0 is accepted otherwise H_0 is rejected and alternative hypothesis H_a may be accepted.

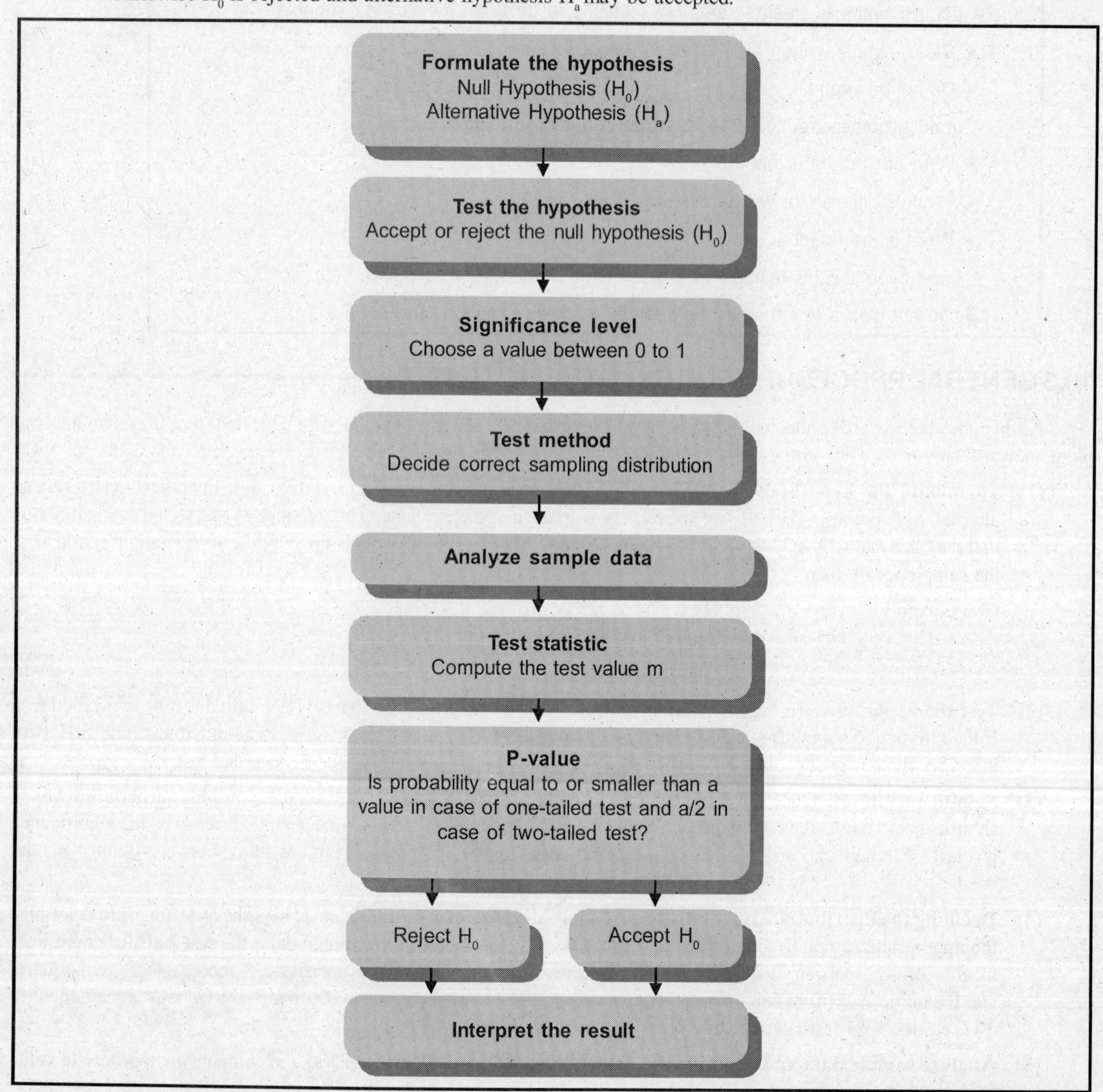

Fig. 10.1: Flow Diagram for Hypothesis Testing

10.4 BASIC CONCEPTS OF HYPOTHESIS TESTING

A **statistical hypothesis** is an assumption about a population parameter. This assumption may or may not be true. The best way to determine whether a statistical hypothesis is true would be to examine the entire population. Since that is often impractical, researchers typically examine a random sample from the population. If sample data are not consistent with the statistical hypothesis, the hypothesis is rejected.

A. Null Hypothesis and Alternative Hypothesis

The **null hypothesis,** denoted by H_0, is usually the hypothesis that sample observations result purely from chance. The hypothesis testing requires that the null hypothesis be considered true until it is proved false on the basis of results observed from the sample data. The null hypothesis is always expressed in the form of mathematical statement which includes the sign ($\leq$, =, $\geq$) making a claim regarding the specific value of the population parameter. That is:

$$H_0: \mu\ (\leq, =, \geq)\ \mu_0$$

where μ is population mean and μ_0 represents the hypothesized value of μ.

The **alternative hypothesis,** denoted by H_a or H_1 is the hypothesis that sample observations are influenced by some non-random cause. An alternative hypothesis must be true when the null hypothesis is found to be false. In other words, the alternative hypothesis states that specific population parameter value is not equal to the value stated in the null hypothesis and written as:

$$H_a: \mu \neq \mu_0$$

Consequently $H_a: \mu < \mu_0$ or $H_a: \mu > \mu_0$

Null Hypothesis and Alternative Hypothesis

Null Hypothesis	Alternative Hypothesis
$H_0: \mu = \mu_0$	$H_a: \mu \neq \mu_0$
$H_0: \mu \leq \mu_0$	$H_a: \mu > \mu_0$
$H_0: \mu \geq \mu_0$	$H_a: \mu < \mu_0$

Hypothesis	Name of the Hypothesis
$\mu = \mu_0$	Simple or Specific Hypothesis
$\mu \neq \mu_0$	Composite or Non-specific Hypothesis
$\mu > \mu_0$	
$\mu < \mu_0$	

B. Level of Significance (α)

The level of significance usually denoted as α (alpha), is a statistical term that tells how sure you are that a difference or relationship exists, so that the results obtained should not influence the choice of the decision makers. It is specified in terms of the probability of null hypothesis H_0 being wrong. In other words, the level of significance defines the likelihood of rejecting a null hypothesis when it is true, i.e., it is the risk a decision-maker takes of rejecting the null hypothesis when it is really true.

Steps in Testing for Statistical Significance

(1) State the Research Hypothesis.

(2) State the Null Hypothesis.

(3) Select a probability of error level (alpha level).

(4) Select and compute the test for statistical significance.

(5) Interpret the results.

Table 10.3: Procedure Used to Test for Significance

Statistic is higher than the critical value	Statistic is lower than the critical value
1. Your finding is significant.	1. Your finding is not significant.
2. You reject the null hypothesis.	2. You fail to reject the null hypothesis.
3. The probability is small that the difference or relationship happened by chance, and p is less than the critical alpha level (p < alpha).	3. The probability is high that the difference or relationship happened by chance, and p is greater than the critical alpha level (p > alpha).

C. Acceptance and Rejection Region

All possible values under the sampling distribution curve of the test-statistic is divided into two mutually exclusive regions. These regions are called the acceptance region and the rejection (critical) region.

The **acceptance region** is a range of values of the sample statistic spread around the null hypothesized population parameter. If value of the sample statistic fall within the limits of acceptance region, the null hypothesis is accepted, otherwise it is rejected.

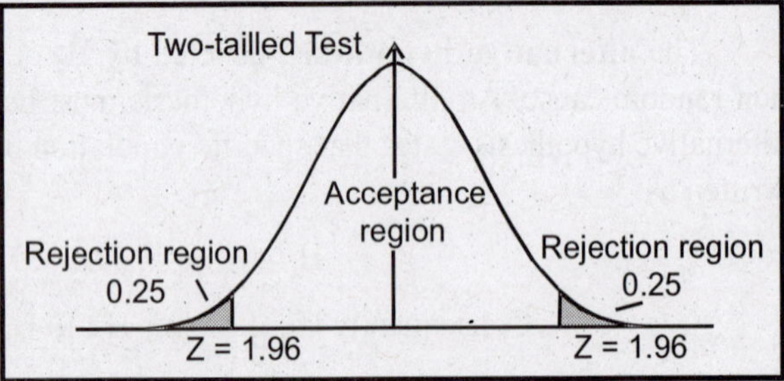

The **rejection region** is the range of sample statistic values within which if values of the sample statistics falls (i.e., outside the limits of the acceptance region), then null hypothesis is rejected.

The value of the sample statistic that separates the regions of acceptance and rejection is called **critical value.**

The size of the rejection region is directly related to the level of precision to make decisions about a population parameter. Decision rules concerning null hypothesis are as follows:

- If prob (H_0 is true) $\leq \alpha$, then reject H_0
- If prob (H_0 is true) $> \alpha$, then accept H_0

D. Test Statistics

The test of significance or test statistics are classified into two categories: (1) Parametric test and (2) Non-parametric test. Parametric tests are more powerful because their data are derived from interval and ratio measurements. Non-parametric tests are used to test hypotheses nominal and ordinal data.

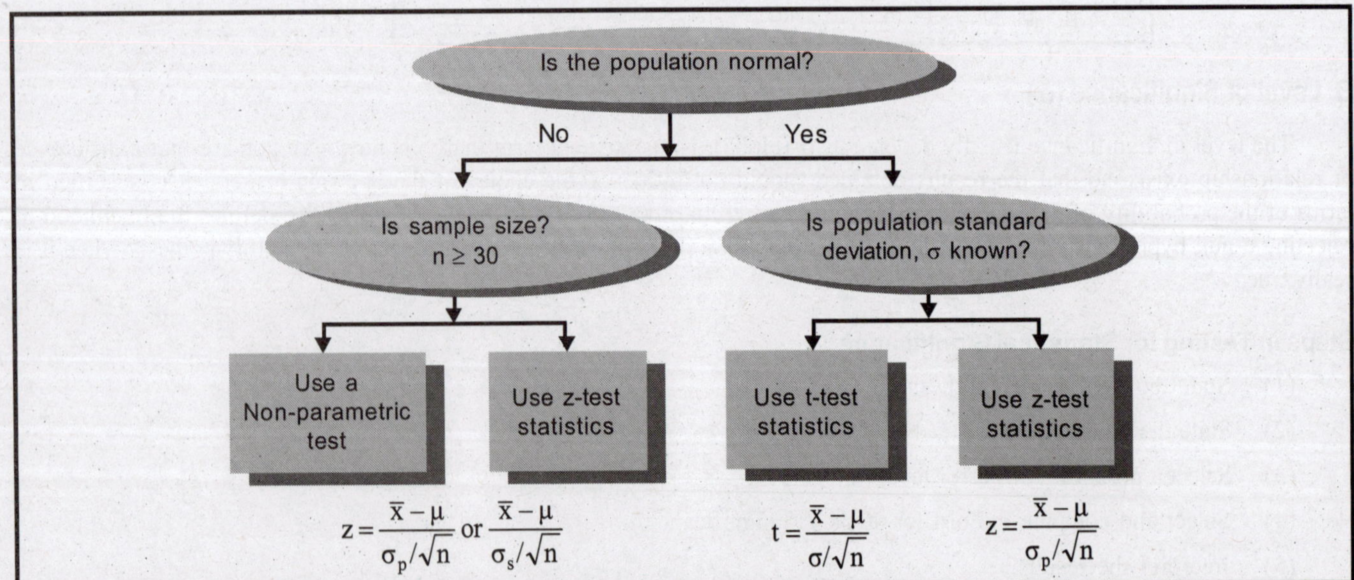

Choice of the Test Statistics

E. Decision Errors – Type One Error and Type Two Error

Two types of errors can result from a hypothesis test.

- **Type I error:** A Type I error occurs when the researcher rejects a null hypothesis when it is true. The probability of committing a Type I error is called the **significance level**. This probability is also called **alpha**, and is often denoted by α.
- **Type II error:** A Type II error occurs when the researcher fails to reject a null hypothesis that is false. The probability of committing a Type II error is called **Beta**, and is often denoted by β. The probability of *not* committing a Type II error is called the **Power** of the test.

Table 10.4: Errors in Hypothesis Testing

Decision	States of Nature	
	Null Hypothesis (H_0) is true	Alternative Hypothesis (H_a) is true
Accept Null Hypothesis	Right decision	Wrong decision Type II Error (β)
Reject Null Hypothesis	Wrong decision Type I Error (α)	Right decision

F. One-tailed and Two-tailed Tests

One-tailed Test: A test of a statistical hypothesis, where the region of rejection is on only one side of the sampling distribution, is called a **one-tailed test.** For example, suppose the null hypothesis states that the mean is less than or equal to 10. The alternative hypothesis would be that the mean is greater than 10. The region of rejection would consist of a range of numbers located on the right side of sampling distribution; that is, a set of numbers greater than 10.

H_0: $\mu \leq$ 10 and H_a: $\mu > 10$ (Right-tailed test)

or H_0: $\mu \geq$ 10 and H_a: $\mu < 10$ (Left-tailed test)

Two-tailed Test: A test of a statistical hypothesis, where the region of rejection is on both sides of the sampling distribution, is called a **two-tailed test.** For example, suppose the null hypothesis states that the mean is equal to 10. The alternative hypothesis would be that the mean is less than 10 or greater than 10. The region of rejection would consist of a range of numbers located on both sides of sampling distribution; that is, the region of rejection would consist partly of numbers that were less than 10 and partly of numbers that were greater than 10.

H_0: $\mu = 10$ and H_a: $\mu \neq 10$ (Two tailed test)

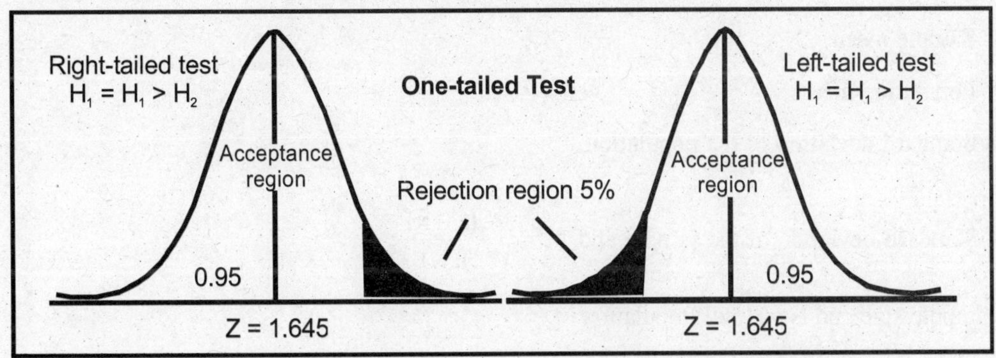

Table 10.5: One-tailed and Two-tailed Table

Set	Null Hypothesis	Alternative Hypothesis	Number of Tails
1	$\mu = \mu_0$	$\mu \neq \mu_0$	Two
2	$\mu \geq \mu_0$	$\mu < \mu_0$	One
3	$\mu \leq \mu_0$	$\mu > \mu_0$	One

Table 10.6: Critical Values for Sample Statistic z

Rejection	Level of Significance, α per cent			
Region	$\alpha = 0.10$	$\alpha = 0.05$	$\alpha = 0.01$	$\alpha = 0.005$
One-tailed region	± 1.28	± 1.64	± 2.33	± 2.58
Two-tailed region	± 1.64	± 1.96	± 2.58	± 2.81

10.5 HYPOTHESIS TESTING WITH LARGE SAMPLE (N > 30)

10.5.1 Hypothesis Testing for Single Population Mean

Case 1: *If standard deviation σ of the population is known, population is normal and infinite, then the z-test is given by:*

$$z = \frac{\bar{x} - \mu}{\sigma_p/\sqrt{n}}$$

Case 2: *If standard deviation of the population is not known, population is normal and infinite, then the z-test is given by:*

$$z = \frac{\bar{x} - \mu}{\sigma_s/\sqrt{n}}$$

Case 3: *If standard deviation σ of the population is known, population is normal and finite, then the z-test is given by:*

$$z = \frac{\bar{x} - \mu}{\sigma_p/\sqrt{n}} \times \frac{1}{\sqrt{(N-n)/(N-1)}}$$

where, $\bar{x}$ = Sample mean

μ = Population mean

σ_p = Standard deviation of the population

σ_s = Standard deviation of the sample and $\sigma_s = \sqrt{\frac{\Sigma(x-\bar{x})^2}{n-1}}$

n = Sample size and N = Total Population

Decision Rules:

Table 10.7: Decision Rule

Two-tailed Test	One-tailed and Left-tailed Test	One-tailed and Right-tailed Test
$H_0: \mu = \mu_0$ and $H_a: \mu \neq \mu_0$ (Two-tailed test)	$H_0: \mu \geq \mu_0$ and $H_a: \mu < \mu_0$ (Two-tailed test)	$H_0: \mu \leq \mu_0$ and $H_a: \mu > \mu_0$ (Two-tailed test)
Accept H_0, if $\lvert z_{Calculation}\rvert \leq \lvert z_{Critical}\rvert$ Or Accept H_0, if $-z_{\alpha/2} < z_{cal} < z_{\alpha/2}$ (Table value of z at $\alpha/2$)	Accept H_0, if $\lvert z_{Calculation}\rvert \leq \lvert z_{Critical}\rvert$ Or Accept H_0, if $z_{cal} > -z_{\alpha}$ (Table value of z at α)	Accept H_0, if $\lvert z_{Calculation}\rvert \leq \lvert z_{Critical}\rvert$ Or Accept H_0, if $z_{cal} < z_{\alpha}$ (Table value of z at α)
Reject H_0, if $\lvert z_{Calculation}\rvert \geq \lvert z_{Critical}\rvert$ Or Reject H_0, if $z_{cal} \leq -z_{\alpha/2}$ or $z_{cal} \leq z_{\alpha/2}$ (Table value of z at $\alpha/2$)	Reject H_0, if $\lvert z_{Calculation}\rvert \geq \lvert z_{Critical}\rvert$ Or Reject H_0, if $z_{cal} \leq -z_{\alpha}$ (Table value of z at α)	Reject H_0, if $\lvert z_{Calculation}\rvert \geq \lvert z_{Critical}\rvert$ Or Rejectt H_0, if $z_{cal} \leq z_{\alpha}$ (Table value of z at α)

Example 10.1:

A sample of 100 members is found to have a mean of 5 cm. Can it be reasonably regarded as a simple sample from a large population with mean 4 cm and standard deviation 3 cm? Test at 5% level of significance.

Solution:

1. **Formulate the hypotheses.** The first step is to state the null hypothesis and an alternative hypothesis.

   Null hypothesis: H_0: $\mu = 4$ cm

   Alternative hypothesis: H_a: $\mu \neq 4$ cm (Two-tailed test)

2. **Formulate an analysis plan.** For this analysis, $\bar{x} = 5$ cm., $\sigma_P = 3$ cm, n = 100 and the significance level is, $\alpha = 5\%$. The test method is a one-sample z-test because sample size, n > 30.

3. **Analyze sample data.** Assuming the population to be normal and test statistic z is:

$$z = \frac{\bar{x} - \mu}{\sigma_p/\sqrt{n}} = \frac{5-4}{3/\sqrt{100}} = \frac{1}{0.3} = 3.33$$

   Since H_a is two-sided and the rejection regions at 5% level of significance which comes to as under, normal curve area table: Then the critical value is:

   The critical value, $|z_{\alpha/2}| = \pm 1.96$

4. **Interpret results.** Since the calculated value of z is 3.33 which is greater than the critical values, i.e., 1.96. Hence, the null hypothesis H_0 is rejected.

Example 10.2:

Mrs. Bijayalaxmi, an agent of LIC, has claimed that the average age of policyholders who insured through her is less than the average for all agents, which is 32 years. A sample of 100 policyholders who has insured through her gave an average

age of 30 years. Assumes a standard error of 5 years do you think that her claim is justifiable? Use at 5% level of significance to test the claim?

Solution:

1. **Formulate the hypotheses.**

   Null hypothesis: H_0: $\mu = 32$ years

   Alternative hypothesis: H_a: $\mu < 32$ years (One-tailed Left-tailed test)

2. **Formulate an analysis plan.** For this analysis, $\bar{x} = 30$ years, $\sigma_p/\sqrt{n} = 5$ years, and the significance level is, $\alpha = 5\%$. The test method is a one-sample z-test because sample size, $n > 30$.

3. **Analyze sample data.** Assuming the population to be normal and test statistic z is:

$$z = \frac{\bar{x} - \mu}{\sigma_p/\sqrt{n}} = \frac{30 - 32}{5} = -0.4$$

   Since H_a is one-sided and the rejection regions at 5% level of significance which comes to as under, normal curve area table. Then the critical value is:

   The critical value, $|z_\alpha| = \pm 1.64$

4. **Interpret results.** Since the calculated value of z is –0.4, this is more than the critical value, i.e., –1.64. Hence the null hypothesis H_0 is accepted. The alternative hypothesis H_a: $\mu < 32$ years. We conclude that the claim made by the insurance agent is not justifiable.

Example 10.3:

MRF Company finds that tyre life in normally distributed with a mean of 40,000 kms and standard deviation of 3,000 kms. It is behind that a change in the production process with result in a better product and the MRF has develops a new tyre. A sample of 64 new tyres has been selected. MRF has from that the mean life of these new tyres is 41,000 kms. Can it be concluded that the new tyres is significantly better than the old one?

Solution:

1. **Formulate the hypotheses.**

   Null hypothesis: H_0: $\mu = 40{,}000$ kms

   Alternative hypothesis: H_a: $\mu > 40{,}000$ kms (One-tailed Right-tailed test)

2. **Formulate an analysis plan.** For this analysis, $\bar{x} = 41{,}000$ kms, $\sigma_p = 3000$ kms, $n = 64$ and the significance level is, $\alpha = 5\%$. The test method is a one-sample z-test because sample size, $n > 30$.

3. **Analyze sample data.** Assuming the population to be normal and test statistic z is:

$$z = \frac{\bar{x} - \mu}{\sigma_p/\sqrt{n}} = \frac{41000 - 40000}{3000/\sqrt{64}} = \frac{1000}{375} = 2.67$$

   Since H_a is one-sided and the rejection regions at 5% level of significance which comes to as under, normal curve area table. Then the critical value is:

   The critical value, $|z_\alpha| = \pm 1.64$

4. **Interpret results.** Since the calculated value of z is 2.67, this is more than the critical value, i.e., 1.64. Hence, the null hypothesis H_0 is rejected. The alternative hypothesis H_a is that $\mu > 40{,}000$ kms is accepted. We conclude that the new tyre is significantly better than the old one.

Example 10.4:

An inventor has developed a new, energy-efficient lawn mower engine. He claims that the engine will run continuously for 5 hours (300 minutes) on a single gallon of regular gasoline. Suppose a simple random sample of 50 engines is tested. The engines run for an average of 295 minutes, with a standard deviation of 20 minutes. Test the null hypothesis that the mean run-time is 300 minutes against the alternative hypothesis that the mean run-time is not 300 minutes. Use a 0.05 level of significance. (Assume that run-times for the population of engines are normally distributed.)

Solution:

1. **Formulate the hypotheses.**

   Null hypothesis: H_0: $\mu = 300$

   Alternative hypothesis: H_a: $\mu \neq 300$ (Two-tailed test)

2. **Formulate an analysis plan.** For this analysis, $\overline{x} = 295$ min, $\sigma_p = 20$ min., n = 50 and the significance level is, $\alpha = 5\%$. The test method is a one-sample z-test because sample size, n > 30.

3. **Analyze sample data.** Assuming the population to be normal and test statistic z is:

$$z = \frac{\overline{x} - \mu}{\sigma_p / \sqrt{n}} = \frac{295 - 300}{20/\sqrt{50}} = \frac{-5}{2.828} = -1.768$$

   Since H_a is two-sided and the rejection regions at 5% level of significance which comes to as under, normal curve area table. Then the critical value is:

   The critical value, $|z_{\alpha/2}| = \pm 1.96$

4. **Interpret results.** Since the calculated value of z is –1.768, this is more than the critical value, i.e., –1.96 (or $-z_{x/2} = -1.96 < z_{cal} = -1.768$). Hence, the null hypothesis H_0 is accepted.

Example 10.5:

An ambulance service claims that it takes on the average 7.5 minutes to reach its destination in emergency calls. To check on this claim, the agency which licenses ambulance services has then timed on 32 emergency calls, getting a mean of 8.1 minutes with standard deviation of 1.5 minutes. Does this constitute evidence that the figure claimed is too low at the 1 per cent significance level?

Solution:

1. **Formulate the hypotheses.**

   Null hypothesis: H_0: $\mu = 7.5$ minutes

   Alternative hypothesis: H_a: $\mu \neq 7.5$ minutes (Two-tailed test)

2. **Formulate an analysis plan.** For this analysis, $\overline{x} = 8.1$ minutes, $\sigma_s = 1.5$ minutes, n = 32 and the significance level is, $\alpha = 1\%$. The test method is a one-sample z-test because sample size, n > 30.

3. **Analyze sample data.** Assuming the population to be normal and test statistic z is:

$$z = \frac{\overline{x} - \mu}{\sigma_s / \sqrt{n}} = \frac{8.1 - 7.5}{1.5/\sqrt{32}} = \frac{0.6}{0.26} = 2.26$$

   Since H_a is two-sided and the rejection regions at 1% level of significance which comes to as under, normal curve area table. Then the critical value is:

   The critical value, $|z_{\alpha/2}| = \pm 2.58$

4. **Interpret results.** Since the calculated value of z is 2.26, this is less than the critical value, i.e., 2.58. Hence, the null hypothesis H_0 is accepted. Hence, we conclude that, there is no difference between the average time observed and claim.

Example 10.6:

The mean lifetime of a sample of 200 light bulbs produced by a company is found to be 1000 hours with a standard deviation of 100 hours. Test the hypothesis that the mean lifetime of the bulbs produced in general is higher than the mean life of 970 hours at $\alpha = 0.01$ level of significance.

Solution:

1. **Formulate the hypotheses.**

   Null hypothesis: H_0: $\mu < 970$ hours

   Alternative hypothesis: H_a: $\mu > 970$ hours (One-tailed Right-tailed test)

2. **Formulate an analysis plan.** For this analysis, $\overline{x} = 1{,}000$ hours, $\sigma_s = 100$ hours, n = 200 and the significance level is, $\alpha = 1\%$. The test method is a one-sample z-test because sample size, $n > 30$.

3. **Analyze sample data.** Assuming the population to be normal and test statistic z is:

$$z = \frac{\overline{x} - \mu}{\sigma_s / \sqrt{n}} = \frac{1000 - 970}{100/\sqrt{200}} = \frac{30}{7.07} = 4.24$$

   Since H_a is one-sided and the rejection regions at 1% level of significance which comes to as under, normal curve area table. Then the critical value is:

   The critical value, $|z_\alpha| = \pm 2.33$

4. **Interpret results.** Since the calculated value of z is 4.24, this is more than the critical value, i.e., 2.33. Hence, the null hypothesis H_0 is rejected. The alternative hypothesis H_a is that $\mu > 970$ hours is accepted. Hence, we conclude that the mean lifetime of bulbs produced by the company may be higher than 970 hours.

Example 10.7:

In a population of 25 units of equal size under Steel Industries, which are experiencing labour turnover problems. The past records show that the mean of the distribution of annual turnover is 350 employees, with a standard deviation of 70 employees. A sample of 10 of these units is taken at random which gives a mean of annual turnover as 320 employees. Is the sample mean consistent with the population mean? Test at 1% level.

Solution:

1. **Formulate the hypotheses.**

   Null hypothesis: H_0: $\mu = 350$ employees

   Alternative hypothesis: H_a: $\mu \neq 350$ employees (Two-tailed test)

2. **Formulate an analysis plan.** For this analysis, $\overline{x} = 320$ employees, $\sigma_s = 70$ employees, n = 10, N = 25 and the significance level is, $\alpha = 1\%$. The test method is a one-sample z-test because sample size, $n > 30$.

3. **Analyze sample data.** Assuming the population to be normal and test statistic z is:

$$z = \frac{\overline{x} - \mu}{\sigma_p / \sqrt{n}} \times \frac{1}{\sqrt{(N-n)/(N-1)}}$$

$$= \frac{320 - 350}{\frac{70}{\sqrt{10}}} \times \frac{1}{\sqrt{(25-10)/(25-1)}}$$

$$= \frac{-30}{15.87} = -1.89$$

Since H_a is two-sided and the rejection regions at 1% level of significance which comes to as under, normal curve area table. Then the critical value is:

The critical value, $|z_{\alpha/2}| = \pm 2.58$

4. **Interpret results.** Since the calculated value of z is –1.89, this is more than the critical value, i.e., –2.58 (or $-z_{\alpha/2} = -2.58 < z_{cal} = -1.89$). Hence, the null hypothesis H_0 is accepted. Hence, we conclude that, the sample mean is consistent with population mean, i.e., the population mean 350 is supported by the sample results.

10.5.2 Hypothesis Testing for Difference between Two Population Mean

If we have two independent populations each having its mean and standard deviation as:

Population	Mean	Standard Deviation (σ)
1	μ_1	σ_1
2	μ_2	σ_2

then the hypothesis testing concepts, whether there is any significant difference between the means of these populations. Suppose the large sample size n_1 and n_2 be drawn from the first and second population respectively. Let the sample means be $\bar{x}_1$ and $\bar{x}_2$. The z-test statistics used to determine the difference between the population mean $(\mu_1 - \mu_2)$ is based on the difference between the sample mean $(\bar{x}_1 - \bar{x}_2)$.

Case 1: *If standard deviation of the populations is known, and when two samples are drawn from the different population, then the z-test is given by:*

$$z = \frac{(\bar{x}_1 - \bar{x}_2)}{\sqrt{\dfrac{\sigma_{p_1}{}^2}{n_1} + \dfrac{\sigma_{p_2}{}^2}{n_2}}}$$

Case 2: *When two samples are drawn from the same population* and if $\sigma_{p_1}{}^2 = \sigma_{p_2}{}^2$, *then z-test is given by:*

$$z = \frac{(\bar{x}_1 - \bar{x}_2)}{\sigma_p\sqrt{\dfrac{1}{n_1} + \dfrac{1}{n_2}}}$$

Case 3: *When two samples are drawn from different populations and if standard deviation* σ_{p_1} *and* σ_{p_2} *of each of the populations is not known, then the z-test is given by:*

$$z = \frac{(\bar{x}_1 - \bar{x}_2)}{\sqrt{\dfrac{\sigma_{s_1}{}^2}{n_1} + \dfrac{\sigma_{s_2}{}^2}{n_2}}}$$

where, $\sigma_{s_1} = \sqrt{\dfrac{\Sigma(x - \bar{x}_1)^2}{n-1}}$ and $\sigma_{s_2} = \sqrt{\dfrac{\Sigma(x - \bar{x}_2)^2}{n-1}}$

Case 4: *When two samples are drawn from the same population and* σ_p *is not known, then z-test is given by:*

$$z = \frac{(\bar{x}_1 - \bar{x}_2)}{\sigma_{s1.2}\sqrt{\dfrac{1}{n_1} + \dfrac{1}{n_2}}}$$

where, $\sigma_{s_{1.2}} = \sqrt{\dfrac{n_1(\sigma_{s_1}{}^2 + D_1{}^2) + n_2(\sigma_{s_2}{}^2 + D_2{}^2)}{n_1 + n_2}}$

and $D_1 = \overline{x}_1 - \overline{x}_{1.2}, D_2 = \overline{x}_2 - \overline{x}_{1.2}, \overline{x}_{1.2} = \dfrac{(n_1\overline{x}_1 + n_2\overline{x}_2)}{n_1 + n_2}$

Example 10.8:

A man buys 100 electric bulbs of "Bajaj" and 100 electric bulbs of "Philips". He finds that "Bajaj" bulbs gave an average life of 1500 hours with standard deviation of 60 hours and "Philips" bulbs gave an average life of 1600 hours with standard deviation 80 hours. Is there a significant difference in the mean life of the two makes of bulls?

Solution:

1. **Formulate the hypotheses.**

   Null hypothesis: H_0: $\mu_1 = \mu_2$

   Alternative hypothesis: H_a: $\mu_1 \neq \mu_2$ (Two-tailed test)

   where, μ_1 and μ_2 = mean of the Bajaj and Philips, respectively.

2. **Formulate an analysis plan.** For this analysis, $\overline{x}_1$ = 1500 hours, σ_{p1} = 60 hours, n_1 = 100 and $\overline{x}_2$ = 1600 hours, σ_{p2} = 80 hours, n_2 = 100, and the significance level is, α = 5%. The test method is a two-sample z-test because sample size, n_1 and n_2 > 30.

3. **Analyze sample data.** Assuming the population to be normal and test statistic z is:

$$z = \frac{(\overline{x}_1 - \overline{x}_2)}{\sqrt{\dfrac{\sigma_{p_1}{}^2}{n_1} + \dfrac{\sigma_{p_2}{}^2}{n_2}}} = \frac{1500 - 1520}{\sqrt{\dfrac{(60)^2}{100} + \dfrac{(80)^2}{100}}} = \frac{-20}{100} = -0.2$$

   Since H_a is two-sided and the rejection regions at 5% level of significance which comes to as under, normal curve area table. Then the critical value is:

   The critical value, $|z_{\alpha/2}| = \pm 1.96$

4. **Interpret results.** Since the calculated value of z is –0.2, this is more than the critical value, i.e., –1.96 (or $-z_{\alpha/2} = -1.96 < z_{cal} = -0.2$). Hence, the null hypothesis H_0 is accepted. Hence, we conclude that mean life of the two makes is almost same, difference is due to sampling error.

Example 10.9:

The means of two random samples of 100 and 200 are 57 inches and 68 inches respectively. Can the samples be regarded to have been drawn from the same population of standard deviation 9 inches? Test at 5% level of significance.

Solution:

1. **Formulate the hypotheses.**

   Null hypothesis: H_0: $\mu_1 = \mu_2$

   Alternative hypothesis: H_a: $\mu_1 \neq \mu_2$ (Two-tailed test)

   where, υ_1 and μ_2 = means of two populations, respectively.

2. **Formulate an analysis plan.** For this analysis, n_1 = 100, $\overline{x}_1$ = 57 inches, n_2 = 200, $\overline{x}_2$ = 68 inches and σ_p = 9 inches, and the significance level is, α = 5%. The test method is a two-sample z-test because sample size, n_1 and n_2> 30.

3. **Analyze sample data.** Assuming the population to be normal and test statistic z is:

$$z = \frac{(\bar{x}_1 - \bar{x}_2)}{\sigma_p \sqrt{\frac{1}{n_1} + \frac{1}{n_2}}} = \frac{57 - 68}{9\sqrt{\frac{1}{100} + \frac{1}{200}}} = \frac{-11}{1.102} = -9.98$$

Since H_a is two-sided and the rejection regions at 5% level of significance which comes to as under, normal curve area table. Then the critical value is:

The critical value, $|z_{\alpha/2}| = \pm 1.96$

4. **Interpret results.** Since the calculated value of z is –9.98, this is less than the critical value, i.e., –1.96 ((or $-z_{\alpha/2} = -1.96 > z_{cal} = -9.98$). Hence, the null hypothesis H_0 is rejected. Hence, we conclude that the difference between means of two samples is statistically not significant.

Example 10.10:

A firm believes that the tyres produced by Process A on an average last longer than tyres produced by Process B. To test this belief, random samples of tyres produced by the two processes were tested and the results are:

Process	Sample Size	Average Lifetime (in Km)	Standard Deviation (in Km)
A	50	21,000	800
B	60	20,000	1,000

Is there evidence at 1% level of significance that the firm is correct in its belief?

Solution:

1. **Formulate the hypotheses.**

   Null hypothesis: H_0: $\mu_1 = \mu_2$

   Alternative hypothesis: H_a: $\mu_1 \neq \mu_2$ (Two-tailed test)

   where, α_1 and μ_2 = average life of the tyres produced by process A and B respectively.

2. **Formulate an analysis plan.** For this analysis, n_1 = 50, $\bar{x}_1$ = 20,000 km, σ_{s1} = 800 km, and n_2 = 60, $\bar{x}_2$ = 21,000 km, σ_{s2} = 1000 km, and the significance level is, α = 1%. The test method is a two-sample z-test because sample size, n_1 and $n_2 > 30$.

3. **Analyze sample data.** Assuming the population to be normal and test statistic z is:

$$z = \frac{(\bar{x}_1 - \bar{x}_2)}{\sqrt{\frac{\sigma_{s_1}^2}{n_1} + \frac{\sigma_{s_2}^2}{n_2}}} = \frac{21{,}000 - 20{,}000}{\sqrt{\frac{(800)^2}{50} + \frac{(1{,}000)^2}{60}}} = 5.82$$

Since H_a is two-sided and the rejection regions at 5% level of significance which comes to as under, normal curve area table. Then the critical value is:

The critical value, $|z_{\alpha/2}| = \pm 2.58$

4. **Interpret results.** Since the calculated value of z is 5.82, this is more than the critical value, i.e., 2.58. Hence, the null hypothesis H_0 is rejected. Hence, we conclude that the tyres Produced by process A last longer than Produced by process B.

Example 10.11:

In a sample of 1000, the mean is 17.5 and standard deviation is 2.7. In another sample of 800, the mean is 18 and the standard deviation is 2.5. Assuming that the samples are independent, discuss whether the two samples could have come from populations which have the same standard deviation.

Solution:

1. **Formulate the hypotheses.**

   Null hypothesis: H_0: $\sigma_1 = \sigma_2$

   Alternative hypothesis: H_a: $\sigma_1 \neq \sigma_2$ (Two-tailed test)

   where, the hypothesis that there is no significance difference in the standard deviations of the two samples.

2. **Formulate an analysis plan.** For this analysis, $n_1 = 1000$, $\sigma_1 = 2.7$, and $n_2 = 800$, $\sigma_2 = 2.5$, and the significance level is, $\alpha = 5\%$. The test method is a two-sample z-test because sample size, n_1 and $n_2 > 30$.

3. **Analyze sample data.** Assuming the population to be normal and test statistic z is:

$$z = \frac{(\sigma_1 - \sigma_2)}{\sqrt{\frac{\sigma_1^2}{2n_1} + \frac{\sigma_2^2}{2n_2}}} = \frac{2.7 - 2.5}{\sqrt{\frac{(2.7)^2}{2 \times 1000} + \frac{(2.5)^2}{2 \times 800}}} = \frac{0.2}{0.107} = 1.86$$

   Since H_a is two-sided and the rejection regions at 5% level of significance which comes to as under, normal curve area table. Then the critical value is:

   The critical value, $|z_{\alpha/2}| = \pm 1.96$

4. **Interpret results.** Since the calculated value of z is 1.86, this is less than the critical value, i.e., 1.96. Hence, the null hypothesis H_0 is accepted. Hence, we conclude that the two samples have come from a population which has the same standard deviation.

10.6 HYPOTHESIS TESTING FOR PROPORTION

10.6.1 Hypothesis Testing for Single Population Proportion

The three forms of null hypothesis and alternative hypothesis pertaining to the hypothesized population proportion p are as follows:

Null Hypothesis	Alternative Hypothesis
• H_0: $p = p_0$	• H_1: $p \neq p_0$ (Two-tailed test)
• H_0: $p > p_0$	• H_1: $p < p_0$ (Left-tailed test)
• H_0: $p < p_0$	• H_1: $p > p_0$ (Right-tailed test)

To conduct a test of a hypothesis, it is assumed that the sampling distribution of a proportion follows a standardized normal distribution. Then, using the value of the sample proportion $\overline{p}$ and its standard deviation $\sigma_{\overline{p}}$, we compute the z-test statistic as follows:

$$z = \frac{(\overline{p} - p_0)}{\sigma_{\overline{p}}} = \frac{(\overline{p} - p_0)}{\sqrt{\frac{p_0(1-p_0)}{n}}}$$

where, $\overline{p}$ = the population or sample , $\overline{p} = \frac{\text{Number of successes in the sample}}{\text{Sample size}} = \frac{x}{n}$

p_0 = Population proportion

n = Sample size

Decision Rule

Table 10.8: Decision Rule

Two-tailed Test	One-tailed and Left-tailed Test	One-tailed and Right-tailed Test
H_0: $p = p_0$ and H_a: $p \neq p_0$ (Two-tailed test)	H_0: $p \geq p_0$ and H_a: $p < p_0$ (Two-tailed test)	H_0: $p \leq p_0$ and H_a: $p > p_0$ (Two-tailed test)
Accept H_0, if $\lvert z_{Calculation}\rvert \leq \lvert z_{Critical}\rvert$ Or Accept H_0, if $-z_{\alpha/2} < z_{cal} < z_{\alpha/2}$ (Table value of z at $\alpha/2$)	Accept H_0, if $\lvert z_{Calculation}\rvert \leq \lvert z_{Critical}\rvert$ Or Accept H_0, if $z_{cal} > -z_{\alpha}$ (Table value of z at α)	Accept H_0, if $\lvert z_{Calculation}\rvert \leq \lvert z_{Critical}\rvert$ Or Accept H_0, if $z_{cal} < z_{\alpha}$ (Table value of z at α)
Reject H_0, if $\lvert z_{Calculation}\rvert \geq \lvert z_{Critical}\rvert$ Or Reject H_0, if $z_{\alpha/2} \leq z_{cal} \leq -z_{\alpha/2}$ (Table value of z at $\alpha/2$)	Reject H_0, if $\lvert z_{Calculation}\rvert \geq \lvert z_{Critical}\rvert$ Or Reject H_0, if $z_{cal} \leq -z_{\alpha}$ (Table value of z at α)	Rejectt H_0, if $\lvert z_{Calculation}\rvert \geq \lvert z_{Critical}\rvert$ Or Rejectt H_0, if $z_{cal} \leq z_{\alpha}$ (Table value of z at α)

Example 10.12:

A dice is thrown 49, 152 times and of these 25, 145 yielded either 4, 5, or 6. Is this consistent with the hypothesis that the dice must be unbiased ?

Solution:

1. **Formulate the hypotheses.**
   Null hypothesis: H_0: p = 50%
   Alternative hypothesis: H_a: p = 50% (Two-tailed test)
   where, the hypothesis that the dice is fair, i.e., 50%.
2. **Formulate an analysis plan.** For this analysis, n = 49,152, x = 25,145, p_0 = 0.50 and the significance level is, α = 5%.

   and Sample proportion of success: $\bar{p} = \frac{25 \times 145}{49 \times 152} = 0.512$

   The test method is a two-sample z-test because sample size, n > 30.
3. **Analyze sample data.** Assuming the population to be normal and test statistic z is:

$$z = \frac{(\bar{p} - p_0)}{\sqrt{\frac{p_0(1-p_0)}{n}}} = \frac{(0.512 - 0.50)}{\sqrt{\frac{0.50(1-0.50)}{49 \times 152}}} = \frac{0.012}{0.002} = 6.0$$

Since H_a is two-sided and the rejection regions at 5% level of significance which comes to as under, normal curve area table. Then the critical value is:

The critical value, $\lvert z_{\alpha/2}\rvert = \pm 1.96$

4. **Interpret results.** Since the calculated value of z is 6.0 which is greater than the critical values, i.e., 1.96. Hence, the null hypothesis H_0 is rejected. We conclude that dice is biased.

Example 10.13:

A company manufacturing a certain type of breakfast cereal claims that 60% of all housewives prefer that type to any other. A random sample of 300 housewives contains 165 who do prefer that type. At 5% level of significance, test the claim of the company.

Solution:

1. **Formulate the hypotheses.**

   Null hypothesis: H_0: p = 60%

   Alternative hypothesis: H_a: p < 60% (One-tailed left-tailed test)

2. **Formulate an analysis plan.** For this analysis, n = 300, x = 165, p0 and the significance level is, α = 5%.

   and Sample proportion of success: $\bar{p} = \frac{165}{300} = 0.55$

   The test method is a two-sample z-test because sample size, n > 30.

3. **Analyze sample data.** Assuming the population to be normal and test statistic z is:

$$z = \frac{(\bar{p} - p_0)}{\sqrt{\frac{p_0(1-p_0)}{n}}} = \frac{(0.55 - 0.60)}{\sqrt{\frac{0.60(1-0.60)}{300}}} = \frac{0.05}{0.028} = -1.77$$

   Since H_a is two-sided and the rejection regions at 5% level of significance which comes to as under, normal curve area table. Then the critical value is:

   The critical value, $|z_\alpha| = \pm 1.64$

4. **Interpret results.** Since the calculated value of z is –1.77 which is more than the critical values, i.e., –1.64. Hence, the null hypothesis H_0 is rejected. We conclude that percentage prefering the breakfast cereal is lower than 60 per cent.

10.6.2 Hypothesis Testing for Difference between Two Population Proportion

Let two independent populations each having proportion and standard deviation of an attribute be as follows:

Population	Mean	Standard Deviation (σ)	Sample Size
1	p_1	σ_{p1}	n_1
2	p_2	σ_{p2}	n_2

The null hypothesis that there is no difference between two population proportions is stated as:

H_0: $p_1 = p_2$ or H_0: $p_1 - p_2 = 0$ and H_1: $p_1 \neq p_2$

Thus, the z-test statistic for the difference between two population proportion is stated as:

$$z = \frac{(\bar{p}_1 - \bar{p}_2) - (p_1 - p_2)}{\sigma(\bar{p}_1 - \bar{p}_2)} = \frac{(\bar{p}_1 - \bar{p}_2)}{\sigma(\bar{p}_1 - \bar{p}_2)}$$

where, $\bar{p}_1 - \bar{p}_2$ = difference in sample proportion

$p_1 - p_2$ = difference between two population proportion

$\sigma(\bar{p}_1 - \bar{p}_2)$ = The standard deviation of sampling distribution of $p_1 - p_2$, and is given by

$$\sigma(\bar{p}_1 - \bar{p}_2) = \sqrt{\frac{p_1(1-p_1)}{n_1} + \frac{p_2(1-p_2)}{n_2}}$$

where, $q_1 = (1 - p_1)$ and $q_2 = (1 - p_2)$

If the standard error $\sigma(\bar{p}_1 - \bar{p}_2)$ of difference between sample proportion is not known, then

$$\sigma(\bar{p}_1 - \bar{p}_2) = \sqrt{\bar{p}(1-\bar{p})\left(\frac{1}{n_1} + \frac{1}{n_2}\right)}$$

where, $\bar{p} = \dfrac{(n_1\bar{p}_1 + n_2\bar{p}_2)}{n_1 + n_2}$

Example 10.14:

In a random sample of 1000 persons from Odisha 510 were found to be consumers of cigarettes. In another sample of 800 persons from UP, 480 were found to be consumers of cigarettes. Do the data reveal a significant difference between Odisha and UP so far as the proportion of consumers of cigarettes in concerned. Test the 1% level of significance.

Solution:

1. **Formulate the hypotheses.**

   Null hypothesis: H_0: $p_1 = p_2$

   Alternative hypothesis: H_a: $p_1 \neq p_2$ (Two-tailed test)

2. **Formulate an analysis plan.** For this analysis, n_1 = 1000, $\bar{p}_1$ = 510/1000 = 0.51, and n_2 = 800, $\bar{p}_2$ = 480/800 = 0.60 and the significance level is, α = 1%.

   and $\bar{p} = \dfrac{(n_1\bar{p}_1 + n_2\bar{p}_2)}{n_1 + n_2} = \dfrac{1000 \times 0.51 + 800 \times 0.60}{1000 + 800} = 0.55$

   The test method is a two-sample z-test because sample size, n_1 and $n_2 > 30$.

3. **Analyze sample data.** Assuming the population to be normal and test statistic z is:

   $$z = \frac{(\bar{p}_1 - \bar{p}_2)}{\sigma(\bar{p}_1 - \bar{p}_2)} = \frac{0.51 - 0.60}{0.024} = -3.75$$

   where, $\sigma(\bar{p}_1 - \bar{p}_2) = \sqrt{\bar{p}(1-\bar{p})\left(\frac{1}{n_1} + \frac{1}{n_2}\right)} = \sqrt{0.55(1-0.55)\left(\frac{1}{1000} + \frac{1}{800}\right)} = 0.024$

   Since H_a is two-sided and the rejection regions at 1% level of significance which comes to as under, normal curve area table. Then the critical value is:

   The critical value, $|z_{\alpha/2}| = \pm 2.58$

4. **Interpret results.** Since the calculated value of z is –3.75 which is more than the critical values, i.e., –2.58. Hence, the null hypothesis H_0 is rejected. We conclude that the proportion of consumers of cigarette in the two states is significant.

Example 10.15:

A machine puts out 10 defective units in a sample of 200 units. After the machine is overloaded, it puts out 4 defective units in a sample of 100 units. Has the machine been improved?

Solution:

1. **Formulate the hypotheses.**
   Null hypothesis: H_0: $p_1 < p_2$
   Alternative hypothesis: H_a: $p_1 > p_2$ (One-tailed test)
2. **Formulate an analysis plan.** For this analysis, $n_1 = 200$, $\bar{p}_1 = 10/200 = 0.05$, and $n_2 = 100$, $\bar{p}_2 = 4/100 = 0.04$ and the significance level is, $\alpha = 5\%$.

   $$\text{and } \bar{p} = \frac{(n_1\bar{p}_1 + n_2\bar{p}_2)}{n_1 + n_2} = \frac{200 \times 0.05 + 100 \times 0.04}{200 + 100} = 0.047$$

   The test method is a two-sample z-test because sample size, n_1 and $n_2 > 30$.
3. **Analyze sample data.** Assuming the population to be normal and test statistic z is:

   $$z = \frac{(\bar{p}_1 - \bar{p}_2)}{\sigma_{(\bar{p}_1 - \bar{p}_2)}} = \frac{0.05 - 0.04}{0.026} = 0.385$$

   $$\text{where, } \sigma_{(\bar{p}_1 - \bar{p}_2)} = \sqrt{\bar{p}(1-\bar{p})\left(\frac{1}{n_1} + \frac{1}{n_2}\right)} = \sqrt{0.047(1-0.047)\left(\frac{1}{200} + \frac{1}{100}\right)} = 0.026$$

   Since H_a is two-sided and the rejection regions at 5% level of significance which comes to as under, normal curve area table. Then the critical value is:

   The critical value, $|z_{\alpha/2}| = \pm 1.64$
4. **Interpret results.** Since the calculated value of z is 0.385 which is less than the critical values, i.e., 1.64. Hence, the null hypothesis H_0 is accepted. We conclude that the machine been improved.

10.7 HYPOTHESIS TESTING WITH SMALL SAMPLE (N ≤ 30)

10.5.1 Hypothesis Testing for Single Population Mean

Case 1. *If standard deviation of the population is known, population is normal and infinite, then the t-test is given by*

$$t = \frac{(\bar{x} - \mu)}{\sigma_s/\sqrt{n}}, \text{ with df} = (n-1)$$

Case 2. *If standard deviation of the population is not known, population is normal and finite, then the t-test is given by*

$$t = \frac{(\bar{x} - \mu)}{\sigma_s/\sqrt{n}} \times \frac{1}{\sqrt{(N-n)/(N-1)}}, \text{ with df} = (n-1)$$

where $\bar{x}$ = Sample mean

μ = Population mean

σ_s = Standard deviation of the sample and $\sigma_s = \sqrt{\frac{\Sigma(x - \bar{x})^2}{n-1}}$

n = Sample size and N = Total population

Decision Rule

Table 10.9: Decision Rule

Two-tailed Test	One-tailed and Left-tailed Test	One-tailed and Right-tailed Test
H_0: $\mu = \mu_0$ and H_a: $\mu \neq \mu_0$ (Two-tailed test)	H_0: $\mu \geq \mu_0$ and H_a: $\mu < \mu_0$ (Two-tailed test)	H_0: $\mu \leq \mu_0$ and H_a: $\mu > \mu_0$ (Two-tailed test)
Accept H_0, if $\lvert t_{Calculation}\rvert \leq \lvert t_{Critical}\rvert$ Or Accept H_0, if $-t_{\alpha/2} < t_{cal} < t_{\alpha/2}$ (Table value of t at $\alpha/2$)	Accept H_0, if $\lvert t_{Calculation}\rvert \leq \lvert t_{Critical}\rvert$ Or Accept H_0, if $t_{cal} > -t_{\alpha}$ (Table value of t at α)	Accept H_0, if $\lvert t_{Calculation}\rvert \leq \lvert t_{Critical}\rvert$ Or Accept H_0, if $t_{cal} < t_{\alpha}$ (Table value of t at α)
Reject H_0, if $\lvert t_{Calculation}\rvert \geq \lvert t_{Critical}\rvert$ Or Reject H_0, if $t_{\alpha 2} \leq t_{cal} \leq -t_{\alpha/2}$ (Table value of t at $\alpha/2$)	Reject H_0, if $\lvert t_{Calculation}\rvert \geq \lvert t_{Critical}\rvert$ Or Reject H_0, if $t_{cal} \leq -t_{\alpha}$ (Table value of t at α)	Rejectt H_0, if $\lvert t_{Calculation}\rvert \geq \lvert t_{Critical}\rvert$ Or Rejectt H_0, if $t_{cal} \leq t_{\alpha}$ (Table value of t at α)

Example 10.16:

The average breaking strength of steel rods is 16 thousand kg. For this, sample of 20 rods was tested. The mean and standard deviation obtained were 15 and 2 respectively. Test the significance of the deviation.

Solution:

1. **Formulate the hypotheses.**

   Null hypothesis: H_0: μ = 16 thousand kg

   Alternative hypothesis: H_a: $\mu \neq$ 16 thousand kg (Two-tailed test)

2. **Formulate an analysis plan.** For this analysis, $\bar{x} = 15$, $\sigma_s = 2$, $n = 20$, $df = (20 - 1) = 19$ and the significance level is, $\alpha = 5\%$. The test method is a one-sample *t*-test because sample size, $n < 30$.

3. **Analyze sample data.** Assuming the population to be normal and test statistic *t* is:

$$t = \frac{x - \mu}{\sigma_s/\sqrt{n}} = \frac{15 - 16}{2/\sqrt{20}} = \frac{-1}{0.047} = -2.23$$

   Since H_a is two-sided and the rejection regions at 5% level of significance which comes to as under, normal curve area table. Then the critical value is:

   The critical value, $\lvert t_{\alpha/2}\rvert = \pm 2.16$

4. **Interpret results.** Since the calculated value of *t* is –2.23 this is greater than the critical values, i.e., –2.16. Hence, the null hypothesis H_0 is accepted. We conclude that there is no significant deviation of sample mean.

Example 10.17:

A college named RCM, has 300 students. The Director of RCM thinks that, the average IQ of students at RCM is at least 110. To prove her point, she administers an IQ test to 20 randomly selected students. Among the sampled students, the average IQ is 108 with a standard deviation of 10. Based on these results, should the Director accept or reject her original hypothesis? Assume a significance level of 0.01.

Solution:

1. **Formulate the hypotheses.**

   Null hypothesis: H_0: $\mu \geq 110$

   Alternative hypothesis: H_a: $\mu < 110$ (One-tailed left-tailed test)

2. **Formulate an analysis plan.** For this analysis, $\overline{x} = 108$, $\sigma_s = 10$, n = 20, *df* = (20 – 19) = 19 and the significance level is, α = 1%. The test method is a one-sample *t*-test because sample size, n < 30.

3. **Analyze sample data.** Assuming the population to be normal and test statistic *t* is:

$$t = \frac{\overline{x} - \mu}{\sigma_s/\sqrt{n}} = \frac{108 - 110}{10/\sqrt{20}} = \frac{-2}{2.236} = -0.894$$

   Since H_a is one-sided and the rejection regions at 1% level of significance which comes to as under, normal curve area table. Then the critical value is:

   The critical value, $|t_\alpha| = \pm 2.53$

4. **Interpret results.** Since the calculated value of *t* is –0.894 this is more than the critical values, i.e., –2.53. Hence, the null hypothesis H_0 is accepted. We conclude that director should accept his original hypothesis.

Example 10.18:

Information Company employs a large number of typists in its Head office at Bhubaneswar. It has developed a new training programme for them and claims that it has increased the typing speed by 15 words per minute. A random sample of 9 typists is taken on their speed observed. The company finds that the average increase has been 17 words per minute. The estimated standard deviation is 8 words per minute. Can it be concluded that the company has made a legitimate claim?

Solution:

1. **Formulate the hypotheses.**

   Null hypothesis: H_0: $\mu = 15$

   Alternative hypothesis: H_a: $\mu > 15$ (One-tailed Right-tailed test)

2. **Formulate an analysis plan.** For this analysis, $\overline{x} = 17$, $\sigma_s = 8$, n = 9, *df* = (9 – 1) = 8 and the significance level is, α = 5%. The test method is a one-sample *t*-test because sample size, n < 30.

3. **Analyze sample data.** Assuming the population to be normal and test statistic *t* is:

$$t = \frac{\overline{x} - \mu}{\sigma_s/\sqrt{n}} = \frac{17 - 15}{8/\sqrt{9}} = \frac{2}{2.66} = 0.75$$

   Since H_a is one-sided and the rejection regions at 5% level of significance which comes to as under, normal curve area table. Then the critical value is:

   The critical value, $|t_\alpha| = \pm 1.86$

4. **Interpret results.** Since the calculated value of *t* is 0.75, this is less than the critical values, i.e., 1.86. Hence, the null hypothesis H_0 is accepted. We conclude that the company has made legitimate claim regarding the efficiency of its main training programme.

Example 10.19:

In a population of 20 units of equal size, under Steel Industry which are experiencing labour turnover problems. The past records show that the mean of the distribution of annual turnover is 30 employees, with a standard deviation of 10 employees. A sample of 10 of these units is taken at random which gives a mean of annual turnover as 25 employees. Is the sample mean consistent with the population mean? Test at 5% level.

Solution:

1. **Formulate the hypotheses.**

   Null hypothesis: H_0: $\mu = 30$ employees

   Alternative hypothesis: H_a: $\mu \neq 30$ employees (Two-tailed test)

2. **Formulate an analysis plan.** For this analysis, $\bar{x} = 25$ employees, $\sigma_p = 10$ employees, n = 10, N = 20 and the significance level is, $\alpha = 5\%$. The test method is a one-sample z-test because sample size, $n \leq 30$.

3. **Analyze sample data.** Assuming the population to be normal and test statistic z is:

$$t = \frac{\bar{x}-\mu}{\sigma_s/\sqrt{n}} \times \frac{1}{\sqrt{(N-n)/(N-1)}}$$

$$= \frac{25-30}{\frac{10}{\sqrt{10}}} \times \frac{1}{\sqrt{(20-10)/(20-1)}}$$

$$= \frac{-5}{15.87} = -2.18$$

   Since H_a is two-sided and the rejection regions at 5% level of significance which comes to as under, normal curve area table. Then the critical value is:

   The critical value, $|t_{\alpha/2}| = \pm 2.16$

4. **Interpret results.** Since the calculated value of *t* is –2.18, this is more than the critical value, i.e., –2.16 (or $-t_{\alpha/2} = -2.16 < z_{cal} = -2.18$). Hence the null hypothesis H_0 is accepted. Hence, we conclude that the sample mean is consistent with population mean, i.e., the population mean 30 is supported by the sample results.

10.7.2 Hypothesis Testing for Difference between Two Population Mean

Case 1. *If standard deviation of the population is not known, population is normal and finite, then the t-test is given by*

$$t = \frac{\bar{x}_1 - \bar{x}_2}{\sqrt{\frac{\Sigma(x_1-\bar{x}_1)^2 + \Sigma(x_2-\bar{x}_2)^2}{n_1+n_2-2}}} \times \frac{1}{\sqrt{\frac{1}{n_1}+\frac{1}{n_2}}}$$

with df = $(n_1 + n_2 - 2)$

Or Alternatively,

$$t = \frac{\bar{x}_1 - \bar{x}_2}{\sqrt{\frac{(n_1-1)\sigma_{S_1}^2 + (n_2-1)\sigma_{S_2}^2}{n_1+n_2-2}}} \times \frac{1}{\sqrt{\frac{1}{n_1}+\frac{1}{n_2}}}$$

with df = $(n_1 + n_2 - 2)$ and

$$\sigma_{S_1} = \sqrt{\frac{\Sigma(x_1-\bar{x}_1)^2}{n_1-1}} \text{ and } \sigma_{S_2}\sqrt{\frac{\Sigma(x_2-\bar{x}_2)^2}{n_2-1}}$$

Example 10.20:

In XYZ institute, students were randomly assigned to one of two Math teachers, Mr. Das and Mr. Patra. After the assignment, Mr. Das had 15 students, and Mr. Patra had 12 students. At the end of the year, each class took the same standardized test. Mr. Das's students had an average test score of 78, with a standard deviation of 9; and Mr. Patra's students had an average test score of 85, with a standard deviation of 10. Test the hypothesis that Mr. Das and Mr. Patra are equally effective teachers. Use a 0.10 level of significance.

Solution:

1. **Formulate the hypotheses.**

   Null hypothesis: H_0: $\mu = \mu_2$

   Alternative hypothesis: H_a: $\mu \neq \mu_2$ (Two-tailed test)

2. **Formulate an analysis plan.** For this analysis, $n_1 = 15$, $\bar{x}_1 = 78$, $\sigma_{s1} = 9$, and $n_2 = 12$, $\bar{x}_2 = 85$, $\sigma_{s2} = 10$, $df = (15 + 12 - 2) = 25$, and the significance level is, $\alpha = .10$. The test method is a two-sample *t*-test because sample size, n_1 and $n_2 < 30$.

3. **Analyze sample data.** Assuming the population to be normal and test statistic *t* is:

$$t = \frac{\bar{x}_1 - \bar{x}_2}{\sqrt{\dfrac{(n_1 - 1)\sigma_{s_1}{}^2 + (n_2 - 1)\sigma_{s_2}{}^2}{n_1 + n_2 - 2}}} \times \frac{1}{\sqrt{\dfrac{1}{n_1} + \dfrac{1}{n_2}}}$$

$$= \frac{78 - 85}{\sqrt{\dfrac{(15-1)9 + (12-1)10}{15+12-2}}} \times \frac{1}{\sqrt{\dfrac{1}{15} + \dfrac{1}{12}}}$$

$$= \frac{-10}{\sqrt{9.44}} \times \frac{1}{\sqrt{0.15}} = -8.40$$

   Since H_a is two-sided and the rejection regions at 0.10 level of significance, which comes to as under, normal curve area table. Then the critical value is:

   The critical value, $|t_{\alpha/2}| = \pm 1.708$

4. **Interpret results.** Since the calculated value of *t* is –8.40 this is more than the critical values, i.e., –1.708. Hence, the null hypothesis H_0 is rejected. We conclude that Mr. Das and Mr. Patra are not equally effective teachers.

Example 10.21:

The heat producing capacity of the coal produced by two mines (in million calories per ton) are given below:

Mine 1	5260	5130	5350	5070	5350	5280	5060
Mine 2	4650	4870	6540	6130	6250	5850	6510

Test at 1% level of significance whether the coal produced by two mines have the same average heat producing capacity.

Solution:

1. **Formulate the hypotheses.**

   Null hypothesis: H_0: $\mu_1 = \mu_2$

   Alternative hypothesis: H_a: $\mu_1 \neq \mu_2$ (Two-tailed test)

Table 10.10: Calculation Table

Mine 1 x_1	$(x_1 - \bar{x}_1)$	$(x_1 - \bar{x}_1)^2$	Mine 2 x_2	$(x_2 - \bar{x}_2)$	$(x_2 - \bar{x}_2)^2$
5260	45.72	2090.31	4650	-1178.57	138927.24
5130	-84.28	7103.11	4870	-958.57	918856.44
5350	135.72	18419.91	6540	711.43	506132.64
5070	-144.28	20816.71	6130	301.43	90860.04
5350	135.72	18419.91	6250	421.43	177603.24
5280	65.72	4319.11	5850	21.43	459.24
5060	-154.28	23802.31	6510	681.43	464346.84
Σx_1 = 36500		$\Sigma(x_1 - \bar{x}_1)^2$ = 94971.37	Σx_2 = 40800		$\Sigma(x_2 - \bar{x}_2)^2$ = 2297185.68

$$-x_1 = \frac{\sum x_1}{n_1} = \frac{36500}{7} = 5214.28 \text{ and } -x_2 = \frac{\sum x_1}{n_2} = \frac{40800}{7} = 5828.57$$

$$\sigma_{S_1} = \sqrt{\frac{\sum(x_1 - \bar{x}_1)^2}{n_1 - 1}} = \sqrt{\frac{94971.37}{6}} = \sqrt{15828.56} = 125.81$$

$$\text{and } \sigma_{S_2} = \sqrt{\frac{\sum(x_2 - \bar{x}_2)^2}{n_2 - 1}} = \sqrt{\frac{2297185.68}{6}} = \sqrt{382864.28} = 1839.25$$

2. **Formulate an analysis plan.** For this analysis, $n_1 = 7$, $\bar{x}_1 = 5214.28$, $\sigma_{S_1} = 125.81$, and $n_2 = 7$, $\bar{x}_2 = 5828.57$, $\sigma_{S_2} = 1839.25$, $df = (7 + 7 - 2) = 12$, and the significance level is, $\alpha = 0.01$. The test method is a two-sample *t*-test because sample size, n_1 and $n_2 < 30$.
3. **Analyze sample data.** Assuming the population to be normal and test statistic *t* is:

$$t = \frac{\bar{x}_1 - \bar{x}_2}{\sqrt{\dfrac{(n_1 - 1)\sigma_{S_1}{}^2 + (n_2 - 1)\sigma_{S_2}{}^2}{n_1 + n_2 - 2}}} \times \frac{1}{\sqrt{\dfrac{1}{n_1} + \dfrac{1}{n_2}}}$$

$$= \frac{5214.28 - 5828.57}{\sqrt{\dfrac{(7-1)(125.81)^2 + (7-1)(1839.25)^2}{7+7-2}}} \times \frac{1}{\sqrt{\dfrac{1}{7} + \dfrac{1}{7}}}$$

$$= \frac{-614.29}{\sqrt{\dfrac{94968.93 + 20297043.37}{12}}} \times \frac{1}{\sqrt{0.28}}$$

$$= \frac{-614.29}{\sqrt{1699334.35}} \times \frac{1}{\sqrt{0.28}}$$

$$= \frac{-10}{1303.58} \times \frac{1}{0.529} = -0.014$$

Since H_a is two-sided and the rejection regions at 0.01 level of significance, which comes to as under, normal curve area table. Then the critical value is:

The critical value, $|t_{\alpha/2}| = \pm 3.05$

4. **Interpret results.** Since the calculated value of *t* is –0.014, this is more than the critical values, i.e., –3.05. Hence, the null hypothesis H_0 is rejected. We conclude that the average heat producing capacity of the coal from two mines is different.

10.8 SUMMARY

A hypothesis is an explanation for a phenomenon which can be tested in some way which ideally either proves or disproves the hypothesis. For the duration of testing, the hypothesis is taken to be true, and the goal of the researcher is to rigorously test the terms of the hypothesis. The concept of the hypothesis is a very important part of the **scientific method.** The researcher states a hypothesis to be tested, formulates an analysis plan, analyzes sample data according to the plan, and accepts or rejects the null hypothesis, based on results of the analysis. The test of significance or test statistics are classified into two categories: (1) Parametric test and (2) Non-parametric test. Parametric tests are more powerful because their data are derived from interval and ratio measurements. Non-parametric tests are used to test hypotheses nominal and ordinal data. After deciding the level of significance, hypothesis testing is to determine the appropriate sampling distribution and test statistics. Computed from sample data, the test statistic might be a mean score, proportion, difference between means, difference between proportions, z-score, t-score, chi-square, etc. If sample size (n) more than 30 (i.e., $n > 30$), z-test is applicable and if sample size (n) less than equal to 30 (i.e., $n < 30$), t-test is applicable.

Basic features of Hypothesis are: (1) Is clear and precise, (2) It is capable of being tested, (3) It marks the relationship between variables, (4) It is specific and compact, (5) It is expressed in simple terms, (6) It is consistent, (7) It is amenable to testing and (8) It has empirical evidence.

10.9 KEY TERMS

Hypothesis: A hypothesis is an explanation for a phenomenon which can be tested in some way which ideally either proves or disproves the hypothesis.

Null Hypothesis: The null hypothesis, denoted by H_0, is usually the hypothesis that sample observations result purely from chance. The hypothesis testing requires that the null hypothesis be considered true until it is proved false on the basis of results observed from the sample data.

Alternative Hypothesis: The alternative hypothesis, denoted by H_a or H_1, is the hypothesis that sample observations are influenced by some non-random cause. An alternative hypothesis must be true when the null hypothesis is found to be false.

Level of Significance: The level of significance usually denoted as α (alpha), is a statistical term that tells how sure you are that a difference or relationship exists, so that the results obtained should not influence the choice of the decision makers.

Acceptance Region: The acceptance region is a range of values of the sample statistic spread around the null hypothesized population parameter. If value of the sample statistic fall within the limits of acceptance region, the null hypothesis is accepted, otherwise it is rejected.

Rejection Region: The rejection region is the range of sample statistic values within which if values of the sample statistics falls (i.e., outside the limits of the acceptance region), then null hypothesis is rejected.

Critical Value: The value of the sample statistic that separates the regions of acceptance and rejection is called critical value.

Type I Error: A Type I error occurs when the researcher rejects a null hypothesis when it is true. The probability of committing a Type I error is called the **significance level.** This probability is also called **alpha**, and is often denoted by α.

Type II Error: A Type II error occurs when the researcher fails to reject a null hypothesis that is false. The probability of committing a Type II error is called **Beta**, and is often denoted by β. The probability of *not* committing a Type II error is called the **Power** of the test.

One-tailed Test: A test of a statistical hypothesis, where the region of rejection is on only one side of the sampling distribution, is called a one-tailed test.

Two-tailed Test: A test of a statistical hypothesis, where the region of rejection is on both sides of the sampling distribution, is called a two-tailed test.

10.10 MULTIPLE OBJECTIVE TYPE QUESTIONS

1. Hypothesis must explain the facts that gave rise to the need for explanation.
   (a) True (b) False
2. A good hypothesis provides a reasonable explanation for the unpredicted outcome.
   (a) True (b) False
3. The null hypothesis be consider true until it is proved false on the basis of results observed from the sample data.
   (a) True (b) False
4. The level of significance defines the likelihood of rejecting a null hypothesis when it is true.
   (a) True (b) False
5. A Type I error occurs when the researchers rejects a null hypothesis when it is false.
   (a) True (b) False
6. A Type II error occurs when the researchers rejects a null hypothesis when it is false.
   (b) True (b) False
7. The p-value is the probability of observing a sample statistic as extreme as the test statistic, assuming the null hypothesis is true
   (a) True (b) False
8. The level of significance defines the likelihood of rejecting a null hypothesis when it is true, i.e., it is the risk a decision-maker takes of rejecting the null hypothesis when it is really true.
   (a) True (b) False
9. The acceptance region is a range of values of the population statistic spread around the null hypothesized population parameter.
   (a) True (b) False
10. The rejection region is the range of sample statistic values within which if values of the sample statistics falls (i.e., outside the limits of the acceptance region), then null hypothesis is rejected.
    (a) True (b) False
11. Which of the following factor does not usually affect the width of a confidence interval?
    (a) Sample size (b) Confidence desired
    (c) Variability in the population (d) Population size
12. Which of the following is not a property of the sample mean?
    (a) Unbiased (b) Efficient
    (c) Consistent (d) Standardized
13. Type I error is defined as the probability to:
    (a) Accept the hypothesis when it is true (b) Accept the hypothesis when it is false
    (c) Reject the hypothesis when it is true (d) Reject the hypothesis when it is false

14. If the alternative hypothesis is m1 < m2 , the critical region will be on?
    (a) The left side (b) The right side
    (c) On both side (d) Any of the above
15. Which of the following statements is normally true?
    (a) Acceptance region is more than the critical region
    (b) Acceptance region is less than the critical region
    (c) Acceptance region is equal to the critical region
    (d) There is no relationship between acceptance and critical region
16. Standard error of a sample mean measures the extent to which:
    (a) Sample mean are nearer to the mean (b) Sample means vary from each other
    (c) Sample means are away from the mean (d) All of the above
17. Which one of the following is not a step in conducting a test of significance?
    (a) Set up the null hypothesis (b) Decide the level of significance
    (c) Decide the power of test (d) Decide on the appropriate statistics
18. Which one of the following statements is false?
    (a) α is called Type I error (b) $1 - \alpha$ is called power of the test
    (c) β is called Type II error (d) $1 - \beta$ is called power of the test
19. A sampling distribution is the distribution of a:
    (a) Parameter (b) Mean
    (c) Proportion (d) Statistics
20. The standard deviation of a sample mean is called:
    (a) Sampling error (b) Standard deviation
    (c) Standard error (d) None of the above

Answers to Multiple Objective Type Questions

Questions	1	2	3	4	5	6	7	8	9	10
Answers	T	F	T	T	F	T	T	T	F	T
Questions	11	12	13	14	15	16	17	18	19	20
Answers	c	b	a	a	d	a	c	d	c	d

10.11 CONCEPTUAL QUESTIONS

1. What is a hypothesis? Point out its characteristics.
2. The general procedure of testing hypothesis requires a researcher to adopt several steps. Describe in brief.
3. Discuss the basic concepts of parametric test in testing of hypothesis.
4. Point out the important limitations of testing of hypothesis.
5. Write short notes:
    (a) Null hypothesis
    (b) Alternative hypothesis
    (c) One-tailed and Two-tailed test
    (d) Type one and Type two error

(e) Acceptance and Rejection region

(f) Small sample test

(g) Large sample test

6. A sample of 100 measurements of breaking strength of cotton-threads gave a mean of 7.4 ounces and a S.D. of 1.2 ounces. Find 95% confidence limits for the mean-breaking strength.

7. Mr. Bijay wants to determine the average time to compete a certain job. The past records show that population standard deviation is 10 days. Determine the sample size so that Mr. Bijay may be 95% confident that the sample average remains within +2 days of the average.

8. In a certain city, 480 men out of 800 were found to be smokers. Discuss whether this information supports the view that the majority of men in this city are non-smokers. (Use 95% level of significance for which the critical value of Z is 1.96 given in Standard Normal Area Table)

9. In a sample of 500 T-shirts manufactured by a company, the number of defective T-shirts was found to be 30. The company, however, claimed that only 5% of their product is defective. Test at 5% level of significance whether the claims of the company is tenable.

10. A manufacturer produced flash bulbs in lots of 50,000. The bulbs have a mean flash-intensity of 5,000 lumens, with a standard deviation of 200 lumens. Since the testing is destructive, only 100 bulbs are tested in each lot. 5% risk of rejecting of good bulbs is acceptable.

11. A machine put out 20 imperfect items in a sample of 500. After the machine was overhauled, it put out 5 imperfect items in a batch of 150. Has the machine being improved after overhauling?

12. The mean height of 60 male students who showed above average participation in average athletics was 68.2 inches with a standard deviation of 2.5 inches, while 40 other students which showed no interest in such participation has a mean height of 67.5 inches with a standard deviation of 2.8 inches. Test the hypothesis that male students who participated in college athletics are taller than other male students.

13. A company can claim that the weight of their product is 10 kgs. A sample of 10 items taken from a lot supplied by the company has shown the following weights. 10.2, 9.7, 10.3, 10.0, 9.8, 9.7, 9.6, 9.7, 9.4. Is there any statistical evidence to support the claim of the company about the weight of the item?

14. An IQ Test was administered to 5 persons, before and after they were trained. The points are as follows.

Candidates	I	II	III	IV	V
IQ before training	110	120	123	132	125
IQ after training	120	118	125	136	121

Test whether there is any change in IQ after the training programmes.

15. A soap manufacturing company was distributing a particular brand of soap through a large number of retail shops. Before a heavy advertisement campaign, the mean sales per shop were 140 dozens. After the campaign, a sample of 26 shops was taken and the mean sales figure was found to be 147 dozens with standard deviation. Can you consider the advertisement effective?

16. The average number of articles produced by two machines per day is 300 and 250 with standard deviations 25 and 20 respectively on the basis of records of 25 days production. Can you regard both the machines equally efficient at 1% level of significance?

CHAPTER 11

HYPOTHESIS TESTING: NON-PARAMETRIC TEST

R E S E A R C H M E T H O D O L O G Y

Chapter Outline

Learning Objectives

- *Explain the meaning of Chi-square (χ^2) test and basic concepts in the context of making intelligent decisions.*
- *Discuss the need for Analysis of Variance (ANOVA) in decision making.*
- *Explain the other non-parametric techniques in managerial decisions.*

11.1 CHI-SQUARE (χ^2) TEST/DISTRIBUTION

11.1.1 Meaning of Chi-square (χ^2) Test

A **chi-square test** (also **chi-squared test** or **χ^2 test**) is any statistical hypothesis test in which the sampling distribution of the test statistic is a chi-square distribution when the null hypothesis is true, or any in which this is *asymptotically* true, meaning that the sampling distribution (if the null hypothesis is true) can be made to approximate a chi-square distribution as closely as desired by making the sample size large enough. The Chi-square (χ) test is the most popular non-parametric test/ methods, to test the hypothesis. The symbol χ is the Greek letter "chi". Like other hypothesis testing procedures, the calculated value of χ^2 test statistics is compared with its critical value to know whether the null hypothesis is true.

Generally the *chi-squared statistic* summarizes the discrepancies between the expected number of times each outcome occurs (assuming that the model is true) and the observed number of times each outcome occurs, by summing the squares of the discrepancies, normalized by the expected numbers, over all the categories.

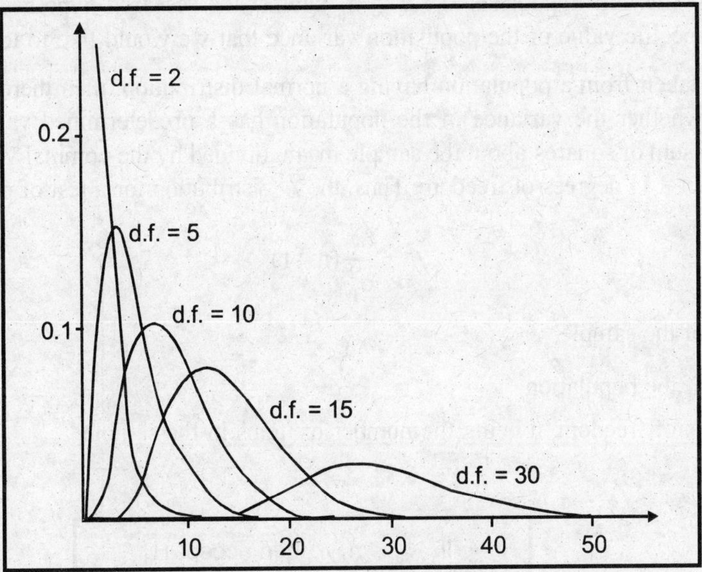

Fig. 11.1: Chi-square (χ^2)

Data used in a chi-square analysis has to satisfy the following conditions:

1. Randomly drawn from the population,
2. Reported in raw counts of frequency,
3. Measured variables must be independent,
4. Observed frequencies cannot be too small, and
5. Values of independent and dependent variables must be mutually exclusive.

11.1.2 Characteristics of the Chi-square Test

1. It is not symmetric.
2. The shape of the chi-square distribution depends upon the degrees of freedom, just like Student's *t*-distribution.
3. As the number of degrees of freedom increases, the chi-square distribution becomes more symmetric as is illustrated in Figure 11.1.
4. The values are non-negative. That is, the values of variables are greater than or equal to 0.

11.2 TYPES OF CHI-SQUARE TEST/DISTRIBUTION

There are three types of chi-square test.

1. **Chi-square test for population variance** which is used to test a hypothesis on a specific value of the population variance.
2. **The Chi-square test for goodness of fit** which compares the expected and observed values to determine how well an experimenter's predictions fit the data.
3. **The Chi-square test for independence** which compares two sets of categories to determine whether the two groups are distributed differently among the categories.

11.2.1 χ^2-test for Population Variance

Chi-square test for population variance is used to test a hypothesis on a specific value of the population variance. Statistically speaking, we test the null hypothesis H_0: $\sigma = \sigma_0$ against the research hypothesis H_1: $\sigma \neq \sigma_0$ where σ is the population mean and σ_0 is a specific value of the population variance that we would like to test for acceptance.

If a sample of size *n* is taken from a population having a normal distribution, then there is a well-known result which allows a test to be made of whether the variance of the population has a predetermined value. The test statistic *t* in this instance could be set to be the sum of squares about the sample mean, divided by the nominal value for the variance then *t* has a chi-square distribution with (n – 1) degrees of freedom. Thus, the χ^2 distribution for a test of population variance is given by:

$$\chi^2 = \frac{\sigma_s^2}{\sigma_p^2}(n-1)$$

where, σ_s^2 = Variance of the sample,

σ_p^2 = Variance of the population

(n – 1) = degrees of freedom, n being the number of items in the sample.

Decision Rule

- If $\chi^2_{cal} < \chi^2_{\alpha/2}$, then accept H_0
- Otherwise reject H_0

Example 11.1:

A random sample of size 25 from a population gives the sample standard deviation of 8.5. Test the hypothesis that the population standard deviation is 10 at 5% level of significance.

Solution:

1. **Formulate the hypotheses:**

   Null hypothesis: H_0: σ_p = 10 (The population standard deviation).

   Alternative hypothesis: H_a: $\sigma_p \neq$ 10.
2. **Formulate an analysis plan:** For the analysis: n = 25, σ_s = 8.5, Degree of freedom = 25 – 1 = 24 and Level of significance, α = 5%.
3. **Analyze sample data:** The χ^2 distribution for a test of population variance is given by:

   $$\chi^2 = \frac{\sigma_s^2}{\sigma_p^2}(n-1) = \frac{(8.5^2)(25-1)}{10^2} = 17.34$$

   The critical value of $\chi^2 : \left|\chi^2_{\alpha/2}\right|$ = 36.415
4. **Interpret results:** Since the calculated value of χ^2 = 17.34 which is less than the critical values, i.e., χ^2 = 36.415. Hence the null hypothesis H_0 is accepted. We conclude that the population variance is 10.

11.2.2 χ^2-test for Goodness of Fit

Chi-square test for testing goodness of fit is used to decide whether there is any difference between the observed (experimental) value and the expected (theoretical) value. *Goodness of fit* means how well a statistical model fits a set of observations. A measure of *goodness of fit* typically summarizes the discrepancy between observed values and the values expected under the model in question. Such measures can be used in statistical hypothesis testing, e.g., to test for normality of residuals, to test whether two samples are drawn from identical distributions.

This distribution may also be used for judging the significance of difference between observed and expected frequencies and also as a test of goodness of fit. The generalized shape of χ^2 distribution depends upon the degrees of freedom and the χ^2 distribution value is:

$$\chi^2 = \sum_{i=1}^{n} \frac{(O_i - E_i)^2}{E_i}$$

where, O_i = an observed frequency;

E_i = an expected (theoretical) frequency, asserted by the null hypothesis;

n = the number of cells in the table.

Procedure:

Step 1: State the null and alternative hypotheses

H_0: No difference between the observed and expected set of frequencies.

H_a: There is a difference.

Step 2: Select a random sample and record the observed frequencies (O values) for each category.

Step 3: Calculate the expected frequencies (E values) in each category by multiplying the category probability by the sample size.

Step 4: Compute the value of test statistics:

Step 5: Using a level of significance α and = (n – 1), find the critical value of χ^2.

Step 6: Compare the calculated and critical value of χ^2.

Step 7: Decision rule:

- If, $\chi^2_{cal} < \chi^2_{\alpha/2}$, then accept H_0
- Otherwise reject H_0

Example 11.2:

The number of scooter accidents per week in a certain town were as: 12, 8, 20, 2, 14, 10, 15, 6, 9 and 4. Are these frequencies in agreement with the belief that accident conditions were the same during this 10-week period?

Solution:

1. **Formulate the hypotheses:**

   Null hypothesis: H_0: Accident were same during the period.

   Alternative hypothesis: H_a: Accident were not same during the period.

2. **Formulate an analysis plan:**

   The number of scooter accidents per week in a certain town were as: 12, 8, 20, 2, 14, 10, 15, 6, 9 and 4. Thus, expected number of accidents per week:

$$E = \frac{(12+8+20+2+14+10+15+6+9+4)}{10} = 10$$

And df = 10 – 1= 9 and Level of significance, α = 5%.

3. **Analyze sample data:**

O	E	(O – E)²	(O – E)²/E
12	10	4	0.40
8	10	4	0.40
20	10	100	10.00
2	10	64	6.40
14	10	16	1.60
10	10	0	0.00
15	10	25	2.50
6	10	16	1.60
9	10	1	0.10
4	10	36	3.60
		Total	**26.60**

The critical value of $\chi^2 : |\chi^2_{\alpha/2}|$ = 16.918

4. **Interpret results:** Since the calculated value of χ^2 = 26.60 which is more than the critical values, i.e., χ^2 = 16.918. Hence, the null hypothesis H_0 is rejected.

Example 11.3:

A sample analysis of examination results of 500 students was made. It was found that 220 students had failed, 170 had secured the third class, 90 were placed in second class and 20 got a first class. Are these figures commensurate with the general examination result which is in the ratio of 4 : 3 : 2 : 1 for the various categories respectively?

Solution:

1. **Formulate the hypotheses:**

   Null hypothesis: H_0: No difference in observed and expected results.

   Alternative hypothesis: H_a: Difference in observed and expected results.

2. **Formulate an analysis plan:**

   Degree of freedom = 10 – 1 = 9 and Level of significance, α = 5%.

3. **Analyze sample data:**

Category	O	E	(O – E)²	(O – E)²/E
Failed	220	500(4/10) = 200	400	2.00
3rd Class	170	500(3/10) = 150	400	2.67
2nd Class	90	500(2/10) = 100	100	1.00
1st Class	20	500(1/10) = 50	900	18.00
			Total	**23.67**

The critical value of $\chi^2 : |\chi^2_{\alpha/2}|$ = 7.81

4. **Interpret results.** Since the calculated value of $\chi^2 = 23.67$ which is more than the critical values, i.e., $\chi^2 = 7.81$. Hence, the null hypothèses H_0.

11.2.3 χ^2-test for Independence

Chi-square test for independence is used to determine the relationship between two variables of a sample. In this context, independence means that the two factors are not related. Suppose N observations are considered and classified according to two characteristics say A and B. We may be interested to test whether the two characteristics are independent. In such a case, we can use Chi-square test for independence of two attributes.

Procedure:

Step 1: State the null and alternative hypotheses

H_0: No difference between the observed and expected set of frequencies.

H_a: There is a difference.

Step 2: Select a random sample and record the observed frequencies ('O' values) for each category.

Step 3: Calculate the expected frequencies ('E' values) for each cell:

$$E = \frac{\text{Raw Total} \times \text{Column Total}}{\text{Grand Total}}$$

Step 4: Compute the value of test statistics:

$$\chi^2 = \sum_{i=1}^{n} \frac{(O_i - E_i)^2}{E_i}$$

Step 5: Using a level of significance α and = $(\pi - 1) \times (c - 1)$, find the critical value of χ^2.

where, r = Number of rows and c = Number of columns.

Step 6: Compare the calculated and critical value of χ^2.

Step 7: Decision rule:

- If, $\chi^2_{cal} < \chi^2_{\alpha/2}$, then accept H_0
- Otherwise reject H_0

Example 11.4:

In a anti-malaria campaign in a certain area, quinine was administered to 1000 persons out of a total population of 4000. The number of fever cases reported is shown below:

Treatment	Fever	No Fever	Total
Quinine	150	1250	1400
No Quinine	350	2250	2600
Total	500	3500	**4000**

Discuss the usefulness of quinine in checking malaria.

Solution:

1. **Formulate the hypotheses:**

   Null hypothesis: H_0: The quinine is not effective in checking area.

   Alternative hypothesis: H_a: The quinine is effective in checking area.

2. **Formulate an analysis plan:**

   The contingency table is of size 2 × 2, the degree of freedom would be (2 – 1) (2 – 1) = 1 and Level of significance, $\alpha = 5\%$.

   The expected frequencies can be determined as follows:

$$E_{11} = \frac{\text{Row Total} \times \text{Column Total}}{\text{Grand Total}} = \frac{1400 \times 500}{4000} = 175$$

$$E_{12} = \frac{\text{Row Total} \times \text{Column Total}}{\text{Grand Total}} = \frac{1400 \times 3500}{4000} = 1225$$

$$E_{21} = \frac{\text{Row Total} \times \text{Column Total}}{\text{Grand Total}} = \frac{2600 \times 500}{4000} = 325$$

$$E_{22} = \frac{\text{Row Total} \times \text{Column Total}}{\text{Grand Total}} = \frac{2600 \times 3500}{4000} = 2275$$

   The contingency table of expected frequencies is as follows:

Treatment	Fever	No Fever	Total
Quinine	175	1225	1400
No Quinine	325	2275	2600
Total	500	3500	**4000**

3. **Analyze sample data:**

O	E	$(O - E)^2$	$(O - E)^2/E$
150	175	625	3.571
1250	1225	625	0.510
350	325	625	1.920
2250	2275	625	0.274
		Total	**6.275**

   The critical value of $\chi^2 : \left|\chi^2_{\alpha/2}\right| = 3.84$

4. **Interpret results:** Since the calculated value of $\chi^2 = 6.275$ which is more than the critical values, i.e., $\chi^2 = 3.84$. Hence, the null hypothesis H_0 is rejected.

Example 11.5:

Two hundred randomly selected adults were asked whether TV shows as a whole are preliminary entertaining, educational, or a waste of time (only one answer could be chosen). The respondents were categorized by gender. Their responses are given in the following table:

Gender	Options			Total
	Entertaining	Educational	West of Time	
Female	52	28	30	110
Male	28	12	50	90
Total	80	40	80	**200**

Is the evidence convincing that there is a relationship between gender and opinion in the population interest?

Solution:

1. **Formulate the hypotheses:**

   Null hypothesis: H_0: The opinion of adults is independent of gender.

   Alternative hypothesis: H_a: The opinion of adults is not independent of gender.

2. **Formulate an analysis plan:** The contingency table is of size 2 × 3, the degree of freedom would be (2 – 1) (3 – 1) = 2 and Level of significance, α = 5%.

   The expected frequencies can be determined as follows:

$$E_{11} = \frac{\text{Row Total} \times \text{Column Total}}{\text{Grand Total}} = \frac{110 \times 80}{200} = 44$$

$$E_{12} = \frac{\text{Row Total} \times \text{Column Total}}{\text{Grand Total}} = \frac{110 \times 40}{200} = 22$$

$$E_{14} = \frac{\text{Row Total} \times \text{Column Total}}{\text{Grand Total}} = \frac{110 \times 80}{200} = 44$$

$$E_{21} = \frac{\text{Row Total} \times \text{Column Total}}{\text{Grand Total}} = \frac{90 \times 80}{200} = 36$$

$$E_{22} = \frac{\text{Row Total} \times \text{Column Total}}{\text{Grand Total}} = \frac{90 \times 40}{200} = 18$$

$$E_{23} = \frac{\text{Row Total} \times \text{Column Total}}{\text{Grand Total}} = \frac{90 \times 80}{200} = 36$$

   The contingency table of expected frequencies is as follows:

Gender	Options			Total
	Entertaining	Educational	Waste of Time	
Female	44	22	44	**110**
Male	36	18	36	**90**
Total	**80**	**40**	**80**	**200**

3. **Analyze sample data:**

O	E	(O – E)²	(O – E)²/E
52	44	64	1.454
28	22	36	1.636
30	44	196	4.455
28	36	64	1.777
12	18	36	2.000
50	36	196	5.444
		Total	**16.766**

The critical value of $\chi^2 : |\chi^2_{\alpha/2}| = 5.99$

4. **Interpret results:** Since the calculated value of $\chi^2 = 16.766$ which is more than the critical values, i.e., $\chi^2 = 5.99$. Hence, the null hypothesis H_0 is rejected. We conclude that the opinion of adults is not independent of gender.

11.3 ANALYSIS OF VARIANCE (ANOVA)

11.3.1 Meaning of ANOVA

Analysis of variance (ANOVA) is a collection of statistical models, and their associated procedures, in which the observed variance in a particular variable is partitioned into components attributable to different sources of variation. In its simplest form, ANOVA provides a statistical test of whether or not the means of several groups are all equal, and therefore generalizes *t*-test to more than two groups. ANOVAs are helpful because they possess an advantage over a two-sample t-test. Doing multiple two-sample t-tests would result in an increased chance of committing a type I error. For this reason, ANOVAs are useful in comparing three or more means. ANOVA is a test whose goal is to assess the plausibility of the hypothesis stating that the means of these normal distributions are indeed equal.

More generally, we have *k* groups of observations known to have been generated by *k* independent normal distributions with identical variances and respective means $\mu_1, \mu_2, \ldots\ldots\ldots\mu_k$. The groups need not have the same size.

ANOVA will test:

- The null hypothesis H_0: $\mu_1, \mu_2, \ldots\ldots\ldots\mu_k$ against
- The alternative hypothesis H_a: at least one of the means is different from the others.

The following are few terms that will be used during discussion on analysis of variance (ANOVA):

1. A *sampling plan of experimental deign* is the way that a sample is selected from the population under study and determines the amount of information in the sample.
2. An *experimental unit* is the objective on which a measurement is taken. Any experimental conditions imposed on an experimental unit provide effect on the response.
3. A *factor or criterion* is an independent variable whose values are controlled and varied by the researchers.
4. A *level* is the intensity setting of a factor.
5. A *treatment or population* is a specific combination of factors levels.
6. The *response* is the dependent variable being measured by the researchers.

11.3.2 ANOVA Approach

The first step in the analysis of variance is to partition the total variation in the sample data into the following two component variations in such a way that it is possible to estimate the contribution of factors that may cause variation.

1. The amount of variation *among the sample means* or the variation attributable to the difference among samples means. The variation is either on account of difference in treatment or due to element of chance. The difference is denoted by SSC or SSTR.
2. The amount of variation *within the sample observations*. This difference is considered due to chance causes or experimental (random) errors. The difference in the values of various elements in a sample due to chance is called an estimate and denoted as SSE.

The observations in the sample data may be classified according to *one factor* (criterion) or *two factors* (criterion). The classification according to one factor and two factors are called *one-way classification* and *two-way classification*, respectively. The calculations for total variation and its components may be carried out in each of the two types of classifications by: *(i) direct method, (ii) short-cut method, and (iii) coding method.*

11.4 ANOVA TECHNIQUE

11.4.1 One-way ANOVA

In one-way ANOVA, we consider only one factor and then observe that the reasons for said factor to be important is that several possible types of sample can occur within that factor. We then determine if there are differences within that factor.

Steps for Testing Hypothesis

Step 1: State null and alternative hypothesis:

Null hypothesis H_0: $\mu_1 = \mu_2 = \mu_3 = \ldots\ldots = \mu_k$

Alternative Hypothesis H_a: $\mu_1 \neq \mu_2 \neq \mu_3 \neq \ldots\ldots \neq \mu_k$

Step 2: Calculate variation between sample mean:

1. **Calculate the mean of each sample, i.e.,**

   $\bar{x}_1, \bar{x}_2, \bar{x}_3, \ldots\ldots\ldots\bar{x}_k$, of all k samples.

2. **Calculate the mean of the sample means:**

$$\bar{\bar{x}} = \frac{\bar{x}_1 + \bar{x}_2 + \ldots.. \bar{x}_k}{\text{No. of sample (k)}} = \frac{T}{n}$$

where, T = Grand total of all observations

n = Number of observations in k samples

3. **Calculate the sum of squares for variance between the samples, (or SS between):**

$$\text{SS between} = \sum_{j=1}^{r} n_j(\bar{x}_j - \bar{\bar{x}})^2$$

$$\text{SS between} = n_1(\bar{x}_1 - \bar{\bar{x}})^2 + n_2(\bar{x}_2 - \bar{\bar{x}})^2 + \ldots. + n_k(\bar{x}_k - \bar{\bar{x}})^2$$

Step 3: Calculate variation within sample:

1. **Calculate the mean of each sample, i.e.,**

   $\bar{x}_1, \bar{x}_2, \bar{x}_3, \ldots\ldots\ldots\bar{x}_r$, of all k samples.

2. **Calculate the sum of squares for variance within the samples (or SS within):**

$$\text{SS within} = \sum_{i=1}^{k}\sum_{j=1}^{n}(\bar{x}_{ij} - \bar{\bar{x}})^2$$

SS within = $\sum_i (x_{1i} - \bar{x}_1)^2 + \sum_i (x_{2i} - \bar{x}_2) + ... + \sum_i (x_{ki} - \bar{x}_k)^2$

i = 1, 2, 3, ...

This sum is also called the *sum of squares for error, i.e., SSE = SS Total – SS between.*

Step 4: Calculate the total variance:

1. Total variation is represented by the sum of squares total (SS total) and equal to the sum of the squared difference between each sample value from the grand mean $\bar{\bar{\chi}}$.

   SS total = $\sum (x_{ij} - \bar{\bar{x}})^2$, i = 1, 2, ... and j = 1, 2, ...

   This total should be equal to: SS for total variance = SS between + SS within

   and (n – 1) = (k – 1) + (n – k)

Step 5: Calculate average variation between and within samples and Mean Square:

When the sum of squares are divided by their associated degrees of freedom, we get the following variances of mean square:

$$\text{MS between} = \frac{\text{SS between}}{k-1}, \text{ MS within} = \frac{\text{SS within}}{n-k} \text{ and MSE} = \frac{\text{SSE}}{k-r}$$

Step 6: Calculate F-ratio:

$$\text{F ratio} = \frac{\text{SS between}/(k-1)}{\text{SS within}/(n-k)} = \frac{\text{MS between}}{\text{MS within}}$$

This ratio is used to judge whether the difference among several sample means is significant or is just a matter of sampling fluctuations. For this purpose we look into the table; giving the value of F for given degrees of freedom at different levels of significance.

Step 7: Set up a ANOVA table:

Table 11.1: ANOVA Table: One-way

Sources of Variation	Sum of Square (SS)	Degree of Freedom (d.f.)	Mean Squares (MS)	F-value
Between Samples	SS between	k – 1	Ms between = $\frac{\text{SS between}}{k-1}$	F = $\frac{\text{MS between}}{\text{MS within}}$
Within Samples	SS within	n – k	MS between = $\frac{\text{SS within}}{n-k}$	
Total	**SS total**	**n – 1**		

Decision Rules:

- Reject H_0 if the calculated value of F > its critical value of $F_{\alpha(k-1, n-k)}$
- Otherwise accept H_0.

Or

- If $F_{cal} < F_{criticalvalue}$, accept null hypothesis H_0.
- Otherwise Reject H_0.

Short-cut Method:

The values of SS between and SS within (SSE) can be calculated by applying the following short-cut methods:

(a) Calculate the grand total of all observations in samples, T is given by:

$$T = \Sigma x_1 + \Sigma x_2 + ... + \Sigma x_k$$

(b) Calculate the correction factor, CF is given by:

$$CF = \frac{T^2}{n}; \; n = n_1 + n_2 + ... + n_k$$

(c) Find the sum of the squares of all observations in samples from each of k samples and subtract CF from this sum to obtain the total sum of the squares of squares of deviations SS total:

$$\text{SS total} = (\Sigma x_1^2 + \Sigma x_2^2 + ... + \Sigma x_k^2) - CF = \sum_{i=1}^{k} \sum_{j=1}^{n} x_{ij}^2 - CF$$

$$\text{SS between} = \frac{(\Sigma x_j)^2}{n_j} - CF$$

and SS within = SS total – SS between

Coding Method

The coding method is based on the fact that the F-test statistic used in the analysis of variance is the ratio of variances without unit of measurement. Thus, the value does not change if an appropriate constant value is either multiplied, subtracted or added to each observations in the sample data. This adjustment reduces the magnitude of numerical values in the sample data and reduces computational time to calculate f-value without any change.

Example 11.6:

A XYZ manufacturing company has purchased three new machines of different makes and wishes to determine whether one of them is faster than the others in producing a certain output. Four hourly production, figures are observed at random from each machine and the results are given below:

Observations	M_1	M_2	M_3
1	28	31	30
2	32	37	28
3	30	38	26
4	34	42	28

Use analysis of variance and determine whether the machines are significantly different in their mean speed.

Solution:

Step 1: Formulate the hypothesis:

Null hypothesis H_0: Machines are not significantly different in their mean speed.

Alternative Hypothesis H_a: Machines are significantly different in their mean speed.

Step 2: Calculate the mean of each of these samples:

$$\bar{x}_1 = \frac{28 + 32 + 30 + 34}{4} = 31$$

$$\bar{x}_2 = \frac{31+37+38+42}{4} = 37$$

$$\bar{x}_3 = \frac{30+28+26+28}{4} = 28$$

Mean of the sample means $\bar{\bar{x}} = \dfrac{34+37+28}{3} = 32$

Step 3: Calculate SS between, SS within and SS total variance

$$\text{SS between} = n_1(\bar{x}_1 - \bar{\bar{x}})^2 + n_2(\bar{x}_2 - \bar{\bar{x}})^2 + ... + n_k(\bar{x}_k - \bar{\bar{x}})^2$$
$$= 4(31 - 32)^2 + 4(37 - 32)^2 + 4(28 - 32)^2$$
$$= 4 + 100 + 64 = 168$$

$$\text{SS within} = \sum_i (x_{1i} - \bar{x}_1)^2 + \sum_i (x_{2i} - \bar{x}_2)^2 + ... + \sum_i (x_{ki} - \bar{x}_k)^2$$
$$= (28 - 31)^2 + (32 - 31)^2 + (30 - 31)^2 + (34 - 31)^2$$
$$+ (31 - 37)^2 + (37 - 37)^2 + (38 - 37)^2 + (42 - 37)^2$$
$$+ (30 - 28)^2 + (28 - 28)^2 + (26 - 28)^2 + (28 - 28)^2$$
$$= 20 + 62 + 8 = 90$$

$$\text{SS total} = \sum (x_{ij} - \bar{\bar{x}})^2, \; i = 1, 2, ... \text{ and } j = 1, 2, ...$$
$$= (28 - 32)^2 + (32 - 32)^2 + (30 - 32)^2 + (34 - 32)^2$$
$$+ (31 - 32)^2 + (37 - 32)^2 + (38 - 32)^2 + (42 - 32)^2$$
$$+ (30 - 32)^2 + (28 - 32)^2 + (26 - 32)^2 + (28 - 32)^2$$
$$= 24 + 162 + 72 = 258$$

SS total = SS between + SS within = 168 + 90 = 258

Step 4: Set-up ANOVA Table:

ANOVA Table: One-way

Sources of Variation	Sum of Squares (SS)	Degree of Freedom (d.f.)	Mean Squares (MS)	F_{cal}- value	$F_{critical}$- value at 5% F(2,9)
Between Samples	168	3 – 1 = 2	MS between = $\frac{168}{2}$ = 84	F = $\frac{84}{10}$ = 8.4	**F (2,9) = 4.26**
Within Samples	90	12 – 3 = 9	MS within = $\frac{90}{9}$ = 10		
Total	**258**	**12 – 1 = 1**			

Step 5: Interpret the result:

Since the calculated value of F is 8.4, this is more than its critical value of 4.26 at $\alpha = 5\%$, with d.f. at $df_1 = v_1 = 2$ and $df_2 = v_2 = 9$. Hence, we reject the hypothesis H_0. We conclude that, the machines are significantly different in their mean speed.

Example 11.7:

There are three main brands of a certain ice-cream. A sample of 120 packets sold is examined and found to be allocated among four groups A, B, C, and D, and brands I, II and III, as shown below:

Brand	Group			
	A	B	C	D
Brand I	0	4	8	15
Brand II	5	8	13	6
Brand III	18	19	11	13

Is there any significant difference in brand preference?

Solution:

Step 1: Formulate the hypothesis:

Null hypothesis H_0: There is no significance difference in brand preference.

Alternative Hypothesis H_a: There is significance difference in brand preference.

Step 2: Calculate the Correction Factor:

Calculation Table

Sample 1		Sample 2		Sample 3	
Brand I		Brand II		Brand III	
(x_1)	x_1^2	(x_2)	x_2^2	(x_3)	x_3^2
0	0	5	25	18	324
4	16	8	64	19	361
8	64	13	169	11	121
15	225	6	36	13	169
27	305	32	294	61	975

T = Total of the values of individual items in the sample = 120.

So, Correction factor (CF) $= \frac{T^2}{n} = \frac{120^2}{12} = 1200$

Step 3: Calculate SS between, SS within and SS total variance and SS residual:

SS total $= (\Sigma x_1^2 + \Sigma x_2^2 + \Sigma x_3^2) - CF$

$= 305 + 294 + 975 = 1574 - 1200 = 374$

SS between $= \frac{(\Sigma x_j)^2}{n_j} - CF = \left[\frac{27^2}{4} + \frac{32^2}{4} + \frac{61^2}{4}\right] - 1200$

$= 13685 - 1200 = 168.5$

and SS within = SS total – SS between = 374 – 168.5 = 205.5

Step 4: Set-up ANOVA Table:

ANOVA Table: One-way

Sources of Variation	Sum of Square (SS)	Degree of Freedom (d.f.)	Mean Squares (MS)	F_{cal}-value	$F_{critical}$-value at 5% F(2,9)
Between Samples	168.5	3 – 1 = 2	MS between = $\frac{168.5}{2}$ = 84.25	F = $\frac{84.52}{22.83}$ = 3.69	**F (2,9) = 4.26**
Within Samples	205.5	12 – 3 = 9	MS within = $\frac{205.5}{9}$ = 22.83		
Total	**374**	**12 – 1 = 1**			

Step 5: Interpret the result:

Since the calculated value of F is 3.69, this is less than its critical value of 4.26 at α = 5%, with d.f. at $df_1 = v_1 = 2$ and $df_2 = v_2 = 9$. Hence, we accept the null hypothesis H_0. We conclude that, there is no significant difference in brand preference.

11.4.2 Two-way ANOVA

In one-way ANOVA, the partitioning of the total variation in the sample data is done into two components: (i) Variation among the samples due to different samples and (ii) Variation within the samples due to random error. ANOVA technique in context of two-way design when repeated values are not there. As we do not have repeated values, we cannot directly compute the sum of squares within samples as we had done in the case of one-way ANOVA. Therefore, we have to calculate this residual or error variation by subtraction, once we have calculated the sum of squares for total variance and for variance between varieties of one treatment as also for variance between varieties of the other treatment.

Steps for Testing Hypothesis

Step 1: Calculation the Correction Factor:

Correction factor = $\frac{T^2}{n}$

T = Total of the values of individual items in the sample.

Step 2: Calculate the sum of squares of deviations for total variance:

$$\text{SS total} = \sum x_{ij}^2 - \frac{T^2}{n}$$

Step 3: Calculate the sum of squares between the columns treatment:

$$\text{SS between treatment } \sum \frac{T_j^2}{n_j} - \frac{T^2}{n}, \ j = \text{column}$$

Step 4: Calculate the sum of squares between the rows treatment:

$$\text{SS between rows treatment } \sum \frac{T_j^2}{n_j} - \frac{T^2}{n}, \ j = \text{row}$$

Step 5: Calculate the sum of squares residual or error:

SS residual or error = SS total (SS between columns + SS between rows)

Step 6: Calculate the degree of freedom:

Degree of freedom between columns = c – 1

Degree of freedom between rows = r – 1

Degree of freedom for residual or error = (c – 1) (r – 1)

Degree of freedom total variance = cr – 1

where, c = number of columns and r = number of rows

Step 7: Set up the ANOVA Table:

Table 11.2: ANOVA Table: Two-way

Sources of Variation	Sum of Square (SS)	Degree of Freedom (d.f.)	Mean Squares (MS)	F-value
Between columns	SS between columns	c – 1	$\frac{\text{SS between columns}}{c-1}$	$\frac{\text{MS between columns}}{\text{MS residual or error}}$
Between Rows	SS Between Rows	r – 1	$\frac{\text{SS between rows}}{r-1}$	$\frac{\text{MS between rows}}{\text{MS residual or error}}$
Residual or error	SS total – (between columns + SS between rows)	(c – 1) (r – 1)	$\frac{\text{SS residual or error}}{(c-1)(r-1)}$	
Total	**SS total**	**cr –1**		

Decision Rule:

- Reject H_0 if the calculated value of F > its critical value of $F_{\alpha(k-1, n-k)}$
- Otherwise accept H_0.

Or

- If $F_{cal} < F_{critical\ value}$, accept null hypothesis H_0.
- Otherwise Reject H_0.

Example 11.8:

The following table gives the number of LCD computers sold by 3 salesmen in four months January, February, March and April:

Month	Salesman		
	A	B	C
January	3	3	3
February	6	5	5
March	8	7	4
April	7	5	4

Is there a significant difference in the sales made by the four salesmen? Is there a significant difference in the sales made during different months?

Solution:

Step 1: Formulate the Hypothesis:

Null hypothesis H_0: There is no significant difference between sales made by four salesmen.

Alternative Hypothesis H_a: There is significant difference between sales made by four salesmen.

Step 2: Calculate the Correction Factor:

Calculation Table

Month	Salesman			Row Total
	A	B	C	
January	3	3	3	9
February	6	5	5	16
March	8	7	4	19
April	7	5	4	16
Column Total	**24**	**20**	**16**	**60**

T = Total of the values of individual items in the sample = 60.

So, Correction factor (CF) $= \frac{T^2}{n} = \frac{60^2}{12} = 300$

Step 3: Calculate SS between, SS within and SS total variance and SS residual:

$$\text{SS total} = \sum x_{ij}^2 - \frac{T^2}{n}$$

$$= 3^2 + 3^2 + 3^2 + 6^2 + 5^2 + 5^2 + 8^2 + 7^2 + 4^2 + 7^2 + 5^2 + 4^2 - 300$$

$$= 332 - 300 = 32$$

$$\text{SS between columns treatment} = \sum \frac{T_j^2}{n_j} - \frac{T^2}{n},\ j = \text{column}$$

$$= \left[\frac{24^2}{4} + \frac{20^2}{4} + \frac{16^2}{4}\right] - 300 = 308 - 300 = 8$$

$$\text{SS between rows treatment} = \sum \frac{T_i^2}{n_i} - \frac{T^2}{n},\ i = \text{row}$$

$$= \left[\frac{9^2}{3} + \frac{16^2}{3} + \frac{19^2}{3} + \frac{16^2}{3}\right] - 300 = 318 - 300 = 18$$

SS residual or error = SS total – (SS between columns + SS between rows) = 32 – (8 + 18) = 6

Step 4: Set-up ANOVA Table:

ANOVA Table: Two-way

Sources of Variation	Sum of Square (SS)	Degree of Freedom (d.f.)	Mean Squares (MS)	F_{cal}-value	$F_{critical}$-value at 5% F(2,9)
Between Columns	8	3 – 1 = 2	$\frac{8}{2} = 4$	$F_1 = \frac{4}{1} = 4$	$F_1(2,6) = 5.14$
Between Rows	18	4 – 1 = 3	$\frac{18}{3} = 6$	$F_2 = \frac{6}{1} = 6$	$F_2(3,6) = 4.76$
Residual or Error	6	(3 – 1)(4 – 1) = 6	$\frac{6}{6} = 1$		
Total	32	12 – 1 = 11			

Step 5: Interpret the result:

(a) The calculated value of $F_1 = 4$, this is less than its critical value of 5.14 at $\alpha = 5\%$, with d.f. at $df_1 = v_1 = 2$ and $df_2 = v_2 = 6$. Hence, we accept the null hypothesis H_0. We conclude that, sales made by the salesman do not differ significantly.

(b) Since the calculated value of $F_2 = 6$, this is more than its critical value of 4.76 at $\alpha = 5\%$, with d.f. at $df_1 = v_1 = 3$ and $df_2 = v_2 = 6$. Hence, we reject the hypothesis H_0. We conclude that, sales made during different months differ significantly.

Example 11.9:

Perform a two-way ANOVA on the data given below:

Plots of Land	Treatment A	B	C	D
1	38	40	41	39
2	45	42	49	36
3	40	38	42	42

Use the coding method for subtracting 40 from the given numbers.

Solution:

Step 1: After subtracting 40 from the given numbers, the following table is:

Plots of Land	Treatment A	B	C	D
1	-2	0	1	-1
2	5	2	9	-4
3	0	-2	2	2

Step 2: Calculate the Correction Factor:

Calculation Table

Plots of Land	Treatment				Row Total
	A	B	C	D	
1	–2	0	1	–1	–2
2	5	2	9	–4	12
3	0	–2	2	2	2
Column Total	3	0	12	–3	12

T = Total of the values of individual items in the sample = 60.

So, Correction factor (CF) = $\frac{T^2}{n} = \frac{12^2}{12} = 12$

Step 3: Calculate SS between, SS within and SS total variance and SS residual:

$$\text{SS total} = \sum x_{ij}^2 - \frac{T^2}{n}$$

$$= (-2)^2 + 0^2 + 1^2 + (-1)^2 + 5^2 + 2^2 + 9^2 + (-4)^2 + 0^2 + (-2)^2 + 2^2 + 2^2 - 12$$

$$= 144 - 12 = 132$$

$$\text{SS between columns treatment} = \sum \frac{T_j^2}{n_j} - \frac{T^2}{n},\ j = \text{column}$$

$$= \left[\frac{3^2}{3} + \frac{0^2}{3} + \frac{12^2}{3} + \frac{(-3)^2}{3}\right] - 12 = 54 - 12 = 48$$

$$\text{SS between rows treatment} = \sum \frac{T_i^2}{n_i} - \frac{T^2}{n},\ i = \text{row}$$

$$= \left[\frac{(-2)^2}{4} + \frac{12^2}{4} + \frac{2^2}{4}\right] - 12 = 38 - 12 = 26$$

SS residual or error = SS total – (SS between columns + SS between rows) = 132 – (42 + 26) = 64

Step 4: Set-up ANOVA Table:

ANOVA Table: Two-way

Sources of Variation	Sum of Square (SS)	Degreeof Freedom (d.f.)	Mean Squares (MS)	F_{cal}-value	$F_{critical}$-value at 5% F(2,9)
Between Columns	42	4 – 1 = 3	$\frac{42}{3} = 14$	$F_1 = \frac{14}{10.67} = 1.1312$	**$F_1(3,6) = 4.76$**
Between Rows	26	3 – 1 = 2	$\frac{26}{2} = 13$	$F_2 = \frac{13}{10.67} = 1.218$	**$F_2(2,6) = 5.14$**
Residual or Error	64	(4 – 1) (3 – 1) = 6	$\frac{64}{6} = 10.67$		
Total	**132**	**12 – 1 = 11**			

Step 5: Interpret the result:

(a) The calculated value of $F_1 = 1.312$, this is less than its critical value of 4.76 at $\alpha = 5\%$, with d.f. at $df_1 = v_1 = 3$ and $df_2 = v_2 = 6$. Hence, we accept the null hypothesis H_0.

(b) Since the calculated value of $F_2 = 1.218$, this is less than its critical value of 5.14 at $\alpha = 5\%$, with d.f. at $df_1 = v_1 = 2$ and $df_2 = v_2 = 6$. Hence, we accept the hypothesis H_0.

11.4.3 ANOVA in Latin-square Design

Latin-square design is an experimental design has a wide variety of application in industrial, agricultural, educational, medical, marketing and sociological experimentation. For the Latin-square design, the treatments are so allocated among the plots that no treatment occurs, more than once in any one row or any one column. Through the elimination of row and column effects from the within treatment variation, the residual or error variance may be considerably reduced. The ANOVA technique in case of Latin-square design remains more or less the same as we have already stated in case of a two-way design, expecting the fact that the variance is splitted into four parts as under.

(i) Variance between columns;

(ii) Variance between rows;

(iii) Variance between varieties;

(iv) Residual variance.

An experiment with a Latin-square design can be conducted with any one of the possible arrangements of Latin-squares. A square is said to be standard of the 1st row and 1st column are ordered alphabetically or numerically.

2 × 2 Latin-square		3 × 3 Latin-square			4 × 4 Latin-square			
A	B	A	B	C	A	B	C	D
B	A	B	C	A	B	C	D	A
		C	A	B	C	D	A	B
					D	A	B	C

Table 11.3: ANOVA Table: Latin-square Design

Sources of Variation	Sum of Square (SS)	Degreeof Freedom (d.f.)	Mean Squares (MS)	F-value
Between columns	SS between Columns	c – 1	$\frac{\text{SS between columns}}{c-1}$	$\frac{\text{MS between columns}}{\text{MS residual or error}}$
Between Rows	SS between Rows	r – 1	$\frac{\text{SS withing row}}{r-1}$	$\frac{\text{MS between rows}}{\text{MS residual or error}}$
Between Varieties	SS between Varieties	v – 1	$\frac{\text{SS withing row}}{v-1}$	$\frac{\text{MS between varieties}}{\text{MS residual or error}}$
Residual Error	SS total – (SS between columns + SS between roes + SS between Varieties)	(c – 1) (c – 2)	$\frac{\text{SS residual or error}}{(c-1)(c-2)}$	
Total	SS total	N – 1		

Example 11.10:

Present your conclusions after doing analysis of variance to the following results of the Latin-square design experiment conducted in respect of five fertilizers which were used on plots of different fertility.

A 28	D 20	C 25	B 20
D 21	C 23	B 21	A 19
B 21	A 18	D 20	C 18
C 20	B 20	A 23	D 17

Solution:

Step 1: Set up the coded table:

Using the coding method, we subtract 20 from the figures given in each of the small squares and obtain the coded figures as under:

		Columns				Row Totals
		1	2	3	4	
Rows	1	A 8	D 0	C 5	B 0	13
	2	D 1	C 3	B 1	A -3	4
	3	B 1	A -2	D 0	C -2	-3
	4	C 0	B 0	A 3	D -3	0
Column Totals		10	1	9	- 6	T = 14

Step 2: Squaring the coded figures in various columns and rows:

		Squares of Coded Figures				
		Columns				Sum of Squares
		1	2	3	4	
Rows	1	C 64	B 0	A 25	D 0	89
	2	A 1	D 9	C 1	B 9	20
	3	B 1	A 4	D 0	C 4	9
	4	D 0	C 0	B 9	A 9	18
Sum of Squares		66	13	35	22	T = 136

Step 3: Calculate the correction factors:

$$\text{Correction factor (CF)} = \frac{T^2}{n} = \frac{14^2}{16} = 12.25$$

Step 4: Calculate SS between columns and SS between rows and SS total variance:

$$\text{SS total} = \sum x_{ij}^2 - \frac{T^2}{n} = 136 - 12.5 = 123.5$$

$$\text{SS between columns treatment} = \sum \frac{T_j^2}{n_j} - \frac{T^2}{n},\ j = \text{column}$$

$$= \left[\frac{10^2}{4} + \frac{1^2}{4} + \frac{9^2}{4} + \frac{(-6)^2}{4}\right] - 12.25 = 54.5 - 12.25 = 42.25$$

$$\text{SS between rows treatment} = \sum \frac{T_i^2}{n_i} - \frac{T^2}{n},\ i = \text{row}$$

$$= \left[\frac{13^2}{4} + \frac{4^2}{4} + \frac{(-3)^2}{4} + \frac{0^2}{4}\right] - 12.25 = 48.5 - 12.25 = 36.25$$

Step 5: Calculate SS between varieties:

For finding the SS between varieties, we would first rearrange the coded data in the following:

Different Fertilizer	Different Fertilities				Total (T)
	I	II	III	IV	
A	8	0	5	0	13
B	1	3	1	-3	2
C	1	-2	0	-2	-3
D	0	0	3	-3	0

$$\text{SS between varieties} = \sum \frac{T_v^2}{n_v} - \frac{T^2}{n}$$

$$= \left[\frac{13^2}{4} + \frac{2^2}{4} + \frac{(-3)^2}{4} + \frac{0^2}{4}\right] - 12.25 = 45.5 - 12.25 = 33.25$$

Step 6: Calculate SS for residual variance:

SS for residual variance = 123.5 – (42.25 + 36.25 + 33.25) = 11.75

Step 7: Calculate the degree of freedom:

Degree of freedom between columns = c – 1 = 4 – 1 = 3

Degree of freedom between rows = r – 1 = 4 – 3 = 3

Degree of freedom between varieties = v – 1 = 4 – 1 = 3

Degree of freedom for residual or error = (c –1) (c – 2) = (4 – 1) (4 – 2) = 6

Degree of freedom total variance = n – 1 = 16 – 1 = 15

where, c = no. of columns, r = no. of rows and v = no. of varieties

Step 8: Set up a ANOVA Table:

ANOVA Table: Latin-square Design

Sources of Variation	Sum of Square (SS)	Degree of Freedom (d.f.)	Mean Squares (MS)	F_{cal}-value	$F_{critical}$-value at 5% F(2,9)
Between Columns	42.25	4 – 1 = 3	$\frac{42.25}{3} = 4.08$	$F_1 = \frac{4.08}{1.95} = 20.9$	**$F_1(3,6) = 4.76$**
Between Rows	36.25	4 – 1 = 3	$\frac{36.25}{3} = 12.08$	$F_2 = \frac{12.08}{1.95} = 6.19$	**$F_2(3,6) = 4.76$**
Between Varieties	33.25	4 – 1 = 3	$\frac{33.25}{3} = 11.08$	$F_3 = \frac{11.08}{1.95} = 5.98$	**$F_3(3,6)=4.76$**
Residual or Error	11.75	(4 – 1) (4 – 2) = 6	$\frac{11.75}{6} = 1.95$		
Total	**123.5**	**16 – 1 = 15**			

Step 9: Interpret the Result:

(a) The calculated value of $F_1 = 2.09$, this is less than its critical value of 4.76 at $\alpha = 5\%$, with d.f. at $df_1 = v_1 = 3$ and $df_2 = v_2 = 6$. Hence, we accept the null hypothesis H_0.

(b) The calculated value of $F_2 = 6.19$, this is more than its critical value of 4.76 at $\alpha = 5\%$, with d.f. at $df_1 = v_1 = 3$ and $df_2 = v_2 = 6$. Hence, we reject the hypothesis H_0.

(c) The calculated value of $F_3 = 5.68$, this is more than its critical value of 4.76 at $\alpha = 5\%$, with d.f. at $df_1 = v_1 = 3$ and $df_2 = v_2 = 6$. Hence, we reject the hypothesis H_0.

From the above three results, we conclude that, the variance between rows and variance between varieties are significant and variance between columns is not significant at 5% level of significance.

11.5 OTHER NON-PARAMETRIC TEST (OR DISTRIBUTION FREE TEST)

Many statistical tests require that your data follow a normal distribution. Sometimes this is not the case. In some instances, it is possible to transform the data to make them follow a normal distribution; in others this is not possible or the sample size might be so small that it is difficult to ascertain whether or not the data a normally distributed. In such cases, it is necessary to use a statistical test that does not require the data to follow a particular distribution. Such test is called a non-parametric or distribution free test.

When to Use It?

For a statistical method, it must satisfy at least one of the following conditions:

1. The data are counts or frequencies of different types of outcomes.
2. The data are measured on a nominal scale and ordinal scale.
3. The assumptions required for the validity of the corresponding parametric procedure are not met or cannot be verified.
4. The sample size is small.
5. The measurements are imprecise.
6. There are outliers and/or extreme values in the data, making the median more representative than the mean.
7. The method can be used with interval or ratio data when no assumption can be made about the population probability distribution.

11.5.1 Sign Test

The sign test is the simplest and one of the easiest non-parametric tests. Count the number of positive values (larger than hypothesized median), the number of negative values (smaller than the hypothesized median), and test whether there are significantly more positives (or negatives) than expected. The Sign test belongs to the confirmatory types of statistical tests. Most statistical tests require data to follow the normal distribution. Many times, it is possible to transform data so that it follows the normal distribution; however sometimes it is not possible, or sometimes the statistical sample size is so small that it becomes difficult to identify if the data is normally distributed or not. In such scenarios, it becomes necessary to use a form of statistical testing, where it is not necessary for the data to be normally distributed.

The Sign Test is a non-parametric statistical test whereby very few assumptions are taken about the nature of the distribution being tested. This statistics hypothesis test works on the theory that there are equal probabilities of two outcomes. Instead of magnitude, this non-parametric test works on the direction of + and - sign of the observation. Since, there are just two choices, i.e., + or –, so the null proportion is taken as p = 0.5. The sign test is used to test the null hypothesis that the median of a distribution is equal to some value.

Table 11.4: Test the Null Hypothesis

Test	Null Hypothesis, H_0	Alternate Hypothesis, H_a
Left-tailed	H_0: Median = M_0	H_a: Median < M_0
Two-tailed	H_0: Median = M_0	H_a: Median $\neq$ M_0
Right-tailed	H_0: Median = M_0	H_a: Median > M_0

M_0 is the hypothesized population median.

Types of Sign Tests:

A. **One Sample Sign Test:** In this test, the hypothesis is set up in a way that + and – signs are the values of the random variables that have equal size.

B. **Two Sample Sign Test (or Paired Test):** It is also known as an alternative to the paired sample statistical t-test. In this case, the + and – signs are used in the paired sample test or in the before/after study. The null hypothesis is set up in a way that either of the + and – signs are of equal size or the population mean values are equal to the sample mean value.

A. One Sample Sign Test

The one sample sign test is a non-parametric equivalent to the parametric one sample t-test. The one sample sign is a non-parametric test of population location (median) and also calculates the corresponding point estimate and confidence interval. Its parametric counterpart is the one sample z and one sample t-tests. Non-parametric tests do not make assumptions that the population is from a specific distribution. Therefore, its results are more robust than a parametric test when such assumptions are violated.

Assumptions:

1. Data is non-normally distributed, even after log transforming.
2. This test makes no assumption about the shape of the population distribution.
3. This test can handle a data set that is non-symmetric, that is skewed either to the left or the right.

Test Procedure:

Hypothesis: H_0: Differences between the median population

H_a: No differences between the median populations

Test Statistics: Let r^+ be the number of positive differences and r^- the number of negative differences and X denotes the number of positive difference, then X has binomial distribution with parameters n and p, i.e., $X \sim B(n, p)$ $(p = \frac{1}{2} = 0.5)$. The null and alternative hypothesis is:

Case 1: H_0: p = 0.5 and H_a: p > 0.5 (One-tailed)

Critical Value: Critical value for the test is obtained from the table for given value of n and at desired level of significance (α)

Decision Rule: If $r^+ \geq r_\alpha$ Reject H_0, where r_α stands for α% critical point of the binomial distribution with small integer such that

$$P(X \geq r) = \sum_{k=r}^{n} \binom{n}{k} (0.5)^n \leq \alpha, \text{ where } r = \max(r^+, r^-)$$

Alternatively: If P ($X \leq r^-$) = α, the H_0 is rejected.

Case 2: H_0: p = 0.5 and H_a: p < 0.5 (One-tailed)

Critical Value: Critical value for the test is obtained from the table for given value of n and at desired level of significance (α).

Decision Rule: If $r^+ = r_a$ Reject H_0, where r_α stands for lower α% critical point of the binomial distribution with larger integer such that

$$p(x \geq r) = \sum_{k=0}^{r} \binom{n}{k} (0.5)^n \leq \alpha, \text{ wherer } = \max(r^+, r^-)$$

Alternatively: If P ($X > r^-$) = a, the H_0 is rejected.

Case 3: H_0: p = 0.5 and H_a: p $\neq$ 0.5 (Two-tailed)

Critical Value: Critical value for the test is obtained from the table for given value of n and at desired level of significance (α).

Decision Rule: If $r^+ = r_{\alpha/2}$ and if $r^+ = R_{\alpha/2}$ Reject H_0, where $r_{\alpha/2}$ stands for $\alpha/2$ % critical point of the binomial distribution with small and larger integer such that

$$\sum_{r_{\alpha/2}}^{n} \binom{n}{k} (0.5)^n \leq \alpha/2 \text{ and } \sum_{0}^{R_{\alpha/2}} \binom{n}{k} (0.5)^n \leq \alpha/2$$

Alternatively: If P ($X \leq r^+$) = $\alpha/2$, the H_0 is rejected.

Alternative Method

Let r^+ be the number of positive differences and r^- the number of negative differences, then

$r = \min (r^+, r^-)$

Case 1:	For two-sided test If $r \leq r_\alpha$ Reject H_0, in favour of p $\neq$ 0.5.
Case 2:	For one-sided test (i) If r- d" $r_á$ Reject H_0, in favour of p > 0.5. (ii) If r^+ d" $r_á$ Reject H_0, in favour of p < 0.5.

For Large Sample: When sample size is greater than 25, the critical value r_c can be obtained using a normal distribution approximation.

$$r_z = Z = \frac{(X = r) - np}{\sqrt{np(1-p)}}, \text{ where } r = \text{Max}(r^+, r^-)$$

P-value Method:

1. Choose r = Max (r^+, r^-)
2. Choose table of binomial distribution to find probability of observing a value of r or higher, assuming p = 0.05.
   (a) If the test is one sided, this is P-value.
   (b) If the test is two sided, double the probability obtained in (i) to obtained P-value.

Example 11.11 (Small Sample):

Number of order in a particular day, received by a manager from a random sample of 10 restaurants in the city of Bhubaneswar are 15, 20, 12, 18, 25, 16, 23, 10, 14 and 24. Use the sign test at 5% level of significance to test the hypothesis that H_0: M = 17 against alternative hypothesis H_a: M < 17.

Solution:

Hypothesis: H_0: M = 17 and H_a: M < 17 (One-tailed Test)

Calculation:

Restaurant	Order Received	Sign of Difference
1	15	–
2	20	+
3	12	–
4	18	+
5	25	+
6	16	–
7	23	+
8	10	–
9	14	–
10	24	+

r^+ = Number of (+) signs = 5

r^- = Number of (–) signs = 5

n = Total no. of students = 10

Critical Value: At 5% level of significance, i.e., α = 5% with n = 10, the critical value r_α (from the Table) is, i.e., $r_\alpha = 1$.

Decision Rule: Since $r^+ = 5 \geq r_\alpha = 1$, we cannot reject the null hypothesis. Hence H_0 is accepted.

Example 11.12 (Small Sample):

In the City Club in Bhubaneswar, playing five rounds of game of 11 professional total scores are 281, 283, 291, 274, 284, 284, 276, 285, 283, 280, and 282. Use the sign test at 5% level of significance to test the null hypothesis that professional gamers average M = 285 for five rounds against the alternative hypothesis M > 285.

Solution:

Hypothesis: H_0: M = 285 and H_a: M > 285 (One-tailed Test)

Calculation:

Professionals	Total Scores	Sign of Difference
1	281	–
2	283	–
3	291	+
4	274	–
5	284	–
6	289	+
7	276	–
8	285	0 (Discard)
9	283	–
10	280	–
11	282	–

r^+ = Number of (+) signs = 2

r^- = Number of (–) signs = 8

n = Total no. of professionals = 10

Critical Value: At 5% level of significance, i.e., $\alpha = 5\%$ with n = 10, the critical value r_α (from the Table) is 1, i.e., $r_\alpha = 1$.

Decision Rule: Since $r^- = 8 \geq r_\alpha = 1$, the null hypothesis H_0 must be rejected. We conclude that the professional gamers average is less than 285 for five round of game.

Example 11.13 (Small Sample):

A recent article in the school newspaper reported that the typical credit card debt of a student is ₹ 500. Professor Das claims that the median credit card debt of students at BB College is different from ₹ 300. To test this claim, he obtains a random sample of 20 students enrolled at the college and asks them to disclose their credit card debt.

Students	Credit Card Debt	Students	Credit Card Debt
1	6000	11	250
2	0	12	580
3	200	13	1000
4	0	14	0
5	400	15	0
6	1060	16	200
7	0	17	400
8	1200	18	800
9	200	19	700
10	250	20	1000

Solution:

Hypothesis: (Two-tailed Test)

H_0: Median = 300 (the median credit card debt of students)

H_a: Median ≠ 300

Calculation:

Students	Credit Card Debt	Sign of Difference	Students	Credit Card Debt	Sign of Difference
1	6000	+	11	250	–
2	0	–	12	580	+
3	200	–	13	1000	+
4	0	–	14	0	–
5	400	–	15	0	–
6	1060	+	16	200	–
7	0	–	17	400	–
8	1200	+	18	800	+
9	200	–	19	700	+
10	250	–	20	1000	+

r^+ = Number of (+) signs = 8

r^- = Number of (–) signs = 12

$r = \text{Min}(r^+, r^-) = 8$

n = Total no. of students = 20

Critical Value: At 5% level of significance, i.e., $\alpha = 5\%$ with n = 20, the critical value r_α (from the Table) is 5, i.e., $r_\alpha = 5$.

Decision Rule: Since $r = 8 \geq r_\alpha = 5$, we cannot reject the null hypothesis H_0. We conclude that students do not disclose their credit card debt.

Example 11.14 (Large Sample):

A sports reporter claims that the median weight of offensive linemen in the NFL is greater than 300 pounds. He obtains a random sample of 30 offensive linemen and obtains the data shown in following Table. Test the reporter's claim at the $\alpha = 0.1$ level of significance.

Linemen	Weight	Linemen	Weight	Linemen	Weight
1	285	11	326	21	312
2	310	12	310	22	329
3	300	13	297	23	320
4	300	14	301	24	300
5	320	15	315	25	311
6	308	16	332	26	286
7	310	17	305	27	309
8	293	18	340	28	292
9	329	19	242	29	287
10	293	20	310	30	305

Solution:

Hypothesis: (One-tailed Test)

H_0: Median = 300 (the median weight of offensive linemen)

H_a: Median > 300 (Right-tailed Test)

Calculation:

Linemen	Weight	Sign of Difference	Linemen	Weight	Sign of Difference
1	285	–	16	332	+
2	310	+	17	305	+
3	300	0	18	340	+
4	300	0	19	242	–
5	320	+	20	310	+
6	308	+	21	312	+
7	310	+	22	329	+
8	293	–	23	320	+
9	329	+	24	300	0
10	293	–	25	311	+
11	326	+	26	286	–
12	310	+	27	309	+
13	297	–	28	292	–
14	301	+	29	287	–
15	315	+	30	305	+

r^+ = Number of (+) signs = 19

r^- = Number of (–) signs = 8

0 = 03

r = Max (r^+, r^-) = 19

n = Total no of students = 30 - 3 = 27

$$r_z = \frac{(X = r) - np}{\sqrt{np(1-p)}} = \frac{19 - 27 \times 0.5}{\sqrt{27 \times 0.5(1-0.5)}} = -1.92$$

Critical Value: At 10% level of significance, i.e., $\alpha = 0.1$ with n = 27, the critical value r_α (from the Table) is –1.28, i.e., $r_\alpha = -1.28$.

Decision Rule: Since $r_z = -1.92 < r_\alpha = -1.28$, we would reject the null hypothesis H_0. We conclude that the median weight of offensive linemen should be more than 300.

B. Two Sample Sign Test (or Paired Test):

The sign test has important applications in problems which deal with paired data. In many situations, comparison of effect of two treatments is of interest but observations occur in pairs. Thus the two samples are not truly random. Because of such pairwise dependence, ordinary two sample tests are not appropriate. In such situations when one member of the pair is associated with the treatment A and the other treatment B, non-parametric sign test has wide applicability.

Test Procedure:

Hypothesis: H_0: No difference in the effect of treatment A and B

H_1: A is better than B

Test Statistics: Let r^+ be the number of '–' signs. Each observation is denoted by a '+' sign if it is more than the previous observation and by a '–' sign if it is less than the previous observation. Total number of runs up (+) and down (–) is counted. In case two values are equal , the concerning pair is discarded. If i^{th} pair of observation is denoted by (x_i, y_i) where x is the effect of treatment A and y to B, then the the response difference $D_i = x_i - y_i$.

Critical Value: Critical value r_c corresponding to n, the number of pairs, is given in table. Significance level is given by α_1 as critical region is one-sided (left-tailed).

Decision Rule: If $r \leq r_c$ reject H_0, Otherwise accept H_0.

Ties Values: In case two values of a pair are equal, reject that pair and reduce the number of observations accordingly.

Note: In case alternative H_1 is that there is some difference in effect of A and B, r represents either the number of negative signs or the number of positive signs whichever turn out to be smaller. A critical region is two-sided and significance level is given α_2 for finding r_c.

Example 11.15:

In a market study, two brands of lemonade were compared. Each of 50 judges tested two samples, one of brand A and one of brand B with the following results: 35 preferred brand A, 10 preferred B, and 5 could not tell the difference. Thus, n = 45 and S = 10. Assuming $\alpha_1 = 5\%$, critical value $r_c = 16$ from Table. Since $r < r_c$, we reject H_0 of no difference in favour of the alternative H_a that the brand A is preferred.

Example 11.16:

The table below shows the hours of relief provided by two analgesic drugs in 12 patients suffering from arthritis. Is there any evidence that one drug provides longer relief than the other?

Case	Drug A	Drug B	Case	Drug A	Drug B
1	2.0	3.5	7	14.9	16.7
2	3.6	5.7	8	6.6	6.0
3	2.6	2.9	9	2.3	3.8
4	2.6	2.4	10	2.0	4.0
5	7.3	9.9	11	6.8	9.1
6	3.4	3.3	12	8.5	20.9

Solution:

Hypothesis: H_0: Evidence for a difference between the two treatments

H_a: No evidence for a difference between the two treatments

Calculation:

Case	Drug A	Drug B	Difference (B – A)	Sign of Difference
1	2.0	3.5	1.50	+
2	3.6	5.7	2.10	+
3	2.6	2.9	0.30	+
4	2.6	2.4	–0.20	–
5	7.3	9.9	2.60	+
6	3.4	3.3	–0.10	–
7	14.9	16.7	1.80	+
8	6.6	6.0	–0.60	–
9	2.3	3.8	1.50	+
10	2.0	4.0	2.00	+
11	6.8	9.1	2.30	+
12	8.5	20.9	12.40	+

In this case, our null hypothesis is that the median difference is zero. Actual differences (Drug B – Drug A) are:

+1.5, +2.1, +0.3, "0.2, +2.6, –0.1, +1.8, –0.6, +1.5, +2.0, +2.3, +12.4

Actual median difference is 1.65 hours. We have $r^+ = 9$, $r^- = 3$, $n = 12$, $r = \max(r^-, r^+) = 9$. Therefore, our two-sided P-value (from binomial tables) is $p = 0.146$. We would conclude that there is no evidence for a difference between the two treatments.

11.5.2. Wilcoxon Signed-rank Test (for Matched Pairs)

The **Wilcoxon signed-rank test** is a non-parametric statistical hypothesis test used when comparing two related samples or repeated measurements on a single sample to assess whether their population means differ (i.e., it is a paired difference test). It can be used as an alternative to the paired Student's t-test when the population cannot be assumed to be normally distributed or the data is on the ordinal scale. In consequence, the test is sometimes referred to as the Wilcoxon *T* test, and the test statistic is reported as a value of *T*.

Signed-rank test are useful where there is some kind of pairing between observations in the two samples. When observations are measured data, signed-rank test is more efficient then sign test as it takes account of the magnitude of the observed differences, if the differences between the response of the two treatments A and B is to be tested.

Hypothesis: H_0: No difference in the effect of the treatment A and B

H_a: Treatment A is better than B

Test Statistics: T represents the sum of ranks with negative signs. For calculating T, obtain the differences $D_i = x_i - y_i$, where x_i's are response of treatment A and y_i's of treatment B. Rank the absolute values of differences. Smallest give rank 1. Ties are assigned average ranks. Assign to each rank sign of observed difference. Obtain the sum of negative ranks.

Critical Value: T_c is given in Table for n no. of pairs. Significance level is given by α_1 as critical region is one-sided.

Decision Rule: $T \le T_c$, reject H_0. Otherwise accept H_0.

Tied Value: Discard the pair for which difference = 0 and reduce n accordingly. Equal differences are assigned average ranks.

Large Samples Sizes: For sample sizes larger than 25, the test statistics z is given below.

where, $Z = \dfrac{T - Ur}{\sigma r}$

$$\text{Mean} = U_r = \frac{n(n+1)}{4}$$

and Standard Deviation $= \sigma_r = \sqrt{n(n+1)(2n+1)/24}$

where, n = (no. of given matched pairs) – (no. of dropped out pairs, if any)

Example 11.17:

Blood pressure reading of ten patients before and after meditation for reducing the blood pressure as following:

Patient	1	2	3	4	5	6	7	8	9	10
Before Treatment A	86	84	78	90	92	77	89	90	90	86
After Treatment B	80	80	92	79	92	82	88	89	92	83

Test the null hypothesis of no effect against the alternative that medication is effective.

Solution:

Hypothesis: H_0: There is no difference in the effect of the treatment A and B

H_a: There is difference in the effect of the treatment A and B

Calculation:

Patient	1	2	3	4	5	6	7	8	9	10
Before Treatment A	86	84	78	90	92	77	89	90	90	86
After Treatment B	80	80	92	79	92	82	88	89	92	83
Differences	6	4	–14	11	0	–5	1	1	–2	3
Rank	7	5	9	8	Discard	6	1.5	1.5	3	4
Rank with Sign	+	+	–	+	Discard	–	+	+	–	+

Rank sum of negative differences = 3 + 6 + 9 = 18.

Critical Value: Since value of test statistics T = 18. For n = 9 and α_1 = 5%, T_c = 8 (from Table).

Decision Rule: Since $T > T_c$, null hypothesis H_0 is rejected. We conclude that, no effect of meditation is accepted.

Example 11.18:

An experiment is conducted to judge the effect of brand name on quality preparation. 16 subjects are recruited for the purpose and are asked to state and compare two samples of product on a set of a scale items judge to be ordinal. The following data are obtained:

Pair	1	2	3	4	5	6	7	8	9	10	11	12	13	14	15	16
Brand A	73	43	47	53	58	47	52	58	38	61	56	56	34	55	65	75
Brand B	51	41	43	41	47	32	24	58	43	53	52	57	44	57	40	68

Test the hypothesis, using Wilcoxon matched-pairs test, that there is no difference between the perceived qualities of the two samples. Use 5% level of significance.

Solution:

Hypothesis: H_0: There is no difference the perceived quality of two samples A and B

H_a: There is difference the perceived quality of two samples A and B

Calculation:

Pair	1	2	3	4	5	6	7	8	9	10	11	12	13	14	15	16
Brand A	73	43	47	53	58	47	52	58	38	61	56	56	34	55	65	75
Brand B	51	41	43	41	47	32	24	58	43	53	52	57	44	57	40	68
Difference	22	2	4	12	11	15	28	0	–5	8	4	–1	–10	–2	25	7
Rank	13	2.5	4.5	11	10	12	15	Discard	6	8	4.5	1	9	2.5	14	7
Rank with Sign	+	+	+	+	+	+	+	Discard	–	+	+	–	–	–	+	+

Rank sum of negative differences = 4 + 11 + 15 = 30.

Critical Value: Since value of test statistics T = 30. For n = 15 and α_1 = 5%, T_c = 25 (from Table).

Decision Rule: Since $T > T_c$, null hypothesis H_0 is rejected. We conclude that, there is difference between the perceived qualities of the two samples.

11.5.3 Run Test

A ***run*** is a series of consecutive points that are either all above or all below the regression curve. Another way of saying this is that a run is a consecutive series of points whose residuals are either all positive (+) or all negative (–). The run test (also called Wald-Wolfowitz test after Abraham Wald and Jacob Wolfowitz) is a non-parametric statistical test that checks a randomness hypothesis for a two-valued data sequence. These parameters do not depend on the "fairness" of the process generating the elements of the sequence in the sense that '+'s and '–'s must have equal probabilities, but only on the assumption that the elements are independent and identically distributed. If the amount of runs is significantly higher or lower than expected, the hypothesis of statistical independence of the elements may be rejected. More precisely, it can be used to test the hypothesis that the elements of the sequence are mutually independent.

Run Tests can be Used to Test

1. The randomness of a distribution, by taking the data in the given order and marking with + the data greater than the median, and with – the data less than the median. (Numbers equaling the median are omitted.)
2. Whether a function fits well to a data set, by marking the data exceeding the function value with + and the other data with – For this use, the runs test, which takes into account the signs but not the distances, is complementary to the chi-square test, which takes into account the distances but not the signs.

A. Run Test for Randomness

Run test is used for examining whether or not a set of observations constitutes a random sample from an infinite population. Test for randomness is of major importance because the assumption of randomness underlies statistical inference. In addition, tests for randomness are important for time series analysis.

Assumptions in Run Test of Randomness:

1. **Data order:** Run test of randomness assumes that data is entered in order (not grouped).
2. **Numeric data:** Run test of randomness assumes that data is in numeric form. This is a compulsory condition for run test, because in numeric form, it is easy to assign run to that particular value.
3. **Data level:** In run test or randomness, we assume that data should be in order. But if data is not in ordered form, then the researcher has to assign a value. These values are one of the following: mean, median, mode or a cut point. By assigning one of these values, data can be ordered.
4. **Distribution:** Run test of randomness is a non-parametric test. Hence, this test does not assume any distribution like any other parametric test.

Test Procedure:

Hypothesis: H_0: Sample values come from a random sequence

H_a: Sample values come from a non-random sequence

Test Statistics: Let r be the number of runs (a run is a sequence of signs of same kind bounded by signs of other kind). For finding the number of runs, the observations are listed in their order of occurrence. Each observation is denoted by a '+' sign if it is more than the previous observation and by a '–' sign if it is less than the previous observation. Total number of runs up (+) and down (–) is counted. Too few runs also indicate that the sequence is not random and too many runs also indicate that the sequence is not random.

Critical Value: Critical value for the test is obtained from the table for given value of n and at desired level of significance (α). Let this value is r_c.

Decision Rule: If r_c (lower) $\leq r \leq r_c$ (upper), accept H_0. Otherwise reject H_0.

Tied Values: If an observation is equal to its preceding observation, it is denoted by zero. While counting the number of runs, ignore it and reduce the value of n accordingly.

Large Sample Sizes: When sample size is greater than 25, the critical value r_c can be obtained using a normal distribution approximation.

The critical values for two-sided test at 5% level of significance are:

r_c (lower) = $\mu - 1.96\ \sigma$

r_c (upper) = $\mu + 1.96\ \sigma$

The critical values for one-sided test at 5% level of significance are:

r_c (left-tailed) = $\mu - 1.65\ \sigma$, if $r \leq r_c$, Reject H_0

r_c (right-tailed) = $\mu + 1.65\ \sigma$, if $r \geq r_c$, Reject H_0

where,

$$\mu = \frac{2n-1}{3} \text{ and } \sigma = \sqrt{\frac{16n-29}{90}}$$

Example 11.19:

Data on value of imports of selected agricultural production inputs from India by a county (in million dollars) during recent 12 years is given below:

5.2	5.5	3.8	2.5	8.3	2.1	1.7	10.0	10.0	6.9	7.5	10.6

Is the sequence random?

Solution:

Hypothesis: H_0: Sequence is random

H_a: Sequence is not random

Calculation:

5.2	5.5	3.8	2.5	8.3	2.1	1.7	10.0	10.0	6.9	7.5	10.6
	+	–	–	+	–	–	+	+	–	+	+

Here n = 11, the number of runs r = 7.

Critical Value: Critical n values for α = 5% (two-sided test) from the table are r_c (lower) = 4 and r_c (upper) = 10.

Decision Rule: Since r_c (lower) $\leq r \leq r_c$ (upper), i.e., $4 \leq 7 \leq 10$, H_0 is accepted. We conclude that the sequence is random.

B. Wald-Wolfowitz Two-sample Run Test

A "run" of a sequence is a maximal non-empty segment of the sequence consisting of adjacent equal elements. For example, the sequence "++++---+++--++++++----" consists of six runs, three of which consist of '+' sign and the others of '–' sign. If '+' and '–' alternate randomly, the number of runs in the sequence *n* for which it is given that there are n_1 occurrences of + and n_2 occurrences of – (so $n = n_1 + n_2$) is a random variable.

Wald-Wolfowitz Two-sample Run Test is used to examine whether two random samples come from populations having same distribution. This test can detect differences in averages or spread or any other important aspect between the two populations. This test is efficient when each sample size is moderately large (greater than or equal to 10).

Procedure:

Hypothesis: H_0: Two samples come from populations having same distribution

H_a: Two samples come from populations having different distributions

Test Statistics: Let r denote the number of runs. To obtain r, list the $n_1 + n_2$ observation from two samples in order of magnitude. Denote observations from one sample by 'x' and other by 'y'. Count the number of runs.

Critical Value: Difference in location results in few runs and difference in spread also result in few numbers of runs. Consequently, critical region for this test is always one-sided. The critical value to decide whether or not the number of runs is few is obtained from the table. The table gives critical value r_c for n_1 (size of sample 1) and n_2 (size of sample 2) at 5% level of significance.

Tied Values: In case x and y observations have same value, place the observation x(y) first if run of x(y) observation is counting.

Large Samples Sizes: For sample sizes larger than 20, critical value r_c is given below.

$r_c = \mu - 1.96\,\sigma$ at 5% level of significance

where

$$\text{Mean} = \mu = 1 + \frac{2n_1n_2}{n_1 + n_2}$$

and

$$\text{Variance} = \sigma^2 = \frac{2n_1n_2(2n_1n_2 - n_1 - n_2)}{(n_1 + n_2)^2(n_1 + n_2 - 1)}$$

Example 11.20:

To determine if a new hybrid seeding produces a bushier flowering plant, following data was collected. Examine if the data indicate that new hybrid products larger shrubs than current variety?

Shrubs Girth (in inches)								
Hybrid	x	31.8	32.8	39.2	36	30	34.5	37.4
Current Variety	y	35.5	27.6	21.3	24.8	36.7	30	

Solution:

Hypothesis: H_0: x and y populations are identical

H_1: There is some difference in girth of x and y shrubs

Calculation:

21.3	24.8	27.6	30.0	30.0	31.8	32.8	34.5	35.5	36.0	36.7	37.4	39.2
y	y	y	y	x	x	x	x	y	x	y	x	x

Test Statistics: r = 6 (Total number of runs).

Critical Value: For $n_1 = 7$ and $n_2 = 6$, critical value r_c at 5% level of significance is 3.

Decision Rule: Since $r > r_c$, we accept H_0 and conclude that x and y have identical distribution.

11.5.4 Mann-Whitney U Test

The **Mann-Whitney *U*** test (**Mann-Whitney-Wilcoxon (MWW)** or **Wilcoxon rank-sum test**) is a non-parametric statistical hypothesis test for assessing whether two independent samples of observations have equally large values. It is one of the most well-known non-parametric significance tests. It was proposed initially by Frank Wilcoxon in 1945, for equal sample sizes, and extended to arbitrary sample sizes and in other ways by Henry Mann and his student Donald Ransom Whitney in 1947.

Assumptions

1. All the observations from both groups are *independent* of each other.
2. The responses are *ordinal* or continuous measurements (i.e., one can at least say, of any two observations, which is the greater).
3. Under the null hypothesis, the distributions of both groups are equal, so that the probability of an observation from one population (X) exceeding an observation from the second population (Y) equals the probability of an observation

from *Y* exceeding an observation from *X*, that is, there is a symmetry between populations with respect to probability of random drawing of a larger observation.

4. Under the alternative hypothesis, the probability of an observation from one population (*X*) exceeding an observation from the second population (*Y*) (after correcting for ties) is not equal to 0.5. The alternative may also be stated in terms of a one-sided test, for example: $P(X > Y) + 0.5\ P(X = Y) > 0.5$.

Procedure:

Hypothesis: H_0: Two samples come from identical populations

H_a: Two samples are not identical (different populations)

Test Statistics:

The test involves the calculation of a statistic, usually called *U*, whose distribution under the null hypothesis is known. In the case of small samples, the distribution is tabulated, but for sample sizes above 20 there is a good approximation using the normal distribution. Some books tabulate statistics equivalent to *U*, such as the sum of ranks in one of the samples, rather than *U* itself. First, arrange all the observations into a single-ranked series. That is, rank all the observations without regard to which sample they are in.

For Small Sample:

1. Choose the sample for which the ranks seem to be smaller (The only reason to do this is to make computation easier). Call this "sample 1," and call the other sample "sample 2."
2. Taking each observation in sample 1, count the number of observations in sample 2 that have a smaller rank (count a half for any that are equal to it). The sum of these counts is *U*.

For Large Sample:

1. Add up the ranks for the observations which came from sample 1. The sum of ranks in sample 2 follows by calculation, since the sum of all the ranks equals N(N + 1)/2 where N is the total number of observations.
2. U is then given by:

$$U_1 = R_1 - \frac{n_1(n_1+1)}{2}$$

where n_1 is the sample size for sample 1, and R_1 is the sum of the ranks in sample 1.
and

$$U_2 = R_2 - \frac{n_2(n_2+1)}{2}$$

where n_2 is the sample size for sample 2, and R_2 is the sum of the ranks in sample 2.

The smaller value of U_1 and U_2 is the one used when consulting significance tables. The sum of the two values is given by:

$$U_1 + U_2 = R_1 - \frac{n_1(n_1+1)}{2} + R_2 - \frac{n_2(n_2+1)}{2}$$

where $R_1 + R_2 = N(N + 1)/2$ and $N = n_1 + n_2$, and the sum is

$U_1 + U_2 = n_1 n_2$

The work test-statistics, i.e., *U*, which is a measurement of the difference between the ranked observations of the two samples as under:

$$U = n_1 n_2 + \frac{n_1(n_1+1)}{2} - R_1$$

where n_1 and n_2 are the sample sizes and R_1 is the sum of ranks assigned to the values of the first sample.

Normal Approximation

For large samples, U is approximately *normally distributed.* In that case, the standardized value

$$Z = \frac{U - m_U}{\sigma_U}$$

where m_U and σ_U are the mean and standard deviation of U, is approximately a standard normal deviate whose significance can be checked in tables of the normal distribution. m_U and σ_U are given by:

$$\text{Mean} = m_U = \frac{n_1 n_2}{2}$$

and

$$\text{Standard Deviation} = \sigma_U = \sqrt{\frac{n_1 n_2 (n_1 + n_2 + 1)}{12}}$$

and

$$\text{Upper limit} = \mu_U + z\sigma_U \text{ and Lower limit} = \mu_U - z\sigma_U$$

Decision Rule:

If n_1 and n_2 are sufficiently large (i.e., both more than 8), the sampling distribution of U can be approximated closely with normal distribution and the limits of the acceptance region can be determined in the usual way at the given level of significance. But if either n_1 or n_2 is so small that the normal curve approximation to the sampling distribution of U cannot be used, then the exact tests may be based on special tables, i.e., Wilcoxon's unpaired distribution.

Case 1: One-sided test

For H_0: $\mu_1 = \mu_2$ and H_a: $\mu_1 > \mu_2$

If U_1 and $U_2 < U_\alpha$ (Critical Value), Reject H_0 for large value of U_1 or small value of U_2.

For H_0: $\mu_1 = \mu_2$ and H_a: $\mu_1 < \mu_2$

If U_1 and $U_2 < U_\alpha$ (Critical Value), Reject H_0 for small values of U_1.

Case 2: Two-sided test

For H_0: $\mu_1 = \mu_2$ and H_a: $\mu_1 \neq \mu_2$

If Min $(U_1, U_2) > U_\alpha$ (Critical Value), the null hypothesis H_0 is accepted.

Otherwise, H_0 is rejected.

Example 11.21:

Suppose that *Aesop* is dissatisfied with his *classic experiment* in which one *tortoise* was found to beat one *hare* in a race, and decides to carry out a significance test to discover whether the results could be extended to tortoises and hares in general. He collects a sample of 6 tortoises and 6 hares, and makes them all run his race at once. The order in which they reach the finishing post (their rank order, from first to last crossing the finish line) is as follows, writing T for a tortoise and H for a hare:

T H H H H H T T T T T H

What is the value of U?

Solution:

Direct Method:

We take each tortoise in turn, and count the number of hares it is beaten by, getting 0, 5, 5, 5, 5, 5, which means $U = 25$. Alternatively, we could take each hare in turn, and count the number of tortoises it is beaten by. In this case, we get 1, 1, 1, 1, 1, 6. So $U = 6 + 1 + 1 + 1 + 1 + 1 = 11$. Note that the sum of these two values for U is 36, which is 6×6.

Indirect Method:

The sum of the ranks achieved by the tortoises is $1 + 7 + 8 + 9 + 10 + 11 = 46$.

Therefore $U = 46 - (6 \times 7)/2 = 46 - 21 = 25$.

The sum of the ranks achieved by the hares is $2 + 3 + 4 + 5 + 6 + 12 = 32$, leading to

$U = 32 - 21 = 11$.

Example 11.22:

The mark obtained by two batches of students, MBA and PGDM in final examination taken after the completion of training. Use U-test with $\alpha = 2\%$ to test the null hypothesis that the samples are drawn from identical distributions against the alternative that the distributions differ in location only.

Batch MBA	25	30	27	31	20	22	28	32
Batch PGDM	21	32	26	27	23	18		

Solution:

Null Hypothesis: H_0: The samples are drawn from identical distributions

H_a: The samples are not identical

Calculation: From the given data n_1 (Batch MBA) = 8 and n_2 (Batch PGDM) = 6, so $n_1 + n_2 = 14$

Arrange all the 14 observations in ascending order and assign the rank.

Sample in Ascending Order	Rank	Name of Related Sample
18	1	PGDM
20	2	MBA
21	3	PGDM
22	4	MBA
23	5	PGDM
25	6	MBA
26	7	PGDM
27	8.5	MBA
27	8.5	PGDM
28	10	MBA
30	11	MBA
31	12	MBA
32	13.5	MBA
32	13.5	PGDM

From the above table,

The sum of the ranks assigned the sample MBA or $R_1 = 2 + 4 + 6 + 8.5 + 10 + 11 + 12 + 13.5 = 64$

The sum of the ranks assigned the sample PGDM or $R_2 = 1 + 3 + 5 + 7 + 8.5 + 13.5 = 38$

So, $R_1 + R_2 = 64 + 38 = 102$

$$U_1 = R_1 - \frac{n_1(n_1+1)}{2} = 64 - \frac{8(8+1)}{2} = 64 - 36 = 28$$

$$U_2 = R_2 - \frac{n_2(n_2+1)}{2} = 38 - \frac{6(6+1)}{2} = 38 - 21 = 17$$

Hence, Min (U_1, U_2) = Min (28, 17) = 17

Critical Value: From the Table, for larger sample size $n_1 = 8$ and smaller sample size $n_2 = 6$ for two-tailed test at the level 2%, the critical value is 4.

Decision: Since, Min (U_1, U_2) = Min (28, 17) = 17, which is greater than the 4. So null hypothesis H_0 is accepted. We conclude that the null hypothesis that the samples are drawn from identical distributions against the alternative.

Alternatively:

Calculation:

For $R_1 = 64$, $n_1 = 8$ and $n_2 = 6$

$$U = n_1 n_2 + \frac{n_1(n_1+1)}{2} - R_1 = 8 \times 6 + \frac{8(8+1)}{2} - 64 = 20$$

$$\text{Mean} = m_U = \frac{n_1 n_2}{2} = \frac{8 \times 6}{2} = 24$$

and

$$\text{Standard Deviation} = \sigma_U = \sqrt{\frac{n_1 n_2 (n_1 + n_2 + 1)}{12}}$$

$$= \sqrt{\frac{8 \times 6(8+6+1)}{12}} = \sqrt{60} = 7.74$$

As the alternative hypothesis is that the means of two samples are not equal, a two-tailed test is appropriate. According to acceptance region, 2% of level of significance is given. So, the z value for 0.49 of the area under normal distribution is 2.32. The limits of acceptance region:

Upper limit = $\mu_U + z\sigma_U = 24 + 2.32 \times 7.74 = 41.95$

and Lower limit = $\mu_U + z\sigma_U = 24 - 2.32 \times 7.74 = 6.04$

Decisions: As the observe value of U is 20, which is lies between the acceptance region, so null hypothesis H_0 is accepted. We conclude that the null hypothesis that the samples are drawn from identical distributions against the alternative.

Similarly, U statistics under U_2 is given by:

$$U = n_1 n_2 + \frac{n_2(n_2+1)}{2} - R_2 = 8 \times 6 + \frac{6(6+1)}{2} - 38 = 31$$

The value of U lies between the acceptance region and conclusion remains the same.

Comparison to Student's t-test

The U test is useful in the same situations as the independent samples Student's t-test, and the question arises of which should be preferred.

Ordinal data: U remains the logical choice when the data are ordinal but not interval scaled, so that the spacing between adjacent values cannot be assumed to be constant.

Robustness: As it compares the sums of ranks, the Mann-Whitney test is less likely than the t-test to spuriously indicate significance because of the presence of outliers, i.e., Mann-Whitney is more robust.

Efficiency: When normality holds, MWW has an (asymptotic) efficiency of $3/\pi$ or about 0.95 when compared to the t test. For distributions sufficiently far from normal and for sufficiently large sample sizes, the MWW can be considerably more efficient than the t.

11.5.5 Median Test

Mood's **Median test** is a special case of *Pearson's chi-square test*. It is a *non-parametric test* that tests the *null hypothesis* that the *medians* of the *populations* from which two *samples* are drawn are identical. The data in each sample are assigned to two groups, one consisting of data whose values are higher than the median value in the two groups combined, and the other consisting of data whose values are at the median or below. A Pearson's chi-square test is then used to determine whether the observed frequencies in each group differ from expected frequencies derived from a *distribution* combining the two groups.

The test has low *power* (efficiency) for moderate to large sample sizes, and is largely regarded as obsolete. To test whether or not two samples come from same population, median test is used. It is more efficient than the run test but each sample should be of size 10 at least.

Procedure:

Hypothesis: H_0: Two samples come from populations having same distribution

H_a: Two samples come from populations having different distributions

Test Statistics: To test the value of test statistics two samples of sizes n_1 and n_2 are combined. Median M of the combined sample of size $n = n_1 + n_2$ is obtained. Number of observations below and above the median M for each sample is determined. This is then analyzed as a 2×2 contingency table in the manner given below.

Table 11.5: Contingency Table

	Number of Observation		
	Sample 1	Sample 2	Total
Above Median	a	b	a + b
Below Median	c	d	c + d
Total	$a + c = n_1$	$b + d = n_2$	$n = a + b + c + d$

$$N^2 \text{ (Chi-square)} = \frac{(ab - bc)^2 (a + b + c + d)}{(a + c)(b + d)(a + b)(c + d)}$$

Decision Rule: If $N^2 \geq Nc^2$, reject H_0 otherwise accept H_0.

Tied values: Ties are ignored and n is adjusted accordingly.

Note: This test can be extended to k samples with number of observations below and above the combined median M from a $2 \times k$ contingency table.

Example 11.23:

A private bank is interested in finding out whether the customers belonging to two groups differ in their satisfaction level. The two groups are customers belonging to current account holders and savings account holders. A random sample of

20 customers of each category was interviewed regarding their perceptions of the bank's service quality using Likert-type (ordinal scale) statements. A score of "1" represents very dissatisfied and a score of "5" represents very satisfied. The compiled aggregate scores for each respondent in each group are tabulated be given below:

Current Account	Savings Account
79	85
86	80
40	50
50	55
75	65
38	50
70	63
73	75
50	55
40	45
20	30
80	85
55	65
61	80
50	55
80	75
60	65
30	50
70	75
50	62

What are your conclusions regarding the satisfaction level of these two groups?

Solution:

Hypothesis: H_0: There is no difference between the current account holders and savings account holders in the perceived satisfaction level.

H_a: There is difference between the current account holders and savings account holders in the perceived satisfaction level.

Calculation:

The first task in the median test is to obtain the grand median. Arrange the combined data of both the groups in the descending order of magnitude. That is rank them from the highest to the lowest. Select the middle most observation in the ranked data. In this case, median is the average of 20th and 21st observation in the array that has been arranged in the descending order of magnitude.

Descending Order	Rank	Descending Order	Rank
86	1	61	21
85	2.5	60	22
85	2.5	55	24.5
80	5.5	55	24.5
80	5.5	55	24.5
80	5.5	55	24.5
80	5.5	50	30
79	8	50	30
75	10.5	50	30
75	10.5	50	30
75	10.5	50	30
75	10.5	50	30
73	13	50	30
70	14.5	45	34
70	14.5	40	35.5
65	17	40	35.5
65	17	38	37
65	17	30	38.5
63	19	30	38.5
62	20	20	40

Grand median is the average of 20th and 21st observation = (62 + 61)/2 = 61.5. Please note that in the above table, average rank is taken whenever the scores are tied. The next step is to prepare a contingency table of two rows and two columns. The cells represent the number of observations that are above and below the grand median in each group. Whenever some observations in each group coincide with the median value, the accepted practice is to first count the observations that are strictly above grand median and put the rest under below grand median. In other words, below grand median in such cases would include less than or equal to grand median.

Scores of Current Account Holders and Savings Account Holders as Compared with Grand Median

	Current Account Holders	Savings Account Holders	Marginal Total
Above Grand Median	8 (a)	12 (b)	20 (a + b)
Below Grand Median	12 (c)	8 (d)	20 (c + d)
Marginal Total	20 (a + c)	20 (b + d)	40 (a + b + c + d) = n

The test statistic to be used is given by:

$$N^2 \text{ (Chi-square)} = \frac{(ab - bc)^2 (a + b + c + d)}{(a + c)(b + d)(a + b)(c + d)} = 0.90$$

Critical Value: Critical value of chi-square for 1 d.f. at 5% level of significance = 3.84 (from the table).

Decision Rule: Since the computed chi-square value (0.90) is less than critical value of chi-square (3.84), we have no convincing evidence to reject the null hypothesis. Thus, the data are consistent with the null hypothesis that there is no difference between the current account holders and savings account holders in the perceived satisfaction level.

Example 11.24:

Two randomly selected samples of Utkal University students were asked to read and then evaluate a short story written by a new author. One sample was told that the author was from Quebec, while the second sample was told the author was from Ontario. The following evaluations were obtained ... a higher score indicating a more favorable evaluation. Assume this is ordinal level data and apply the median test to determine whether there is significant difference between the medians of these groups. Were student evaluations of the short story influenced by the cultural background of its authors?

Sample 1	Sample 2
6	6
5	8
1	8
1	2
3	5
4	6
3	3
6	8
5	6
5	8
1	2
3	2
5	6
6	8
6	4
3	3

Solution:

Hypothesis: H_0: Student evaluations were not influenced by the cultural background of the author.

H_a: student evaluations were influenced by the cultural background of the author.

Calculation:

The first task in the median test is to obtain the grand median. Arrange the combined data of both the groups in the descending order of magnitude. That is rank them from the highest to the lowest. Select the middle most observation in the ranked data. In this case, median is the average of 16th and 17th observation in the array that has been arranged in the descending order of magnitude.

Descending Order of Higher Score

Descending Order	Rank	Descending Order	Rank
8	3	5	16
8	3	5	16
8	3	4	19.5
8	3	4	19.5
8	3	3	23.5
6	9.5	3	23.5
6	9.5	3	23.5
6	9.5	3	23.5
6	9.5	3	23.5

6	9.5	3	23.5
6	9.5	2	28
6	9.5	2	28
6	9.5	2	28
5	16	1	31
5	16	1	31
5	16	1	31

Grand median is the average of 16th and 17th observation = (5 + 5)/2 = 5. Please note that in the above table, average rank is taken whenever the scores are tied. The next step is to prepare a contingency table of two rows and two columns. The cells represent the number of observations that are above and below the grand median in each group. Whenever some observations in each group coincide with the median value, the accepted practice is to first count the observations that are strictly above grand median and put the rest under below grand median. In other words, below grand median in such cases would include less than or equal to grand median.

	Sample 1	**Sample 2**	**Marginal Total**
Above Grand Median	12(a)	9(b)	21(a + b)
Below Grand Median	4(c)	7(d)	11(c + d)
Marginal Total	16(a + c)	16(b + d)	32(a + b + c + d) = n

The test statistic to be used is given by:

$$N^2 \text{ (Chi-square)} = \frac{(ab - bc)^2 (a + b + c + d)}{(a + c)(b + d)(a + b)(c + d)} = 3.236$$

Critical Value: Critical value of chi-square for 1 d.f., at 5% level of significance = 3.84 (from the table).

Decision Rule: Since the computed chi-square value (3.236) is less than critical value of chi-square (3.841). Hence, we cannot reject the null hypothesis and must conclude that student evaluations were not influenced by the cultural background of the author.

Some Commonly Used Statistical Tests

Normal Theory Based Test	**Corresponding Non-parametric Test**	**Purpose of Test**
1. t-test for independent samples	1. Mann-Whitney U test; Wilcoxon rank-sum test	1. Compares two independent samples
2. Paired t-test	2. Wilcoxon matched pairs signed-rank test	2. Examines a set of differences
3. Pearson correlation coefficient	3. Spearman rank correlation coefficient	3. Assesses the linear association between two variables.
4. One-way analysis of variance (F test)	4. Kruskal-Wallis analysis of variance by ranks	4. Compares three or more groups
5. Two-way analysis of variance	5. Friedman Two-way analysis of variance	5. Compares groups classified by two different factors

11.6 ADVANTAGES AND DISADVANTAGES OF NON-PARAMETRIC TEST

Advantages

(1) Non-parametric test make less stringent demands of the data. For standard parametric procedures to be valid, certain underlying conditions or assumptions must be met, particularly for smaller sample sizes. The one-sample t-test, for example, requires that the observations be drawn from a normally distributed population. For two independent samples, the t-test has the additional requirement that the population standard deviations be equal. If these assumptions/conditions are violated, the resulting P-values and confidence intervals may not be trustworthy. However, normality is not required for the

Wilcoxon signed-rank or rank sum tests to produce valid inferences about whether the median of a symmetric population is 0 or whether two samples are drawn from the same population.

(2) Non-parametric procedures can sometimes be used to get a quick answer with little calculation.

Two of the simplest non-parametric procedures are the sign test and median test. The *sign test* can be used with paired data to test the hypothesis that differences are equally likely to be positive or negative, (or, equivalently, that the median difference is 0). For small samples, an exact test of whether the proportion of positives is 0.5 can be obtained by using a binomial distribution. For large samples, the test statistic is

$(\text{Plus} - \text{Minus})^2/(\text{Plus} + \text{Minus})$,

where *plus* is the number of positive values and *minus* is the number of negative values. Under the null hypothesis that the positive and negative values are equally likely, the test statistic follows the chi-square distribution with 1 degree of freedom. Whether the sample size is small or large, the sign test provides a quick test of whether two paired treatments are equally effective simply by counting the number of times each treatment is better than the other.

Example: 15 patients given both treatments A and B to test the hypothesis that they perform equally well. If 13 patients prefer A to B and 2 patients prefer B to A, the test statistic is $(13 - 2)^2/(13 + 2)$ [= 8.07] with a corresponding P-value of 0.0045. The null hypothesis is therefore rejected.

The ***median test*** is used to test whether two samples are drawn from populations with the same median. The median of the combined data set is calculated and each original observation is classified according to its original sample (A or B) and whether it is less than or greater than the overall median. The chi-square test for homogeneity of proportions in the resulting 2×2 table tests whether the population medians are equal.

(3) Non-parametric methods provide an air of objectivity when there is no reliable (universally recognized) underlying scale for the original data and there is some concern that the results of standard parametric techniques would be criticized for their dependence on an artificial metric. For example, patients might be asked whether they feel *extremely uncomfortable/ uncomfortable/neutral/comfortable/very comfortable*. What scores should be assigned to the comfort categories and how do we know whether the outcome would change dramatically with a slight change in scoring? Some of these concerns are blunted when the data are converted to ranks.

(4) A historical appeal of rank tests is that it was easy to construct tables of exact critical values, provided there were no ties in the data. The same critical value could be used for all data sets with the same number of observations because every data set is reduced to the ranks 1, ..., *n*. However, this advantage has been eliminated by the ready availability of personal computers.

(5) Sometimes the data do not constitute a random sample from a larger population. The data in hand are all there are. Standard parametric techniques based on sampling from larger populations are no longer appropriate. Because there are no larger populations, there are no population parameters to estimate. Nevertheless, certain kinds of non-parametric procedures can be applied to such data by using *randomization models*.

Disadvantages

Such a strong case has been made for the benefits of non-parametric procedures that some might ask why parametric procedures aren't abandoned entirely in favor of non-parametric methods!

The major disadvantage of non-parametric techniques is contained in its name. Because the procedures are *non-parametric*, there are no parameters to describe and it becomes more difficult to make quantitative statements about the actual difference between populations. (For example, when the sign test says two treatments are different, there's no confidence interval and the test doesn't say by how much the treatments differ.) However, it is sometimes possible with the right software to compute estimates (and even confidence intervals!) for medians, differences between medians. However, the calculations are often too tedious for pencil-and-paper. A computer is required. As statistical software goes though its various iterations, such confidence intervals may become readily available.

The second disadvantage is that non-parametric procedures throw away information! The sign test, for example, uses only the signs of the observations. Ranks preserve information about the order of the data but discard the actual values. Because information is discarded, non-parametric procedures can never be as powerful (able to detect existing differences) as their parametric counterparts when parametric tests can be used.

11.7 SUMMARY

A **chi-square test (χ^2 test)** is any **statistical hypothesis test** in which the **sampling distribution** of the test statistic is a **chi-square distribution** when the **null hypothesis** is true, or any in which this is *asymptotically* true, meaning that the sampling distribution (if the null hypothesis is true) can be made to approximate a chi-square distribution as closely as desired by making the sample size large enough. The Chi-square (χ^2) test is the most popular non-parametric tests/method, to test the hypothesis. Chi-square analysis has to satisfy the following conditions: (1) Randomly drawn from the population, (2) Reported in raw counts of frequency, (3) Measured variables must be independent, (4) Observed frequencies cannot be too small, and (5) Values of independent and dependent variables must be mutually exclusive. Characteristics of the Chi-square Test: (1) It is not symmetric, (2) The shape of the chi-square distribution depends upon the degrees of freedom, just like Student's *t*-distribution, (3) As the number of degrees of freedom increases, the chi-square distribution becomes more symmetric and (4) The values are non-negative. That is, the values of variable are greater than or equal to 0. There are three types of chi-square test. (1) *Chi square test for population variance* which is used to test a hypothesis on a specific value of the **population variance,** (2) *The Chi-square test for goodness of fit* which compares the expected and observed values to determine how well an experimenter's predictions fit the data and (3) *The Chi-square test for independence* which compares two sets of categories to determine whether the two groups are distributed differently among the categories.

Analysis of variance (ANOVA) is a collection of **statistical models,** and their associated procedures, in which the observed **variance** in a particular variable is partitioned into components attributable to different sources of variation. In its simplest form, ANOVA provides a **statistical test** of whether or not the **means** of several groups are all equal, and therefore generalizes **t-test** to more than two groups. ANOVAs are helpful because they possess an advantage over a two-sample t-test. The first step in the analysis of variance is to partition the total variation in the sample data into the following two component variations in such a way that it is possible to estimate the contribution of factors that may cause variation: (1) The amount of variation *among the sample means* or the variation attributable to the difference among samples means. The variation is either on account of difference in treatment or due to element of chance. The difference is denoted by SSC or SSTR and (2) The amount of variation *within the sample observations*. This difference is considered due to chance causes or experimental (random) errors. The difference in the values of various elements in a sample due to chance is called an estimate and denoted as SSE. The observations in the sample data may be classified according to *one factor* (criterion) or *two factors* (criterion). The classification according to one factor and two factors are called *one-way classification* and *two-way classification*, respectively. The calculations for total variation and its components may be carried out in each of the two types of classifications by: *(i) direct method, (ii) short-cut method, and (iii) coding method.*

11.8 KEY TERMS

Chi-square Test: A chi-square test (χ^2 test) is any **statistical hypothesis test** in which the **sampling distribution** of the test statistic is a **chi-square distribution** when the **null hypothesis is** true, or any in which this is *asymptotically* true, meaning that the sampling distribution (if the null hypothesis is true) can be made to approximate a chi-square distribution as closely as desired by making the sample size large enough.

Chi-square Test for Population Variance: *Chi-square test for population variance* which is used to test a hypothesis on a specific value of the **population variance.**

The Chi-square Test for Goodness of Fit: *The Chi-square test for goodness of fit* which compares the expected and observed values to determine how well an experimenter's predictions fit the data.

The Chi-square Test for Independence: *The Chi-square test for independence* which compares two sets of categories to determine whether the two groups are distributed differently among the categories.

Analysis of Variance (ANOVA): ANOVA is a collection of **statistical models,** and their associated procedures, in which the observed **variance** in a particular variable is partitioned into components attributable to different sources of variation.

One-way ANOVA: In one-way ANOVA, consider only one factor and then observe that the reasons for said factor to be important are that several possible types of sample can occur within that factor.

Two-way ANOVA: The partitioning of the total variation in the sample data is done into two components: (i) Variation among the samples due to different samples and (ii) Variation within the samples due to random error. ANOVA technique in context of two-way design when repeated values are not there.

Latin-square Design: Latin-square design is an experimental design; the treatments are allocated among the plots that no treatment occurs, more than once in any one row or any one column.

11.8 MULTIPLE OBJECTIVE TYPE QUESTIONS

1. The Chi-square test for independence which compares two sets of categories to determine whether the two groups are distributed differently among the categories.
   (a) True (b) False
2. If a sample of size n is taken from a population having a normal distribution, then there is a well-known result which allows a test to be made of whether the variance of the population has a predetermined value.
   (a) True (b) False
3. Goodness of fit means how well a statistical model fits a set of populations.
   (a) True (b) False
4. Chi-square test for independence is used to determine the relationship between two variables of a sample.
   (a) True (b) False
5. Chi-square is a collection of statistical models, and their associated procedures, in which the observed variance in a particular variable is partitioned into components attributable to different sources of variation.
   (a) True (b) False
6. The coding method is based on the fact that the z-test statistic used in the analysis of variance is the ratio of variances without unit of measurement.
   (a) True (b) False
7. Latin-square design is an experimental design used frequently in agricultural research.
   (a) True (b) False
8. The Sign Test is a non-parametric statistical test whereby very few assumptions are taken about the nature of the distribution being tested.
   (a) True (b) False
9. Signed-rank test are useful where there is some kind of pairing between observations in the one sample.
   (a) True (b) False
10. Run test is used for examining whether or not a set of observations constitutes a random sample from an infinite population.
    (a) True (b) False
11. Chi-square analysis has to be satisfied which of the following conditions?
    (a) Randomly drawn from the population (b) Reported in raw counts of frequency
    (c) Measured variables must be independent (d) All of the above
12. In one-way ANOVA, the partitioning of the total variation in the sample data is done into which components?
    (a) Variation among the samples due to different samples
    (b) Variation within the samples due to random error
    (c) Both (a) and (b)
    (d) None of the above

13. The ANOVA technique in case of Latin-square design remains more or less the same as we have already stated in case of a two-way design, expecting the fact that the variance is splitted into which part?
    (a) Variance between columns (b) Variance between rows
    (c) Variance between varieties (d) All of the above
14. Most of the non-parametric methods utilize measurements on:
    (a) Interval scale (b) Ordinal scale
    (c) Nominal scale (d) Both (c) and (d)
15. In tests using rank methods, the null hypothesis is rejected if the calculated value:
    (a) Exceeds the tabulated value (b) Is less than the tabulated value
    (c) Is either less or more than the tabulated value (d) All the above
16. A "run" is defined as
    (a) Succession of values with '+' sign (b) Succession of values with '–' sign
    (c) Succession of values with the same sign (d) All the above
17. Mann-Whitney 'U' test is used for testing:
    (a) Equality of two means (b) Equality of more than two means
    (c) Equality of three means (d) Equality of two sets of rankings
18. Kolmogorow-Smirnov have evolved tests for:
    (a) Goodness of fit of a distribution (b) Comparing two populations
    (c) Both (a) and (b) (d) None of these
19. Median test is used:
    (a) Sample should be at least 10 (b) Sample should be more than 10
    (c) Any sample (d) All of the above
20. The non-parametric test that is analogous to the One-way ANOVA is the:
    (a) Kruskal-Wallis test (b) Friedman test
    (c) Mann-Whitney test (d) None of the above

Answers to Multiple Objective Type Questions

Questions	1	2	3	4	5	6	7	8	9	10
Answers	T	T	F	T	F	F	T	T	F	T
Questions	11	12	13	14	15	16	17	18	19	20
Answers	d	c	d	d	b	c	d	c	a	d

11.10 CONCEPTUAL QUESTIONS

1. What is the meaning of chi-square test? What are their characteristics?
2. Explain the different types of Chi-square test with suitable example.
3. What is ANOVA? Describe briefly the techniques of analysis of variance for one-way and two-way classifications.
4. State the basic assumptions of analysis of variance.
5. Write short notes:
    (a) Chi-square test for population variance
    (b) The Chi-square test for goodness of fit

(c) The Chi-square test for independence which compares

(d) Latin-square design

(e) Coding method

(f) Significance of ANOVA

6. A certain drug was administered to 456 males out of a total 720 in a certain locality to test its efficiency against typhoid. The incidence of typhoid is shown below. Find out the effectiveness of the drug against the disease.

	Inflation	No inflation	Total
Administering the Drug	144	312	**456**
Without Administering the Drug	192	72	**264**
Total	**336**	**384**	**720**

7. A sample analysis of examination result of 500 students was made. It was found that 180 students had failed, 170 had secured a third class, 110 were placed in second class and 40 got a first class. Are those figures commensurate with the general examination result which is in the ratio 4 : 3 : 1 for the various categories respectively?

8. The following table gives the number of screws declared fit and also unfit by three inspectors X, Y and Z. Test the hypothesis that the proportion of screws declared unfit by three inspectors are same.

Inspector	**Number of Screws**			**Total No. of Screws**
	X	**Y**	**Z**	
Fit Screws	50	47	56	**153**
Screws Unfit	5	14	8	**27**
Total	**55**	**61**	**64**	**180**

9. The following table gives the number of aircraft accidents that occurred during the various days of the week. Find whether the accidents are uniformly distributed over the week ($X2_{6,005}$ = 12.55).

Day	Sun	Mon	Tue	Wed	Thu	Fri	Sat
No. of Accidents	14	16	8	20	11	9	14

10. A market analyst took a sample of 20 markets in Odisha to determine, how much variation is there in the price of peanut butter. Sample mean X = 70 and sample standard deviation = 7 from the 20 prices which were quoted to him for from samples of peanut butter. Find a 95% confidence interval for the standard deviation of all the markets.

11. The following table gives the monthly sales (in thousand) of a certain firm in three states by its four salesman:

States	**Salesman**				**Total**
	S1	S2	S3	S4	
Odisha	6	5	5	8	24
Bihar	8	9	6	5	28
West Bengal	10	7	8	9	34
Total	24	21	19	22	86

Set up the analysis of variance table for the above information.

12. A Company planned to compare four programs for training employees to achieve a certain manual assignment. Twenty fresh employees are randomly allocated to the training programs, with 5 in each program. At the conclusion of the training period, a examination is conducted to know how fast trainees can complete the task. The number of times the task is completed per minute is traced for each trainee, with the subsequent results:

Observation	Program 1	Program 2	Program 3	Program 4
1	9	10	12	9
2	12	6	14	8
3	14	9	11	11
4	11	9	13	7
5	13	10	11	8

Prepare the one-way and two-way ANOVA result.

APPENDIX 11.1

What Statistical Test Do I Need?

Deciding on appropriate statistical methods for your research:

What is your research question?

Which variables will help you answer your research question and which is the dependent variable?

What type of variables are they?

Which statistical test is most appropriate? Should a parametric or non-parametric test be used?

Comparing	Dependent variable	Independent variable	Parametric test (Dependent variable is Normally distributed)	Non-parametric test
The means of two independent groups	Continuous/scale	Categorical/nominal	Independent t-test	Mann-Whitney test
The means of 2 paired (matched) samples e.g., weight before and after a diet for one group of subjects	Continuous/scale	Time variable (time 1 = before, time 2 = after)	Paired t-test	Wilcoxon signed rank test
The means of 3 + independent groups	Continuous/scale	Categorical/nominal	One-way ANOVA	Kruskal-Wallis test
The 3+ measurements on the same subject	Continuous/scale	Time variable	Repeated measures ANOVA	Friedman test
Relationship between 2 continuous variables	Continuous/scale	Continuous/scale	Pearson's Correlation Coefficient	Spearman's Correlation Coefficient (also use for ordinal data)
Predicting the value of one variable from the value of a predictor variable	Continuous/scale	Any	Simple Linear Regression	
Assessing the relationship between two categorical variables	Categorical/nominal	Categorical/nominal		Chi-squared test

Examples:

- **Are height and weight related?** Both are continuous variables so Pearson's Correlation Coefficient would be appropriate if the variables are both normally distributed.
- **Can height predict weight?** You cannot determine height from weight but you could estimate weight given height so height is the continuous independent variable. Simple linear regression will help decide if weight is a good predictor of height and produce an equation to predict weight given an individual's height.
- **Is Diet 1 better than Diet 2?** A researcher would randomly allocate subjects to two groups with one group following Diet 1 and the other Diet 2. Weight would be taken before and after the diet and the mean weight lost compared for the two groups. The dependent variable 'weight lost' is continuous and the independent variable is the group the subject is in which is categorical. If the data is normally distributed, use the independent t-test, if not use the Mann-Whitney test.
- **Are patients taking treatment A more likely to recover than those on treatment B?** Both 'Treatment' (A or B) and 'Recovery' (Yes or No) are categorical variables so the Chi-squared test is appropriate.

CHAPTER 12

MULTIVARIATE ANALYSIS

Chapter Outline

Learning Objectives

- *Explain the concept of association that takes place between a dependent variable and a set of independent variables.*
- *Describe the various multivariate procedures available to analyze associative data in the context of any research problem.*
- *Interpret the findings of multivariate analysis in any research study.*
- *Use a particular technique of multivariate analysis suitable for a particular business research problem.*

12.1 MEANING OF MULTIVARIATE ANALYSIS

The subject of multivariate analysis deals with the statistical analysis of the data collected on more than one (response) variable. These variables may be correlated with each other, and their statistical dependence is often taken into account when analyzing such data. In fact, this consideration of statistical dependence makes multivariate analysis somewhat different in approach and considerably more complex than the corresponding univariate analysis, when there is only one response variable under consideration.

Response variables under consideration are often described as random variables and since their dependence is one of the things to be accounted for in the analyses, these response variables are often described by their joint probability distribution. This consideration makes the modeling issue relatively manageable and provides a convenient framework for scientific analysis of the data. Multivariate normal distribution is one of the most frequently made distributional assumptions for the analysis of multivariate data. However, if possible, any such consideration should ideally be dictated by the particular context. Also, in many cases, such as when the data are collected on a nominal or ordinal scales, multivariate normality may not be an appropriate or even viable assumption.

In the real world, most data collection schemes or designed experiments will result in multivariate data. A few examples of such situations are given below.

Example 1: During a survey of households, several measurements on each household are taken. These measurements, being taken on the same household, will be dependent. For example, the education level of the head of the household and the annual income of the family are related.

Example 2: During a production process, a number of different measurements such as the tensile strength, brittleness, diameter, etc. are taken on the same unit. Collectively such data are viewed as multivariate data.

Example 3: On a sample of 100 cars, various measurements such as the average gas mileage, number of major repairs, noise level, etc. are taken. Also each car is followed for the first 50,000 miles and these measurements are taken after every 10,000 miles. Measurements taken on the same car at the same mileage and those taken at different mileage are going to be correlated. In fact, these data represent a very complex multivariate analysis problem.

Most of the problems stated above require (at least for the convenience of modeling and for performing statistical tests) the assumption of multivariate normality. There are however, several other aspects of multivariate analysis such as factor analysis, cluster analysis, etc., which are largely distribution free in nature.

12.2 MULTIVARIATE DATA ANALYSIS

Multivariate Data Analysis refers to any statistical technique used to analyze data that arises from more than one variable. This essentially models reality where each situation, product, or decision involves more than a single variable. The information age has resulted in masses of data in every field. Despite the quantum of data available, the ability to obtain a clear picture of what is going on and make intelligent decisions is a challenge. When available information is stored in database tables containing rows and columns, Multivariate Analysis can be used to process the information in a meaningful fashion.

Multivariate Analysis Methods Typically Used for

1. Consumer and market research
2. Quality control and quality assurance across a range of industries such as food and beverage, paint, pharmaceuticals, chemicals, energy, telecommunications, etc.
3. Process optimization and process control
4. Research and development

With Multivariate Analysis, you can

1. Obtain a summary or an overview of a table. This analysis is often called Principal Components Analysis or Factor Analysis. In the overview, it is possible to identify the dominant patterns in the data, such as groups, outliers, trends, and so on. The patterns are displayed as two plots.

2. Analyze groups in the table, how these groups differ, and to which group individual table rows belong. This type of analysis is called Classification and Discriminate Analysis
3. Find relationships between columns in data tables, for instance relationships between process operation conditions and product quality. The objective is to use one set of variables (columns) to predict another, for the purpose of optimization, and to find out which columns are important in the relationship. The corresponding analysis is called Multiple Regression Analysis or Partial Least Squares (PLS), depending on the size of the data table.

12.2.1 How a Multivariate Analysis Works?

A multivariate analysis enables you to avoid the problem of multiple tests that would arise if you tested the effect of each independent variable on each dependent variable separately. Another way to handle the same problem is to use the Bonferroni method to correct for multiple tests. For some problems, the Bonferroni method is much more powerful than a multivariate test, and for other problems the reverse is true. To understand when a multivariate test is likely to outperform the Bonferroni method and when it is not, it helps to understand in more detail how the multivariate approach tests a hypothesis.

Consider first a problem with no covariates. When there is just one dependent variable Y, an ordinary multiple regression finds the linear function of the independent variables that correlates maximally with Y. That correlation is called the multiple correlation R. The size of R (or some equivalent statistic, such as a residual sum of squares) is used to test the null hypothesis of no relation between Y and any of the independent variables.

That concept is extended to the multivariate case as follows. The computer program derives two linear functions — a linear function of the X's, and a separate linear function of the Y's — such that the two functions correlate maximally with each other. That maximum correlation is called the first canonical correlation between the X and Y sets. This canonical correlation would be 0 only if all the aforementioned $p \times q$ simple correlations were 0. That would virtually never be true in a sample. But just as the size of a sample's simple correlation can be used to test a null hypothesis about the population value of the correlation, so can the sample value of the canonical correlation be used to test the null hypothesis that all $p \times q$ simple XY correlations are zero.

Now consider the more general case in which you use the multivariate approach to test the null hypothesis that there is no relation between several independent variables X_1, X_2, etc. and several dependent variables Y_1, Y_2, etc., when several covariates C_1, C_2, etc. are controlled. In effect a multivariate analysis will foilow a three-step process:

1. Regress each independent variable on the set of covariates and save in memory the residuals in that regression. Call these variables $X_1.C$ (the portion of X_1 independent of the C variables), $X_2.C$, etc.
2. Similarly derive $Y_1.C$, $Y_2.C$, etc. by regressing Y_1, Y_2, etc. on the C variables.
3. Find the canonical correlation between the two sets of variables derived in steps 1 and 2. This partial canonical correlation is the principal statistic used to test the hypothesis of interest.

12.3 MULTIVARIATE ANALYSIS TECHNIQUES

Multivariate Techniques are Defined as Following:

1. Correlation Analysis
2. Regression Analysis
3. Factor Analysis
4. Cluster Analysis
5. Discriminant Analysis
6. Multivariate Analysis of Variance (MANOVA)
7. Multidimensional Scaling (MDS)
8. Correspondence Analysis
9. Conjoint Analysis
10. Canonical Correlation
11. Structural Equation Modeling

12.4 CORRELATION ANALYSIS

Correlation is a statistical technique that can show whether and how strongly pairs of variables are related. Correlation refers to any of a broad class of statistical relationships involving dependence. Following aspects are considered in examining the statistical relationship between two or more variables.

- Is there an association between two or more variables? If yes, what is the form and degree of that relationship?
- Is the relationship strong or significant enough to arrive at a desirable conclusion?
- Can the relationship be used for predictive purpose, that is, to predict the most likely value of a dependent variable corresponding to the given value of independent variable or variables?

Correlation is a technique which measures the strength of association between two variables. Both the variables *X* and *Y* may be random or may be that one variable is independent (non-random) and the other to be correlated are dependent. When the changes in one variable appear to be linked with the changes in the other variable, the two variables are said to be correlated. When the two variables are meaningfully related and both increase or both decrease simultaneously, then the correlation is termed as positive. If increase in any one variable is associated with decrease in the other variable, the correlation is termed as negative or inverse. Suppose marks in Mathematics are denoted by *X* and marks are Statistics are denoted by *Y*. If small values of *X* appear with small values of *Y* and large values of *X* come with large values of *Y*, then correlation is said to be positive. If *X* stands for marks in English and *Y* stands for marks in Mathematics, it is possible that small values of *X* appear with large values of *Y*. It is a case of negative correlation.

12.4.1 Types of Correlations

Positive Correlation

The correlation in the same direction is called positive correlation. If one variable increase, other also increases and if one variable decrease, other also decreases. For example, the length of an iron bar will increase as the temperature increases. For example:

Price	10	15	20	25
Supply	100	110	115	130

Price	40	30	20	10
Supply	150	140	115	100

Negative Correlation

The correlation in opposite direction is called negative or inverse correlation. If one variable increase, other decrease and *vice versa*. For example, the volume of gas will decrease as the pressure increase or the demand of a particular commodity increases as price of such commodity decrease. For example:

Price	10	15	20	25
Demand	100	90	80	60

Price	40	30	20	10
Demand	60	80	90	100

No or Zero Correlation

If there is no relationship between the two variables such that the value of one variable change and the other variable remain constant, it is called no or zero correlation.

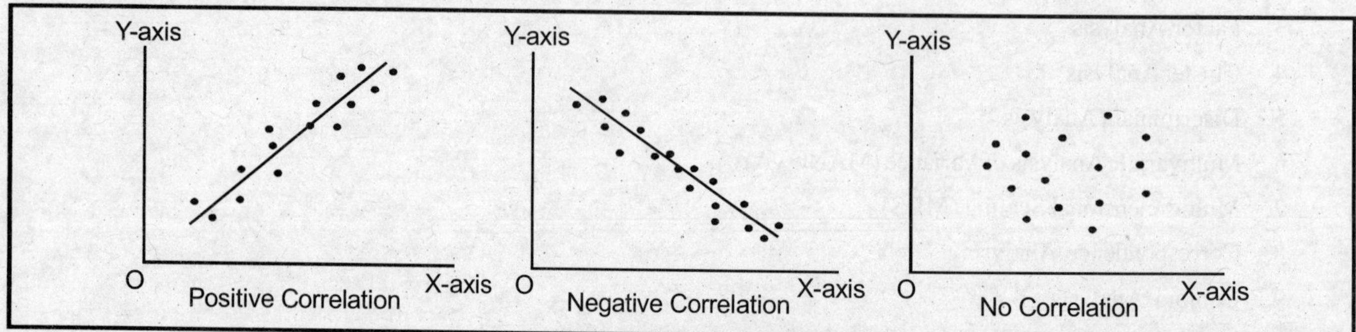

Fig. 12.1: Types of Correlation

Perfect Correlation

If there is any change in the value of one variable, the value of the other variable also changes in a fixed proportion, then the correlation between them is said to be perfect correlation. It is indicated numerically as **+1** and **–1**.

1. If the values of both the variables move in same direction with fixed proportion, it is called perfect positive correlation. It is indicated numerically as **+1**.
2. If the values of both the variables move in opposite direction with fixed proportion, it is called perfect negative correlation. It is indicated numerically as **–1**.

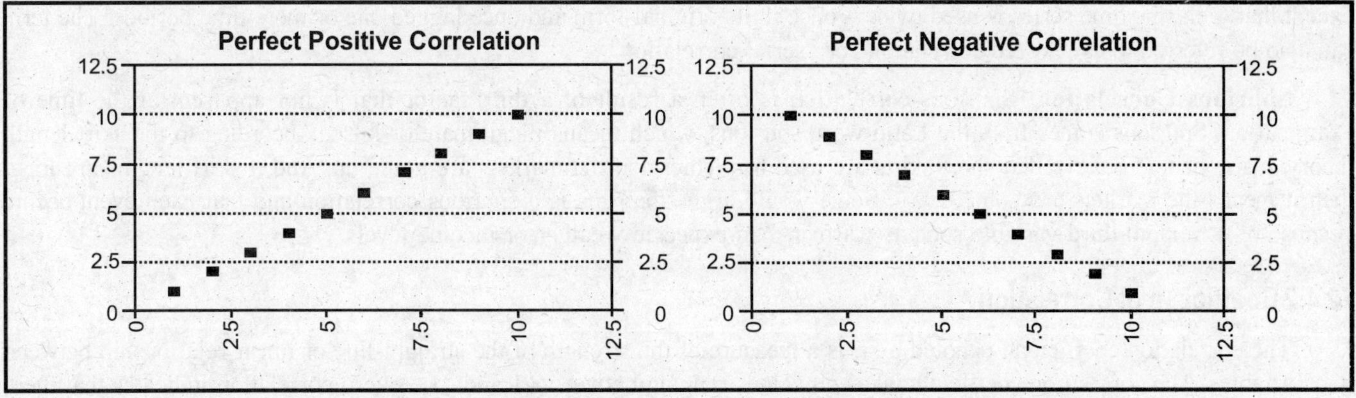

Fig. 12.2: Perfect Positive and Negative Correlation

Linear Correlation

Correlation is said to be linear if the ratio of change is constant. The amount of output in a factory is doubled by doubling the number of workers is the example of linear correlation.

In other words, it can be defined as if all the points on the scatter diagram tends to lie near a line which look like a straight line, the correlation is said to be linear, as shown in the figure.

Non-linear (Curvilinear) Correlation

Correlation is said to be non-linear if the ratio of change is not constant. In other words it can be defined as if all the points on the scatter diagram tends to lie near a smooth curve, the correlation is said to be non-linear (curvilinear), as shown in the figure.

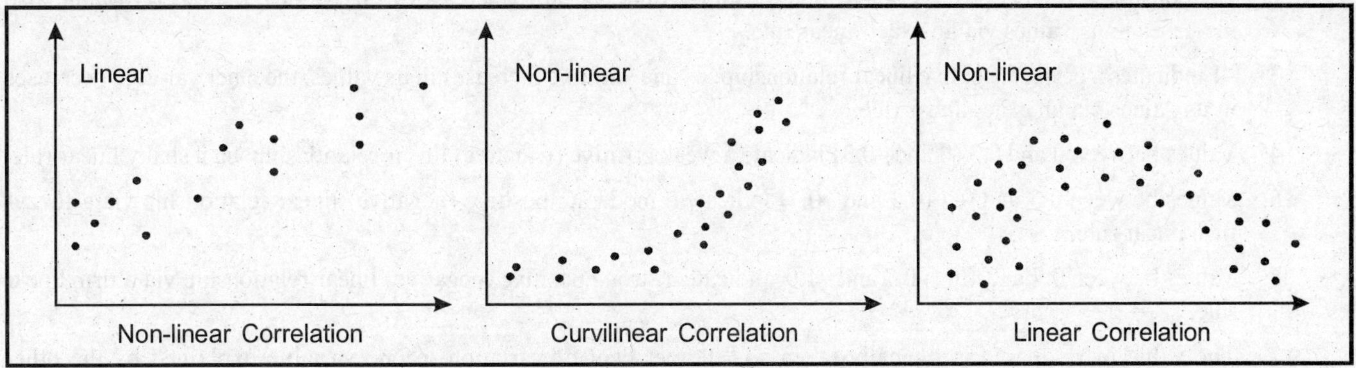

Fig. 12.3: Liner and Non-linear Correlation

Simple Correlation: If only two variables are chosen to study the correlation between them, the correlation is called as simple correlation.

Partial Correlation: In partial correlation, two variables are chosen to study the correlation between them, but the effect of other influencing variables is kept constant.

Multiple Correlations: In multiple correlation, the relationship between more than three variables are considered simultaneously for study.

Cross Correlation: A statistical measure timing the movements and proximity of alignment between two different information sets of a series of information. Cross correlation is generally used when measuring information between two different time series. The range of the data is –1 to 1 such that the closer cross correlation value is to 1, the more closely the information sets are.

Autocorrelation: A mathematical representation of the degree of similarity between a given time series and a lagged version of itself over successive time intervals. It is the same as calculating the correlation between two different time series, except that the same time series is used twice – once in its original form and once lagged one or more time periods. The term can also be referred to as "lagged correlation" or "serial correlation".

Spurious Correlation: Spurious correlation is often a result of a third factor that is not apparent at the time of examination. Spurious comes from the Latin word spurious, which means illegitimate or false. According to the skirt length theory, many people believe that short skirts are used to predict that the markets are going up. And if skirt lengths are long, then it means the markets are going down. Some would argue that this is a spurious correlation and that each event occurs because of a random third variable such as warmer-than-expected weather or income levels.

12.4.2 Coefficient of Correlation

The correlation coefficient, denoted by r, is a measure of the strength of the straight-line or linear relationship between two variables. The correlation coefficient takes on values ranging between +1 and –1. A zero correlation indicates that there is no relationship between the variables. A correlation of –1 indicates a perfect negative correlation, meaning that as one variable goes up, the other goes down. A correlation of +1 indicates a perfect positive correlation, meaning that both variables move in the same direction together.

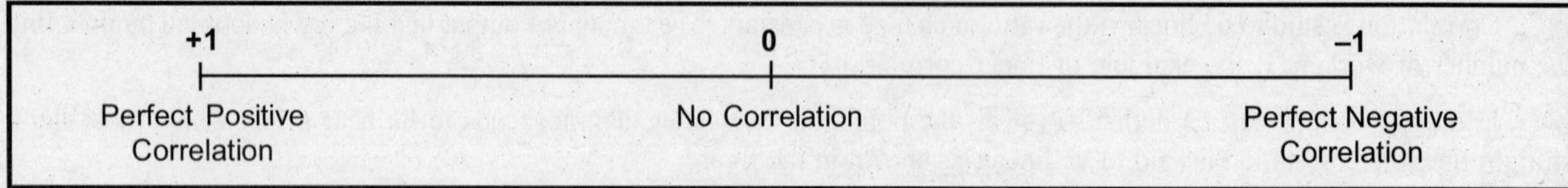

Fig. 12.4: Coefficient of Correlation

The following points are the accepted guidelines for interpreting the correlation coefficient:

1. 0 indicates no linear relationship.
2. +1 indicates a perfect positive linear relationship: as one variable increases in its values, the other variable also increases in its values via an exact linear rule.
3. –1 indicates a perfect negative linear relationship: as one variable increases in its values, the other variable decreases in its values via an exact linear rule.
4. Values between 0 and 0.3 (0 and –0.3) indicate a weak positive (negative) linear relationship via a shaky linear rule.
5. Values between 0.3 and 0.7 (0.3 and –0.7) indicate a moderate positive (negative) linear relationship via a fuzzy-firm linear rule.
6. Values between 0.7 and 1.0 (–0.7 and –1.0) indicate a strong positive (negative) linear relationship via a firm linear rule.
7. The value of r squared is typically taken as "the per cent of variation in one variable explained by the other variable," or "the per cent of variation shared between the two variables."
8. Linearity Assumption. The correlation coefficient requires that the underlying relationship between the two variables under consideration is linear. If the relationship is known to be linear, or the observed pattern between the two variables appears to be linear, then the correlation coefficient provides a reliable measure of the strength of the linear relationship. If the relationship is known to be non-linear, or the observed pattern appears to be non-linear, then the correlation coefficient is not useful, or at least questionable.

Properties of Coefficient of Correlation

1. The correlation coefficient is symmetrical with respect to X and Y, i.e., $r_{XY} = r_{YX}$
2. The correlation coefficient is the geometric mean of the two regression coefficients. $r = \sqrt{b_{YX} \times b_{XY}}$ or $r = \sqrt{b \times d}$
3. The correlation coefficient is independent of origin and unit of measurement, i.e., $r_{XY} = r_{UV}$
4. The correlation coefficient lies between –1 and +1, i.e., $-1 \le r \le +1$.

12.4.3 Methods of Correlation Analysis

The method of correlation opened new vistas for quantitative social science. The notion of causality as the sole explanatory principle of events was broadened to include the notion of association between events. Expectation was born that these quantified associations would be elaborated into homological networks, encompassing relationships between elements of complex systems. As the association between events becomes stronger, the probability that those events are also influenced by unknown factors lessens. The correlation coefficient denoted by r, and linear relationship between two variables which takes on values between –1 and +1.

The following methods of finding the correlation coefficient between two variables x and y:

1. Scatter Diagram Method
2. Karl Pearson's Coefficient of Correlation Method
3. Spearman's Rank Correlation Method
4. Concurrent Deviation Method

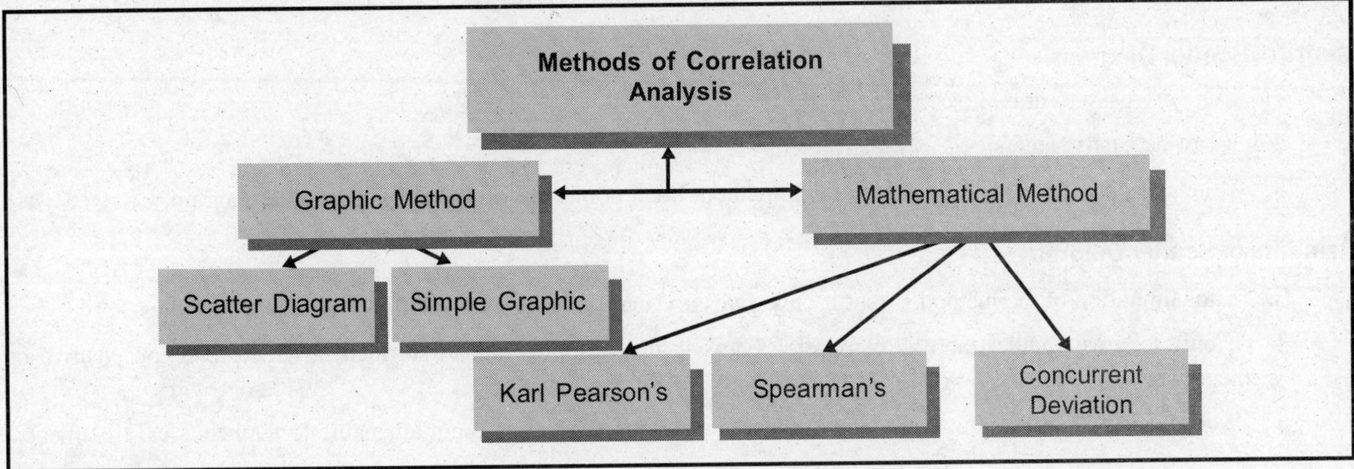

Fig. 12.5: Methods of Correlation Analysis

Scatter Diagram Methods

A Scatter Diagram examines the relationship between data collected for two different characteristics. Although the Scatter Diagram cannot determine the cause of such a relationship, it can show whether or not such a relationship exists, and if so, just how strong it is. The analysis produced by the Scatter Diagram is called Regression Analysis.

1. Correlation is positive when the values increase together, and
2. Correlation is negative when one value decreases as the other increases
   - 1 is a perfect positive correlation
   - 0 is no correlation (the values don't seem linked at all)
   - –1 is a perfect negative correlation

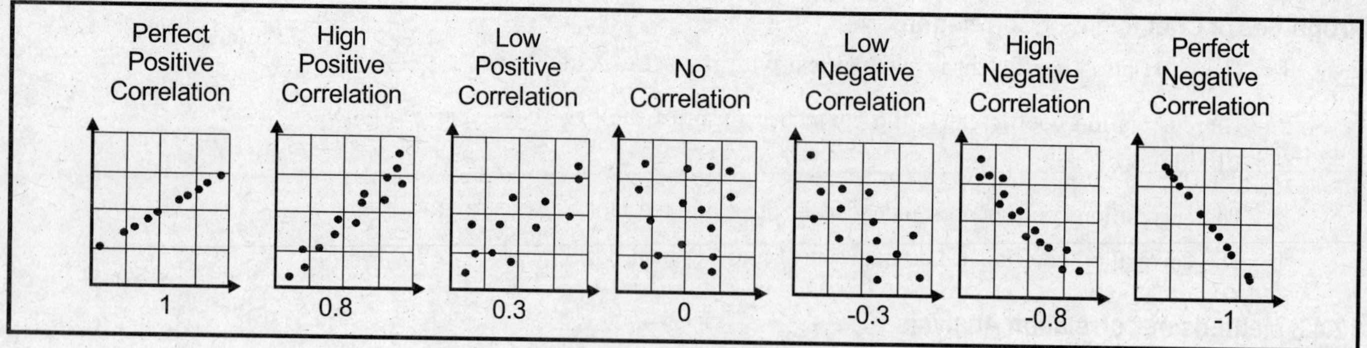

Fig. 12.6: Scatter Diagram of Correlation

Interpret the Data

Scatter diagrams will generally show one of seven possible correlations between the variables:

1. **Strong Positive Correlation:** The value of Y clearly increases as the value of X increases.
2. **Strong Negative Correlation:** The value of Y clearly decreases as the value of X increases.
3. **Moderate Positive Correlation:** The value of Y increases moderately as the value of X increases.
4. **Moderate Negative Correlation:** The value of Y decreases moderately as the value of X increases.
5. **Weak Positive Correlation:** The value of Y increases slightly as the value of X increases.
6. **Weak Negative Correlation:** The value of Y decreases slightly as the value of X increases.
7. **No Correlation:** There is no demonstrated connection between the two variables.

Merits of Scatter Diagram

1. It is very easy to draw a scatter diagram.
2. It can be easily understood and interpreted.
3. Values of extreme items do not affect this method. Such points are always isolated in the diagram.

Demerits of Scatter Diagram

The major limitation of the method is that it only gives a visual picture of the relationship of two variables.

1. It only tells us whether there is correlation between the variables, and if so, then in which direction positive or negative.
2. It does not give an idea about the precise degree of relationship as it is not amenable to mathematical treatment.

12.4.4 Karl Pearson' Coefficient of Correlation

Karl Pearson's Product Moment Correlation Coefficient or simply Pearson's Correlation Coefficient for short, is one of the important methods used in Statistics to measure correlation between two variables. Karl Pearson was a British mathematician, statistician, lawyer and a eugenicist. He established the discipline of mathematical statistics. He founded the world's first statistics department in the University of London in the year 1911. The correlation between two variables X and Y, which are measured using Pearson's Coefficient, give the values between +1 and –1. When measured in population, the Pearson's Coefficient is designated the value of Greek letter rho (ρ). But, when studying a sample, it is designated the letter r. It is therefore sometimes called Pearson's r. Pearson's coefficient reflects the linear relationship between two variables. As mentioned above if the correlation coefficient is +1, then there is a perfect positive linear relationship between variables, and if it is –1 then there is a perfect negative linear relationship between the variables. And 0 denotes that there is no relationship between the two variables. The degrees –1, +1 and 0 are theoretical results and are not generally found in normal circumstances. That means the results cannot be more than –1, +1. These are the upper and the lower limits.

Karl Pearson's Coefficient of correlation r is given by:

$$r = \frac{\text{Covariance}(x, y)}{\sqrt{\text{var } x}\sqrt{\text{var } y}} = \frac{\text{Cov}(x, y)}{\sigma_x \sigma_y}$$

where, $\text{cov}(x, y) = \frac{1}{n}\Sigma(x-\bar{x})(y-\bar{y})$

$$\sigma_x = \sqrt{\frac{\Sigma(x-\bar{x})^2}{n}}, \text{ on variable x.}$$

and $\sigma_y = \sqrt{\frac{\Sigma(y-\bar{y})^2}{n}}$, on variable y.

Substituting the value of cov (x, y), σ_x and σ_y, on the above formula, r is given by:

$$r = \frac{\frac{1}{n}\Sigma(x-\bar{x})(y-\bar{y})}{\sqrt{\frac{\Sigma(x-\bar{x})^2}{n}}\sqrt{\frac{\Sigma(y-\bar{y})^2}{n}}}$$

$$\text{Or } r = \frac{\Sigma(x-\bar{x})(y-\bar{y})}{\sqrt{\Sigma(x-\bar{x})^2}\sqrt{\Sigma(y-\bar{y})^2}}$$

$$\text{Or } r = \frac{\Sigma dx\, dy}{\sqrt{\Sigma dx^2}\sqrt{\Sigma dy^2}}$$

where, $dx = x - \bar{x}$ and $dy = y - \bar{y}$

$$\text{Or } r = \frac{n\Sigma xy - (\Sigma x)(\Sigma y)}{\sqrt{n\Sigma x^2 - (\Sigma x)^2}\sqrt{n\Sigma y^2 - (\Sigma y)^2}}$$

For Ungroup data,

$$r = \frac{n\Sigma d_x d_y - (\Sigma d_x)(\Sigma d_y)}{\sqrt{n\Sigma {d_x}^2 - (\Sigma d_x)^2}\sqrt{n\Sigma {d_x}^2 - (\Sigma d_y)^2}}$$

where, $d_x = x - A$ and $d_y = x - B$, A and B are assumed mean of x and y.

For Group data,

$$r = \frac{n\Sigma fd_x fd_y - (\Sigma fd_x)(\Sigma fd_y)}{\sqrt{n\Sigma {fd_x}^2 - (\Sigma fd_x)^2}\sqrt{n\Sigma {fd_x}^2 - (\Sigma fd_y)^2}}$$

Assumptions:

1. **Independent of case:** Cases should be independent to each other.
2. **Distribution:** Variables of the correlation should be normally distributed.
3. **Linear relationship:** Two variables should be linearly related to each other, or if we plot the value of variables on a scatter diagram, it should yield a relatively straight line.

Properties:

1. **Limit:** Coefficient values lie between +1 to –1.
2. **Pure number:** It is independent of the unit of measurement. For example, if one variable's unit of measurement is in inches and the second variable is in quintals, even then, Pearson's correlation coefficient value does not change.
3. **Symmetric:** Correlation of the coefficient between two variables is symmetric. This means between X and Y or Y and X, the value of coefficient will remain the same.

Degree of Correlation:

1. **Perfect:** If the value is near ± 1, then it said to be a perfect correlation.
2. **High degree:** If the value lies between ± 0.75 and ± 1, then it is said to be a high degree of correlation.
3. **Moderate degree:** If the value lies between ± 0.25 and ± 0.75, then it is said to be moderate degree of correlation.
4. **Low degree:** When the value lies between 0 and ± 0.25, then it is said to be a low degree of correlation.
5. **No correlation:** When the value is zero.

Interpretation of Pearson's Coefficient of Correlation

The sign of the correlation coefficient determines whether the correlation is positive or negative. The magnitude of the correlation coefficient determines the strength of the correlation. Although there are no hard and fast rules for describing correlational strength, I [hesitatingly] offer these guidelines:

1. $0 < |r| < .3$ weak correlation
2. $.3 < |r| < .7$ moderate correlation
3. $|r| > 0.7$ strong correlation

For example, r = –0.849 suggests a strong negative correlation.

Merits and Limitations of Pearson's Coefficient of Correlation

The chief merit of this coefficient is that it not only gives an idea about the covariation of the two series but also indicates the direction of relationship. Thus, this Coefficient measures both the degree and direction of the correlation between two variables.

It is the most widely used method of studying relationship between interrelated phenomena. However, it suffers from certain limitations also. These are:

1. It assumes a linear relationship between the variables even though it may not be there.
2. It is liable to be misinterpreted, as a high degree of correlation. It does not necessarily mean very close relationship between the variables.
3. It is tedious to calculate.
4. It is unduly affected by the values of extreme items. For example if the values of x-series are 1, 2, 3, 4, 5 and the corresponding values of y-series are 5, 4, 3, 2, 1, the Coefficient of Correlation between them would be zero. However, if we add one more value in the x-series and its value is 100 and add one more value in the y-series and its value is 120, the Coefficient of Correlation of these six pairs of values would be +.99. Thus, the addition of a single set of large figures has boosted up the correlation from zero to +.99.

Example 12.1:

Calculate Karl Pearson's coefficient of correlation between expenditure on advertising and sales from the following the data given below.

Advertising Expenses ('000 ₹)	39	65	62	90	82	75	25	98	36	78
Sales (Lakh ₹)	47	53	58	86	62	68	60	91	51	84

Solution:

Table 12.1: Calculations for Correlation Coefficient

x	y	dx = x − $\bar{x}$	dy = y − $\bar{y}$	dx²	dy²	$d_x d_y$
39	47	-26	-19	676	361	494
65	53	0	-13	0	169	0
62	58	-3	-8	9	64	24
90	86	25	20	625	400	500
82	62	17	-4	289	16	-68
75	68	10	2	100	4	20
25	60	-40	-6	1600	36	240
98	91	33	25	1089	625	825
36	51	-29	-15	841	225	435
78	84	13	18	169	324	234
Σx = 650	Σy = 660	Σdx = 0	Σdy = 0	Σdx² = 5398	Σdy² = 2224	Σdxdy = 2704

$$\bar{x} = \frac{\sum x}{n} = \frac{650}{10} = 65 \text{ and } \bar{y} = \frac{\sum y}{n} = \frac{660}{10} = 66$$

The Karl Pearson's correlation coefficient

$$r = \frac{\sum d_x d_y}{\sqrt{\sum dx^2}\sqrt{\sum dy^2}} = \frac{2704}{\sqrt{5398}\sqrt{2224}} = \frac{2704}{3464.84} = 0.0784$$

Interpretation: Since the value of r = 0.0784 is positive, therefore the expenditure on advertising and sales are positively correlated to the extent of 0.0784. Hence, we conclude that expenditure on advertising increases, the sales also slightly increases.

Example 12.2:

The following table gives indices of industrial production and number of registered unemployed people. Calculate the value of the correlation coefficient.

Year	**2001**	**2002**	**2003**	**2004**	**2005**	**2006**	**2007**	**2008**
Production	100	102	104	107	105	112	103	99
Unemployed	15	12	13	11	12	12	19	26

Solution:

Table 12.2: Calculation for Correlation Coefficient

Year	Production x	Unemployed y	$d_x = x - \bar{x}$	$d_y = y - \bar{y}$	d_x^2	d_y^2	$d_x d_y$
2001	100	15	-4	0	16	0	0
2002	102	12	-2	-3	4	9	6
2003	104	13	0	-2	0	4	0
2004	107	11	3	-4	9	16	-12

2005	105	12	1	-3	1	9	-3
2006	112	12	8	-3	64	9	-24
2007	103	19	-1	4	1	16	-4
2008	99	26	-5	11	25	121	-55
	$\Sigma x = 832$	$\Sigma y = 120$	$\Sigma d_x = 0$	$\Sigma d_y = 0$	$\Sigma d_x^2 = 120$	$\Sigma d_y^2 = 184$	$\Sigma d_x d_y = -92$

$$\bar{x} = \frac{\Sigma x}{n} = \frac{832}{8} = 104 \text{ and } \bar{y} = \frac{\Sigma y}{n} = \frac{120}{8} = 15$$

The Karl Pearson's correlation coefficient

$$r = \frac{n\Sigma d_x d_y - (\Sigma d_x)(\Sigma d_y)}{\sqrt{n\Sigma dx^2 - (\Sigma d_x)^2}\sqrt{n\Sigma d_x{}^2 - (\Sigma d_y)^2}}$$

$$= \frac{8 \times -92}{\sqrt{8 \times 120}\sqrt{8 \times 184}} = \frac{-92}{10.95 \times 13.56} = \frac{-92}{148.58} = -0.619$$

Interpretation: Since the coefficient of correlation r = –0.619 is moderately negative, it indicates that there is a moderately large inverse correlation between the two variables. Hence, we conclude that as the production index increases, the numbers of unemployed decreases and *vice versa.*

Example 12.3:

The following table gives the frequency according to the marks, obtained by 67 students in an intelligence test. Measure the degree of relationship between age and marks:

	Age in Year				
Test Marks	**18**	**19**	**20**	**21**	**Total**
200-250	4	4	2	1	11
250-300	3	5	4	2	14
300-350	2	6	8	5	21
350-400	1	4	6	10	21
Total	10	19	20	18	**67**

Solution:

Age of student and marks obtained by them be represented by variables x and y respectively.

Table 12.3: Calculation for Correlation Coefficient

y	x → / d_y ↓ d_x	18 (-1)	19 (0)	20 (1)	21 (2)	Total f_y	fd_y	fd_y^2	$fd_x d_y$
200-250	-1	4 (4)	4 (0)	2 (-2)	1 (-2)	11	-11	11	0
250-300	0	3 (0)	5 (0)	4 (0)	2 (0)	14	0	0	0
300-350	1	2 (-2)	6 (0)	8 (8)	5 (10)	21	21	21	16
350-400	2	1 (-2)	4 (0)	6 (12)	10 (40)	21	42	44	50
Total $_x$f		10	19	20	18	n = 67	$\Sigma fd_y = 52$	$\Sigma fd_y^2 = 116$	$\Sigma fd_x d_y = 66$
Σfd_x		-10	19	20	18	$\Sigma fd_x = 46$			
Σfd_x^2		10	0	20	72	$\Sigma fd_x^2 = 102$			
$\Sigma fd_y d_x$		0	0	18	48	$\Sigma fd_y d_x = 66$			

where $d_x = x - 19$ and $d_y = (m - 275)/50$

The Karl Pearson's correlation coefficient

$$r = \frac{n\sum fd_x fd_y - (\sum fd_x)(f\sum d_y)}{\sqrt{n\sum fd_x{}^2 - (\sum fd_x)^2}\sqrt{n\sum fd_x{}^2 - (\sum fd_y)^2}}$$

$$= \frac{67\times 66 - 46\times 52}{\sqrt{67\times 120 - (46)^2}\sqrt{67\times 116\times (52)^2}}$$

$$= \frac{2030}{\sqrt{4718}\sqrt{5068}} = \frac{2030}{68.68\times 71.19} = 0.415$$

Interpretation: Since the value of r = 0.415 is positive, therefore age of students and marks obtained in an intelligence test are positively correlated to the extent of 0.415. Hence, we conclude that as the age of student's increases, score of marks in intelligence test also increases.

12.4.5 Standard and Probable Error in Coefficient of Correlation

The standard error of a correlation coefficient is used to determine the confidence intervals around a true correlation of zero. If your correlation coefficient falls outside of this range, then it is significantly different than zero. The standard error can be calculated for interval or ratio-type data (i.e., only for Pearson's product moment correlation).

$$\text{Standard Error} = SE_r = \frac{1\times r^2}{\sqrt{n}}$$

where, r = Correlation coefficient

n = Sample Data

The significance (probability) of the correlation coefficient is determined from the t-statistic. The probability of the t-statistic indicates whether the observed correlation coefficient occurred by chance if the true correlation is zero. In other words, it asks if the correlation is significantly different than zero. When the t-statistic is calculated for Spearman's rank difference correlation coefficient, there must be at least 30 cases before the t-distribution can be used to determine the probability. If there are fewer than 30 cases, you must refer to a special table to find the probability of the correlation coefficient.

After the calculation of coefficient of correlation, the next thing is to find out the extent to which is dependable. For this purpose, the probable error of the coefficient of correlation is calculated. The formula for finding out the probable error of the Karl Pearson's coefficient of correlation is:

$$\text{Probable Error} = PE_r = 0.6745\ SE_r = 0.6745 \times \frac{1 \times r^2}{\sqrt{n}}$$

Interpretation:

1. If the value of r is less than the probable error, there is no evidence of correlation.
2. If the value of r is more than six times of the probable error, it is significant correlation.
3. If the probable error is not much and if the coefficient of correlation is .5 or more, it is generally considered to be significant.
4. Probable error as a measure for interpreting coefficient of correlation should be used only when the number of pairs of observations is large. If n is small, probable error may give misleading conclusions.
5. Probable error as a measure for interpreting coefficient of correlation should be used only when a sample study is being made and the sample is unbiased and representative. With the help of sample studies, the correlation in the universe is estimated.

12.4.6 The Coefficient of Determination

The coefficient of determination is a measure of how well a statistical model is likely to predict future outcomes. Interpreting Coefficient of Correlation is the calculation of Coefficient of Determination which is the square of Coefficient of Correlation or r^2 is the square of the sample correlation coefficient between outcomes and predicted values. The reason of the Coefficient of Determination is a better measure lies in the fact that it tells us about the effect of the independent variable on the dependent variable. For example if the Coefficient of Correlation between price and supply is + .8, it does not mean that 80 per cent of the variation in supply is due to change in price. However, if we calculate the Coefficient of Determination or r^2 which in this case would be (+.8)2 or +.64, it means that 64% of the variation in supply are on account of changes in price. This is a very important property of the Coefficient of Determination.

Finding the coefficient of determination takes only three steps:

Step 1: Find the correlation coefficient, r.

Step 2: Square the correlation coefficient.

Step 3: Convert the correlation coefficient to a percentage.

$$\text{Coefficient of Determination} = r^2 = \frac{\text{Explained Variance}}{\text{Total Variance}}$$

and Coefficient of Non-determination = $1 - r^2$

Interpretation of Coefficient of Determination

1. If $r^2 = 0$, then no variation in y can be explained by the variable x (where x is no value in predicting the value y). There is no association between x and y.

2. If $r^2 = 1$, then the value of y are completely explained by the variable x. There is perfect association between x and y.
3. If $0 \leq r^2 \leq 1$, the degree of explained variation y as a result of variation in values of x depends on the value of r^2. If r^2 is closer to 0, low proportion of variation in y is explained by x. If r^2 is closer to 1, the variable x can predict the actual value of the variable y.

Coefficient of correlation is not always a cause and effect relationship. It is only covariance which may or may not be in the nature of cause and effect. As such the coefficient of correlation must be very carefully interpreted. It should also be noted that r^2 or Coefficient of determination is always a positive figure. As such it does not indicate the direction of relationship. The direction of relationship is indicated by the coefficient of correlation only which can be as we have seen, either positive or negative.

12.4.7 Spearman's Rank Correlation Coefficient

Sometimes such problems are faced where it is possible to arrange the various items of a series in serial order but the quantitative measurement of their value is difficult; for example, it is possible for a class teacher to arrange his students in ascending or descending order of intelligence, even though intelligence cannot be measured quantitatively. No doubt, the quantitative study about the intelligence of students can be made by holding an examination and assigning them marks, but this method can never be said to be infallible. There are many such attributes which are incapable of quantitative measurements; for example, honesty, character, morality, etc. If it is desired to have a study of association between two such attributes, say intelligence and beauty the Karl Pearson's Coefficient of Correlation cannot be calculated as these attributes cannot be assigned definite values. However, there is a method by which we can study correlation between such attributes. This method was developed by the British psychologist Charles Edward Spearman in the year 1904.

In this method, x and y variables denote the rank of the attributes A and B. In case of a study of correlation between intelligence and beauty, we can pick up 10 or 20 or any other number of individuals and first arrange them in order of their rank according to intelligence — beginning with the most intelligent person whose rank would be 1 and going down in order till the rank of the last person is indicated. Similarly, we can arrange these individuals again in order of rank according to beauty — the most beautiful person getting Rank No. 1 and going down to the last person who is the least beautiful. In this way, we will have two sets of ranks for these two attributes. If 10 individuals are arranged like this, we will have ranks from 1 to 10 for each attribute. Once this is done, we can find out a Coefficient of Correlation between these two series.

Spearman's Rank Correlation Coefficient R, is given by:

$$R = 1 - \frac{6\sum d^2}{n(n^2 - 1)}$$

where, R = Spearman's Rank Correlation coefficient

$d = R_1 - R_2$, difference of the ranks of the same individual in the two attributes

R_1 = Rank of observations with respect to first variable

R_2 = Rank of observations with respect to second variable

n = Number of paired observations.

The value of the Coefficient is interpreted in the same way as that of the Pearson's Coefficient of Correlation. Its value also ranges between –1 and +1. When correction is – 1, it indicates complete agreement in the order of ranks between the two attributes (the most intelligent being the most beautiful also and so on). If correlation is it indicates complete disagreement in the order of ranks (the most intelligent being the one who is, the least beautiful.)

There are three types of problems in calculating this coefficient:

A. When actual ranks are given.

B. When actual ranks are not given.

C. When actual ranks are equal.

Merits of Spearman's Rank Correlation Coefficient

1. Since in this method Σd or the sum of the differences between R_1, and R_2 is always equal to zero, it provides a check on the calculation.
2. Since Spearman's Rank Correlation is the same thing as Karl Pearson's Coefficient of Correlation between ranks, it can be interpreted in the same way as Karl Pearson's Coefficient of correlation.
3. Rank correlation unlike Karl Pearson's Coefficient of Correlation does not assume normality in the universe from which the sample has been taken.
4. Rank Correlation is very easy to understand and apply. However, Pearson's Coefficient is based on a set of full information while Spearman's Coefficient is based only on the ranks. The values of obtained by these two methods would generally differ.
5. Spearman's Rank method is the only way of studying correlation between qualitative data which cannot be measured in figures but can be arranged in serial order.

Demerits of Spearman's Rank Correlation Coefficient

1. The method cannot be used in two-way frequency tables or bivariate frequency distribution.
2. It can be conveniently used only when n is small say 30, otherwise calculation become tedious.

A. When Actual Ranks are Given

Example 12.4:

The rank of 15 students in two subjects A and B are given below. The two numbers within brackets denote the ranks of students in A and B subjects respectively:

(1, 10), (2, 7), (3, 2), (4, 6), (5, 4), (6, 8), (7, 3), (8, 1), (9, 11), (10, 15), (11, 9), (12, 5), (13, 14), (14, 12), (15, 13).

Find the Spearman's rank correlation coefficient.

Solution:

Table 12.4: Calculation of Spearman's Correlation of Coefficient

Rank in A (R_1)	Rank in B (R_2)	$d = R_1 - R_2$	d^2
1	10	-9	81
2	7	-5	25
3	2	1	1
4	6	-2	4
5	4	1	1
6	8	-2	4
7	3	4	16
8	1	7	49
9	11	-2	4
10	15	-5	25
11	9	2	4
12	5	7	49
13	14	-1	1
14	12	2	4
15	13	2	4
			$\Sigma d^2 = 272$

Spearman's Rank Correlation Coefficient R, is given by:

$$R = 1 - \frac{6\sum d^2}{n(n^2 - 1)}$$

$$= 1 - \frac{6 \times 272}{15(15^2 - 1)}$$

$$= 1 - \frac{1632}{3360} = 1 - 0.4857 = 0.5143$$

Interpretation: Since the value of R = 0.5143 is positive, therefore the moderate degree positive correlation between performance of students in two subjects.

B. When Actual Ranks are Not Given

Example 12.5:

Calculate Spearman's rank correlation coefficient between expenditure on advertisement cost and sales from the following the data:

Advertisement Cost ('000 ₹)	39	65	62	90	82	75	25	98	36	78
Sales (Lakh ₹)	47	53	58	86	62	68	60	91	51	84

Solution:

Table 12.5: Calculation for Rank Correlation Coefficient

Advertisement Cost (X)	Sales (Y)	Rank of X (R_1)	Rank of Y (R_2)	$d = R_1 - R_2$	d^2
39	47	8	10	-2	4
65	53	6	8	-2	4
62	58	7	7	0	0
90	86	2	2	0	0
82	62	3	5	-2	4
75	68	5	4	1	1
25	60	10	6	4	16
98	91	1	1	0	0
36	51	9	9	0	0
78	84	4	3	1	1
				$\Sigma d = 0$	$\Sigma d^2 = 30$

Spearman's Rank Correlation coefficient R, is given by:

$$R = 1 - \frac{6\sum d^2}{n(n^2 - 1)}$$

$$= 1 - \frac{6 \times 30}{10(10^2 - 1)}$$

$$= 1 - \frac{180}{990} = 1 - 0.1819 = 0.8181$$

Interpretation: Since the value of r = 0.8181 is positive, therefore the expenditure on advertising and sales are positively correlated to the extent of 0.0784. Hence, we conclude that expenditure on advertising increases, the sales also increases.

C. When Actual Ranks are Equal

Spearman rank correlation coefficient R is given by:

$$R = 1 - \frac{6\left\{\sum d^2 + \frac{1}{12}(m_1^3 - m_1) + \frac{1}{12}(m_2^3 - m_2) + \ldots\right\}}{n(n^2 - 1)}$$

Example 12.6:

Obtain the rank correlation coefficient between the variables X and Y from the following data:

X	50	55	65	50	55	60	50	65	70	75
Y	110	110	115	125	140	115	130	120	115	160

Solution:

Table 12.6: Calculation for Rank Correlation Coefficient

X	Y	Rank of X (R_1)	Rank of Y (R_2)	$d = R_1 - R_2$	d^2
50	110	2	1.5	0.5	0.25
55	110	4.5	1.5	3.0	9.00
65	115	7.5	4	3.5	12.25
50	125	2	7	-5.0	25.00
55	140	4.5	9	-4.5	20.25
60	115	6	4	2.0	4.00
50	130	2	8	-6.0	36.00
65	120	7.5	6	1.5	2.25
70	115	9	4	5.0	25.00
75	160	10	10	0.0	00.00
					$\Sigma d^2 = 134$

From the table, it may be noted that for variable x, 50 is repeated thrice ($m_1 = 3$), 55 is repeated twice ($m_2 = 2$), and 65 is repeated thrice ($m_3 = 2$). For variable y, 110 is repeated twice ($m_4 = 2$) and 115 thrice ($m_5 = 3$).

Spearman's Rank Correlation coefficient R, is given by:

$$R = 1 - \frac{6\left\{\sum d^2 + \frac{1}{12}(m_1^3 - m_1) + \frac{1}{12}(m_2^3 - m_2) + \frac{1}{12}(m_3^3 - m_3) + \frac{1}{12}(m_4^3 - m_4) + \frac{1}{12}(m_5^3 - m_5)\right\}}{n(n^2 - 1)}$$

$$R = 1 - \frac{6\left\{134 + \frac{1}{12}(3^3 - 3) + \frac{1}{12}(2^3 - 2) + \frac{1}{12}(2^3 - 2) + \frac{1}{12}(2^3 - 2) + \frac{1}{12}(3^3 - 3)\right\}}{10(10^2 - 1)}$$

$$R = 1 - \frac{6\{134 + 2 + 0.5 + 0.5 + 0.5 + 2\}}{990} = 1 - \frac{887}{990} = 1 - 0.845 = 0.155$$

Interpretation: Since the value of R = 0.155 is positive, therefore the result shows a weak positive association between variables x and y.

12.4.8 Coefficient of Concurrent Deviations Method

Sometimes it is desired to study the correlation between two series in a very casual manner and in such cases no particular attention is needed so far as precision is concerned. In such cases, it is enough to calculate the coefficient of concurrent deviations. In this method, correlation is calculated between the direction of deviations and not their magnitudes. As such only the direction of deviations is taken into account in the calculation of this coefficient, and their magnitude is ignored.

To calculate the coefficient of concurrent deviations, the deviation are not calculated from any average or by the method of moving averages but only their direction from the previous period is noted down. The formula for the calculation of coefficient of concurrent deviations is given below:

Coefficient of concurrent deviations

$$r_c = \pm\sqrt{\pm\frac{(2c-n)}{n}}$$

where, r_c stands for the coefficient of concurrent deviations, c for the number of pairs of concurrent deviations and n for the number of pairs of deviations. The value of this coefficient of correlation also varies between 1. The plus and minus signs given in the formula should be carefully noted. If the value of (2c – n)/n) is negative, its square root cannot be calculated and so a minus sign is placed before the sign of the root so that the square root may be calculated and the minus sign may be kept before the value of the coefficient of correlation.

Steps in the calculation of this coefficient of concurrent deviations are:

1. Find out the direction of change of x-variable. It means find out whether the second figure in the series is more than the first figure, if it is so the direction is. If the second figure is less than the first, the direction is —. If both the figures are equal, the direction is 0. Similarly, find the direction of the third figure from the second, of the fourth figure from the third and so on. It is denoted by (d_x).
2. Find out the direction of change of y-variable in the same manner as discussed above. It is denoted by (d_y).
3. Multiply dx and dy and determine the value of c, which would be the number of positive products of dxdy (x–) or (x+).
4. Use the formula given above to obtain the value of the coefficient or r.

Merits and Demerits of Concurrent Deviation Method

This method is the easiest way of calculating correlation, and is very convenient when the number of pairs of observations is very large.

The chief demerit is that it is only a very rough indicator of correlation and further it does not differentiate between small and big deviation, e.g., if x increases from 100 to 1,000 the sign indicating change would be + and if the change is from 100 to 110, then also the sign of change would be +, without taking into account the magnitude of change.

Example 12.7:

Calculate Coefficient of Concurrent Deviation from the following data:

Supply	65	40	35	75	63	80	35	20	80	60	50
Demand	60	55	50	56	30	70	40	35	80	75	80

Solution:

Table 12.7: Calculation of Coefficient of Concurrent Deviations

Supply (X)	Sign of the deviation from preceding value (d_x)	Demand (Y)	Sign of the deviation from preceding value (d_y)	Product deviations ($d_x d_y$)
65		60		
40	-	55	-	+
35	-	50	-	+
75	+	56	+	+
63	-	30	-	+
80	+	70	+	+
35	-	40	-	+
20	-	35	-	+
80	+	80	+	+
60	-	75	-	+
50	-	80	+	-

n = Number of pair of deviations = 11 – 1 = 10

c = Number of pairs of deviations having like signs = 9

Coefficient of concurrent deviations

$$r_c = \pm\sqrt{\pm\frac{(2c-n)}{n}} = \pm\sqrt{\pm\frac{(2\times 9-10)}{10}} = \pm\sqrt{\pm 0.8}$$

Since 2c – n = 8, is positive, we take positive sign inside and outside the square root so that:

$$r_c = \pm\sqrt{\pm 0.8} = 0.89$$

12.5 REGRESSION ANALYSIS

Regression takes a group of random variables, thought to be predicting Y, and tries to find a mathematical relationship between them. This relationship is typically in the form of a straight line (linear regression) that best approximates all the individual data points. Regression is often used to determine how much specific factors such as the price of a commodity, interest rates, particular industries or sectors influence the price movement of an asset.

Linear regression attempts to model the relationship between two variables by fitting a linear equation to observed data. One variable is considered to be an explanatory variable, and the other is considered to be a dependent variable. For example, a modeler might want to relate the weights of individuals to their heights using a linear regression model. Before attempting to fit a linear model to observed data, a modeler should first determine whether or not there is a relationship between the variables of interest. A scatter plot can be a helpful tool in determining the strength of the relationship between two variables. If there appears to be no association between the proposed explanatory and dependent variables (i.e., the scatter plot does not indicate any increasing or decreasing trends), then fitting a linear regression model to the data probably will not provide a useful model. A valuable numerical measure of association between two variables is the correlation coefficient, which is a value between –1 and 1 indicating the strength of the association of the observed data for the two variables.

The two basic types of regression are linear regression and multiple regressions. Linear regression uses one independent variable to explain and/or predict the outcome of Y, while multiple regression use two or more independent variables to predict the outcome.

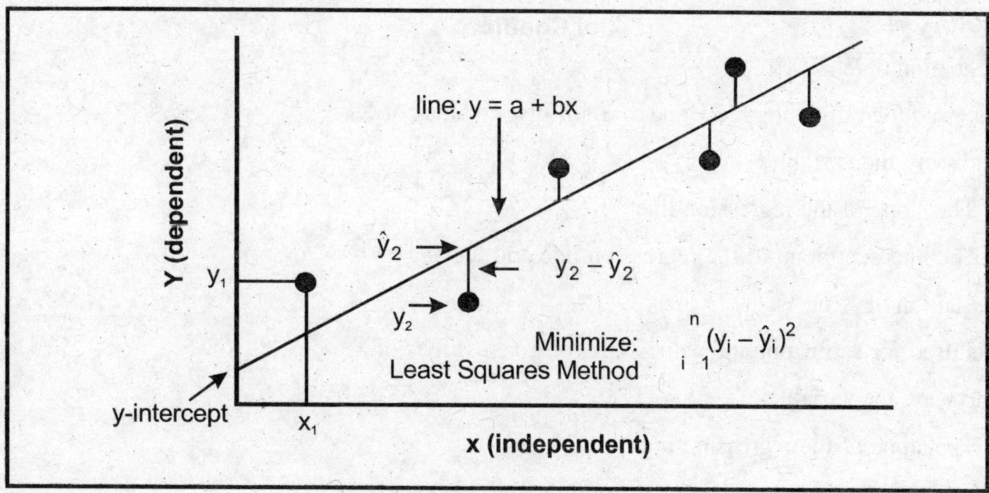

Fig. 12.7: Regression Line

12.5.1 Scatter Plot

A scatter plot is a useful summary of a set of bivariate data (two variables), usually drawn before working out a linear correlation coefficient or fitting a regression line. It gives a good visual picture of the relationship between the two variables, and aids the interpretation of the correlation coefficient or regression model. A scatter plot is often employed to identify potential associations between two variables, where one may be considered to be an explanatory variable (such as years of education) and another may be considered a response variable (such as annual income). A **positive association** between education and income would be indicated on a scatter plot by a upward trend (positive slope), where higher incomes correspond to higher education levels and lower incomes correspond to fewer years of education. A **negative association** would be indicated by the opposite effect (negative slope), where the most highly educated individuals would have lower incomes than the least educated individuals. Or, there might not be any notable association, in which case a scatter plot would not indicate any trends whatsoever. The following plots demonstrate the appearance of positively associated, negatively associated, and non-associated variables:

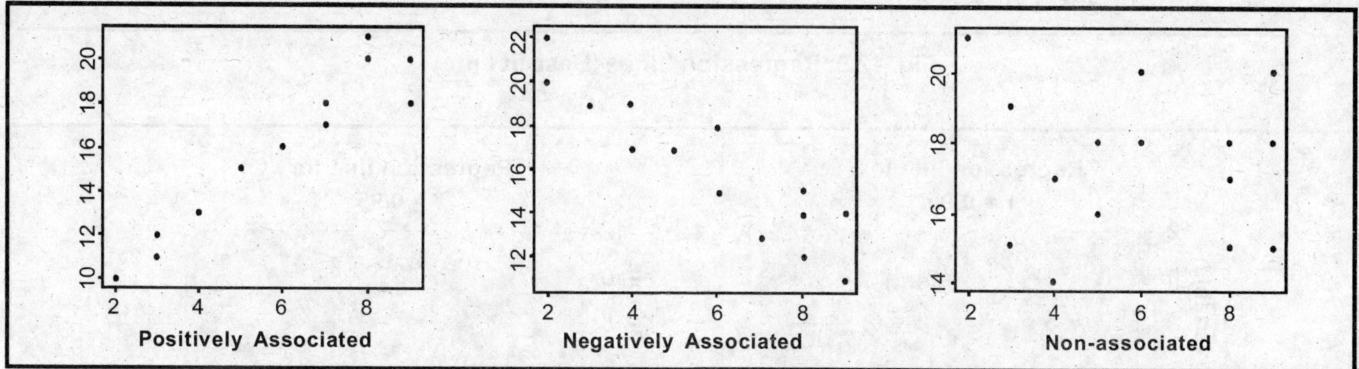

Fig. 12.8: Scatter Plot of Regression

12.5.2 Simple Linear Regression

Regression analysis is most often used for prediction. The goal in regression analysis is to create a mathematical model that can be used to predict the values of a dependent variable based upon the values of an independent variable. In other words, we use the model to predict the value of Y when we know the value of X. (The dependent variable is the one to be predicted). Correlation analysis is often used with regression analysis because correlation analysis is used to measure the strength of association between the two variables X and Y.

In regression analysis involving one independent variable and one dependent variable, the values are frequently plotted in two dimensions as a scatter plot. The scatter plot allows us to visually inspect the data prior to running a regression analysis. Simple linear regression analysis finds the straight line that best fits the data. When the dependence of the variable is represented by a straight line, then it is called linear regression, otherwise it is said to be non-linear or curvilinear regression.

Line of Regression

Regression equation of Y on X:

Y = a + bx is used for estimating the value of Y for given values of X.

where, x and y are the variables

b = The slope of the regression line

a = The intercept point of the regression line and the Y-axis

Regression equation of X on Y:

X = a + by is used for estimating the value of X for given values of Y.

where, x and y are the variables

b = The slope of the regression line

a = The intercept point of the regression line and the X-axis

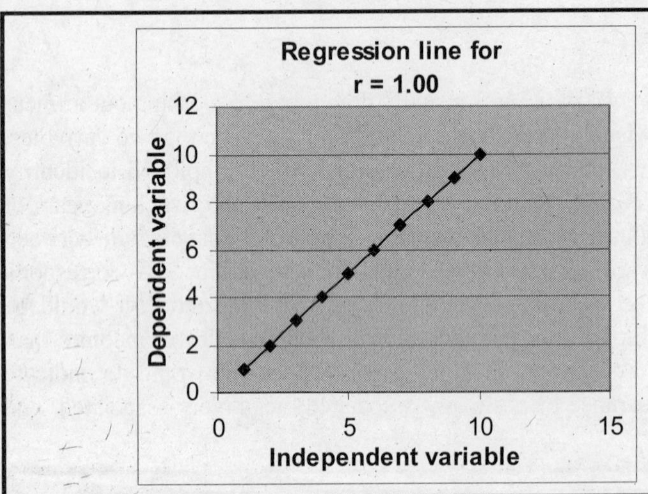

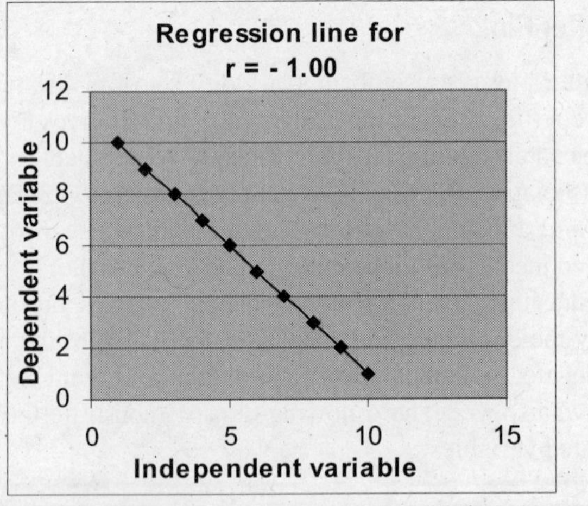

Fig. 12.9: Regression Lines (Best-fit Line)

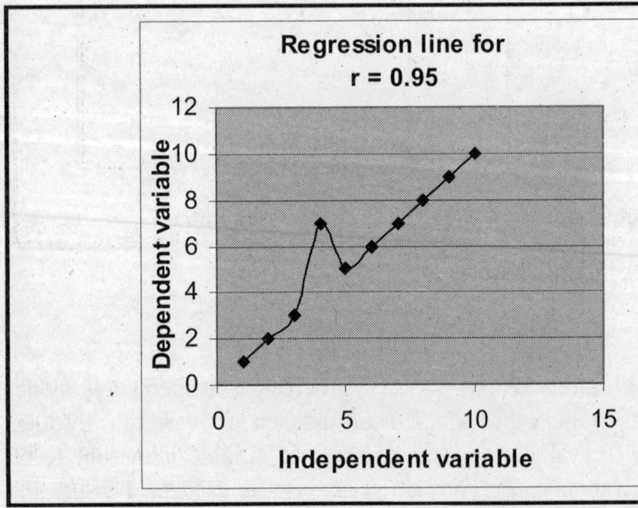

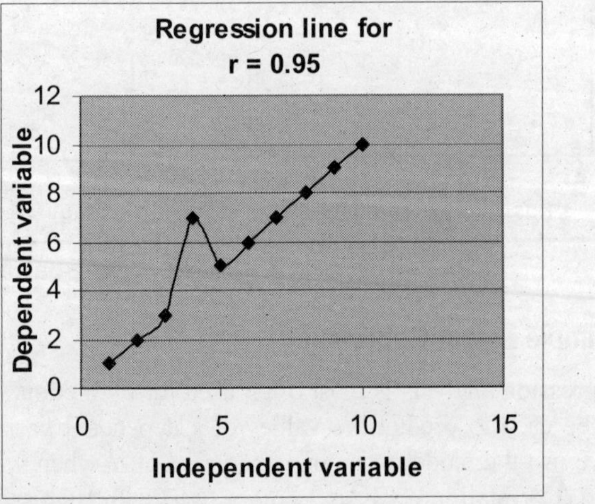

Fig. 12.10: Change in Best-fit Line

Regression Equations by Methods of Least-square

To calculate the values a and b from the line of regression Y on X, the normal equation is given by:

$$\Sigma Y = na + b\Sigma X$$

$$\Sigma XY = n\Sigma X + b\Sigma X^2$$

where, b = The slope of the regression line

a = The intercept point of the regression line and the Y-axis

n = Number of values or elements

X = First Score

Y = Second Score

ΣXY = Sum of the product of first and Second Scores

ΣX = Sum of First Scores

ΣY = Sum of Second Scores

ΣX^2 = Sum of square First Scores

After solving these equations for a and b, the values of a and b are substituted in the regression equation, Y = a + bX.

Alternatively, a and b values can be calculated by the following formula:

$$b = \frac{n\sum xy - (\sum x)(\sum y)}{(n\sum x^2 - (\sum x)^2} \text{ and } a\bar{Y} - b\,\bar{X}$$

where, $x = X - \bar{X}$ and $y = Y - \bar{Y}$

Regression Coefficient in Terms of Correlation Coefficient

Correlation Coefficient, r is given by:

$$r = \sqrt{b_{xy} \times b_{yx}}$$

Regression Coefficient Y on X is given by:

$$b_{xy} = \frac{n\sum xy - (\sum x)(\sum y)}{(n\sum x^2 - (\sum x)^2}$$

Regression Coefficient X on Y is given by:

$$b_{yx} = \frac{n\sum xy - (\sum x)(\sum y)}{(n\sum y^2 - (\sum y)^2}$$

where, $x = X - \bar{X}$ and $y = Y - \bar{Y}$

Example 12.8:

Fit a regression line to estimate the increase in sales revenue expected from an increase of 8% in advertising expenditure.

Advertising Expenditure	1	3	4	6	8	9	11	14
Sales Revenue	1	2	2	4	6	8	8	9

Solution:

Assume the sales revenue (Y) is dependent on advertising expenditure (X). The normal equations are:

$$\Sigma Y = na + b\Sigma X \text{ and } \Sigma XY = n\Sigma X + b\Sigma X^2$$

Table 12.8: Calculation Table

Sales Revenue (Y)	Advertising Expenditure (X)	X^2	XY
1	1	1	1
2	3	9	6
2	4	16	8
4	6	36	24
6	8	64	48
8	9	81	72
8	11	121	88
9	14	196	126
$\Sigma Y = 40$	$\Sigma X = 56$	$\Sigma X^2 = 524$	$\Sigma XY = 373$

$\Sigma Y = na + b\Sigma X$ or $40 = 8a + 56b$

and $\Sigma XY = n\Sigma X + b\Sigma X^2$ or $373 = 56a + 524b$

Solving these equations, we get $a = 0.072$ and $b = 0.704$.

Substituting these values in the regression equation

$Y = a + bX = 0.072 + 0.704\ (X)$

For X = 8%, increase in advertising expenditure, the estimated increase in sales revenue will be

$Y = 0.072 + 0.704\ (0.08) = 0.1283 = 12.83\%$

Example 12.9:

A panel of judges P and Q graded seven dramatic performances by independently awarding marks as follows:

Performance	1	2	3	4	5	6	7
Marks by P	45	41	43	40	44	42	46
Marks by Q	41	37	39	35	36	38	40

The eighth performance which judge Q could not attend was awarded 37 marks by judge P. If judge Q had also been present, how many marks would be expected to have been by him to eighth performance?

Solution:

Let us assume marks awarded by the judge P as X and judge Q as Y. Since we have to estimate the marks that would have been awarded by judge Q, we shall fit a line of regression of Y on X to the given data:

Table 12.9: Calculation Table

X	Y	$x = X - \bar{X}$	$y = Y - \bar{Y}$	x^2	y^2	xy
45	41	3	3	9	9	9
41	37	-1	1	1	1	-1
43	39	1	-1	1	1	-1
40	35	-3	-2	9	4	6
44	36	0	2	0	4	0
42	38	-2	0	4	0	0
46	40	2	4	4	16	8
$\Sigma X = 301$	$\Sigma Y = 226$	$\Sigma x = 0$	$\Sigma y = 7$	$\Sigma x^2 = 28$	$\Sigma y^2 = 35$	$\Sigma xy = 21$

From the table, we have

$$\bar{X} = \frac{\sum X}{n} = \frac{301}{7} = 43 \text{ and } \bar{Y} = \frac{\sum Y}{n} = \frac{226}{7} = 38$$

Further,

$$b = \frac{n\sum xy - (\sum x)(\sum y)}{(n\sum x^2 - (\sum x)^2} = \frac{7\times 21 - 0\times 7}{7\times 28 - 0} = \frac{147}{196} = 0.75$$

and $a = \bar{Y} - b\bar{X} = 38 - 0.75 \times 43 = 5.75$

Substituting these values in the regression equation

$Y = a + bX = 5.75 + 0.75\ (X)$

For X = 37,

$Y = 5.75 + 0.75\ (37) = 33.5$ Marks

Hence, it is expected that the judge Q would have awarded 33.5 marks to the eighth performance.

Example 12.10:

The following data gives the scores and sales made by nine salesmen during a certain period:

Salesmen	1	2	3	4	5	6	7	8	9
Test Score	80	50	80	40	70	50	60	50	60
Weekly Sales	60	30	70	50	60	30	60	40	50

Calculate the correlation coefficient between test scores and sales.

Solution:

Assume the weekly sales (Y) is dependent variables and test scores (X) is independent variables.

Table 12.10: Calculation Table

X	**Y**	**$x = X - \bar{X}$**	**$y = Y - \bar{Y}$**	**x^2**	**y^2**	**xy**
80	60	20	10	400	100	200
50	30	-10	-20	100	400	200
80	70	20	20	400	400	400
40	50	-20	0	400	0	0
70	60	10	10	100	100	100
50	30	-10	-20	100	400	200
60	60	0	10	0	100	0
50	40	-10	-10	100	100	100
60	50	0	0	0	0	0
$\Sigma X = 540$	$\Sigma Y = 450$	$\Sigma x = 0$	$\Sigma y = 0$	$\Sigma x^2 = 1600$	$\Sigma y^2 = 1600$	$\Sigma xy = 1200$

From the table, we have

$$\bar{X} = \frac{\sum X}{n} = \frac{540}{9} = 60 \text{ and } \bar{Y} = \frac{\sum Y}{n} = \frac{450}{9} = 50$$

Regression Coefficient Y on X is given by:

$$b_{yx} = \frac{n\sum xy - (\sum x)(\sum y)}{(n\sum x^2 - (\sum x)^2} = \frac{9 \times 1200}{9 \times 1600} = 0.75$$

Regression Coefficient X on Y is given by:

$$b_{yx} = \frac{n\sum xy - (\sum x)(\sum y)}{(n\sum y^2 - (\sum y)^2} = \frac{9 \times 1200}{9 \times 1600} = 0.75$$

Correlation Coefficient, r is given by:

$$r = \sqrt{b_{xy} \times b_{yx}} = \sqrt{0.75 \times 0.75} = 0.075$$

12.5.3 Multiple Regression Analysis

Multiple regression analysis is the most commonly utilized multivariate technique. It examines the relationship between a single metric dependent variable and two or more metric independent variables. The technique relies upon determining the linear relationship with the lowest sum of squared variances; therefore, assumptions of normality, linearity, and equal variance are carefully observed. The beta coefficients (weights) are the marginal impacts of each variable, and the size of the weight can be interpreted directly. Multiple regression analysis is often used as a forecasting tool.

Multiple regression requires two or more predictor variables, and this is why it is called multiple regression. The multiple regression equation explained above takes the following form:

$$y = b_1x_1 + b_2x_2 + \ldots + b_nx_n + C$$

Here, b_is (i = 1, 2 … n) are the regression coefficients, which in multiple regression represents the value at which the criterion variable changes when the predictor variable changes.

Multiple regression in SPSS is done by selecting "analyze" from the menu. Then, from analyze, select "regression," and from regression select "linear." You can then perform multiple regression..

These terminologies are as follows:

The beta value in multiple regression is used in measuring how effectively the predictor variable influences the criterion variable. In multiple regression, it is measured in terms of standard deviation.

R, in multiple regression, is the measure of association between the observed value and the predicted value of the criterion variable. R Square, or R^2, in multiple regression is the square of the measure of association which indicates the per cent of overlap between the predictor variables and the criterion variable. Adjusted R^2 in multiple regression is an estimate of the R^2 if you used this model with a new data set.

Assumptions of Multiple Regression

1. There should be proper specification of the model in multiple regression. This means that only relevant variables must be included in the multiple regression model. This means that in multiple regression the model should be reliable.
2. Linearity must be assumed in multiple regression. This means that in multiple regression, the model should be linear in nature.
3. Normality must be assumed in multiple regression. This means that in multiple regression, variables must have normal distribution.
4. Homoscedasticity must be assumed in multiple regression. This means that in multiple regression, the variance is constant across all levels of the predicted variable.

Multiple regression analysis is a method for explanation of phenomena and prediction of future events. A coefficient of correlation between variables X and Y is a quantitative index of association between these two variables. In its squared form, as a coefficient of determination, indicates the amount of variance (information) in the criterion variable Y which is accounted for by the variation in the predictor variable X. A multivariate counterpart of the coefficient of determination is the coefficient of multiple determination, R_2. In multiple regression analysis, the set of predictor variables X_1, X_2, ..., Xn is used to explain variability of the criterion variable Y. Initially, a matrix of correlations R is computed for all variables involved in the analysis. This matrix can be conceptualized as a super matrix, containing sub matrices, Rxx, Rxy, Ryx and a scalar number.

$$R = \begin{bmatrix} Rxx & Rxy \\ Ryx & 1 \end{bmatrix}$$

An intuitive approach to the multiple regression analysis is to sum the correlations between the predictor variables and the criterion variable to obtain an index of the overall relationship between the predictor variables and the criterion variable. However, such a sum is often greater than one, suggesting that simple summation of the coefficients of correlations is not a correct procedure to employ. As a matter of fact, a simple summation of squared coefficient of correlations between the predictor variables and the criterion variable is the correct procedure, but only in the special case when the predictor variables are orthogonal. If the predictors are related, their inter-correlations must be removed that only the unique contributions of each predictor toward explanation of the criterion are included. Thus, the fundamental equation of the multiple regression analysis is

$$R^2 = Ryx\ Rxx^{-1}\ Rxy$$

The expression on the left side signifies the coefficient of multiple determinations. The expressions on the right side are the transposed matrix of cross-correlations, the matrix of inter-correlations to be inverted, and the matrix of cross-correlations. The pre-multiplication of the matrix of cross-correlations by its transpose changes the coefficients of correlation into coefficients of determination. The function of the inverted matrix of the inter-correlations is to remove the redundant variance from the matrix of inter-correlations of the predictor set of variables

The fundamental equation of regression analysis contains two distinct operations. The first operation is the post-multiplication of the transpose of cross-correlations by the inverse of inter-correlations, resulting in the matrix of beta weights B

$$B = Ryx\ Rxx^{-1}$$

The second operation is the pre-multiplication of the cross-correlations, by the beta weights, resulting in the coefficient of multiple determinations

$$R^2 = B\ Rxy$$

Notice that in the case of the multiple regressions, sub-matrices of cross-correlations and beta weights are in reality vectors. As you will realize later, the convention of signifying both the matrices and the vectors by capital letters facilitates the discussion of canonical analysis of which the multiple regression is a special case.

Example 12.11:

Let us consider a hypothetical example of the multiple regression analysis, consisting of two predictor variables X and a criterion variable Y. As an example, you may consider scores on an aptitude test and scores on test of motivation as predictors of academic performance.

	X_1	X_2	Y
S_1	2	3	1
S_2	1	1	2
S_3	5	2	3
S_4	4	4	4
S_5	3	5	5

The corresponding super matrix of inter- and cross-correlations was computed as

$$R = \left[\begin{array}{cc|c} 1 & .30 & .50 \\ .30 & 1 & .70 \\ \hline .50 & .70 & 1 \end{array}\right]$$

The first question is whether the matrix of inter-correlations is invertible. Its determinant, computed as (1)(1)-(.30)(.30), equals .91; the matrix is not singular and can be inverted by changing signs of the off-diagonal elements and dividing by the determinant.

$$R_{\alpha}^{-1} = \begin{bmatrix} 1.00/.91 - .30/.91 \\ -.30/.91\ 1.00/.91 \end{bmatrix}$$

$$R_{\alpha}^{-1} \begin{bmatrix} 1.10 - .33 \\ -.33\ 1.10 \end{bmatrix} R_{\alpha}^{-1} = \begin{bmatrix} 1.10 - .33 \\ -.33\ 1.10 \end{bmatrix}$$

The standard partial regression coefficients (beta weights), are computed as

$$B = [.50\ .70] \begin{bmatrix} 1.10 - .33 \\ -.33\ 1.10 \end{bmatrix} = [(.55 - .53)(-.17 + .77)]$$

with resulting vector of beta weights

$$B = [.32\ .60]^{B=[.32\ .60]}$$

The coefficient of the multiple determinations is computed as

$$R^2 = [.32\ .60] \begin{bmatrix} .50 \\ .70 \end{bmatrix}_{R^2} = [.32\ .60] \begin{bmatrix} .50 \\ .70 \end{bmatrix}$$

This operation weights the cross-correlations by the beta weights as

$$R^2 = .32(.50) + .60(.70)^{R^2} = 32(.50) + .60(.70)$$

The coefficient of multiple determinations equals .16 + .42 which equals .58. The coefficient of multiple correlations R is obtained by taking a square root of the coefficient of multiple determinations and equals .76. For our hypothetical experiment, we can conclude that 58 per cent of variability in the academic achievement is explained by the students' scores on the test of aptitude and the test of motivation.

12.5.4 Logistic Regression Analysis

Sometimes referred to as "choice models," this technique is a variation of multiple regression analysis that allows for the prediction of an event. It is allowable to utilize non-metric (typically binary) dependent variables, as the objective is to arrive at a probabilistic assessment of a binary choice. The independent variables can be either discrete or continuous. A contingency table is produced, which shows the classification of observations as to whether the observed and predicted events match. The sum of events that were predicted to occur which actually did occur and the events that were predicted not to occur which actually did not occur, divided by the total number of events, is a measure of the effectiveness of the model. This tool helps predict the choices consumers might make when presented with alternatives.

In statistics, **logistic regression** (sometimes called the **logistic model** or logit **model**) is used for prediction of the probability of occurrence of an event by fitting data to a logit function logistic curve. It is a generalized linear model used for binomial regression. Like many forms of regression analysis, it makes use of several predictor variables that may be either numerical or categorical. For example, the probability that a person has a heart attack within a specified time period might be predicted from knowledge of the person's age, sex and body mass index. Logistic regression is used extensively in the medical and social sciences fields, as well as marketing applications such as prediction of a customer's propensity to purchase a product or cease a subscription.

An explanation of logistic regression begins with an explanation of the logistic function:

$$f(x) = \frac{e^z}{(e^z + 1)} = \frac{1}{(1 + e^{-z})}$$

A graph of the function is shown in figure 1. The input is *z* and the output is *f*(*z*). The logistic function is useful because it can take as an input any value from negative infinity to positive infinity, whereas the output is confined to values between 0 and 1. The variable z represents the exposure to some set of independent variables, while $f(z)$ represents the probability of a particular outcome, given that set of explanatory variables. The variable z is a measure of the total contribution of all the independent variables used in the model and is known as the logit.

The variable z is usually defined as

$$z = \beta_0 + \beta_1 x_1 + \beta_2 x_2 + \ldots.. + \beta_k x_k$$

where β_0 is called the "intercept" and β_1, β_2, β_3 and so on, are called the "regression coefficients" of x_1, x_2, x_3 respectively. The intercept is the values of z when the value of all independent variables is zero (e.g., the value of z in someone with no risk factors). Each of the regression coefficients describes the size of the contribution of that risk factor. A positive regression coefficient means that the explanatory variable increases the probability of the outcome, while a negative regression coefficient means that the variable decreases the probability of that outcome; a large regression coefficient means that the risk factor strongly influences the probability of that outcome; while a near-zero regression coefficient means that the risk factor has little influence on the probability of that outcome.

Logistic regression is a useful way of describing the relationship between one or more independent variables (e.g., age, sex, etc.) and a binary response variable, expressed as a probability, that has only two possible values, such as death ("dead" or "not dead").

Example 12.12:

The application of a logistic regression may be illustrated using a fictitious example of death from heart disease. This simplified model uses only three risk factors (age, sex, and blood cholesterol level) to predict the 10-year risk of death from heart disease. This is the model that we fit:

$\beta_0 = -5.0$ (the intercept)

$\beta_1 = +2.0$

$\beta_2 = -1.0$

$\beta_3 = +1.2$

x_1 = age in years, above 50

x_2 = sex, where 0 is male and 1 is female

x_3 = cholesterol level, in mmcl/L above 5.0

which means the model is

$$\text{Risk of death} = \frac{1}{(1+e^{-z})}$$

where, $z = -5.0 + 2.0x_1 - 1.0x_2 + 1.2x_3$

In this model, increasing age is associated with an increasing risk of death from heart disease (z goes up by 2.0 for every year over the age of 50), female sex is associated with a decreased risk of death from heart disease (z goes down by 1.0 if the patient is female), and increasing cholesterol is associated with an increasing risk of death (z goes up by 1.2 for each 1 mmol/L increase in cholesterol above 5 mmol/L).

We wish to use this model to predict Nathan Petrelli's risk of death from heart disease. He is 50 years old and his cholesterol level is 7.0 mmol/L. Nathan Petrelli's risk of death is therefore

$$\frac{1}{(1+e^{-z})} = .07$$

where, z= –5.0 + +2.050 – 50 + –1.00 + + 1.2 (7.0 – 5.0)

This means that by this model, Nathan Petrelli's risk of dying from heart disease in the next 10 years is 0.07 (or 7%).

12.6 FACTOR ANALYSIS

When there are many variables in a research design, it is often helpful to reduce the variables to a smaller set of factors. This is an independence technique, in which there is no dependent variable. Rather, the researcher is looking for the underlying structure of the data matrix. Ideally, the independent variables are normal and continuous, with at least three to five variables loading onto a factor. The sample size should be over 50 observations, with over five observations per variable. Multi-collinearity is generally preferred between the variables, as the correlations are key to data reduction. Kaiser's Measure of Statistical Adequacy (MSA) is a measure of the degree to which every variable can be predicted by all other variables. An overall MSA of .80 or higher is very good, with a measure of under .50 deemed poor.

Essential Features of Factor Analysis

1. It is a multivariate technique where initially a large number of variables are considered.
2. The large number of variables are reduced to a small number of factors.
3. Selection of variables constituting a factor is made on the basis of total variation accounted for by them.
4. It also provides a measure of correlation. A large number of response about a large number of variables are used to identify the highly correlated variables which constitute a factor.
5. The variables constituting a factor are highly correlated with one another but not correlated with other factor.
6. For each factor, judgment has to be exercised to determine the theme of the factor.
7. Factor models are based on the assumption of linear relationship.

Application of Factor Analysis

Early efforts and contribution towards the development of concept and application of factor useful mathematical basis for explaining human behavior and abilities. Factor analysis was used for psychological tests, such as IQ test, personality test for different groups of persons, etc. Gradually, it was picked up by other disciplines such as Economics, Sociology, Commerce, Management, etc. Various uses and applications of factor analysis are:

1. Reduction in the Number of Variables: Factor analysis reduces the number of explanatory variables taken initially to a small number of independent factors. This reduced data overload and the cost of analysis. At the same time, more useful variables can be distinctly identified.

2. Determination of Latent Factors: Factor analysis identifies latent factors which determine the relationship among a set of observed values. For example, the growth of firm is influenced by a number of factors such as, new investment, quality of management, quality of product, market environment, credit policy, etc. Factor analysis can be used to identify the variables influencing the growth of a firm.

3. Determination of Latent Relationship: Factor analysis identifies the latent relationship among various groups of variables under observation. If a certain relationship exists but is not clearly observable, it can be highlighted by factor analysis.

4. Determination of Grouping of Factors: Sometimes, it may be desired to group various factors on the basis of their common characteristics. Factor analysis can be used for such a grouping of the factors.

5. Determination of Cluster of Observations: Factor analysis can be used for determining the cluster among the observations based on a survey.

6. Developing of Composite Indicators: Factor analysis can be used for developing composite indicators for the comparison of two situations or two periods in some respect. Composite indicators are considered very useful in economic research.

7. Market Research Including Determination of Consumer Preference: In the field of market research, determination of consumers' preference for different products can be done through factor analysis. The analysis not only throws light on consumers' preference, which may be very useful in identifying the market trend, but also provides knowledge about crucial attributes of the product that determine consumers' preference. This knowledge can be useful in:

- Improving the quality of the product, as greater attention may be given to key variables in production.
- Planning more effective advertising campaigns.
- Control of quality, etc.

Such a study can be undertaken for one product or a group of products. In case of single product, the attributes of the product expected to influence the choice of consumers are identified. Then taking a sample of product users, the consumers may be asked to give their rating of the product based on each of its attribute on a five/six/ten-point differential scale. Finally, with analysis the attributes influencing the choice can be identified.

Assumptions of Factor Analysis

1. A factor in a linear combination of variables under study. It describes a group of variables in relation to several others and the relationship is linear.
2. The number of factors is considerably small than the number of variables. Thus, out of large number of variables considered, a small number of factors are determined. These factors account for a large percentage of the total variance among the variables considered.
3. The factors are derived so as to minimize the correlation between them. Thus, the highly correlated variables are combined within a single factor.
4. The variables allotted to a factor are nearly independent of the variables allocated to other factors.
5. The factors are derived in such a manner that the percentage of total variance explained by the variables and included in successive factors is maximized.

Terminology in Factor Analysis

Factor analysis has certain unique terms. It may be useful to understand their meaning and significance for understanding its methodology and applications. Important terms used in factor analysis are:

1. Factor: A factor is weighted linear combination of the variables under study. It accounts for several observed variables. The output of factor analysis is in terms of factor. One or more of these factors are considered for analysis depending upon the nature and object of the study.

2. Factor Loading: Factor loading (factor variable correlation) are values indicating the extent of closeness of relationship among variable constituting a factor. These are useful in understanding the meaning of factor. In the interpretation of factor loading its absolute size, ignoring algebraic signs (plus or minus), is considered.

3. Factor Scores: Factor scores are the coefficient of the factors.

4. Commonality (h^2): Commonality indicates the extent a variable has been accounted for by underlying factor taken together. Higher the value of commonality, higher the variable has been considered by the factor and lower of it left out. It is worked out in respect of all the variables included in the factors one by one separately as:

Commonality (h^2) of ith variable = Factor loading off i^{th} variable in Factor A2 + Factor loading of ith variable on Factor B2.

5. Eigen Value: The sum of squares of factor loading relating to a factor is known as Eigen value or latent root. It indicates the relative importance of factor in accounting for the set of variables considered in the analysis.

6. Total Sum of Squares: The total of Eigen values of all the factors extracted is known as total sum of squares. Total sum of squares divided by the number of variables included in the factor indicates the extent to which the factor accounts for the variables. If the variables considered are different from each other, this index is low. But if the variables considered fall into one or more of the groups and the factors extracted account for these groups, the index is high.

7. Factor Rotation: Rotation of factors is done to reveal different structures in the data. Though different rotations give different results, from statistical point of view, these are taken as equal, not superior or inferior to others. For final interpretation, however, the correct rotation should be identified and selected. If the factors are independent, orthogonal rotation is done. But if the factors are correlated, then an oblique rotation is done. On factor rotation, the commonality remains unaffected but the Eigen value changes.

There are two main factor analysis methods:

1. Centroid Method/Common Factor Analysis
2. Principal Component Analysis

12.6.1 Centroid Method/Common Factor Analysis

The centroid method of factor analysis was developed by L.L. Thurston. This method was commonly used till 1950, before the use of electronic computers became widespread. In centroid method, the sum of loading are maximized ignoring their mathematical signs. The linear combination of all weights is taken between +1 and –1.

Step by Step Treatment of Data **in Centroid Method is as given below:**

1. First, for the given observations, standard scores are determined. From these scores, statistics such as mean, standard deviation and coefficient of correlation between the variables are determined. Product moment method can be conveniently used for calculations. The coefficients of correlation are arranged in the form of a correlation matrix *r*.
2. The centroid method requires that the weights for all the variables are positive. Thus, in case the correlation matrix obtained is a positive manifold (i.e., ignoring and the diagonal elements if for each variable the sum of positive correlations is large than the sum of negative correlations), the correlation matrix is used as such for extracting the first centroid factor. But in case the correlation matrix is not a positive manifold, then a reflected correlation matrix is obtained.
3. From the correlation matrix/reflected correlation matrix first, centroid factor is obtained as under:
   - For each column of correlation matrix, sum of coefficients including the diagonal unity are obtained.
   - From the above, by adding all the figures in the row, sum of column sums (T) is obtained.
   - First Centroid Factor Loading (F_1) are obtained by dividing the sums of the coefficients in the columns by square root of sum of column sums (T).
4. Then the second centroid factor is obtained as under:
   - A matrix of factor cross products (Q) is obtained by multiplying the elements of first centroid factor for each variable by elements of first centroid factor for all other variables.
   - From the above first, matrix of residual coefficients (R_1) is obtained by subtracting the factor cross products (Q_1) from their respective coefficients of correlation in correlation matrix (r). In case some of the residuals in the matrix of residual coefficients (R_1) are negative, a reflected matrix of the residual coefficients (r_1) is obtained.

   For each column of the reflected residual, coefficients (r_1) sum is obtained. Dividing these, sums by square root of sum of column sums, second centroid (F_2) is obtained.
5. Third, fourth and subsequent centroid factors are extracted by following the procedures, as explained in step (4) above.
6. After factoring, vectors of centroid factors are arranged in a table and commonalty (h^2) for all the variables and Eigen values for all the factors are obtained. The commonality (h^2) is the sum of squares of factor loading for the variable. The Eigen values are sum of squares of loading for each factor as well as the commonality.
7. From Eigen values, proportion of total variance explained and proportion of common variance explained by each factor is determined. Proportion of total variance explained is determined by dividing the Eigen value of a factor by the number of variables considered. The proportion of common variance explained is obtained by dividing the Eigen value for the factor by the Eigen value of the commonality.

Example 12.13:

From the following correlation matrix (r) relating to six variables, obtain the first two centroid factors, commonality for each variable and eigen value for each factor and comment on the results.

Variables	1	2	3	4	5	6
1	1.00	0.55	0.43	0.32	0.28	0.36
2		1.00	0.50	0.25	0.31	0.32
3			1.00	0.39	0.25	0.33
4				1.00	0.43	0.49
5					1.00	0.44
6						1.00

Solution:

As the given correlation matrix (r) is a positive manifold, the first centroid factor (A) is calculated as under:

Table 12.11: First Centroid Factor (A)

	1	2	3	4	5	6
1	1.00	0.55	0.43	0.32	0.28	0.36
2	0.55	1.00	0.50	0.25	0.31	0.32
3	0.43	0.50	1.00	0.39	0.25	0.33
4	0.32	0.25	0.39	1.00	0.43	0.49
5	0.28	0.31	.025	0.43	1.00	0.44
6	0.36	0.32	0.33	0.49	0.44	1.00
Column Sums	2.94	2.93	2.90	2.88	2.71	2.94 + 17.30 + T^2 (T = 4.16)

Table 10.12: Matrix of Factor Cross Products

Factor Loading	**0.707**	**0.704**	**0.697**	**0.692**	**0.651**	**0.707**
0.707	0.4998	0.4977	0.4928	0.4892	0.4603	0.4998
0.704	0.4977	0.4956	0.4907	0.4872	0.4583	0.4977
0.697	0.4928	0.4907	0.4858	0.4823	0.4537	0.4928
0.692	0.4892	0.4972	0.4823	0.4789	0.4505	0.4892
0.651	0.4603	0.4583	0.4537	0.4505	0.4238	0.4602
0.707	0.4998	0.7977	0.4928	0.4892	0.4603	0.4998

Table 10.13: Matrix of Residual Coefficients (R_1)

	1	2	3	4	5	6
1	0.5002	0.0523	0.0623	0.1692	0.1803	0.1398
2	0.0523	0.5044	0.0093	0.2372	0.1483	0.1777
3*	0.0628	0.0093	0.5142	0.0923	0.2037	0.1628
4*	0.1692	0.2372	0.0923	0.5211	0.0205	0.0008
5*	0.1803	0.1483	0.2037	0.0205	0.5762	0.0203
6*	0.1398	0.1777	0.1628	0.0008	0.0203	0.5002
Column	1.1046	1.1292	1.0451	1.0411	1.1493	1.0016 T = 6.4709 = 2.5438
Second Centroid Factor (B)	0.4342	0.4439	–0.4108	–0.4093	–0.4518	–0.3937
These variables are reflected.						

Table 12.14: Determination of Commonalities (h^2) and Eigen Values

Variables	**Factor Loadings**		**Commonality (h^2)**
	Centroid Factor A	Centroid Factor B	
1	0.707	0.4342	(0.707)2 + (0.4342)2 = 0.6883
2	0704	0.4439	(0.704)2 + (0.4439)2 = 0.6926
3	0.697	–0.4108	(0.697)2 + (0.4108)2 = 0.654

4	0.692	–0.4093	(0.692)2 + (0.4093)2 = 0.6464
5	0.651	–0.4518	(0.651)2 + (0.4518)2 = 0.627
6	0.707	–0.3937	(0.707)2 + (0.3937)2 = 0.6548
Eigen Values	2.8837+	1.0809	= 3.964
Proportion of Total Variance Explained	0.4806+	0.1802	= 0.6608(66.3%)
Proportion of Common Variance Explained	0.7274+	0.2726	= 1.0000(100%)

12.6.2 Principal Component Analysis

Common factor analysis is used to look for the latent (underlying) factors, whereas principal component analysis is used to find the fewest number of variables that explain the most variance. The first factor extracted explains the most variance. Typically, factors are extracted as long as the Eigen values are greater than 1.0 or the Scree test visually indicates how many factors to extract. The factor loadings are the correlations between the factor and the variables. Typically, a factor loading of four or higher is required to attribute a specific variable to a factor. An orthogonal rotation assumes no correlation between the factors, whereas an oblique rotation is used when some relationship is believed to exist.

Principal component method of factor analysis was developed by H. Hotelling. This makes certain improvements over the centroid method. It is a widely used method. A principal component is linear combination of variables contributing maximum total variance. Thus, first principal component is linear combination of variables contributing the maximum to total variance. Second principal component unrelated with the first is linear combination of variables contributing second maximum to residual variance, and so on. Sum of variances of all principal components taken together is equal to the sum of variance of all variables considered.

In the principal components method, all the factors are arranged as per the values of their coefficients (aij, i = 1, 2, 3, …, n) from the highest positive to the highest negative and principal factors are identified. Thus, k observed variables are described linearly in terms of R new uncorrected (orthogonal) components/factor (F_1, F_2, F_3, ………, F_p), and combination of variables with largest percentage variance are selected, such that first principal component is one with the maximum variance, the second principal component is one with the next maximum variance and so on.

Step by step treatment of data in principal component method is as under:

1. Statistics such as mean, standard deviation and coefficient of correlation between pairs of variables are obtained from the given set of observations.
2. The coefficients of correlation are arranged in the form of a correlation matrix (r) in case the correlation matrix is not positive manifold, a reflected matrix of the coefficients (r') is obtained.
3. From correlation matrix/reflected correlation matrix, the first principal component is obtained as under:
   - For each column, sum of correlation coefficients including the diagonal elements is obtained. The vector of column sums is referred to as:

$$Ua_1 = \left(\sqrt{\sum_{1=1}^{k} a_1 + a_2 + ... + ak}\right)$$

   - A normalization factor is obtained for normalization of column sums (Vector 1). The normalization factor is square root of the sum of squares of all the column sums:

$$Ua_1 = \left(\sqrt{\sum_{1=1}^{k} Ua_{12} + Ua_{22} + ... + Uak_2}\right)$$

   - The elements of normalized column sums (Va_1) are multiplied by their respective coefficients in various rows of the correlation matrix/reflected correlation matrix (r or r') one by one starting with first row and ending with the last row of the matrix and the sum of these products is put at the end of the row. The resultant vector is referred to as Ua_2.
   - A normalization factor is obtained for normalization of row sums (Vector Ua_2). The normalization factor is square root of the sum of squares of all the elements of the vector Ua_2.

$$\left(\sqrt{\sum_{l=1}^{k} k\,Ua_{12}{}^{2} + Ua_{22}{}^{2} + \ldots + Uak_{2}{}^{2}}\right)$$

- The elements of the vector Ua_2 are divided by the normalization factor. This normalized vector is referred to as Va_2.
- Vector Va_1 is compared with Va_2. If the two vectors are nearly identical, it is called convergence. In case there is no convergence, the third vector is processed again till convergence occurs.

  Once convergence occurs, first principal component is extracted. For this, various elements of vector Va are multiplied by square root of normalization factor of vector Ua_2. The products constitute the elements of First Principal Component (F_1).

4. For extracting second principal component, the vector of first principal component is further processed as under:
   - A matrix of factor cross products is obtained by multiplying all the elements of the vector of First Principal Component by its all other elements including itself one by one. These products presented in the form of matrix are referred to as first matrix of factor cross products (Q_1).
   - Various elements of the matrix of factor cross products (Q_1) are subtracted from the respective elements of the matrix of correlation coefficient (r) one by one. The residuals presented in the form of matrix are referred to as first matrix of residual coefficients (R_1).
   - In case any of the residual coefficients is negative, it is reflected and a matrix of reflected residual coefficients is obtained. This is referred to as first matrix of reflected residual coefficients (R'_1).
5. From the first matrix of reflected residual coefficients (R_1), second principal component is extracted under:
   - Sum of residual components for each column-wise sum of residual components is referred to as:

     $$Ub_1 = \left(\sum_{l=1}^{1} Ub_1\right)$$

   - A normalization factor for the vector of sums of residual coefficients is obtained. The normalization factor (NF) is square root of the sum of squares of all the column sums.
   - The column sums are normalized by dividing the elements of vector Ub_1 by normalization factor (NF) one by one. The normalized column sums so obtained is referred to as Vb_1.
   - The elements of vector Ub_1 are multiplied by their respective coefficients in each row of the first reflected matrix of residual coefficients (R_1) one by one, starting with first row and ending with last row. The vector of sum of products placed at the end of row is referred to as Ub_2.
   - For normalization of the elements of the vector Ub_2, a normalization factor (NF) is obtained by extracting square root of the sum of squares of all the elements of vector Ub_2. Various elements of the vector Ub_2 are divided by the normalization factor one by one. The resultant vector is referred to as a new normalized vector Vb_2.
   - If the elements of the two vectors (Vb_1 and Vb_2) are identical, it is taken as convergence. In case there is no convergence, the trial vectors are processed again and again till convergence occurs.
   - Second principal component (F_2) is extracted by multiplying the elements of vector V_b by square root of the normalization factor of Vb_2.
6. The method for extracting second principal components is followed for extracting third, fourth and subsequent principal components.
7. Finally, a matrix of factor loadings, commonalities of variables considered, Eigen values of factors and proportion of variance explained by factors is obtained. The commonality (h_2) for a variable is sum of squares of elements of principal component for that variable. An Eigen value is sum of loading for each principal component/factor as well as commonality.

   The proportion of total variance explained is determined by dividing Eigen value of a factor by the number of variables considered. The proportion of common variance explained is obtained by dividing the Eigen value of the factor by the Eigen value of the commonality.

Example 12.14:

From the following correlation matrix (r) of six variables, compute first two principal component factors, their Eigen values and commonality for the variables. Also determine the proportion of total variance and common variance explained by each of the two component factors:

Variable	1	2	3	4	5	6
	1.000	0.704	0.707	0.428	0.357	0.862
	0.704	1.000	0.387	0.425	0.379	0.642
	0.707	0.387	1.000	0.579	0.342	0.862
	0.428	0.425	0.579	1.000	0.375	0.427
	0.357	0.379	0.342	0.375	1.000	0.643
	0.862	0.642	0.862	0.427	0.643	1.000

Solution:

Since the given correlation matrix is a positive manifold, first principal component factor is worked out as under:

Table 12.15: First Principal Component Factor

Variable	1	2	3	4	5	6	Ua_2	Normalized Vector
								$Va_2 = Ua_2NF@$
1	1.000	0.704	0.707	0.428	0.357	0.862	1.705	0.452
2	0.704	1.000	0.387	0.425	0.379	0.642	1.452	0.385
3	0.707	0.387	1.000	0.579	0.342	0.862	1.625	0.431
4	0.428	0.425	0.579	1.000	0.375	0.427	1.286	0.341
5	0.357	0.379	0.342	0.375	1.000	0.643	1.232	0.326
6	0.862	0.642	0.862	0.427	0.643	1.000	1.848	0.490
Column Sums (Ua_1)		4.058	3.537	3.8774	3.23	3.096	4.436	
Normalized Vector (Va_1) Ua_2/ NF** =	0.443	0.387	0.424	0.353	0.338	0.485		

** Normalization Factor for (Ua_1)*

Normalized Factor Ua_1 = (4.058)2 + (3.537)2 + (3.877)2 + (3.234)2 + (3.096)2 + (4.436)2

= 83.73 = 9.15**

Normalized Factor Ua_2 = (1.705)2 + (1.452)2 + (1.625)2 + (1.286)2 + (1.232)2 + (1.848)2

= 14.243 = 3.774 @

Comparing Va_1 and Va_2, we find that the two vectors are nearly equal, so convergence has occurred. Hence, first principal component is extracted.

Table 12.16: Extraction of First Principal Component

Variable	Characteristics	X (Va)	Normalizing Factor of Ua_2 or 3.774	-	First Component (F1)
1	0.443	X	1.943	-	0.861
2	0.387	X	1.945	-	0.752
3	0.424	X	1.943	-	0.824
4	0.353	X	1.943	-	0.686
5	0.338	X	1.943	-	0.657
6	0.485	X	1.943	-	0.942

Table 12.17: First Matrix of Cross Products (Q_1)

First Principal Component	0.861	0.752	0.824	0.686	0.657	0.942
0.861	0.741	0.647	0.709	0.591	0.566	0.811
0.752	0.647	0.566	0.620	0.516	0.494	0.708
0.824	0.709	0.620	0.679	0.565	0.541	0.776
0.686	0.591	0.516	0.565	0.471	0.451	0.646
0.657	0.566	0.494	0.541	0.451	0.432	0.619
0.942	0.811	0.708	0.776	0.646	0.619	0.887

Table 12.18: First Matrix of Residual Coefficients (R_1)

Variable	0.861	0.752	0.824	0.686	0.657	0.942
1	0.259	0.057	–0.002	–0.163	–0.209	0.51
2	0.057	0.434	–0.233	–0.091	–0.115	–0.066
3	–0.002	–0.233	0.321	0.014	–0.199	0.086
4	–0.163	–0.091	0.014	0.529	–0.076	–0.219
5	–0.209	–0.115	–0.199	–0.076	0.568	0.024
6	0.051	–0.006	0.086	–0.219	0.024	0.133

Table 12.19: Reflected Matrix of Residual Coefficients (R'_1) and Extraction of Second Principal Component

	1	2	3	4	5	6	Ua_2	Normalized Vector $Va_2 = Ua_2NF@$
	0.259	0.057	0.002	0.163	0.209	0.051	0.309	0.322
	*0.057	0.434	0.233	0.091	0.115	0.066	0.416	0.433
	*0.002	0.233	0.321	0.014	0.199	0.086	0.355	0.369
	*0.163	0.091	0.014	0.529	0.076	0.219	0.445	0.463
	*0.209	0.115	0.199	0.529	0.568	0.024	0.531	0.553
	0.051	0.066	0.086	0.219	0.024	0.113	0.224	0.233
Column (Ub1) sums	0.741	0.996	0.855	1.092	1.191	0.559		

Normalized Vector Vb_1 – Ub/NF**	0.325	-0.437	-0.375	-0.47	-0.523	0.245		•

** Normalization Factor (Ub_1)*

Normalized Factor Ub_1* = (0.741)2 + (0.996)2 + (0.855)2 + (1.092)2 + (1.191)2 + (0.599)2
= 5.195 = 2.279

@Normalized Factor Ub_2 = (0.309)2 + (0.416)2 + (0.355)2 + (0.445)2 + (0.531)2 + (0.224)2
= 0.924 = 0.961

As vectors Vb_1 and Vb_2 are nearly equal, convergence has occurred. Hence, Vb_1 is taken as characteristics vector Vb.

Table 12.20: Extraction of Second Principal Component

Variables (V_b)	Characteristics	X	Normalizing Vector = Vb_1 or 0.961	-	Second Principal Component (F2)
1	0.325	X	0.98	-	0.319
2	–0.437	X	0.98	-	–0.428
3	–0.375	X	0.98	-	–0.368
4	–0.479	X	0.98	-	–0.469
5	–0.523	X	0.98	-	–0.513
6	0.245	X	0.98	-	0.240

Table 12.21: Matrix of Factor Loading, Commonality and Eigen Values

Variables	Factor Loadings		Commonality (h^2)
	First Principal Component	Second Principal Component	
1	0.861	0.319	$(0.861)^2 + (0.319)^2 = 0.843$
2	0.752	–0.428	$(0.752)^2 + (–0.428)^2 = 0.749$
3	0.824	–0.368	$(0.824)^2 + (–0.368)^2 = 0.814$
4	0.686	–0.469	$(0.686)^2 + (–0.469)^2 = 0.691$
5	0.657	–0.513	$(0.657)^2 + (–0.513)^2 = 0.714$
6	0.942	0.240	$(0.942)^2 + (0.240)^2 = 0.945$
Eigen Values			= 3.775 0.981 = 4.75
Proportion of Total Variance			0.629 0.164 = 0.793
Proportion of Common Variance			0.794 0.206 = 1.000

12.7 CLUSTER ANALYSIS

The purpose of cluster analysis is to reduce a large data set to meaningful subgroups of individuals or objects. The division is accomplished on the basis of similarity of the objects across a set of specified characteristics. Outliers are a problem with this technique, often caused by too many irrelevant variables. The sample should be representative of the population, and it is desirable to have uncorrelated factors. There are three main clustering methods: hierarchical, which is a tree like process appropriate for smaller data sets; non-hierarchical, which requires specification of the number of clusters a priori; and a combination of both. There are four main rules for developing clusters: the clusters should be different, they should be reachable, they should be measurable, and the clusters should be profitable (big enough to matter). This is a great tool for market segmentation.

Characteristic Features of Cluster Analysis

Some of the typical characteristic features of cluster analysis are as follows:

- Cluster analysis determines internal homogeneity, i.e., the similarity existing among the respondents or items.
- Cluster analysis also determines external heterogeneity, i.e., the similarity existing among the respondents or items.
- Generally a large data set, i.e., a large number of variables and a large number of respondents are used for cluster analysis.
- Cluster analysis can be done in case of metric as well as non-metric data.
- The methodology of cluster analysis is simple. In case only two variables are under consideration, clusters can be formed by simple observation method, after plotting the responses on a graph. However, in case more than two variables are under consideration, use of some mathematical model and computer program becomes necessary for the analysis of data.
- Cluster analysis has a wide range of applications. It is used in theoretical as well as applied research.

Objects of Cluster Analysis

The main object of cluster analysis is to identify different groups (or clusters) of respondents, such a while the respondents in one cluster are all similar to one another, these are different from the respondents in other clusters.

Cluster analysis is also concerned with determining interdependence among the variables considered in a study, especially within different subsets of respondents.

Example 12.15:

A group of 12 respondents were asked to mark their preference for a particular game in each of the two sets. The first set included 10 games arranged as indoor-outdoor. The second set included 10 games arranged as very easy to most rugged. The preferences of the respondents are given below

Respondent	Variable 1 Indoor-Outdoor	Variable 2 Easy-rugged
A	2	1
B	2	5
C	2	6
D	3	5
E	5	8
F	8	2
G	9	2
H	9	3
I	10	9
J	10	4
K	10	8
L	10	10

Identify the cluster of respondents by showing the values on a graph.

Solution:

For identification of clusters, the preferences have been marked on a graph. On the one side of the graph, variable 1 (x_1) is shown and on the other variable 2 (x_2) is shown. Drawing circles the cluster have been marked.

It may be observed from the above that respondents A, B, C, and D, respondents F, G, H and J and respondents I, K and L form three distinct clusters with common characteristics.

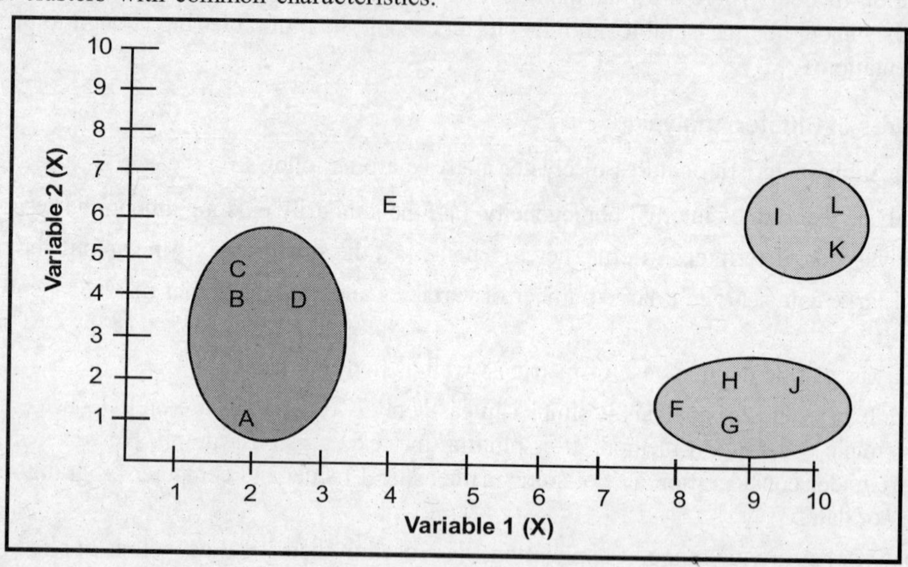

12.8 DISCRIMINANT ANALYSIS

The purpose of discriminant analysis is to correctly classify observations or people into homogeneous groups. The independent variables must be metric and must have a high degree of normality. Discriminant analysis builds a linear discriminant function, which can then be used to classify the observations. The overall fit is assessed by looking at the degree to which the group means differ (Wilkes Lambda or D2) and how well the model classifies. To determine which variables have the most impact on the discriminant function, it is possible to look at partial F values. The higher the partial F, the more impact that variable has on the discriminant function. This tool helps categorize people, like buyers and non-buyers.

Discriminant analysis is a statistical technique that is used to classify the dependent variable between two or more categories. Discriminant analysis also has a regression technique, which is used for predicting the value of the dependent categorical variable.

In discriminant analysis, we predict the value of two categories. When the category of a dependent variable is more than two, it will simply be an extension of the simple discriminant analysis called the multiple discriminant analysis. Multiple discriminant analysis and **MANOVA** are considered to be similar because both tests share many similar assumptions and tests.

The F test (Wilkes Lambda) is used to test whether or not the discriminant model is significant as a whole. If the F test shows the overall significance of the model, then the individual variables are accessed to see which variable will move the significance from the group mean.

Discriminant analysis also has several assumptions, such as multiple linear regressions, linear relationships, homoscedastic relationships, untruncated interval data, etc. Logistic regression is the alternative technique and it is frequently used in place of discriminant analysis when data does not meet the assumptions.

Discriminant analysis is a technique for classifying a set of observations into predefined classes. The purpose is to determine the class of an observation based on a set of variables known as predictors or input variables. The model is built based on a set of observations for which the classes are known. This set of observations is sometimes referred to as the training set. Based on the training set, the technique constructs a set of linear functions of the predictors, known as discriminant functions, such that $L = b_1x_1 + b_2x_2 + ? + b_nx_n + c$, where the b's are discriminant coefficients, the x's are the input variables or predictors and c is a constant.

These discriminant functions are used to predict the class of a new observation with unknown class. For a k class problem, k discriminant functions are constructed. Given a new observation, all the k discriminant functions are evaluated and the observation is assigned to class i if the ith discriminant function has the highest value.

Key Terms and Concepts

Discriminating variables: Discriminating variables are independent variables that are used to predict the dependent variable. These variables are also called the predictors.

The criterion variable: Dependent variables are also called the criterion variables.

Discriminant function: The linear combination of the discriminating (independent) variable is called the discriminant function. For example,

$$L = b_1x_1 + b_2x_2 + ? + b_nx_n + c$$

where L = discriminant function, b_1 = discriminant coefficients, x = independents variables, and c = constants

Number of discriminant functions: For the two groups, there is one discriminant analysis function. For multivariate discriminant analysis, there will be g – 1 discriminant function.

The Eigen values: This is also called characteristic root, which tells us the variance explained by each discriminant function.

The discriminant score: By applying discriminant formulas, the value that comes is called the discriminant score. This discriminant score helps us to classify the group category.

Cutoff: This is the value which divides the group value into two parts. When the value of the discriminant score is at the negative side of the cutoff point, then the group will fall into a lower category, and when it is at the positive side, the group will be at a higher category.

Unstandardized discriminant coefficients: Unstandardized discriminant coefficients are simply like the regression beta, which is used to predict the discriminate score. Standardized discriminant coefficients are used to compare the relative importance of the independent variables.

Tests of Significance

Wilkes Lambda: The overall model significance of the discriminant function is tested by the Wilkes Lambda test. If the overall model is significant, then the F test is used to test whether or not the individual variable means differ from the group mean function.

Assumptions in Discriminant Analysis

1. **Independence:** Each case should be independent of each other. Correlated data cannot be used in discriminant analysis.
2. **Adequate sample size:** There must be at least two cases for each category of the dependent variable. However, it is recommended that there should be at least four or five times as many cases as independent variables.
3. **Interval data:** In discriminant analysis, there should be an interval data for independent variable.
4. **Variance:** No independents have a zero standard deviation in one or more of the groups formed by the dependent.
5. **Random error:** Error terms are assumed to be randomly distributed.
6. **Homogeneity of variances:** Variance with each group of independent variables should be equal.
7. **Absence of perfect multicollinearity:** There should be no perfect multicollinearity between the independent variables.
8. **Assumes linearity:** The discriminant functions should be linear and related to each other.
9. **Normally distributed:** The predictor variable should be normally distributed.

12.9 MULTIVARIATE ANALYSIS OF VARIANCE (MANOVA)

This technique examines the relationship between several categorical independent variables and two or more metric dependent variables. Whereas analysis of variance (ANOVA) assesses the differences between groups (by using T tests for two means and F tests between three or more means), MANOVA examines the dependence relationship between a set of dependent measures across a set of groups. Typically, this analysis is used in experimental design, and usually a hypothesized relationship between dependent measures is used. This technique is slightly different in that the independent variables are categorical and the dependent variable is metric. Sample size is an issue, with 15-20 observations needed per cell. However, too many observations per cell (over 30) and the technique loses its practical significance. Cell sizes should be roughly equal, with the largest cell having less than 1.5 times the observations of the smallest cell. That is because, in this technique, normality of the dependent variables is important. The model fit is determined by examining mean vector equivalents across groups. If there is a significant difference in the means, the null hypothesis can be rejected and treatment differences can be determined.

12.10 MULTIDIMENSIONAL SCALING (MDS)

The purpose of MDS is to transform consumer judgments of similarity into distances represented in multidimensional space. This is a decompositional approach that uses perceptual mapping to present the dimensions. As an exploratory technique, it is useful in examining unrecognized dimensions about products and in uncovering comparative evaluations of products when the basis for comparison is unknown. Typically, there must be at least four times as many objects being evaluated as dimensions. It is possible to evaluate the objects with non-metric preference rankings or metric similarities (paired comparison) ratings. Kruskal's Stress measure is a "badness of fit" measure; a stress percentage of 0 indicates a perfect fit, and over 20% is a poor fit. The dimensions can be interpreted either subjectively by letting the respondents identify the dimensions or objectively by the researcher.

12.11 CORRESPONDENCE ANALYSIS

This technique provides for dimensional reduction of object ratings on a set of attributes, resulting in a perceptual map of the ratings. However, unlike MDS, both independent variables and dependent variables are examined at the same time. This technique is more similar in nature to factor analysis. It is a compositional technique, and is useful when there are many attributes and many companies. It is most often used in assessing the effectiveness of advertising campaigns. It is also used when the attributes are too similar for factor analysis to be meaningful. The main structural approach is the development of a contingency (crosstab) table. This means that the form of the variables should be non-metric. The model can be assessed by examining the Chi-square value for the model. Correspondence analysis is difficult to interpret, as the dimensions are a combination of independent and dependent variables.

12.12 CONJOINT ANALYSIS

Conjoint analysis is often referred to as "trade-off analysis," since it allows for the evaluation of objects and the various levels of the attributes to be examined. It is both a compositional technique and a dependence technique, in that a level of preference for a combination of attributes and levels is developed. A part-worth, or utility, is calculated for each level of each attribute, and combinations of attributes at specific levels are summed to develop the overall preference for the attribute at each level. Models can be built that identify the ideal levels and combinations of attributes for products and services.

12.13 CANONICAL CORRELATION

The most flexible of the multivariate techniques, canonical correlation simultaneously correlates several independent variables and several dependent variables. This powerful technique utilizes metric independent variables, unlike MANOVA, such as sales, satisfaction levels, and usage levels. It can also utilize non-metric categorical variables. This technique has the fewest restrictions of any of the multivariate techniques, so the results should be interpreted with caution due to the relaxed assumptions. Often, the dependent variables are related, and the independent variables are related, so finding a relationship is difficult without a technique like canonical correlation.

12.14 STRUCTURAL EQUATION MODELING

Unlike the other multivariate techniques discussed, structural equation modeling (SEM) examines multiple relationships between sets of variables simultaneously. This represents a family of techniques, including LISREL, latent variable analysis, and confirmatory factor analysis. SEM can incorporate latent variables, which either are not or cannot be measured directly into the analysis. For example, intelligence levels can only be inferred, with direct measurement of variables like test scores, level of education, grade point average, and other related measures. These tools are often used to evaluate many scaled attributes or to build summated scales.

Each of the multivariate techniques described above has a specific type of research question for which it is best suited. Each technique also has certain strengths and weaknesses that should be clearly understood by the analyst before attempting to interpret the results of the technique. Current statistical packages (SAS, SPSS, S-Plus, and others) make it increasingly easy to run a procedure, but the results can be disastrously misinterpreted without adequate care.

12.15 SUMMARY

Multivariate Data Analysis refers to any statistical technique used to analyze data that arises from more than one variable. This essentially models reality where each situation, product, or decision involves more than a single variable. The information age has resulted in masses of data in every field analysis methods typically used for: (1) Consumer and market research, (2) Quality control and quality assurance across a range of industries such as food and beverage, paint, pharmaceuticals, chemicals, energy, telecommunications, etc., (3) Process optimization and process control and (4) Research and development.

A multivariate analysis enables you to avoid the problem of multiple tests that would arise if you tested the effect of each independent variable on each dependent variable separately. To understand when a multivariate test is likely to outperform the Bonferroni method and when it is not, it helps to understand in more detail how the multivariate approach tests a hypothesis. Multivariate techniques are defined as following: (1) Multiple Regression Analysis, (2) Logistic Regression Analysis, (3) Factor Analysis, (4) Cluster Analysis, (5) Discriminant Analysis, (6) Multivariate Analysis of Variance (MANOVA), (7) Multidimensional Scaling (MDS), (8) Correspondence Analysis, (9) Conjoint Analysis, (10) Canonical Correlation and (11) Structural Equation Modeling.

12.16 KEY TERMS

Multivariate Analysis: Multivariate analysis deals with the statistical analysis of the data collected on more than one (response) variable. These variables may be correlated with each other, and their statistical dependence is often taken into account when analyzing such data.

Multivariate Data Analysis: Multivariate Data Analysis refers to any statistical technique used to analyze data that arises from more than one variable. This essentially models reality where each situation, product, or decision involves more than a single variable.

Multiple Regression: Multiple regression analysis is the most commonly utilized multivariate technique. It examines the relationship between a single metric dependent variable and two or more metric independent variables.

Logistic Regression Analysis: Logistic regression analysis is a variation of multiple regression analysis that allows for the prediction of an event.

Factor Analysis: Factor analysis is often helpful to reduce the variables to a smaller set of factors. This is an independence technique, in which there is no dependent variable.

Factor Loading: Factor loading (factor variable correlation) are values indicating the extent of closeness of relationship among variable constituting a factor.

Commonality (h_2): indicates the extent a variable has been accounted for by underlying factor taken together.

Eigen Value: The sum of squares of factor loading relating to a factor is known as Eigen value or latent root. It indicates the relative importance of factor in accounting for the set of variables considered in the analysis.

Cluster Analysis: Cluster analysis is to identify different groups (or clusters) of respondents, such a while the respondents in one cluster are all similar to one another, these are different from the respondents in other clusters.

Discriminant Analysis: Discriminant analysis is a statistical technique that is used to classify the dependent variable between two or more categories. Discriminant analysis also has a regression technique, which is used for predicting the value of the dependent categorical variable.

Multidimensional Scaling (MDS): MDS is to transform consumer judgments of similarity into distances represented in multidimensional space. This is a decompositional approach that uses perceptual mapping to present the dimensions.

12.17 MULTIPLE OBJECTIVE TYPE QUESTIONS

1. Correlation is a technique which measures the strength of association between two variables.
   (a) True (b) False
2. If there is no relationship between the two variables such that the value of one variable change and the other variable remain constant, it is called no or zero correlation.
   (a) True (b) False
3. In multiple correlation, the relationship between more than two variables are considered simultaneously for study.
   (a) True (b) False
4. Correlation results cannot be more than –1 and +1.
   (a) True (b) False
5. The standard error of a correlation coefficient is used to determine the confidence intervals around a true correlation of one.
   (a) True (b) False
6. Interpreting Coefficient of Correlation is the calculation of Coefficient of Determination which is the square of Coefficient of Correlation or r^2 is the square of the sample correlation coefficient between outcomes and predicted values.
   (a) True (b) False
7. Spearman's Rank method is the only way of studying correlation between quantitative data which cannot be measured in figures but can be arranged in serial order.
   (a) True (b) False
8. Linear regression attempts to model the relationship between two variables by fitting a linear equation to observed data.
   (a) True (b) False
9. When the dependence of the variable is represented by a straight line, then it is called non-linear regression, otherwise it is said to be non-linear or curvilinear regression.
   (a) True (b) False
10. Multivariate analysis deals with the statistical analysis of the data collected on more than two (response) variables.
    (a) True (b) False
11. Which of the following are the merits of Scatter Diagram?
    (a) It is very easy to draw a scatter diagram (b) It can be easily understood and interpreted
    (c) Both (a) and (b) (d) None of the above
12. Correlation coefficient is a measure of:
    (a) Relationship between two variables (b) Linear relationship between two variables
    (c) Independence between two variables (d) Dependence between two variables
13. If correlation coefficient between two variables is uncertain, it implies that
    (a) $r = +1$ (b) $r = -1$
    (c) $r = 0$ (d) $r = 0.5$

14. Which type of data is not suited for calculation of Pearson' correlation coefficient?
    (a) Nominal (b) Ordinal
    (c) Interval (d) Ratio
15. We should expect negative correlation while studying relationship between
    (a) Income and expenditure of family (b) Price and demand of a product
    (c) Sales and profit of a company (d) None of the above
16. If coefficient of determination is 0.81, the correlation coefficient is:
    (a) +0.9 (b) –0.9
    (c) ±0.9 (d) None of the above
17. If the correlation coefficient between the sales of a company and promotional expenses are reported to be high, which of the following values of r is more likely to be true?
    (a) –0.9 (b) +0.6
    (c) +0.85 (d) +0.8
18. Which of the following are the essential features of factor analysis
    (a) It is a multivariate technique where initially a large number of variables are considered
    (b) The large number of variables is reduced to a small number of factors
    (c) Selection of variables constituting a factor is made on the basis of total variation accounted for by them
    (d) All of the above
19. Which of the following are the characteristics of cluster analysis?
    (a) Cluster analysis determines internal homogeneity
    (b) Cluster analysis also determines external heterogeneity,
    (c) Both (a) and (b)
    (d) None of the above
20. Discriminate analysis is a technique for classifying a set of observations into which classes?
    (a) Defined (b) Predefined
    (c) Well-defined (d) All of the above

Answers to Multiple Objective Type Questions

Questions	1	2	3	4	5	6	7	8	9	10
Answers	T	T	F	T	F	T	F	T	F	F
Questions	11	12	13	14	15	16	17	18	19	20
Answers	c	b	c	a	b	c	c	d	c	b

12.18 CONCEPTUAL QUESTIONS

1. What do you mean by multivariate analysis and multivariate data analysis? How a multivariate analysis work?
2. What are the important multivariate techniques? Explain the important characteristic of each one.
3. What is multiple regression? Write its importance.
4. What is Factor Analysis? Point out its essential features and applications.
5. What is the principal component method of Factor Analysis? Explain.
6. What is Cluster Analysis? Point out its objectives and its characteristics.

7. Given the following correlation matrix R, relating to six variables with unities in the diagonal spaces:

		Variables					
		1	2	3	4	5	6
	1	1.00	0.55	0.43	0.32	0.28	0.36
	2		1.00	0.50	0.25	0.31	0.32
Variables	3			1.00	0.39	0.25	0.33
	4				1.00	0.43	0.49
	5					1.00	0.44
	6						1.00

Using centroid method of factor analysis, work out the first and second centroid factors from the above information.

8. Write short notes:
   (a) Logistic Regression Analysis
   (b) Discriminant Analysis
   (c) Multivariate Analysis of Variance (MANOVA)
   (d) Multidimensional Scaling (MDS)
   (e) Correspondence Analysis
   (f) Conjoint Analysis
   (g) Canonical Correlation
   (h) Structural Equation Modeling

CHAPTER 13

BASIC CONCEPTS OF SPSS

RESEARCH METHODOLOGY

Chapter Outline

Learning Objectives

- *Explain the meaning and basic operations in SPSS.*
- *Discuss the need of SPSS in decision making.*
- *Explain the actual process of SPSS in research and its role in managerial decisions.*

13.1 WHAT IS SPSS?

***SPSS** (Statistical Package for the Social Sciences) is a software program developed in the late 1960s by graduate students at Stanford University. Although initially created to manage a large survey research project of citizen participation in seven nations, the package quickly gained popularity, and was greatly enhanced over the next few years. In 1985, a microcomputer version of SPSS for IIBM-compatible personal computers was introduced, which included many of the most popular features of the mainframe version of SPSS. Today, there are more than one million users of SPSS in academic, business, government, and non-profit organizations.

SPSS is a full-featured data analysis program that offers a variety of applications including database management and reporting, statistical analysis, and graphics. The SPSS program runs on a wide variety of mainframe, mini, and microcomputers.

SPSS is a comprehensive and flexible statistical analysis and data management system. SPSS can take data from almost any type of file and use them to generate tabulated reports, charts, and plots of distributions and trends, descriptive statistics, and conduct complex statistical analysis. SPSS is available from several platforms; Windows, Macintosh, and the UNIX systems.

SPSS for Windows brings the full power of the mainframe version of SPSS to the personal computer environment. It will enable you to perform many analysis on your PC that were once possible only on much larger machines. SPSS for Windows provides a user interface that makes statistical analysis more intuitive for all levels of users. Simple menus and dialog box selections make it possible to perform complex analysis without typing a single line of command syntax. The built-in SPSS Data Editor offers a simple and efficient spreadsheet-like utility for entering data and browsing the working data file. High-resolution, presentation-quality charts and plots can be created and edited. Using the SPSS Viewer, you can handle the output with greater flexibility. SPSS for Windows also reads data files from a variety of file formats including Excel, SAS, and Stata.

13.2 BASIC OPERATIONS IN SPSS

- **The SPSS Data Editor.** This is the sphere of SPSS into which data are entered and subsequently edited and defined. It is made up of two screens: the Data Viewer and the Variable Viewer. You move between these two viewers by selecting the appropriate tab at the bottom of the screen.
- **The Data Viewer.** This is the spreadsheet into which your data are entered. When you start up SPSS, the Data Viewer will be facing you.
- **The Variable Viewer.** This is another spreadsheet, but this one displays information about each of the variables and allows you to change that information. It is the platform from which you provide for each variable such information as; the variable name; a variable level; and value levels (see below).
- **The Output.** When you perform an analysis or produce a diagram (called a 'chart' in SPSS), your output will be deposited here. The Output Viewer superimposes itself over the Data Editor after an analysis has been performed or a chart generated.
- **A Variable Name.** This is the name that you give to a variable, e.g., gender. The name must be no more than eight characters. Until you give a variable a name, it will be referred to as var00001, etc. When the variable has been given a name, it will appear in the column for that variable in the Data View window. It is generated from the Variable Viewer.
- **A Variable Label.** This is a label that you can give to a variable but which is not restricted to eight characters. Spaces can be used, e.g., reasons for visiting. The Level will appear in any output you generate. It is generated from the Variable Viewer.
- **A Value Label.** This is a label that you can attach to code that has been used when entering data for all types of variables other than interval/ratio variable. Thus, for var00001, we would attach the label male to 1 and female to 2. When you generate output, such as a frequency table or chart, the levels for each value will be presented. This makes the interpretation of output easier. It is generated from the Variable Viewer.
- **Missing Values.** When you do not have data for a particular variable when entering data for a case, you must specify how you are denoting missing values for that variable. Missing values are generated from the Variable Viewer.
- **Record.** A procedure that allows codes or numbers to be changed. It is especially helpful when you need to combine groups of people — for example, when producing age bands.
- **Compute.** A procedure that allows you to combine two or more variables to form a new variable.

- **Analyze.** This is the point on the menu bar above the Data Editor from which you choose (via a drop-down menu) which method of analysis you want to select. Note that, whenever an item on a menu appears with a right-pointing arrowhead after it, this means that, if you select that option, a further menu will follow on.
- **Graphs.** This is the point on the menu bar above the Data Editor from which you choose (via a drop-down menu) which chart you want to select.
- **Chart Editor.** When you produce a graph, you can edit it with the Chart Editor. To activate this editor, double-click anywhere in the graph. A small chart editor window will appear and your main graph will appear opaque until you exit the Editor. From the Editor, you can make various changes and enhancements to your graph.

13.3 GETTING STARTED IN SPSS

To start SPSS, double click on the **spsswin** icon on your computer screen. If there is no icon, → the Start button in the bottom left hand corner of your screen. From the menu of programs, → **SPSS for Windows.** A follow-on menu will appear, from which you should select **SPSS 16.0 for Windows.** When SPSS loads, you may be faced with an opening dialog box with the title "What do you want to do?' and a list of options. Many users prefer to disable this opening box. It is not important in relation to the following exposition, so → Cancel. You will then be faced with the **SPSS Data Editor.** This is made up of two components: Data View and Variable View. The Data Editor displays the contents of the active data file. The information in the Data Editor consists of variables and cases.

- In Data View, columns represent variables, and rows represent cases (observations).
- In Variable View, each row is a variable, and each column is an attribute that is associated with that variable.

Variables are used to represent the different types of data that you have compiled. A common analogy is that of a survey. The response to each question on a survey is equivalent to a variable. Variables come in many different types, including numbers, strings, currency, and dates. Data can be entered into the Data Editor, which may be useful for small data files or for making minor edits to larger data files.

13.1.1 Entering Numeric Data in the Data Viewer

The SPSS Data Viewer

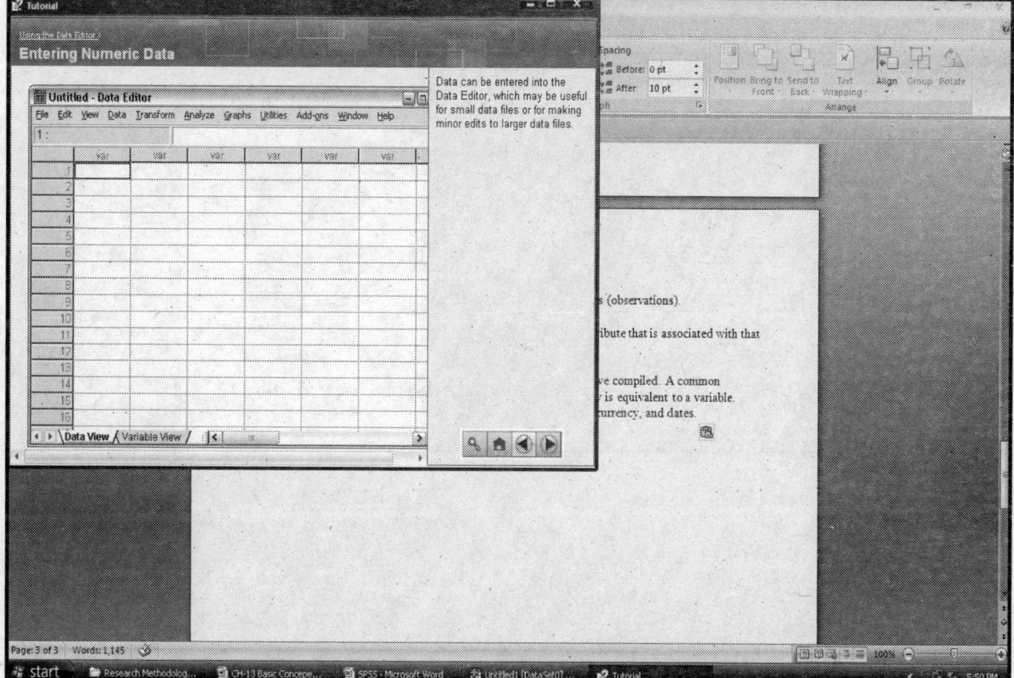

- Click the Variable View tab at the bottom of the Data Editor window.

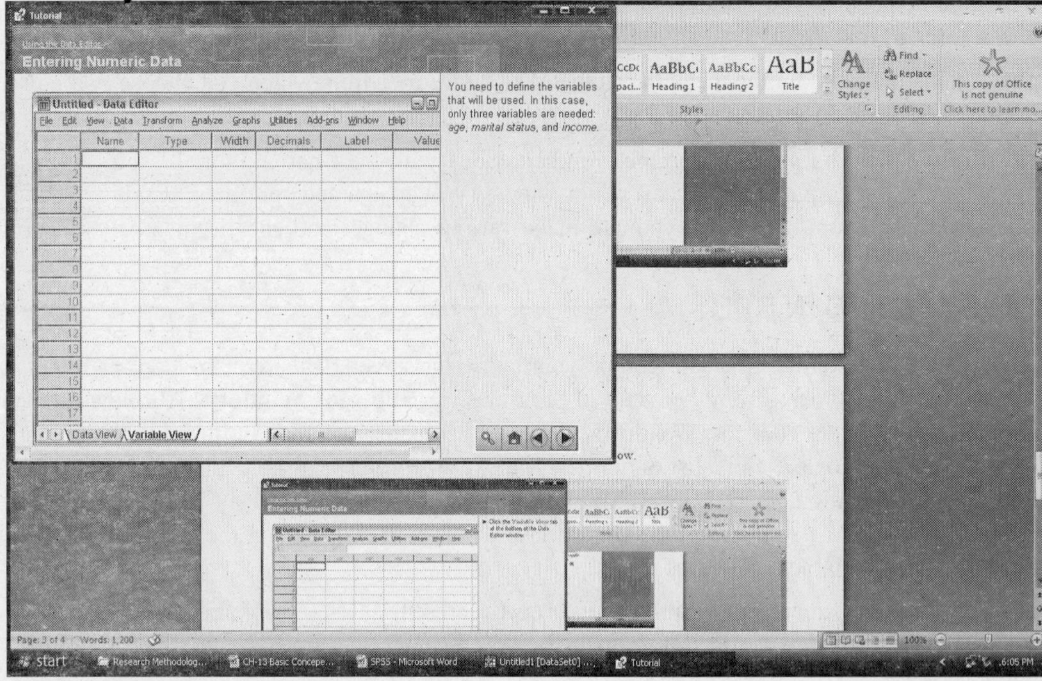

- If you need to define the variables that will be used. In this case, only three variables are needed. Suppose the three variables are: age, marital status, and income.
- In the first row of the first column, type age.
- In the second row, type marital.
- In the third row, type income.

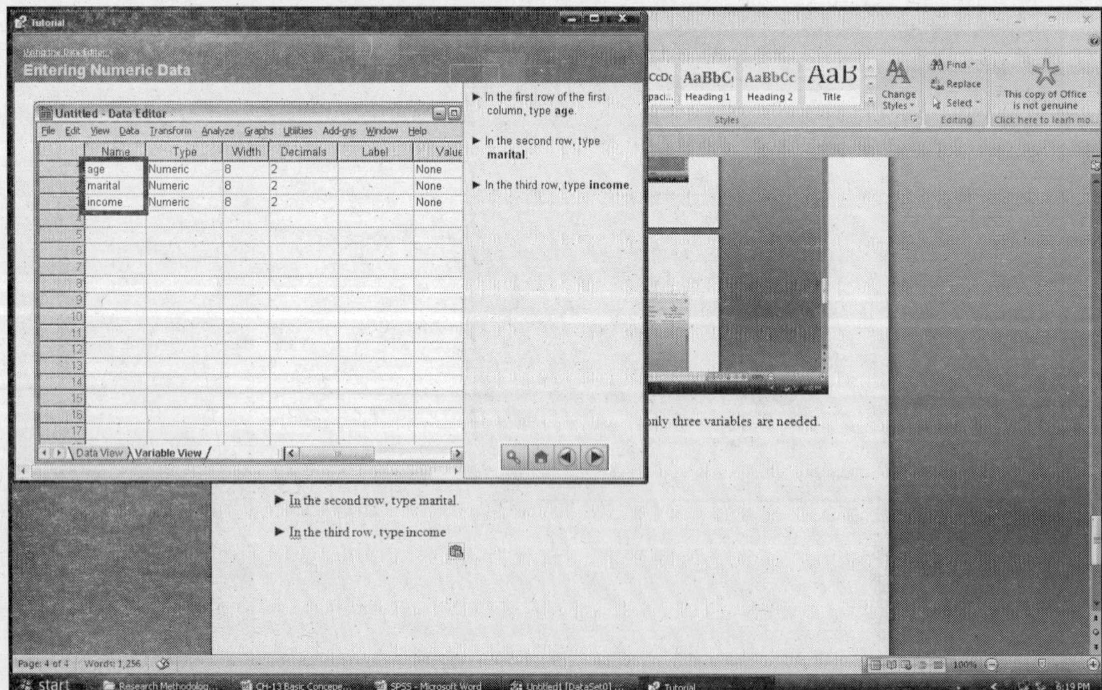

- Then, new variables are automatically given a Numeric data type.
- If you don't enter variable names, unique names are automatically created. However, these names are not descriptive and are not recommended for large data files.

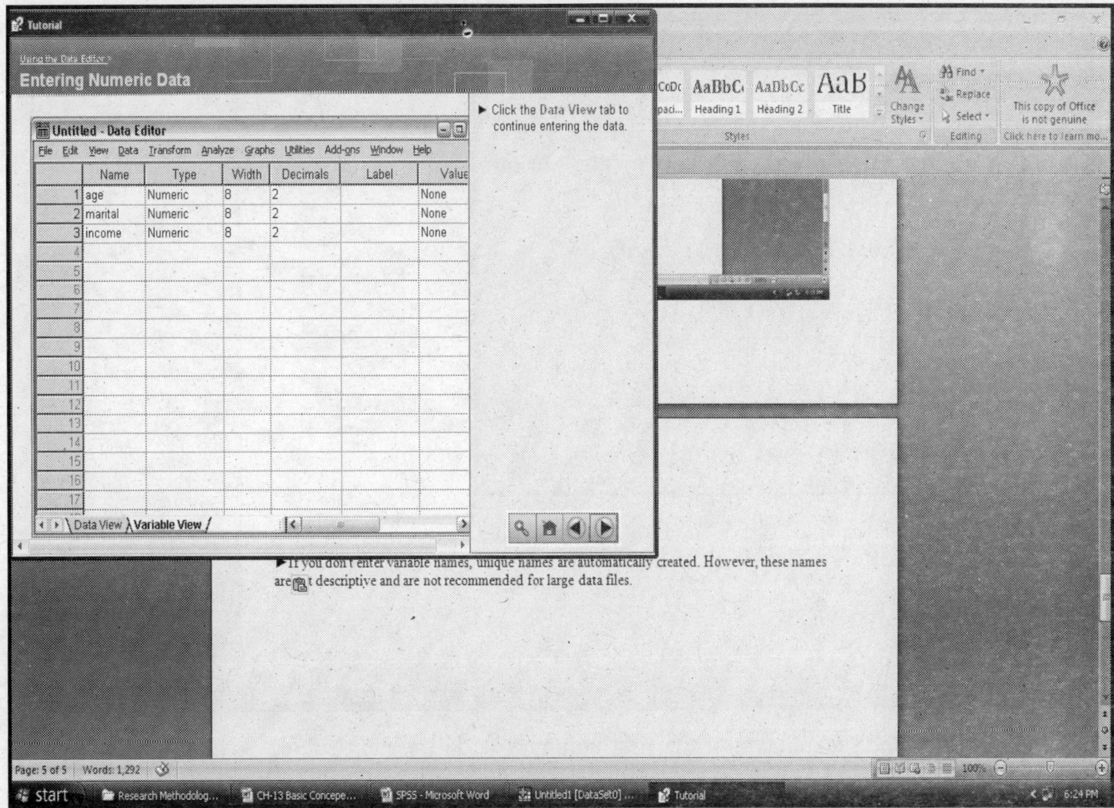

- Click the Data View tab to continue entering the data. The names that you entered in Variable View are now the headings for the first three columns in Data View.
- Begin entering data in the first row, starting at the first column.

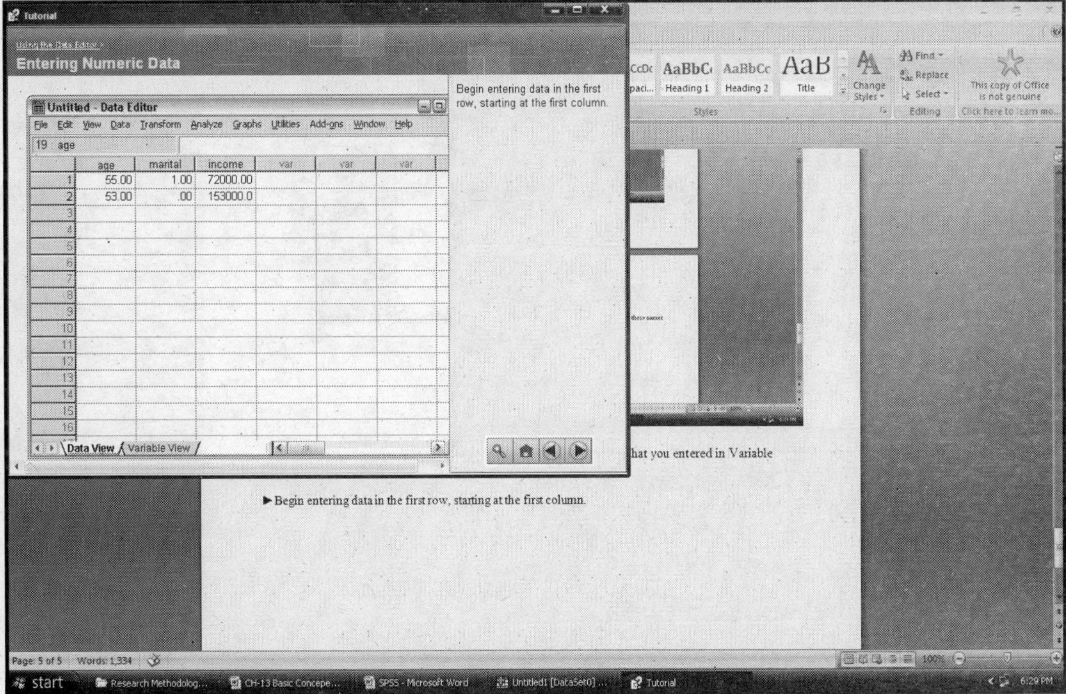

- In the age column, type 55.
- In the marital column, type 1.
- In the income column, type 72000.

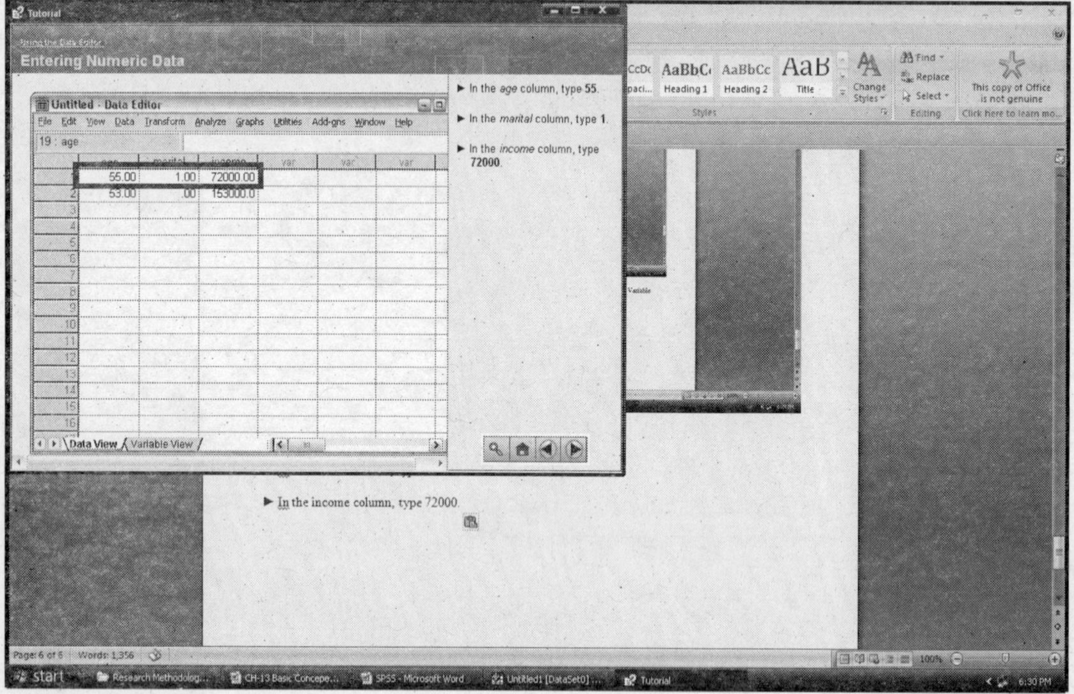

- Move the cursor to the second row of the first column to add the next subject's data.
- In the age column, type 53.
- In the marital column, type 0.
- In the income column, type 153000.

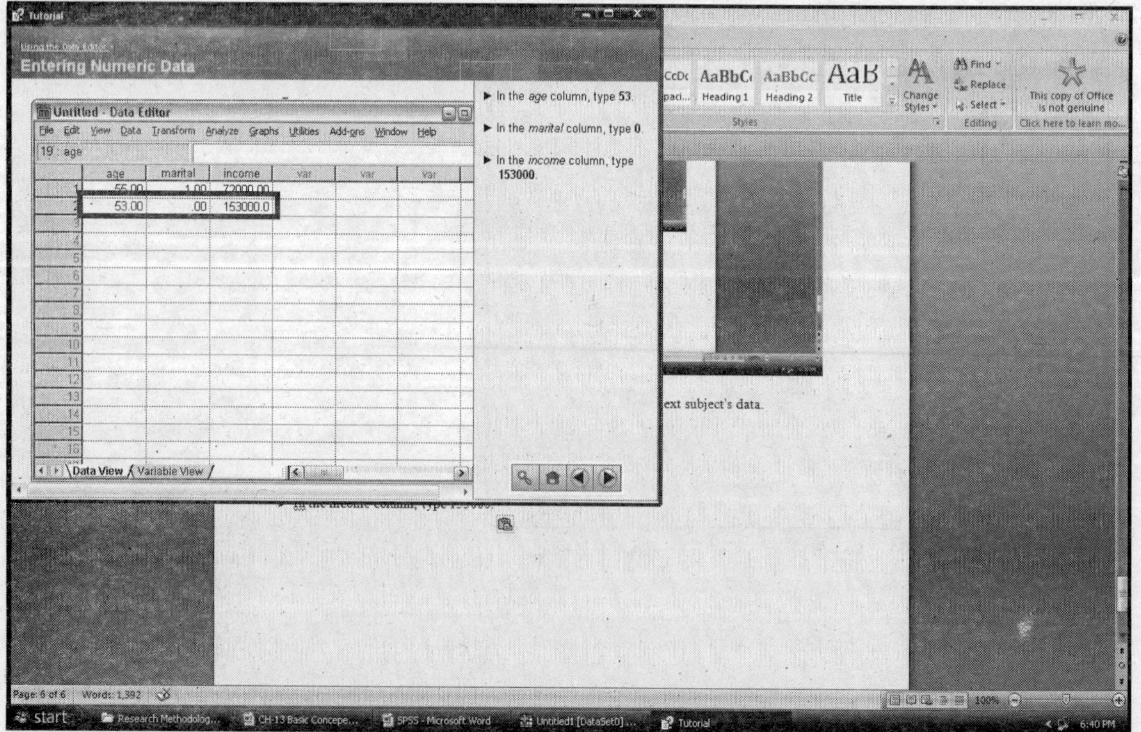

- Currently, the age and marital columns display decimal points, even though their values are intended to be integers. To hide the decimal points in these variables:
- Click the Variable View tab at the bottom of the Data Editor window.

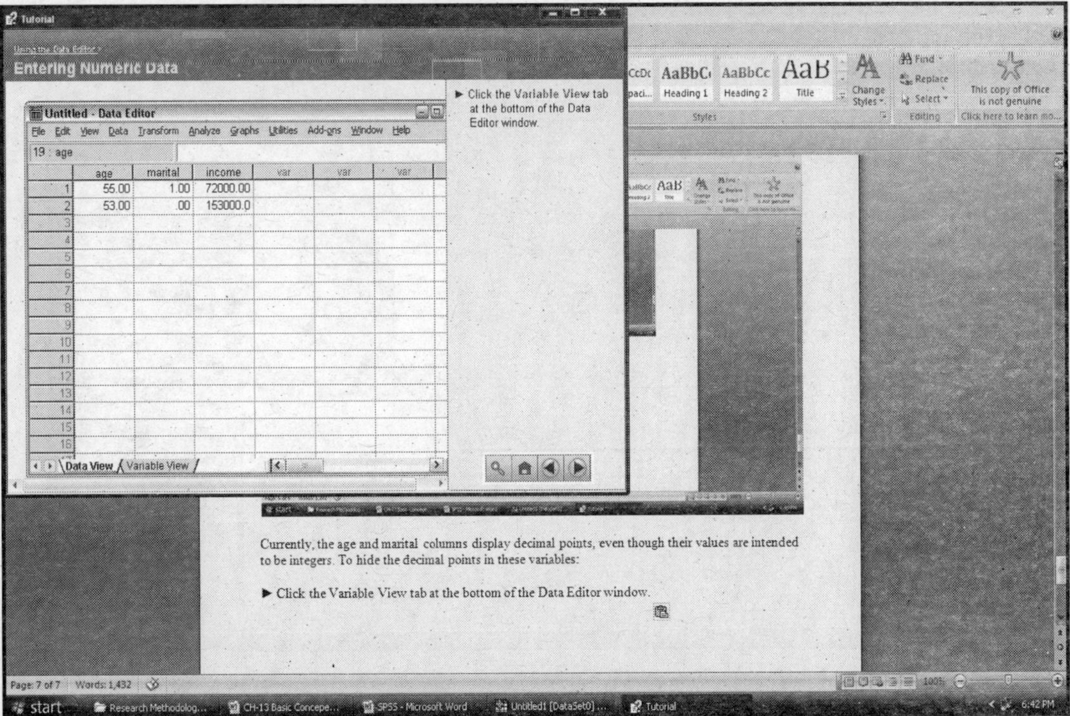

- In the Decimals column of the age row, type 0 to hide the decimal.
- In the Decimals column of the marital row, type 0 to hide the decimal.

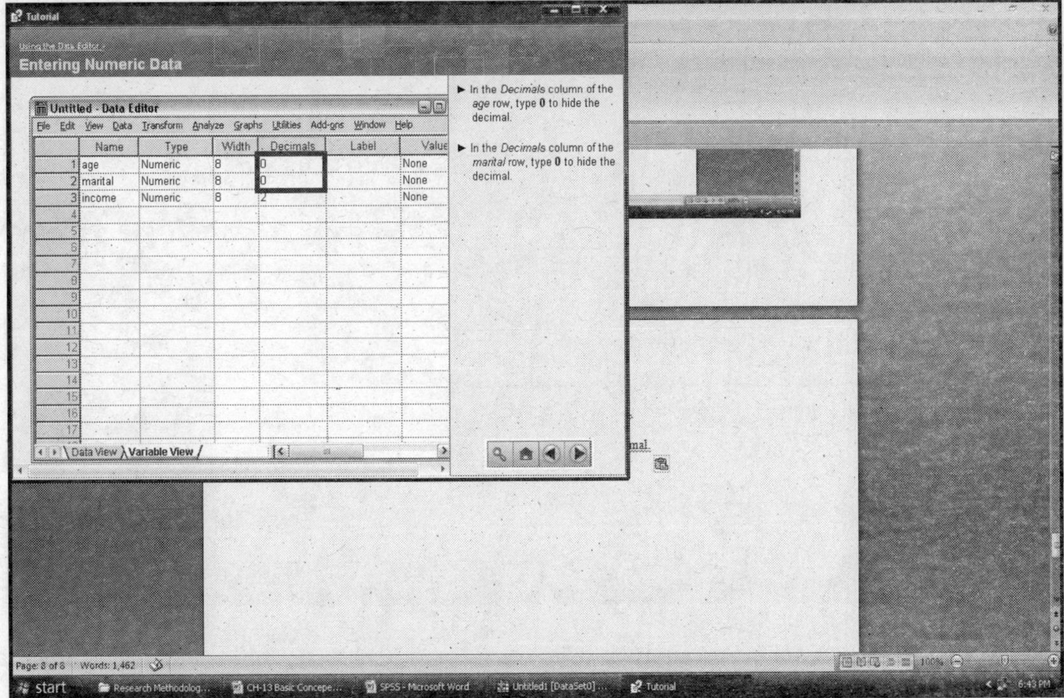

13.3.2 Entering String Data

- Non-numeric data, such as strings of text, can also be entered into the Data Editor.
- Click the Variable View tab at the bottom of the Data Editor window.

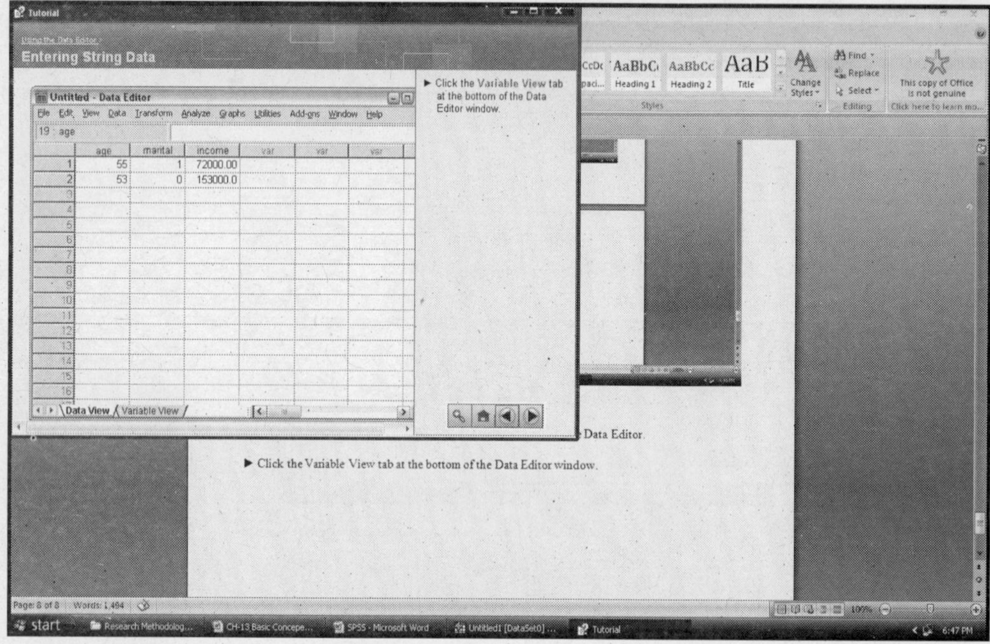

- In the first cell of the first empty row, type sex for the variable name.

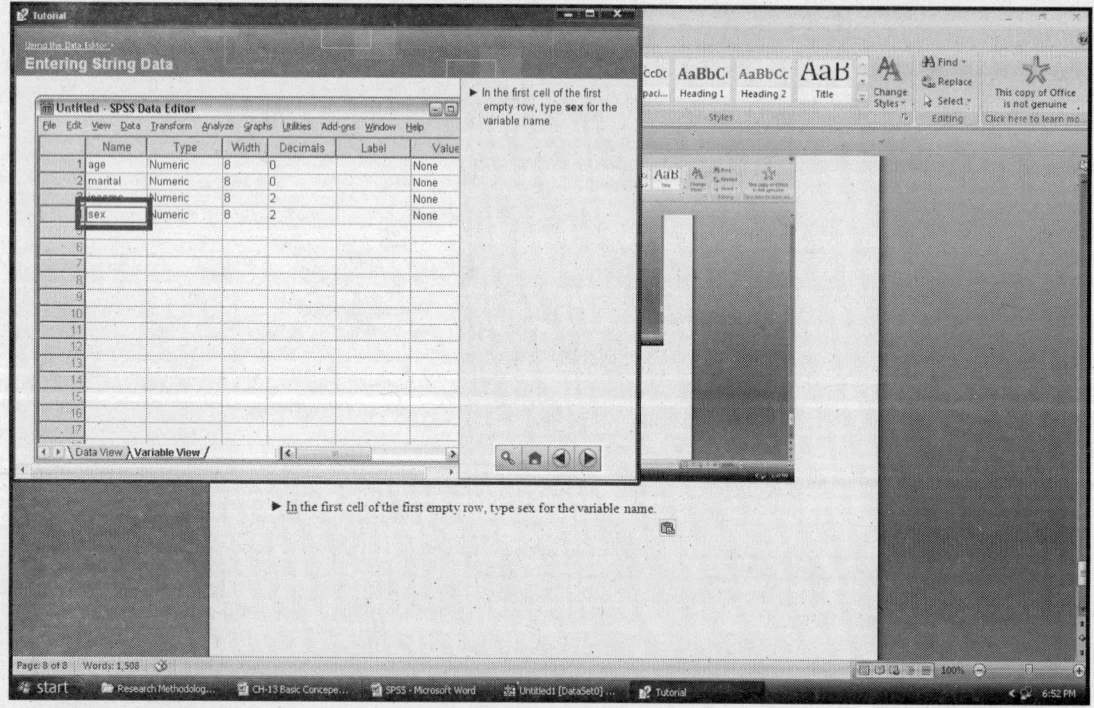

- Click the Type cell next to your entry.
- Click the button on the right side of the Type cell to open the Variable Type dialog box.

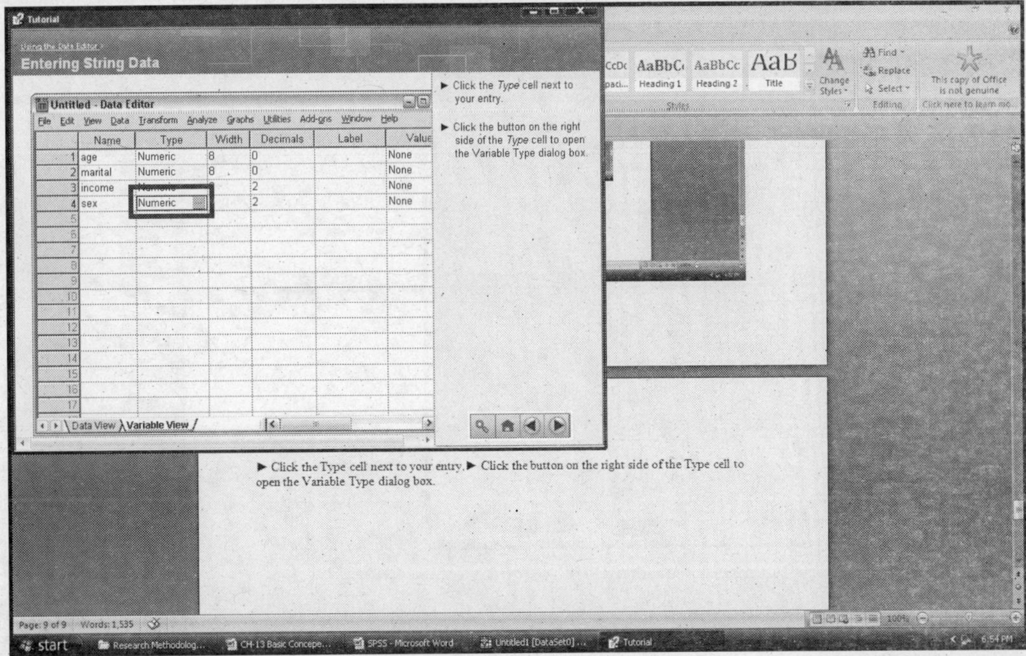

- Select String to specify the variable type.
- Click OK to save your selection and return to the Data Editor.

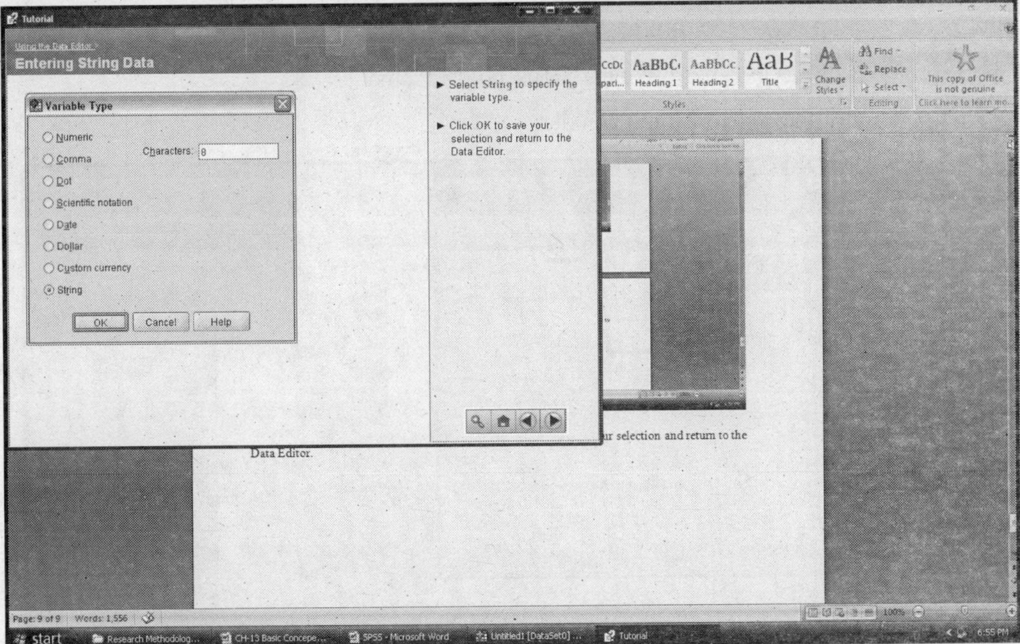

13.3.3 Defining Data and Adding Variable Labels

In addition to defining data types, you can also define descriptive variable labels and value labels for variable names and data values. These descriptive labels are used in statistical reports and charts.

Labels are meant to provide descriptions of variables. These descriptions are often longer versions of variable names. Labels can be up to 255 bytes. These labels are used in your output to identify the different variables.

- Click the Variable View tab at the bottom of the Data Editor window.

- In the Label column of the age row, type Respondent's Age.
- In the Label column of the marital row, type Marital Status.

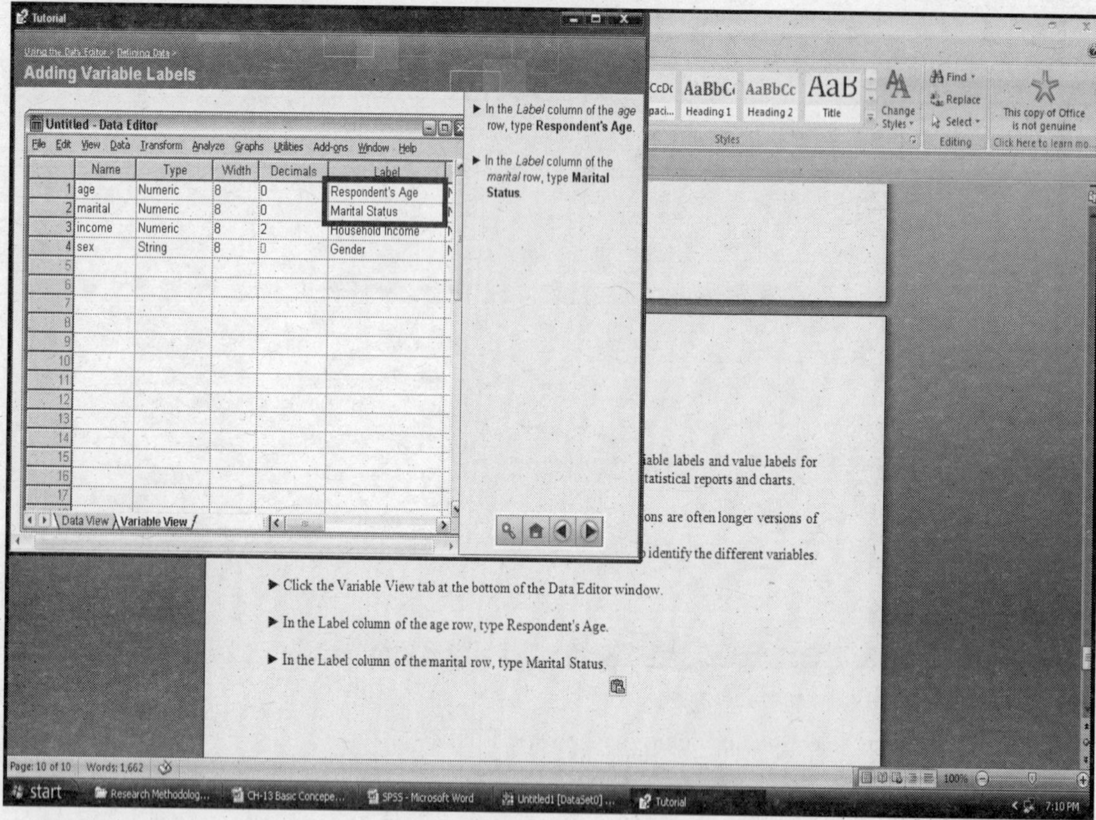

- In the Label column of the income row, type Household Income.
- In the Label column of the sex row, type Gender.

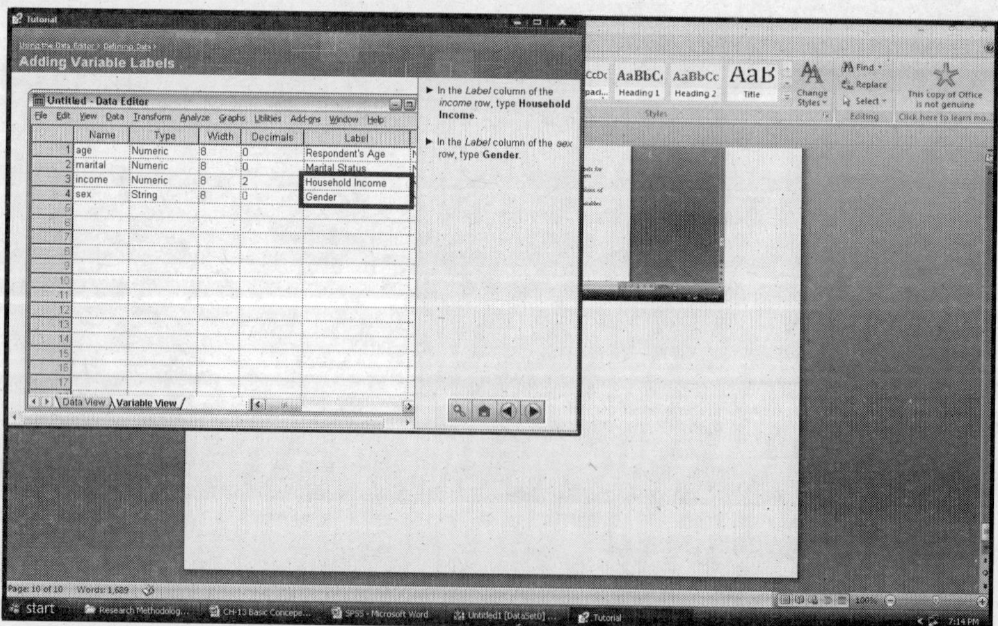

13.3.4 Changing Variable Type and Format

The Type column displays the current data type for each variable. The most common data types are numeric and string, but many other formats are supported. In the current data file, the income variable is defined as a numeric type.

- Click the Type cell for the income row, and then click the button on the right side of the cell to open the Variable Type dialog box.
- Select Dollar.

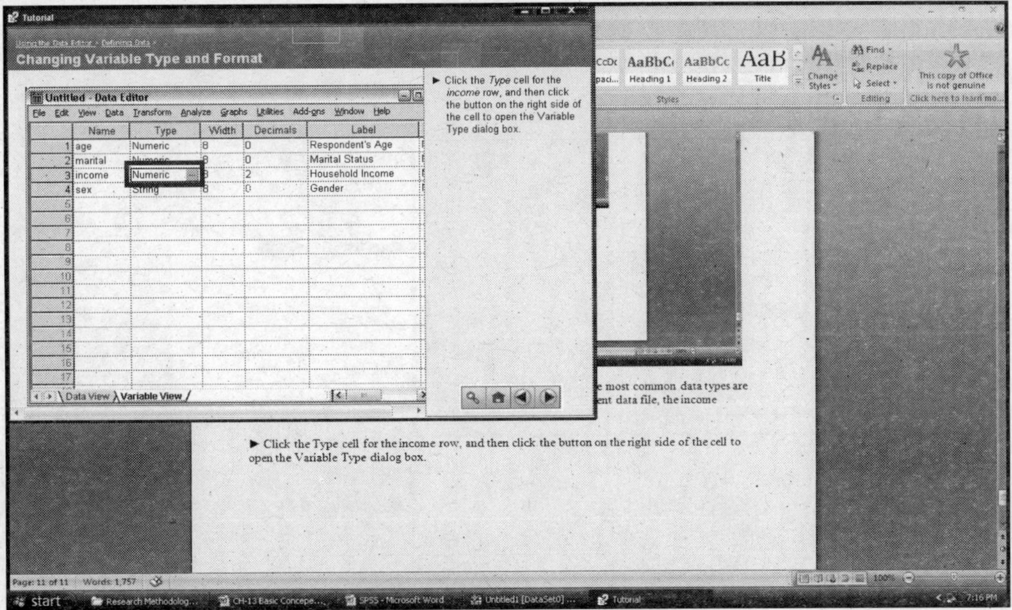

The formatting options for the currently selected data type are displayed.

- For the format of the currency in this example, select $###,###,###.
- Click OK to save your changes.

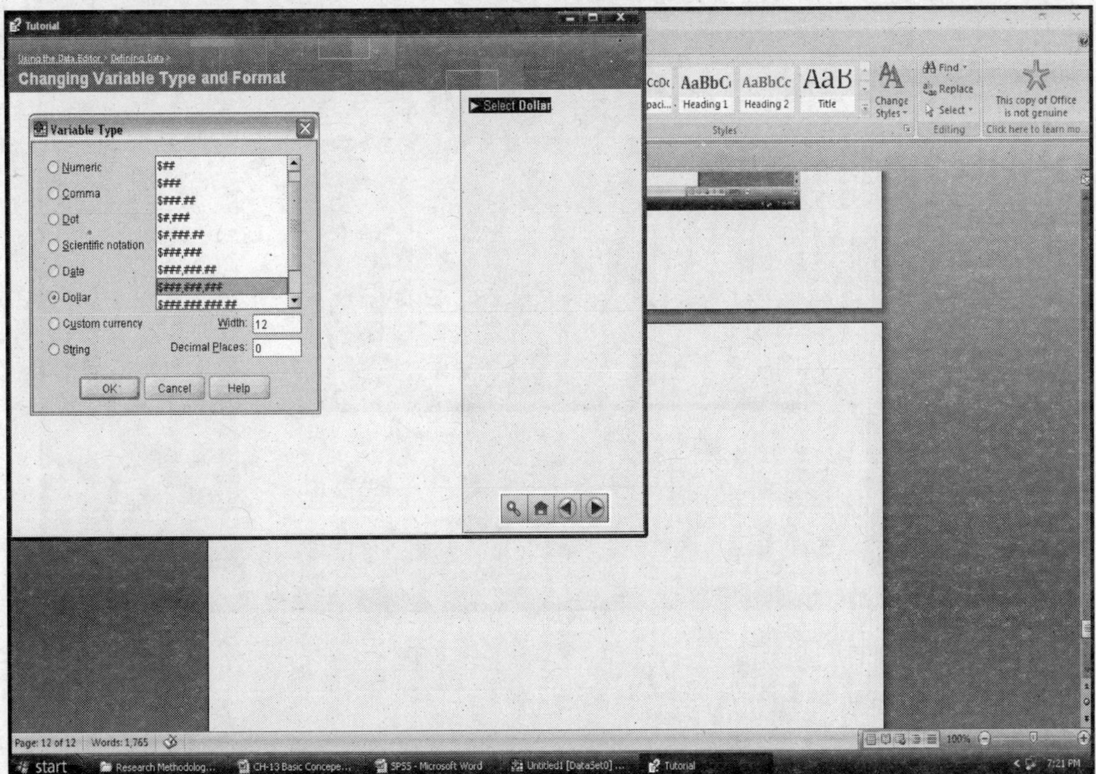

13.3.5 Adding Value Labels for Numeric Variables

Value labels provide a method for mapping your variable values to a string label. In this example, there are two acceptable values for the marital variable. A value of 0 means that the subject is single, and a value of 1 means that he or she is married.

- Click the Values cell for the marital row, and then click the button on the right side of the cell to open the Value Labels dialog box.

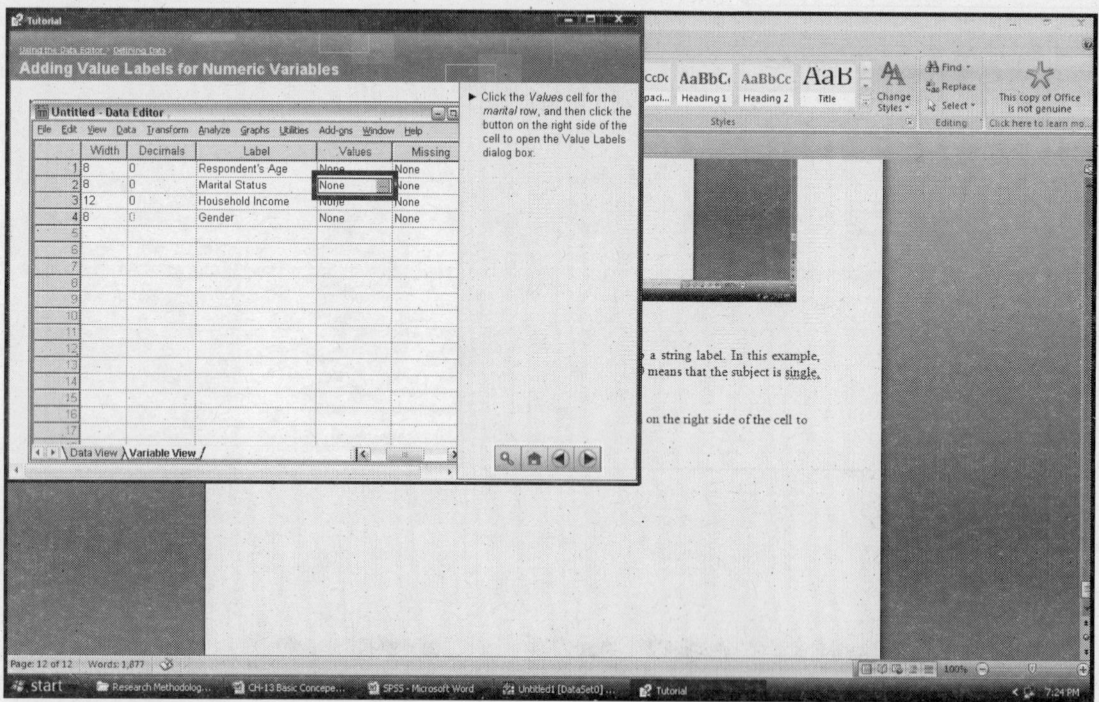

The value is the actual numeric value. The value label is the string label that is applied to the specified numeric value.

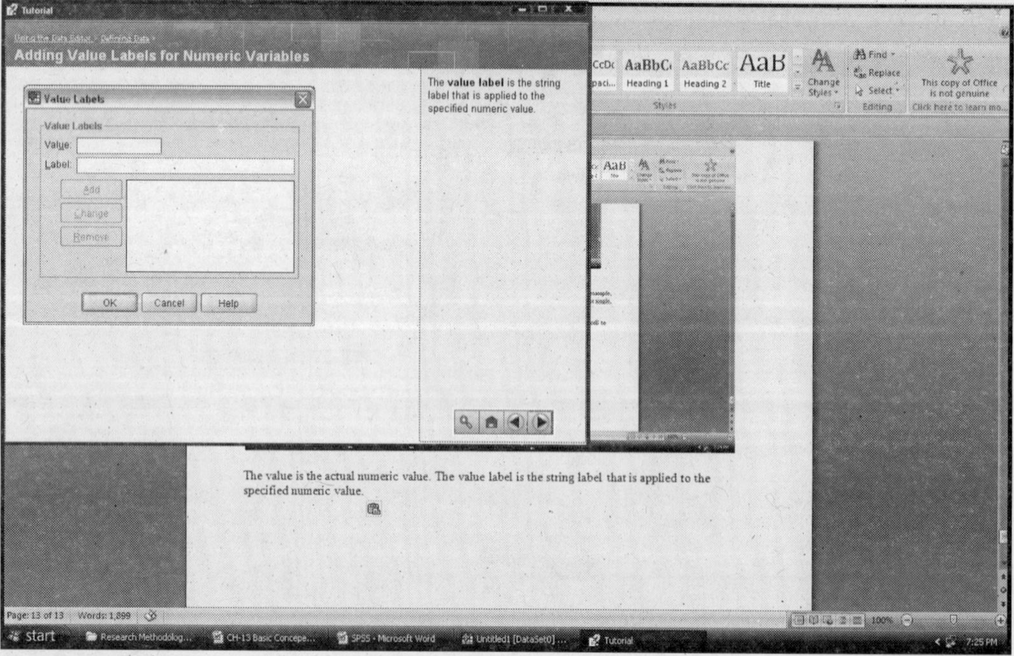

- Type 0 in the Value field.
- Type Single in the Label field.
- Click Add to add this label to the list.

- Type 1 in the Value field, and type Married in the Label field.
- Click Add, and then click OK to save your changes and return to the Data Editor.

These labels can also be displayed in Data View, which can make your data more readable.

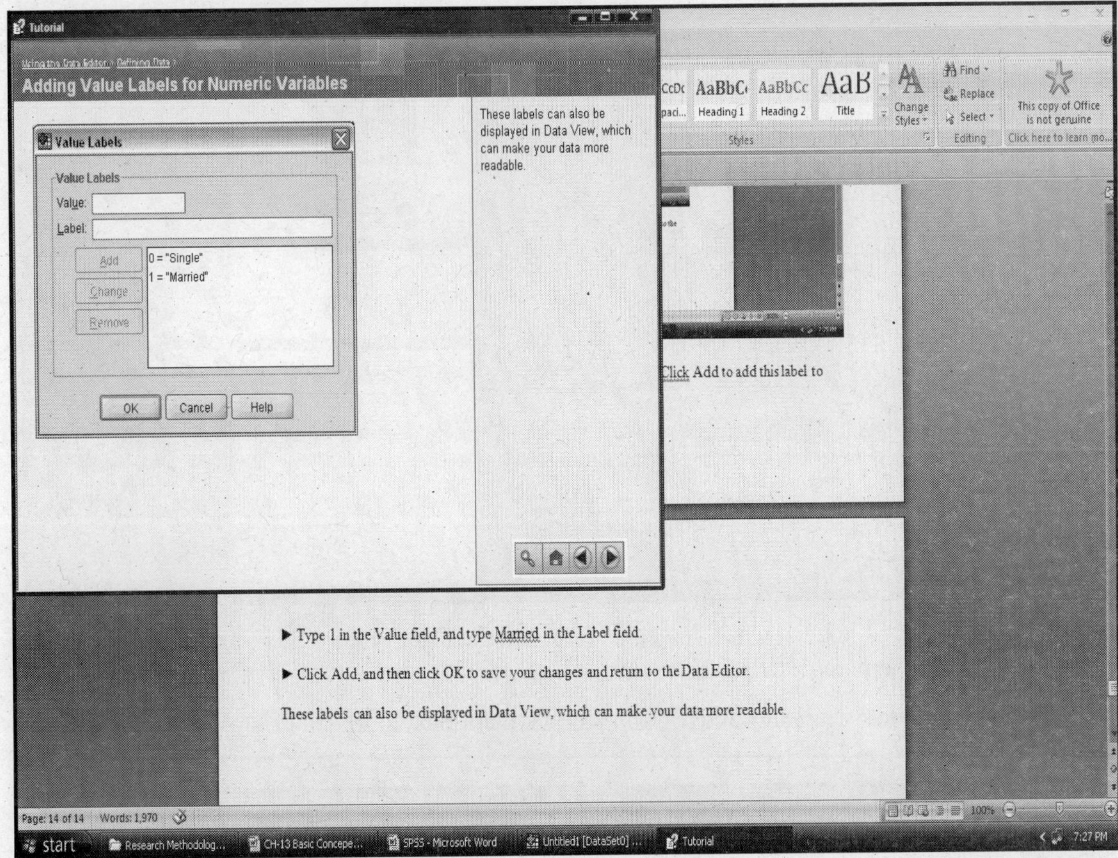

- Click the Data View tab at the bottom of the Data Editor window.

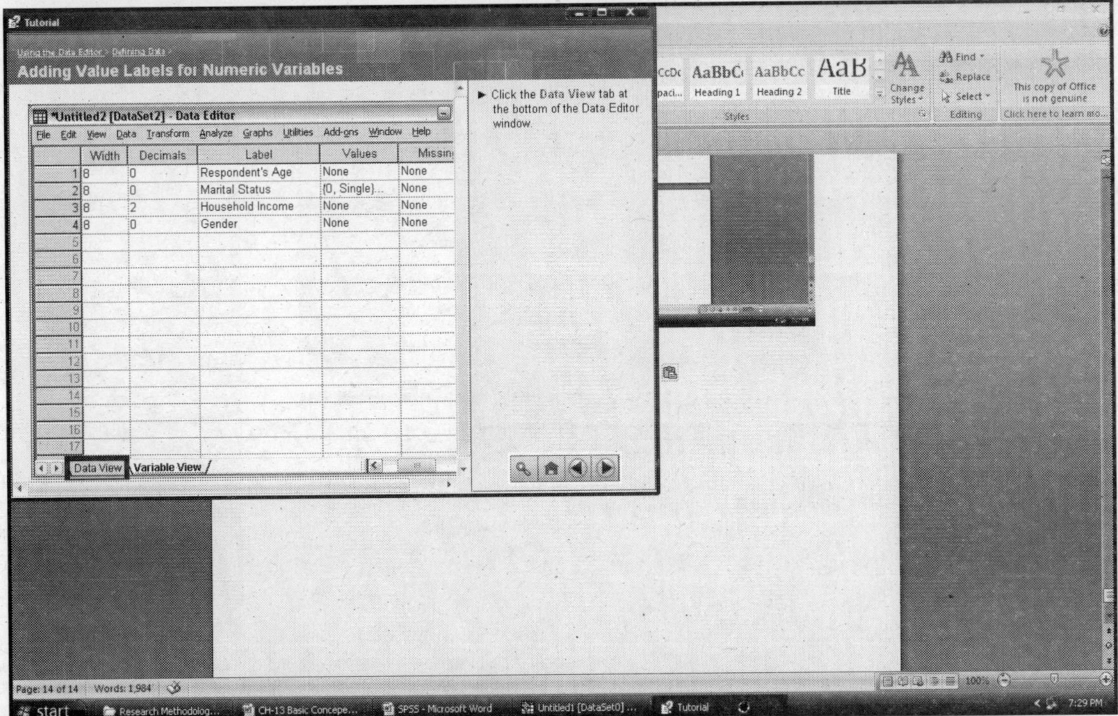

- From the menus, choose View Value Labels.

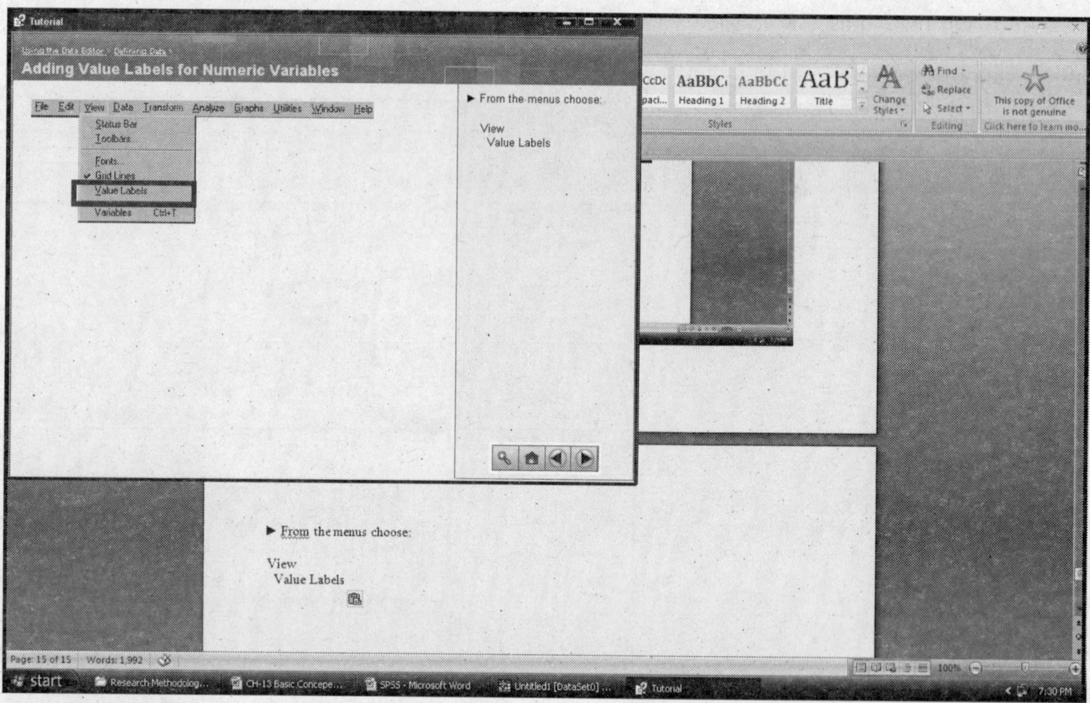

The labels are now displayed in a list when you enter values in the Data Editor. This setup has the benefit of suggesting a valid response and providing a more descriptive answer.

If the Value Labels menu item is already active (with a check mark next to it), choosing Value Labels again will turn off the display of value labels.

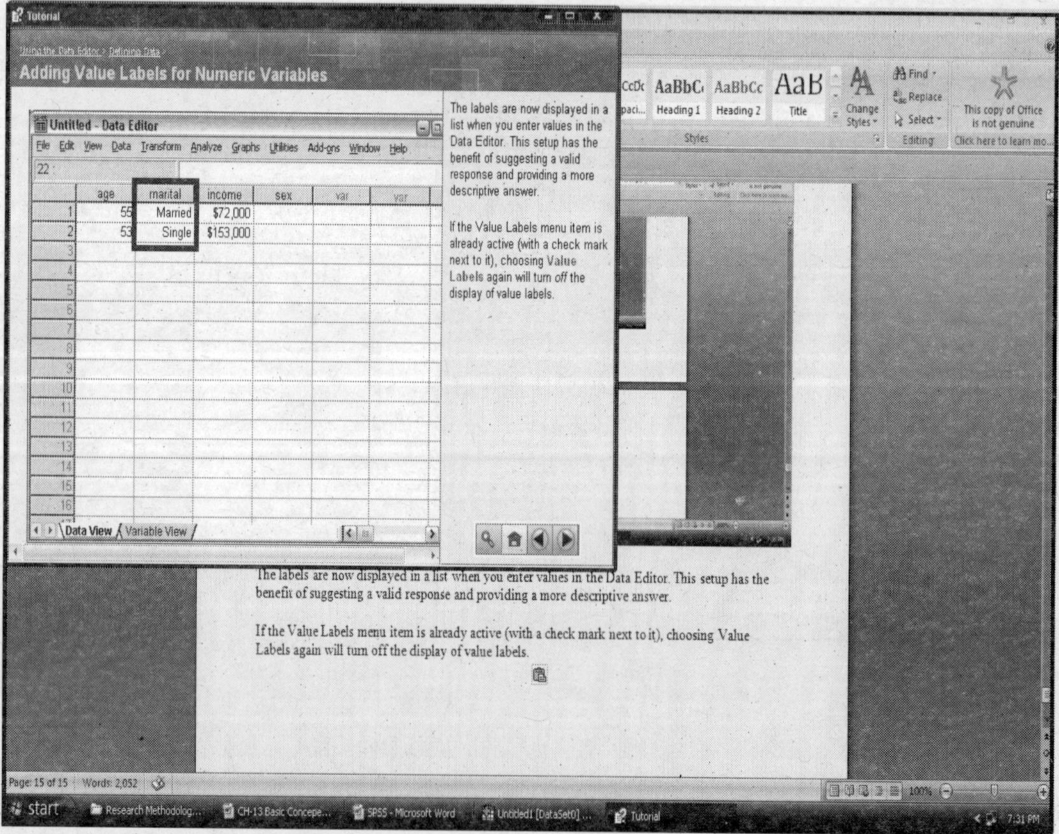

String variables may require value labels as well. For example, your data may use single letters, M or F, to identify the sex of the subject. Value labels can be used to specify that M stands for Male and F stands for Female.

- Click the Variable View tab at the bottom of the Data Editor window.
- Click the Values cell in the sex row, and then click the button on the right side of the cell to open the Value Labels dialog box.

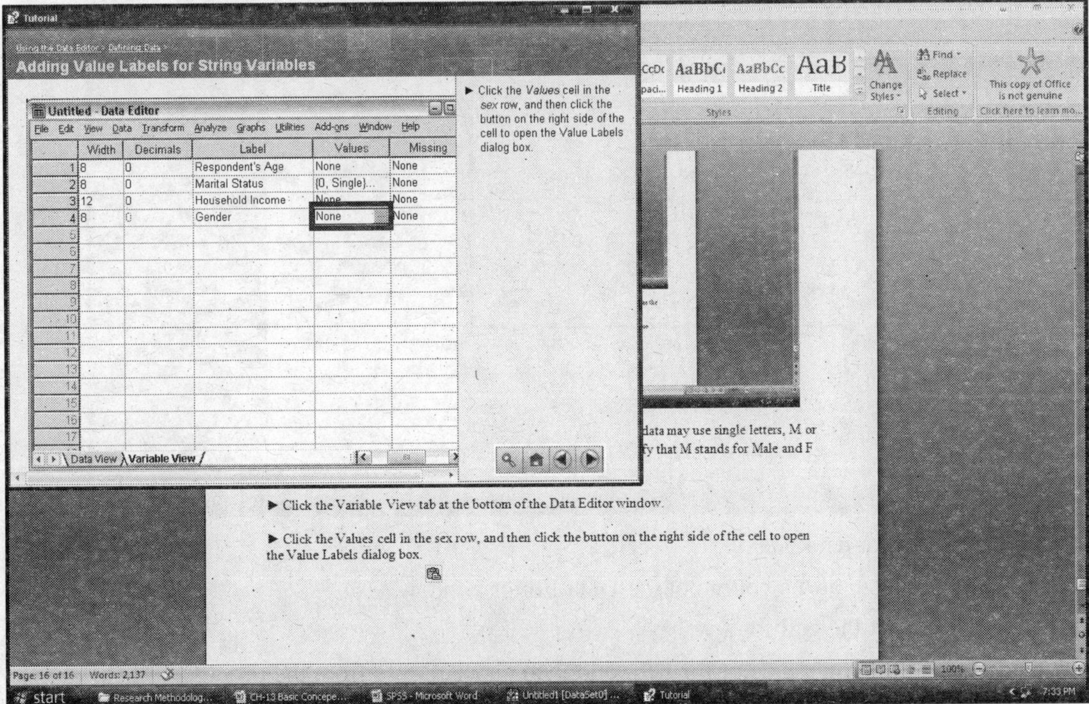

- Type F in the Value field, and then type Female in the Label field.
- Click Add to add this label to your data file.

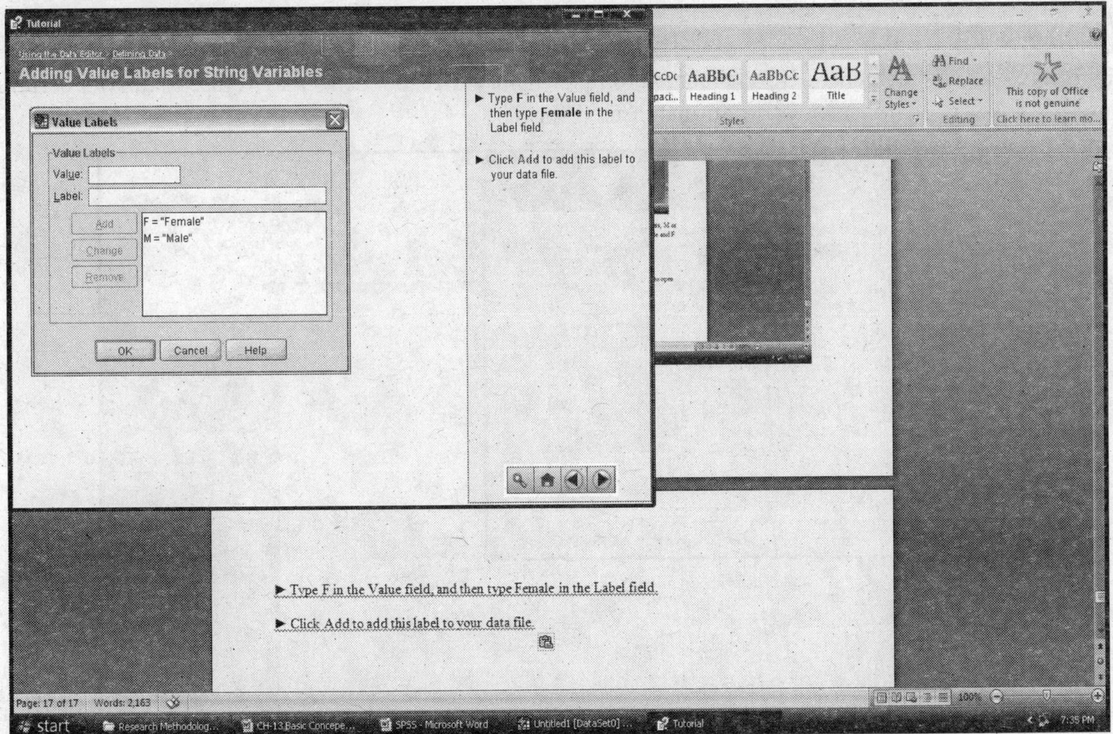

- Type M in the Value field, and type Male in the Label field.
- Click Add, and then click OK to save your changes and return to the Data Editor. Because string values are case sensitive, you should be consistent. A lowercase m is not the same as an uppercase M.

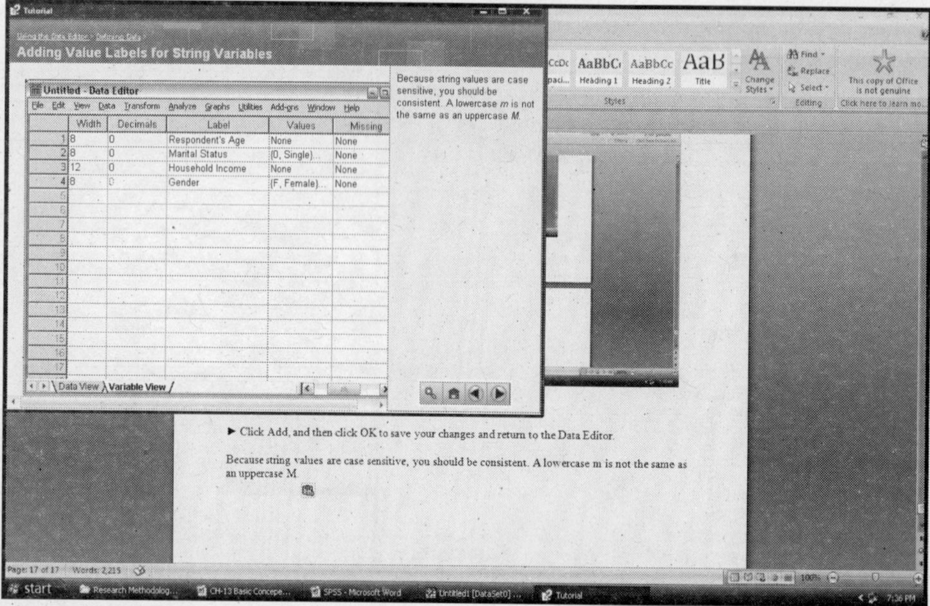

You can use value labels for data entry.

- Click the Data View tab at the bottom of the Data Editor window.
- In the first row, select the cell for sex.
- Click the button on the right side of the cell, and then choose Male from the drop-down list.
- In the second row, select the cell for sex.
- Click the button on the right side of the cell, and then choose Female from the drop-down list.

Only defined values are listed, which ensures that the entered data are in a format that you expect.

13.3.6 Handling Missing Data

Missing or invalid data are generally too common to ignore. Survey respondents may refuse to answer certain questions, may not know the answer, or may answer in an unexpected format.

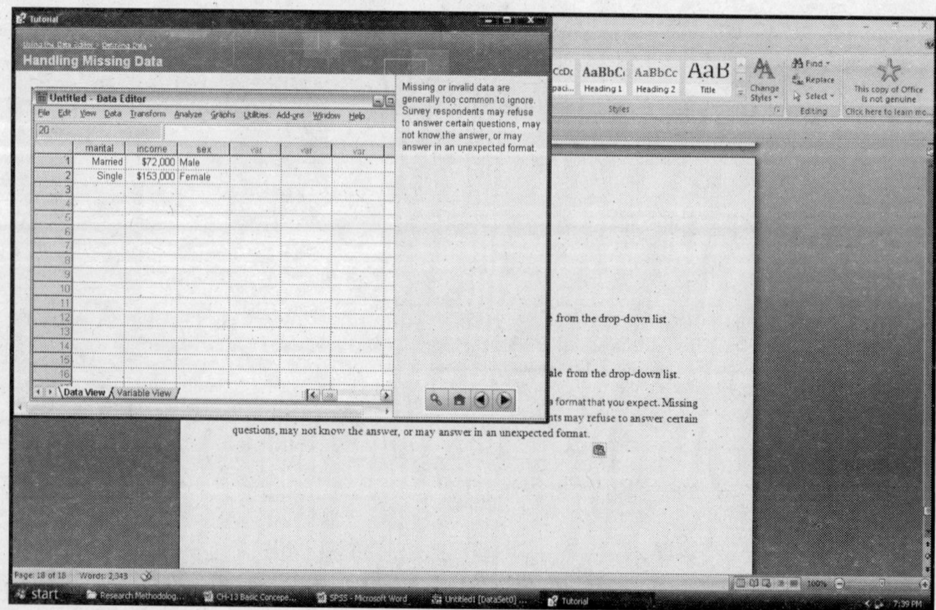

If you don't filter or identify these data, your analysis may not provide accurate results. For numeric data, empty data fields or fields containing invalid entries are converted to system-missing, which is identifiable by a single period. The reason a value is missing may be important to your analysis.

- Click the Variable View tab at the bottom of the Data Editor window.

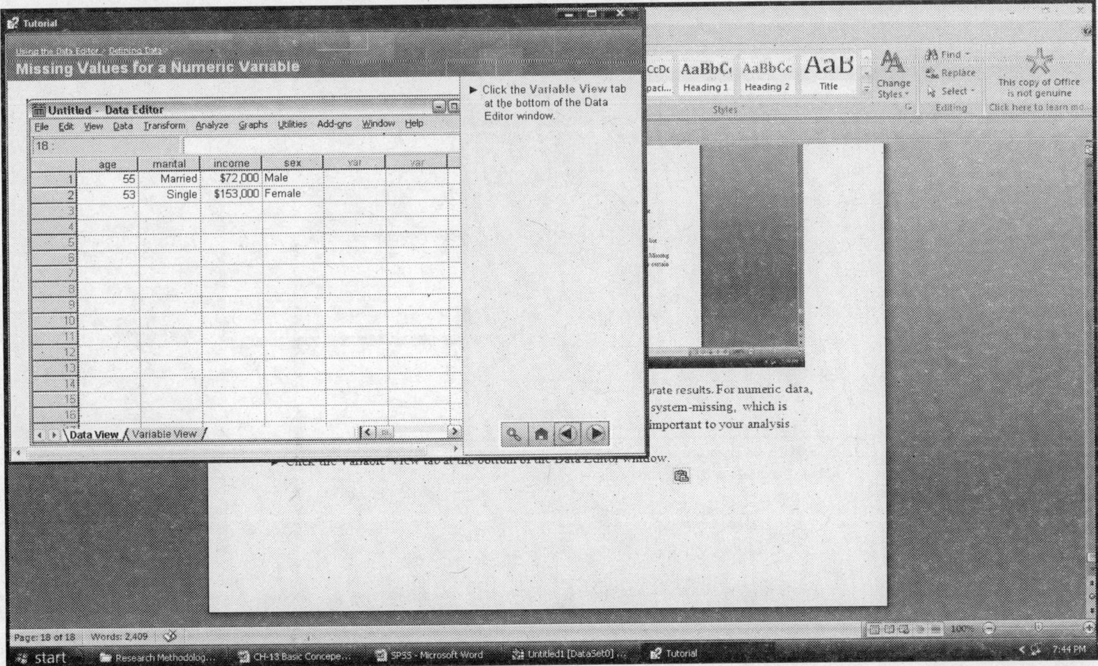

13.3.7 Missing Values for a Numeric Variable

- Click the Missing cell in the age row, and then click the button on the right side of the cell to open the Missing Values dialog box.

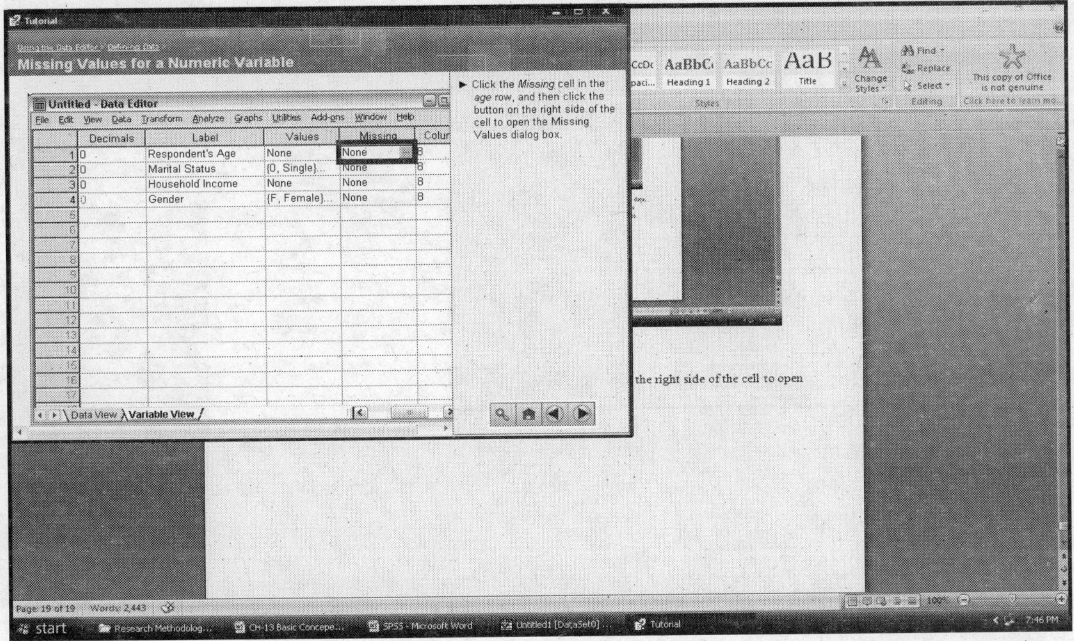

In this dialog box, you can specify up to three distinct missing values, or you can specify a range of values plus one additional discrete value.

- Select Discrete missing values.
- Type 999 in the first text box and leave the other two text boxes empty.
- Click OK to save your changes and return to the Data Editor.

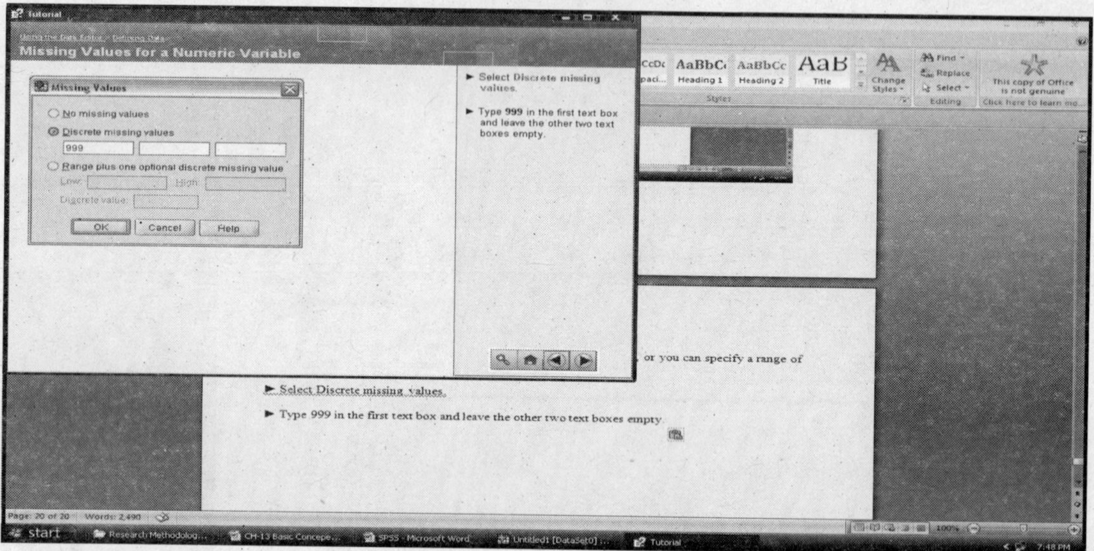

Now that the missing data value has been added, a label can be applied to that value.

- Click the Values cell in the age row, and then click the button on the right side of the cell to open the Value Labels dialog box.

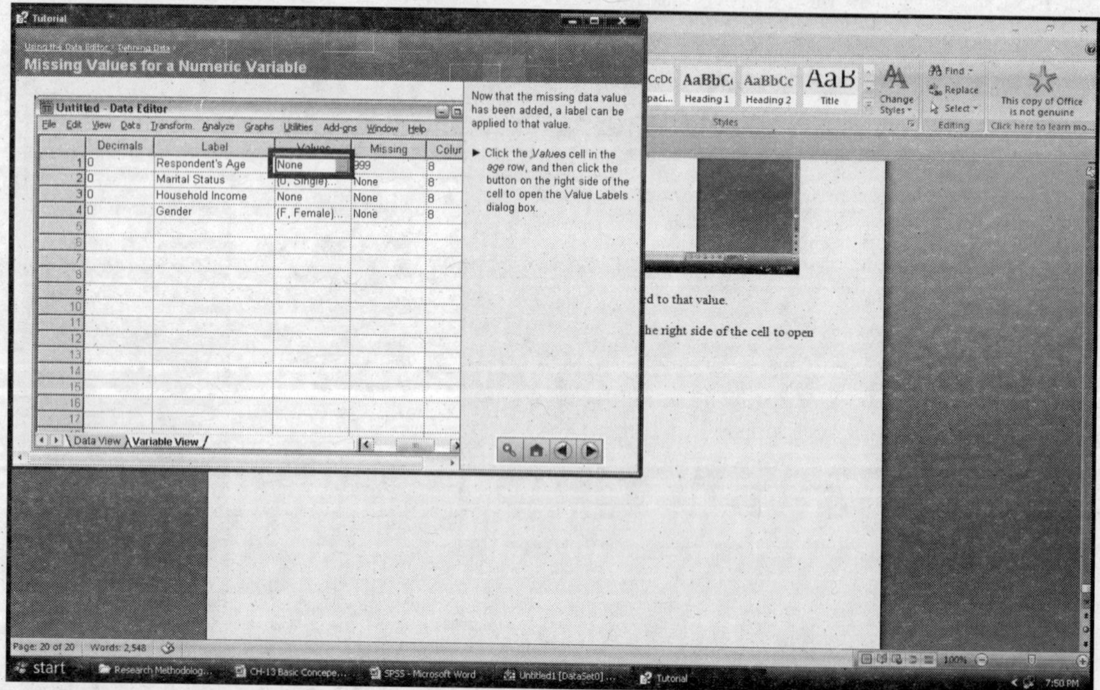

- Type 999 in the Value field.
- Type No Response in the Label field.
- Click Add to add this label to your data file.
- Click OK to save your changes and return to the Data Editor.

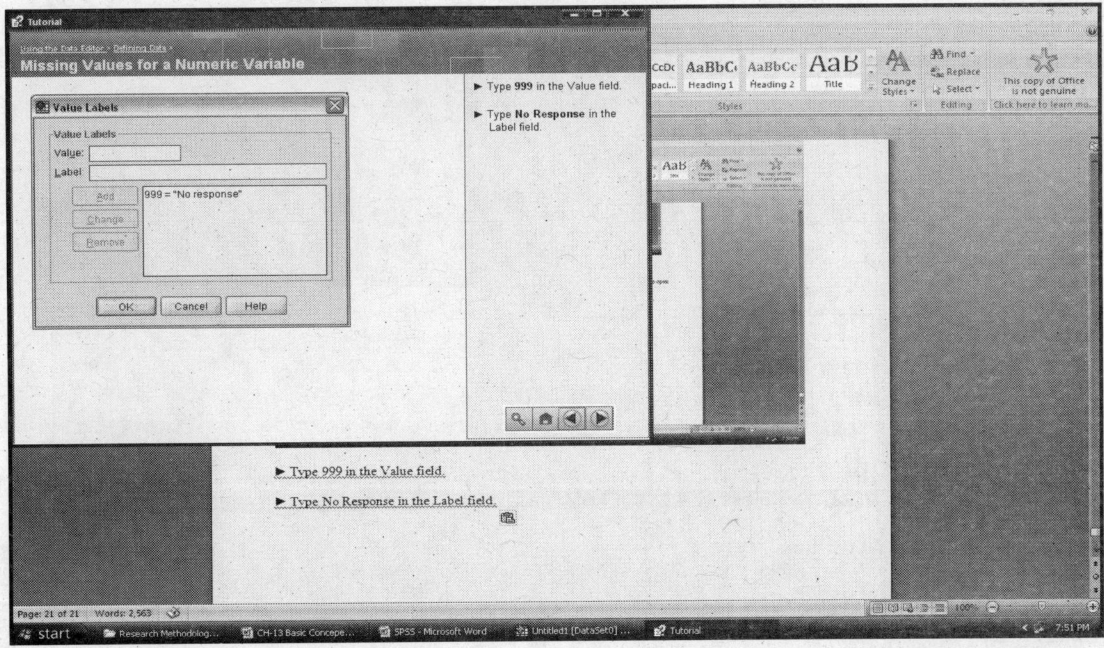

13.3.8 Missing Values for a String Variable

Missing values for string variables are handled similarly to the missing values for numeric variables. However, unlike numeric variables, empty fields in string variables are not designated as system-missing. Rather, they are interpreted as an empty string.

- Click the Variable View tab at the bottom of the Data Editor window.

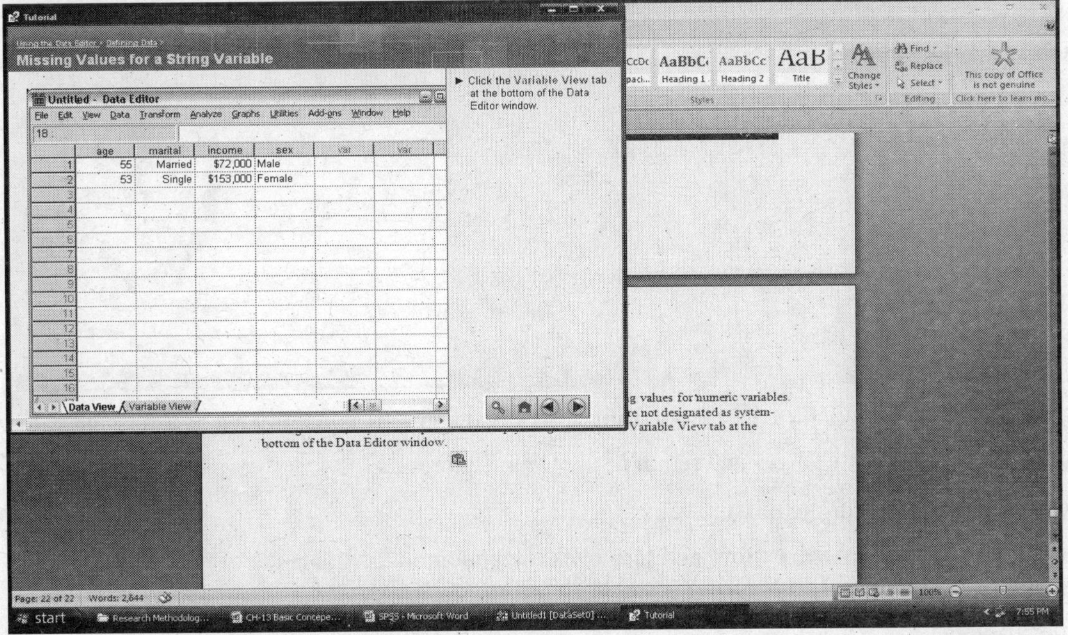

- Click the Missing cell in the sex row, and then click the button on the right side of the cell to open the Missing Values dialog box.

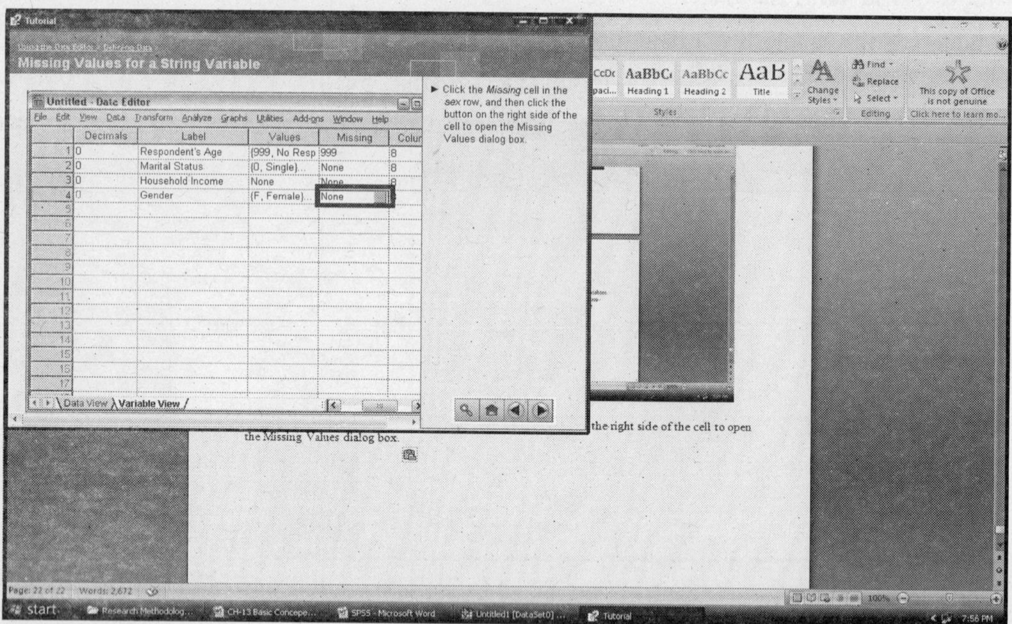

- Select Discrete missing values.
- Type NR in the first text box.

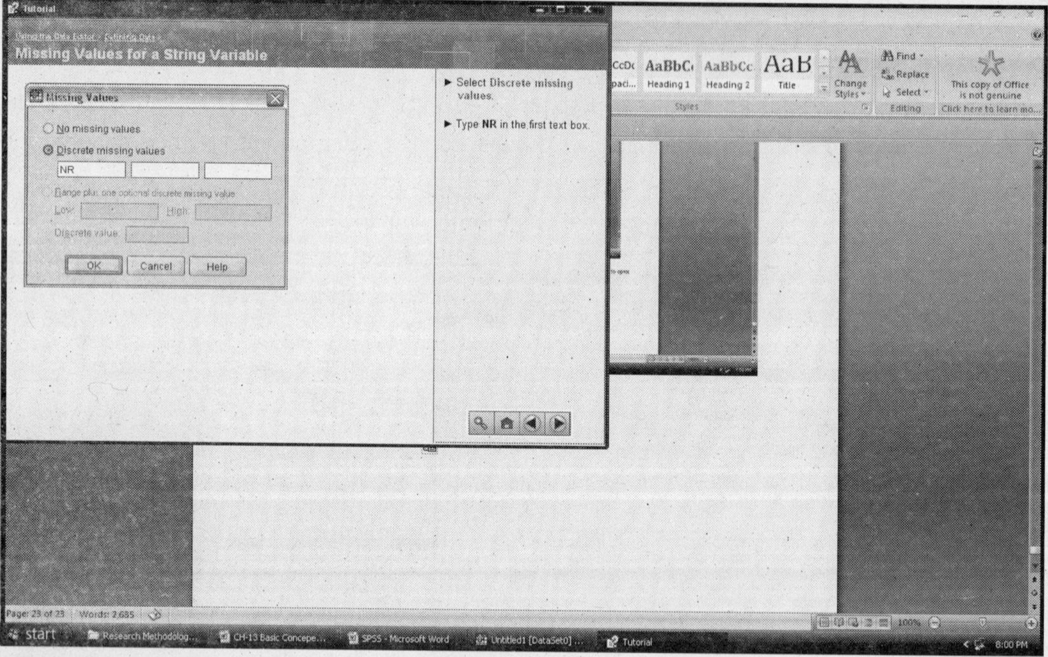

Missing values for string variables are case sensitive. So, a value of NR is not treated as a missing value.

- Click OK to save your changes and return to the Data Editor.

Now, you can add a label for the missing value.

- Click the Values cell in the sex row, and then click the button on the right side of the cell to open the Value Labels dialog box.
- Type NR in the Value field.
- Type No Response in the Label field.

- Click Add to add this label to your project.
- Click OK to save your changes and return to the Data Editor.

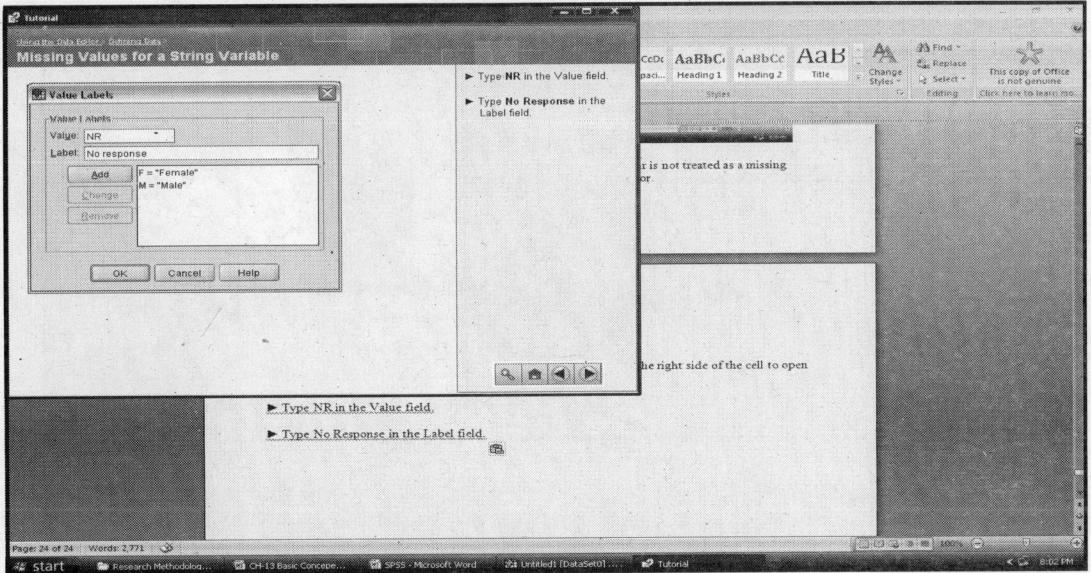

13.3.9 Copying and Pasting Variable Attributes

After you've defined variable attributes for a variable, you can copy these attributes and apply them to other variables.

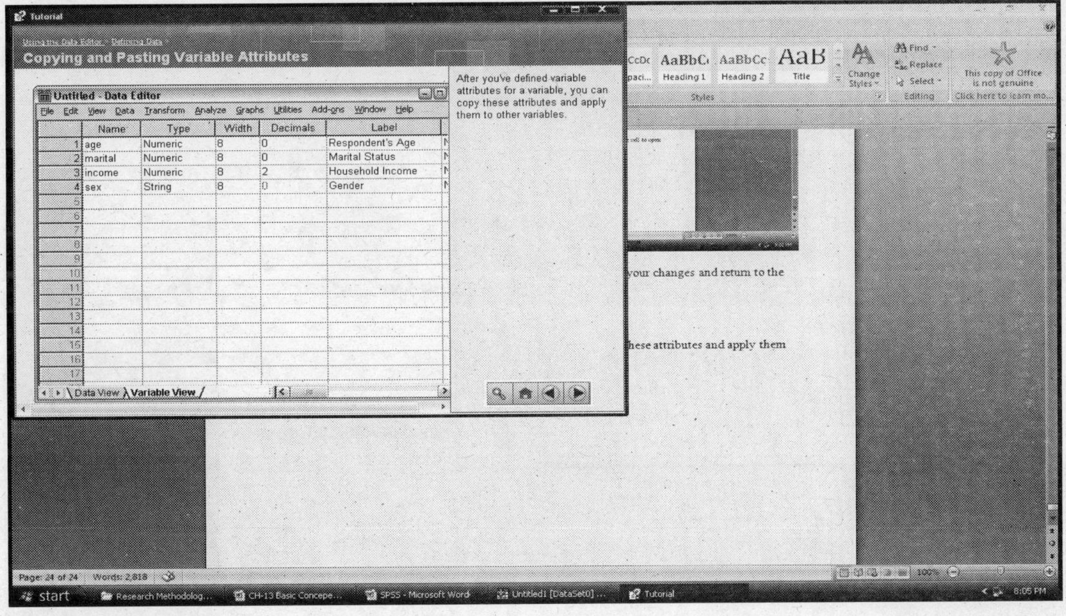

- In Variable View, type agewed in the first cell of the first empty row.
- In the Label column, type Age Married.

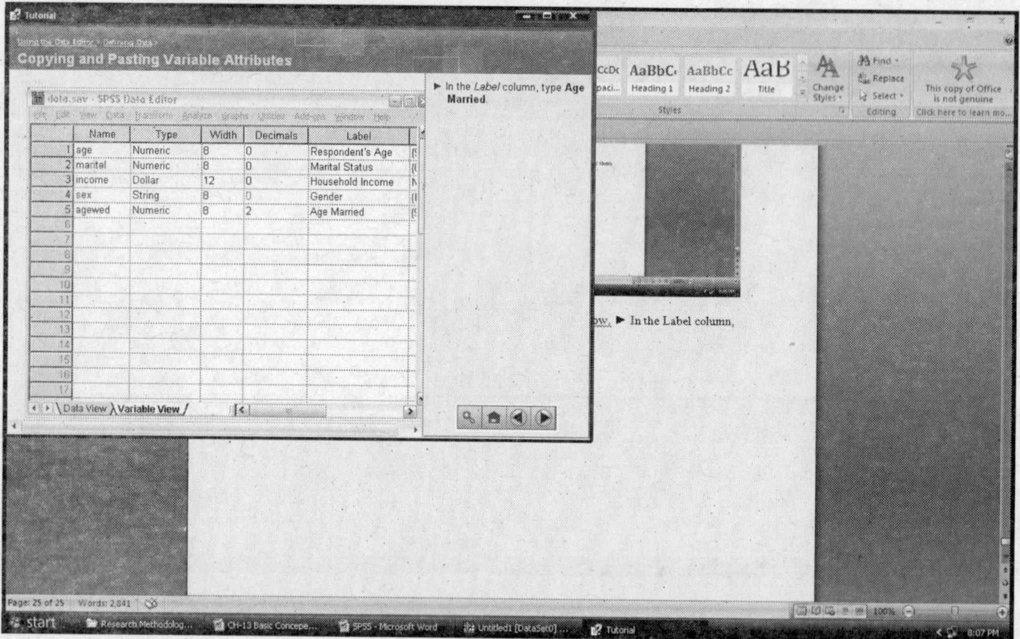

- Click the Values cell in the age row.
- From the menus, choose Edit Copy.

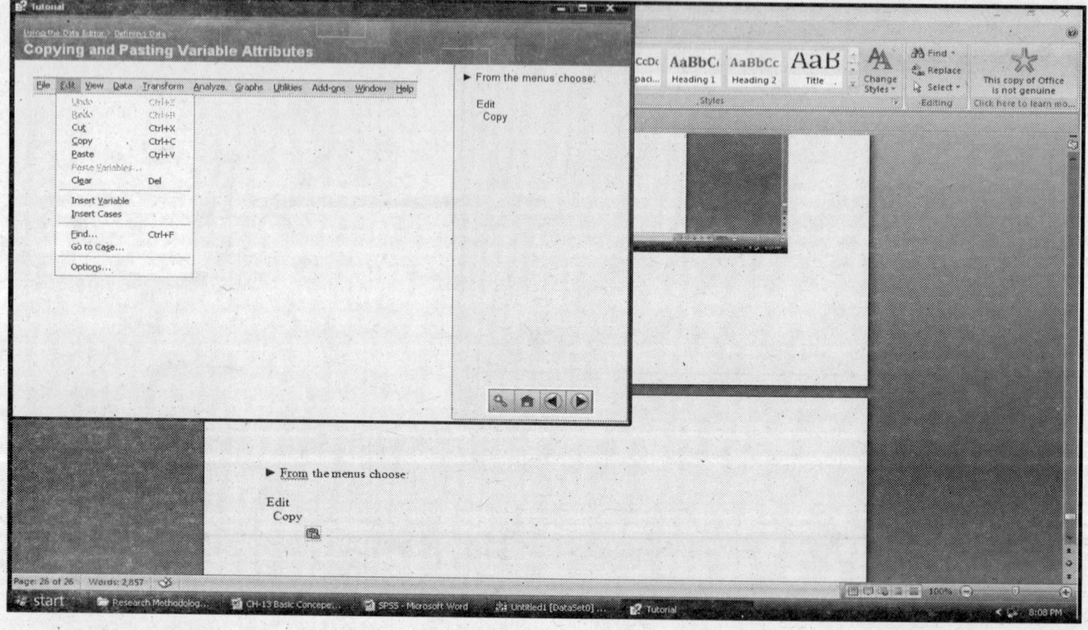

- Click the Values cell in the agewed row.

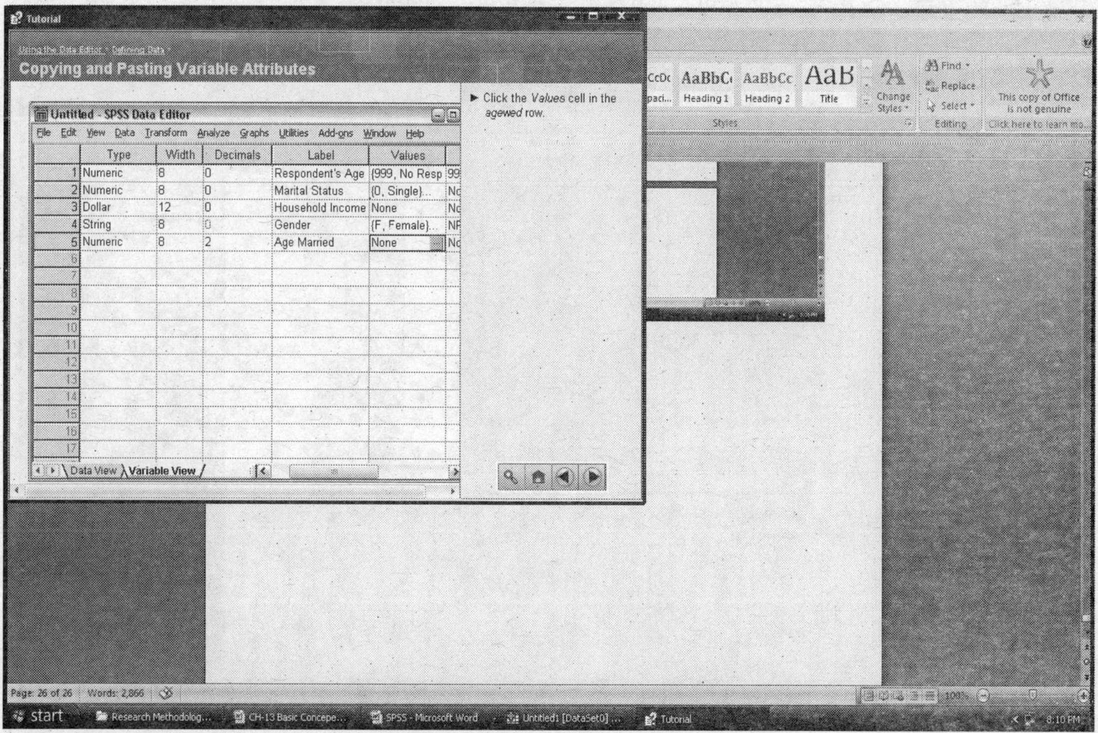

- From the menus, choose
  Edit Paste.

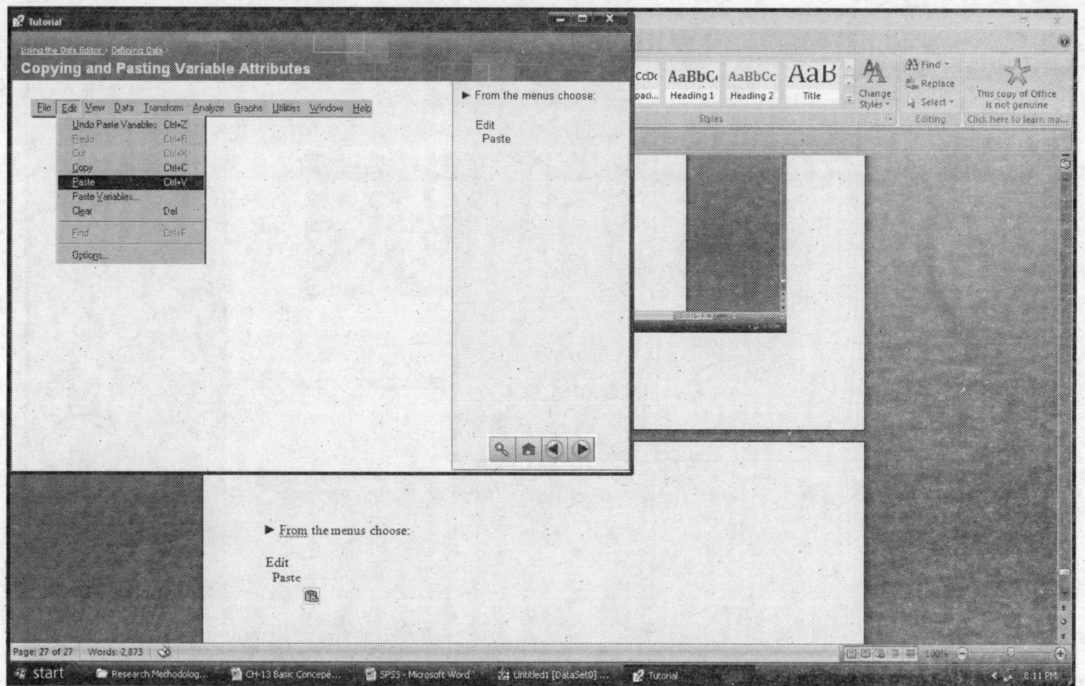

The defined values from the age variable are now applied to the agewed variable. To apply the attribute to multiple variables, simply select multiple target cells (click and drag down the column).

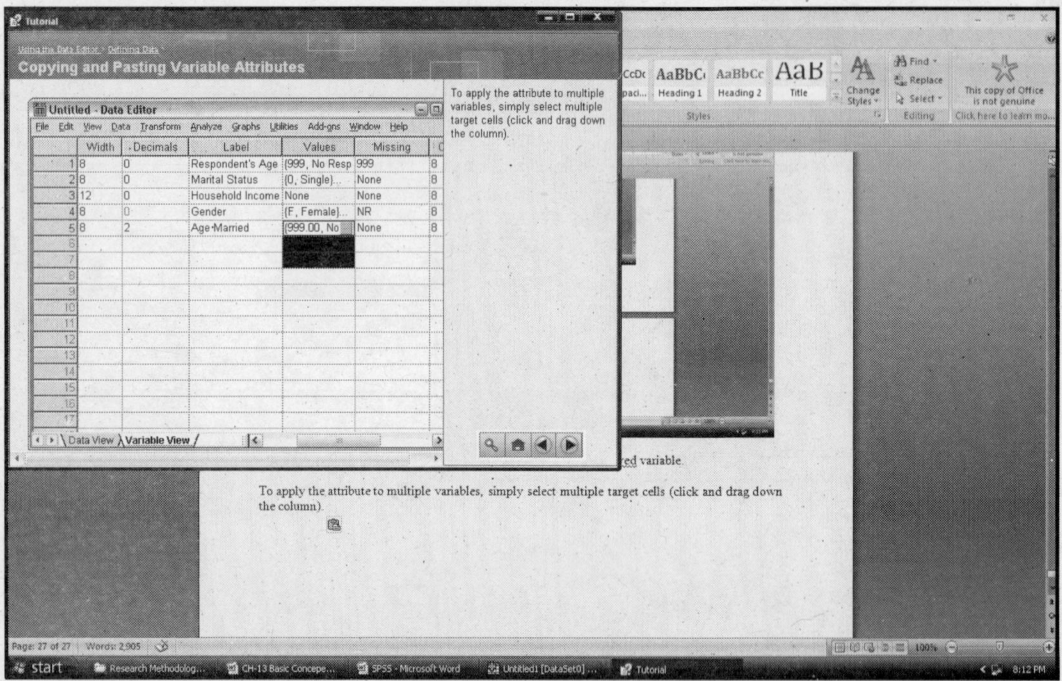

When you paste the attribute, it is applied to all of the selected cells. New variables are automatically created if you paste the values into empty rows. To copy all attributes from one variable to another variable:

- Click the row number in the marital row.

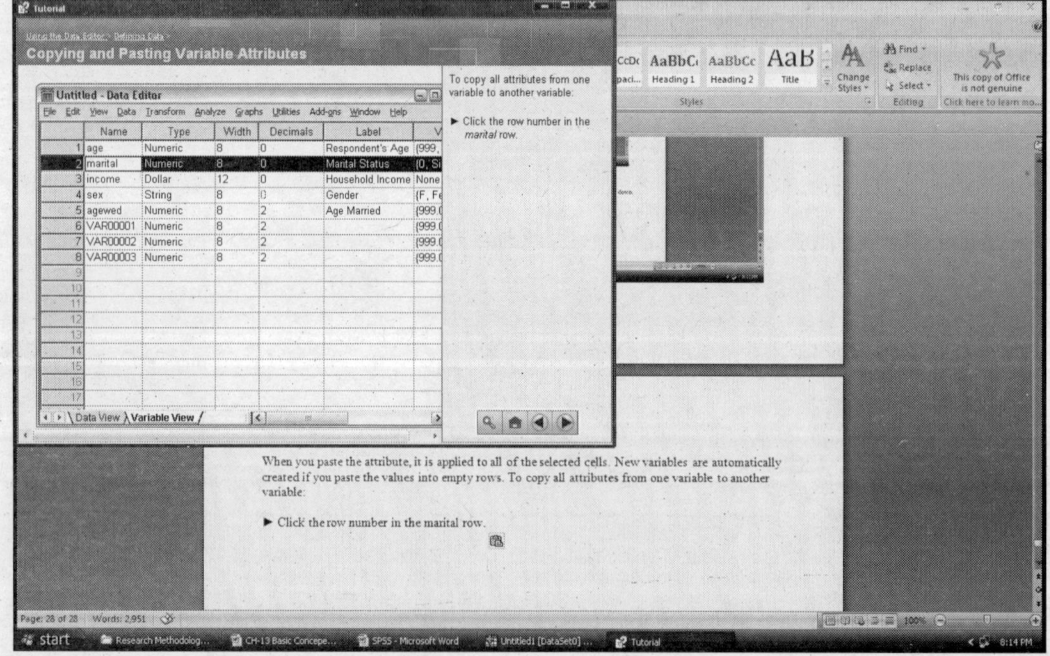

- From the menus, choose Edit and Copy.

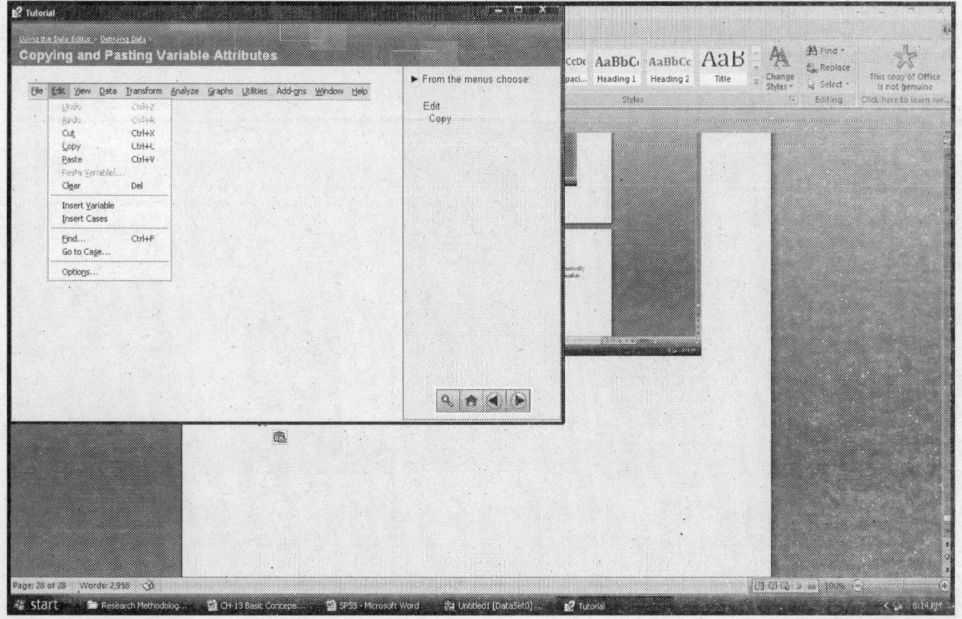

- Click the row number of the first empty row.
- From the menus, choose Edit and Paste.

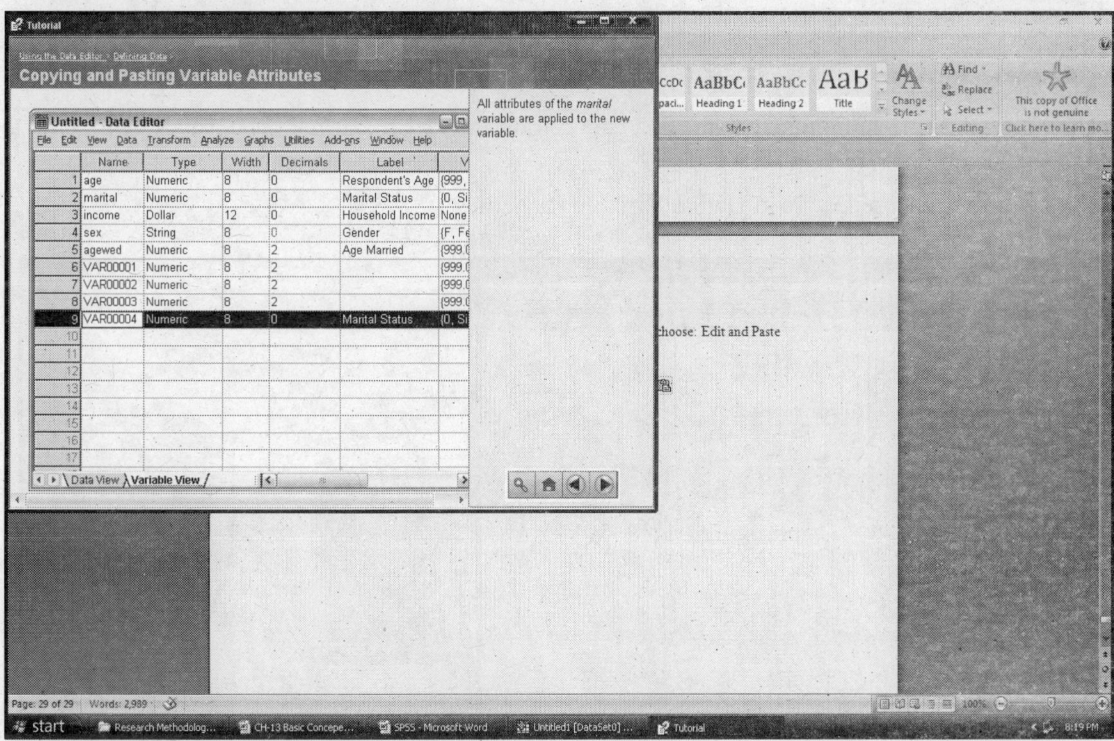

All attributes of the marital variable are applied to the new variable.

13.3.10 Defining Variable Properties for Categorical Variables

For categorical (nominal, ordinal) data, you can use Define Variable Properties to define value labels and other variable properties. The Define Variable Properties process:

- Scans the actual data values and lists all unique data values for each selected variable.

- Identifies unlabeled values and provides an "auto-label" feature.
- Provides the ability to copy defined value labels from another variable to the selected variable or from the selected variable to additional variables. This data file already has defined value labels, so we will enter a value for which there is no defined value label.

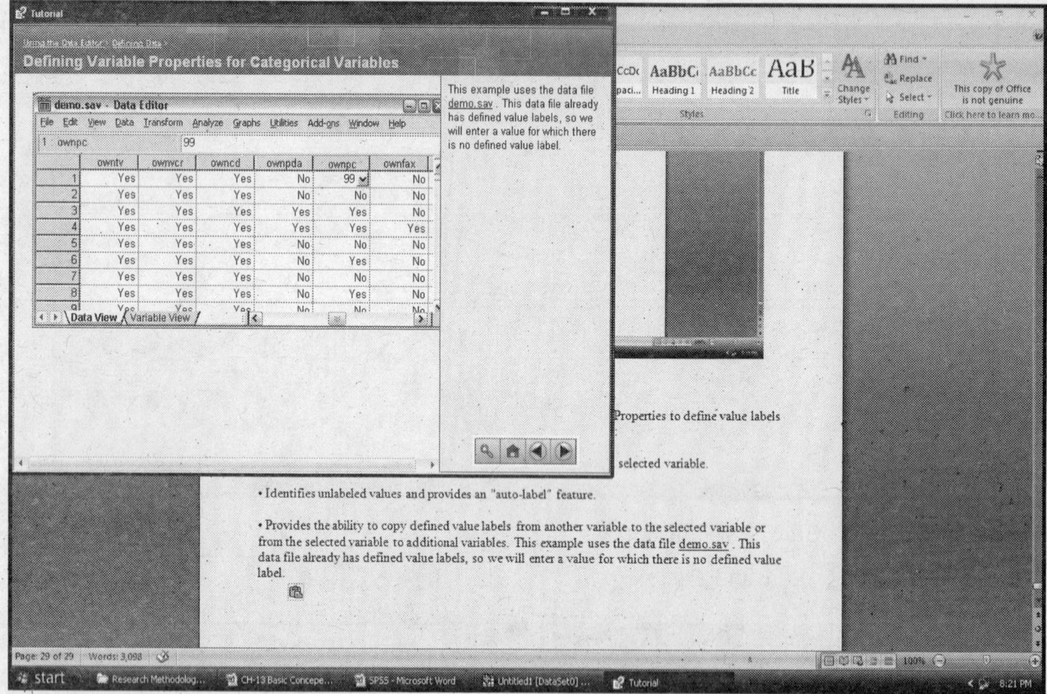

- In Data View of the Data Editor, click the first data cell for the variable ownpc (you may have to scroll to the right), and then enter 99.
- From the menus, choose Data and Define Variable Properties.

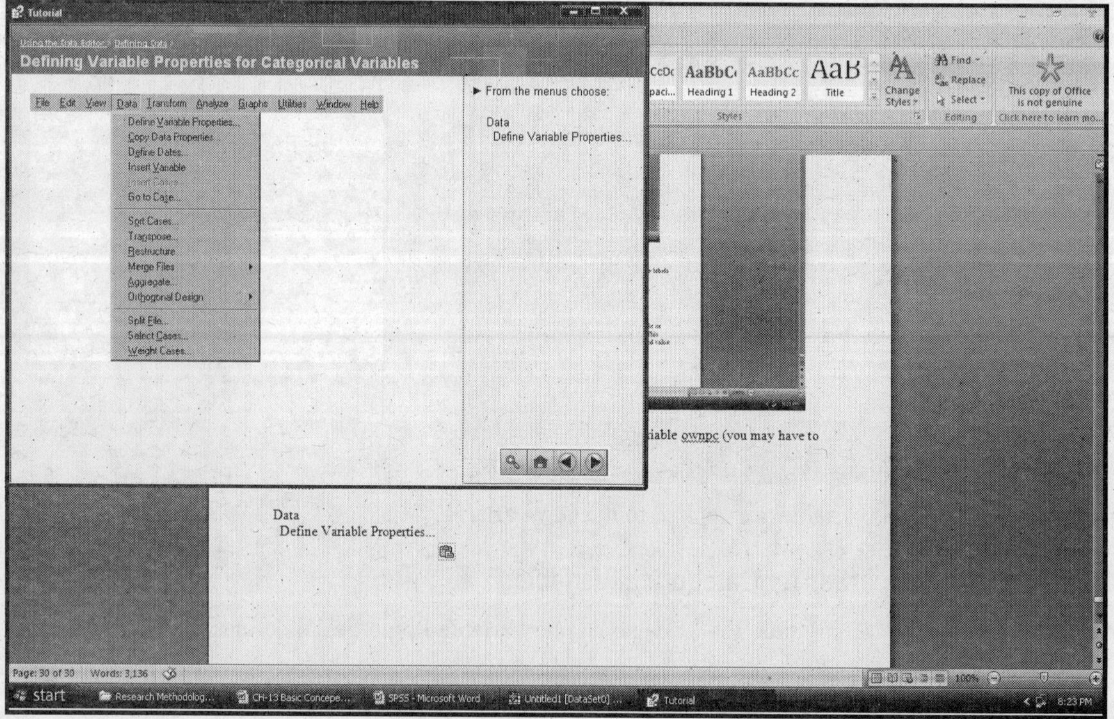

In the initial Define Variable Properties dialog box, you select the nominal or ordinal variables for which you want to define value labels and/or other properties.

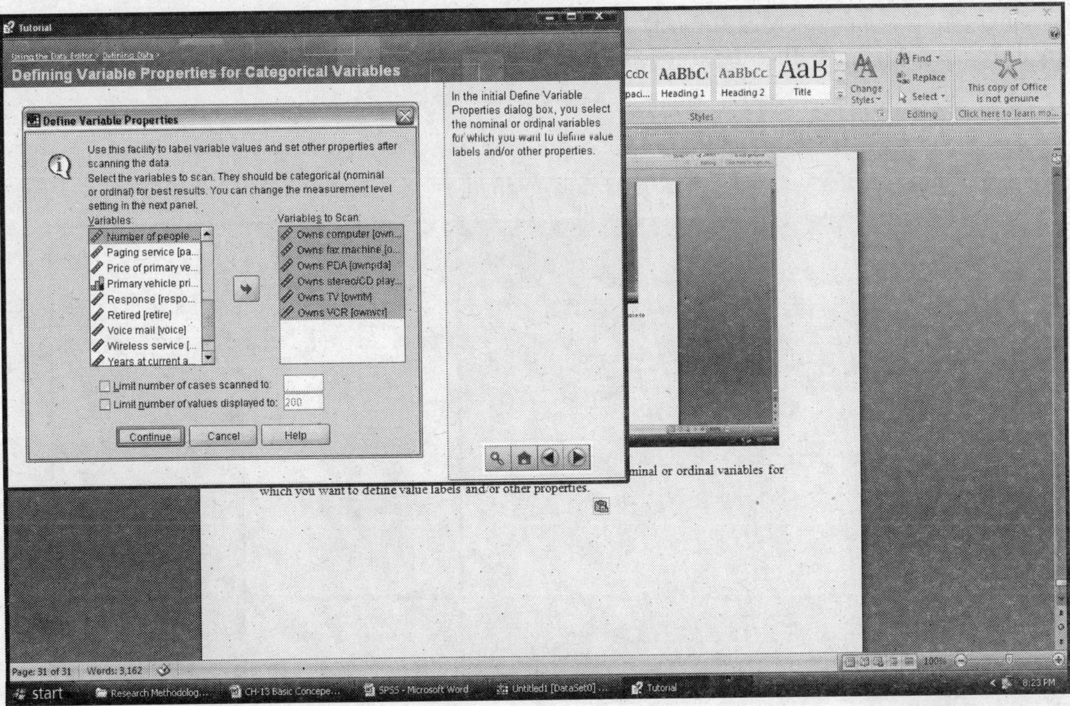

- Drag and drop Owns computer [ownpc] through Owns VCR [ownvcr] into the Variables to Scan list.

You might notice that the measurement level icons for all of the selected variables indicate that they are scale variables, not categorical variables. All of the selected variables in this example are really categorical variables that use the numeric values 0 and 1 to stand for No and Yes, respectively — and one of the variable properties that we'll change with Define Variable Properties is the measurement level.

- Click Continue.
- In the Scanned Variable List, select owner.

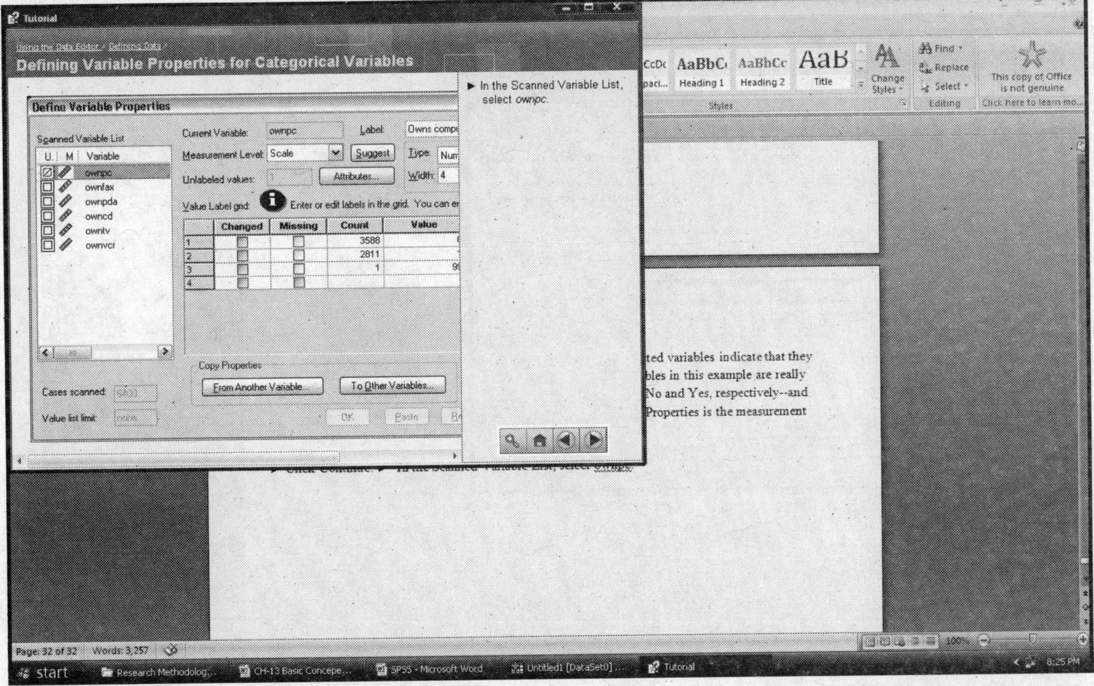

The current level of measurement for the selected variable is scale. You can change the measurement level by selecting a level from the drop-down list, or you can let Define Variable Properties suggest a measurement level.

- Click Suggest. The Suggest Measurement Level dialog box is displayed. Because the variable doesn't have very many different values and all of the scanned cases contain integer values, the proper measurement level is probably ordinal or nominal.
- Select Ordinal, and then click Continue.

The measurement level for the selected variable is now ordinal.

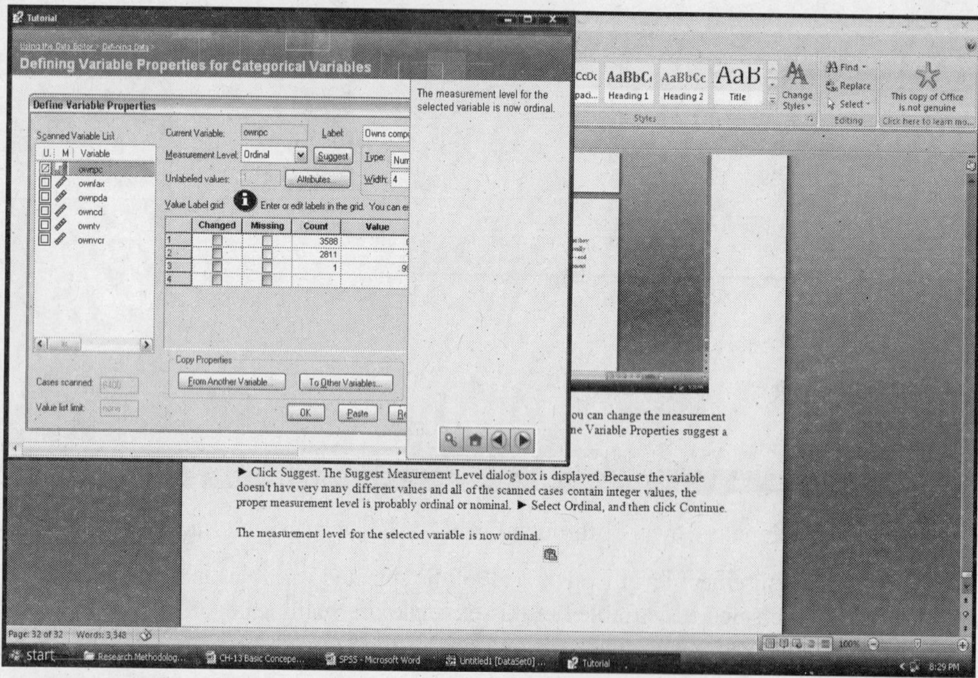

The Value Label grid displays all of the unique data values for the selected variable, any defined value labels for these values, and the number of times (count) that each value occurs in the scanned cases. The value that we entered in Data View, 99, is displayed in the grid. The count is only 1 because we changed the value for only one case, and the Label column is empty because we haven't defined a value label for 99 yet.

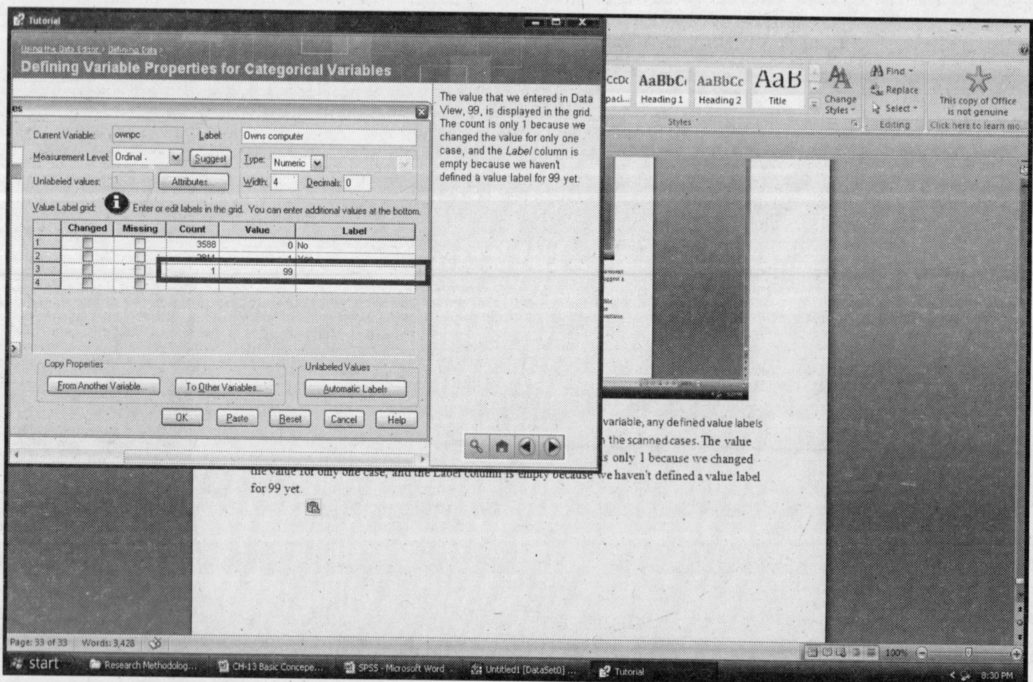

The X in the first column of the Scanned Variable List also indicates that the selected variable has at least one observed value without a defined value label.

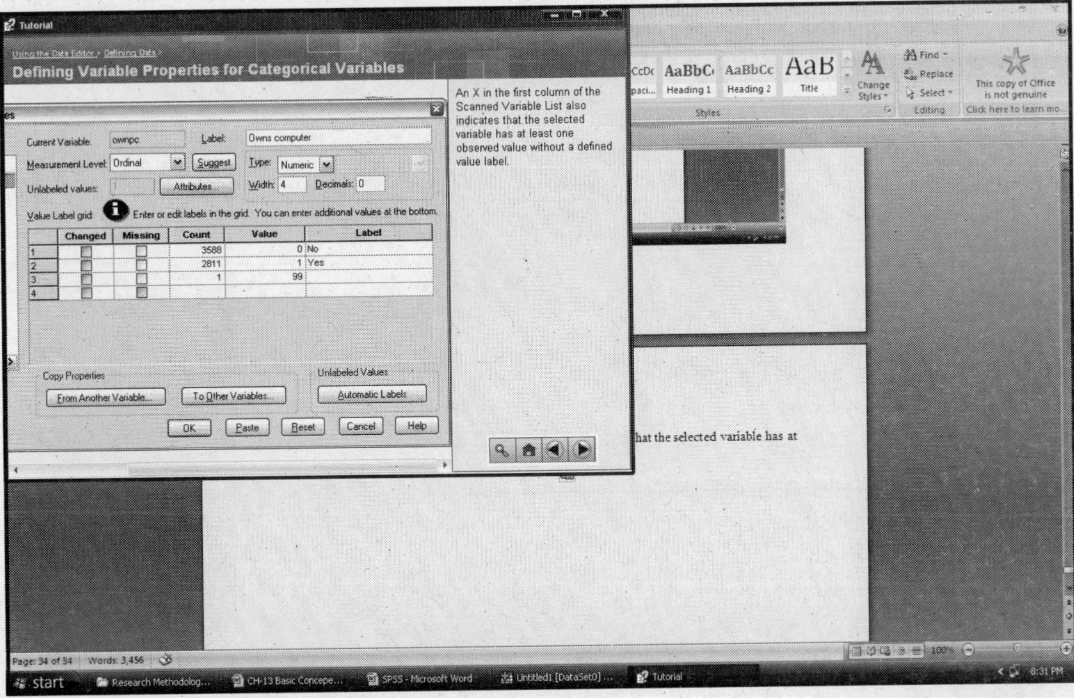

- In the Label column for the value of 99, enter No answer.

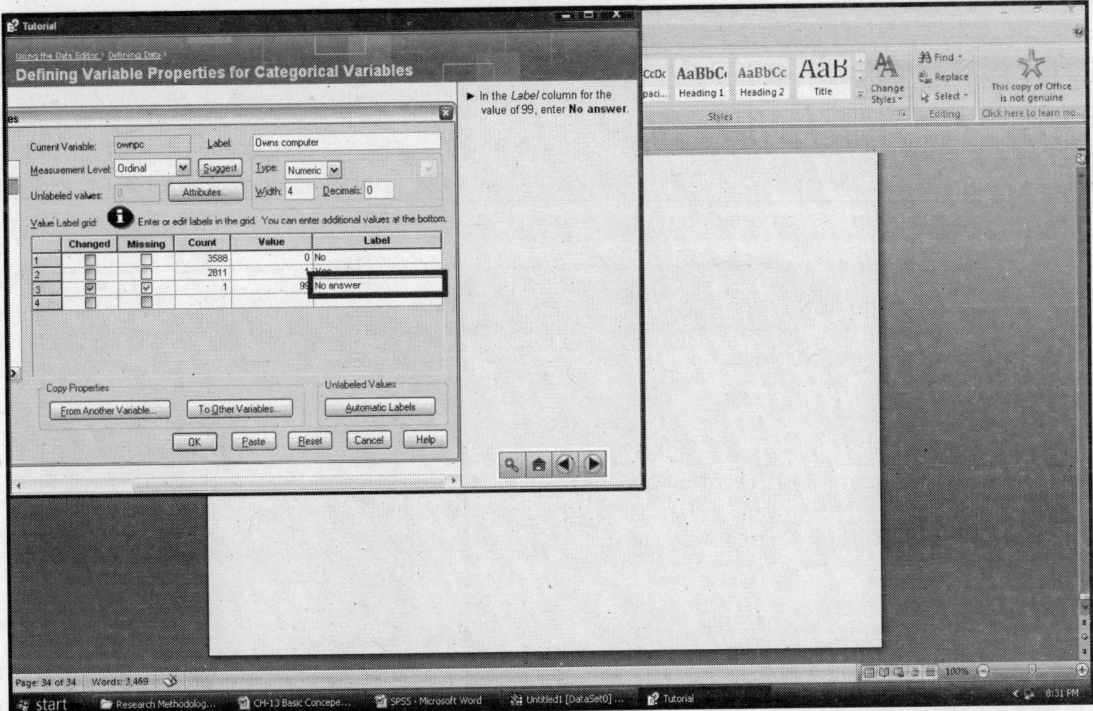

- Check the box in the Missing column for the value 99 to identify the value 99 as user-missing.

Data values that are specified as user-missing are flagged for special treatment and are excluded from most calculations.

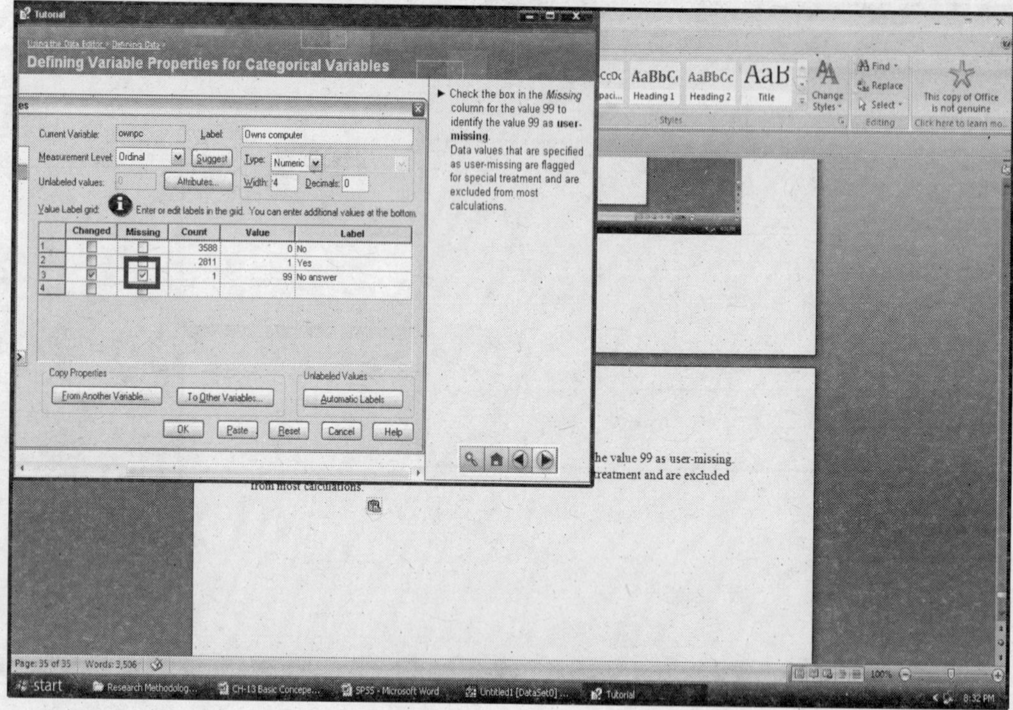

Before we complete the job of modifying the variable properties for owner, let's apply the same measurement level, value labels, and missing values definitions to the other variables in the list.

- In the Copy Properties area, click 'To Other Variables'.
- In the Apply Labels and Level dialog box, select all of the variables in the list, and then click Copy.

If you select any other variable in the Scanned Variable List of the Define Variable Properties main dialog box now, you will see that they are all ordinal variables, with a value of 99 defined as user-missing and a value label of No answer.

- Click OK to save all of the variable properties that you have defined.

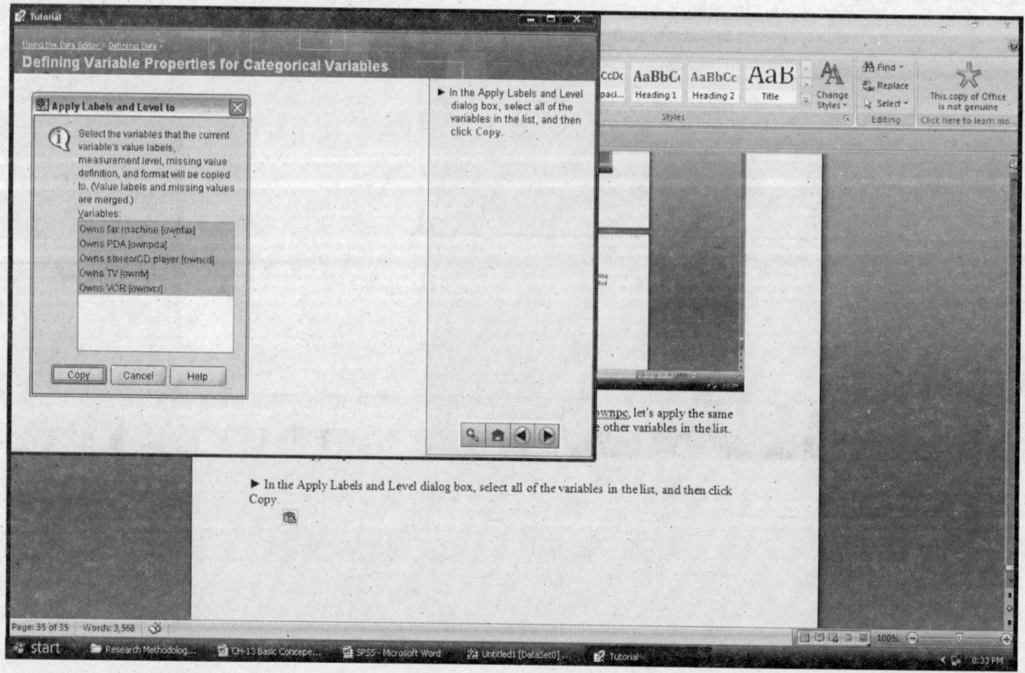

If you select any other variable in the Scanned Variable List of the Define Variable Properties main dialog box now, you'll see that they are all ordinal variables, with a value of 99 defined as user-missing and a value label of No answer. Click OK to save all of the variable properties that you have defined.

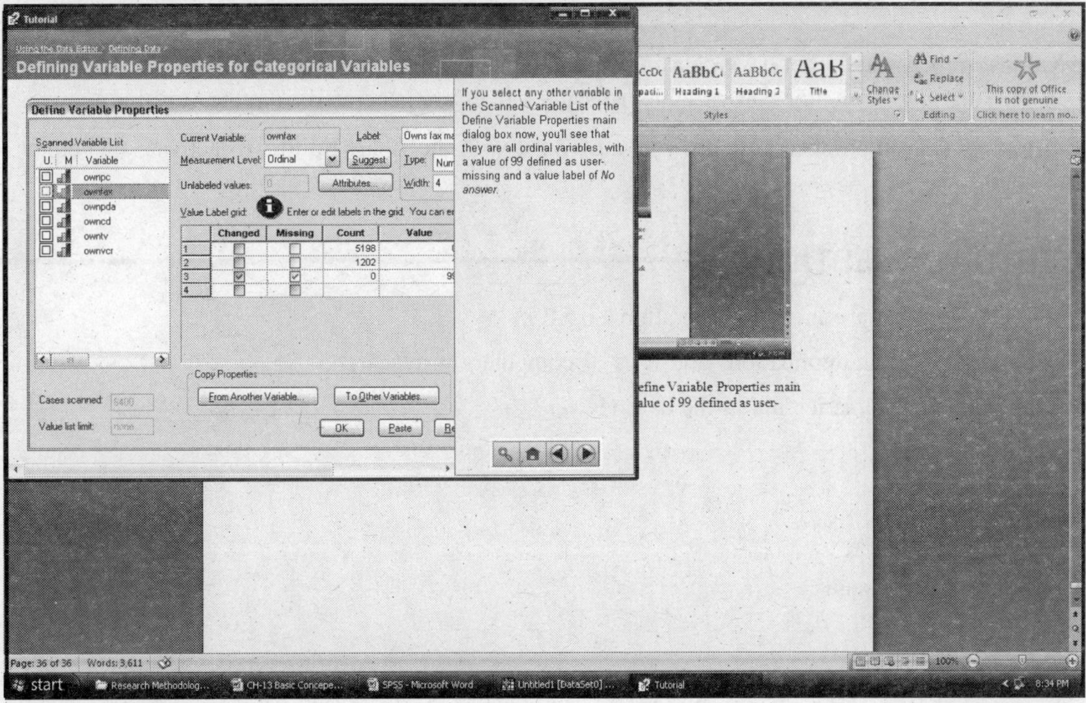

13.4 SUMMARY

SPSS is a full-featured data analysis program that offers a variety of applications including database management and reporting, statistical analysis, and graphics. The SPSS program runs on a wide variety of mainframe, mini, and microcomputers.

SPSS is a comprehensive and flexible statistical analysis and data management system. SPSS can take data from almost any type of file and use them to generate tabulated reports, charts, and plots of distributions and trends, descriptive statistics, and conduct complex statistical analyses. SPSS is available from several platforms; Windows, Macintosh, and the UNIX systems.

SPSS for Windows brings the full power of the mainframe version of SPSS to the personal computer environment. It will enable you to perform many analyses on your PC that were once possible only on much larger machines. SPSS for Windows provides a user interface that makes statistical analysis more intuitive for all levels of users. Simple menus and dialog box selections make it possible to perform complex analyses without typing a single line of command syntax. The built-in SPSS Data Editor offers a simple and efficient spreadsheet-like utility for entering data and browsing the working data file. High-resolution, presentation-quality charts and plots can be created and edited. Using the SPSS Viewer, you can handle the output with greater flexibility. SPSS for Windows also reads data files from a variety of file formats including Excel, SAS, and Stata.

13.5 KEY TERMS

SPSS: SPSS is a full-featured data analysis program that offers a variety of applications including database management and reporting, statistical analysis, and graphics.

The SPSS Data Editor: This is the sphere of SPSS into which data are entered and subsequently edited and defined.

The Data Viewer: This is the spreadsheet into which your data are entered. When you start up SPSS, the Data Viewer will be facing you.

The Variable Viewer: This is another spreadsheet, but this one displays information about each of the variables and allows you to change that information.

The Output: The Output Viewer superimposes itself over the Data Editor after an analysis has been performed or a chart generated.

Missing Values: When you do not have data for a particular variable when entering data for a case, you must specify how you are denoting missing values for that variable. Missing values are generated from the Variable Viewer.

Chart Editor: When you produce a graph, you can edit it with the Chart Editor. To activate this editor, double-click anywhere in the graph.

13.6 CONCEPTUAL QUESTIONS

1. What is SPSS? What are the basic operations in SPSS?
2. Describe the important applications and uses of computers in research.
3. How can you enter numeric data in the data viewer?
4. Write short notes:
   (a) String data
   (b) Numeric Variables
   (c) Handling missing data
   (d) Missing values
   (e) Categorical variables

CHAPTER 14

DATA ANALYSIS WITH SPSS

Chapter Outline

Learning Objectives

- *Discuss the need of SPSS in research for decision making.*
- *Explain the various table and charts for data analysis with SPSS for managerial decisions.*
- *Analysis the various statistical techniques with SPSS.*

14.1 GENERATING A FREQUENCY TABLE

How to Produce a Frequency Table?
SPSS Commands:

Step 1:	Data entered into a data file in SPSS. *[See Plate 14.1.1]*
Step 2:	Click the button **Analyze** on the SPSS menu bar [→ **Descriptive Statistics** → **Frequencies**] and opens the frequencies dialog box. *[See Plate 14.1.2]*
Step 3:	On the dialog box, select variable(s) for analyze and clicking on the right arrow to send selected variable(s) into **Variable(s) List.** *[See Plate 14.1.2]*
Step 4:	Click OK, the table will appear in the Output Viewer. *[See Plate 14.1.3].*

Note that in the Frequencies dialog box, variables that have been assigned labels will appear in terms of their variable labels, but those that have not been assigned labels will appear in terms of their variable names. This is a feature of all dialog boxes produced via Analyze and Graphs.

Example 14.1:

Consider the following set of 15 scores which were obtained by asking a class of students their shoe size, shoe width, and sex (male or female).

Shoe Size	10.5	6.0	9.5	8.5	7.0	10.5	8.5	6.5	9.5	7.0	7.5	9.0	6.5	7.5	
Shoe Width	B	B	D	A	B	C	C	D	B	C	B	B	D	A	B
Gender	M	F	M	F	F	M	F	M	F	M	F	M	M	F	M

Solution:

Step 1: Data entered into a data file in SPSS appears as follows:

Plate: 14.1.1

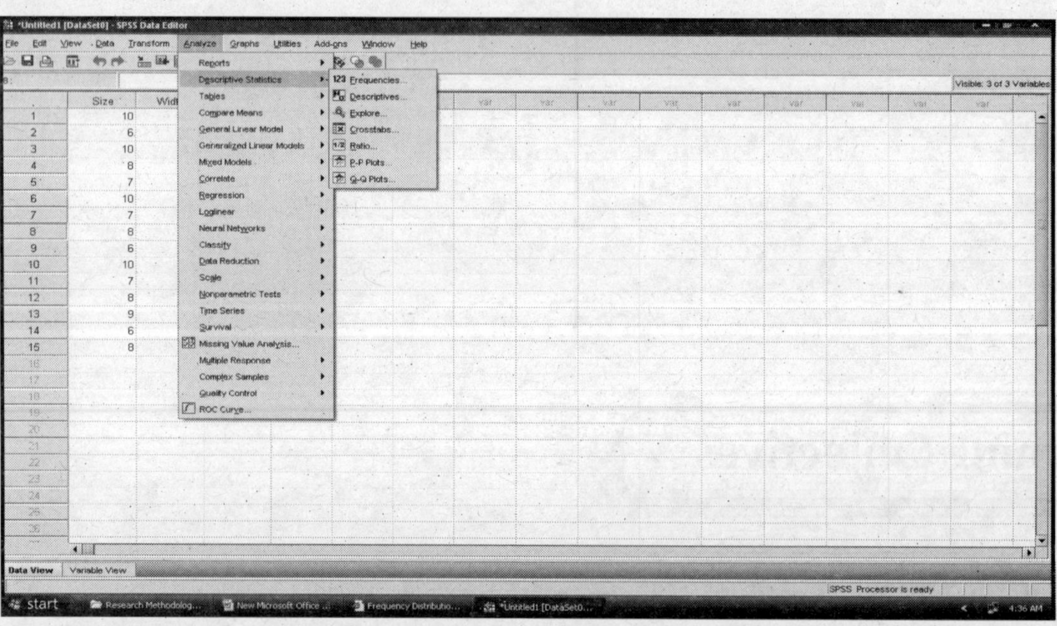

Step 2: Select variable(s) for analyze and clicking on the right arrow to send selected variable(s) into **Variable(s) List.**

The Frequency Dialog Box

Plate: 14.1.2

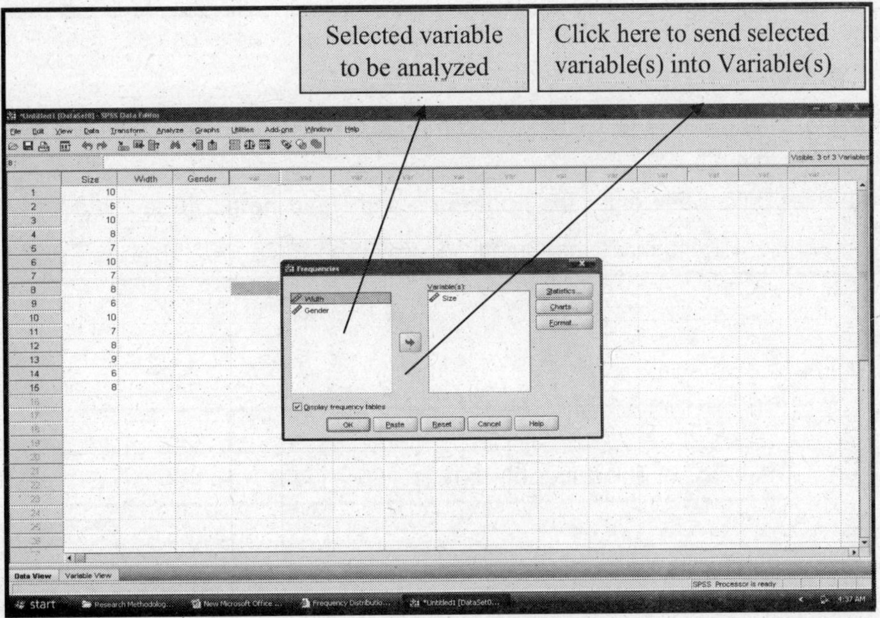

Step 3: Click OK, view the Output Viewer with Frequency Table.

Plate: 14.1.3

The Output Viewer with Frequency Table

Number of cases in each category

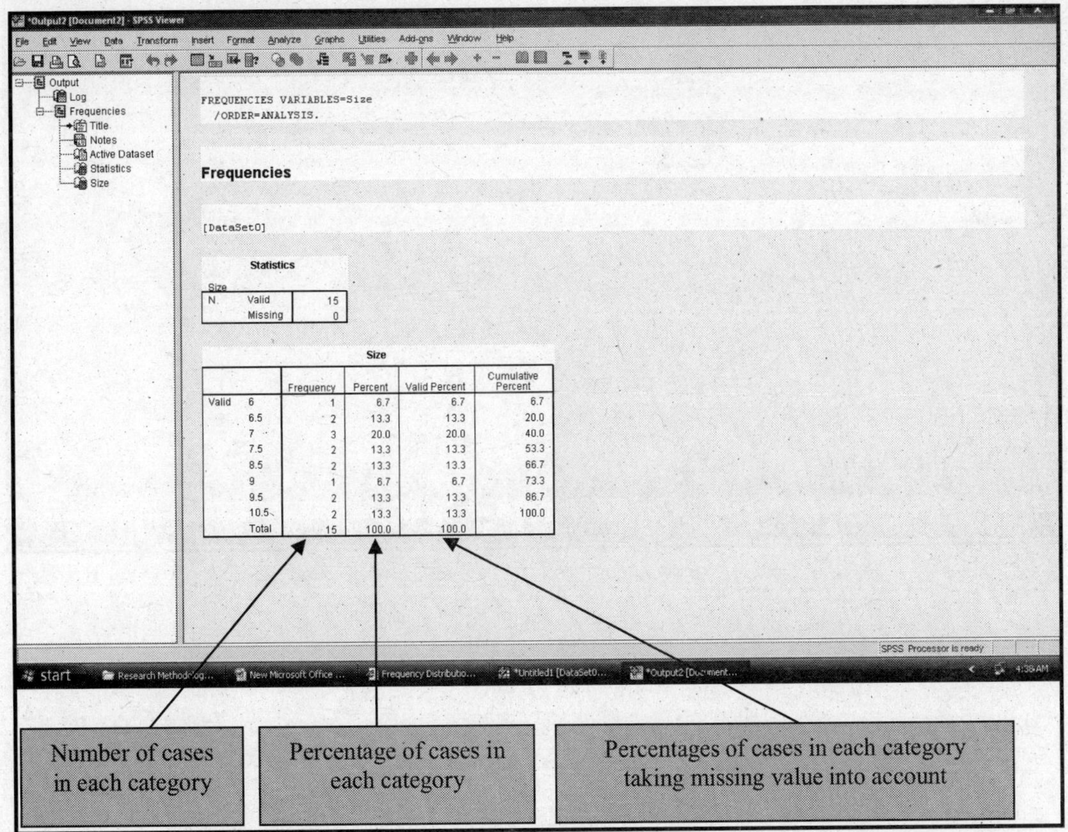

		Frequency	Percent	Valid Percent	Cumulative Percent
Valid	6	1	6.7	6.7	6.7
	6.5	2	13.3	13.3	20.0
	7	3	20.0	20.0	40.0
	7.5	2	13.3	13.3	53.3
	8.5	2	13.3	13.3	66.7
	9	1	6.7	6.7	73.3
	9.5	2	13.3	13.3	86.7
	10.5	2	13.3	13.3	100.0
	Total	15	100.0	100.0	

14.2 GENERATING A BAR CHART

How to Produce a Bar Diagram?
SPSS Commands:

Step 1:	Data entered into a data file in SPSS → Click the button in Graphs options. [See Plate 14.2.1]
Step 2:	Select the Graph → Click **Bar Chart.** [See Plate 14.2.2]
Step 3:	Select variable(s) for analyze → Clicking on the right arrow to send selected variable(s) into **Variable(s) List.** [See Plate 14.2.3]
Step 4:	Clicking the titles button and enter the **Footnotes** and **Head notes.** [See Plate 14.2.4.]
Step 5:	Click OK; the table will appear in the Output Viewer. [See Plate 14.2.5].

Example 14.2:

Draw the bar chart from the following data:

Production Units	A	B	C	D	E
Total No. of Production	50	90	40	100	80

Solution:

Step 1: Data entered into a Data file in SPSS and click the button in Graphs Option.

Plate: 14.2.1

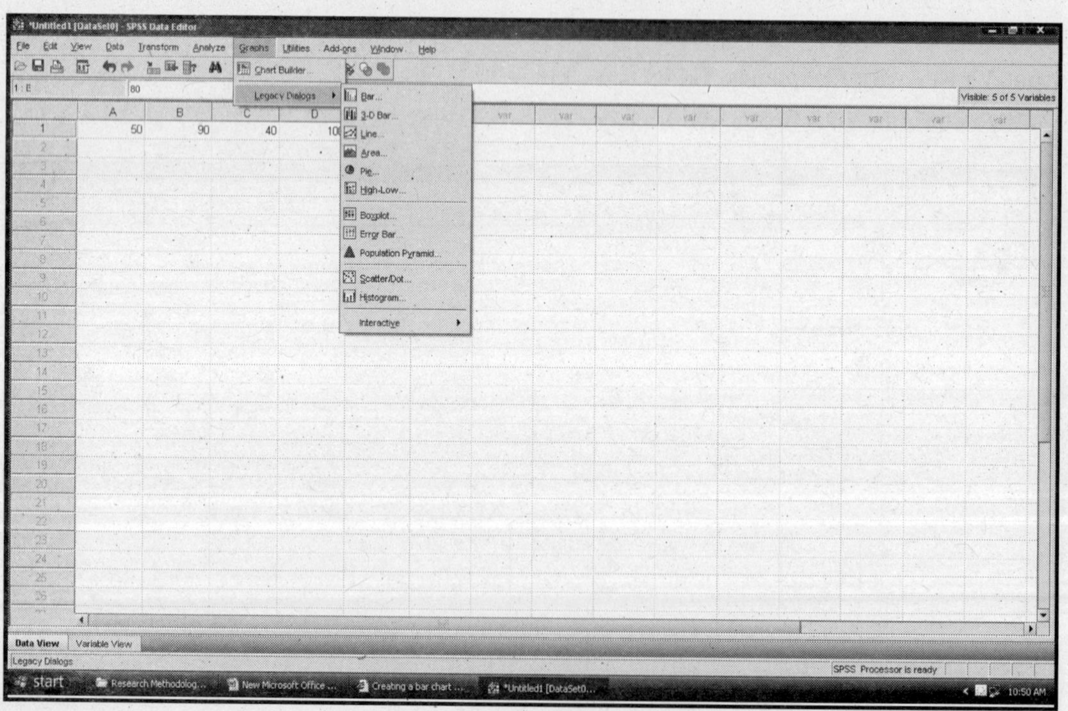

Step 2: Select the graph from Bar chart table.

Plate: 14.2.2

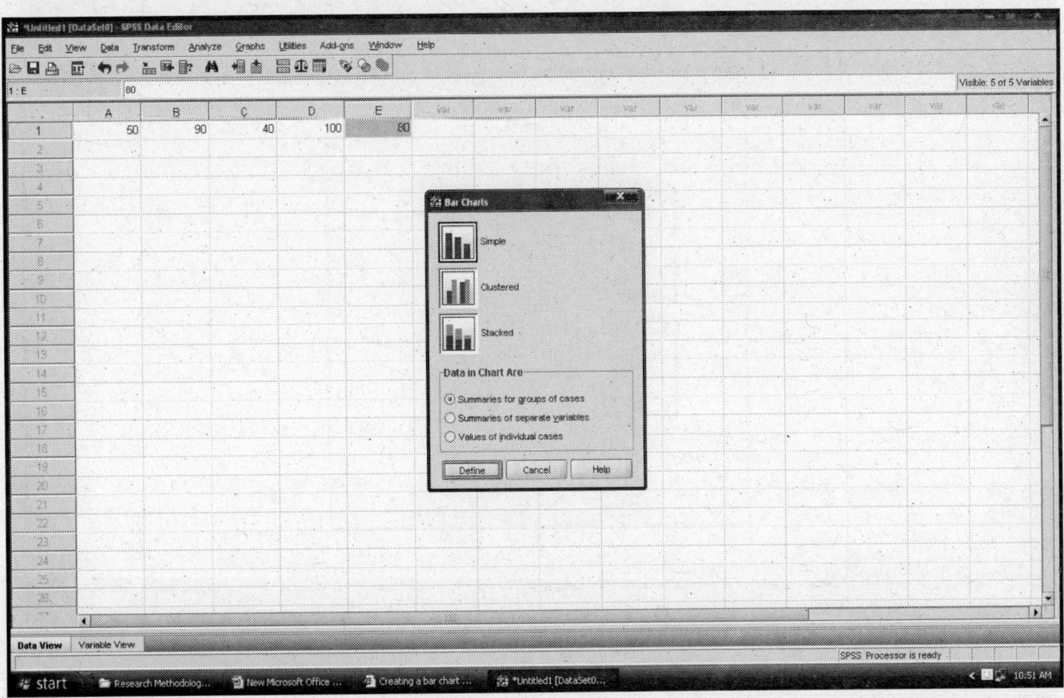

Step 3: Select variable(s) for analyze and clicking the right arrow to send selected Variable(s) into variable(s) List.

Plate: 14.2.3

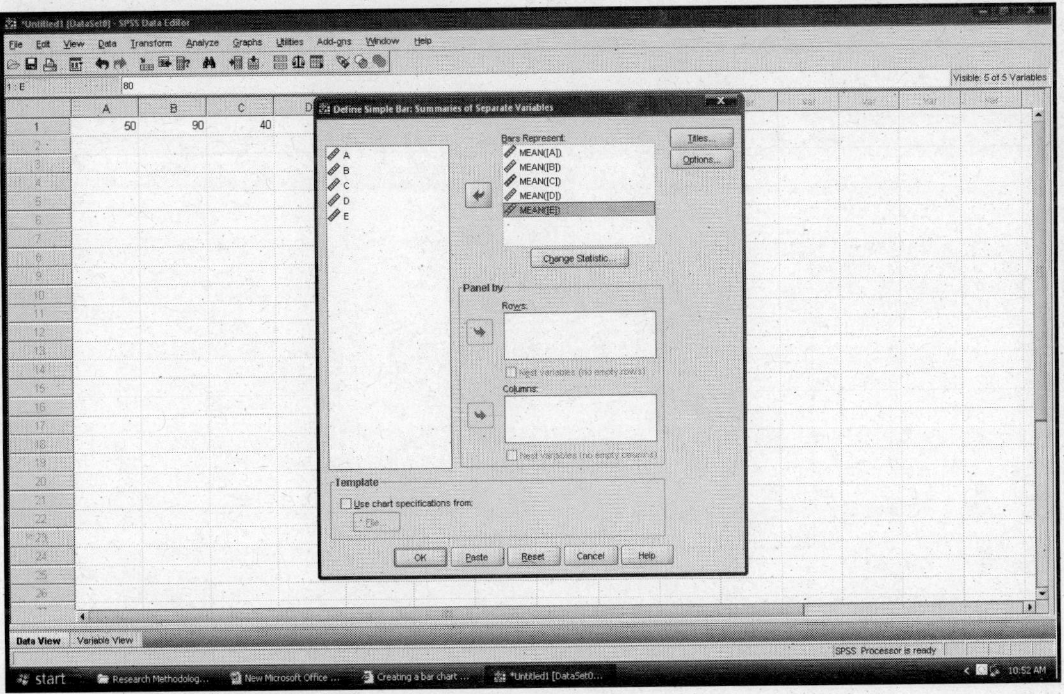

Step 4: Click the titles Button and enter the Footnotes and Head notes.

Plate: 14.2.4

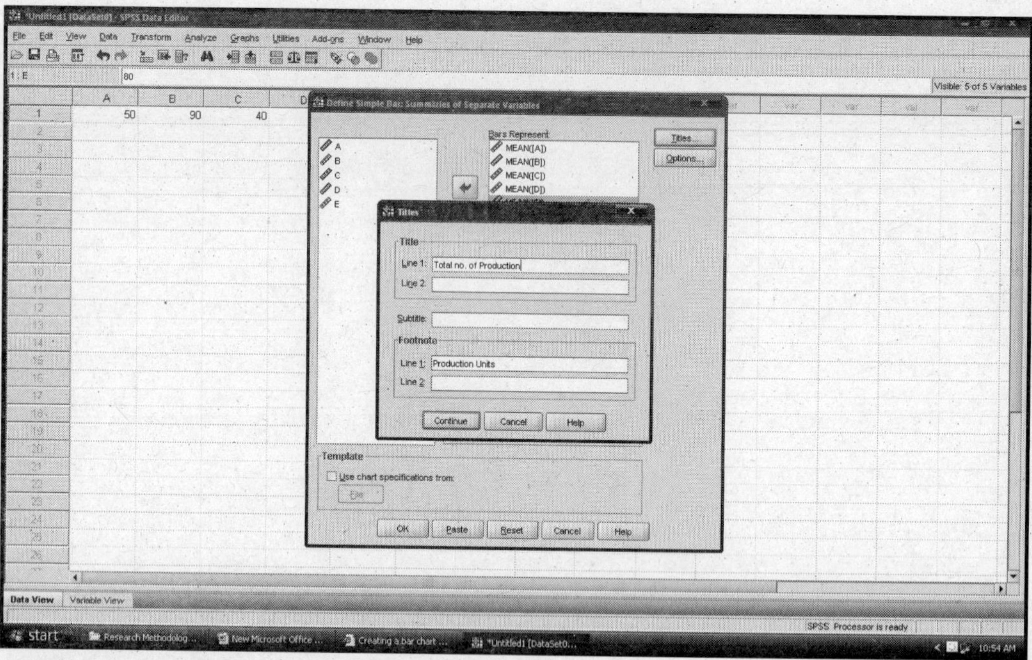

Step 5: Click OK, the table will appear in the Output Viewer.

Plate: 14.2.5

Bar Diagram

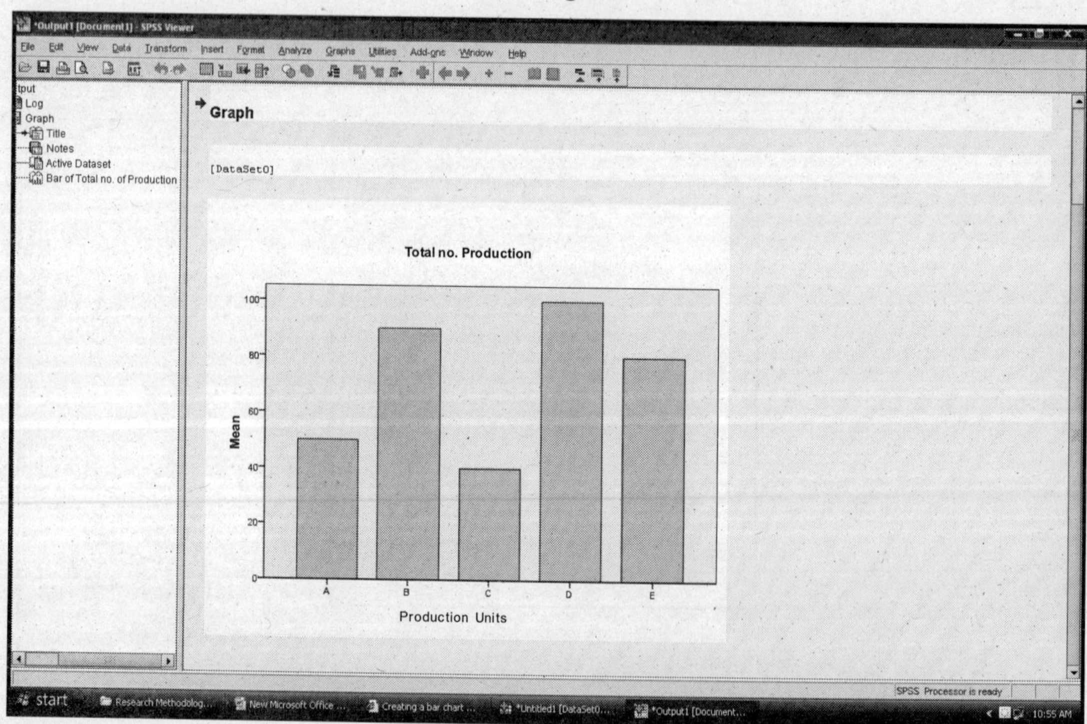

14.3 GENERATING A PIE CHART

How to Produce a Pie Chart?
SPSS Commands:

Step 1: Data entered into a data file in SPSS → Click the button in **Graphs options.** [See Plate 14.3.1]

Step 2: Select Pie Button → Click → Choose value of individual cases → Click the Define button. [See Plate 14.3.2]

Step 3: Select the Case number. [See Plate 14.3.2]

Step 4: Click OK; the table will appear in the Output Viewer. [See Plate 14.3.3]

Step 5: Double click above the pie chart and select the element. [See Plate 14.3.4]

Step 6: Click the Show data levels. [See Plate 14.3.5]

Example 14.3:

In a survey 43% people like the flower Rose and 18% people like Jasmine, 33% people like Sunflower and 6% of people like Tulips. For this survey information, draw a pie chart.

Solution:

Step 1: Data entered into a Data file in SPSS and click the button in Graphs Option.

Plate: 14.3.1

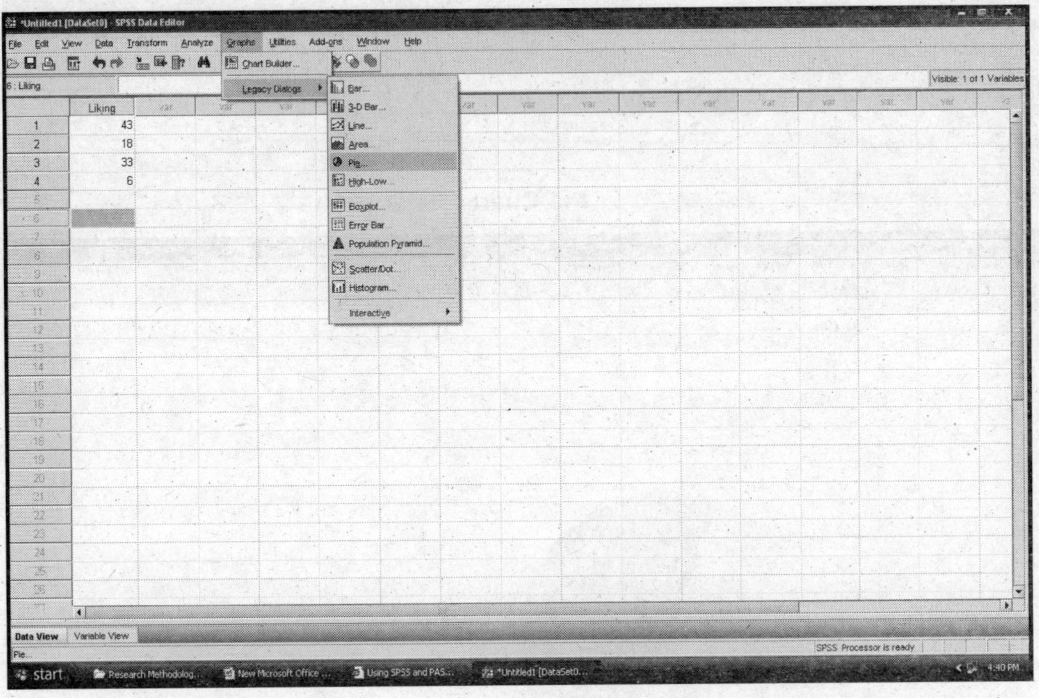

Step 2: Click the pie button, choose value of individual cases and click the Define button.

Plate: 14.3.2

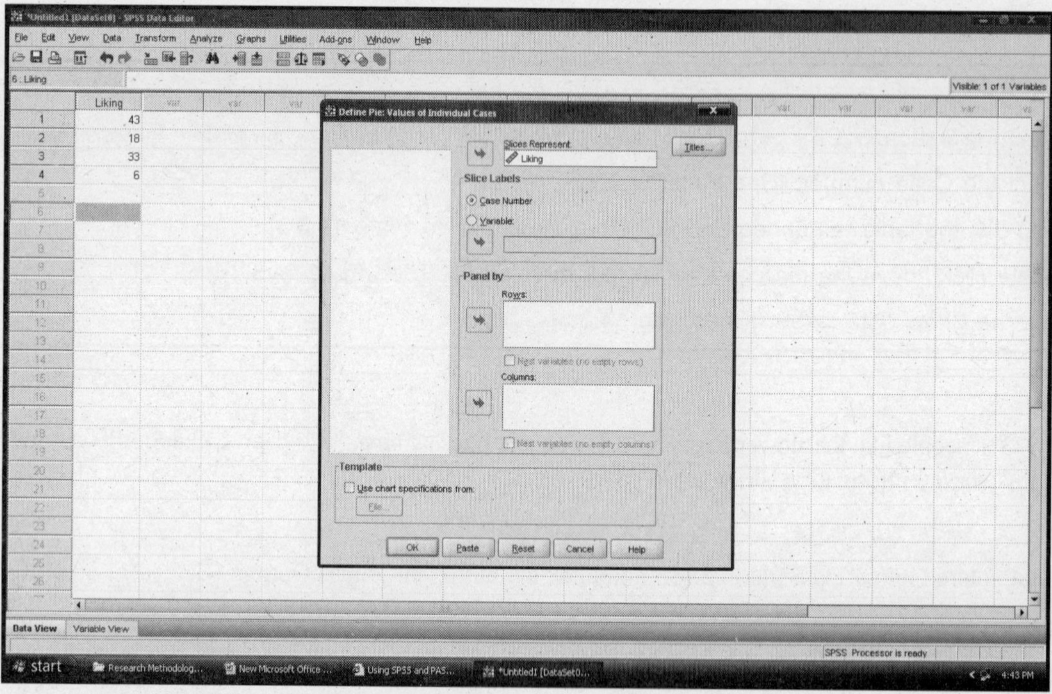

Step 3: Select the Case number and click OK.

Plate: 14.3.3

Pie Chart

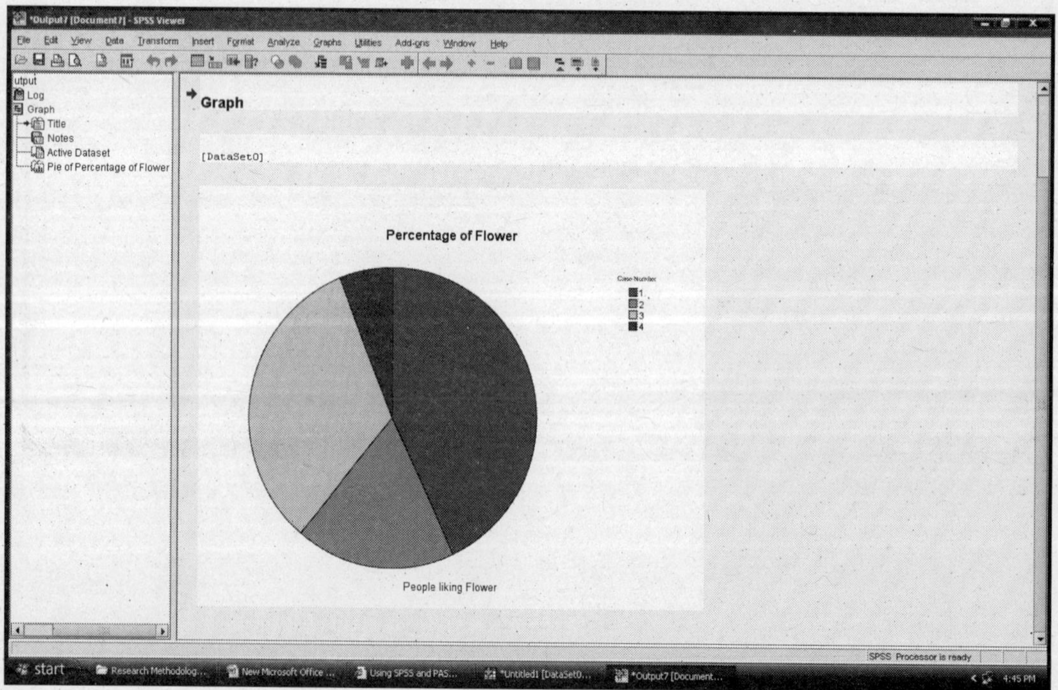

Step 4: Double click above the pie chart and select the element.

Plate: 14.3.4

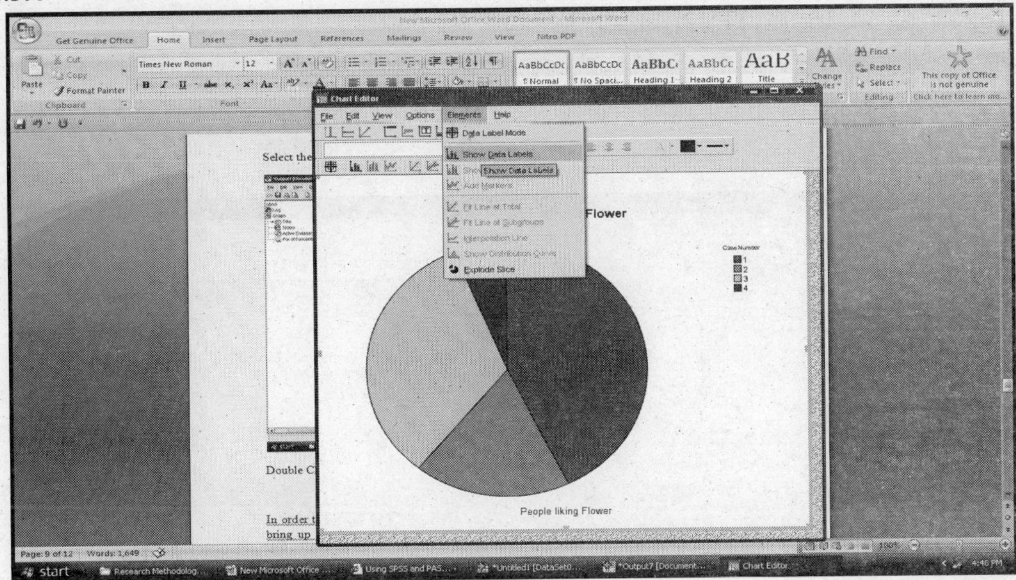

Step 5: Click the Show data levels.

Plate: 14.3.5

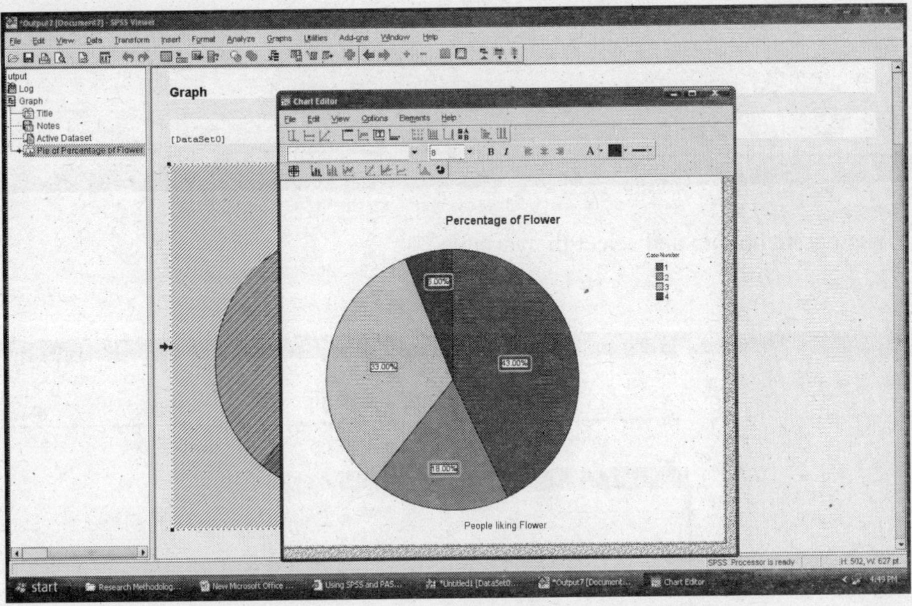

Your chart will be in colour, but, if you only have access to a monochrome printer, you can change your pie chart into patterns, which allows the slices to the clearer. This can be done through the Chart Editor.

14.4 GENERATING A HISTOGRAM

How to Produce a Histogram?
SPSS Commands:

Step 1:	Data entered into a data file in SPSS → Click the button in Graphs option. [See Plate 14.4.1]
Step 2:	Select the Button **Histogram** → Click. [See Plate 14.4.2]
Step 3:	Select variable(s) for analyze and clicking the right to send selected variable(s) into **Variable(s) List.** [See Plate 14.4.3]
Step 4:	Select the Display normal curve. [See Plate 14.4.3]
Step 5:	Click OK; the table will appear in the Output Viewer. [See Plate 14.4.3]

Example 14.4:

From the following data, draw the Histogram.

14, 13, 12, 14, 15, 12, 14, 16, 15, 14, 13, 14, 13, 15.

Solution

Step 1: Data entered into a Data file in SPSS and click the button in Graphs Option.

Plate: 14.4.1:

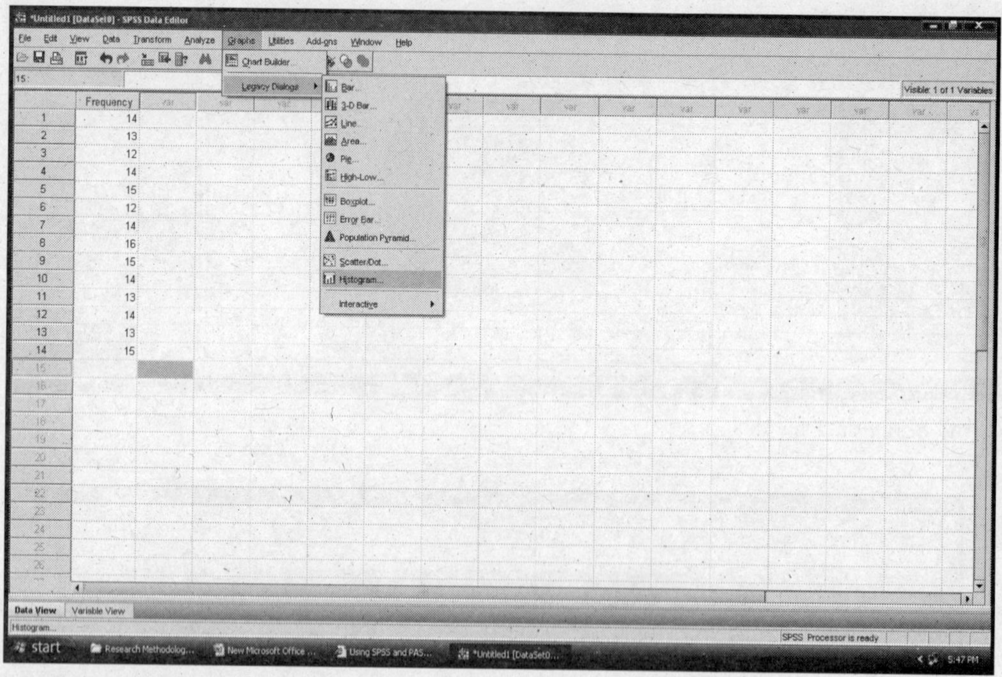

Step 2: Click the Histogram bottom and select the variable.

Plate: 14.4.2

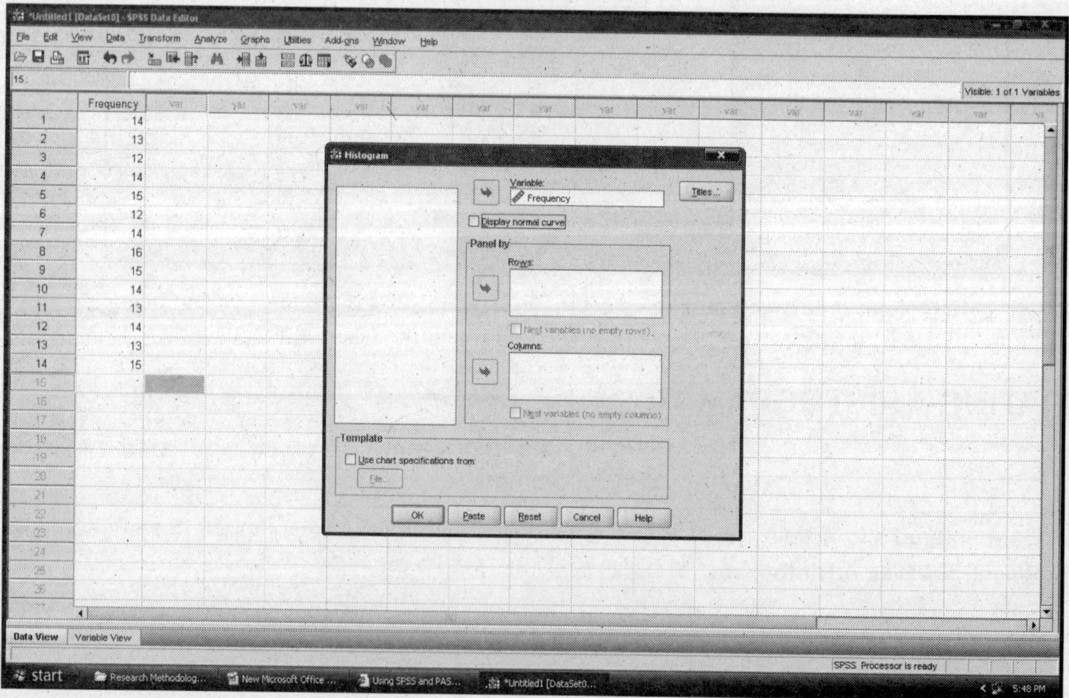

Step 3: Select the Display normal curve and click OK.

Plate: 14.4.3

Histogram

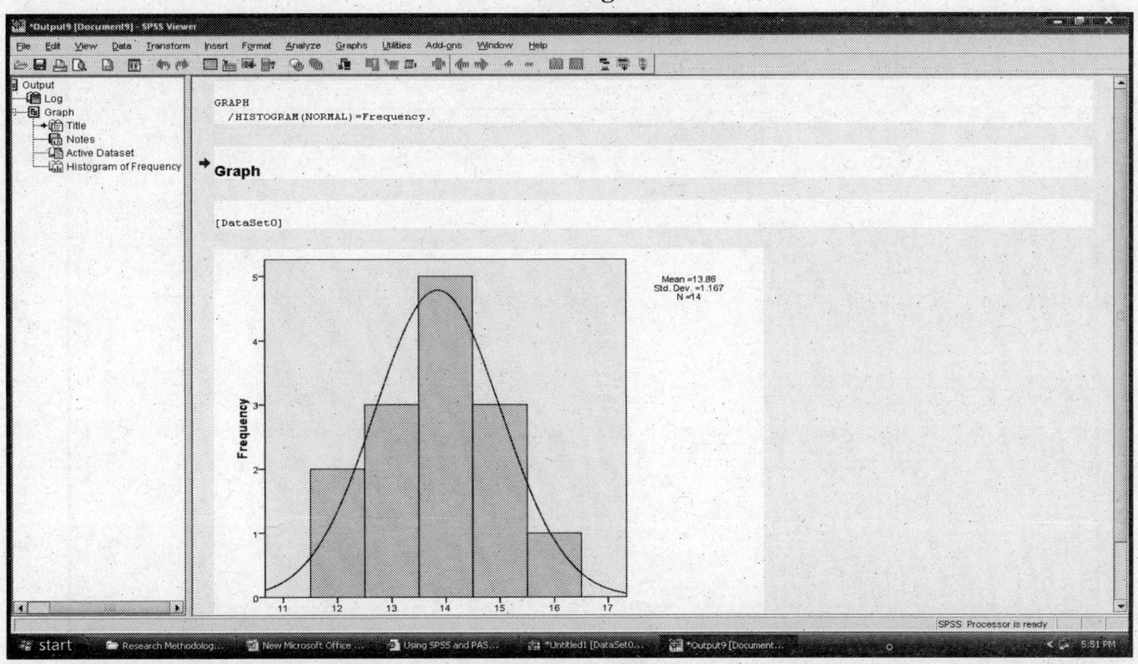

In order to generate a histogram for an interval/ratio variable like age, → Graphs → Histogram.... And then select the relevant variable and place it below Variable. This procedure will generate a histogram whose age bands are defined by the software. By double clicking on the diagram, the histogram can be edited using the Chart Editor. For example, colours can be changed or patterns inserted.

14.5 GENERATING ARITHMETIC MEAN, MEDIAN, STANDARD DEVIATION AND RANGE

How to Produce the Mean, Median, Standard Deviation and Range?
SPSS Commands:

Step 1: Data entered into a data file in SPSS → Click the button Analyze. [See Plate 14.5.1]

Step 2: Select Descriptive Statistics → Explore [opens the Explore dialog box]. [See Plate 14.5.2]

Step 3: Select variable(s) for analyze and clicking the right to send selected variable(s) into **Variable(s) List.** [See Plate 14.5.2]

Step 4: Click OK; the table will appear in the Output Viewer. [See Plate 14.5.3]

Example 14.5:

Ages of the 12 peoples are given. Calculate the arithmetic mean, median, standard deviation, and range from the following data:

Age	20	21	30	35	40	45	60	52	36	25	22	18

Solution:

Step 1: Data entered into a Data file in SPSS and click the button Analyze.

Plate: 14.5.1

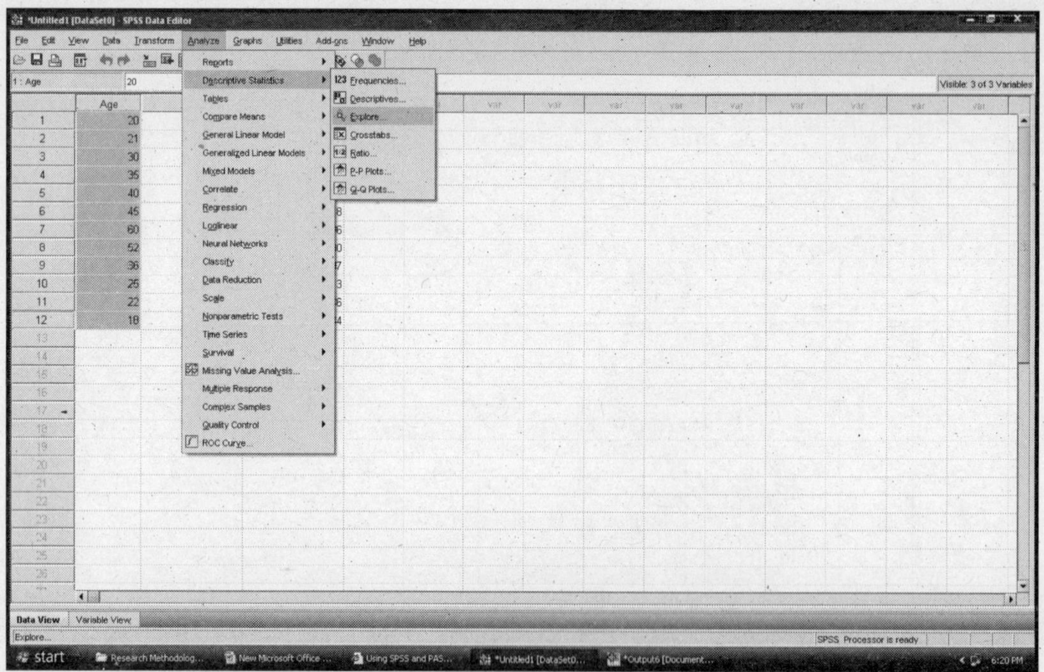

Step 2: Select Descriptive Statistics → Explore [opens the Explore dialog box].

Step 3: Select variable(s) for analyze and click here to send selected variable(s) into **Variable(s) List.**

Plate: 14.5.2

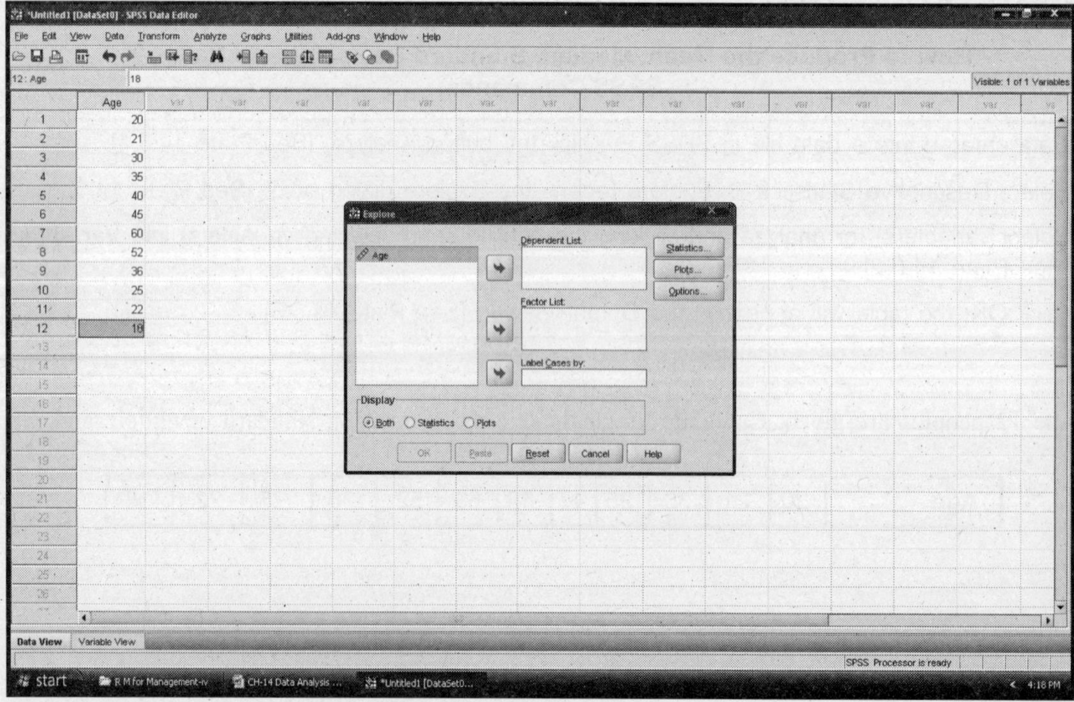

Step 4: Click OK.

Plate: 14.5.3

Contingency Table

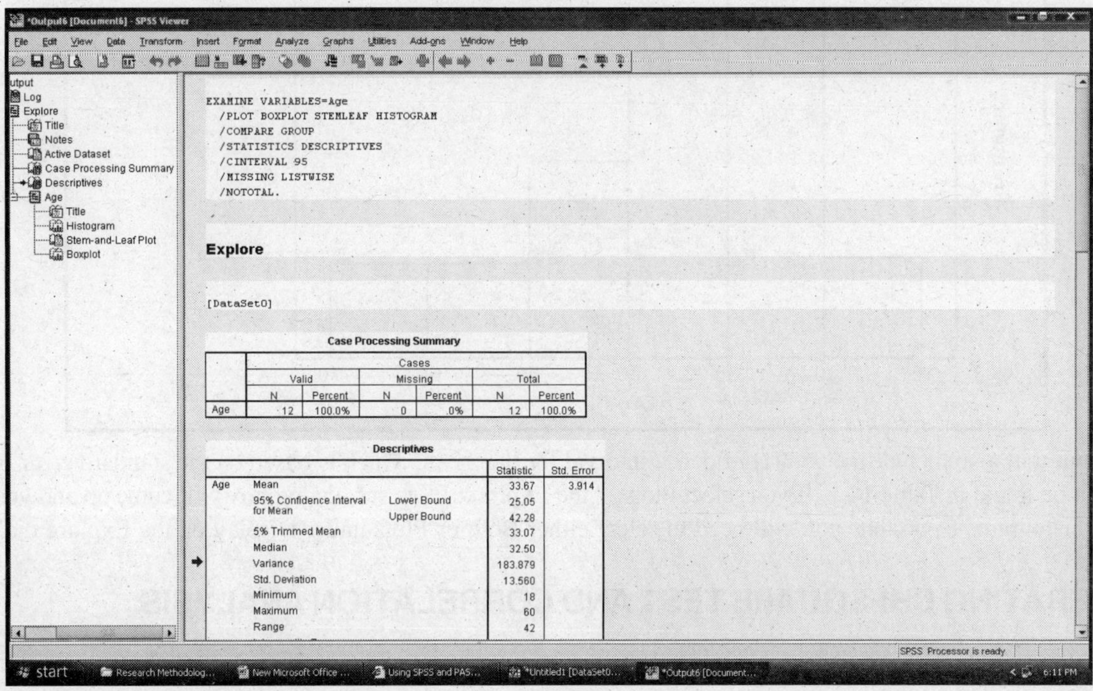

Detail Results from SPSS

Table 14.1: Case Processing Summary

	Cases					
	Valid		Missing		Total	
	N	Per cent	N	Per cent	N	Per cent
Age	12	100.0%	0	.0%	12	100.0%

Table 14.2: Descriptive Statistic

		Statistics	Std. Error
Age	Mean	33.67	3.914
	95% Confidence Interval for Mean		
	Lower Bound	25.05	
	Upper Bound	42.28	
	5% Trimmed Mean	33.07	
	Median	32.50	
	Variance	183.879	
	Standard Deviation	13.560	
	Minimum	18	
	Maximum	60	
	Range	42	
	Interquartile Range	22	
	Skewness	.675	.637
	Kurtosis	-.504	1.232

Histogram

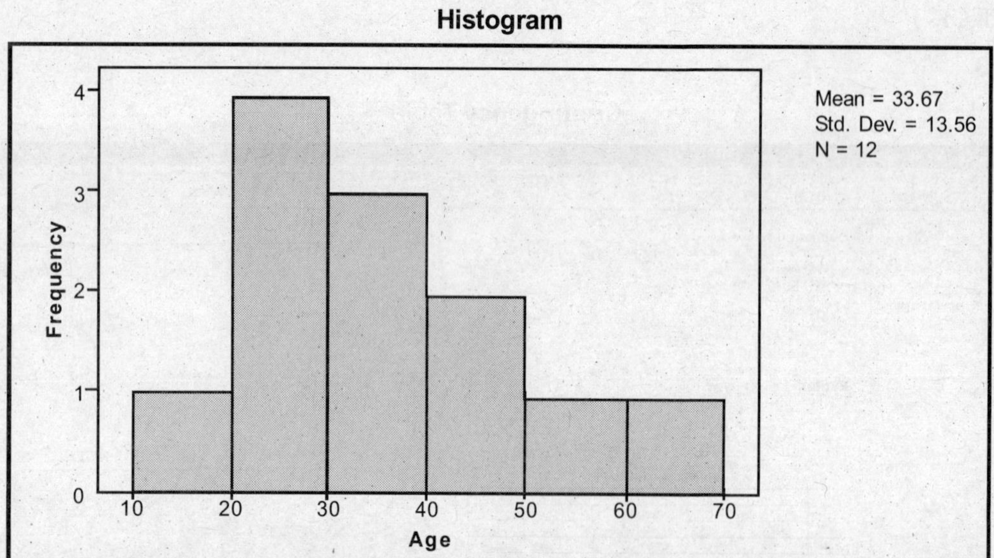

The output will also include the 95% confidence interval for the mean, which is based on the standard error of the mean. The output can be found in Table 14.1. If you select Plots….the Explore: Plots sub-dialog box will come up and you can select to generate a histogram. To do this, you will need to select either Both or Plots under Display on the Explore dialog box.

14.6 GENERATING CHI-SQUARE TEST AND CORRELATION ANALYSIS

In order to generate a contingency table, along with a Chi-square test and Correlation, the following procedure should be followed:

How to Generate a Contingency Table? (Chi-square and Correlation)
SPSS Commands:

Step 1: Data entered into a data file in SPSS → Click the button Analyze. [See Plate 14.6.1]

Step 2: Select Descriptive Statistics → crosstabs......[opens the Crosstabs dialog box]. [See Plate 14.6.2]

Step 3: Select variable(s) for analyze. [See Plate 14.6.3]

Step 4: Click Statistics button and Select Chi-square and Correlation and Continue [See Plate 14.6.4]

Step 5: Click OK; the table will appear in the Output Viewer. [See Plate 14.6.5]

Example 14.6:

Find the Chi-square and Correlation from the following data:

Age	20	21	30	35	40	45	60	52	36	25	22	18
Weight	45	48	50	65	60	62	58	65	68	62	58	48

Solution:

Step 1: Select Age and Weight in Variable Viewer and data entered into a Data file in SPSS and click the button Analyze.

Plate 14.6.1

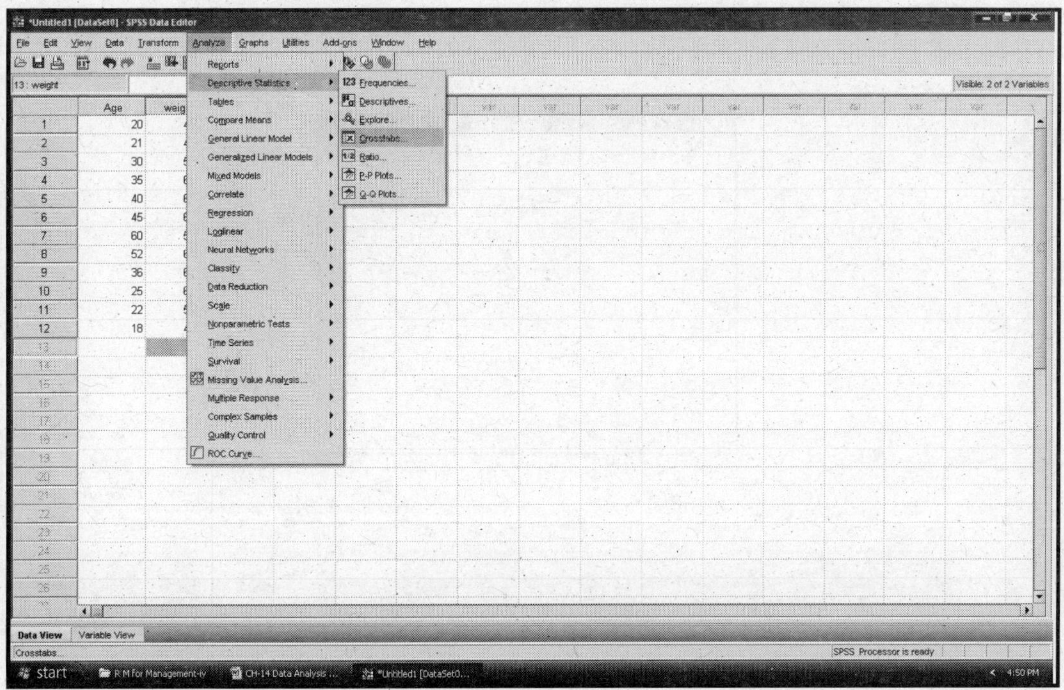

Step 2: Analyze → Descriptive Statistics → Crosstabs……[opens the Crosstabs dialog box]

Plate 14.6.2

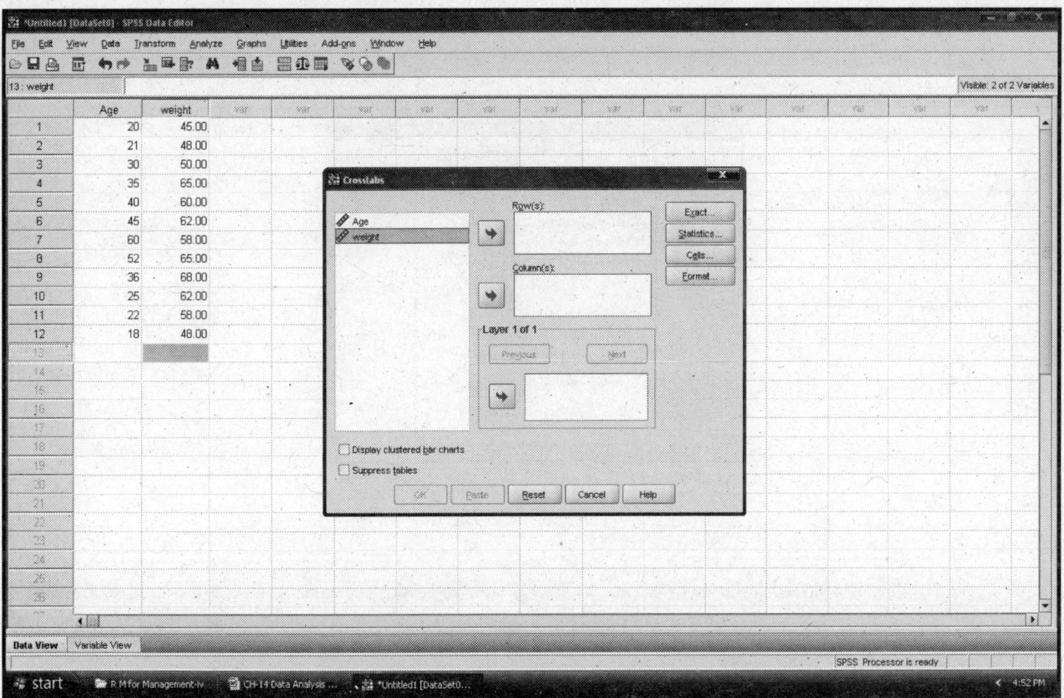

Step 3: Select the variables for analysis as Age for Row and Weight for Column.

Plate: 14.6.3

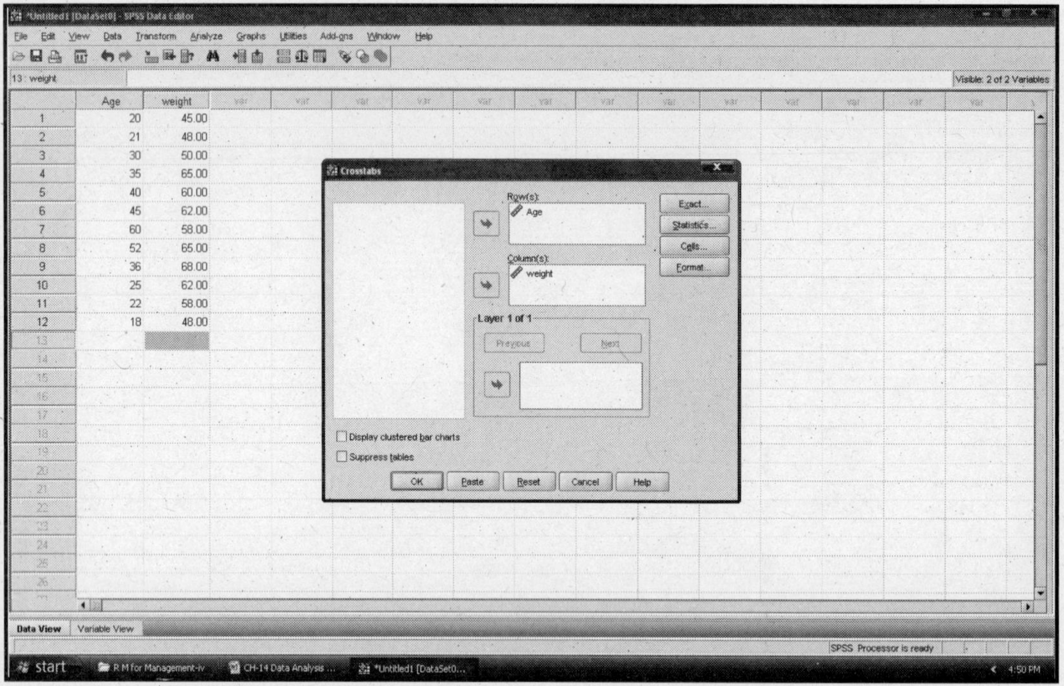

Step 4: Click Statistics button and select Chi-square and Correlation and continue.

Plate: 14.6.4

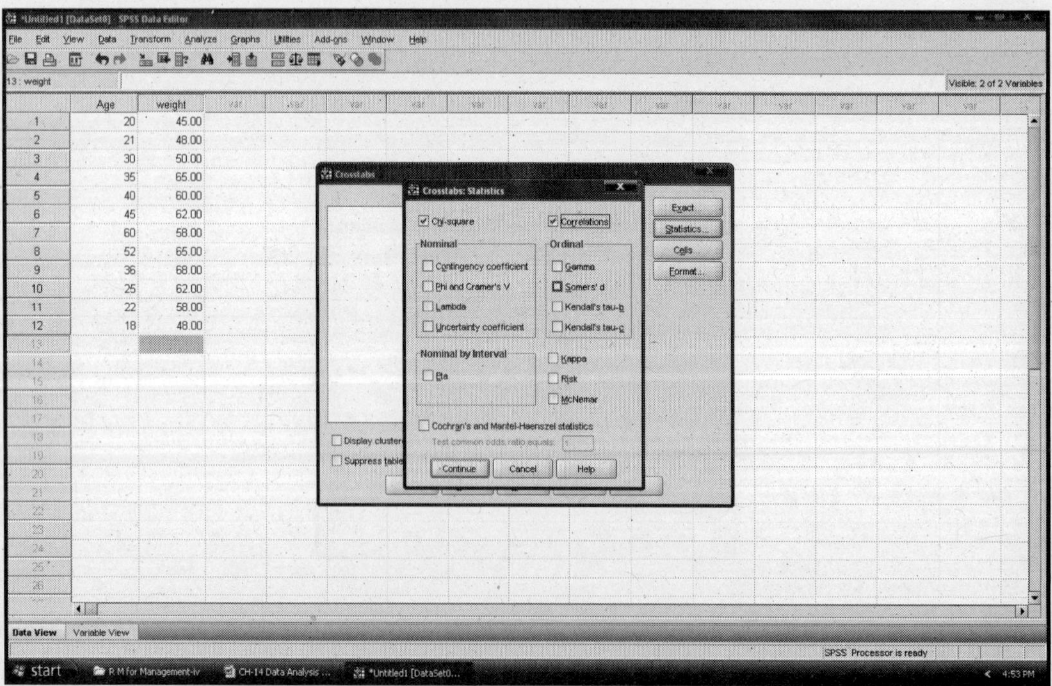

Step 5: Click OK.

Plate: 14.6.5

Contingency Table

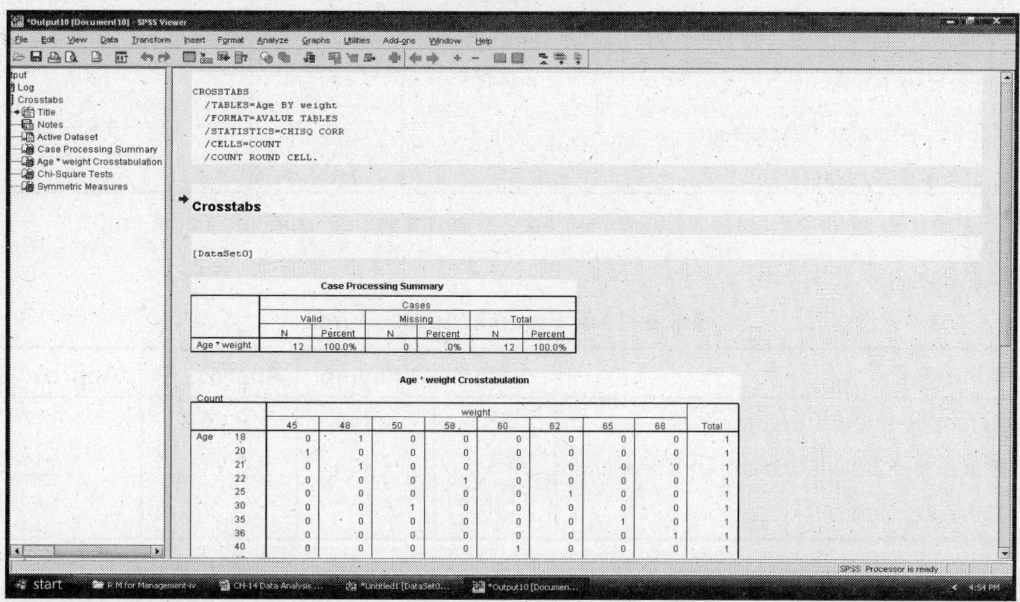

Detail Results from SPSS:

Table 14.3: Case Processing Summary

	Cases					
	Valid		Missing		Total	
	N	Per cent	N	Per cent	N	Per cent
Age * Weight	12	100.0%	0	.0%	12	100.0%

Cross Tabulation

Table 14.4: Age * Weight Cross Tabulation

Count										
		Weight								Total
		45	48	50	58	60	62	65	68	
Age	18	0	1	0	0	0	0	0	0	1
	20	1	0	0	0	0	0	0	0	1
	21	0	1	0	0	0	0	0	0	1
	22	0	0	0	1	0	0	0	0	1
	25	0	0	0	0	0	1	0	0	1
	30	0	0	1	0	0	0	0	0	1
	35	0	0	0	0	0	0	1	0	1
	36	0	0	0	0	0	0	0	1	1
	40	0	0	0	0	1	0	0	0	1
	45	0	0	0	0	0	1	0	0	1
	52	0	0	0	0	0	0	1	0	1
	60	0	0	0	1	0	0	0	0	1
Total		1	2	1	2	1	2	2	1	12

Chi-square

Table 14.5: Chi-square Tests

	Value	df	Asymp. Sig. (2-sided)
Pearson Chi-square	84.000[a]	77	.274
Likelihood Ratio	48.547	77	.995
Linear-by-Linear Association	3.734	1	.053
N of Valid Cases	12		

a. 96 cells (100.0%) have expected count less than 5. The minimum expected count is .08.

Symmetric Measures

Table 14.6: Symmetric Measures

Std. Error[a]	Value	Asymp.	Approx. T[b]	Approx. Sig.
Interval by Interval Pearson's R	583	.148	2.267	.047[c]
Ordinal by Ordinal Spearman Correlation	651	.203	2.715	.022[c]
N of Valid Cases	12			

(a) Not assuming the null hypothesis.

(b) Using the asymptotic standard error assuming the null hypothesis.

(c) Based on normal approximation.

14.7 GENERATING REGRESSION ANALYSIS

SPSS Commands:

Step 1: Data entered into a data file in SPSS → Click the button Analyze.

Step 2: Click on Regression and followed by linear.

Step 3: Select a dependent variable by clicking on the arrow leading to the dependent box after highlighting the appropriate variable from the list of variables on the left side.

Step 4: Select independent variables to be included in the regression model in the same way, transferring them from left side to the right side box by clicking on the arrow leading to the box called independent variables.

Step 5: Select the METHOD in the same dialog box.

Step 6: Select OPTIONS, if need additional output options.

Step 7: Click OK from the main dialogue box to get the regression output.

Example 14.7:

Consider the data on the quantity demand and the price of a commodity over a twelve-year period as in the given below:

Year	2000	2001	2002	2003	2004	2005	2006	2007	2008	2009	2010	2011
Demand	80.0	65.0	70.0	75.0	60.0	65.0	90.0	102.0	108.0	50.0	55.0	75.0
Price	8.0	6.0	7.0	6.0	8.0	7.0	7.0	5.0	4.0	3.0	9.0	6.0

(a) Find out the correlation coefficient between the quantity demand and price and interpret.

(b) Compute coefficient of determination (r^2) and interpret.

(c) Estimate the linear regression equation of demand on price and interpret.

Solution:

Data for SPSS Format:

Year	Demand	Price
2000	80.0	8.0
2001	65.0	6.0
2002	70.0	7.0
2003	75.0	6.0
2004	60.0	8.0
2005	65.0	7.0
2006	90.0	7.0
2007	102.0	5.0
2008	108.0	4.0
2009	50.0	3.0
2010	55.0	9.0
2011	75.0	6.0

Descriptive Statistics

Table 14.7: Descriptive Statistics

	Mean	Std. Deviation	N
Demand	74.5833	17.94161	12
Price	6.3333	1.72328	12

Correlation Matrix

Table 14.8: Correlations

		Demand	Price
Pearson Correlation	Demand	1.000	-.283
	Price	-.283	1.000
Sig. (1-tailed)	Demand	.	.186
	Price	.186	.
N	Demand	12	12
	Price	12	12

Model Summary

Table 14.9: Model Summary

Model	R	R Square	Adjusted R Square	Std. Error of the Estimate
1	.283[a]	.080	-.012	18.04669

a. Predictors: (Constant), Price

ANOVA

Table 14.10: ANOVA[b]

	Model	Sum of Squares	d.f.	Mean Square	F	Sig.
1	Regression	284.085	1	284.085	.872	.372[a]
	Residual	3256.832	10	325.683		
	Total	3540.917	11			

a. Predictors: (Constant), Price

b. Dependent Variable: Demand

Table 14.11: Coefficient

Model		Unstandardized Coefficients		Standardized Coefficients	t	Sig.
		B	Std. Error	Beta		
1	(Constant)	93.260	20.665		4.513	.001
	Price	-2.949	3.158	–.283	–.934	.372

a. Dependent Variable: Demand

(a) From Table 14.8, the result indicates that the correlation between demand and price is 283, which is same as when the problem is solved out manually. The p-value for the correlation coefficient is 186 (1-tailed) and assume level of significance.

(b) From Table 14.9, the coefficient of determination (r^2) is 0.080. This means that 8% of the variations in the quantity demand are explained by price.

(c) From Table 14.11, the estimated regression equation is:

Demand = 93.26 – –2.949 Price

The intercept and the slope term are 93.26 and –2.949.

14.8 GENERATING ANALYSIS OF VARIANCE (ANOVA) [ONE-WAY]

SPSS Commands

Step 1: Data entered into a data file in SPSS → Click the button Analyze.

Step 2: Click on Compare means and then One-way ANOVA.

Step 3: Select the appropriate variable as the dependent variable and take it to the right hand side box called DEPENDENT list, then select another appropriate variable, i.e., independent variable appears from the list of the variables on the left hand side of the box and click the arrow to the factor box.

Step 4: Then click OPTION followed by DESCRIPTIVES.

Step 5: Click CONTINUE to return to the main dialog box.

Step 6: Click OK to get output for One-way ANOVA.

Example 14.8:

The following data represents the numbers of units produced by three operators during three different sifts:

Sifts	Operators		
	A	B	C
I	6	5	5
II	7	5	4
III	3	3	3
IV	8	7	4

Using 5% level of significance, perform one-way analysis of variance and interpret the result.

Solution:

Data for SPSS format:

Sl. No.	Operators	Sifts
1	6	1
2	5	1
3	5	1

4	7	2
5	5	2
6	4	2
7	3	3
8	3	3
9	3	3
10	8	4
11	7	4
12	4	4

Results of One-way ANOVA

Table 14.12: ANOVA

Operator					
	Sum of Squares	**df**	**Mean Square**	**F**	**Sig.**
Between Groups	18.000	3	6.000	3.429	.073
Within Groups	14.000	8	1.750		
Total	32.000	11			

Interpretation: It could be noted that the results in the above table, the p-value for the problem is 0.073 which is less than the 0.05, the null hypothesis is rejected. We conclude that there is no significance in the number of units produced by three operators during three different sifts.

14.9 GENERATING ANALYSIS OF VARIANCE (ANOVA) [TWO-WAY]

SPSS Commands

Step 1: Data entered into a data file in SPSS → Click the button Analyze.

Step 2: Click on GENERAL LINEAR MODEL followed by UNIVARIATE.

Step 3: Take the appropriate variable as the dependent variable box, and then select another appropriate two variables as FIXED FACTORS. The independent variable is the first factor and the block variable is the second factor.

Step 4: Click MODEL, followed by CUSTOM.

Step 5: Take both the factors one by one to the right hand side box called MODEL.

Step 6: Click CONTIONUE to return to the main dialog box.

Step 7: Click OK to get the output for Two-way ANOVA.

Example 14.9:

The following table presents the number of the defective pieces produced by three workmen operating in turn on three different machines:

Workmen	**Machines**		
	A	**B**	**C**
1	27	34	23
2	29	32	25
3	22	30	22

Conduct a Two-way ANOVA to test at 5% level of significance, whether:

(a) The difference among the means obtained for the three workmen can be attributed to chance.

(b) The difference among the means obtained for the three machines can be attributed to chance.

Solution:

Data for SPSS Format:

X	Machine	Workmen
27	1	1
29	1	2
22	1	3
34	2	1
32	2	2
30	2	3
23	3	1
25	3	2
22	3	3

X = No. of defective pieces

Table 14.13: Between Subject Factors

		N
Machine	1	3
	2	3
	3	3
Workmen	1	3
	2	3
	3	3

Table 14.14: Results for Two-way ANOVA

Tests of Between Subjects Effects

Dependent Variable: X

Source	Type III Sum of Squares	df	Mean Square	F	Sig.
Corrected Model	145.778[a]	4	36.444	13.120	.014
Intercept	6615.111	1	6615.111	2.381E3	.000
Machine	118.222	2	59.111	21.280	.007
Workmen	27.556	2	13.778	4.960	.083
Error	11.111	4	2.778		
Total	6772.000	9			
Corrected Total	156.889	8			

a. R Squared = .929 (Adjusted R Squared = .858)

From the above table, the p-values corresponding to the hypothesis for the machines and workmen are 0.007 and 0.083 respectively. The assumed level of significance is 5%.

Interpretation:

(a) As the p-value corresponding to the hypothesis for the machines is less than the level of significance, the null hypothesis in such cases is rejected. That means the average number of defects for various machines is different.

(b) As the p-value corresponding to the hypothesis for the workmen is more than the level of significance, the null hypothesis in such cases is accepted. We conclude that the average number of defectives items produced by the three workmen does not vary significantly.

14.10 SPSS COMMANDS FOR OTHER TEST

14.10.1. SPSS Command for One Sample t-Test

Step 1: Data entered into a data file in **SPSS.**

Step 2: Click on **Analysis** at the SPSS menu bar.

Step 3: Click on **Compare Means** followed by **One sample t-test**.

Step 4: Take the concerned variable from left to the right hand side box.

Step 5: Specify the test value which is the hypothesized value.

14.10.2. SPSS Command for Independent Sample t-Test

Step 1: Data entered into a data file in **SPSS.**

Step 2: Click on **Analysis** at the SPSS menu bar.

Step 3: Click on **Compare Means** followed by **Independent sample t-test**.

Step 4: Take the concerned variable from left to the right hand side box.

Step 5: Select the **Grouping variable** in the same way transfer it to the right side box.

Step 6: Define the codes for the two groups by clicking on **Define Groups**, just below the **Grouping Variable** and typing in the code.

Step 7: Click OK to get the output for independent sample t-test.

14.10.3. SPSS Command for Paired Sample t-Test

Step 1: Data entered into a data file in **SPSS.**

Step 2: Click on **Analysis** at the SPSS menu bar.

Step 3: Click on **Compare Means** followed by **Paired sample t-test**.

Step 4: Select two variables from left to the right hand side box.

Step 5: Click OK to get the output for paired sample t-test.

14.10.4. SPSS Commands for RUN Test

Step 1: Data entered into a data file in **SPSS.**

Step 2: Click on **Analysis** at the SPSS menu bar.

Step 3: Click on **Non-parametric Statistics** followed by **Runs**.

Step 4: Take the concerned variable to the right hand side box.

Step 5: Tick on **Median** or **Mean** depending upon which one you want it as your cut-off value.

14.10.5. SPSS Commands for Mann-Whitney U Test

Step 1: Data entered into a data file in **SPSS.**

Step 2: Click on **Analysis** at the SPSS menu bar.

Step 3: Click on **Non-parametric Statistics** followed by **Two Independent Samples**.

Step 4: Take the test variable to the right hand side box and coded grouping variables followed by define groups.

Step 5: Click **Mann-Whitney U Test.**

Step 6: Click OK to get the output for MANN-WHITNEY U TEST.

14.10.6. SPSS Commands for the Wilcoxon Matched Pair Rank Sum Test

Step 1: Data entered into a data file in **SPSS.**

Step 2: Click on **Analysis** at the SPSS menu bar.

Step 3: Click on **Non-parametric Statistics** followed by **Two Related Samples**.

Step 4: Take two variables simultaneously in the right hand side box.

Step 5: Click **Wilcoxon Test.**

Step 6: Click OK to get the output for WILCOXON MATCHED PAIR RANK SUM TEST.

14.10.7. SPSS Commands for the Kruskal-Wallis Test

Step 1: Data entered into a data file in **SPSS.**

Step 2: Click on **Analysis** at the SPSS menu bar.

Step 3: Click on **Non-parametric Statistics** followed by **K Independent Samples**.

Step 4: Take two variables simultaneously in the right hand side box and below that click the box of **Define Groups** and give **minimum and maximum** coded value.

Step 5: Click **KruskaL-Wallis Test**.

Step 6: Click OK to get the output for KRUSKAL-WALLIS TEST.

14.10.8. SPSS Commands for Factor Analysis

Step 1: Data entered into a data file in **SPSS.**

Step 2: Click on **Analysis** at the SPSS menu bar.

Step 3: Click on **Data Reduction** followed by FACTOR.

Step 4: Select all the variables required for the factor analysis from the dialog box by clicking right arrow to transfer them from the variable list.

Step 5: Click on **Extraction** in the lower part of the dialog box. (1) Select **"Principal Component"** as the method. (2) Select **"Unrotated Factor Solution"** from **Display**. (3) Select **"Eigen values over 1"** from **Extract**. (4) Choose **"Correlation Matrix"** from **Analyse**. (5) Click Continue.

Step 6: Click on **Rotation** in the main dialog box. (1) Select **Varimax** from the options under **Method**. (2) Click Continue.

Step 7: Click on **Descriptive** in the main dialog box. (1) Select **KMO and Bartlett's** Test. (2) Click Continue.

Step 8: Click on **Scores** and Click on **Save as Variable**. (1) Select Method as **Regression**. (2) Click on **Display Factor Score Coefficient**.

Step 9: Click OK to get the FACTOR ANALYSIS output.

14.10.9. SPSS Commands for Cluster Analysis

Two-step Cluster Analysis

Step 1: Data entered into a data file in **SPSS.**

Step 2: Click on **Analysis** at the SPSS menu bar.

Step 3: Click on **Classify** followed by **Two-step Cluster**.

Step 4: Select all the variables required for the cluster analysis from the dialog box by clicking right arrow to transfer them from the variable list into the Continuous and Categorical Variable Box.

Step 5: Select **Euclidian** for the Distance Measures and Select **Long Likelihood** for the Categorical and Mix.

Step 6:	Select **Akaike's Information Criterion** (AIC) for Clustering Creation.
Step 7:	Select **Determine Automatically** (Default 15) for Number of Cluster.
Step 8:	Click on **Plots** and Select **Cluster Pie-Chart**.
Step 9:	Click on **Output** and Select **Descriptive** by Cluster and Cluster Frequencies.
Step 10:	Click OK to get the CLUSTER ANALYSIS output.

K-Means Cluster Analysis

Step 1:	Data entered into a data file in **SPSS.**
Step 2:	Click on **Analysis** at the SPSS menu bar.
Step 3:	Click on **Classify** followed by **K-Means Cluster**.
Step 4:	Select all the variables required for the cluster analysis from the dialog box by clicking right arrow to transfer them from the variable list and select the number of Cluster.
Step 5:	Select **Options** in the Display Box and in the top of window, in the Statistics Box. Select **Initial Cluster Centers, ANOVA,** and **Cluster Information** in each cases. Click Continue.
Step 6:	Go to **Save** and Click on **Save Cluster Membership**.
Step 9:	Click OK to get the CLUSTER ANALYSIS output.

Hierarchical Cluster Analysis

Step 1:	Data entered into a data file in **SPSS.**
Step 2:	Click on **Analysis** at the SPSS menu bar.
Step 3:	Click on **Classify** followed by Hierarchical Cluster.
Step 4:	Select all the variables required for the cluster analysis from the dialog box by clicking right arrow to transfer them from the variable list.
Step 5:	Select **Cases, Statistics** and **Plots** in the Display Box.
Step 6:	Click on **Method** in the main dialog box. (1) Select **"Between Group Linkages"**. (2) In the Measure Box check the scale as **"Interval"** or **"Count"** or **"Binary"**. (3) Once the measure is selected, the option for calculating distance for the measure would get activated. (4) For Interval Data, select **Squared Euclidian Distance**. Click Continue. (5) For Binary Data select **Simple Matching Coefficient**. Click Continue. (6) For Count Data, select **Chi-Square**, Click Continue.
Step 7:	Click on **Statistics** in the main dialog box. Select **Agglomeration Schedule**. Click Continue.
Step 8:	Click on **Plots** in the main dialog box. Select **Dendrogram.** Select **"All Cluster"** in ICICLE box and Select **"Vertical"** in Orientation box. Click Continue.
Step 9:	Click OK to get the CLUSTER ANALYSIS output.

14.10.10 SPSS Commands for Discriminant Analysis

Step 1:	Data entered into a data file in **SPSS.**
Step 2:	Click on **Analysis** at the SPSS menu bar.
Step 3:	Click on **Classify** followed by **Discriminant.**
Step 4:	Select all the variables required for the Discriminant analysis from the dialog box by clicking right arrow to transfer them from the Grouping variable box list.
Step 5:	Define the range of values of the grouping variable by clicking on **Define Range** just below the grouping variable Box. Fill the minimum and maximum values (0 and 1). Then Click Continue.

Step 6: Select all the Independent variables for discriminant analysis from the variable list by clicking on the arrow which transfer them to the Independent box on the right.

Step 7: Just below the Independent box select **"Enter independent together"** if you want all the selected independent variables (that are in the box) in the discriminant model or select **"Use Stepwise Method"**.

Step 8: Click on **Statistics** in the main dialog box. Select **Means** and **Univariate ANOVAs** under **Descriptive.** Select **"Unstandardized"** under function **Coefficient** and Select **Within Group Correlation** under **Matrix.** Click Continue.

Step 9: Click on **Classify** on the lower part of the main dialog box. Select **Summary Table** and **Leave-one-out Classification** under the heading **Display**. This gives Classification table or Confusion Matrix. Click Continue.

Step 10: Click on **Save** and Select **Predicted Group Membership** and **Discriminant Scores.**

Step 11: Click OK to get the DISCRIMINANT ANALYSIS output.

14.11 SUMMARY

SPSS is a comprehensive and flexible statistical analysis and data management system. SPSS can take data from almost any type of file and use them to generate tabulated reports, charts, and plots of distributions and trends, descriptive statistics, and conduct complex statistical analyses. SPSS is available from several platforms; Windows, Macintosh, and the UNIX systems. Data analysis of SPSS represents how to generate frequency table, graphs and various statistical techniques like mean median, mode, correlation, regression, level of significance etc.

14.12 CONCEPTUAL QUESTIONS

1. Draw the bar chart from the following data.

Section	A	B	C	D	E	F	G	H
No. of Students	50	60	70	40	60	50	100	80

2. In a survey, 45% people like Rose and 15% people like Jasmine and 35% people like Lotus, 35% of people like Tulips. For this survey information, draw a pie chart.
3. From the following data, draw the Histogram.

   24, 23, 22, 24, 25, 31, 22, 29, 19, 24, 26, 25, 24, 23, 24, 23, 25, 28, 30.
4. Ages of the 15 peoples are given. Calculate the arithmetic mean, median, standard deviation, and range from the following data:

Age	30	28	40	45	50	45	60	52	36	25	42	27	38	32	33

5. Find the Chi-square and Correlation from the following data:

Age	40	45	50	45	60	52	36	25	42	27	38	32
Weight	65	68	50	66	50	62	58	65	68	62	68	55

6. The quantity demanded and the price of a commodity over a nine-year period are given below:

Year	2003	2004	2005	2006	2007	2008	2009	2010	2011
Demand	60	55	70	65	50	55	80	92	98
Price	6	7	8	6	8	7	6	5	6

   (a) Find out the correlation coefficient between the quantity demanded and price and interpret.

   (b) Compute coefficient of determination (r^2) and interpret.

   (c) Estimate the linear regression equation of demand on price and interpret.

7. The numbers of units produced by three operators during three different shifts are given below:

Shifts	Operators		
	A	B	C
I	3	3	5
II	7	5	3
III	4	6	5
IV	7	8	4

Using 5% level of significance, perform one-way and two-way analysis of variance and interpret the result.

CHAPTER 15

REPORT WRITING

Chapter Outline

Learning Objectives

- *Discuss the subject matter of various types of reports.*
- *Prepare a proposal for any type of report.*
- *Review and edit the draft of a report.*
- *Distinguish between various parts of a report.*
- *Explain the different parts of a report.*
- *Instruct the typist as to how he/she should go about writing the report.*
- *Distinguish between various components of presentation skills.*
- *Suggestion to a presenter about the care she has to take while presenting a report.*

15.1 MEANING OF A REPORT

A report is a clearly structured document that presents information about an investigation that one has undertaken. It is a self-explanatory statement of facts relating to a specific subject and serves the purpose of providing information for decision-making and follow-up actions. It is a systematic presentation of ascertained facts about a specific event/subject. Report is a summary of findings and recommendations about a particular matter/problem. Report is for the guidance of higher authorities including company executives and directors. Reports facilitate timely decisions and follow-up measures.

15.2 TYPES OF REPORTS

After thorough study, collection of all relevant facts and information and proper scrutiny and analysis of a problem relating to past or present, submission of the conclusions supported by statements and other relevant data etc. is called a report, which offers suggestions for solution of the problem studied.

The following are the two bases of classifying the reports:

1. According to function
   - Analytical Report
   - Informational Report
   - Research reports
2. According to formality:
   - Statutory report
   - Non-statutory or voluntary report
   - Routine Report
   - Special Report
   - Technical Report
   - Popular Report

15.2.1 Analytical Reports

These reports contain facts along with analytical explanations offered by the reporter himself or may be asked for by the one who is seeking the report. Such reports contain the narration of facts, collected data and information, classified and tabulated data and also explanatory note followed by the conclusions arrived at or interpretations. A company chairman may ask for a report on falling trends in sale in a particular area. He will in this case be naturally interested in knowing all the details including that of opinion of any of the investigator.

15.2.2 Informational Reports

These reports present facts about certain given activity in detail without any note or suggestions. Whatever is gathered is reported without giving anything by way of either explanation or any suggestion. A vice-chancellor asking about the number of candidates appearing at a particular examination naturally seeks only information of the fact (candidates taking up the examination) of course without any comment. Generally, such reports are of routine nature. Sometimes they may fall under statutory routine category. A company registrar asking for allotment return within the stipulate period is nothing but informational routine, falling under statutory but routine report.

15.2.3 Research Reports

These reports are based on some research work conducted by either an individual or a group of individuals on a given problem. Indian Oil Company might have asked its research division to find some substitute for petrol, and if such a study is conducted then a report shall be submitted by the research division detailing its findings and then offering their own suggestions, including the conclusions at which the division has arrived at as to whether such a substitute is there and if it is there can the same be put to use with advantage and effectiveness. All details shall naturally be asked and has to be given. In fact, such a report is the result of a research.

15.2.4 Statutory Reports

These reports are to be presented according to the requirements of a particular law or a rule or a custom that now has become a rule. The auditor reports to company registrar has to be submitted as per the requirements of country legal requirement. A return on compensation paid to factory workers during a period by a factory has to be submitted to competent authorities periodically. These reports are generally prepared in the prescribed form as the rules have prescribed.

15.2.5 Non-statutory Reports

These reports are not in the nature of legal requirements or rules. These reports are required to be prepared and submitted: (i) for the administrative and other conveniences, (ii) for taking decisions in a matter, (iii) for policy formulations, (iv) for projecting the future or (v) anything alike so that efficient and smooth functioning may be assured and proper and necessary decision may be taken.

15.2.6 Routine Reports

These reports are required to be prepared and submitted periodically on matters required by the organization so as to help the management of the organization to take decisions in the matters relating to day-to-day affairs. The main objectives of routine reports are to let the management know as to what is happening in the organization, what is its progress where the deviation lies, what measures have been taken in solving the problems and what to do so that the organization may run smoothly and efficiently. Routine reports are generally brief. They only give the facts. No comments or explanations are usually offered in such reports. Generally, forms are prescribed for preparation and submission of such reports.

15.2.7 Special Reports

Such a type of report is specially required to be prepared and submitted on matters of special nature. Due to an accident, a death of the foreman has occurred in a factory. The factory manager may ask for a detail report from the head foreman. Such a report is classified as special reports. These reports contain not only facts and details but they may contain suggestions, comments and explanations as well.

15.2.8 Technical Reports

Elements of a Technical Report

1. Title
2. Abstract (Executive Summary)
3. Introduction
4. Theory and Analysis
5. Experimental Procedures/Methodology
6. Results and Discussion
7. Conclusion(s)
8. Acknowledgments
9. References
10. Appendix

In the technical report, the main emphasis is on: (i) the methods employed, (ii) assumptions made in the course of the study, and (iii) the detailed presentation of the findings including their limitations and supporting data.

A general outline of a technical report can be as follows:

1. **Summary of results:** A brief review of the main findings just in two or three pages.
2. **Nature of the study:** Description of the general objectives of study, formulation of the problem in operational terms, the working hypothesis, the type of analysis and data required, etc.
3. **Methods employed:** Specific methods used in the study and their limitations. For instance, in sampling studies, we should give details of sample design, viz., sample size, sample selection, etc.

4. **Data:** Discussion of data collected, their sources, characteristics and limitations. If secondary data are used, their suitability to the problem at hand be fully assessed. In case of a survey, the manner in which data were collected be fully described.
5. **Analysis of data and presentation of findings:** The analysis of data and presentation of the findings of the study with supporting data in the form of tables and charts be fully narrated. This, in fact, happens to be the main body of the report usually extending over several chapters.
6. **Conclusions:** A detailed summary of the findings and the policy implications drawn from the results be explained.
7. **Bibliography:** Bibliography of various sources consulted be prepared and attached.
8. **Technical appendices:** Appendices be given for all technical matters relating to questionnaire, mathematical derivations, elaboration on particular technique of analysis and the like.
9. **Index:** Index must be prepared and be given invariably in the report at the end.

15.2.9 Popular Reports

The popular report is one which gives emphasis on simplicity and attractiveness. The simplification should be sought through clear writing, minimization of technical, particularly mathematical, details and liberal use of charts and diagrams. Attractive layout along with large print, many sub-headings, even an occasional cartoon now and then is another characteristic feature of the popular report. Besides, in such a report, emphasis is given on practical aspects and policy implications.

We give below a general outline of a popular report.

1. **The findings and their implications:** Emphasis in the report is given on the findings of most practical interests and on the implications of these findings.
2. **Recommendations for action:** Recommendations for action on the basis of the findings of the study is made in this section of the report.
3. **Objective of the study:** A general review of how the problem arises is presented along with specific objectives of the project under study.
4. **Methods employed:** A brief and non-technical description of the methods and techniques used, including a short review of the data on which the study is based, is given in this part of the report.
5. **Results:** This section constitutes the main body of the report wherein the results of the study are presented in clear and non-technical terms with liberal use of all sorts of illustrations such as charts, diagrams and the likes.
6. **Technical appendices:** More detailed information on methods used, forms, etc. is presented in the form of appendices. But the appendices are often not detailed if the report is entirely meant for general public.

There can be several variations of the form in which a popular report can be prepared. The only important thing about such a report is that it gives emphasis on simplicity and policy implications from the operational point of view, avoiding the technical details of all sorts to the extent possible.

15.3 SIGNIFICANCE OF REPORT

In the modern business scenario, reports play a major role in the progress of business. Reports are the backbone to the thinking process of the establishment and they are responsible, to a great extent, in evolving an efficient or inefficient work environment. The significance of the reports include:

1. Reports present adequate information on various aspects of the business.
2. All the skills and the knowledge of the professionals are communicated through reports.
3. Reports help the top line in decision making.
4. A true and balanced report also helps in problem solving.
5. Reports communicate the planning, policies, and other matters regarding an organization to the masses.
6. News reports play the role of ombudsman and levy checks and balances on the establishment.

15.4 CHARACTERISTICS OF REPORT

1. **Complete and Compact Document:** Report is a complete and compact written document giving updated information about a specific problem.
2. **Systematic Presentation of Facts:** Report is a systematic presentation of facts, figures, conclusions and recommendations. Report writers closely study the problem under investigation and prepare a report after analyzing all relevant information regarding the problem. Report is supported by facts and evidences. There is no scope for imagination in a report which is basically a factual document.
3. **Prepared in Writing:** Reports are usually in writing. Writing reports are useful for reference purpose. It serves as complete, compact and self-explanatory document over a long period. Oral reporting is possible in the case of secret and confidential matters.
4. **Provides Information and Guidance:** Report is a valuable document which gives information and guidance to the management while framing future policies. It facilitates planning and decision making. Reports are also useful for solving problems faced by a business enterprise.
5. **Self-explanatory Document:** Report is a comprehensive document and covers all aspects of the subject matter of study. It is a self-explanatory and complete document by itself.
6. **Acts as a Tool of Internal Communication:** Report is an effective tool of communication between top executives and subordinate staff working in an organization. It provides feedback to employees and to executives for decision making. Reports are generally submitted to higher authorities. It is an example of upward communication. Similarly, reports are also sent by company executives to the lower levels of management. This is treated as downward communication. In addition, reports are also sent to shareholders and others connected with the company. It may be pointed out that report writing/preparation acts as a backbone of any system of communication.
7. **Acts as Permanent Record:** A report serves as a permanent record relating to certain business matter. It is useful for future reference and guidance.
8. **Time-consuming and Costly Activity:** Report writing is a time-consuming, lengthy and costly activity as it involves collection of facts, drawing conclusion and making recommendations.

15.5 REPORT HEADING AND BODY OF THE REPORT

1. **Title:** The title should tell the reader what the report is about.
2. **Acknowledgements:** Briefly thank people who assisted you in compiling and writing up the information in the report.
3. **Abstract, Executive Summary or Synopsis:** Many readers will only read this abstract so it needs to be informative, clear and brief. It provides an accurate summary of the content of the report. The first sentence should articulate the main aim or question explored in the report. It should also outline the approach to the research, the main theories applied, and the most important findings or results of the research.
4. **Table or List of Contents:** A list is the main sections/headings of the report and the page number on which they first appear. One should be able to generate this automatically from a styled MSWord document after they have completed the rest of the report.
5. **List of Tables and Illustrations:** It is a list of any illustrations, graphs, charts, maps and the page number on which they first appear.
6. **Introduction:** A report is set within a context of background information to illustrate the relevance or importance of the research. The research aims are stated: what is it the research will explore or demonstrate? Areas that may need to be covered in the introduction include:
   - (a) **Background:** The significance of the report and why it was commissioned.
   - (b) **Purpose:** Is to be stated clearly and succinctly.
   - (c) **Scope:** What issues were covered, what were omitted?
   - (d) **Research:** How the data was obtained (e.g., interviews, surveys, literature review)?
   - (e) **Definition of Terms:** Specific terms or concepts that need to be clarified or defined.

7. **Literature Review:** A brief summary of the most significant writings and major research findings in the field of investigation using APA format is presented. Evaluating the major works/findings and connecting them to one's own work, to show how one will draw upon or depart from the literature in the research.
8. **Materials and Methods:** States/defines the methods used to conduct the research (quantitative/qualitative; primary/ secondary) and briefly provides a rationale for why this method was employed. Describes the conditions under which the research was conducted, number of participants, how they were selected, duration of the experiment etc.
9. **Results:** Presentation of the main findings of the research, using sub-headings where appropriate. Results can be ordered chronologically, or in any other appropriate way.
10. **Discussion of Results:** In this section analysis of findings at length, and provision of an explanation for why those results were obtained is presented. Researcher may state whether or not the results confirmed the initial hypothesis, whether they were expected, and their possible significance. Presentation of findings or arguments is done in a logical manner according to the subject matter. Options, alternatives or responses to specific situations or issues may also be presented in this section.
11. **Conclusions:** Summary of the purpose of the report, the methodology or theories employed, the key points or findings of the report and the significance of those findings are presented here. Don't introduce any new points, or information or new sources. Recommendations can be put here if a specific section for them is not intended.
12. **Recommendations:** Suggesting ways in which problems identified in the report may be resolved in this part. They should be given in a numbered list and should be feasible and realistic. Information on how they can be implemented should also be given. There should be a logical relationship between the results and the recommendations, and all recommendations should clearly spring from previously discussed material.
13. **Reference List:** An alphabetical list of the sources referred to in the body of the report comprise this section. Use APA end-text referencing for sources quoted, paraphrased or referred to in-text. Only include sources mentioned in the report.
14. **Appendices:** This is for material you consider important but that interferes with the flow of your discussion; for example, data, calculations, surveys, transcripts, graphics, maps, questionnaires, pamphlets etc. referred to in-text. Number each item starting each item on a new page. Only include items mentioned in the report.

15.6 SECTION AND STAGES OF REPORT

The following table shows the most common sections typically contained in the two different types of reports and the various parts or stages making up each section. The headings in a report are used to identify the content of each section and stage.

Table 15.1: Sections and Stages of a Report and the Headings

Sections	Stages	Headings	
		Analytical Reports	Practical/Scientific Reports
Preliminary Section – Provides the context and background information		**Title Page**	Title Page
		Table of Contents	Table of Contents (if required)
		Executive Summary/Abstract	Abstract/Synopsis
Main Section or body of the report – Presents the key aspects of the report: what was done, what was found, what this means	***Stage 1*** Introduces this section	**Introduction**	Introduction
			Materials and Methodology
	Stage 2 Presents the findings and your analysis of these	**(Headings identifying the aspect dealt with in each sub-section)**	Results
			Discussion

	Stage 3 States the implications of the findings and analysis	**Conclusion**	Conclusion
		Recommendations (if required)	
Supplementary Section – Contains extra information		**References/ Bibliography**	References/ Bibliography
		Appendices	Appendices

15.7 MEANING OF RESEARCH REPORT

Purpose

The first step in all research reports is to identify the purpose. All research reports are designed to gather knowledge to make a more informed decision before investing money into a concept, to determine the direction of a business venture or to decide whether to eliminate a product or service. Identifying the purpose of the report helps to direct the approach of the research-gathering efforts. The report may sell an idea or change management's mind about an idea. Reports can also be used to identify and rectify a problem within a company.

Gathering Information

It is important to first collect data that has already been collected by other sources. Published reports from research firms such as Plunkett and Forrester can be reviewed to avoid doubling efforts already made. Sales invoices, customer information and other internal documentation you have can also be used. First-hand data should be gathered by asking the questions that haven't already been answered. It should also be collected if the information available is outdated. Interviews and questionnaires of consumers are among the most used methods to gather information.

Statistical Research

Statistical research attempts to learn how much of the population uses certain products, predict trends involving the product, and identify the audience that buys the product. This form of research is also called descriptive research and is generally used to understand what impact a product may have on the target market. Descriptive research could be used to establish a control group for future research studies the company may commission.

Exploratory Research

Exploratory research is a strictly information-gathering form of developing a research report. This method is used when the problem hasn't been identified. It helps clarify the best way to collect data, choose subjects to study and research models. Secondary data, such as expert opinions and previous studies, are the primary source of information. Case studies and data gathered through focus groups are also used.

Causal Research

Causal research begins at the point at which the previous research gathered has helped the researchers to develop a hypothesis. The causal research is the testing phase for the hypothesis developed. An editor of Entrepreneur Magazine says that this research is important because, "Popular opinion and procedures are not necessarily reliable guides to best practices." In his summation, causal research is the method to test the assumptions of exploratory research and descriptive research.

15.8 MEANING OF REPORT WRITING

The basic aim of the report is to communicate the objectives of the work done, the procedures used in sufficient detail so that the work can be reproduced, discussion of results, and conclusions. It should give a list of symbols used, and references that have been cited in the body of the report. It should have appendices that contain all the details of data, and an example of calculation of quantities that have been reported in the body of the report but that had to be obtained from the observations or raw data. Appendices can also contain other details relevant to the report but which would hinder the flow of presentation if they were included in the main body of the report.

15.9 DIFFERENT STEPS IN REPORT WRITING

1. Logical Analysis of the Subject Matter

It is the first step which is primarily concerned with the development of a subject. There are two ways in which to develop a subject: (a) Logically and (b) Chronologically. The logical development is made on the basis of mental connections and associations between the one thing and another by means of analysis. Logical treatment often consists in developing the material from the simple possible to the most complex structures. Chronological development is based on a connection or sequence in time or occurrence. The directions for doing or making something usually follow the chronological order.

2. Preparation of the Final Outline

It is the next step in writing the research report. "outlines are the framework upon which long written works are constructed. They are an aid to the logical organization of the material and a reminder of the points to be stressed in the report."

3. Preparation of the Rough Draft

This follows the logical analysis of the end preparation of the final outline. Such a step is of utmost importance for the researcher now sits to write down what he has done in the context of his research study. He will write down the procedure adopted by him in collecting the material for his study along with various limitations faced by him, the technique of analysis adopted by him, the broad findings and generalization and the various suggestions he wants to offer regarding the problem concerned.

4. Rewriting and Polishing of the Rough Draft

This step happens to be the most difficult part of all formal writing. Usually, this step requires more time than the writing of the rough draft. The careful revision makes the difference between a mediocre and a good piece of writing. While rewriting and polishing, one should check the report for weaknesses in logical development or presentation.

The researcher should also "see whether or not the material, as it is presented, has unity and cohesion; does the report stand upright and firm and exhibit a definite pattern, like a marble arch? Or does it resemble an old wall of moldering cement and loose bricks." In addition, the researcher should give due attention to the fact that in his rough draft he has been consistent or not. He should check the mechanics of writing – grammar, spelling and usage.

5. Preparation of the Final Bibliography

Next in order comes the task of the preparation of the final bibliography. The bibliography, which is generally appended to the research report, is a list of books in some way pertinent to the research which has been done. It should contain all those works which the researcher has consulted. The bibliography should be arranged alphabetically and may be divided into two parts; the first part may contain the names of books and pamphlets, and the second part may contain the names of magazines and newspaper articles. Generally, this pattern of bibliography is considered convenient and satisfactory from the point of view of the reader, though it is not the only way of presenting bibliography. The entries in bibliography should be made adopting the following order:

For books and pamphlets, the order may be as under:

(1) Name of author, last name first

(2) Title, underlined to indicate italics

(3) Number of volumes

(4) Place, publisher, and date of publication

Example: Mahalaxmi, S., Research Methodology, New Delhi, Sagar Publishing House Pvt. Ltd., 2010.

For magazines and newspapers, the order may be as under:

(1) Name of the author, last name first.

(2) Title of article, in quotation marks.

(3) Name of periodical, underlined to indicate italics.

(4) The volume or volume and numbers.

(5) The date of the issue.

(6) The pagination.

Example:

Singh P.R., "International Money Flows", The Yojona, Bhubaneswar, December, 2010, p. 555.

The above examples are just the samples for bibliography entries and may be used, but one should also remember that they are not the only acceptable forms. The only thing important is that, whatever method one selects, it must remain consistent throughout the report.

6. Writing the Final Draft

This constitutes the last step. The final draft should be written in a concise and objective style and in simple language, avoiding vague expressions such as "it seems", "there may be", and the like. While writing the draft, the researcher must avoid abstract terminology and technical jargon. Illustration and examples based on common experiences must be incorporated in the final draft as they happen to be most effective in communicating the research findings to others. A research report should not be dull, but must enthuse people and maintain interest and must show originality. It must be remembered that every report should be an attempt to solve some intellectual problem and must contribute to the solution of the problem and must add to the knowledge of both the researcher and the reader.

15.10 BUSINESS REPORT WRITING

Report writing is an essential skill for professionals in almost every field. Each kind of report has its characteristics. An enquiry report or a survey report is essentially a fact-finding report and should bring out the facts clearly. A Directors' Report, on the other hand, is the detailing of the developments or the progress relating to the business organization during a particular period. A committee report may not only bring out facts and figures, but also cover the alternative viewpoints expressed by the members and final recommendations. Notwithstanding these features specific to the reports, there are certain essential features for good report writing:

1. Issue in Perspective

The first essential for any good report is to bring out the issue in its proper perspective emphasizing the pros and cons. Be it a progress report; a survey report, an analytical report or an enquiry report, the subject should be presented in an unbiased and objective manner. Both the positive and negative aspects of the issues studied should be covered in the report.

2. Authoritative Facts and Figures

The report writer should ensure that the facts and figures quoted in the report are authentic and reliable. The data quoted in the report is likely to be made use of by several other individuals and agencies. When the data quoted is taken from secondary sources, care should be taken to see that the sources are reliable and cross-verified.

3. Maintain a Judicial Approach

The report writer should keep to measurable facts and verifiable details. Impressionistic statements and inaccuracies will have to be avoided. A good report calls for an effective assessment based on authentic facts and figures. Human errors, biases and any kind of selective reporting have no place in report writing. Good reports are those where the report writer maintains non-partisan attitude.

4. In-depth Analysis

Any report that does not go into the details of the subject studied may turn out to be peripheral requiring additional information. The reporting authority or the report writer, as the case may be, should make it a point to meticulously go about collecting all related information for inclusion in the report.

5. Alternative Viewpoints

The purpose of a report is to get the facts in proper perspective. There should be an intention to get the inputs or views from different persons who are in a position to throw light on the subject or incident under study. Although the final recommendations may be based on a consensus or majority view, the fact that some other views were also expressed during the course of deliberations or enquiries should also be mentioned.

6. Appropriate Annexure

Most reports contain relevant annexure, which cover additional information which is pertinent to the matter dealt within the body of the report. Such annexure normally includes charts, graphs, relevant statistics, and questionnaires and so on. Care should be taken to ensure that any such charts, maps and tables are relevant to the matter under study and enhance understanding.

15.11 RESEARCH REPORT WRITING

A comprehensive layout of the research report should comprise: (A) Preliminary pages, (B) The main text, and (C) The end matter.

Let us deal with them separately.

(A) Preliminary Pages

In its preliminary pages the report should carry a title and date, followed by acknowledgements in the form of 'Preface' or 'Foreword'. Then there should be a table of contents followed by list of tables and illustrations so that the decision-maker or anybody interested in reading the report can easily locate the required information in the report.

(B) Main Text

The main text provides the complete outline of the research report along with all details. Title of the research study is repeated at the top or the first page of the main text and then follows the other details on pages numbered consecutively, beginning with the second page. Each main section of the report should begin on a new page. The main text of the report should have the following sections: (i) Introduction; (ii) Statement of findings and recommendations; (iii) The results; (iv) The implications drawn from the results; and (v) The summary.

1. Introduction

The purpose of introduction is to introduce this research project to the readers. It should contain a clear statement of the objectives of research, i.e., enough background should be given to make clear to the reader why the problem was considered worth investigating. A brief summary of other relevant research may also be stated so that the present study can be seen in that context. The hypotheses of study, if any, and the definitions of the major concepts employed in the study should be explicitly stated in the introduction of the report.

The methodology adopted in conducting the study must be fully explained. The scientific reader would like to know in detail about such things: How was the study carried out? What was its basic design? If the study was an experimental one, then what were the experimental manipulations? If the data were collected by means of questionnaires or interview, schedule is usually given in an appendix. If measurements were based on observation, then what instructions were given to the observers? Regarding the sample used in the study the reader should be told: Who were the subjects? How many were there? How were they selected?

All these questions are crucial for estimating the probable limits of generalizability of the findings. The statistical analysis adopted must also be clearly stated. In addition to all this, the scope of the study should be stated and the boundary lines be demarcated. The various limitations, under which the research project was completed, must also be narrated.

2. Statement of Findings and Recommendations

After introduction, the research report must contain a statement of findings and recommendations in non-technical language so that it can be easily understood by all concerned. If the findings happen to be extensive, at this point they should be put in the summarized form.

3. Results

A detailed presentation of the findings of the study, with supporting data in the form of tables and charts together with a validation of results, is the next step in writing the main text of the report. This generally comprises the main body of the report, extending over several chapters. The result section of the report should contain statistical summaries and reductions of the data rather than the raw data. All the results should be presented in logical sequence and split into readily identifiable sections. All relevant results must find a place in the report. But how one is to decide about what is relevant is the basic question. Quite often, guidance comes primarily from the research problem and from the hypotheses, if any, with which the study was concerned. But ultimately the researcher must rely on his own judgment in deciding the outline of his report. "Nevertheless, it is still necessary that he states clearly the problem with which he was concerned, the procedure by which he worked on the problem, the conclusions at which he arrived, and the bases for his conclusions."

4. Implications of the Results

Toward the end of the main text, the researcher should again put down the results of his research clearly and precisely. He should state the implications that flow from the results of the study, for the general reader is interested in the implications for understanding the human behaviour. Such implications may have three aspects as stated below:

(a) A statement of the inferences drawn from the present study which may be expected to be applied in similar circumstances.

(b) The conditions of the present study which may limit the extent of legitimate generalizations of the inferences drawn from the study.

(c) The relevant questions that still remain unanswered or new questions raised by the study along with suggestions for the kind of research that would provide answers for them.

It is considered a good practice to finish the report with a short conclusion with summaries that recapitulate the main points of the study. The conclusion drawn from the study should be clearly related to the hypotheses that were stated in the introductory section. At the same time, a forecast of the probable future of the subject and an indication of the kind of research which needs to be done in that particular field is useful and desirable.

5. Summary

It has become customary to conclude the research report with a very brief summary, resting in brief the research problem, the methodology, the major findings and the major conclusions drawn from the research results.

(C) End Matter

At the end of the report, appendices should be enlisted in respect of all technical data such as questionnaires, sample information, mathematical derivations and the likes. Bibliography of sources consulted should also be given. Index (an alphabetical listing of names, places and topics along with the numbers of the pages in a book of report on which they are mentioned or discussed) should invariably be given at the end of the report. The value of index lies in the fact that it works as a guide to the reader for the contents in the report.

15.12 THE ANALYTICAL RESEARCH REPORT

The analytical report examines a problem or issue and recommends an action. Some analytical reports function as proposals that identify or define problems and argue for specific ways of resolving them. Other analytical reports are feasibility studies that examine proposed solutions and determine their practicality.

Analytical reports are written by experts, often working in teams. The reports generally require that these experts:

- use their professional skills to define an issue, making the study large enough in scope to identify all the factors that bear on the problem and using a standard professional methodology,
- know or learn how such issues have been resolved in other cases, inside and outside their own company; and
- accommodate constraints like cost, time, company policy, union contracts, local and federal law.

The completed report will have at least three groups of readers:

- Experts, who will be asked to validate the scope of the study, the data collected, the methodology used, and the practicality of the solution
- Managers who ordered the study, and will consider the significance of the problem identified in the study, the practicality of the solution in terms of cost, duration, and affect on other operations, and the judgment of the experts asked to validate the report
- Managers from other units of the company, who will be asked to validate the results from their own perspectives such as whether the solution conforms to environmental or tax law or whether the company has adequate personnel to staff it.

Elements of Reports

Parts of the report, in order, are

1. ***Letter or Memo of Transmittal*** (not actually part of the report but included with the report)
2. ***Title Page***
   - Title of the report
   - Name of the person, department, or company commissioning the report
   - Date submitted
   - Authors and their corporate or departmental affiliation
   - The title of the report should be long enough to describe the report's contents (two-line titles are acceptable) and incorporate the keywords from the report to allow indexing and retrieval.
3. ***Executive Summary***

   The executive summary will be read by the executive who commissioned the report and in many cases, this is the only part of the report that he or she will read. Staff members will analyze and read the rest of the report.

   The executive summary is always one paragraph long and contains the following:
   - an identification of the problem addressed in the report
   - a brief description of the significance of the problem to the company
   - a very brief description of the solution
   - a very brief description of the time and funds required to implement the solution

   Executive summaries do not contain explanations or justifications because there is no space for them; a partial explanation is worse than none at all. Note that the executive summary is not a complete summary. Many key parts of the report are not mentioned. It is also not an "abstract." Abstracts are written by experts for other experts who use them for research purposes. Abstracts place primary emphasis on the scope of the study and the methodology used.
4. ***Table of Contents***

   Tables of contents are necessary only when the report is more than ten pages long or has many separate parts. The table of contents generally is not included in a five-page report because the readers can skim the report to find content as easily as they can use the table of contents. But the table of contents generally is included in a ten-page report because the readers can generally locate information in a table of contents more quickly than they can skim ten pages.

5. ***Table of Figures***

Tables of figures are necessary only when the report has a number of charts, graphs, or line drawings and the readers will be accessing them non-sequentially.

6. ***Glossary of Terms***

Glossaries are necessary only in those rare cases when the report will use a number of terms that are not familiar to the reader.

7. ***Body***

Presents the findings of the primary and secondary research using an appropriateorganizational plan with logical and parallel headings; uses proper documentation with appropriate and accurate paraphrasing and summarizing.

8. ***Conclusion***

Conclusions are a natural extension of the report and complete its logic. The "Conclusions" section can be of any length and is always written in paragraphed prose. The conclusions are a separate part of the report, always labeled "Conclusions." The conclusion section need not begin on a new page of the report.

9. ***Recommendations***

The recommendations are a separate part of the report, always labeled "Recommendations." They always form a separate page.

10. ***Appendices***

Appendices are put at the end of the report and are labeled "A" through "Z." They are referenced in the report itself, generally with a sentence in parentheses. Appendices are used to hold independent data or documents needed to explain or support points made in the report. For example, if the report recommends purchasing a safety device to improve a machine's operation, an appendix would contain a manufacturer's specification sheet describing the device. If the report recommended a department reorganization and change of titles and salaries, an appendix would contain.

11. ***Bibliography***

The bibliography lists the published documents that are referenced in the report itself. It is always placed on a separate page and is labeled "Bibliography."

List only physical documents rather than Web pages in bibliographies. Report readers must be able to order the cited published document at any later time, but Web pages disappear or change over time. When you need to reference Web-based data, download and print the information and include it as an appendix.

Since most reports do not include references to published documents, bibliographies are relatively uncommon.

12. ***Page Numbering***

The system for numbering pages is standard for all reports and is slightly different from the system used in other documents.

- Pages are always numbered and numbers are most often placed at the bottom of the page, either centered or in the right corner.
- If readers will be working with multiple reports at the same time or if you expected the report to be disassembled, use "footer" instead of just a number. The footer, which you create in your word processing program applies to each page, always includes the page number, and can also contain the title, the report date, the draft number, or other useful information.
- The letter of transmittal is not part of the numbering sequence because it is not strictly part of the report.
- The title page is page 1 of the report, but the number is not put on the page.
- The table of contents is page 2, and the number is put on the page.
- All other pages through the end of the bibliography are numbered sequentially.
- The appendices have independent numbering systems; appendices are lettered in sequence, and each appendix is internally numbered. So, the first appendix is "Appendix A"; the second is "Appendix B" and so on. If Appendix A has four pages and Appendix B has three pages, the pages are labeled A-1, A-2, A-3, A-4, B-1, B-2, B-3. The "Table of C" "Table of F."

15.13 SUMMARY

A report is a clearly structured document that presents information about an investigation that you have undertaken. It is a self-explanatory statement of facts relating to a specific subject and serves the purpose of providing information for decision-making and follow-up actions. It is a systematic presentation of ascertained facts about a specific event/subject. Report is a summary of findings and recommendations about a particular matter/problem. Following are the two bases of classifying the reports: (According to function) (1) Analytical Report, (2) Informational Report and (3) Research reports. (According to formality) (1) Statutory report, (2) Non-statutory or voluntary report, (3) Routine Report, (4) Special Report, (5) Technical Report and (6) Popular Report. The basic aim of the report is to communicate the objectives of the work done, the procedures used in sufficient detail so that the work can be reproduced, discussion of results, and conclusions. It should give a list of symbols used, and references that have been cited in the body of the report. It should have appendices that contain all the details of data.

Report writing is an essential skill for professionals in almost every field. Each kind of report has its characteristics. An enquiry report or a survey report is essentially a fact-finding report and should bring out the facts clearly. A comprehensive layout of the research report should comprise: (A) Preliminary pages, (B) The main text, and (C) The end matter. The analytical report examines a problem or issue and recommends an action. Some analytical reports function as proposals that identify or define problems and argue for specific ways of resolving them. Other analytical reports are feasibility studies that examine proposed solutions and determine their practicality.

15.14 KEY TERMS

Report: A report is a clearly structured document that presents information about an investigation that you have undertaken. It is a self-explanatory statement of facts relating to a specific subject.

Analytical Report: These reports contain facts along with analytical explanations offered by the reporter himself or may be asked for by the one who is seeking the report.

Informational Report: These reports present facts about certain given activity in detail without any note or suggestions. Whatever is gathered is reported without giving any thing by way of either explanation or any suggestion.

Research Report: These reports are based on some research work conducted by either an individual or a group of individuals on a given problem.

Statutory Report: These reports are to be presented according to the requirements of a particular law or a rule or a custom now has become a rule.

Non-statutory Report: These reports are not in the nature of legal requirements or rules.

Routine Report: These reports are required to be prepared and submitted periodically on matters required by the organization so as to help the management of the organization to take decisions in the matters relating to day-to-day affairs.

Technical Report: In the technical report, the main emphasis is on: (i) the methods employed, (ii) assumptions made in the course of the study, (iii) the detailed presentation of the findings including their limitations and supporting data.

Popular Report: The popular report is one which gives emphasis on simplicity and attractiveness. The simplification should be sought through cleat writing, minimization of technical, particularly mathematical, details and liberal use of charts and diagrams.

Exploratory Research: Exploratory research is a strictly information-gathering form of developing a research report. This method is used when the problem hasn't been identified.

Causal Research: Causal research begins at the point at which the previous research gathered has helped the researchers to develop a hypothesis. The causal research is the testing phase for the hypothesis developed.

Report Writing: The basic aim of the report writing is to communicate the objectives of the work done, the procedures used in sufficient detail so that the work can be reproduced, discussion of results, and conclusions.

15.14 MULTIPLE OBJECTIVE TYPE QUESTIONS

1. Report is a summary of findings and recommendations about a particular matter/problem.
   (a) True (b) False
2. Informational Report present facts about certain given activity in detail without any note or suggestions.
   (a) True (b) False
3. Routine Report are required to be prepared and submitted periodically on matters required by the organization so as to help the management of the organization to take decisions in the matters relating to day-to-day affairs.
   (a) True (b) False
4. The analytical report is one which gives emphasis on simplicity and attractiveness.
   (a) True (b) False
5. Exploratory research is a strictly information-gathering form of developing a research report. This method is used when the problem hasn't been identified.
   (a) True (b) False
6. Causal research begins at the point at which the previous research gathered has helped the researchers to develop a hypothesis.
   (a) True (b) False
7. In the preliminary pages, the report should carry a title and date, followed by acknowledgements in the form of 'Preface' of 'Foreword'.
   (a) True (b) False
8. After introduction, the research report must contain a statement of findings and recommendations in non-technical language so that it can be easily understood by all concerned.
   (a) True (b) False
9. Popular reports are feasibility studies that examine proposed solutions and determine their practicality.
   (a) True (b) False
10. Glossaries are necessary only in those rare cases when the report will use a number of terms that are not familiar to the reader.
    (a) True (b) False
11. Which of the following report is to be presented according to the requirements of a particular law or a rule or a custom?
    (a) Analytical (b) Informational
    (c) Statutory (d) All of the above
12. The significance of the reports includes:
    (a) Reports present adequate information on various aspects of the business
    (b) All the skills and the knowledge of the professionals are communicated through reports
    (c) Reports help the top line in decision making
    (d) All of the above
13. Which type of research report are designed to gather knowledge to make a more informed decision before investing money into a concept, to determine the direction of a business venture or to decide whether to eliminate a product or service?
    (a) Popular (b) Analytical
    (c) Informational (d) All

14. Which research attempts to learn how much of the population uses certain products, predict trends involving the product, and identify the audience that buys the product?
    (a) Statistical Research (b) Popular Research
    (c) Observational Research (d) None of the above
15. Which research is a strictly information-gathering form of developing a research report?
    (a) Exploratory (b) Causal
    (c) Statistical (d) None of these above
16. Which of the following is an essential feature of business report writing?
    (a) Issue in prospective (b) In-depth analysis
    (c) Appropriate Annexure (d) All of the above
17. A comprehensive layout of the research report should comprise
    (a) Preliminary pages (b) The main text
    (c) The end matter (d) All of the above
18. Analytical reports are written by which of the following?
    (a) Team member (b) Expert of the team member
    (c) Analyst (d) None of the above
19. Which of the following must specify what estimation procedure(s) you used?
    (a) Validity (b) Reliability
    (c) Both (a) and (b) (d) None of these
20. Which one is the first section of the research paper?
    (a) Abstract (b) Introduction
    (c) Methodology (d) Analysis

Answers to Multiple Objective Type Questions

Questions	1	2	3	4	5	6	7	8	9	10
Answers	T	T	T	F	T	T	T	T	F	T
Questions	11	12	13	14	15	16	17	18	19	20
Answers	c	d	d	a	a	d	d	b	b	a

15.16 CONCEPTUAL QUESTIONS

1. What is the meaning of report? Describe the different types of report.
2. Distinguish between technical report and popular report.
3. What are the significance and characteristics of the report?
4. Describes the layout of a research report, covering all relevant points.
5. What are the section and stages of the report?
6. Explain the meaning of research report and report writing.
7. Enumerate the different steps of report writing.
8. How can you write business report? Explain.
9. What points will you keep in mind while preparing a research report? Explain.
10. How can you write analytical report? Discuss briefly each of the points.

11. "Report writing is more an art that hinges upon practice and experience". Discuss.
12. Write short notes:
    (a) Analytical report
    (b) Informational report
    (c) Research reports
    (d) Statutory report
    (e) Non-statutory or voluntary report
    (f) Routine report
    (g) Special report
    (h) Technical report
    (i) Popular report
    (j) Characteristics of good research report
    (k) Importance of research report

CASE STUDY QUESTIONS

Chapter Outline

Case Study – 1: Juice VJ_{100}
Case Study – 2: Small Cafe
Case Study – 3: Star MRSI
Case Study – 4: Management Education
Case Study – 5: Improving Employee's Performance
Case Study – 6: Flexible Work Arrangements
Case Study – 7: Pritam Manufacturing Co., Inc
Case Study – 8: Sales Performance
Case Study – 9: Employee Attitude-Performance
Case Study – 10: Movie Theater
Case Study – 11: Attitude towards Fast Food Items
Case Study – 12: Restaurant Food vs. Fast Food
Case Study – 13: Brand Preference
Case Study – 14: Preference of the First Food
Case Study – 15: Good Health and Bad Health
Case Study – 16: Success and Failure of Small Business
Case Study – 17: Small Car Manufacturing Company
Case Study – 18: Telecom Industry

Case Study – 1

Juice VJ_{100}

Testy Soup Company India has marked its presence with significant achievements and today commands a market leadership status. The story of success is based on dedication to nature, corporate and process hygiene, dynamic leadership and commitment to our partners and stakeholders. Over the years, Testy Soup Company overseas business has successfully transformed from being a small operation into a multi-location business spreading through the Middle East, North Africa, West Africa and South Asia.

VJ_{100} is a 100% vegetable juice drink produced and marketed by the Testy Soup Company. The juice drink made from concentrate with added ingredients, provides a full serving of vegetables and is a natural source of beta carotene. VJ_{100}'s ingredient include tomato juice from concentrate; reconstituted vegetable juice blend, made from water and concentrated juices of carrots, clearly, beets, parsley, lettuce, watercress and spinach; salt; vitamin C; flavoring and citric acid. The drink contains no fat or cholesterol and it is a good source of vitamins A and C.

VJ_{100} has for many years had a large share of the tomato and vegetable juice market. However, sale had begun to slip, so the company decided it needed to conduct consumer research that would enable it to develop a new advertising campaign.

Questions:

1. What research objectives should marketers at VJ_{100} establish?
2. What research methods would be most appropriate to accomplish these objectives?

Case Study – 2

Small Cafe

The ability to come up with a business idea can be transformed into a viable business, where ideas supported by feasibility and a business plan can then be sold to interested investors, firms, and interested parties for a lump sum or a management contract, or as agreed. Business ideas, if introduced at the right time, when demand for such service or a product introduced by the idea is expected to surge, can lead to a very profitable business. Business ideas are always available through different sources; however, it is the application applied on these ideas, and timing makes all the difference in failure or success.

After discussing some good business ideas, Rabin and Ronald have decided that their best option is to open a small cafe. They believe that their background and experience in the hospitality industry will help them to succeed. Ronald is keen to start up the business straight away and has already found what he thinks is a good location. However, Rabin is not so sure and wants to spend more time researching the market before they commit to anything. Rabin can see the benefits in being fully prepared before investing time and money into starting the business.

Questions:

1. Explain why you think Rabin and Ronald should conduct market research before starting up their business. What could they find out by researching their market?
2. Describe some methods that Rabin and Ronald could use to learn more about their potential customers, competitors and business location.

Case Study – 3

Star MRSI

Star Market Research Service Inc. (MRSI) is dedicated, experienced marketing research professionals. Over the last 35 years, he has developed a range of consumer research solutions to deliver consumer insights to clients across industries, and an extensive toolbox of consumer research services. MRSI team that has the expertise of your industry and the understanding of your business challenges to know which solutions and marketing research tools will deliver the most effective findings. MSRI use this knowledge to pull consumer insights from marketing research data to tell the story and provide with clear, actionable direction from which to make strategic business decisions.

MSRI has four business units: Campbell Marketing Research, Star Satisfaction Associates, Star Strategic Consulting Group and Star Training and Development Center. MSRI provides a number of management consultant services to clients around the world. Services including product testing, brand equity research, pricing research, market segmentation, image and positioning studies and a wide range of other marketing research services. Campbell has been providing market research service to XYZ Companies since 1971. Star has tremendous depth of experience in all forms of research designs, including telephone, internet, mail and mall intercept.

Star Market research procedures are typical of those of suppliers of custom research studies. A client may come to Campbell indicating it has a marketing "problem". Campbell will spend some time investing the problem and then submit a research proposal to the client. If the client approves the proposal, Campbell conducts the fieldwork and prepares a research report.

Questions:

1. Outline the steps in the survey research process.
2. How might a company like Campbell help a client in each step of the survey research process?

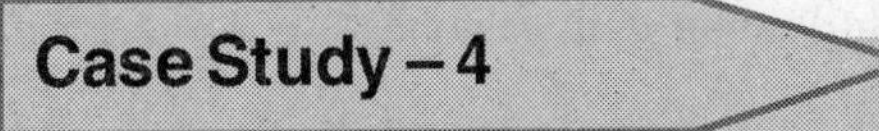

Case Study – 4 Management Education

Management is a much sought-after field for Indians. Today, the best and brightest students want to study management because it is a sure way to well-paid jobs with great prospects for advancement. In 2008-09, there were over 102,000 students studying for a Masters of Business Administration or its equivalent. But are management schools up to the challenge of providing able recruits to companies that need them the most?

The short answer is no. Many of the 2,000 or so management schools recognized by the All India Council for Technical Education (AICTE) have minimal faculty, most of whom have little practical experience in management and who undertake little research of decent quality. Also, a scant 250-300 management schools allow themselves to be rated — something that would make for easy assessment. Management schools should be at the apex of management education, for older students with work experience, but that isn't so today.

Moreover, instead of focusing just on B-schools, it is vital to improve other education streams like commerce education, and management orientation in professional courses like accounting and secretarial studies. These constitute the base for the thousands of managers in Indian enterprises who need grounding to make an early and positive contribution as managers.

However, the most serious problem with management today concerns the placement of B-School graduates. In 2007, there were 12,500 or so unlisted companies in India — including public sector firms, banks, financial enterprises and service companies. The top 75 of these compare with the best of the listed companies. Most of the others, however, show poor performance in sales growth, profit ratios and consistency in overall performance — but that is where management graduates should be found playing a positive role.

Having been associated with over 35 companies over the decades, I have noticed that most holders of MBA degrees are targeting — and are targeted by — consultancy firms, multinationals and finance outfits. The huge requirement of the rest of industry, including infrastructure services, real estate, small-scale units, NBFCs and educational organizations, amongst others, are largely met by graduates and postgraduates in commerce, economics and engineering.

The small number of management graduates in relation to the total need produces another problem. It makes many of them feel superior and arrogant. They complete MBAs in their early 20s and often get multiple job offers. Monthly remunerations can get as high as ₹ 5 lakh a month. These schools are evaluated by the media, employers and students based on how quickly students get placed and how big their pay packets are. Thus, greed is inculcated at an age when idealism should be.

Sumantra Ghoshal identified this, saying: "We as business school faculty — need to own up (that)... it is our theories and ideas that have done much to strengthen the management practices we are all so loudly condemning." Recent excesses in the US and elsewhere, especially in the financial sector, involved many MBAs and had roots in ideas developed in business schools.

If managers seek ever-more inventive ways of boosting share prices, paying themselves over the odds for doing so and offloading the costs on to society, they are just doing what B-School courses on strategy, transaction cost economics and agency theory have taught them — which is to maximize the value of a company, product and themselves. Management education must focus on society and social good, not merely on building corporate bottom lines at any cost.

Questions:

1. What is the management decision problem in this case?
2. How would you translate the management decisions problem into research problem?

Case Study – 5

Improving Employee's Performance

Bill was a 41 year-old professional who I "inherited" in my new team of five people. He had been in his position for about 10 years. Bill was a nice guy who often did enough to get by and avoided serious complaints. When he wanted, he performed very well. This was relatively rare. Too often, his work was insufficient — lack of follow-up with customers, computational errors, being somewhat rude with others, missing deadlines.

When asked how he was doing, he emphasized his accomplishments and compliments he had received. If asked about substandard work, he was very skillful at avoiding responsibility. He saw himself as a better-than-average employee who deserved recognition and good raises. His previous manager had not addressed the performance issues, which reinforced Bill's opinion of himself and made my job much more difficult.

As his boss, I could have done nothing since there were a lot of "Bills" in the organization and my manager wasn't concerned. In fact, he was more concerned about having unhappy employees than having high productivity. Still, I decided to see how Bill's performance could be improved. The other employees' performance on the team was consistently better than his, though not so much that it was a point of contention. The other employees wanted to keep the peace and not deal with Bill's ire. He did not hesitate to confront others. It worked for him.

Questions:

1. Evaluate the research design in this case.
2. What changes, if any, would you make in the observation form?

Case Study – 6

Flexible Work Arrangements

Employees have shown a great desire for flexible work arrangements (FWAs). National data reveals that nearly 80% of workers say they would like to have more ûexible work options and would use them if there were no negative consequences at work. However, most workers do not have access to flexible work arrangements and barriers to their effective implementation persist in many organizations as the following nationally representative employer-based survey data reveals:

- 32% of employers do not allow any workers to change their starting and quitting times, and 67% do not allow all or most employees to do so;
- 61% do not allow any workers to control which shifts they work;
- 47% do not allow any employees to move from full time to part-time and back again while remaining in the same position, and 79% do not allow most or all employees to do so;

- 54% do not allow any workers to share jobs; 66% do not allow any employees to work part of the work week at home on either an occasional or a regular basis; and
- 61% do not allow any workers to work a compressed work week for at least part of the year.

Many businesses have responded and various studies indicate both a growth in flexible work options and an expanded understanding of their relevance to workforce recruitment, morale, production, and retention. However, to the extent that flexibility is available, access differs considerably across occupations with managerial, administrative and professional workers having the most flexibility.

Uniform information on FWA characteristics, access and utilization is not available across job sectors and occupations. Most publicly available literature on the implementation of FWAs is employer-based and tends to emphasize the processes through which companies develop and market their flexible arrangements and only minimally describes the specific details of actual policies and their use. To the extent that these programs have been documented, several themes emerge. The catalyst for change often begins with employees.

Companies may learn of employee dissatisfaction through a survey or a needs-assessment, or supervisors may be approached by individual employees with compelling requests for flexible work. Occasionally, the process begins at the top; in these cases, companies may be trying to address a systemic problem like high turnover rates or absenteeism.

While some flexible work arrangements have formal written policies with specific eligibility and utilization parameters, many others rely upon individual negotiations with willing managers who exercise explicit or permissive scopes of discretionary decision-making. The scope of coverage can be broad or specific to categories of workers. Many of the references we found to FWAs suggest their availability to all workers at a given company; although this was not something we could confirm. Other corporate information made it clear that certain types of occupational groups were excluded from participation in FWAs (such as manufacturing units).

Even when FWAs are part of official company policies, managerial commitment to the benefit and discretion in its approval significantly impacts actual use. Public and private studies indicate that the following contribute to improved adoption of flexible arrangements across job settings: leadership at the highest levels; written policies and broad dissemination to workers; implementation training for decisional managers; and review and enforcement mechanisms including employee surveys, utilization data collection and review, and managerial performance assessments. Available literature suggests that some of the most successful programs are those that are developed jointly by employees and company management.

Questions:

1. What are the primary information needs of the company?
2. What type of research design should be used in this study?

Case Study – 7 Pritam Manufacturing Co., Inc.

Pritam Manufacturing Company, Inc. began operations in 1950 in Bhubaneswar, Odisha producing road maintenance equipment. Today, Pritam continues to produce high-quality highway maintenance equipment including a full line of salt and sand spreaders, vacuum leaf loaders, and catch basin cleaners.

In 1999, Treasurer, saw a considerable increase in the cost of electricity for the plant that could not be explained by changes in production levels or equipment.

When contacted, the utility company agreed to test the accuracy of the two electric meters for the plant, but its tests showed the meters to be accurate. The utility company also installed advanced metering equipment to measure demand and consumption in 15-minute intervals. This metering data produced reams of paper, but still no explanation for the increased costs that were now averaging over ₹ 1,000 per month.

Questions:

1. Name the sampling design that is being used in the study.
2. What research methods would be most appropriate to accomplish these objectives?

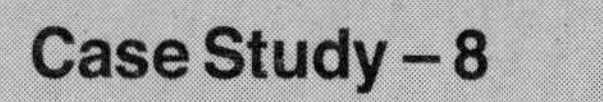

Case Study – 8

Sales Performance

The Background

The right product for the right customers in the right market would seem to be all that a company could need for success. That is, unless, it was stumbling over its own inadequate systems, procedures and processes. While expending enormous energy struggling to get through its own swamp, the company was losing market share to its competitors in a rapidly growing market; a double whammy. The company's marketing and sales operations and administrative tools were woefully outdated, having served it well in earlier years in a less dynamic and less competitive market. Everyone sort of knew everyone else, including the prospects and customers, and tracking and managing things was relatively easily accomplished.

The Company

The company was an independent marketer of petroleum products and services headquartered in San Francisco. It had three separate businesses under one roof, each handling different deliverables. However, all of the sales were generated through a six person field sales force, and part-time inside sales/customer service person.

Their Issue

The resulting impact of several issues was a zero per cent growth rate across all product lines. The external environmental influences the company faced included significantly increased competition, increasing cost of sales, and ever-demanding agency regulations governing the handling and transportation of many of their products. These were facts of life over which the company had absolutely no control. Even more significantly, their own internal infrastructure characteristics combined to produce constraints on their operations. Their processes were poorly documented and relied heavily on the experience of a few key people to keep their system running. Secondly, their technology was virtually non-existent insofar as their systems capability to track and measure sales activity and results was concerned. System inadequacy was also apparent in their general inability to efficiently and effectively communicate prospect and customer information to their sales personnel. Finally, the company's sales resources were stretched too thin to perform even an adequate job ... let alone generate exceptional performance.

Customer Manufacturing Group's Role

As the result of some initial fact finding, CMG was asked to evaluate and recommend process solutions in two key areas: (1) The separate and combined responsibilities and activities of the company's inside sales and field sales personnel, and; (2) The information handling technology with which the company could monitor, track, and communicate all aspects of its prospect and customer buying activity

Question:

1. Design for analyze the case and find out the critical performance of the selling process.

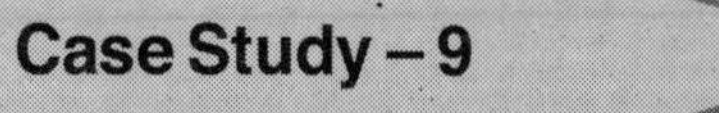

Case Study – 9

Employee Attitude-Performance

Employee attitude survey was commissioned by the UK parent company of a Danish subsidiary. The Danish subsidiary had been acquired by the UK company two years earlier.

Prior to the acquisition, the subsidiary was a privately held exclusive distributor of the parent's products in the Danish and broader Scandinavian markets. The subsidiary's customers were dealers, not end-users.

The former owners of the subsidiary had remained in the company in the capacity of Directors for a transition period. Subsequently, the former owners had been replaced by a British Managing Director (who was not fluent in the Danish language) and his senior team.

The official operating language of the company worldwide is English. Management are required to be fluent in English, whatever their nationality and mother tongue.

It had been identified by the company previously that the Danish staff and, to a somewhat lesser extent the Danish customers perceived the senior management team to be ignorant of Danish business culture, practices, and the nature of the Danish domestic market. Reportedly, it was felt locally also that the UK parent was "remote, unsupportive, and generally unsympathetic to the needs of its subsidiary."

Whether real or not, these perceptions had taken on a 'life of their own' and seemed linked to the presence of friction and lessened company performance. The Danish company was ailing financially anyway and these issues did not help the parent's objective of turning its subsidiary around. The UK parent had reached the point of considering the closure of its Danish subsidiary company.

The UK Board of the parent company decided though to adopt a completely open mind and to fully explore its options before reaching any decision. They decided to find out what the 'real issues' were. Hence, the UK Board commissioned this study (together with a psychological audit of the capabilities and style of the management conducted in tandem by us, alongside an internal commercial audit of the business).

Questions:

1. Indicate the employee attitude survey in the above cases.
2. How factors which were impeding organizational performance, morale and development were identified and addressed to the benefit of the organization, its people and other stakeholders?

Case Study – 10 Movie Theater

The primary benefit of staggering movie times is that it provides a steady flow of patrons into the theater to purchase their refreshments before their particular move starts. If all of the movies started at the same time or if only one or two screens were available, then the concession stand would experience a large amount of downtime while the movies were running and suffer a significant rush just before the movies started. Staggered times in multi-screen theaters allow the concession stand to be staffed more consistently with fewer employees who experience a steady flow of customers than would be necessary during a rush if all of the movies started at the same time.

Secondarily, an additional benefit of staggering movie times and keeping the flow of customers constant is that prepared foods will be fresher that if they had to be prepared in advance of a rush or have been sitting while a movie is running. All of these factors contribute to greater customer satisfaction (shorter wait, fresher food, etc.) with their overall theater experience.

I don't think movie going is often an impulse decision, so the main benefit to locating a multi-screen movie theater at a shopping mall is the increased exposure that the theater will have to mall patrons who may take note of what movies are showing and make plans to return to see a particular film. Also, if a patron shows up for a showing of a film and finds it to be sold out, having the shopping mall nearby may give them an alternative activity while they wait for the next showing.

Questions:

1. Which method of data collection is appropriate for above case analysis?
2. What are the benefits of the staggered movie times allowed by multiple screens?
3. What is the benefit to a multi-screen theater of locating at a shopping mall?

Case Study – 11

Attitude towards Fast Food Items

Introduction

Restaurants have been around in some form for most of human civilization. But they usually catered to travelers. As far back as ancient Greece and Rome, inns and taverns generally served food to people who had a reason to be away from home. This trend continued until relatively recently. Although taverns and coffee houses were popular places to gather and share beverages in the 17th century, the idea of eating out for fun didn't take off in Western society until the late 18th century. Although McDonald's was the first restaurant to use the assembly-line system, some people think of White Castle as the first fast food chain. White Castle was founded in 1921 in Wichita, Kansas. At the time, most people considered the burgers sold at fairs, circuses, lunch counters and carts to be low quality. Many people thought hamburger came from slaughterhouse scraps and spoiled meat. It is hard to imagine fast food without drive-through windows. Drive-troughs existed in the 1930s, and many drive-in restaurants had some form of drive-up window. However, the speaker systems commonly used to place drive-through orders didn't hit the scene until the 1950s. The double drive-through, used by many busy fast-food restaurants, debuted in the 1980s. Today, many people eat fast food instead of homemade food. The reason is that fast food is fast, cheap and convenient. This fast food culture started in India in the late eighties and became very popular. Many people believe that fast food is synonymous with the American lifestyle and it originates from the US. However, much fast food is European in origin, with a considerable history. Fast food affects a community in many aspects. It is mainly geared towards the younger end of the market. The preparation and service times are relatively quick in case of fast food. Fast food can be clearly distinguished from snack/confectionery items by its perishable nature.

Objective:

1. The objective of this research is to find out the condition of "University Students Attitude towards Fast Food Items in India".

Methodology

This research is based on both secondary and primary source. The secondary sources of data include books and research articles written on Fast food and the younger. Most of the data required for the study were collected from primary source through structured questionnaire.

Questions:

1. Prepare a questionnaire for collecting the information and analyze the case.
2. What are the conditions of University student's attitude towards fast food items?

Case Study – 12

Restaurant Food vs. Fast Food

(t- Test)

Pritam Enterprises has a restaurant in Bhubaneswar Odisha serving only lunch and dinner with high quality food at premium prices. The top management of the restaurant observes that the total sales revenues of the restaurants have been more at the rate of 2% only for the last two years. A meeting of the senior management personnel was called to discuss the issue. Some of them were of the opinion that young customers in the age group of 15 to 40 were switching to fast food. Further, they were of the view that the trend mainly is among people belonging to high income-group and to familiar where both partners were economically employed.

In the series of meeting with top management, it was decided they got a survey conducted for a comparative study to understand the preference of people for restaurant food and fast food. A sample of 30 respondents was chosen.

The following questions were asked incorporating the attributes:

Sl. No	Parameter	Restaurant Food (R_i)	Fast Food (F_j)
1	Taste		
2	Menu Variety		
3	Cost		
4	Quality Ingredients		
5	Hygiene		
6	Service Quality		
7	Total Time Taken		

The survey data on a sample of 30 respondents is given below:

Resp. No.	R_1	R_2	R_3	R_4	R_5	R_6	R_7	F_1	F_2	F_3	F_4	F_5	F_6	F_7
1	3	2	3	2	3	3	4	4	4	4	3	3	4	4
2	2	4	4	3	3	3	4	4	4	4	3	2	4	4
3	3	3	2	3	4	2	3	4	4	4	2	2	2	2
4	2	1	3	3	3	3	4	4	3	4	2	3	4	3
5	4	4	4	4	3	3	3	2	2	2	3	4	3	4
6	2	2	3	3	3	3	4	4	4	4	4	2	2	2
7	1	1	1	1	3	4	5	4	4	2	3	2	3	2
8	2	2	3	3	3	3	4	2	2	2	3	3	3	4
9	3	4	4	3	4	3	4	4	3	4	3	1	3	3
10	1	3	3	2	2	3	3	4	3	4	2	1	3	4
11	1	1	3	1	1	1	5	4	4	4	2	1	4	4
12	5	4	5	2	2	3	5	4	3	3	1	1	2	4
13	2	1	1	2	3	4	3	4	3	3	2	3	3	3
14	1	1	4	3	2	2	5	4	4	2	3	1	3	3
15	3	3	3	4	4	4	4	4	4	4	4	2	3	2
16	1	1	3	2	2	3	4	4	4	2	2	2	3	3
17	1	1	3	2	2	3	4	4	4	2	2	2	3	2
18	3	4	4	3	4	4	4	1	1	1	1	1	1	2
19	3	2	4	3	3	2	4	4	4	2	2	2	3	1
20	1	2	4	4	3	4	5	5	4	2	3	2	4	3
21	1	1	1	2	2	2	1	4	4	5	3	3	4	2
22	1	1	2	1	2	2	4	4	4	4	3	1	4	4
23	3	4	5	3	2	5	4	4	5	3	2	2	4	4

24	1	2	2	2	2	3	4	4	2	3	3	2	4	4
25	3	3	3	3	3	3	3	4	4	4	3	3	3	3
26	2	3	3	2	3	4	3	5	5	2	3	2	2	3
27	3	2	3	2	4	3	2	4	3	4	4	3	2	2
28	3	4	4	4	4	4	4	2	2	3	3	3	3	4
29	3	3	2	3	4	3	3	5	5	4	3	2	3	2
30	2	2	4	3	3	4	3	5	4	4	3	3	3	5

Questions:

1. By using pare sample t-test, identify the parameters on which the first food has an edge over the restaurant food.
2. Based on the results obtained, what are your recommendations?

Case Study – 13

Brand Preference

(Chi-Square Test)

This case study, a bivariate cross-tabulation to understand the brand preference between the Age and Cigarette Brand.

Methodology

1. A data set consisting of 25 respondents. The data was mainly constructed to find the relationship between the dependent and independent variable.
2. Age was taken as the independent variable and choice of Cigarette as dependent variable. Five brands of cigarette were considered as the different choice for the respondents.
3. The age group was coded into five categories as 1 to 5 and the brands of cigarette were coded into five categories and the coding are as follows:

Independent Variable

Age	Coding
≤20	1
21-30	2
31-40	3
41-50	4
>50	5

Dependent Variables

Different Brand	Coding
A – Gold Flake	1
B – Wills Flake	2
C – King Size	3
D – Wills Filter	4
E – Classic Menthol	5

Input Data

Serial No.	Age	Age Code	Cigarette	Brand Code
1	≤20	1	A	1
2	≤20	1	C	3
3	≤20	1	A	1
4	≤20	1	D	4

5	≤20	1	E	5
6	21-30	2	B	2
7	21-30	2	C	3
8	21-30	2	D	4
9	21-30	2	A	1
10	21-30	2	A	1
11	31-40	3	B	2
12	31-40	3	C	3
13	31-40	3	D	4
14	31-40	3	B	2
15	31-40	3	A	1
16	41-50	4	B	2
17	41-50	4	B	2
18	41-50	4	A	1
19	41-50	4	A	1
20	41-50	4	C	3
21	>50	5	D	4
22	>50	5	E	5
23	>50	5	C	3
24	>50	5	B	2
25	>50	5	A	1

Questions:

1. Analysis the cross tabulation by SPSS.
2. Calculate the contingency coefficient.
3. Find out the association between the variables and interpret the result.

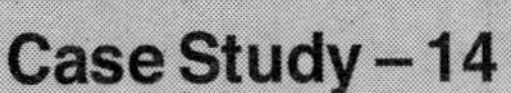

Case Study – 14 Preference of the First Food

(Chi-Square Test)

Pritam Enterprises has a restaurant in Bhubaneswar Odisha serving only lunch and dinner with high quality food at premium prices. The top management of the restaurant observes that the total sales revenues of the restaurants have been more at the rate of 2% only for the last two years. A meeting of the senior management personnel was called to discuss the issue. Some of them were of the opinion that young customers in the age group of 15 to 40 were switching to fast food. Further, they were of the view that the trend mainly is among people belonging to high income-group and to familiar where both partners were economically employed.

In the series of meeting which top management had, it was decided to lunch a fast food joint with restaurant which already present. However, before starting the fast food joint, they got a survey conducted to understand the preference of people for fast food. A sample of 60 respondents was chosen. Following table gives the data on select variables.

1. First column indicates the respondent's number.
2. Second column indicates the preferences for first food (on 5 point scale).

Preferences for First Food	Code
Very much preferred	5
Preferred	4
Natural	3
Not preferred	2
Not at all preferred	1

3. Third column indicates the actual age of the respondents.
4. Fourth column of the table indicates the household income.

Household Income	Code
Less than ₹ 25,000.00	1
₹ 25,000.00 – ₹ 50,000.00	2
More than ₹ 50,000.00	3

5. Fifth column indicates the respondent gender.

   (a) Male = 1 (b) Female = 2

Data on Selected Variables for first food:

Resp. No.	Preference	Age	Income	Gender	Resp. No.	Preference	Age	Income	Gender
1	4	30	1	2	31	3	41	1	1
2	2	46	2	1	32	5	42	2	1
3	3	37	3	1	33	1	61	3	1
4	4	22	3	2	34	2	31	1	1
5	3	26	1	2	35	1	19	3	1
6	4	47	3	2	36	3	20	1	1
7	3	45	1	2	37	4	29	3	2
8	2	50	1	1	38	3	26	2	1
9	2	54	2	2	39	4	31	3	1
10	5	26	3	2	40	4	28	3	2
11	3	41	2	2	41	3	29	1	1
12	2	51	1	1	42	2	32	2	2
13	1	49	1	1	43	4	26	2	1
14	5	31	3	1	44	5	19	2	1
15	3	46	2	1	45	4	41	3	1
16	4	26	1	1	46	2	20	1	1
17	5	31	3	1	47	3	36	2	2
18	4	35	2	1	48	4	31	3	1

19	5	32	3	2	49	5	28	1	2
20	1	46	2	2	50	2	54	1	1
21	2	24	1	1	51	1	52	2	1
22	4	22	3	1	52	3	46	1	2
23	4	18	3	1	53	2	21	2	1
24	2	46	1	1	54	4	21	3	2
25	2	38	1	1	55	5	18	3	1
26	1	47	1	2	56	5	29	2	2
27	2	54	2	2	57	4	51	3	1
28	5	50	3	2	58	1	52	2	2
29	4	46	3	1	59	2	46	2	2
30	1	46	2	2	60	2	31	1	2

Questions:

1. Cross-tabulate the above two groups against gender and interpret result.
2. Prepare cross-tabulation table of the above-mentioned groups of preference for first food with age and interpret the result.
3. Again cross-tabulate preference for fast food against the income and interprets the result.

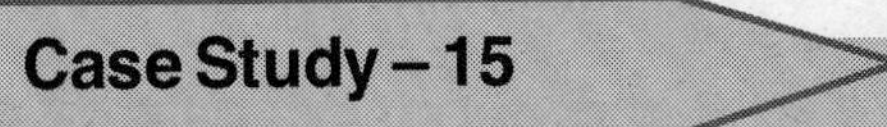

Case Study – 15 — Good Health and Bad Health

(ANOVA)

As part of a long-term study of individuals 65 years of age or older, sociologist and physicians at the Kalinga Medical Center in upstate Bhubaneswar investigated the relationship between geographic location and depression. A sample of 60 individuals all in reasonably good health, was selected; 20 individuals were residents of Balasore, 20 were residents of Bhubaneswar, and 20 were residents of Sambalpur. Each of the individuals sampled was given a standardized test to measure depression. The data collected follow; higher test scores indicate higher levels of depression. These data are available on the disk in the medical file.

A second part of the study considered the relationship between geographic location and depression for individuals 65 years of age or older who had a chronic health condition such as arthritis, hypertension, and/or heart ailment. A sample of 60 individuals with such conditions was identified. Again 20 were residents of Balasore, 20 were residents of Bhubaneswar, and 20 were residents of Sambalpur the levels of depression recorded for this study follow. These data are available on the data disk in the file Medical.

Data from Medical 1

Balasore	Bhubaneswar	Sambalpur
3	8	10
7	11	7
7	9	3
3	7	5
8	8	11
8	7	8

Data from Medical 2

Balasore	Bhubaneswar	Sambalpur
13	14	10
12	9	12
17	15	15
17	12	18
20	16	12
21	24	14

8	8	4
5	4	3
5	13	7
2	10	8
6	6	8
2	8	7
6	12	3
6	8	9
9	6	8
7	8	12
5	5	6
4	7	3
7	7	8
3	8	11

16	18	17
14	14	8
13	15	14
17	17	16
12	20	18
9	11	17
12	23	19
15	19	15
16	17	13
15	14	14
13	9	11
10	14	12
11	13	13
17	11	11

Questions:

1. Use analysis of variance (One-way and Two-way) on data set 1 (Good Health). State the hypotheses being tested. What are your conclusions?
2. Use analysis of variance (One-way and Two-way) on data set 2 (Chronic Bad Health). State the hypotheses being tested. What are your conclusions?

Case Study – 16

Success and Failure of Small Business

(Factor Analysis)

A study aimed to determining the reasons for success or failure of small business. A sample of 50 entrepreneurs was asked to indicate the perceived areas of strength of their organizations. Their responses identified 7 variables rated on five point scale.

Five-point Scale

Organizational Strength	Code
Very strong	5
Strong	4
Natural/Normal	3
Weak	2
Very weak	1

Variables

V_1 = Location of the Firm

V_2 = Product Quality

V_3 = Pricing of the Product

V_4 = Customer Service

V_5 = Innovation in Product

V_6 = Cost control

V_7 = Employee Productivity

Data on Selected Variables for Small Business:

Resp. No.	V_1	V_2	V_3	V_4	V_5	V_6	V_7
1	5.00	5.00	4.00	5.00	3.00	4.00	3.00
2	5.00	5.00	5.00	5.00	5.00	5.00	5.00
3	4.00	3.00	4.00	3.00	3.00	3.00	3.00
4	3.00	5.00	5.00	4.00	4.00	4.00	4.00
5	4.00	5.00	4.00	5.00	4.00	5.00	5.00
6	5.00	5.00	3.00	4.00	4.00	5.00	5.00
7	4.00	4.00	4.00	5.00	4.00	5.00	4.00
8	4.00	4.00	4.00	4.00	4.00	4.00	4.00
9	4.00	4.00	5.00	4.00	2.00	2.00	2.00
10	2.00	5.00	5.00	5.00	5.00	5.00	5.00
11	4.00	4.00	4.00	5.00	4.00	4.00	4.00
12	2.00	5.00	4.00	5.00	4.00	5.00	4.00
13	4.00	4.00	3.00	4.00	4.00	4.00	4.00
14	3.00	3.00	4.00	4.00	4.00	5.00	4.00
15	5.00	4.00	3.00	5.00	4.00	5.00	3.00
16	5.00	5.00	3.00	4.00	4.00	5.00	4.00
17	5.00	4.00	4.00	4.00	4.00	3.00	4.00
18	4.00	4.00	5.00	5.00	3.00	3.00	3.00
19	4.00	3.00	4.00	4.00	4.00	4.00	3.00
20	1.00	5.00	4.00	4.00	5.00	5.00	5.00
21	4.00	4.00	4.00	5.00	5.00	4.00	4.00
22	4.00	5.00	5.00	5.00	5.00	5.00	4.00
23	4.00	4.00	4.00	4.00	4.00	4.00	4.00
24	4.00	4.00	5.00	5.00	3.00	4.00	3.00
25	3.00	3.00	3.00	3.00	3.00	3.00	3.00
26	3.00	5.00	3.00	3.00	4.00	4.00	4.00
27	5.00	4.00	2.00	4.00	3.00	5.00	4.00
28	4.00	4.00	3.00	4.00	4.00	5.00	4.00
29	5.00	4.00	3.00	4.00	3.00	5.00	4.00
30	5.00	5.00	3.00	5.00	3.00	4.00	3.00
31	5.00	4.00	2.00	4.00	2.00	5.00	4.00
32	5.00	4.00	1.00	5.00	3.00	4.00	2.00

33	5.00	4.00	3.00	4.00	2.00	5.00	4.00
34	5.00	4.00	2.00	5.00	4.00	4.00	3.00
35	5.00	5.00	4.00	5.00	3.00	5.00	5.00
36	5.00	4.00	2.00	4.00	3.00	4.00	4.00
37	5.00	5.00	1.00	5.00	4.00	5.00	3.00
38	5.00	4.00	3.00	5.00	3.00	5.00	5.00
39	5.00	4.00	1.00	5.00	2.00	5.00	2.00
40	5.00	5.00	2.00	4.00	3.00	4.00	3.00
41	5.00	3.00	1.00	3.00	3.00	5.00	4.00
42	5.00	4.00	3.00	4.00	4.00	4.00	2.00
43	5.00	4.00	1.00	5.00	3.00	5.00	4.00
44	4.00	5.00	2.00	1.00	5.00	5.00	2.00
45	4.00	4.00	4.00	4.00	2.00	4.00	2.00
46	4.00	4.00	4.00	4.00	4.00	4.00	4.00
47	3.00	3.00	4.00	4.00	4.00	4.00	4.00
48	5.00	5.00	5.00	4.00	5.00	5.00	5.00
49	5.00	4.00	4.00	4.00	4.00	5.00	4.00
50	4.00	5.00	3.00	4.00	4.00	4.00	4.00

Questions:

1. Conduct a factor analysis to identify the reasons for success or failure of small business.
2. What are the implications for the decision-maker in this case?

Small Car Manufacturing Company

(Factor Analysis)

The Indian automobile market is largely contributed by the small cars. Small cars in India are the most common mode of personal vehicles. The use of small cars as a reliable mode of private transportation system is well suitable to the economic state and transport conditions in India. In various cities of the country, the use of small cars has been popular due to narrow roads, excellent fuel economy of these cars, and price of these small cars.

There are some prominent small car manufacturing companies both from India and abroad, who have established their production, sales, and service centers in the country. Maruti, Suzuki, Hyundai, TATA, and GM are some of the small car manufacturers in India. TATA, one of the major international automobile companies has brought the recent sensation to launch the most inexpensive car of the world. Priced at ₹ 1 lakh, the TATA Nano is expected to hit the Indian automobile market early in the year 2009. This will remarkably change the popularity of small cars among Indian automobile lovers. In recent future, one of the famous Indian two-wheeler and three-wheeler manufacturers, Bajaj Motors, has also announced to launch a small car for the Indian automobile market. Apart from this, Honda Motors and Reva Electric Car company has also launched various models of small cars in the Indian small car market.

One new car manufacturing company aiming to released a small car into the market. For this purpose, he has surveyed twenty-five respondents about their perceptions and image attributes of small cars. Ten questions are asked to each of them. All answered on scale of 1 to 5 (5 = completely agree, 1 = completely disagree).

Variables

1. Reasonable price
2. More mileage
3. Easy to maintain and service
4. Comfortable to seat
5. Driving pleasure
6. Convenience feature
7. Space for luggage
8. Attractive colors
9. After sale service
10. Safety

Data on Selected Variables for Small Car:

Resp. No.	Price	Mileage	Service	Comfort	Driving	Feature	Space	Colors	Sale	Safety
1	5.00	2.00	1.00	1.00	5.00	3.00	4.00	5.00	1.00	1.00
2	5.00	2.00	2.00	2.00	4.00	3.00	2.00	4.00	2.00	2.00
3	5.00	2.00	1.00	4.00	5.00	5.00	2.00	5.00	5.00	1.00
4	5.00	3.00	2.00	4.00	4.00	4.00	2.00	3.00	5.00	2.00
5	3.00	4.00	5.00	4.00	4.00	3.00	4.00	3.00	5.00	4.00
6	3.00	4.00	5.00	4.00	2.00	3.00	2.00	3.00	2.00	4.00
7	3.00	4.00	5.00	4.00	2.00	3.00	2.00	4.00	2.00	4.00
8	3.00	5.00	5.00	4.00	2.00	3.00	2.00	5.00	2.00	4.00
9	3.00	5.00	5.00	4.00	2.00	2.00	3.00	5.00	3.00	4.00
10	3.00	4.00	5.00	3.00	2.00	4.00	3.00	5.00	3.00	3.00
11	3.00	4.00	4.00	3.00	2.00	4.00	3.00	5.00	3.00	3.00
12	2.00	5.00	4.00	2.00	5.00	5.00	2.00	5.00	2.00	4.00
13	2.00	4.00	4.00	2.00	4.00	4.00	2.00	4.00	2.00	4.00
14	2.00	4.00	2.00	2.00	4.00	4.00	2.00	4.00	2.00	2.00
15	2.00	4.00	2.00	2.00	4.00	4.00	2.00	4.00	2.00	4.00
16	4.00	5.00	4.00	4.00	5.00	5.00	4.00	5.00	4.00	4.00
17	4.00	4.00	4.00	4.00	4.00	4.00	4.00	4.00	4.00	4.00
18	4.00	3.00	4.00	4.00	5.00	5.00	4.00	5.00	4.00	4.00
19	4.00	3.00	4.00	4.00	5.00	5.00	4.00	5.00	4.00	4.00
20	4.00	3.00	4.00	4.00	4.00	4.00	4.00	4.00	4.00	4.00
21	3.00	3.00	3.00	3.00	3.00	3.00	3.00	3.00	3.00	3.00
22	3.00	4.00	3.00	3.00	4.00	4.00	3.00	4.00	3.00	3.00
23	2.00	5.00	2.00	2.00	5.00	5.00	2.00	5.00	2.00	2.00
24	2.00	5.00	2.00	2.00	5.00	5.00	2.00	5.00	2.00	2.00
25	1.00	4.00	1.00	1.00	4.00	4.00	1.00	4.00	1.00	1.00

Questions:

1. Conduct a factor analysis to identify the variables, which are to be considered.
2. What are the implications for the decision-maker in this case?

Case Study – 18

Telecom Industry

(Cluster Analysis)

Problem

India is today one of the largest telecom markets in the world. The growth of Indian telecommunication sector is highly driven by supportive government policies, emerging new technologies and changing consumer behavior. In the mobile telecom sector, vast competition has emerged. So, the subscribers now have the various alternatives to choose according to their convenience. Obviously, customers prefer a particular brand on the basis of some criteria. Therefore, to survive in the industry, the companies have to identify the factor related to customer satisfaction and loyalty.

Scope of the Study

Factors affecting customer satisfaction in telecom industry explores profiles of the target market of mobile phones and as well it identifies the relationship between consumer perceptions, price promotion with product quality perception and customer satisfaction in the mobile market.

Objective of the Study

To identify the variables that affects the customer satisfaction in the telecommunication industry.

Type of Research

Exploratory Research

Data Collection Method

Primary data has been collected through a questionnaire containing several types of questions for respondents' profile, usage background and satisfaction measurement.

Questionnaire Design

Section A: Personnel information. For example: age, profession, income and monthly usage etc.

Section B: Satisfaction measurement question. There were 10 variables (services) in Likert rating scales ranging from highly satisfied (1) and highly dissatisfied (5).

Independent Variables

1. Network coverage (X_1)
2. Network Quality (X_2)
3. Customer support (X_3)
4. Complaint Management (X_4)
5. Availability of customer service station (X_5)
6. Price (X_6)
7. Bill payment System (X_7)
8. Value-added service (X_8)
9. Internet service (X_9)
10. Promotional offer (X_{10})

Telecom sector has done this market research with 30 respondents who answered the above questionnaire. The input data matrix is shown below in Table:

Resp. No.	X_1	X_2	X_3	X_4	X_5	X_6	X_7	X_8	X_9	X_{10}
1	2	4	3	2	3	4	2	2	2	2
2	2	4	5	2	4	3	3	2	3	2
3	1	2	3	1	2	2	4	1	2	1
4	2	3	4	4	3	3	3	3	3	2
5	3	5	1	3	2	4	2	3	3	2
6	1	2	2	2	3	2	1	3	2	1
7	3	2	2	1	3	2	2	2	2	3
8	1	2	3	2	4	1	1	3	2	1
9	1	1	5	4	4	3	2	4	3	3
10	4	4	3	2	4	5	1	2	5	3
11	2	4	3	2	3	4	2	2	2	2
12	2	4	5	2	4	3	3	2	3	2
13	1	2	3	1	2	2	4	1	2	1
14	3	3	2	1	2	1	3	1	1	3
15	3	2	3	5	4	2	1	3	4	2
16	2	2	2	1	1	3	2	3	4	2
17	3	3	2	1	2	1	3	1	1	3
18	3	2	3	5	4	2	1	3	4	2
19	2	2	2	1	1	3	2	3	4	2
20	2	4	1	2	1	4	2	4	4	2
21	4	4	1	3	5	5	1	5	4	2
22	2	4	1	2	1	4	2	4	4	2
23	4	4	1	3	5	5	1	5	4	2
24	1	1	5	4	4	3	2	4	3	3
25	2	3	4	4	3	3	3	3	3	2
26	3	5	1	3	2	4	2	3	3	2
27	1	2	2	2	3	2	1	3	2	1
28	3	2	2	1	3	2	2	2	2	3
29	2	3	3	2	4	3	2	2	2	4
30	4	4	3	3	3	3	3	5	2	5

Questions:

1. Conduct a quick clustering on the data and arrive at a two-cluster solution.
2. Interpret and name of the cluster.
3. What are the implications for the decision-maker in this case?

References

1. Aaker, David A., V. Kumar and George S. Day, Marketing Research, 7th Edition, John Wiley and Sons, 2001.
2. Aaker, Kumar and Day, Marketing Research. 7th Edition, John Wiley and Sons Inc, 2000.
3. Adams, John, Hafiz T.A. Khan, Robert Raeside and David White, Research Methods for Graduate Business and Social Studies. Response, New Delhi, 2007.
4. Aggarwal, L.N. and Diwan, Parag, Research Methodology and Management Decisions, Global Business Press, New Delhi, 1997.
5. Beri, G.C., Marketing Research., 3rd Edition, Tata McGraw-Hill Publishing Company Ltd., New Delhi, 2000.
6. Bhattacharyya Deepak Kumar, Research Methodology, Excel Books, New Delhi, 2006.
7. Burns Robert B., Introduction to Research Methods, Sage Publications, London, 200.
8. Chawla, D. and Sondhi, N., Research Methodology – Concepts and Cases, 1st Edition, Vikash Publishing House Pvt. Ltd., New Delhi, 2011.
9. Cooper R., Donald, Business Research Methods, Tata McGraw-Hill Publishing Company Ltd., New Delhi, 2006.
10. Dwivedi, R.S., Research Methods in Behavioral Sciences, MacMillan India Ltd., Delhi, 1997.
11. Easwaran, Sunanda and Sharmila J. Singh, Marketing Research – Concepts, Practices and Cases, Oxford University Press, New Delhi, 2006.
12. Emory, Willam C., Business Research Methods, Richard D. Irwin, IIlinois, 1976.
13. Gay, L.R., Research Methods for Business and Management, Macmillan Publishing Company, New York, 1992.
14. Gilbert, A. Churchill, Jr. and Dawn Lacobuchi, Marketing Research Methodological Foundations, 8th Edition, Thompson South-Western, New Delhi, 2002.
15. Green, Paul E. and Donald S. Tull, Research for Marketing Decisions, 4th Edition, Prentice-Hall of India Pvt. Ltd., New Delhi, 2006.
16. Keller, Gerald, Statistics for Management and Economics, 7th Edition, South-Western Cengage Learning, Ohio, 2005.
17. Kinnear, Thomas C. and James R. Taylor, Marketing Research: An Applied Approach, 5th Edition, McGraw-Hill, Inc., New York, 1996.
18. Kothari, C.R., Research Methodology – Methods and Techniques, 2nd Revised Edition, New Age Publisher (P) Ltd., New Delhi, 2004.
19. Krishnaswami, O.R. and Rangnathan, M., Methodology of Research in Social Sciences, 2nd Revised Edition, Himalaya Publishing House, New Delhi, 2008.
20. Kumar Ranjit, Research Methodology – A Step by Step Guide for Beginners, 2nd Edition, Pearson Publication, New Delhi, 2006.
21. Majhi, P.R. and Khatua P.K., Research Methodology for Management, 1st Edition, Himalaya Publishing House, New Delhi, 2011.
22. Malhotra, Naresh K., Marketing Research – An Applied Orientation, Pearson Education, New Delhi, 2002.
23. McBurney, Donald H., Research Methods, 5th Edition, Thomson Wadsworth Publication, 2006.
24. Michael, V.P., Research Methodology in Management, Himalaya Publishing House, Mumbai, 2000.
25. Murthy, C., Research Methodology, 1st Edition, Vrinda Publication Pvt. Ltd., New Delhi, 2009.
26. Nagundkar, Rajendra, Marketing Research (Text and Cases), Tata McGraw-Hill Publishing Company Ltd., New Delhi, 2002.

27. Nation, Jack, R., Research Methods, Prentice-Hall, New Jersey, 1997.

28. Paneerselvam, R., Research Methodology, Prentice-Hall of India Pvt. Ltd., 2004.

29. Parasuraman, A., Dhruv Grewal and Krishnan, R., Marketing Research, Biztantra, New Delhi, 2004.

30. Sauderes, Lewis and Thornhill. Research Methods for Business Student. Pearson Education, New Delhi, 2003.

31. Sekharan, Uma, Research Methods for Business: A Skill Building Approach, John Wiley and Sons (Asia) Pvt. Ltd., Singapore, 2003.

32. Shajahan, S., Marketing Research – Concepts and Practices in India, Macmillan India Ltd., New Delhi, 2005.

33. Sharma, J.K., Business Statistics. Pearson Education, New Delhi, 2006.

34. Sontakki, C. N. Marketing Research, Himalaya Publishing House, New Delhi, 2006.

35. Swain, A.K.P.C., A Text Book of Research Methodology, 2nd Revised Edition, Kalyani Publishing House, New Delhi, 2008.

36. Tripathi, P.C., A Text Book of Research Methodology in Social Sciences, Sultan Chand and Sons, New Delhi, 2005.

37. Trochim, Willium M., Research Methods, Biztantra, New Delhi, 2003.

38. Tull, Donald S. and Del I Hawkins, Marketing Research: Measurement and Method, 6th Edition, Prentice-Hall of India Pvt. Ltd., New Delhi, 1993.

39. Zikmund, Willium G., Business Research Methods, 5th Edition, Dryden Press, Harcourt Brace College Publishers, 1997.

Index

Table 1: Area Under Normal Curve between 0 and z

The table is the proportion under the entire curve which is between z = 0 and a positive value of z. Areas for negative values for z are obtained by symmetry.

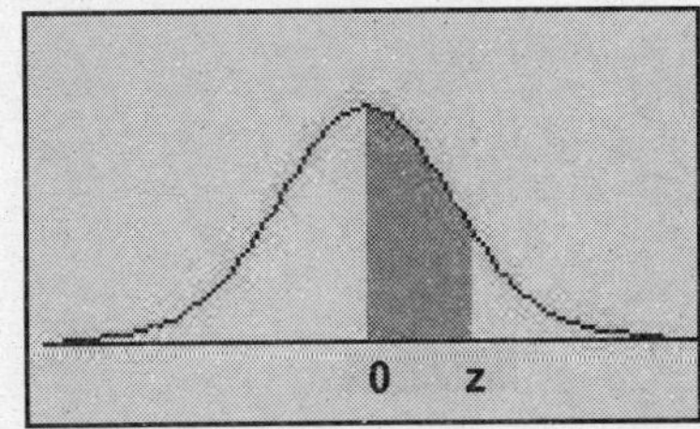

Areas of a Standard Normal Distribution

Z	0.00	0.01	0.02	0.03	0.04	0.05	0.06	0.07	0.08	0.09
0.0	0.0000	0.0040	0.0080	0.0120	0.0160	0.0199	0.0239	0.0279	0.0319	0.0359
0.1	0.0398	0.0438	0.0478	0.0517	0.0557	0.0596	0.0636	0.0675	0.0714	0.0753
0.2	0.0793	0.0832	0.0871	0.0910	0.0948	0.0987	0.1026	0.1064	0.1103	0.1141
0.3	0.1179	0.1217	0.1255	0.1293	0.1331	0.1368	0.1406	0.1443	0.1480	0.1517
0.4	0.1554	0.1591	0.1628	0.1664	0.1700	0.1736	0.1772	0.1808	0.1844	0.1879
0.5	0.1915	0.1950	0.1985	0.2019	0.2054	0.2088	0.2123	0.2157	0.2190	0.2224
0.6	0.2257	0.2291	0.2324	0.2357	0.2389	0.2422	0.2454	0.2486	0.2517	0.2549
0.7	0.2580	0.2611	0.2642	0.2673	0.2704	0.2734	0.2764	0.2794	0.2823	0.2852
0.8	0.2881	0.2910	0.2939	0.2967	0.2995	0.3023	0.3051	0.3078	0.3106	0.3133
0.9	0.3159	0.3186	0.3212	0.3238	0.3264	0.3289	0.3315	0.3340	0.3365	0.3389
1.0	0.3413	0.3438	0.3461	0.3485	0.3508	0.3531	0.3554	0.3577	0.3599	0.3621
1.1	0.3643	0.3665	0.3686	0.3708	0.3729	0.3749	0.3770	0.3790	0.3810	0.3830
1.2	0.3849	0.3869	0.3888	0.3907	0.3925	0.3944	0.3962	0.3980	0.3997	0.4015
1.3	0.4032	0.4049	0.4066	0.4082	0.4099	0.4115	0.4131	0.4147	0.4162	0.4177
1.4	0.4192	0.4207	0.4222	0.4236	0.4251	0.4265	0.4279	0.4292	0.4306	0.4319
1.5	0.4332	0.4345	0.4357	0.4370	0.4382	0.4394	0.4406	0.4418	0.4429	0.4441
1.6	0.4452	0.4463	0.4474	0.4484	0.4495	0.4505	0.4515	0.4525	0.4535	0.4545
1.7	0.4554	0.4564	0.4573	0.4582	0.4591	0.4599	0.4608	0.4616	0.4625	0.4633
1.8	0.4641	0.4649	0.4656	0.4664	0.4671	0.4678	0.4686	0.4693	0.4699	0.4706
1.9	0.4713	0.4719	0.4726	0.4732	0.4738	0.4744	0.4750	0.4756	0.4761	0.4767
2.0	0.4772	0.4778	0.4783	0.4788	0.4793	0.4798	0.4803	0.4808	0.4812	0.4817
2.1	0.4821	0.4826	0.4830	0.4834	0.4838	0.4842	0.4846	0.4850	0.4854	0.4857
2.2	0.4861	0.4864	0.4868	0.4871	0.4875	0.4878	0.4881	0.4884	0.4887	0.4890
2.3	0.4893	0.4896	0.4898	0.4901	0.4904	0.4906	0.4909	0.4911	0.4913	0.4916
2.4	0.4918	0.4920	0.4922	0.4925	0.4927	0.4929	0.4931	0.4932	0.4934	0.4936
2.5	0.4938	0.4940	0.4941	0.4943	0.4945	0.4946	0.4948	0.4949	0.4951	0.4952
2.6	0.4953	0.4955	0.4956	0.4957	0.4959	0.4960	0.4961	0.4962	0.4963	0.4964
2.7	0.4965	0.4966	0.4967	0.4968	0.4969	0.4970	0.4971	0.4972	0.4973	0.4974
2.8	0.4974	0.4975	0.4976	0.4977	0.4977	0.4978	0.4979	0.4979	0.4980	0.4981
2.9	0.4981	0.4982	0.4982	0.4983	0.4984	0.4984	0.4985	0.4985	0.4986	0.4986
3.0	0.4987	0.4987	0.4987	0.4988	0.4988	0.4989	0.4989	0.4989	0.4990	0.4990

Table 2: Critical Values of Student's t-Distribution

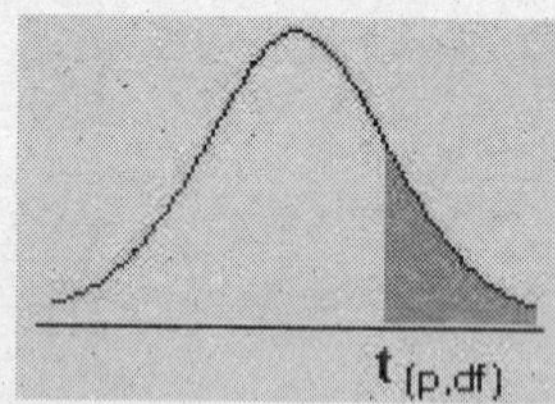

Level of Significance for Two-tailed Test								
Degree of freedom	0.80	0.50	0.20	0.10	0.05	0.02	0.01	0.001
Level of Significance for One-tailed Test								
Degree of freedom	0.40	0.25	0.10	0.05	0.025	0.01	0.005	0.0005
1	0.324920	1.000000	3.077684	6.313752	12.70620	31.82052	63.65674	636.6192
2	0.288675	0.816497	1.885618	2.919986	4.30265	6.96456	9.92484	31.5991
3	0.276671	0.764892	1.637744	2.353363	3.18245	4.54070	5.84091	12.9240
4	0.270722	0.740697	1.533206	2.131847	2.77645	3.74695	4.60409	8.6103
5	0.267181	0.726687	1.475884	2.015048	2.57058	3.36493	4.03214	6.8688
6	0.264835	0.717558	1.439756	1.943180	2.44691	3.14267	3.70743	5.9588
7	0.263167	0.711142	1.414924	1.894579	2.36462	2.99795	3.49948	5.4079
8	0.261921	0.706387	1.396815	1.859548	2.30600	2.89646	3.35539	5.0413
9	0.260955	0.702722	1.383029	1.833113	2.26216	2.82144	3.24984	4.7809
10	0.260185	0.699812	1.372184	1.812461	2.22814	2.76377	3.16927	4.5869
11	0.259556	0.697445	1.363430	1.795885	2.20099	2.71808	3.10581	4.4370
12	0.259033	0.695483	1.356217	1.782288	2.17881	2.68100	3.05454	4.3178
13	0.258591	0.693829	1.350171	1.770933	2.16037	2.65031	3.01228	4.2208
14	0.258213	0.692417	1.345030	1.761310	2.14479	2.62449	2.97684	4.1405
15	0.257885	0.691197	1.340606	1.753050	2.13145	2.60248	2.94671	4.0728
16	0.257599	0.690132	1.336757	1.745884	2.11991	2.58349	2.92078	4.0150
17	0.257347	0.689195	1.333379	1.739607	2.10982	2.56693	2.89823	3.9651
18	0.257123	0.688364	1.330391	1.734064	2.10092	2.55238	2.87844	3.9216
19	0.256923	0.687621	1.327728	1.729133	2.09302	2.53948	2.86093	3.8834
20	0.256743	0.686954	1.325341	1.724718	2.08596	2.52798	2.84534	3.8495
21	0.256580	0.686352	1.323188	1.720743	2.07961	2.51765	2.83136	3.8193
22	0.256432	0.685805	1.321237	1.717144	2.07387	2.50832	2.81876	3.7921
23	0.256297	0.685306	1.319460	1.713872	2.06866	2.49987	2.80734	3.7676
24	0.256173	0.684850	1.317836	1.710882	2.06390	2.49216	2.79694	3.7454
25	0.256060	0.684430	1.316345	1.708141	2.05954	2.48511	2.78744	3.7251
26	0.255955	0.684043	1.314972	1.705618	2.05553	2.47863	2.77871	3.7066
27	0.255858	0.683685	1.313703	1.703288	2.05183	2.47266	2.77068	3.6896
28	0.255768	0.683353	1.312527	1.701131	2.04841	2.46714	2.76326	3.6739
29	0.255684	0.683044	1.311434	1.699127	2.04523	2.46202	2.75639	3.6594
30	0.255605	0.682756	1.310415	1.697261	2.04227	2.45726	2.75000	3.6460
inf	0.253347	0.674490	1.281552	1.644854	1.95996	2.32635	2.57583	3.2905

Table 3: Critical Values of Chi-square (x^2) Distribution

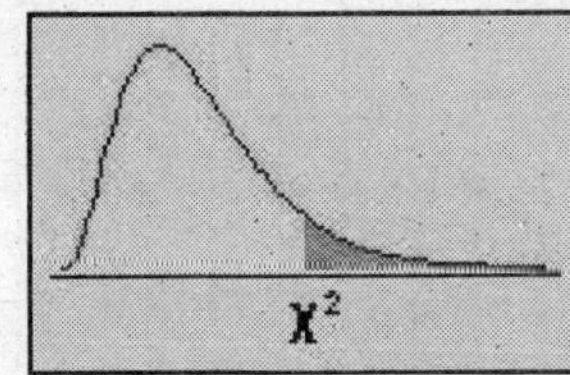

Degree of Freedom	.990	.950	.900	.750	.500	.250	.100	.050	.025	.010
1	0.00016	0.00393	0.01579	0.10153	0.45494	1.32330	2.70554	3.84146	5.02389	6.63490
2	0.02010	0.10259	0.21072	0.57536	1.38629	2.77259	4.60517	5.99146	7.37776	9.21034
3	0.11483	0.35185	0.58437	1.21253	2.36597	4.10834	6.25139	7.81473	9.34840	11.34487
4	0.29711	0.71072	1.06362	1.92256	3.35669	5.38527	7.77944	9.48773	11.14329	13.27670
5	0.55430	1.14548	1.61031	2.67460	4.35146	6.62568	9.23636	11.07050	12.83250	15.08627
6	0.87209	1.63538	2.20413	3.45460	5.34812	7.84080	10.64464	12.59159	14.44938	16.81189
7	1.23904	2.16735	2.83311	4.25485	6.34581	9.03715	12.01704	14.06714	16.01276	18.47531
8	1.64650	2.73264	3.48954	5.07064	7.34412	10.21885	13.36157	15.50731	17.53455	20.09024
9	2.08790	3.32511	4.16816	5.89883	8.34283	11.38875	14.68366	16.91898	19.02277	21.66599
10	2.55821	3.94030	4.86518	6.73720	9.34182	12.54886	15.98718	18.30704	20.48318	23.20925
11	3.05348	4.57481	5.57778	7.58414	10.34100	13.70069	17.27501	19.67514	21.92005	24.72497
12	3.57057	5.22603	6.30380	8.43842	11.34032	14.84540	18.54935	21.02607	23.33666	26.21697
13	4.10692	5.89186	7.04150	9.29907	12.33976	15.98391	19.81193	22.36203	24.73560	27.68825
14	4.66043	6.57063	7.78953	10.16531	13.33927	17.11693	21.06414	23.68479	26.11895	29.14124
15	5.22935	7.26094	8.54676	11.03654	14.33886	18.24509	22.30713	24.99579	27.48839	30.57791
16	5.81221	7.96165	9.31224	11.91222	15.33850	19.36886	23.54183	26.29623	28.84535	31.99993
17	6.40776	8.67176	10.08519	12.79193	16.33818	20.48868	24.76904	27.58711	30.19101	33.40866
18	7.01491	9.39046	10.86494	13.67529	17.33790	21.60489	25.98942	28.86930	31.52638	34.80531
19	7.63273	10.11701	11.65091	14.56200	18.33765	22.71781	27.20357	30.14353	32.85233	36.19087
20	8.26040	10.85081	12.44261	15.45177	19.33743	23.82769	28.41198	31.41043	34.16961	37.56623
21	8.89720	11.59131	13.23960	16.34438	20.33723	24.93478	29.61509	32.67057	35.47888	38.93217
22	9.54249	12.33801	14.04149	17.23962	21.33704	26.03927	30.81328	33.92444	36.78071	40.28936
23	10.19572	13.09051	14.84796	18.13730	22.33688	27.14134	32.00690	35.17246	38.07563	41.63840
24	10.85636	13.84843	15.65868	19.03725	23.33673	28.24115	33.19624	36.41503	39.36408	42.97982
25	11.52398	14.61141	16.47341	19.93934	24.33659	29.33885	34.38159	37.65248	40.64647	44.31410
26	12.19815	15.37916	17.29188	20.84343	25.33646	30.43457	35.56317	38.88514	41.92317	45.64168
27	12.87850	16.15140	18.11390	21.74940	26.33634	31.52841	36.74122	40.11327	43.19451	46.96294
28	13.56471	16.92788	18.93924	22.65716	27.33623	32.62049	37.91592	41.33714	44.46079	48.27824
29	14.25645	17.70837	19.76774	23.56659	28.33613	33.71091	39.08747	42.55697	45.72229	49.58788
30	14.95346	18.49266	20.59923	24.47761	29.33603	34.79974	40.25602	43.77297	46.97924	50.89218

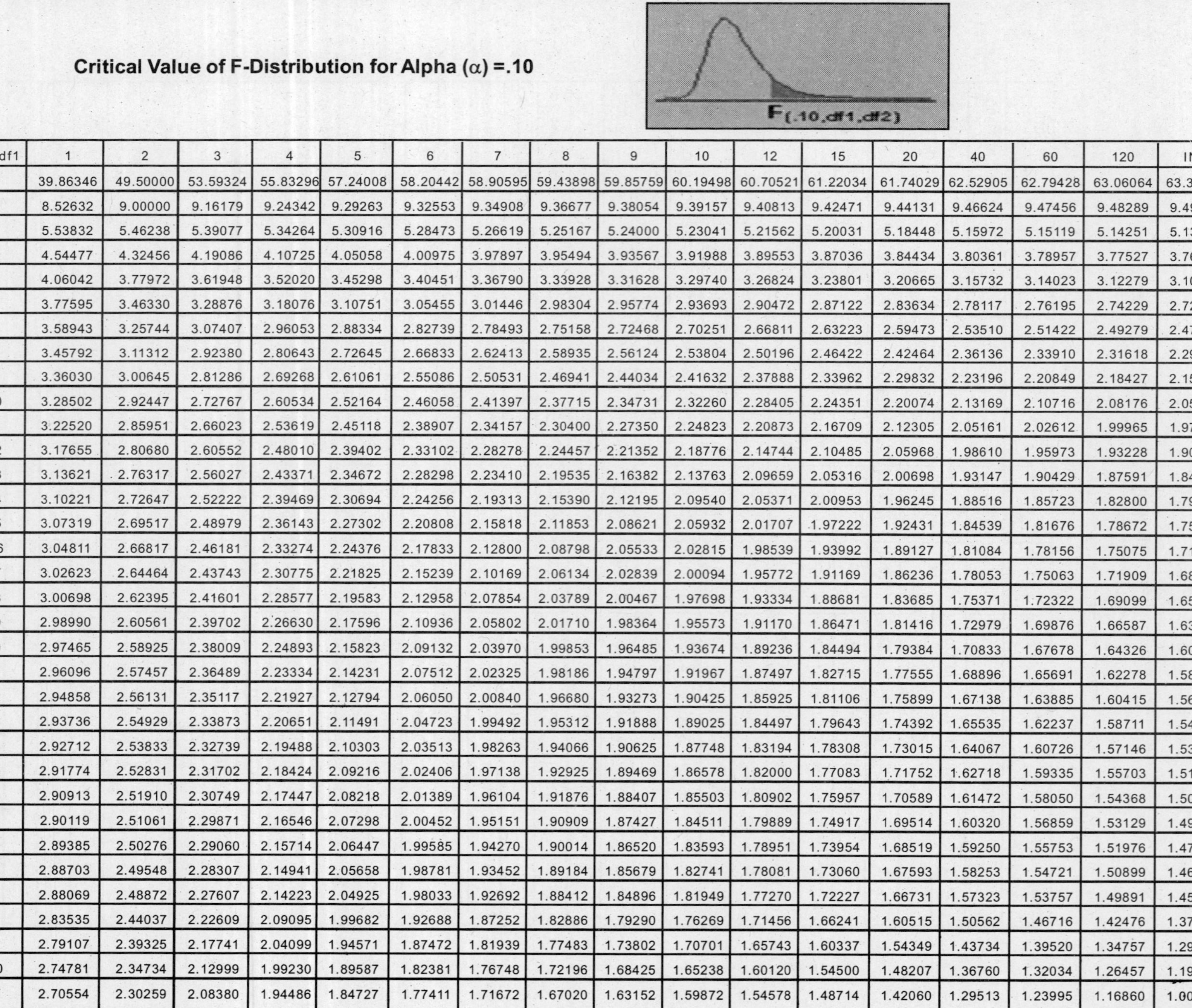

Critical Value of F-Distribution for Alpha (α) =.10

df2/df1	1	2	3	4	5	6	7	8	9	10	12	15	20	40	60	120	INF
1	39.86346	49.50000	53.59324	55.83296	57.24008	58.20442	58.90595	59.43898	59.85759	60.19498	60.70521	61.22034	61.74029	62.52905	62.79428	63.06064	63.32812
2	8.52632	9.00000	9.16179	9.24342	9.29263	9.32553	9.34908	9.36677	9.38054	9.39157	9.40813	9.42471	9.44131	9.46624	9.47456	9.48289	9.49122
3	5.53832	5.46238	5.39077	5.34264	5.30916	5.28473	5.26619	5.25167	5.24000	5.23041	5.21562	5.20031	5.18448	5.15972	5.15119	5.14251	5.13370
4	4.54477	4.32456	4.19086	4.10725	4.05058	4.00975	3.97897	3.95494	3.93567	3.91988	3.89553	3.87036	3.84434	3.80361	3.78957	3.77527	3.76073
5	4.06042	3.77972	3.61948	3.52020	3.45298	3.40451	3.36790	3.33928	3.31628	3.29740	3.26824	3.23801	3.20665	3.15732	3.14023	3.12279	3.10500
6	3.77595	3.46330	3.28876	3.18076	3.10751	3.05455	3.01446	2.98304	2.95774	2.93693	2.90472	2.87122	2.83634	2.78117	2.76195	2.74229	2.72216
7	3.58943	3.25744	3.07407	2.96053	2.88334	2.82739	2.78493	2.75158	2.72468	2.70251	2.66811	2.63223	2.59473	2.53510	2.51422	2.49279	2.47079
8	3.45792	3.11312	2.92380	2.80643	2.72645	2.66833	2.62413	2.58935	2.56124	2.53804	2.50196	2.46422	2.42464	2.36136	2.33910	2.31618	2.29257
9	3.36030	3.00645	2.81286	2.69268	2.61061	2.55086	2.50531	2.46941	2.44034	2.41632	2.37888	2.33962	2.29832	2.23196	2.20849	2.18427	2.15923
10	3.28502	2.92447	2.72767	2.60534	2.52164	2.46058	2.41397	2.37715	2.34731	2.32260	2.28405	2.24351	2.20074	2.13169	2.10716	2.08176	2.05542
11	3.22520	2.85951	2.66023	2.53619	2.45118	2.38907	2.34157	2.30400	2.27350	2.24823	2.20873	2.16709	2.12305	2.05161	2.02612	1.99965	1.97211
12	3.17655	2.80680	2.60552	2.48010	2.39402	2.33102	2.28278	2.24457	2.21352	2.18776	2.14744	2.10485	2.05968	1.98610	1.95973	1.93228	1.90361
13	3.13621	2.76317	2.56027	2.43371	2.34672	2.28298	2.23410	2.19535	2.16382	2.13763	2.09659	2.05316	2.00698	1.93147	1.90429	1.87591	1.84620
14	3.10221	2.72647	2.52222	2.39469	2.30694	2.24256	2.19313	2.15390	2.12195	2.09540	2.05371	2.00953	1.96245	1.88516	1.85723	1.82800	1.79728
15	3.07319	2.69517	2.48979	2.36143	2.27302	2.20808	2.15818	2.11853	2.08621	2.05932	2.01707	1.97222	1.92431	1.84539	1.81676	1.78672	1.75505
16	3.04811	2.66817	2.46181	2.33274	2.24376	2.17833	2.12800	2.08798	2.05533	2.02815	1.98539	1.93992	1.89127	1.81084	1.78156	1.75075	1.71817
17	3.02623	2.64464	2.43743	2.30775	2.21825	2.15239	2.10169	2.06134	2.02839	2.00094	1.95772	1.91169	1.86236	1.78053	1.75063	1.71909	1.68564
18	3.00698	2.62395	2.41601	2.28577	2.19583	2.12958	2.07854	2.03789	2.00467	1.97698	1.93334	1.88681	1.83685	1.75371	1.72322	1.69099	1.65671
19	2.98990	2.60561	2.39702	2.26630	2.17596	2.10936	2.05802	2.01710	1.98364	1.95573	1.91170	1.86471	1.81416	1.72979	1.69876	1.66587	1.63077
20	2.97465	2.58925	2.38009	2.24893	2.15823	2.09132	2.03970	1.99853	1.96485	1.93674	1.89236	1.84494	1.79384	1.70833	1.67678	1.64326	1.60738
21	2.96096	2.57457	2.36489	2.23334	2.14231	2.07512	2.02325	1.98186	1.94797	1.91967	1.87497	1.82715	1.77555	1.68896	1.65691	1.62278	1.58615
22	2.94858	2.56131	2.35117	2.21927	2.12794	2.06050	2.00840	1.96680	1.93273	1.90425	1.85925	1.81106	1.75899	1.67138	1.63885	1.60415	1.56678
23	2.93736	2.54929	2.33873	2.20651	2.11491	2.04723	1.99492	1.95312	1.91888	1.89025	1.84497	1.79643	1.74392	1.65535	1.62237	1.58711	1.54903
24	2.92712	2.53833	2.32739	2.19488	2.10303	2.03513	1.98263	1.94066	1.90625	1.87748	1.83194	1.78308	1.73015	1.64067	1.60726	1.57146	1.53270
25	2.91774	2.52831	2.31702	2.18424	2.09216	2.02406	1.97138	1.92925	1.89469	1.86578	1.82000	1.77083	1.71752	1.62718	1.59335	1.55703	1.51760
26	2.90913	2.51910	2.30749	2.17447	2.08218	2.01389	1.96104	1.91876	1.88407	1.85503	1.80902	1.75957	1.70589	1.61472	1.58050	1.54368	1.50360
27	2.90119	2.51061	2.29871	2.16546	2.07298	2.00452	1.95151	1.90909	1.87427	1.84511	1.79889	1.74917	1.69514	1.60320	1.56859	1.53129	1.49057
28	2.89385	2.50276	2.29060	2.15714	2.06447	1.99585	1.94270	1.90014	1.86520	1.83593	1.78951	1.73954	1.68519	1.59250	1.55753	1.51976	1.47841
29	2.88703	2.49548	2.28307	2.14941	2.05658	1.98781	1.93452	1.89184	1.85679	1.82741	1.78081	1.73060	1.67593	1.58253	1.54721	1.50899	1.46704
30	2.88069	2.48872	2.27607	2.14223	2.04925	1.98033	1.92692	1.88412	1.84896	1.81949	1.77270	1.72227	1.66731	1.57323	1.53757	1.49891	1.45636
40	2.83535	2.44037	2.22609	2.09095	1.99682	1.92688	1.87252	1.82886	1.79290	1.76269	1.71456	1.66241	1.60515	1.50562	1.46716	1.42476	1.37691
60	2.79107	2.39325	2.17741	2.04099	1.94571	1.87472	1.81939	1.77483	1.73802	1.70701	1.65743	1.60337	1.54349	1.43734	1.39520	1.34757	1.29146
120	2.74781	2.34734	2.12999	1.99230	1.89587	1.82381	1.76748	1.72196	1.68425	1.65238	1.60120	1.54500	1.48207	1.36760	1.32034	1.26457	1.19256
inf	2.70554	2.30259	2.08380	1.94486	1.84727	1.77411	1.71672	1.67020	1.63152	1.59872	1.54578	1.48714	1.42060	1.29513	1.23995	1.16860	1.00000

Critical Value of F-Distribution for Alpha (α) =.05

F (.05,df1,df2)

df2/df1	1	2	3	4	5	6	7	8	9	10	12	15	20	40	60	120	INF
1	161.4476	199.5000	215.7073	224.5832	230.1619	233.9860	236.7684	238.8827	240.5433	241.8817	243.9060	245.9499	248.0131	251.1432	252.1957	253.2529	254.3144
2	18.5128	19.0000	19.1643	19.2468	19.2964	19.3295	19.3532	19.3710	19.3848	19.3959	19.4125	19.4291	19.4458	19.4707	19.4791	19.4874	19.4957
3	10.1280	9.5521	9.2766	9.1172	9.0135	8.9406	8.8867	8.8452	8.8123	8.7855	8.7446	8.7029	8.6602	8.5944	8.5720	8.5494	8.5264
4	7.7086	6.9443	6.5914	6.3882	6.2561	6.1631	6.0942	6.0410	5.9988	5.9644	5.9117	5.8578	5.8025	5.7170	5.6877	5.6581	5.6281
5	6.6079	5.7861	5.4095	5.1922	5.0503	4.9503	4.8759	4.8183	4.7725	4.7351	4.6777	4.6188	4.5581	4.4638	4.4314	4.3985	4.3650
6	5.9874	5.1433	4.7571	4.5337	4.3874	4.2839	4.2067	4.1468	4.0990	4.0600	3.9999	3.9381	3.8742	3.7743	3.7398	3.7047	3.6689
7	5.5914	4.7374	4.3468	4.1203	3.9715	3.8660	3.7870	3.7257	3.6767	3.6365	3.5747	3.5107	3.4445	3.3404	3.3043	3.2674	3.2298
8	5.3177	4.4590	4.0662	3.8379	3.6875	3.5806	3.5005	3.4381	3.3881	3.3472	3.2839	3.2184	3.1503	3.0428	3.0053	2.9669	2.9276
9	5.1174	4.2565	3.8625	3.6331	3.4817	3.3738	3.2927	3.2296	3.1789	3.1373	3.0729	3.0061	2.9365	2.8259	2.7872	2.7475	2.7067
10	4.9646	4.1028	3.7083	3.4780	3.3258	3.2172	3.1355	3.0717	3.0204	2.9782	2.9130	2.8450	2.7740	2.6609	2.6211	2.5801	2.5379
11	4.8443	3.9823	3.5874	3.3567	3.2039	3.0946	3.0123	2.9480	2.8962	2.8536	2.7876	2.7186	2.6464	2.5309	2.4901	2.4480	2.4045
12	4.7472	3.8853	3.4903	3.2592	3.1059	2.9961	2.9134	2.8486	2.7964	2.7534	2.6866	2.6169	2.5436	2.4259	2.3842	2.3410	2.2962
13	4.6672	3.8056	3.4105	3.1791	3.0254	2.9153	2.8321	2.7669	2.7144	2.6710	2.6037	2.5331	2.4589	2.3392	2.2966	2.2524	2.2064
14	4.6001	3.7389	3.3439	3.1122	2.9582	2.8477	2.7642	2.6987	2.6458	2.6022	2.5342	2.4630	2.3879	2.2664	2.2229	2.1778	2.1307
15	4.5431	3.6823	3.2874	3.0556	2.9013	2.7905	2.7066	2.6408	2.5876	2.5437	2.4753	2.4034	2.3275	2.2043	2.1601	2.1141	2.0658
16	4.4940	3.6337	3.2389	3.0069	2.8524	2.7413	2.6572	2.5911	2.5377	2.4935	2.4247	2.3522	2.2756	2.1507	2.1058	2.0589	2.0096
17	4.4513	3.5915	3.1968	2.9647	2.8100	2.6987	2.6143	2.5480	2.4943	2.4499	2.3807	2.3077	2.2304	2.1040	2.0584	2.0107	1.9604
18	4.4139	3.5546	3.1599	2.9277	2.7729	2.6613	2.5767	2.5102	2.4563	2.4117	2.3421	2.2686	2.1906	2.0629	2.0166	1.9681	1.9168
19	4.3807	3.5219	3.1274	2.8951	2.7401	2.6283	2.5435	2.4768	2.4227	2.3779	2.3080	2.2341	2.1555	2.0264	1.9795	1.9302	1.8780
20	4.3512	3.4928	3.0984	2.8661	2.7109	2.5990	2.5140	2.4471	2.3928	2.3479	2.2776	2.2033	2.1242	1.9938	1.9464	1.8963	1.8432
21	4.3248	3.4668	3.0725	2.8401	2.6848	2.5727	2.4876	2.4205	2.3660	2.3210	2.2504	2.1757	2.0960	1.9645	1.9165	1.8657	1.8117
22	4.3009	3.4434	3.0491	2.8167	2.6613	2.5491	2.4638	2.3965	2.3419	2.2967	2.2258	2.1508	2.0707	1.9380	1.8894	1.8380	1.7831
23	4.2793	3.4221	3.0280	2.7955	2.6400	2.5277	2.4422	2.3748	2.3201	2.2747	2.2036	2.1282	2.0476	1.9139	1.8648	1.8128	1.7570
24	4.2597	3.4028	3.0088	2.7763	2.6207	2.5082	2.4226	2.3551	2.3002	2.2547	2.1834	2.1077	2.0267	1.8920	1.8424	1.7896	1.7330
25	4.2417	3.3852	2.9912	2.7587	2.6030	2.4904	2.4047	2.3371	2.2821	2.2365	2.1649	2.0889	2.0075	1.8718	1.8217	1.7684	1.7110
26	4.2252	3.3690	2.9752	2.7426	2.5868	2.4741	2.3883	2.3205	2.2655	2.2197	2.1479	2.0716	1.9898	1.8533	1.8027	1.7488	1.6906
27	4.2100	3.3541	2.9604	2.7278	2.5719	2.4591	2.3732	2.3053	2.2501	2.2043	2.1323	2.0558	1.9736	1.8361	1.7851	1.7306	1.6717
28	4.1960	3.3404	2.9467	2.7141	2.5581	2.4453	2.3593	2.2913	2.2360	2.1900	2.1179	2.0411	1.9586	1.8203	1.7689	1.7138	1.6541
29	4.1830	3.3277	2.9340	2.7014	2.5454	2.4324	2.3463	2.2783	2.2229	2.1768	2.1045	2.0275	1.9446	1.8055	1.7537	1.6981	1.6376
30	4.1709	3.3158	2.9223	2.6896	2.5336	2.4205	2.3343	2.2662	2.2107	2.1646	2.0921	2.0148	1.9317	1.7918	1.7396	1.6835	1.6223
40	4.0847	3.2317	2.8387	2.6060	2.4495	2.3359	2.2490	2.1802	2.1240	2.0772	2.0035	1.9245	1.8389	1.6928	1.6373	1.5766	1.5089
60	4.0012	3.1504	2.7581	2.5252	2.3683	2.2541	2.1665	2.0970	2.0401	1.9926	1.9174	1.8364	1.7480	1.5943	1.5343	1.4673	1.3893
120	3.9201	3.0718	2.6802	2.4472	2.2899	2.1750	2.0868	2.0164	1.9588	1.9105	1.8337	1.7505	1.6587	1.4952	1.4290	1.3519	1.2539
inf	3.8415	2.9957	2.6049	2.3719	2.2141	2.0986	2.0096	1.9384	1.8799	1.8307	1.7522	1.6664	1.5705	1.3940	1.3180	1.2214	1.0000

Critical Value of F-Distribution for Alpha (α) =.025

df2/df1	1	2	3	4	5	6	7	8	9	10	12	15	20	40	60	120	INF
1	647.7890	799.5000	864.1630	899.5833	921.8479	937.1111	948.2169	956.6562	963.2846	968.6274	976.7079	984.8668	993.1028	1005.598	1009.800	1014.020	1018.258
2	38.5063	39.0000	39.1655	39.2484	39.2982	39.3315	39.3552	39.3730	39.3869	39.3980	39.4146	39.4313	39.4479	39.473	39.481	39.490	39.498
3	17.4434	16.0441	15.4392	15.1010	14.8848	14.7347	14.6244	14.5399	14.4731	14.4189	14.3366	14.2527	14.1674	14.037	13.992	13.947	13.902
4	12.2179	10.6491	9.9792	9.6045	9.3645	9.1973	9.0741	8.9796	8.9047	8.8439	8.7512	8.6565	8.5599	8.411	8.360	8.309	8.257
5	10.0070	8.4336	7.7636	7.3879	7.1464	6.9777	6.8531	6.7572	6.6811	6.6192	6.5245	6.4277	6.3286	6.175	6.123	6.069	6.015
6	8.8131	7.2599	6.5988	6.2272	5.9876	5.8198	5.6955	5.5996	5.5234	5.4613	5.3662	5.2687	5.1684	5.012	4.959	4.904	4.849
7	8.0727	6.5415	5.8898	5.5226	5.2852	5.1186	4.9949	4.8993	4.8232	4.7611	4.6658	4.5678	4.4667	4.309	4.254	4.199	4.142
8	7.5709	6.0595	5.4160	5.0526	4.8173	4.6517	4.5286	4.4333	4.3572	4.2951	4.1997	4.1012	3.9995	3.840	3.784	3.728	3.670
9	7.2093	5.7147	5.0781	4.7181	4.4844	4.3197	4.1970	4.1020	4.0260	3.9639	3.8682	3.7694	3.6669	3.505	3.449	3.392	3.333
10	6.9367	5.4564	4.8256	4.4683	4.2361	4.0721	3.9498	3.8549	3.7790	3.7168	3.6209	3.5217	3.4185	3.255	3.198	3.140	3.080
11	6.7241	5.2559	4.6300	4.2751	4.0440	3.8807	3.7586	3.6638	3.5879	3.5257	3.4296	3.3299	3.2261	3.061	3.004	2.944	2.883
12	6.5538	5.0959	4.4742	4.1212	3.8911	3.7283	3.6065	3.5118	3.4358	3.3736	3.2773	3.1772	3.0728	2.906	2.848	2.787	2.725
13	6.4143	4.9653	4.3472	3.9959	3.7667	3.6043	3.4827	3.3880	3.3120	3.2497	3.1532	3.0527	2.9477	2.780	2.720	2.659	2.595
14	6.2979	4.8567	4.2417	3.8919	3.6634	3.5014	3.3799	3.2853	3.2093	3.1469	3.0502	2.9493	2.8437	2.674	2.614	2.552	2.487
15	6.1995	4.7650	4.1528	3.8043	3.5764	3.4147	3.2934	3.1987	3.1227	3.0602	2.9633	2.8621	2.7559	2.585	2.524	2.461	2.395
16	6.1151	4.6867	4.0768	3.7294	3.5021	3.3406	3.2194	3.1248	3.0488	2.9862	2.8890	2.7875	2.6808	2.509	2.447	2.383	2.316
17	6.0420	4.6189	4.0112	3.6648	3.4379	3.2767	3.1556	3.0610	2.9849	2.9222	2.8249	2.7230	2.6158	2.442	2.380	2.315	2.247
18	5.9781	4.5597	3.9539	3.6083	3.3820	3.2209	3.0999	3.0053	2.9291	2.8664	2.7689	2.6667	2.5590	2.384	2.321	2.256	2.187
19	5.9216	4.5075	3.9034	3.5587	3.3327	3.1718	3.0509	2.9563	2.8801	2.8172	2.7196	2.6171	2.5089	2.333	2.270	2.203	2.133
20	5.8715	4.4613	3.8587	3.5147	3.2891	3.1283	3.0074	2.9128	2.8365	2.7737	2.6758	2.5731	2.4645	2.287	2.223	2.156	2.085
21	5.8266	4.4199	3.8188	3.4754	3.2501	3.0895	2.9686	2.8740	2.7977	2.7348	2.6368	2.5338	2.4247	2.246	2.182	2.114	2.042
22	5.7863	4.3828	3.7829	3.4401	3.2151	3.0546	2.9338	2.8392	2.7628	2.6998	2.6017	2.4984	2.3890	2.210	2.145	2.076	2.003
23	5.7498	4.3492	3.7505	3.4083	3.1835	3.0232	2.9023	2.8077	2.7313	2.6682	2.5699	2.4665	2.3567	2.176	2.111	2.041	1.968
24	5.7166	4.3187	3.7211	3.3794	3.1548	2.9946	2.8738	2.7791	2.7027	2.6396	2.5411	2.4374	2.3273	2.146	2.080	2.010	1.935
25	5.6864	4.2909	3.6943	3.3530	3.1287	2.9685	2.8478	2.7531	2.6766	2.6135	2.5149	2.4110	2.3005	2.118	2.052	1.981	1.906
26	5.6586	4.2655	3.6697	3.3289	3.1048	2.9447	2.8240	2.7293	2.6528	2.5896	2.4908	2.3867	2.2759	2.093	2.026	1.954	1.878
27	5.6331	4.2421	3.6472	3.3067	3.0828	2.9228	2.8021	2.7074	2.6309	2.5676	2.4688	2.3644	2.2533	2.069	2.002	1.930	1.853
28	5.6096	4.2205	3.6264	3.2863	3.0626	2.9027	2.7820	2.6872	2.6106	2.5473	2.4484	2.3438	2.2324	2.048	1.980	1.907	1.829
29	5.5878	4.2006	3.6072	3.2674	3.0438	2.8840	2.7633	2.6686	2.5919	2.5286	2.4295	2.3248	2.2131	2.028	1.959	1.886	1.807
30	5.5675	4.1821	3.5894	3.2499	3.0265	2.8667	2.7460	2.6513	2.5746	2.5112	2.4120	2.3072	2.1952	2.009	1.940	1.866	1.787
40	5.4239	4.0510	3.4633	3.1261	2.9037	2.7444	2.6238	2.5289	2.4519	2.3882	2.2882	2.1819	2.0677	1.875	1.803	1.724	1.637
60	5.2856	3.9253	3.3425	3.0077	2.7863	2.6274	2.5068	2.4117	2.3344	2.2702	2.1692	2.0613	1.9445	1.744	1.667	1.581	1.482
120	5.1523	3.8046	3.2269	2.8943	2.6740	2.5154	2.3948	2.2994	2.2217	2.1570	2.0548	1.9450	1.8249	1.614	1.530	1.433	1.310
inf	5.0239	3.6889	3.1161	2.7858	2.5665	2.4082	2.2875	2.1918	2.1136	2.0483	1.9447	1.8326	1.7085	1.484	1.388	1.268	1.000

Critical Value of F-Distribution for Alpha (α) =.01

df2/df1	1	2	3	4	5	6	7	8	9	10	12	15	20	40	60	120	INF
1	4052.181	4999.500	5403.352	5624.583	5763.650	5858.986	5928.356	5981.070	6022.473	6055.847	6106.321	6157.285	6208.730	6286.782	6313.030	6339.391	6365.864
2	98.503	99.000	99.166	99.249	99.299	99.333	99.356	99.374	99.388	99.399	99.416	99.433	99.449	99.474	99.482	99.491	99.499
3	34.116	30.817	29.457	28.710	28.237	27.911	27.672	27.489	27.345	27.229	27.052	26.872	26.690	26.411	26.316	26.221	26.125
4	21.198	18.000	16.694	15.977	15.522	15.207	14.976	14.799	14.659	14.546	14.374	14.198	14.020	13.745	13.652	13.558	13.463
5	16.258	13.274	12.060	11.392	10.967	10.672	10.456	10.289	10.158	10.051	9.888	9.722	9.553	9.291	9.202	9.112	9.020
6	13.745	10.925	9.780	9.148	8.746	8.466	8.260	8.102	7.976	7.874	7.718	7.559	7.396	7.143	7.057	6.969	6.880
7	12.246	9.547	8.451	7.847	7.460	7.191	6.993	6.840	6.719	6.620	6.469	6.314	6.155	5.908	5.824	5.737	5.650
8	11.259	8.649	7.591	7.006	6.632	6.371	6.178	6.029	5.911	5.814	5.667	5.515	5.359	5.116	5.032	4.946	4.859
9	10.561	8.022	6.992	6.422	6.057	5.802	5.613	5.467	5.351	5.257	5.111	4.962	4.808	4.567	4.483	4.398	4.311
10	10.044	7.559	6.552	5.994	5.636	5.386	5.200	5.057	4.942	4.849	4.706	4.558	4.405	4.165	4.082	3.996	3.909
11	9.646	7.206	6.217	5.668	5.316	5.069	4.886	4.744	4.632	4.539	4.397	4.251	4.099	3.860	3.776	3.690	3.602
12	9.330	6.927	5.953	5.412	5.064	4.821	4.640	4.499	4.388	4.296	4.155	4.010	3.858	3.619	3.535	3.449	3.361
13	9.074	6.701	5.739	5.205	4.862	4.620	4.441	4.302	4.191	4.100	3.960	3.815	3.665	3.425	3.341	3.255	3.165
14	8.862	6.515	5.564	5.035	4.695	4.456	4.278	4.140	4.030	3.939	3.800	3.656	3.505	3.266	3.181	3.094	3.004
15	8.683	6.359	5.417	4.893	4.556	4.318	4.142	4.004	3.895	3.805	3.666	3.522	3.372	3.132	3.047	2.959	2.868
16	8.531	6.226	5.292	4.773	4.437	4.202	4.026	3.890	3.780	3.691	3.553	3.409	3.259	3.018	2.933	2.845	2.753
17	8.400	6.112	5.185	4.669	4.336	4.102	3.927	3.791	3.682	3.593	3.455	3.312	3.162	2.920	2.835	2.746	2.653
18	8.285	6.013	5.092	4.579	4.248	4.015	3.841	3.705	3.597	3.508	3.371	3.227	3.077	2.835	2.749	2.660	2.566
19	8.185	5.926	5.010	4.500	4.171	3.939	3.765	3.631	3.523	3.434	3.297	3.153	3.003	2.761	2.674	2.584	2.489
20	8.096	5.849	4.938	4.431	4.103	3.871	3.699	3.564	3.457	3.368	3.231	3.088	2.938	2.695	2.608	2.517	2.421
21	8.017	5.780	4.874	4.369	4.042	3.812	3.640	3.506	3.398	3.310	3.173	3.030	2.880	2.636	2.548	2.457	2.360
22	7.945	5.719	4.817	4.313	3.988	3.758	3.587	3.453	3.346	3.258	3.121	2.978	2.827	2.583	2.495	2.403	2.305
23	7.881	5.664	4.765	4.264	3.939	3.710	3.539	3.406	3.299	3.211	3.074	2.931	2.781	2.535	2.447	2.354	2.256
24	7.823	5.614	4.718	4.218	3.895	3.667	3.496	3.363	3.256	3.168	3.032	2.889	2.738	2.492	2.403	2.310	2.211
25	7.770	5.568	4.675	4.177	3.855	3.627	3.457	3.324	3.217	3.129	2.993	2.850	2.699	2.453	2.364	2.270	2.169
26	7.721	5.526	4.637	4.140	3.818	3.591	3.421	3.288	3.182	3.094	2.958	2.815	2.664	2.417	2.327	2.233	2.131
27	7.677	5.488	4.601	4.106	3.785	3.558	3.388	3.256	3.149	3.062	2.926	2.783	2.632	2.384	2.294	2.198	2.097
28	7.636	5.453	4.568	4.074	3.754	3.528	3.358	3.226	3.120	3.032	2.896	2.753	2.602	2.354	2.263	2.167	2.064
29	7.598	5.420	4.538	4.045	3.725	3.499	3.330	3.198	3.092	3.005	2.868	2.726	2.574	2.325	2.234	2.138	2.034
30	7.562	5.390	4.510	4.018	3.699	3.473	3.304	3.173	3.067	2.979	2.843	2.700	2.549	2.299	2.208	2.111	2.006
40	7.314	5.179	4.313	3.828	3.514	3.291	3.124	2.993	2.888	2.801	2.665	2.522	2.369	2.114	2.019	1.917	1.805
60	7.077	4.977	4.126	3.649	3.339	3.119	2.953	2.823	2.718	2.632	2.496	2.352	2.198	1.936	1.836	1.726	1.601
120	6.851	4.787	3.949	3.480	3.174	2.956	2.792	2.663	2.559	2.472	2.336	2.192	2.035	1.763	1.656	1.533	1.381
inf	6.635	4.605	3.782	3.319	3.017	2.802	2.639	2.511	2.407	2.321	2.185	2.039	1.878	1.592	1.473	1.325	1.000

Table 5A: Critical Values for the Sign Test

n = total number of + and – signs combined

n	.005 (one tail) .01 (two tails)	.01 (one tail) .02 (two tails)	.025 (one tail) .05 (two tails)	.05 (one tail) .10 (two tails)
1	*	*	*	*
2	*	*	*	*
3	*	*	*	*
4	*	*	*	*
5	*	*	*	0
6	*	*	0	0
7	*	0	0	0
8	0	0	0	1
9	0	0	1	1
10	0	0	1	1
11	0	1	1	2
12	1	1	2	2
13	1	1	2	3
14	1	2	2	3
15	2	2	3	3
16	2	2	3	4
17	2	3	4	4
18	3	3	4	5
19	3	4	4	5
20	3	4	5	5
21	4	4	5	6
22	4	5	5	6
23	4	5	6	7
24	5	5	6	7
25	5	6	7	7

Notes:

1. * indicated that it is not possible to get a value in critical region.
2. Reject the null hypothesis if the number of the less frequent sign (x) is the less than or equal to the value in the table.
3. For values of n greater than 25, a normal approximation is used with

$$Z = \frac{(x + 0.5) - \left(\frac{n}{2}\right)}{\frac{\sqrt{n}}{2}}$$

From M.F. Triola, Elementary Statistics, 10 ed., Pearson Addison Wesley, Boston, MA, 2006, p. 781.

Table 5B: Critical Values of T for the Sign Test

Level of Significance α					Level of Significance α				
Two-sided	0.10	0.05	0.02	0.01	Two-sided	0.10	0.05	0.02	0.01
One-sided	0.05	0.025	0.01	0.005	One-sided	0.05	0.025	0.01	0.005
n					n				
1	-	-	-	-	31	11	13	15	17
2	-	-	-	-	32	12	14	16	16
3	-	-	-	-	33	11	13	15	17
4	-	-	-	-	34	12	14	16	16
5	5	-	-	-	35	11	13	15	17
6	6	6	-	-	36	12	14	16	18
7	7	7	7	-	37	11	13	17	17
8	6	8	8	8	38	12	14	16	18
9	7	7	9	9	39	13	15	17	17
10	8	8	10	10	40	12	14	16	18
11	7	9	9	11	45	13	15	17	19
12	8	8	10	10	46	14	16	18	20
13	7	9	11	11	49	13	15	19	19
14	8	10	10	12	50	14	16	18	20
15	9	9	11	11	55	15	17	19	21
16	8	10	12	12	56	14	16	18	20
17	9	9	11	13	59	15	17	19	21
18	8	10	12	12	60	14	18	20	22
19	9	11	11	13	65	15	17	21	23
20	10	10	12	14	66	16	18	20	22
21	9	11	13	13	69	15	19	23	25
22	0	12	12	14	70	16	18	22	24
23	9	11	13	15	75	17	19	23	25
24	10	12	14	14	76	16	20	22	24
25	11	11	13	15	79	17	19	23	25
26	10	12	14	14	80	16	20	22	24
27	11	13	13	15	89	17	21	23	27
28	10	12	14	16	90	18	20	24	26
29	11	13	15	15	99	19	21	25	27
30									

Kanji, Gopal K., 100 Statistical Tests. London: Sage Publication Ltd., 1993.

Table 6: Critical Values of the Wilcoxon Signed Ranks Test

n	Two-Tailed Test		One-tailed Test	
	α = .05	α = .01	α = .05	α = .01
5	-	-	0	-
6	0	-	2	-
7	2	-	3	0
8	3	0	5	1
9	5	1	8	3
10	8	3	10	5
11	10	5	13	7
12	13	7	13	7
13	17	9	21	12
14	21	12	25	15
15	25	15	30	19
16	29	19	35	23
17	34	23	41	27
18	40	27	47	32
19	46	32	53	37
20	52	37	60	43
21	58	42	67	49
22	65	48	75	55
23	73	54	83	62
24	81	61	91	69
25	89	68	100	76
26	98	75	110	84
27	107	83	119	92
28	116	91	130	101
29	126	100	140	110
30	137	109	151	120

Table 7: Critical Values of *r* in the Runs Test*

Given in the tables are various values of *r* for values of *m* and *n* less than or equal to 20. For the one-sample runs test, any observed value of *r* which is less than or eqaul to the smaller value, or is greater than or equal to the larger value in a pair is significant at the α = .05 level.

m \ n	2	3	4	5	6	7	8	9	10	11	12	13	14	15	16	17	18	19	20
2											2 -	2 -	2 -	2 -	2 -	2 -	2 -	2 -	2 -
3					2 -	2 -	2 -	2 -	2 -	2 -	2 -	2 -	2 -	3 -	3 -	3 -	3 -	3 -	3 -
4				2 9	2 9	2 -	3 -	3 -	3 -	3 -	3 -	3 -	3 -	3 -	4 -	4 -	4 -	4 -	4 -
5			2 9	2 10	3 10	3 11	3 11	3 -	3 -	4 -	4 -	4 -	4 -	4 -	4 -	4 -	5 -	5 -	5 -
6		2 -	2 9	3 10	3 11	3 12	3 12	4 13	4 13	4 13	4 13	5 -	5 -	5 -	5 -	5 -	5 -	6 -	6 -
7		2 -	2 -	3 11	3 12	3 13	4 13	4 14	5 14	5 14	5 14	5 15	5 15	6 15	6 -	6 -	6 -	6 -	6 -
8		2 -	3 -	3 11	3 12	4 13	4 14	5 14	5 15	5 15	6 16	6 16	6 16	6 16	6 17	7 17	7 17	7 17	7 17
9		2 -	3 -	3 -	4 13	4 14	5 14	5 15	5 16	6 16	6 16	6 17	7 17	7 18	7 18	7 18	8 18	8 18	8 18
10		2 -	3 -	3 -	4 13	5 14	5 15	5 16	6 16	6 17	7 17	7 18	7 18	7 18	8 19	8 19	8 19	8 20	9 20
11		2 -	3 -	4 -	4 13	5 14	5 15	6 16	6 17	7 17	7 18	7 19	8 19	8 19	8 20	9 20	9 20	9 21	9 21
12	2 -	2 -	3 -	4 -	4 13	5 14	6 16	6 16	7 11	7 18	7 19	8 19	8 20	8 20	9 21	9 21	9 21	10 22	10 22
13	2 -	2 -	3 -	4 -	5 -	5 15	6 16	6 17	7 18	7 19	8 19	8 20	9 20	9 21	9 21	10 22	10 22	10 23	10 23
14	2 -	2 -	3 -	4 -	5 -	5 15	6 16	7 17	7 18	8 19	8 20	9 20	9 21	9 22	10 22	10 23	10 23	11 23	11 24
15	2 -	2 -	3 -	4 -	5 -	6 15	6 16	7 18	7 18	8 19	8 20	9 21	9 22	10 22	10 23	11 23	11 24	11 24	12 25
16	2 -	3 -	4 -	4 -	5 -	6 -	6 17	7 18	8 19	8 20	9 21	9 21	10 22	10 23	11 23	11 24	11 25	12 25	12 25
17	2 -	3 -	4 -	4 -	5 -	6 -	7 17	7 18	7 18	9 20	9 21	10 22	10 23	11 23	11 24	11 25	12 25	12 26	13 26
18	2 -	3 -	4 -	5 -	5 -	6 -	7 17	8 18	8 19	9 20	9 21	10 22	10 23	11 24	11 25	12 25	12 26	13 26	13 27
19	2 -	3 -	4 -	5 -	6 -	6 -	7 17	8 18	8 20	9 21	10 22	10 23	11 23	11 24	12 25	12 26	13 26	13 27	13 27
20	2 -	3 -	4 -	5 -	6 -	6 -	7 17	8 18	9 20	9 21	10 22	10 23	11 24	12 25	12 25	13 26	13 27	13 27	14 28

Table 8A: Critical Values for the Wilcoxon/Mann-Whitney Test (U)

Non-directional α = .05 (Directional α = .025)

	n2																			
n1	1	2	3	4	5	6	7	8	9	10	11	12	13	14	15	16	17	18	19	20
1	-	-	-	-	-	-	-	-	-	-	-	-	-	-	-	-	-	-	-	-
2	-	-	-	-	-	-	-	0	0	0	0	1	1	1	1	1	2	2	2	2
3	-	-	-	-	0	1	1	2	2	3	3	4	4	5	5	6	6	7	7	8
4	-	-	-	0	1	2	3	4	4	5	6	7	8	9	10	11	11	12	13	13
5	-	-	0	1	2	3	5	6	7	8	9	11	12	13	14	15	17	18	19	20
6	-	-	1	2	3	5	6	8	10	11	13	14	16	17	19	21	22	24	25	27
7	-	-	1	3	5	6	8	10	12	14	16	18	20	22	24	26	28	30	32	34
8	-	0	2	4	6	8	10	13	15	17	19	22	24	26	29	31	34	36	38	41
9	-	0	2	4	7	10	12	15	17	21	23	26	28	31	34	37	39	42	45	48
10	-	0	3	5	8	11	14	17	20	23	26	29	33	36	39	42	45	48	52	55
11	-	0	3	6	9	13	16	19	23	26	30	33	37	40	44	47	51	55	58	62
12	-	1	4	7	11	14	18	22	26	29	33	37	41	45	49	53	57	61	65	69
13	-	1	4	8	12	16	20	24	28	33	37	41	45	50	54	59	63	67	72	76
14	-	1	5	9	13	17	22	26	31	36	40	45	50	55	59	64	67	74	78	83
15	-	1	5	10	14	19	24	29	34	39	44	49	54	59	64	70	75	80	85	90
16	-	1	6	11	15	21	26	31	37	42	47	53	59	64	70	75	81	86	92	98
17	-	2	6	11	7	22	28	34	39	45	51	57	63	67	75	81	87	93	99	105
18	-	2	7	12	18	24	30	36	42	48	55	61	67	74	80	86	93	99	106	112
19	-	2	7	13	19	25	32	38	45	52	58	65	72	78	85	92	99	106	113	119
20	-	2	8	14	20	27	34	41	48	55	62	69	76	83	90	98	105	112	119	127

Non-directional α = .01 (Directional α = .005)

	n2																			
n	1	2	3	4	5	6	7	8	9	10	11	12	13	14	15	16	17	18	19	20
1	-	-	-	-	-	-	-	-	-	-	-	-	-	-	-	-	-	-	-	-
2	-	-	-	-	-	-	-	-	-	-	-	-	-	-	-	-	-	-	0	0
3	-	-	-	-	-	-	-	-	0	0	0	1	1	1	2	2	2	2	3	3
4	-	-	-			0	0	1	1	2	2	3	3	4	5	5	6	6	7	8
5	-	-	-		0	1	1	2	3	4	5	6	7	7	8	9	10	11	12	13
6	-	-	-	0	1	2	3	4	5	6	7	9	10	11	12	13	15	16	17	18
7	-	-	-	0	1	3	4	6	7	9	10	12	13	15	16	18	19	21	22	24
8	-	-	-	1	2	4	6	7	9	11	13	15	17	18	20	22	24	26	28	30
9	-	-	0	1	3	5	7	9	11	13	16	18	20	22	24	27	29	31	33	36
10	-	-	0	2	4	6	9	11	13	16	18	21	24	26	29	31	34	37	39	42
11	-	-	0	2	5	7	10	13	16	18	21	24	27	30	33	36	39	42	45	46
12	-	-	1	3	6	9	12	15	18	21	24	27	31	34	37	41	44	47	51	54

13	-	-	1	3	7	10	13	17	20	24	27	31	34	38	42	45	49	53	56	60
14	-	-	1	4	7	11	15	18	22	26	30	34	38	42	46	50	54	58	63	67
15	-	-	2	5	8	12	16	20	24	29	33	37	42	46	51	55	60	64	69	73
16	-	-	2	5	9	13	18	22	27	31	36	41	45	50	55	60	65	70	74	79
17	-	-	2	6	10	15	19	24	29	34	39	44	49	54	60	65	70	75	81	86
18	-	-	2	6	11	16	21	26	31	37	42	47	53	58	64	70	75	81	87	92
19	-	0	3	7	12	17	22	28	33	39	45	51	56	63	69	74	81	87	93	99
20	-	0	3	8	13	18	24	30	36	42	46	54	60	67	73	79	86	92	99	105

U_{obt} is the lesser of the two calculated test statistics (U1 and U2). If $U_{obt} \leq U_{crit}$, reject H0.

Dashes (-) indicate that the sample size is too small to reject the Null Hypothesis at the chosen α level.

If n > 20, this table cannot be used. A p can be computed for U_{obt}, using the normal distribution approximation:

$$Z_U = \frac{\left|U_{obt} - \left(\frac{n_1 n_2}{2}\right)\right|}{\sqrt{\frac{n_1 n_2 (n_1 + n_2 + 1)}{12}}}$$

Table 8B: Critical Values for the Mann-Whitney U-Test

Level of significance: 5% (P = 0.05)

Size of the Largest Sample (n2)

Size of the smallest sample (n1)	5	6	7	8	9	10	11	12	13	14	15	16	17	18	19	20	21	22	23	24	25	26	27	28	29	30
3	0	1	1	2	2	3	3	4	4	5	5	6	6	7	7	8	8	9	9	10	10	11	11	12	13	13
4	1	2	3	4	4	5	6	7	8	9	10	11	11	12	13	14	15	16	17	17	18	19	20	21	22	23
5	2	3	5	6	7	8	9	11	12	13	14	15	17	18	19	20	22	23	24	25	27	28	29	30	32	33
6		5	6	8	10	11	13	14	16	17	19	21	22	24	25	27	29	30	32	33	35	37	38	40	42	43
7			8	10	12	14	16	18	20	22	24	26	28	30	32	34	36	38	40	42	44	46	48	50	52	54
8				13	15	17	19	22	24	26	29	31	34	36	38	41	43	45	48	50	53	55	57	60	62	65
9					17	20	23	26	28	31	34	37	39	42	45	48	50	53	56	59	62	64	67	70	73	76
10						23	26	29	33	36	39	42	45	48	52	55	58	61	64	67	71	74	77	80	83	87
11							30	33	37	40	44	47	51	55	58	62	65	69	73	76	80	83	87	90	94	98
12								37	41	45	49	53	57	61	65	69	73	77	81	85	89	93	97	101	105	109
13									45	50	54	59	63	67	72	76	80	85	89	94	98	102	107	111	116	120
14										55	59	64	67	74	78	83	88	93	98	102	107	112	118	122	127	131
15											64	70	75	80	85	90	96	101	106	111	117	122	125	132	138	143
16												75	81	86	92	98	103	109	115	120	126	132	138	143	149	154
17													87	93	99	105	111	117	123	129	135	141	147	154	160	166
18														99	106	112	119	125	132	138	145	151	158	164	171	177
19															113	119	126	133	140	147	154	161	168	175	182	189
20																127	134	141	149	156	163	171	178	186	193	200
21																	142	150	157	165	173	181	188	196	204	212
22																		158	166	174	182	191	199	207	215	223
23																			175	183	192	200	209	218	226	235
24																				192	201	210	219	228	238	247
25																					211	220	230	239	249	258
26																						230	240	250	260	270
27																							250	261	271	282
28																								272	282	293
29																									294	305
[illegible]																										317